Postfix

RICHARD BLUM

201 West 103rd Street, Indianapolis, Indiana 46290

Postfix

Richard Blum

International Standard Book Number: 0-672-32114-9

Library of Congress Catalog Card Number: 2001086075

Printed in the United States of America

First Printing: May 2001

04 03 4 3

Trademarks

All terms mentioned in this book that are known to be trademarks or service marks have been appropriately capitalized. Sams Publishing cannot attest to the accuracy of this information. Use of a term in this book should not be regarded as affecting the validity of any trademark or service mark.

Warning and Disclaimer

Every effort has been made to make this book as complete and as accurate as possible, but no warranty or fitness is implied. The information provided is on an "as is" basis. The author and the publisher shall have neither liability nor responsibility to any person or entity with respect to any loss or damages arising from the information contained in this book.

Associate Publisher
Jeff Koch

Acquisitions Editor
Kathryn Purdum

Development Editor
Hugh Vandivier

Managing Editor
Matt Purcell

Project Editor
Christina Smith

Copy Editor
Kim Cofer

Indexer
Sheila Schroeder

Proofreader
Matt Wynalda

Technical Editor
Robin Anderson

Team Coordinator
Vicki Harding

Interior Designer
Gary Adair

Cover Designer
Alan Clements

Page Layout
Ayanna Lacey

Contents at a Glance

Contents

Part II Installing and Configuring Postfix

About the Author

Rich Blum has worked for the past 12 years as a network and systems administrator for the U.S. Department of Defense at the Defense Finance and Accounting Service. There he has been using Unix operating systems as an FTP server, TFTP server, e-mail server, mail list server, and network monitoring device in a large networking environment. Rich currently serves on the board of directors for Traders Point Christian Schools and is active on the computer support team at the school, supporting a Microsoft network in the classrooms and computer lab of a small K-8 school. Rich has a Bachelor of Science degree in Electrical Engineering and a Master of Science degree in Management, specializing in Management Information Systems, both from Purdue University. When Rich is not being a computer nerd, he is either playing electric bass for the church worship band or spending time with his wife, Barbara, and two daughters, Katie Jane and Jessica.

About the Technical Editor

Robin Anderson graduated cum laude from the University of Maryland, Baltimore County (UMBC) in 1998 with a Bachelor's degree in Computer Science and History. She is currently a Unix SysAdmin Specialist at UMBC in the Office of Information Technology (OIT). She also manages OIT's Operations Support Staff and is a member of the Security Work Group. As an adjunct professor for the UMBC CS/EE department, she developed and taught an undergraduate Unix SysAdmin course.

Robin has earned the GCUX (Unix Administrator) and GCIH (Incident Handling) security certifications from the SANS Institute. She also works with SANS to develop online exam materials and presentations. Robin is currently teaching SANS LevelOne security courses for UMBC's Department of Professional Education and Training.

Dedication

This book is dedicated to my daughters, Katie Jane and Jessica. "Do not merely listen to the word, and so deceive yourselves. Do what it says." James 1:22 (NIV)

Acknowledgments

First, all glory, honor, and praise goes to God, who through His Son all things are possible, and who gave us the gift of eternal life.

I would like to thank all of the great people at Sams Publishing for their help, guidance, and professionalism. Thanks to Katie Purdum, the acquisitions editor, for offering me the opportunity to write this book. Also, many thanks to Hugh Vandivier, the development editor, for guiding this book along, and Christina Smith, the project editor, for making sure everything turned out right.

Kim Cofer, the copy editor, did an excellent job of correcting my poor grammar, and Robin Anderson, the technical editor, did an excellent job of pointing out my technical goofs and setting me straight when necessary. Many thanks to the interior design group at Sams for turning my scribbles into great looking pictures.

Finally, I would like to thank my family. My parents, Mike and Joyce Blum, for their dedication and support and my wife, Barbara, and daughters, Katie Jane and Jessica, for their love, faith, and understanding, especially while I was writing this book.

Tell Us What You Think!

As the reader of this book, *you* are our most important critic and commentator. We value your opinion and want to know what we're doing right, what we could do better, what areas you'd like to see us publish in, and any other words of wisdom you're willing to pass our way.

As an Associate Publisher for Sams Publishing, I welcome your comments. You can fax, e-mail, or write me directly to let me know what you did or didn't like about this book—as well as what we can do to make our books stronger.

Please note that I cannot help you with technical problems related to the topic of this book, and that due to the high volume of mail I receive, I might not be able to reply to every message.

When you write, please be sure to include this book's title and author as well as your name and phone or fax number. I will carefully review your comments and share them with the author and editors who worked on the book.

Fax: 317-581-4770

E-mail: feedback@samspublishing.com

Mail: Jeff Koch
Associate Publisher
Sams Publishing
201 West 103rd Street
Indianapolis, IN 46290 USA

INTRODUCTION

Over the years, the Internet has grown from a research tool to a worldwide communications medium. One of the applications that has grown up with the Internet is e-mail. What was once a convenient method of sending quick messages to mainframe terminal users is now a multimillion-dollar enterprise. As some of the recent e-mail viruses have shown us, many companies cannot do business when their e-mail systems are down.

Home users have also jumped on the e-mail bandwagon. Internet service providers (ISPs) are rapidly popping up all across the world to support the high demand for home e-mail accounts. It is not uncommon these days to find a home where every member of the family has an e-mail account (including the pets).

The challenge for computer professionals is to create systems that can keep up with the demand for e-mail services. Larger, quicker, more secure systems are constantly required to support the growing demand as well as abuse of the e-mail system. Unfortunately, many small and medium-sized businesses, organizations, and ISPs do not have the resources to keep up with the cost of bigger and better e-mail systems. Fortunately for them, alternatives exist.

The Open Source movement has provided many excellent products that can be used by smaller organizations to support e-mail services for little or no cost. Free operating systems such as Linux and FreeBSD can be used as the platform for e-mail servers to support hundreds or even thousands of users. In addition to the operating system, several open source e-mail server software packages are available.

The granddaddy of all free e-mail applications on the Internet is the Sendmail program, developed by the Sendmail Consortium (`http://www.sendmail.org`), and also supported by Sendmail, Inc. (`http://www.sendmail.com`). The Sendmail program has undergone much criticism in its lifetime. When first released, Sendmail contained many backdoors and security blunders. These "features" were understandable, though, because when Sendmail was first released the Internet was a controlled network of a few universities and military sites. As the Internet matured, so did Sendmail. All of the backdoors and security leaks were fixed. Unfortunately, in the process Sendmail became a complicated application that was difficult for the average network administrator to install and maintain.

To compensate for this, many alternative e-mail software packages have been developed. One such package is the Postfix e-mail server package. Wietse Venema developed it while working at the IBM Watson Research Center. It became one of IBM's first excursions into the open source world. Originally created as the Vmailer package and later released under the Postfix title, it quickly became a favorite of mail administrators.

This book takes the network administrator through the process of installing, configuring, and maintaining a Postfix e-mail server. Because many different options are available with Postfix, I added several sections to help the mail administrator configure different features of the Postfix server, such as using external databases along with Postfix.

The first few chapters are devoted to educating novice administrators in how e-mail servers function on the Internet. Often the mail administrator for a small organization has been thrown into the position with little support from the company, and little (if any) training. It is often best to ensure that every reader is using the same terminology and understands the same processes. If you are an advanced mail administrator just wanting to try Postfix, feel free to skip the first few chapters.

How This Book Is Organized

That said, the book is divided into the following sections:

Chapter 1, "E-Mail Services," describes the history of e-mail and defines most of the terms used throughout the book. It shows how Postfix fits into the "big picture" of a complete e-mail server system.

Chapter 2, "Postfix Services," describes the layout of the Postfix server software and how it interacts internally to receive and deliver mail messages.

Chapter 3, "Server Requirements for Postfix," describes the server functionality required to install and run the Postfix software. Because Postfix must run on a Unix operating system, this chapter describes the Linux operating system basics, along with the GNU utilities required to compile and install Postfix.

Chapter 4, "DNS and Postfix," describes the domain name system and how e-mail servers use it to determine where mail is delivered.

Chapter 5, "SMTP and Postfix," describes the Simple Mail Transfer Protocol and how Postfix uses it to deliver messages to remote hosts on the Internet.

The next set of chapters begins the discussion on the Postfix software specifics:

Chapter 6, "Installing Postfix," describes how to download, compile, and install the Postfix software.

Chapter 7, "The `master.cf` Configuration File," Chapter 8, "The `main.cf` Configuration File," and Chapter 9, "Postfix Lookup Tables," describe the format of the Postfix configuration files used to control the behavior of the Postfix server.

Chapter 10, "Using Postfix," describes a simple, no-frills configuration of a Postfix server, whereas Chapter 11, "Using Postfix as an ISP Mail Server," and Chapter 12, "Using Postfix as an Office Mail Server," describe more detailed configuration examples for real-world situations.

Chapter 13, "Postfix Server Administration," describes some basic duties that are required of the mail administrator and Chapter 14, "Migrating from Sendmail to Postfix," outlines some steps that should be followed by mail administrators deciding to migrate existing e-mail server software to Postfix.

Because many mail administrators may not be familiar with the new Maildir mailbox format, Chapter 15, "Using the Maildir Mailbox Format," describes in detail the differences and requirements of Maildir mailboxes.

The section concludes with Chapter 16, "Using MDA Programs with Postfix," which provides information to administrators wanting to use external local mail delivery programs with Postfix.

The last set of chapters describes more advanced features that administrators can use with Postfix once they become comfortable with the basic settings.

Chapter 17, "Using MySQL with Postfix," and Chapter 18, "Using OpenLDAP with Postfix," help the advanced administrator use external open source database packages with Postfix to maintain lookup tables.

Chapter 19, "Using Majordomo with Postfix," Chapter 20, "Using POP3 and IMAP with Postfix," and Chapter 21, "Using SqWebMail with Postfix," show advanced administrators ways to incorporate common external open source software packages with the Postfix server to provide advanced services to their customers.

The final two elements, Chapter 22, "Performance Tuning Postfix," and Chapter 23, "Common Postfix Problems," are intended to help Postfix administrators keep their Postfix servers operating as various types of problems arise.

A Few Disclaimers

This book uses many examples for setting up a Postfix mail server for a fictitious organization. At the time of this writing, none of the example domain names chosen are registered with the Internet Corporation for Assigned Names and Numbers (ICANN). If, by chance, they are registered at the time you read this, there is no association between this book and the owner(s) of the registered domain name(s).

Also, all IP addresses used in this book are for example only. Where possible, public IP addresses are used and should be replaced with the IP addresses that have been assigned to your particular organization. When that is not possible, fictitious IP addresses have been selected and are not associated with any existing IP networks. Please consult your Internet service provider before assigning any IP addresses to your network if it is connected to the Internet.

Conventions Used in This Book

Features in this book include the following:

NOTE

Notes give you comments and asides about the topic at hand, as well as full explanations of certain concepts.

CAUTION

Cautions warn you against making your life miserable and show you how to avoid the pitfalls in networking.

At the end of each chapter, you'll find a handy Summary that sums up the main themes explored in the chapter.

In addition, you'll find various typographic conventions throughout this book:

- *Italic* is used to set apart new terms.
- Commands and variables appear in text in a special `monospaced font`.
- Throughout code listings, I use a **`boldface monospaced type`** to emphasize certain lines.
- Placeholders in syntax descriptions appear in a *`monospaced italic`* typeface. This indicates that you will replace the placeholder with the actual filename, parameter, or other element that it represents.

PART I

Introduction to E-Mail Services and Postfix

CHAPTER 1

E-Mail Services

The use of e-mail has grown significantly over the past few years. What was once considered a luxury item now is almost a necessity, especially in the corporate environment. When personal e-mail use in the home became popular, an entire new industry of Internet service providers (ISPs) was created to provide e-mail services to home Internet users.

As e-mail usage grew, so did e-mail systems. What was once a simple mainframe application suddenly became a monster application that required dedicated hardware and high-speed Internet connectivity. Often large corporations purchased expensive e-mail software packages to support the e-mail environment within the corporation. In addition to complicated server software, many e-mail packages require complicated client software so users can access their mail on servers located on the corporate network.

The increasing demand and complexity of e-mail systems brought about advancements in e-mail protocols. The Simple Mail Transfer Protocol (SMTP) was designed to efficiently transfer messages between remote computers. The Post Office Protocol (POP) and Interactive Mail Access Protocol (IMAP) were designed so that users located remotely from their mail hosts could access messages in their mailboxes.

This chapter describes the history of e-mail services and functions, outlining the functional requirements that have grown as e-mail has matured. Also, this chapter describes the many protocols and software packages used to implement e-mail on the Internet.

Early Mainframe E-Mail Systems

In the beginning, e-mail systems weren't so complicated. The large mainframe environment initiated requirements for messaging systems. E-mail started out as a convenience for mainframe users to contact other users using a simple messaging system.

Mainframe Messages

Figure 1.1 shows an example of the simplest form of message communications. Two mainframe users, each one on a different terminal connected to a common mainframe, wanted to share information between them. The simple solution was to create a system that could send text messages from one user's terminal directly to the terminal display of another user.

The downside to this system was that it required both users to be logged in to the mainframe at the same time. A user could not send messages to users who were not logged in to the system. As mainframe messaging-systems became more popular, users wanted the ability to send messages to other users who weren't logged in to the mainframe. A system of storing messages for individual users was created. Figure 1.2 shows a message storage system.

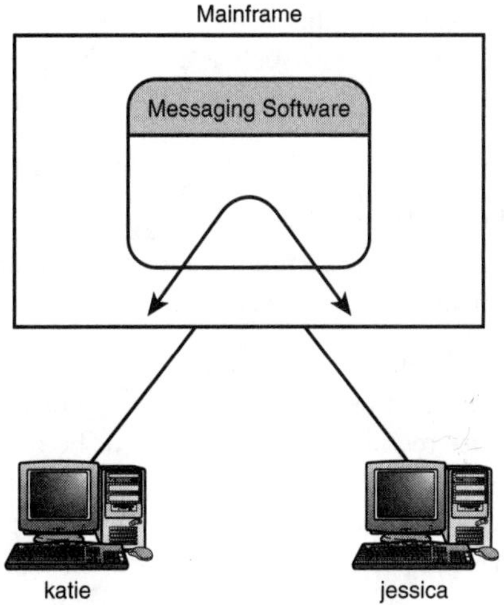

FIGURE 1.1

A mainframe messaging system.

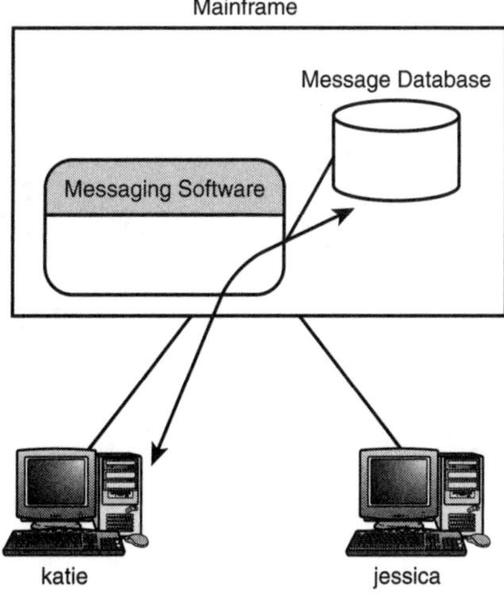

FIGURE 1.2

A mainframe message storage system.

The main advantage of the message storage system was that messages could be saved in a specific location and sent to users when they logged in to the mainframe. Of course, this made the mail software more complicated because it needed to devise a system of storing and recovering messages on the system.

One disadvantage to this system was that it transferred only text messages. No systems were capable of transferring binary data such as executable programs from one user to another.

Multi-Mainframe E-Mail Systems

As mainframes matured, so did their communications systems. Before long, it was possible to transfer data between mainframes using complicated proprietary protocols.

One thing that became a necessity in the multi-mainframe environment was a standard naming convention for hosts and users. As mainframes were added to the communications system, each computer required a unique name to be identified. If the user *katie* wanted to send a message to the user *jessica* on the same mainframe, the messaging software only needed to find jessica's mailbox on the system and place the message there. With multiple mainframes connected together, the messaging software was required to know not only the username, but also on which mainframe the user was located. The possibility also existed that several remote mainframes could contain the same username. This initiated the requirement of a two-part e-mail address. Both the username and mainframe name were required for the messaging system to be able to successfully deliver the message to the right user on the right mainframe. Figure 1.3 shows a diagram for a sample multi-mainframe e-mail system.

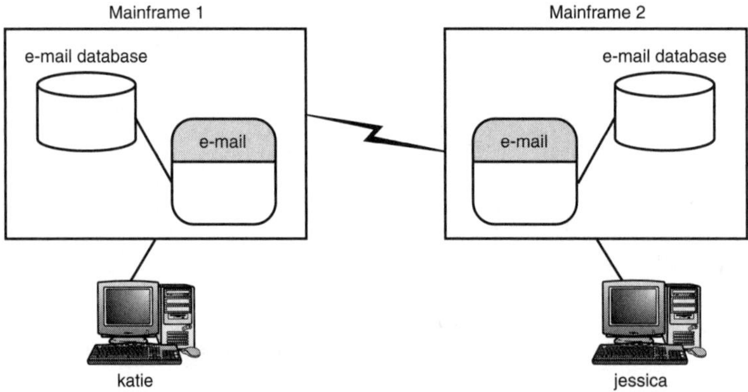

FIGURE 1.3

A multi-mainframe messaging system.

Unix E-Mail Systems

As Unix machines became more popular in replacing mainframes, Unix e-mail systems also became more popular. Unix changed the way e-mail software was approached. One of the main goals of Unix was to modularize software. Instead of having one gigantic program that handled all of the required pieces of a function, smaller programs were created, each program handling a smaller piece of the total functionality of the system. This philosophy was used for e-mail systems. Figure 1.4 shows how e-mail software was modularized in the Unix environment.

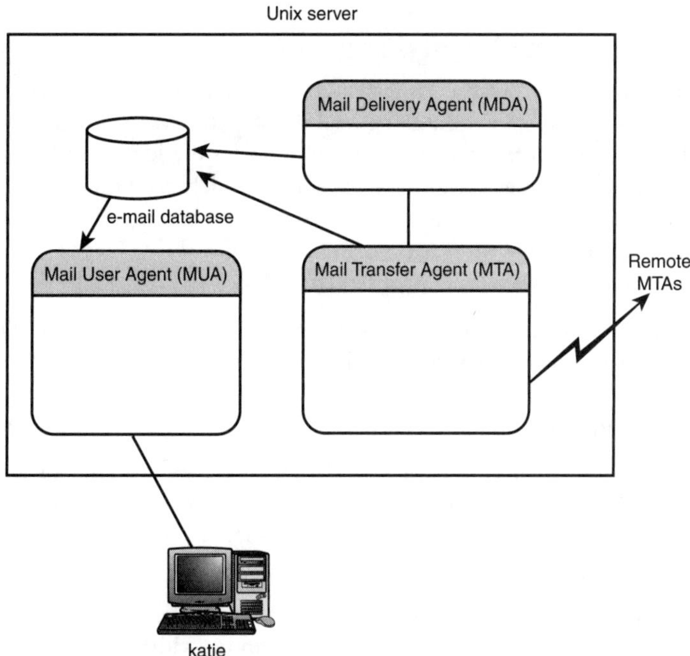

FIGURE 1.4

A Unix modular e-mail environment.

The main portion of the e-mail functionality was located in the Mail Delivery Agent (MDA) software. It was the MDA's responsibility to deliver a message to a user on the local Unix machine. If a message was intended for a user on a remote system, the MDA passed the message off to a Mail Transfer Agent (MTA) program.

The MTA's responsibility was to determine how to connect to the remote host and transfer the message there. Some programs combined the functionality of two agents into one program. Often the MDA and MTA are treated as a single module: Messages for local users are passed to the MDA section, and messages for remote users are passed to the MTA section of the same program.

Another piece of the Unix e-mail puzzle is the Mail User Agent (MUA). The MUA software is responsible for allowing users on remote network clients to read their mailbox messages. With the availability of high-powered network clients, many MUA programs have incorporated fancy graphical front-end designs to help the client read and organize mail messages.

The following sections describe in more detail the different e-mail agents that were implemented in Unix systems.

Unix Mail Transfer Agent Programs

The Mail Transfer Agent software is responsible for transferring both incoming and outgoing mail messages. For each outgoing mail message, the MTA determines the destination of the recipient addresses. If the destination host is the local machine, all the MTA must do is pass the message off to the local MDA for delivery. However, if the destination host is a remote mail server, the MTA must establish a communication method to transfer the message to the remote host. For incoming messages, the MTA must be able to accept connection requests from remote mail servers and receive messages for local users.

The Unix environment has many different types of mail MTA programs. The following sections describe some of the more popular MTAs in use today.

The Sendmail Program

Sendmail is one of the most popular Unix MTAs available. Eric Allman originally wrote the Sendmail suite. The Sendmail Consortium (`http://www.sendmail.org`) currently maintains the source code for it. Eric has moved on to Sendmail, Inc., which provides commercial versions of Sendmail and provides support to the Sendmail Consortium.

Sendmail has gained popularity mainly because it is extremely versatile. Many of the built-in features of Sendmail have become synonymous with e-mail systems: virtual domains, message forwarding, user aliases, mailing lists, and masquerading. Newer e-mail systems (including Postfix) are compared against the functionality of Sendmail. Postfix does support all of these Sendmail functions, which are covered in depth in later chapters.

Sendmail can be used in many different types of e-mail configurations: large corporate Internet e-mail servers, small corporate servers that dial into ISPs, and even standalone workstations that forward mail through a mail hub. Simply changing a few lines in Sendmail's configuration file can change its characteristics and behavior.

Besides being able to change its server characteristics, Sendmail can also parse and handle mail messages according to predefined rule sets. The mail administrator will often want to filter messages depending on particular local site requirements. To do this, that person just needs to add a few new rules to the Sendmail configuration file.

Unfortunately, with versatility comes complexity. Sendmail's large configuration file often becomes overwhelming for beginning mail administrators to handle. Many books have been written to assist the mail administrator in determining the proper configuration file settings for a particular e-mail server application.

The Postfix Program

This book focuses on the Postfix MTA. Wietse Venema wrote Postfix as a complete MTA package. This made Postfix capable of replacing Sendmail (or any other Unix MTA) currently used on any given Unix server.

The main difference between Postfix and Sendmail is Postfix's modularity. Just as the Unix system broke up e-mail functionality between modules, Postfix extends that practice to the MTA program. Postfix uses several different programs to implement the MTA functionality. This allows each modular program to be smaller and quicker than one large monolithic program would be.

Another feature that goes with modularity is security. Postfix requires a separate userid to be added to the mail server. Each module runs under this userid. If an intruder compromises a Postfix module, he most likely will still not be able to break out of the module and gain control of the mail server.

One of the nicest features of Postfix is its simplicity. Instead of one large compiled configuration file, Postfix uses multiple files that use plaintext parameter and value names to define functionality. Most of the parameters used in Postfix default to common-sense values that allow the mail administrator to configure a complete mail server with a minimal amount of effort.

The qmail Program

Another MTA program intended for Unix environments, qmail was written and is maintained by Dan Bernstein (`http://www.qmail.org`). qmail is another complete replacement for Sendmail.

Similar to Postfix, qmail was written as a set of modular programs and uses several different programs to implement the different MTA functions.

qmail requires several different userids to be added to the mail server. Each program module runs under a different userid. If an intruder compromises one module, it most likely will not affect the other modules. The security features of qmail are often touted as its best trait.

Still another feature of qmail is its reliability. As each message enters the qmail system, it is placed in a mail queue. qmail uses a system of mail subdirectories and message states to ensure that each message stored in the message queue is not lost. As an added feature, qmail also can use a specialized user mailbox system that decreases the chance of user messages getting corrupted or lost in the message mailbox.

The smail Program

The smail program is another popular MTA available for the Unix platform. It is maintained by the GNU Project (`http://www.gnu.org`). The GNU Project is a major free software contributor to the Linux and FreeBSD environments and is discussed in more detail in Chapter 3, "Server Requirements for Postfix."

The smail program provides many of the same features as Sendmail. Its claim to fame is that it is much easier to configure than Sendmail. A standard smail configuration file requires fewer than 20 lines of configuration code, which is considerably fewer than Sendmail requires.

One of the nice features of smail is its capability to forward mail messages without using mail queues. The Sendmail, Postfix, and qmail programs place all messages in a queue file to queue them for delivery. For low-volume mail servers, queuing presents an unnecessary delay. The smail program attempts to deliver messages immediately without placing them in a mail queue. Although this works great for low-volume mail servers, unfortunately this method can get bogged down on high-volume mail servers. To compensate, you can also configure the smail program to use mail queues for handling larger volumes of mail.

The exim Program

The University of Cambridge maintains the exim program (`http://www.exim.org`). exim has recently gained popularity because it can be easily configured to restrict hackers and spammers. *Hackers* are people who attempt to break into sites using well-known security holes in software. *Spammers* are people who send out mass quantities of (usually) unwanted e-mails, mostly for advertisement purposes.

The exim program has several configuration files that can contain addresses of known hackers and spammers to restrict any messages from those sites to the mail server. After a hacker or spammer has been identified, his address can be added to the configuration files to prevent any more messages from that address from being received.

Unix Mail User Agent Programs

The Unix e-mail model uses a local mailbox for each user to hold messages for that user. Programs called Mail User Agents (MUAs) became available that could interface with the mailbox format.

The MUAs did not receive messages from remote computers; they only displayed messages that were already placed in the user's mailbox. Throughout the years, many different MUAs have been available for the Unix platform. The following sections describe some of the more popular MUA programs available in Unix.

The `mail` Program

The simplest MUA program is `mail`, which allows users to access their mailboxes to read stored messages, as well as send messages to other mail users, both on the local mail system and on remote mail servers. Listing 1.1 shows a sample `mail` session.

LISTING 1.1 Sample `mail` Program Session

```
$ mail
Mail version 8.1 6/6/93.  Type ? for help.
"/var/spool/mail/rich": 4 messages 4 new
>N  1 barbara@shadrach.isp  Thu Feb 10 18:47 12/417 "This is the first tes"
 N  2 katie@shadrach.isp1.  Thu Feb 10 18:57 12/415 "Second test message"
 N  3 jessica@shadrach.isp  Thu Feb 10 19:23 12/413 "Third test message"
 N  4 mike@shadrach.ispnet  Thu Feb 10 19:42 12/423 "Fourth and final test"
& 1
Message 1:
From barbara@shadrach.isp1.net Thu Feb 10 18:47:05 2000
Date: 10 Feb 2000 23:47:05 -0000
From: barbara@shadrach.isp1.net
To: rich@shadrach.isp1.net
Subject: This is the first test message

Hi, This is a test message

& d
& 2
Message 2:
From katie@shadrach.isp1.net Thu Feb 10 18:57:32 2000
Date: 10 Feb 2000 23:57:32 -0000
From: katie@shadrach.isp1.net
To: rich@shadrach.isp1.net
Subject: Second test message

Hi, this is the second test message

& q
Saved 3 messages in mbox
```

The first line shows the `mail` program being executed with no command-line options. By default, this allows the user to check the messages in his mailbox. After entering the `mail` command, a summary of all of the messages in the user's mailbox is displayed. The location of the users' mailboxes depends on the particular flavor of Unix the mail server is using. On FreeBSD servers, the default mailbox directory location is `/var/mail`, whereas on Linux they are located at `/var/spool/mail`.

Each user has a separate file that contains all of her messages. The filename is usually the system username of the user and is located in the system mailbox directory. Thus, all messages for username *rich* are stored in the file `/var/spool/mail/rich` on a Linux system. As new messages are received for the user, they are appended to the end of the file.

In the `mail` program listing, you can see how summary information for each message is displayed on a single line. This information includes the message number, the sender of the message, the date of the message, and the `Subject:` header of the message. After the summary information, the `mail` program generates an interactive command-line prompt. The user must enter a command to tell the `mail` program how to proceed. By typing a message number, the text of that message is displayed, as shown. Following the message, the next command line shows the user command used to delete a message. By entering the `d` command, the current message number is deleted from the mailbox. At the end of the `mail` session, the user can type the `q` command to exit the `mail` program. Any undeleted messages are moved from the user's mailbox to a special file in the user's home directory. The user can later retrieve messages in this file by using the `-f` option on the `mail` program command line.

The `pine` Program

As advances were made to the Unix environment, MUA programs became fancier. One of the first attempts at graphics on Unix systems was the ncurses graphics library. Using ncurses, a program could manipulate the location of a cursor on the terminal screen and place characters almost anywhere on the terminal.

One MUA program that takes advantage of the ncurses library is the `pine` program. When `pine` is started, it paints a user-friendly menu on the user's terminal screen, as shown in Figure 1.5.

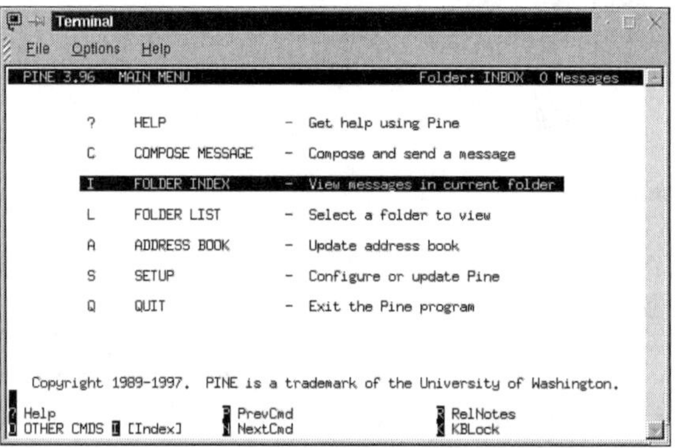

FIGURE 1.5

The `pine` program main menu screen.

The `pine` program assigns any messages in the user's mailbox to a special folder labeled `INBOX`. by default, all new messages appear in the `INBOX`. The user can create separate folders to hold mail that has already been read, thus making message storage and retrieval easier. As you can see from Figure 1.5, `pine` also includes an address book feature, allowing the user to save important e-mail addresses in a single location.

X Window MUA Programs

Almost all Unix systems support the graphical X Window environment. Linux uses the Xfree86 software to run X Window programs on either the system console or a remote X terminal on the network. Many e-mail MUA programs utilize the X Window System to display message information. The `kmail` MUA program can read and send messages from an X Window system using the KDE desktop manager. Figure 1.6 shows a sample `kmail` session screen.

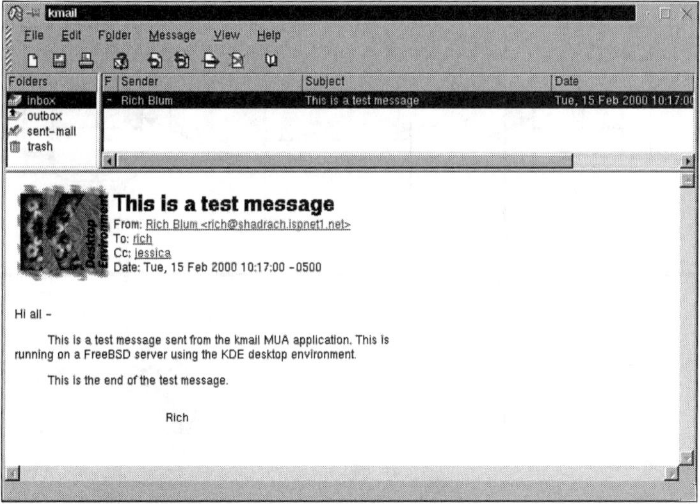

FIGURE 1.6

The `kmail` MUA program main screen.

LAN-Based E-Mail Systems

In the late 1980s, the computer world dramatically changed again with the invention of the personal computer. PCs started popping up in corporations, replacing the dumb terminals that were used to communicate with mainframes and mini-computers.

Many organizations utilize some type of LAN-based network server that allows network workstations to share disk space on the network fileserver. This created a new type of e-mail server that utilized the shared network disk space.

Modern e-mail solutions, such as Microsoft Exchange, Novell GroupWise, and IBM Lotus Notes, utilize programs that access a common disk area that contains the user mailboxes. The mailboxes are often contained within a single database. To access the database, the MUA programs running on the workstations must be able to read and parse the mailbox database. This method almost always uses a proprietary protocol to access the mailboxes in the database.

MTAs often become quite complicated in this kind of environment. Because the e-mail systems use special databases, the method of sending messages to remote systems depends on what the remote system is. If the remote system uses the same type of e-mail system as the sending system, you can use the same proprietary protocol to transfer the message. If the remote system uses a different type of e-mail system, the MTA must be able to convert the message to a standard format and use a standard e-mail protocol (discussed in the following section) to send the message. Figure 1.7 shows an example of a proprietary e-mail system on an office network.

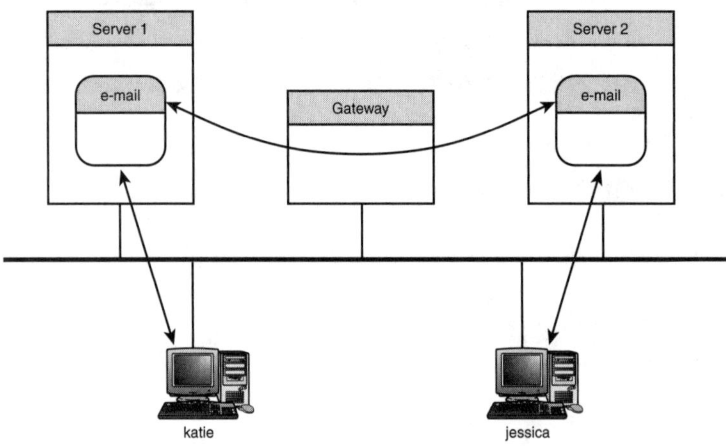

FIGURE 1.7

A LAN-based proprietary e-mail system.

Often with LAN-based e-mail systems, dedicated workstations are required to route messages between destinations. This increases the chance of failure, because there is now additional hardware and software besides the e-mail server involved in the e-mail transfer.

Both Microsoft Exchange and Novell GroupWise require separate software (and often servers) to route mail messages to other types of mail servers. This extra level of complexity lends itself to mail delivery failures and extra administration work.

Another possible problem with proprietary e-mail systems is the mail database. Because all messages are stored in one database, the database increases in proportion to the amount of messages saved on the system. It is not uncommon to see databases over 1GB in size for a small organization. Often in this situation, the database can become corrupt and a database recovery routine must be run. If the routine is unsuccessful, all of the messages in the database are lost.

Microsoft Exchange, Novell GroupWise, and IBM Lotus Notes all use special database utilities for managing the user mail database. To run the database utility, the mail server must be shut down and unavailable to receive new messages. This can create other complications for the mail administrator.

Unix-based systems keep individual mailboxes for each user. If one mailbox becomes corrupt, only one user loses messages. The rest of the users are unaffected. As described earlier, Postfix and qmail even take this one step further by creating user mailbox directories, with each message being a separate file in the directory. Thus, one bad message would not corrupt the entire mailbox.

Proprietary LAN-based e-mail systems are very popular, but they also they tend to be very expensive. As the mail administrator, you should weigh all of the pros and cons involved with purchasing a proprietary e-mail system. Often you can attain the same functionality using a Unix system such as Linux or FreeBSD with open source programs.

E-Mail Protocols

Many protocols have been developed to allow messages to be transferred between mail servers and to allow network clients to read their messages from the mail server. This section describes the protocols that are detailed in this book.

Mail Transfer Agent Protocols

MTAs must be able to transfer messages to remote mail servers. To do this, one MTA package must be able to communicate with another MTA package to move not only the mail message but also the necessary message header information needed to identify the remote user. MTA programs use the following protocols to transfer messages and information between remote hosts.

SMTP

The Simple Mail Transfer Protocol (SMTP) was developed as the primary method to transfer messages across the Internet between MTA servers. Any host connected to the Internet can use SMTP to send a mail message to any other host.

SMTP uses simple commands to establish a connection and to transfer information and data between hosts (thus the word *simple* in its name). Commands consist of a single word with additional information following the command, such as the SMTP command

```
MAIL FROM: <rich@shadrach.ispnet1.net>
```

which identifies to the remote mail server who originated the message. Each command line is transmitted across the Internet in plain ASCII text. After each command, the remote host must send a reply code to the originating host to identify whether the command was successful. Figure 1.8 demonstrates a sample SMTP connection between two hosts.

It is the responsibility of the remote host to interpret the received message and to decide whether to forward it to the appropriate local mailbox. Chapter 5, "SMTP and Postfix," describes the full SMTP protocol.

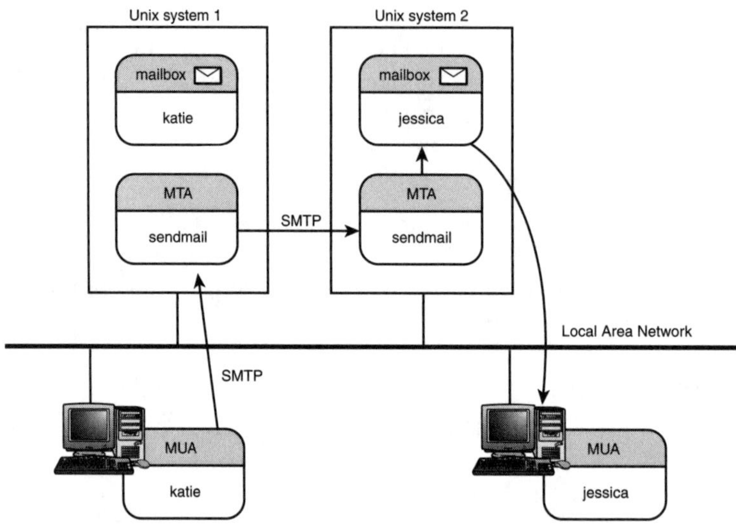

FIGURE 1.8

A sample SMTP connection between two hosts.

To identify remote hosts, SMTP uses the *Domain Name System (DNS)*. DNS is a distributed database on the Internet that (among other things) allows hosts to be uniquely identified by a name as well as an IP address. Each area within the Internet has a DNS server that is responsible for maintaining the DNS database for the area, or zone. Any Internet hosts within that zone that use a registered DNS name have an entry in the database on the DNS server. The entry maps the host's IP address to its official DNS name. Chapter 4, "DNS and Postfix," describes how DNS works and how DNS servers are implemented for zones.

ESMTP

As SMTP became more popular, some shortcomings were identified in the original protocol. Rather than create a new protocol, developers decided to extend the basic SMTP commands with new commands. The new protocol was named the *Extended Simple Mail Transfer Protocol (ESMTP)*. The new functionality of ESMTP has proven more robust and more than capable of supporting the mail transfer environment between MTA hosts for the past several years.

One important function that ESMTP implemented was the capability for MTA hosts to "reverse" the SMTP connection. SMTP was designed to allow only "one-way" communications between MTAs. One local MTA would connect to a remote MTA, transfer any queued mail messages to the remote MTA, and then disconnect. If the remote MTA had any queued messages destined for the originating MTA, it could not transfer them during the SMTP session.

To solve this problem, ESMTP created a new command that allowed an MTA to request a reverse connection. This asked the remote MTA to establish a new SMTP connection to the originating MTA and transfer any queued messages. By establishing a new connection, the remote MTA had a better chance of connecting to the real destination instead of a potential fake. The ESMTP commands are also discussed in more detail in Chapter 5.

LMTP

Another limitation of SMTP that has been addressed is the advent of multiple message recipients. SMTP allows for a single message to be forwarded to multiple recipients on the same host. However, the receiving host sends only one return code back to the SMTP client. The SMTP client has no idea if all of the recipients successfully received the message. It's not until the e-mail user receives a bounce message that he knows something didn't work right.

The *Local Mail Transport Protocol (LMTP)* attempts to remedy this situation by providing a separate return code for each message recipient. If the LMTP server reports any temporary delivery failures for individual recipients, the LMTP client can inform the message queue manager to requeue the message for delivery at a later time.

While LMTP was originally designed for internal mail delivery systems (thus the word *local*), it has been adapted for remote network mail delivery. The Postfix package includes an LMTP server and client implementation that can be used to send messages to other Postfix servers using LMTP. LMTP is described in more detail in Chapter 5.

Mail User Agent Protocols

The MUA protocols allow users to read messages from their mailboxes. On a single-user Unix system, this is not usually a problem: the user is logged in to the system from the console. However, in a multi-user environment, multiple users will need to access their mailboxes to read their messages at the same time. This would be practically impossible to do from a single console screen.

To accommodate this scenario, protocols have been developed to allow remote network users to log in and read messages in their mailboxes on the network mail server. Each user can connect to her mailbox on the mail server through an MUA that resides on her workstation. The MUA uses special protocols to connect to the mail server and manipulate messages in the mailbox. The following sections describe the two most popular MUAs in current use.

The Post Office Protocol

The simplest MUA is the *Post Office Protocol (POP)*. The current version of POP is version 3, thus the term POP3. MUA programs on the workstation use POP3 to access and read messages in the user's mailbox. Figure 1.9 shows an example of a workstation using POP3 to read mail messages.

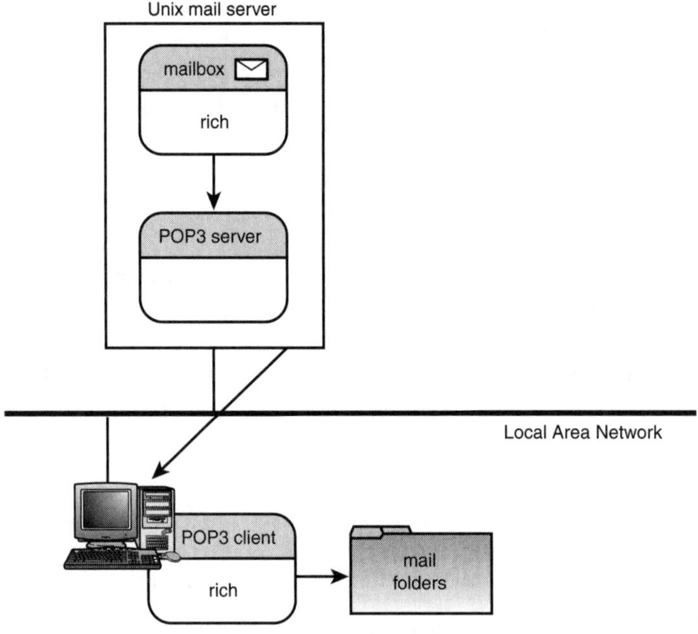

FIGURE 1.9

A sample POP3 connection.

When using POP3, all of the messages for the user are transferred from the user's remote mailbox on the server and stored on the local workstation. Usually, when using POP3, the workstation MUA deletes messages from the server mailbox after initial transfer, thus freeing up space on the mail server.

The Interactive Mail Access Protocol

Another commonly used MUA is the *Interactive Mail Access Protocol (IMAP)*. IMAP is currently at version 4, revision 1, thus the term IMAP4rev1 is often used. MUAs on workstations can use IMAP to remotely manipulate e-mail messages in folders that reside on the mail server. Figure 1.10 shows an example of a workstation using IMAP.

In an IMAP connection, all of the user's mail messages reside on the mail server. Messages are downloaded only for the purpose of displaying the message on the workstation screen. They are not stored on the local workstation. This protocol is useful if the user must access his mailbox from several different computers.

Using POP3, each time the user accesses his mailbox the current messages are downloaded to the workstation used for the access. This could easily distribute messages across several different computers. IMAP prevents this situation by leaving all of the messages on the mail server, no matter which workstation is used to display the messages. Although this is more convenient for the user, it makes the job of the mail administrator more difficult. In this scenario, you must carefully watch disk space on the mail server because it can quickly fill up with undeleted messages.

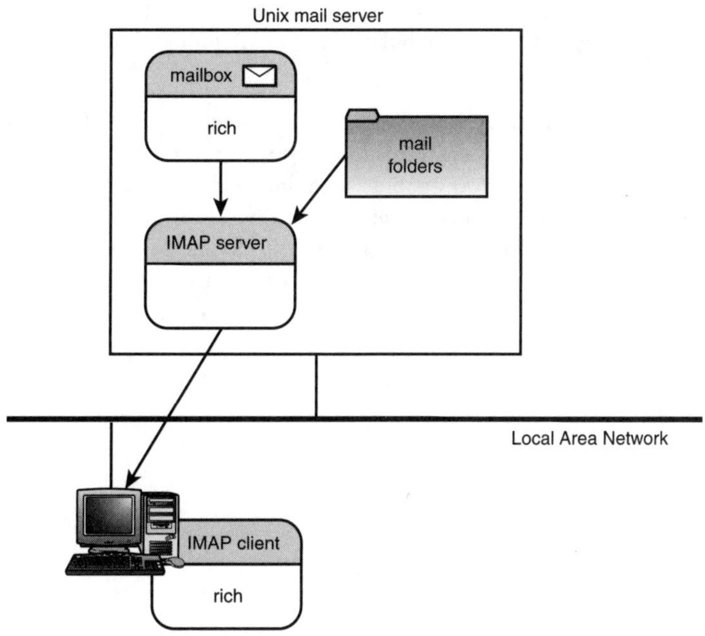

FIGURE 1.10

A sample IMAP connection.

Summary

This chapter discussed the history and functionality of e-mail systems. E-mail systems started out as nothing more than simple messaging systems that allowed users of a mainframe to exchange quick messages between terminals. As mainframes matured, screen messaging became e-mail messaging, and developed increased functionality. E-mail allowed users to send messages to other local users who weren't currently logged in to the system, storing the messages in an area where the other users could retrieve the messages when they logged in. Also, as mainframe networks became mature and allowed inter-mainframe communications, e-mail systems allowed users to send mail messages to users on remote mainframes.

The Unix operating system changed the way e-mail systems operated. Instead of one large e-mail program, the e-mail software was divided into smaller pieces, each piece performing an individual function of the e-mail process. Mail Transfer Agents (MTAs) were used to deliver mail messages to users, both locally and remotely. To deliver messages to remote users, one MTA was required to communicate with another MTA program. Often this communication took place across a network, such as the Internet. To accomplish this communication, protocols were developed that allowed the two MTAs to successfully pass messages and message information between them. The Simple Mail Transfer Protocol (SMTP) became the most popular of the MTA protocols due to its versatility and simplicity.

The other piece of software used in the Unix environment is the Mail User Agent (MUA) program. MUAs allow users to read messages from their mailboxes. With the advent of network-connected workstations came the need for MUAs that ran on remote clients. These MUAs needed protocols that allowed them to read the user mailboxes on the remote mail server. The Post Office Protocol (POP3) and Interactive Mail Access Protocol (IMAP) were developed to allow remote MUAs to access messages on the mail server.

CHAPTER 2

Postfix Services

The Postfix software package is quickly becoming one of the more popular e-mail packages available for Unix systems. Postfix was developed by Wietse Venema in the late 1990s to provide an alternative Mail Transfer Agent (MTA) for standard Unix servers.

The Postfix software can turn a Linux system into a fully functional e-mail server.

For general information about Postfix you can reach the Postfix Web site at `http://www.postfix.org`. There, you can also subscribe to several different mail lists. By subscribing to a Postfix mail list you can keep up-to-date on the latest information about Postfix software improvements.

The MTA package manages messages that come into or leave the mail server. Postfix accomplishes this message tracking by using several different modular programs and a system of mail queue directories. Each program processes messages through the various message queues until they are delivered to their final destination. If at any time the mail server crashes during a message transfer, Postfix can determine which queue the message was last successfully placed in and attempt to continue the message processing.

Postfix was also designed to have higher security, higher reliability, and higher performance than other MTA packages. This kind of built-in quality makes it quite an attractive alternative for e-mail system administrators looking to improve performance.

This chapter details the features and components that make up the Postfix software package. Because Postfix was designed to be a complete Unix MTA mail system, many other software pieces must interact for Postfix to successfully transfer and deliver mail messages. I also explain these pieces.

The Role of Postfix on a Unix Mail Server

The Postfix software package is just one piece of the larger Unix mail server picture. It is best to take a couple of steps back to view the entire e-mail server system before looking at the individual pieces of Postfix.

Figure 2.1 shows a block diagram of how Postfix interacts with other system software packages necessary to transport mail on a Unix mail system.

As shown in Figure 2.1, several pieces of software help Postfix transfer e-mail on the server. To be able to send and receive messages from remote hosts, the Unix server must provide a method to communicate with remote mail hosts. This communication is most often done using either the TCP/IP or UUCP protocols. While the UUCP process uses dial-up modems, the TCP/IP protocol can be used directly across a Local Area Network (LAN) connection, as well as using a dial-up modem connection utilizing the Point-to-Point Protocol (PPP).

Also, once users receive messages from remote hosts, they must have a method to read the messages stored in their mailboxes. The two most common methods are the Post Office Protocol (POP3) and Interactive Mail Access Protocol (IMAP). The following sections describe the pieces that must interact to complete the mail server process.

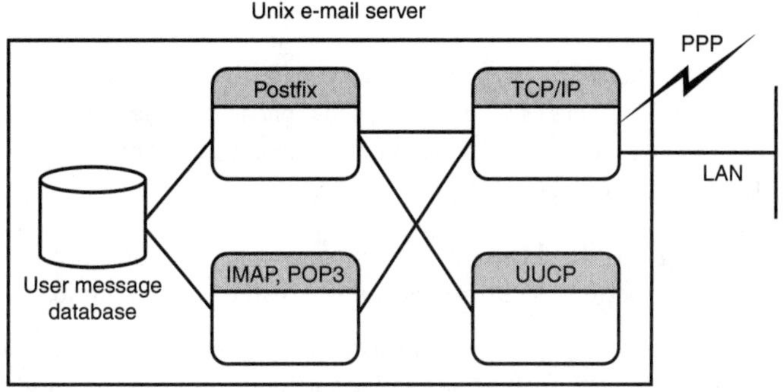

FIGURE 2.1

Block diagram of Postfix on a Unix system.

The TCP/IP Software

For e-mail systems to work, they must be able to talk with one another. For more than two decades now, the TCP/IP protocol has been the protocol of choice for communications between remote computers. All Unix systems support the TCP/IP protocol from both a client and a server perspective. The TCP/IP software is installed by default on most Linux distributions. One easy way to determine whether TCP/IP is configured on your Linux system is to use the `ifconfig` program.

The `ifconfig` program displays and sets TCP/IP address information on the network interfaces of the Linux system. Any user can display the TCP/IP information using `ifconfig`, but only the `root` user can modify the values.

Listing 2.1 shows a sample `ifconfig` output.

LISTING 2.1 Sample `ifconfig` Command Output

```
[nicholas@shadrach nicholas]$ /sbin/ifconfig
eth0      Link encap:Ethernet  HWaddr 00:00:C0:54:62:B0
          inet addr:192.168.1.10  Bcast:192.168.1.255  Mask:255.255.255.0
          UP BROADCAST RUNNING MULTICAST  MTU:1500  Metric:1
          RX packets:11948902 errors:0 dropped:0 overruns:0 frame:0
          TX packets:781365 errors:0 dropped:0 overruns:0 carrier:0
          collisions:239237 txqueuelen:100
          Interrupt:9 Base address:0x310 Memory:e0000-e4000

lo        Link encap:Local Loopback
          inet addr:127.0.0.1  Mask:255.0.0.0
```

LISTING 2.1 Continued

```
UP LOOPBACK RUNNING  MTU:3924  Metric:1
RX packets:817 errors:0 dropped:0 overruns:0 frame:0
TX packets:817 errors:0 dropped:0 overruns:0 carrier:0
collisions:0 txqueuelen:0
```

As shown in Listing 2.1, this Linux system contains two network interfaces. The `eth0` interface is the Ethernet network interface and is assigned an IP address of 192.168.1.10.

The `lo` interface is a special "logical" interface called a *loopback* that is available on Unix systems. A loopback device enables programs on the system to communicate with each other using the TCP/IP protocol. The IP address for a loopback interface is always 127.0.0.1.

The PPP Software

If your Linux system does not have an Ethernet interface that connects directly to the Internet, you will need another method of communication. The cheapest method of host communication used today is dial-up modems. Many home users use dial-up modems to communicate with the remote mail server. Many small businesses also use dial-up modems to communicate efficiently with remote Internet service providers (ISPs).

The most efficient method of dial-up communications using modems is to establish a TCP/IP connection with the remote ISP mail host. PPP is used to transfer TCP/IP packets from the client computer to the ISP host computer. Once the PPP session is established, TCP/IP packets can be transferred between the hosts just as if they were both connected with a LAN (only much slower).

Postfix uses the Simple Mail Transfer Protocol (SMTP) to transfer mail messages across the PPP connection to the remote mail host. SMTP uses the TCP/IP connection established with the PPP connection to transfer mail messages to the mail server. Chapter 5, "SMTP and Postfix," describes SMTP in more detail.

The UUCP Software

In addition to TCP/IP, you can use the older Unix-to-Unix CoPy protocol (UUCP) to establish a communications link with a remote ISP computer. As shown in Figure 2.1, you can use either TCP/IP or UUCP to establish communication with a remote mail server. In fact, you can configure and use both protocols at the same time. Postfix will process messages that have been received from either method. Although many network administrators consider UUCP a "dead" protocol, offices that do not want to have IP connectivity to the Internet choose to transfer mail using the UUCP protocol, often for security reasons.

Configuring the mail server to support UUCP connectivity to remote hosts is not a difficult task. Chapter 11, "Using Postfix as an ISP Mail Server," describes the steps necessary to create a mail server for UUCP clients.

The MUA Server Software

Once Postfix has received the mail messages and placed them in the user mailboxes, the users must be able to read them. For the user to be able to read his messages, he must use a Mail User Agent (MUA) program. If users are remotely located from the e-mail server (as is most often the case), the server must utilize MUA server software to allow remote clients to connect to the mail server and retrieve their mail messages from their mailboxes. These customers require an MUA client program to connect to the remote mail server and retrieve their messages. Most of these types of MUAs utilize user-friendly GUI application programs to assist them in connecting to the ISP and downloading new mail messages.

The POP3 and IMAP protocols allow remote users to read messages stored in their mailboxes on the mail server, as well as forward new messages to remote Internet users via the mail server. The POP3 and IMAP protocols come in several different Unix implementations.

Several MUA server software packages are currently available for the Unix environment, including the popular (and free) `pop3d` and `imapd` programs from the University of Washington. These programs can support several different types of authentication methods.

Chapter 20, "Using POP3 and IMAP with Postfix," details the use of POP3 and IMAP on a mail server.

The Postfix Block Diagram

The Postfix system itself consists of several mail queue directories and executable programs, all interacting with each other to provide mail service. Figure 2.2 shows a block diagram of the core Postfix parts.

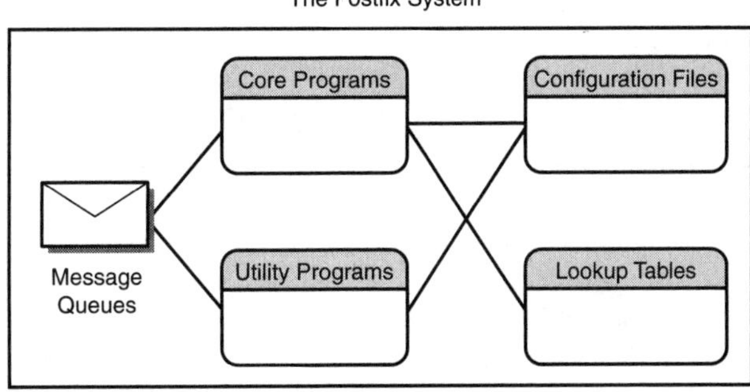

FIGURE 2.2

Block diagram of Postfix.

Each piece of the Postfix block diagram provides a different function for the whole e-mail process. The following sections describe the different pieces of the Postfix block diagram in more detail.

Postfix Core Programs

The Postfix package uses a `master` program that runs as a background process at all times. The `master` program allows Postfix to spawn programs that scan the mail queues for new messages and send them to the proper destinations.

You can configure the core programs to remain running for set times after they are utilized. This allows for the `master` program to reuse a running helper program if necessary, saving processing time. After a set time limit, the helper program quietly stops itself.

Listing 2.2 shows the typical Postfix processes that you should see running on a normal Unix system.

LISTING 2.2 Postfix Background Programs

```
[rich@shadrach ]$ ps ax
  232 con- I+  0:00.34 /usr/sbin/postfix/master
  236 con- I+  0:00.07 qmgr
  237 con- I+  0:00.05 pickup
```

These processes run continually in the background to control mail delivery on the Postfix system. The `master` program controls the overall operation of Postfix and is responsible for starting other Postfix processes as needed. The `qmgr` and `pickup` programs are configured to remain as background processes longer than other core programs. The `pickup` program determines when messages are available to be routed by the Postfix system. The `qmgr` program is responsible for the central message routing system for Postfix.

Table 2.1 shows other core programs in addition to `qmgr` and `pickup` that Postfix uses to transfer mail messages.

TABLE 2.1 Core Postfix Mail Processing Programs

Program	*Description*
`bounce`	Posts a log in the `bounce` message queue for bounced messages and returns the bounced message to the sender. Can also defer mail directed to an unavailable remote host.
`cleanup`	Processes incoming mail headers and places messages in the `incoming` queue.
`error`	Processes message delivery requests from `qmgr`, forcing messages to bounce.
`local`	Delivers messages destined for local users.
`pickup`	Waits for messages in the `maildrop` queue and sends them to the cleanup program to begin processing.
`pipe`	Forwards messages from the queue manager program to external programs.

TABLE 2.1 Continued

Program	*Description*
`postdrop`	Moves an incoming message to the `maildrop` queue when that queue is not writable by normal users.
`qmgr`	Processes messages in the `incoming` queue, determining where and how they should be delivered, and spawns programs to deliver them.
`showq`	Reports Postfix mail queue status.
`smtp`	SMTP client that forwards messages to external mail hosts using the SMTP protocol.
`smtpd`	SMTP server that receives messages from external mail hosts using the SMTP protocol.
`trivial-rewrite`	Receives messages from `cleanup` to ensure header addresses are in a standard format for the `qmgr` program, and used by the `qmgr` program to resolve remote host addresses.

You can control the operation of these core Postfix programs with the `master.cf` configuration file. Each program is listed on a separate line along with its current settings. Listing 2.3 shows a sample `master.cf` file with default settings.

LISTING 2.3 Sample `master.cf` Configuration File

```
# ==========================================================================
# service type  private unpriv  chroot  wakeup  maxproc command + args
#             (yes)   (yes)   (yes)   (never) (50)
# ==========================================================================
smtp      inet  n       -       n       -       -       smtpd
pickup    fifo  n       n       n       60      1       pickup
cleanup   unix  -       -       n       -       0       cleanup
qmgr      fifo  n       -       n       300     1       qmgr
rewrite   unix  -       -       n       -       -       trivial-rewrite
bounce    unix  -       -       n       -       0       bounce
defer     unix  -       -       n       -       0       bounce
smtp      unix  -       -       n       -       -       smtp
showq     unix  n       -       n       -       -       showq
error     unix  -       -       n       -       -       error
local     unix  -       n       n       -       -       local
```

NOTE

The complete `master.cf` configuration file format is described in Chapter 7, "The `master.cf` Configuration File."

Postfix Message Queues

Unlike some other MTA packages, Postfix uses several different queues for managing e-mail messages as they are processed.

Each message queue contains messages in a different message state in the Postfix system. Table 2.2 lists the message queues that are used by Postfix.

TABLE 2.2 Postfix Message Queues

Queue	*Description*
`maildrop`	New messages waiting to be processed, received from local users
`incoming`	New messages waiting to be processed, received from remote hosts, as well as processed messages from local users
`active`	Messages that are ready to be delivered by Postfix
`deferred`	Messages that have failed on an initial delivery attempt and are waiting for another attempt
`mail`	Delivered messages stored for local users to read

If the Postfix system is shut down at any time, messages remain in the last queue in which they were placed. When Postfix is restarted, it automatically begins processing messages from the queues.

NOTE

Future production releases of Postfix are expected to contain an additional message queue called the `flush` queue. This queue is described in more detail later in the section "Postfix: Future Features and Releases."

Postfix Utility Programs

In addition to the Postfix core programs, both Postfix processes and local Postfix users use several utilities to help manipulate and transfer messages.

Table 2.3 shows the standard Postfix utilities.

TABLE 2.3 Postfix Utility Programs

Program	*Description*
`mailq`	Checks the Postfix mail queues for messages and displays the results
`postalias`	Creates, updates, or queries the Postfix alias database
`postcat`	Displays the contents of Postfix queue files
`postconf`	Displays and modifies parameter entries in the `main.cf` configuration file
`postfix`	Controls starting, stopping, and reloading the Postfix system

TABLE 2.3 Continued

Program	*Description*
`postkick`	Sends command requests to running Postfix services
`postlock`	Locks specified Postfix files and executes a specified command
`postlog`	Logs a message to the system logging facility using Postfix-style log messages
`postmap`	Creates or queries a Postfix lookup table
`postsuper`	Performs maintenance on specified Postfix queue directories
`sendmail`	Provides a sendmail-compatible interface for programs to send messages to the `maildrop` queue

Each Postfix utility program plays a different role in either processing mail messages or querying the Postfix system for status information. Postfix core programs use some of the utilities to process mail, whereas the Postfix administrator uses others to manipulate messages and obtain statistics about the running system.

Postfix Configuration Files

The next block in the diagram shown in Figure 2.2 is the Postfix configuration files. The configuration files contain information that the Postfix programs use when processing messages. Unlike some other MTA programs, you can change configuration information while the Postfix server is running and issue a command to have Postfix load the new information without completely downing the mail server.

There are three Postfix configuration files, which are located in a common Postfix directory. Often the default location for this directory is `/etc/postfix`. Usually, all users have access to view the configuration files, while only the `root` user can change values within the files.

Table 2.4 lists the three main Postfix configuration files.

TABLE 2.4 Postfix Configuration Files

File	*Description*
`install.cf`	Contains information from the install parameters used when Postfix was installed
`main.cf`	Contains operational parameters used by the Postfix programs when processing messages
`master.cf`	Contains parameters used by the Postfix `master` program when running core programs

The Postfix operational parameters are set in the `main.cf` file. Postfix parameters have a default value that is implied within the Postfix system. If a parameter value is not present in the `main.cf` file, Postfix presets its value. If a parameter value is present in the `main.cf` file, its contents override the default value.

Two examples of this are the `myhostname` and `mydomain` parameters. If they are not specified in the `main.cf` configuration file, the `myhostname` parameter assumes the results of a `gethostname()` command, while the `mydomain` assumes the domain part of the default `myhostname` parameter.

If the mail administrator does not want to use these values for the mail server, he can specify different values in the configuration file using the following parameters:

```
myhostname = mailserver.smallorg.org
mydomain = smallorg.org
```

When Postfix starts, it recognizes the local mail server as `mailserver.smallorg.org` and the local domain as `smallorg.org`, and it ignores any system set values.

Postfix Lookup Tables

Postfix also uses several lookup tables that can be created by the e-mail administrator. Each lookup table defines parameters that control the delivery of mail within the Postfix system.

Table 2.5 shows the different lookup tables that can be created for Postfix.

TABLE 2.5 Postfix Lookup Tables

Table	*Description*
`access`	Maps remote SMTP hosts to an accept/deny table for security
`aliases`	Maps alternative recipients to local mailboxes
`canonical`	Maps alternative mailbox names to real mailboxes for message headers
`relocated`	Maps an old user mailbox name to a new mailbox name
`transport`	Maps domain names to delivery methods for remote host connectivity and delivery
`virtual`	Maps recipients and domains to local mailboxes for delivery

The mail administrator creates each lookup table as a plain ASCII text file. Once the text file is created, a binary database file is created using the `postmap` command. Postfix uses the binary database file when searching the lookup tables. This helps speed up the lookup process for Postfix.

NOTE

The lookup tables are described in detail in Chapter 9, "Postfix Lookup Tables."

The Postfix Mail Delivery Process

The Postfix software package is different from other MTAs in that it comprises several executable programs that interact with each other and the message queues to transfer messages. Each program has a specific function in the mail delivery process. Figure 2.3 shows a block diagram of the core programs used by Postfix.

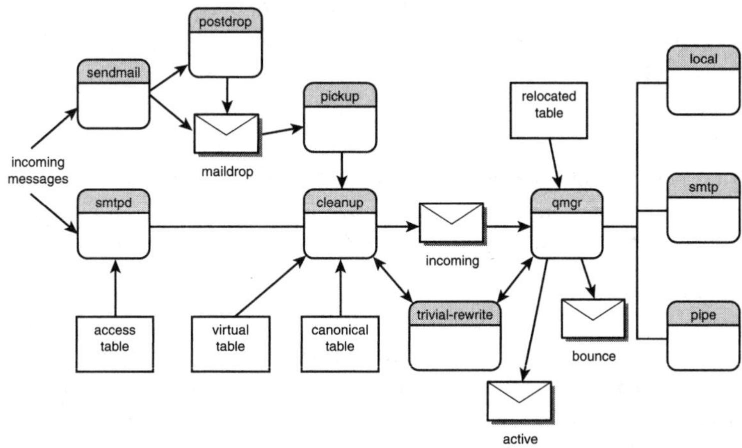

FIGURE 2.3

Internal Postfix block diagram.

As shown in Figure 2.3, the Postfix system uses several different core programs instead of one large program. Each core program has its own function in the total Postfix system shown in Figure 2.3. The following sections describe the functionality of each of the core programs.

Receiving Messages

Postfix can receive new e-mail messages for local users by one of two methods: from other local users (via the local mail queue) or from remote users (via remote MTAs using SMTP). This section describes the Postfix programs that receive messages for local users.

`sendmail`

Although it sounds like a mistake, Postfix really does have a component program called `sendmail`. This program masquerades as the original Unix `sendmail` program to forward messages from local users to the Postfix mail queue.

The reason for the odd name comes from the history of `sendmail` and Unix. In the old days of Unix, the `sendmail` program was the only MTA program available. It was so common that many programs built for Unix were designed exclusively to interface with the `sendmail` program to send messages. This allowed Unix programs to send mail messages without having to include mailing software.

To fully replace the `sendmail` MTA, Postfix needed to provide a suitable interface that would not break any existing mail configurations for other programs. The simple solution was to provide a program that could masquerade as the `sendmail` program but operate using the Postfix mail queues. The Postfix `sendmail` program receives mail messages from local users and either places them directly in the `maildrop` message queue or passes them to the `postdrop` program.

postdrop

Security-conscious mail administrators can use the `postdrop` program as a helper to the `sendmail` program. If the mail administrator uses a world-writable `maildrop` directory, the `sendmail` program can write new messages directly into the `mail` queue.

However, using a world-writable `maildrop` directory presents a serious security risk to the mail server. Postfix provides an alternate solution. The mail administrator can create a special `maildrop` group for the `maildrop` message queue and make it not world-writable. The `postdrop` program must be used to place messages in the `maildrop` directory. Using this scenario, the `sendmail` program must pass messages to the `postdrop` program for them to be placed in the `maildrop` queue.

Figure 2.4 demonstrates this process.

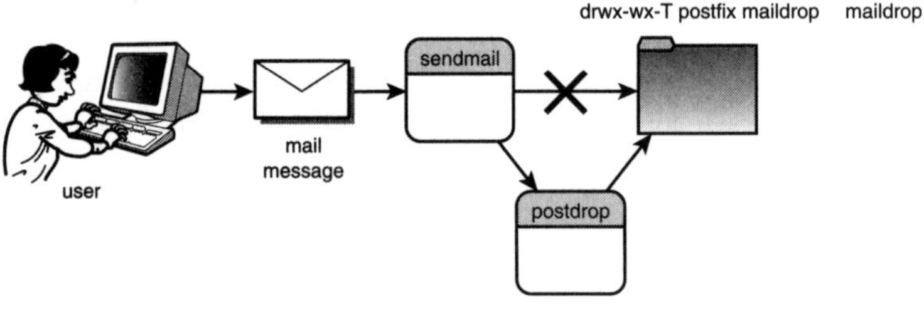

FIGURE 2.4

Using the `postdrop` program with a restricted `maildrop` queue.

As seen in Figure 2.4, the `maildrop` queue is restricted to users who belong to the `maildrop` group. This prevents system users who are not in the group from attempting any tricks with messages in the mail queue. By passing the mail message to the `postdrop` program, the `sendmail` program allows normal messaging programs to insert new mail messages into the `maildrop` message queue.

smtpd

The smtpd program directly receives e-mail messages from remote hosts using the Simple Mail Transfer Protocol (SMTP). SMTP allows hosts using different MTAs to communicate according to a common protocol.

Listing 2.4 demonstrates a sample session between two hosts.

LISTING 2.4 Sample SMTP Session

```
[rich@shadrach]$ telnet localhost 25
Trying 127.0.0.1...
Connected to localhost.
Escape character is '^]'.
220 shadrach.smallorg.org ESMTP Postfix
HELO meshach.ispnet1.net
250 shadrach.ispnet1.net
MAIL FROM: <rich@meshach.ispnet1.net>
250 Ok
RCPT TO: <rich@shadrach.ispnet1.net>
250 Ok
DATA
354 End data with <CR><LF>.<CR><LF>
This is a test message send using the SMTP protocol.
.
250 Ok: queued as 78FC6B3B5
QUIT
221 Bye
Connection closed by foreign host.
You have new mail in /var/spool/mail/rich
[rich@shadrach]$
```

As shown in Listing 2.4, establishing a TCP connection to port 25 connects the remote server to the SMTP process in Postfix. Postfix issues a banner line that is configured within the main.cf configuration file. All communications between the two hosts occur in ASCII text mode. Chapter 5 describes SMTP in more detail as well as how Postfix uses SMTP.

pickup

The pickup program monitors the maildrop message queue. If a new message is received in the maildrop queue, the pickup program reads it and forwards it to the cleanup program to begin the mail process.

Processing Messages

Once Postfix receives the raw message, it must ensure that all addresses used in the e-mail header are recognizable so that the Postfix delivery programs can determine the best method to deliver the message. This section describes the Postfix processing programs that are used to ensure the message header fields are in the proper format.

`cleanup`

Once the `sendmail` or `smtpd` processes have received a message, the `cleanup` program ensures that addresses in the mail message header are in a proper format so Postfix can process the message for delivery.

The standard used for e-mail message header formatting is described in Request For Comment (RFC) 822. The `cleanup` program checks the incoming message to ensure that it is in proper RFC 822 message format.

NOTE

Chapter 5 describes the RFC 822 message format standard.

The `cleanup` program checks the following RFC 822 header fields:

- Insertion of missing From:, Message-ID:, and Date: fields
- Extraction of recipient To:, Cc:, and Bcc: addresses

The `cleanup` program checks Postfix tables for local addresses and also checks the canonical and virtual tables because they may contain information pertinent to rewriting the message addresses. If the message addresses match any entries in either table, the addresses are modified according to the table entries.

Once `cleanup` has finished its processing and has determined that the message contains valid header information, it places the message in the `incoming` message queue. Any messages with invalid headers are discarded and not forwarded for processing and are placed in the `corrupt` message queue.

`trivial-rewrite`

The `trivial-rewrite` program is called if any header addresses are not in the fully qualified domain name (FQDN) standard format (*user@host.domain*). The `trivial-rewrite` program converts the following addresses:

- Remove any source routing information from the header
- Convert UUCP-style *host!user* addresses to *user@host*
- Convert UUCP-style *user%domain* addresses to *user@domain*
- Convert plain *user* address to *user@host*

- Convert *user@host* addresses to *user@host.domain*
- Convert *user@site.* addresses to *user@site*

Once `trivial-rewrite` converts all necessary addresses in the mail header, it returns the message to the `cleanup` program.

The `qmgr` program (discussed in the following section) can also invoke `trivial-rewrite` to resolve unknown header addresses.

qmgr

Once the valid message is rewritten and placed in the `incoming` message queue, the `qmgr` program ensures that the message is delivered to the proper destinations.

Each message is retrieved from the `incoming` queue and placed in the `active` message queue for processing.

Postfix deliberately limits the number of messages that can be in the `active` message queue at one time. This restriction is meant to ensure that Postfix does not overburden the mail server system.

The `qmgr` program then examines message headers and passes them to the appropriate delivery program depending on the destination addresses. Currently, the `qmgr` program can forward messages to the `local`, `smtp`, and `pipe` programs.

Delivering Messages

Once the message has been processed to determine the recipient(s), the message is forwarded to the delivery area. The `qmgr` program forwards a copy of the message to the appropriate delivery program depending on the recipient(s) destination. This section describes the different delivery programs that Postfix supports.

local

The `local` program receives messages from the `qmgr` program that are destined for local users on the mail system. The `local` program checks the `aliases` table and any user `.forward` files before attempting to deliver the message to the local user.

The `local` program can use several delivery methods to send the message to the local user:

- Writing to `sendmail`-style mailboxes located in `/var/spool/mail`
- Writing to `sendmail`-style mailboxes located in the users' `$HOME` directory
- Writing to `qmail`-style `Maildir` mailboxes located in the users' `$HOME` directory
- Invoking a separate mail delivery program such as `procmail` or `binmail`

If the address is found in the Postfix aliases database, it is redirected to the defined mailbox. Also, if the local user has a `.forward` file configured, Postfix forwards the message to the recipient(s) listed in that file.

NOTE

Chapter 10, "Using Postfix," describes the `aliases` and `.forward` files in detail.

`smtp`

The `smtp` program delivers messages destined for users on remote hosts via the SMTP protocol. This process is covered in detail in Chapter 5.

The `smtp` program must also be able to determine the mail host responsible for receiving messages for the destination address. This is often accomplished using the Domain Name System (DNS). This process is covered in detail in Chapter 4, "DNS and Postfix."

`pipe`

The `pipe` program forwards messages to other mail systems on the local mail server. The most common use for this is when forwarding a message to UUCP software for transport across a UUCP network to a remote user.

`bounce`

The `bounce` program processes messages that have been rejected by the intended recipient's mail server. Any error messages received during delivery are appended to the message, and the message is re-addressed to the original sender. Bounced messages are then placed in the `deferred` message queue and wait for processing by the `qmgr` as normal messages. The `qmgr` normally processes messages from the `deferred` message queue at the same rate as messages from the `incoming` message queue.

Inside the Postfix Message Queue System

The Postfix program uses a unique method of queuing received messages for delivery. Unlike other mail programs that create a single mail directory to handle messages, Postfix uses a system of message queue directories to indicate the current state of the message during the queuing and delivery processes.

One feature of Postfix is an advanced capability to recover messages after a mail server crashes. By determining the current queue the message is in, Postfix can restart processing the message and attempt delivery after a server crash.

The following sections describe the Postfix mail queue structure and the message states that each e-mail message must traverse to complete the queuing and delivery processes.

Postfix Message Queue Structure

By default, the Postfix mail queues are located in the `/var/spool/postfix` directory. Each message queue is created as a separate subdirectory within this directory. Each message is stored as a separate file in the subdirectory, using a unique identifier for the filename.

Table 2.6 shows the subdirectories that are used in the Postfix mail queuing system.

TABLE 2.6 Postfix Mail Queue Subdirectories

Directory	*Description*
`active`	Contains messages currently being processed by the Postfix queue manager.
`bounce`	Contains log messages for messages that have permanently failed the delivery attempt.
`corrupt`	Contains messages that are not in the proper Postfix format.
`defer`	Contains log messages for messages that have temporarily failed a delivery attempt. Postfix will attempt another delivery.
`deferred`	Contains messages that have temporarily failed a delivery attempt. Postfix will attempt to process these messages again.
`incoming`	Contains new messages received from remote SMTP hosts.
`maildrop`	Contains new messages received from local users.

The following sections describe the Postfix mail queue subdirectories in more detail.

`active`

The `active` message queue holds messages that are currently being processed by the `qmgr` program. Postfix sets a limit to the number of messages that can be in the `active` queue at any one time. This prevents Postfix from using up resources on the server. The number of messages allowed in the `active` queue at any time can be controlled by a parameter in the `main.cf` configuration file.

`bounce`

The `bounce` message queue contains log files of information about bounced messages. The original message itself is returned to the original sender via the `bounce` program. Each log file in the `bounce` message queue uses the same filename as the original message. The messages in the `bounce` queue allow the Postfix `mailq` program to report the status of any bounced messages waiting in the message queue.

`corrupt`

The `corrupt` message queue holds e-mail messages that `qmgr` could not process. This acts as a broad security check to ensure that local users have not placed any bogus messages in the `maildrop` directory.

`defer`

The `defer` message queue contains message log files that contain information for deferred messages. Again, like the `bounce` queue messages, the Postfix `mailq` program uses these messages to display the status of deferred messages in the `deferred` message queue.

deferred

The `deferred` message queue contains messages that have failed on a delivery attempt. The reason for the delivery failure is documented in a file in the `defer` subdirectory.

Postfix attempts to resend messages in the `deferred` message queue at a later time. If the re-sent messages also fail, Postfix increases the time interval and tries again, up to a set number of times. This process is called the *backoff protocol.*

If, after the set number of delivery attempts, the message still fails, Postfix attempts to bounce the message back to the original sender.

incoming

The `incoming` message queue houses new e-mail messages that have been received from remote SMTP mail servers and from local users. Messages are processed through the `cleanup` program and placed in the `incoming` message queue.

Each message is uniquely identified with a special filename. The filenames are created using the process id (PID) of the `smtpd` service, and the current millisecond from the system clock. This ensures unique filenames for all messages.

maildrop

The `maildrop` message queue contains new messages placed by local users for delivery by the mail system. The `maildrop` directory may be the most controversial part of the Postfix system. One option for installing Postfix allows any user on the mail system to write to the `maildrop` directory. This enables the Postfix `sendmail` program to operate without special privileges and place new messages in the `maildrop` queue. Thereby, a malicious user can try to place data files into the `maildrop` directory. As discussed earlier, Postfix provides the `postdrop` program to solve this problem.

Postfix Message States

Postfix programs and message queues combine to form a well-defined process for handling mail. This process can be divided into five distinct message states. From the time a message is first handed off to Postfix `sendmail` until it is delivered by `local`, it passes through all possible message states. As the message passes from state to state, files are created in the appropriate message queue subdirectories described in the previous section. If at any time the Postfix server crashes, it can determine the last state that a message was in and continue processing the message. This is an extremely good feature of the Postfix system: simple crash tolerance.

The following sections describe the various message states that the mail message traverses before it is delivered to the final destination.

Message State 1: Message Insertion

The first step in e-mail handling is for Postfix to accept new messages from users. As previously discussed, Postfix has two separate methods for receiving new messages: the `maildrop` queue and `smtpd`.

Messages received from local users are placed in the `maildrop` message queue. Either the local user can do this directly using the `sendmail` program (or an MUA that utilizes the `sendmail` program), or the `postdrop` program can do this if the `maildrop` message queue is write protected.

The `smtpd` program receives messages from remote mail hosts using the SMTP protocol. `smtpd` does some basic processing of the incoming message to determine that it is a proper message. The `smtpd` program can also implement filtering to block Unsolicited Commercial E-mail (UCE), also known as *spam*.

NOTE

Chapter 13, "Postfix Server Administration," describes the method of configuring Postfix to implement UCE controls.

If the `smtpd` program accepts the incoming mail message, you can configure `smtpd` to either place it in the `maildrop` message queue or pass it directly to the `cleanup` program for message state 2.

As messages are received for processing, each message is stored in the message queue using a unique filename based on the inode number of the file and the microsecond part of the time of day. This ensures that each new message is assigned a unique filename within the message queue.

Message State 2: Message Header Formatting

Once the message is either successfully stored in the `maildrop` message queue or the `smtpd` program accepts it, it is ready for header address checking. The Postfix system is very picky about the format of addresses in the message header. All message addresses need to use the fully qualified domain name of the sending and receiving hosts, including messages sent to and from local users. Postfix uses the `cleanup` program to accomplish this.

If the incoming messages were placed in the `maildrop` message queue, the `pickup` program determines that a new message is available. It automatically passes the new message to the `cleanup` program to examine the message header addresses. If the message was received using the `smtpd` program, it can be passed directly to the `cleanup` program without using the `maildrop` message queue.

Any incomplete addresses are fixed using the `trivial-rewrite` program. After the messages are put into a standard format, they are ready for message state 3.

Message State 3: Message Storage

In message state 3, an e-mail message is copied to the `incoming` message queue. Each message in this queue is stored as a separate file.

Once an e-mail message is successfully stored in the `incoming` message queue, the Postfix queue manager is ready to process it. This begins message state 4.

Message State 4: Message Queuing and Preprocessing

In message state 4, messages are queued for processing by the Postfix queue manager program, `qmgr`. Messages are transferred from the `incoming` and `deferred` message queues to the `active` message queue. The `active` message queue holds messages that are currently being processed. The `qmgr` program controls how many messages are placed in the `active` message queue from the `incoming` and `deferred` message queues.

The goal of the `qmgr` program is not to overload the mail system. The mail administrator can control the maximum number of messages that can be in the `active` message queue at any one time. This ensures that Postfix does not overload the mail server while processing mass quantities of messages. So, as space becomes available in the `active` message queue, the `qmgr` program adds in one message from the `incoming` message queue and one message from the `deferred` message queue.

Once an e-mail message has been placed in the `active` message queue, it is ready to enter message state 5.

Message State 5: Message Delivery

In message state 5, `qmgr` processes the files in the `active` message queue for delivery to the intended recipients. Each file in the `active` message queue contains addresses of recipients that must receive the message. `qmgr` reads each recipient address and attempts to deliver the message to the appropriate recipient.

When necessary, `qmgr` calls `trivial-rewrite` to resolve domain names for remote hosts.

Messages destined for remote users are passed to Postfix's `smtp` program for delivery. Postfix's `smtp` attempts to deliver messages in a fair and cordial manner. By default, Postfix creates only two concurrent `smtp` sessions with a single remote host. If those connections are successful, it attempts more concurrent connections. This process continues up to the maximum configured number of concurrent `smtp` connections defined for a particular remote host. This prevents Postfix from overwhelming a remote server that may have been down for an extended period of time.

The `smtp` program employs a round-robin technique of connecting to remote hosts. If one host is down for an extended time, e-mail to other hosts is still delivered. Thus, one unavailable host does not dominate all of the remote delivery attempts.

Messages destined for local users are sent to the `local` program. The `local` program checks the `aliases` database and the intended recipient's `.forward` file for delivery instructions.

If the message is determined to be destined for a local system user, the `local` program can directly deliver the message to the user's system mailbox (usually located in `/var/spool/mail`), a special user mailbox (usually `$HOME/Mailbox`), or to a special Maildir-formatted mailbox.

Alternatively, `local` can pass the e-mail message off to yet another Mail Delivery Agent (MDA) such as `binmail` or `procmail`. This allows local users greater flexibility in handling how local messages are delivered and stored in mailboxes.

Messages can also be transferred to other MTAs using the `pipe` program. The `pipe` program allows other programs (such as shell scripts or UUCP programs) the capability to send messages to users.

Problematic E-Mail Messages

In this day of constantly changing e-mail addresses, it is very common for mail messages to be undeliverable. The refused e-mail messages are called *bounced messages*. Postfix handles bounced messages with the `bounce` program. `bounce` creates a system message describing the problem and attempts to send the original e-mail back through the Postfix system to the original sender. Once the e-mail has been redirected, the bounced message is placed in the `incoming` message queue and is processed just like any other new message.

A similar type of mail problem is *deferred messages*. Deferred messages are messages that were undeliverable for a temporary reason, such as a down remote mail server. The intention is that at some time in the future the message may become deliverable.

Postfix allows for this by using the `defer` program. The `defer` program places the original message in the `deferred` message queue.

Postfix uses an exponential backoff algorithm to process deferred messages. This means that each message is retransmitted after a predetermined waiting period. After each successive delivery failure, the wait period is extended. This process is not infinite, of course. It stops at a configured cutoff point.

Postfix and `sendmail`

The granddaddy of all Unix e-mail systems is `sendmail`. Its use has been so widespread that most Unix implementations install it by default. The Postfix system was designed to be a complete replacement for the `sendmail` system: it can perform all functions and offer all the features of `sendmail` on a Unix system. Some of the `sendmail` compatibility features that Postfix supports are

- `.forward` files in the user `$HOME` directories
- System-wide `aliases` table
- System `/var/spool/mail` or `/var/mail` mail delivery directories
- Virtual domains and e-mail handling for multiple hosts

- Mail relaying (and even more importantly, mail relay blocking)
- Support for all standard Unix Mail User Agents (MUAs)

By supporting these `sendmail` features and more, Postfix makes it easy for a mail administrator to completely replace an existing `sendmail` system with a Postfix installation. Chapter 14, "Migrating from Sendmail to Postfix," describes this conversion process.

Postfix: Future Features and Releases

While many Linux distributions include the postfix-19991231 version of Postfix, at the time of this writing, Wietse Venema has released a new production version of Postfix—version release-20010228. There are several new features of the experimental versions that were incorporated in the new release.

This book documents and uses many of the features found in the experimental releases of Postfix that are now part of the production release. This section describes some of the features included in the latest release version of Postfix that were not in the previous release.

Modified `active`, `bounce`, and `deferred` Queues

One item of contention for busy mail servers is the message queues. As new messages are received, they are placed in separate files in the message queues. As more files are stored in the message queues, file handling performance decreases.

It is a well-known fact on Unix systems that accessing files in a directory containing lots of files is slower than accessing fewer files in multiple subdirectories. Using this information, Venema has modified the crucial message queue directories (`active`, `bounce`, and `deferred`), subdividing them into new subdirectories.

Each of the three main queue directories is split into two levels of subdirectories. Each message is placed into a subdirectory based on the first two characters of its filename.

Figure 2.5 demonstrates this layout.

As new messages are received in the message queues, corresponding subdirectories are created. As files are retrieved from the directories, other messages use the subdirectories. Although this structure appears more complicated, it clearly outperforms the old structure in time required to retrieve messages from the message queue.

The `flush` Program and Message Queue

The `flush` program has been added to the Postfix core programs to improve performance for messages retrieved from the Postfix message queues by remote mail systems.

Many ISPs use Postfix to receive mail for small business domains that are not connected to the Internet full time. At predetermined times, the small business mail server connects to the ISP mail server and requests that any messages for its domain be delivered. A common method for doing this is the SMTP ETRN command.

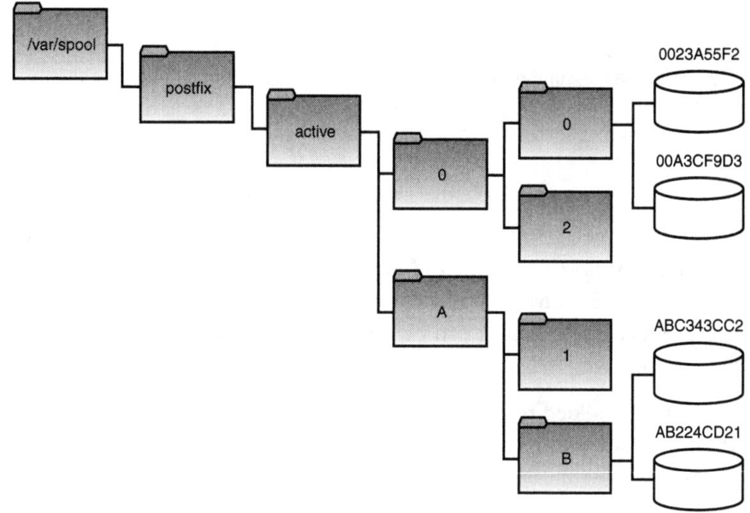

FIGURE 2.5

New message queue directory format.

NOTE

Chapter 5 describes the ETRN command in more detail.

The ETRN command instructs Postfix to establish a new SMTP session with the remote mail server and transfer any messages waiting to be delivered to the domain users. The problem is that the messages destined for the domain are stored along with any other messages in the `deferred` message queue. This requires Postfix to search through *all* of the messages in the `deferred` queue to find the ones destined for the domain listed in the ETRN command.

The `flush` message queue obviates this time-consuming search by using log files and indices. Like the `defer` queue, the `flush` queue maintains log files of messages waiting to be delivered to remote hosts. The key difference is that the messages are also indexed and posted to separate files with names based on the remote domain. When the `smtpd` program receives an ETRN command from a listed domain, the `flush` program is started. The `flush` program reads in the log files in the `flush` message queue for the domain and determines which messages in the `deferred` message queue are destined for the desired domain. This method "front-loads" most of the work, thereby enabling Postfix to send messages to the remote domain much more efficiently.

Domains that are not listed in the `main.cf` configuration file receive queued messages using the standard non-`flush` method.

NOTE

Chapter 22, "Performance Tuning Postfix," discusses the `flush` queue and its configuration parameters in more detail.

LMTP Support

The Local Mail Transport Protocol (LMTP) is a different mail transport protocol described in RFC 2033. LMTP utilizes a set protocol similar to SMTP for delivering messages to the local host. Postfix can be configured to deliver messages to local users using LMTP if desired.

The `lmtp` program is added to support client communications with remote mail servers using LMTP. It is called from the Postfix `master` program and must be have a record defining its behavior in the `master.cf` configuration file.

NOTE

Chapter 5 describes LMTP and how Postfix utilizes LMTP in more detail.

The `spawn` Program

The latest experimental release of Postfix also includes a new program for spawning Internet connections with remote hosts. In a normal Postfix installation, the Unix `inetd` program is used to listen for connection attempts for remote SMTP servers. Over the years there has been much criticism of the `inetd` program.

Many critics claim that it is slow and can be easily crashed using standard Denial-of-Service (DOS) attacks.

To combat this situation, the Postfix program can utilize the `spawn` program. You can configure the `spawn` program to listen to a predetermined network port and spawn a Postfix network program when a connection attempt is detected.

At this time the default Postfix configuration does not use this feature, but it is assumed that Venema will incorporate the `spawn` program in future releases of Postfix.

The `nqmgr` Program

The `nqmgr` program was first introduced in the 20000528 experimental release as a replacement for the standard `qmgr` program. The claim of this new queue manager is that it improves the delivery scheduler of the original queue manager.

One complaint about most MTA programs is that they have poor performance when handling large mailing lists. If your mail site processes a 100,000-user mail list along with normal mail traffic, it could be easy for a single user message to be delayed for several hours while the MTA processes the 100,000-user mail list messages.

To avoid this situation, the `nqmgr` program attempts to intersperse normal mail message traffic within the mail list traffic. This allows for semi-normal mail delivery of individual mail messages while still processing mail list messages.

Summary

You can use the Postfix program as a complete Unix MTA mail system. It has features that make it an attractive e-mail alternative for mail administrators. Postfix's strengths are in higher security, higher reliability, and higher performance than other MTA packages. A Postfix system comprises several different pieces, including software to support TCP/IP, PPP, POP3, and IMAP functionality on the mail server.

The Postfix software itself consists of several different parts. The Postfix package contains several programs that run in background mode to monitor mail queues looking for new messages to send. Also, Postfix can use several utility programs to process messages and retrieve statistics.

The Postfix configuration files configure the Postfix system. Postfix divides the MTA processes into several separate programs, each with individual responsibilities in the mail delivery process. The `smtpd` program is responsible for accepting SMTP connections from remote mail servers, while the `sendmail` program allows local users to send messages through the Postfix system. The `qmgr` program processes the messages as they enter the Postfix mail queue system. `qmgr` uses a unique method of storing messages in the mail queue. The mail queue is divided into several different directories, each directory holding information for the message for a different message state. The `qmgr` program processes the messages in the `active` message queue waiting to be delivered. The `local`, `smtp`, and `pipe` programs are used to deliver messages to users depending on their location. The `smtp` program delivers messages to users on remote mail servers.

You can use the Postfix package as a replacement for the standard Unix Sendmail mail program. It implements the entire standard `sendmail` features on a Unix mail server.

CHAPTER 3

Server Requirements for Postfix

Before you can get your feet wet with Postfix, you must have a server available for it to run on. The Postfix package was written specifically for the Unix platform. Postfix requires several features of the Unix operating system to operate properly. This prevents Postfix from running on a standard Microsoft Windows workstation (even Windows 2000). Fortunately, many Unix implementations are available that can support Postfix.

Novice mail administrators often are not familiar with the operating system that is used for the mail server. This chapter presents a brief description of the Unix operating system that Postfix requires. It also describes one popular free Unix implementation that is available for Postfix: Linux. If you are new to the Unix world and have not yet chosen an operating system to run Postfix on, you may want to read this chapter before deciding.

NOTE

The Postfix package is an extremely robust software package that can run under any Unix operating system. I stress that the operating system used must be an implementation of Unix. Several features of the Postfix system utilize Unix features that are not present on other operating systems. Also, while this chapter discusses only Linux, you have many different Unix systems to choose from that can fully support Postfix.

The Unix Operating System

The core of the Unix operating system is the *kernel*. The kernel must control the hardware and software on the system, allocating hardware when necessary and executing software when required. The kernel is primarily responsible for system memory management, software program management, hardware management, and filesystem management. The following sections describe each of these functions in more detail.

Memory Management

One of the primary functions of the operating system kernel is memory management. Not only does the kernel manage the physical memory available on the server, it can also create and manage *virtual memory*, or memory that does not physically exist in RAM.

It does this by using space on the hard disk, called the *swap space*, and swapping memory locations back and forth from the hard disk to the actual physical memory. This allows the system to think there is more memory available than what physically exists as RAM. The memory locations are grouped into blocks called *pages*. Each page of memory is located either in the physical memory or the swap space. The kernel must maintain a table of the memory pages that indicates which pages are where.

The kernel automatically copies memory pages that have not been accessed for a period of time to the swap space area on the hard disk. When a program wants to access a memory page that has been "swapped out," the kernel must swap out a different memory page and swap in the required page from the swap space. To use virtual memory, you must explicitly create swap space on the hard disk or indicate a special file to be used for swap. This is often done during system installation. The `fdisk` command partitions the installed hard drive on the system. During the partition time, you can create special swap partitions on the disks. The format of the `fdisk` command is

```
fdisk [option] [device]
```

where *`device`* is the hard disk device that is being partitioned. Unix systems use different naming standards for hard disk devices. Table 3.1 shows the Linux hard disk naming standard.

TABLE 3.1 Linux Hard Disk Devices

Device	*Description*
/dev/hd[a-h]	IDE disk drives
/dev/sd[a-p]	SCSI disk drives
/dev/ed[a-d]	ESDI disk drives
/dev/xd[ab]	XT disk drives

The first available drive of a particular type is labeled as drive "a," the second one drive "b," and so on. Within a particular drive, partitions are numbered starting at partition 1. Listing 3.1 shows a sample partition from a Linux system.

LISTING 3.1 Sample `fdisk` Partition Listing

```
[root@shadrach]# /sbin/fdisk /dev/sda

 Command (m for help): p

 Disk /dev/sda: 64 heads, 32 sectors, 521 cylinders
 Units = cylinders of 2048 * 512 bytes

    Device Boot    Start       End    Blocks    Id  System
 /dev/sda1             1       460    471024    83  Linux native
 /dev/sda2           461       521     62464     5  Extended
 /dev/sda5           461       521     62448    82  Linux swap

 Command (m for help): q
```

The first line shows the `fdisk` command being run on the first SCSI disk on the Linux system: `/dev/sda`. `fdisk` is an interactive program that allows the system administrator to manipulate the partition table on the disk drive. You enter the `p` command to print the current partition table. The `/dev/sda5` line shows the partition that is available on the hard drive for the Linux swap area.

After a swap area has been created on a hard drive, the kernel must know that it is available and activate it. The `swapon` program activates memory page swapping. The `swapon` command sets up the virtual memory information in the kernel. This information is lost when the server is rebooted. This requires that the `swapon` command be executed at every boot time. Most Unix distributions allow the `swapon` command to be run from a startup script when the system boots.

On Linux systems, the current status of the virtual memory can be determined by viewing the special `/proc/meminfo` file. Listing 3.2 shows a sample `/proc/meminfo` entry.

LISTING 3.2 Sample `/proc/meminfo` File

```
[root@shadrach]# cat /proc/meminfo
        total:    used:    free:  shared: buffers:  cached:
 Mem:  31535104 29708288  1826816 31817728  3051520 15773696
 Swap: 63942656  2838528 61104128
 MemTotal:        30796 kB
 MemFree:          1784 kB
 MemShared:       31072 kB
 Buffers:          2980 kB
 Cached:          15404 kB
 SwapTotal:       62444 kB
 SwapFree:        59672 kB
```

The first line shows the Linux command used to view the `/proc/meminfo` file. The third line shows that this Linux server has 32MB of physical memory. It also shows that about 18MB is not currently being used. The next line shows that there is about 64MB of swap space memory available on this system. This corresponds with Listing 3.1, which showed a 64MB swap space partition on the `/dev/sda` hard drive.

By default, each process running on the Unix system has its own private memory area. One process cannot access memory being used by another process. No processes can access memory used by the kernel processes. To facilitate data sharing, you can create shared memory segments. Multiple processes can read and write to a common shared memory area. The kernel must maintain and administer the shared memory areas. You can use the `ipcs` command to view the current shared memory segments on the system. Listing 3.3 shows the output from a sample `ipcs` command.

LISTING 3.3 Sample `ipcs` Command Output

```
[root@shadrach]# ipcs -m

 ------ Shared Memory Segments --------
 key        shmid      owner     perms     bytes     nattch    status
 0x00000000 0          rich      600       52228     6         dest
 0x395ec51c 1          oracle    640       5787648   6
```

This shows the ipcs command using the -m option to display just the shared memory segments. Each shared memory segment has an owner who created the segment. Each segment also has standard Unix permissions that set the availability of the segment to other users. The key value allows other users to gain access to the shared memory segment.

Process Management

The Unix operating system handles programs as processes. The kernel controls how processes are managed in the system. The kernel creates the first process, called the init process, to start all other processes on the system. When the kernel starts, the init process is loaded into virtual memory. As each process is started, it is given an area in virtual memory to store data and code that the system will execute.

Some Unix implementations contain a table of terminal processes to start automatically on bootup. On Linux systems, when the init process starts, it reads the file /etc/inittab to determine what processes it must start on the system.

The Unix operating system uses an init system that utilizes run levels. A run level can direct the init process to run only certain types of processes. There are multiple run levels in the Linux operating system and each one can be configured to start different processes.

At run level 1, only the basic system processes are started, along with one console terminal process. This is called *single user mode*, which is most often used for filesystem maintenance. The standard init run level is 3. At this run level, most application software such as network support software is started. Another popular run level in Unix is run level 5, which is where the graphical X Window System software is started for GUI terminals. Notice how the Unix system can control the overall system functionality by controlling the init run level. By changing the run level from 3 to 5, the system can change from a console-based system to an advanced graphical X Window System.

To view the currently active process on the Unix system, you can use the ps command. The format of the ps command is

```
ps [options]
```

where *options* is a list of options that can modify the output of the ps command. Table 3.2 shows the options that are available.

TABLE 3.2 ps Command Options

Option	*Description*
l	Uses the long format to display
u	Uses user format (shows user name and start time)
j	Uses job format (shows process gid and sid)

TABLE 3.2 Continued

Option	*Description*
`s`	Uses signal format
`v`	Uses vm format
`m`	Displays memory information
`f`	Uses "forest" format (displays processes as a tree)
`a`	Shows processes of other users
`x`	Shows processes without a controlling terminal
`S`	Shows child CPU and time and page faults
`c`	Command name for `task_struct`
`e`	Shows environment after command line and a `+`
`w`	Uses wide output format
`h`	Does not display the header
`r`	Shows running processes only
`n`	Shows numeric output for `USER` and `WCHAN`
`txx`	Shows the processes that are controlled by terminal `ttyxx`
`O`	Orders the process listing using sort keys `k1`, `k2`, and so on
`pids`	Shows only the specified `pids`

Lots of options are available to modify the `ps` command output. Listing 3.4 shows a sample output.

LISTING 3.4 Sample ps Command Output

```
[rich@shadrach]$ ps ax
  PID TTY      STAT   TIME COMMAND
    1 ?        S      0:03 init
    2 ?        SW     0:00 [kflushd]
    3 ?        SW     0:00 [kupdate]
    4 ?        SW     0:00 [kpiod]
    5 ?        SW     0:00 [kswapd]
  243 ?        SW     0:00 [portmap]
  295 ?        S      0:00 syslogd
  305 ?        S      0:00 klogd
  320 ?        S      0:00 /usr/sbin/atd
  335 ?        S      0:00 crond
  350 ?        S      0:00 inetd
  365 ?        SW     0:00 [lpd]
  403 ttyS0    S      0:00 gpm -t ms
  418 ?        S      0:00 httpd
  423 ?        S      0:00 httpd
  424 ?        SW     0:00 [httpd]
```

LISTING 3.4 Continued

```
425 ?       SW    0:00 [httpd]
426 ?       SW    0:00 [httpd]
427 ?       SW    0:00 [httpd]
428 ?       SW    0:00 [httpd]
429 ?       SW    0:00 [httpd]
430 ?       SW    0:00 [httpd]
432 ?       S     0:02 /usr/local/jdk1.2.2/bin/i386/green_threads/java org.a
436 ?       SW    0:00 [httpd]
437 ?       SW    0:00 [httpd]
438 ?       SW    0:00 [httpd]
470 ?       S     0:02 xfs -port -1
485 ?       SW    0:00 [smbd]
495 ?       S     0:00 nmbd -D
533 ?       SW    0:00 [postmaster]
538 tty1    SW    0:00 [mingetty]
539 tty2    SW    0:00 [mingetty]
540 tty3    SW    0:00 [mingetty]
541 tty4    SW    0:00 [mingetty]
542 tty5    SW    0:00 [mingetty]
543 tty6    SW    0:00 [mingetty]
544 ?       SW    0:00 [prefdm]
548 ?       S     2:23 /etc/X11/X -auth /usr/X11R6/lib/X11/xdm/authdir/A:0-u
549 ?       SW    0:00 [prefdm]
559 ?       S     0:02 [kwm]
585 ?       S     0:06 kikbd
594 ?       S     0:00 kwmsound
595 ?       S     0:03 kpanel
596 ?       S     0:02 kfm
597 ?       S     0:00 krootwm
598 ?       S     0:01 kbgndwm
611 ?       S     0:00 kcmlaptop -daemon
666 ?       S     0:00 /usr/libexec/postfix/master
668 ?       S     0:00 qmgr -l -t fifo -u
787 ?       S     0:00 pickup -l -t fifo
790 ?       S     0:00 telnetd: 192.168.1.2 [vt100]
791 pts/0   S     0:00 login -- rich
792 pts/0   S     0:00 -bash
805 pts/0   R     0:00 ps ax
```

The first line shows the `ps` command as entered on the command line. Both the `a` and `x` options are used for the output to display all processes running on the system. The first column in the output shows the process ID (or PID) of the process. The third line shows the `init` process started by the kernel. The `init` process is assigned PID 1. All other processes that start after the `init` process are assigned PIDs in numerical order. No two processes can have the same PID.

The third column shows the current status of the process. Table 3.3 lists the possible process status codes.

TABLE 3.3 Process Status Codes

Code	*Description*
D	Uninterruptible sleep
L	Process has pages locked into memory
N	Low priority task
R	Runnable
S	The process has asked for a page replacement (sleeping)
T	Traced or stopped
Z	A defunct (zombie) process
W	Process has no resident pages
<	High priority process

The process name is shown in the last column. Processes that are in brackets (`[ ]`) have been swapped out of memory to the disk swap space due to inactivity. You can see that some of the processes have been swapped out, but most of the running processes have not.

Device Driver Management

Still another responsibility for the kernel is hardware management. Any device that the Unix system must communicate with needs driver code inserted inside the kernel code. The driver code allows the kernel to pass data back and forth to the device. Two methods are used for inserting device driver code in the Unix kernel.

Previously, the only way to insert a device driver code was to recompile the kernel. Each time a new device was added to the system, the kernel code needed to be recompiled. This process became more inefficient as Unix kernels supported more hardware. A better method was developed to insert driver code into the running kernel. The concept of *kernel modules* was developed to allow driver code to be inserted into a running kernel and also removed from the kernel when the device is no longer being used.

Hardware devices are identified on the Unix server as special device files. There are three different classifications of device files:

- Character
- Block
- Network

Character device files can only handle data one character at a time. Most types of modems are character devices. *Block* device files can handle data in large blocks at a time, such as disk drives. *Network* devices use packets to send and receive data. This includes network cards and the special loopback device that allows the Unix system to communicate with itself using common network programming protocols.

Device files are created in the filesystem as *nodes*. Each node has a unique number pair that identifies it to the Unix kernel. The number pair includes a major and a minor device number. Similar devices are grouped into the same major device number. The minor device number identifies the device within the major device numbers. Listing 3.5 shows an example of device files on a Linux server.

LISTING 3.5 Sample Device Listing from a Linux Server

```
[rich@shadrach /dev]$ ls -al sda* ttyS*
 brw-rw----    1 root      disk       8,   0 May  5  1998 sda
 brw-rw----    1 root      disk       8,   1 May  5  1998 sda1
 brw-rw----    1 root      disk       8,  10 May  5  1998 sda10
 brw-rw----    1 root      disk       8,  11 May  5  1998 sda11
 brw-rw----    1 root      disk       8,  12 May  5  1998 sda12
 brw-rw----    1 root      disk       8,  13 May  5  1998 sda13
 brw-rw----    1 root      disk       8,  14 May  5  1998 sda14
 brw-rw----    1 root      disk       8,  15 May  5  1998 sda15
 brw-rw----    1 root      disk       8,   2 May  5  1998 sda2
 brw-rw----    1 root      disk       8,   3 May  5  1998 sda3
 brw-rw----    1 root      disk       8,   4 May  5  1998 sda4
 brw-rw----    1 root      disk       8,   5 May  5  1998 sda5
 brw-rw----    1 root      disk       8,   6 May  5  1998 sda6
 brw-rw----    1 root      disk       8,   7 May  5  1998 sda7
 brw-rw----    1 root      disk       8,   8 May  5  1998 sda8
 brw-rw----    1 root      disk       8,   9 May  5  1998 sda9
 crw-------    1 root      tty        4,  64 Nov 29 16:09 ttyS0
 crw-------    1 root      tty        4,  65 May  5  1998 ttyS1
 crw-------    1 root      tty        4,  66 May  5  1998 ttyS2
 crw-------    1 root      tty        4,  67 May  5  1998 ttyS3
```

This shows the `ls` command being used to display all of the entries for the `sda` and `ttyS` devices. The `sda` device is the first SCSI hard drive, and the `ttyS` devices are the standard IBM PC COM ports. The listing shows all of the `sda` devices that were created on the sample Linux system. Not all are actually used, but they are created in case the administrator needs them. Similarly, the listing shows all of the `ttyS` devices created.

The fifth column is the major device node number. Notice that all of the `sda` devices have the same major device node, 8, and all of the `ttyS` devices use 4. The sixth column is the minor device node number. Each device within a major number has its own unique minor device node number.

The first column indicates the permissions for the device file. The first character of the permissions indicates the type of file. Notice that the SCSI hard drive files are all marked as block (b) files, whereas the COM port device files are marked as character (c) files.

To create a new device node, you can use the `mknod` command. The format of the `mknod` command is

```
mknod [OPTION] NAME TYPE [MAJOR MINOR]
```

where *`NAME`* is the filename and *`TYPE`* is the filetype (character or block). The *`OPTION`* parameter has only one usable option. The `-m` option allows you to set the permissions of the file as it is created. You must be careful to select a unique major and minor device node number pair.

Filesystem Management

Unlike some other operating systems, the Unix kernel can support different types of filesystems to read and write data to hard drives. Currently 16 different filesystem types are available on Linux systems. The kernel must be compiled with support for all types of filesystems that the system will use. Table 3.4 lists the standard filesystems that a Unix system can use to read and write data.

TABLE 3.4 Unix Filesystems

Filesystem	*Description*
`affs`	Amiga filesystem
`ext`	Linux Extended filesystem
`ext2`	Second extended filesystem
`hpfs`	OS/2 high performance filesystem
`iso9660`	ISO 9660 filesystem (CD-ROMs)
`minix`	MINIX filesystem
`msdos`	Microsoft FAT16
`ncp`	Netware filesystem
`nfs`	Network file system
`proc`	Access to system information
`smb`	Samba SMB filesystem
`sysv`	Older Unix filesystem
`ufs`	BSD filesystem
`umsdos`	Unix-like filesystem that resides on top of MS-DOS
`vfat`	Windows 95 filesystem (fat32)
`xia`	Similar to ext2, not used

Any hard drive that a Unix server accesses must be formatted using one of the filesystem types listed in Table 3.4. Formatting a Unix filesystem is similar to formatting an MS-DOS type disk. The operating system must build the necessary filesystem information onto the disk before the disk can be used to store information. The command that Linux uses to format filesystems is the `mkfs` command. The format of the `mkfs` command is

```
mkfs  [ -V ] [ -t fstype ] [ fs-options ] filesys [ blocks ]
```

where *`fstype`* is the type of filesystem to use, and *`blocks`* is the number of blocks to use. The default filesystem type for Linux systems is `ext2`, and the default block count is all blocks available on the partition.

The Linux kernel interfaces with each filesystem using the *Virtual File System (VFS)*. This provides a standard interface for the kernel to communicate with any type of filesystem. VFS caches information in memory as each filesystem is mounted and used.

The Linux Operating System

One popular free Unix implementation is Linux. Linux has gained increasing acceptance in the Unix marketplace as a solid production Unix operating system. The Linux system consists of a core Unix-like kernel and a host of libraries. This section describes the pieces of the Linux operating system.

The Linux Kernel

The development of the Linux kernel has taken on a very rapid pace. Linus Torvalds, creator of Linux, maintains strict control over the Linux kernel, although he accepts change requests from anyone, anywhere. There have been many advances in the Linux kernel design over the years, such as the addition of modules.

The kernel developers use a strict version control system. The format of a kernel release is

```
linux-a.b.c
```

where *`a`* is the major release number, *`b`* is the minor release number, and *`c`* is the patch number. Currently, a convention has been established where odd-numbered minor releases are considered developmental releases, and even-numbered minor releases are considered stable production releases.

At the time of this writing, the current stable production release of the Linux kernel is 2.4.1, whereas the current development release is 2.3.99-pre1. Although version 2.4.2 is the current kernel release, most Linux distributions have not released versions using this kernel.

To determine the kernel version that your Linux system is using, you can use the `uname` command with the `-a` option. Listing 3.6 shows an example of this command using a Mandrake 6.0 Linux system.

LISTING 3.6 Sample uname -a Output

```
[rich@shadrach]$ uname -a
Linux shadrach.smallorg.org 2.2.9-19mdk #1 Wed May 19 19:53:00 GMT 1999
➥ i586 unknown
```

The output from the `uname` command is shown in line 2. The third field shows the specific Linux kernel version used. This example uses the 2.2.9 kernel that was compiled specifically for the Mandrake Linux distribution, thus the extra added `-19mdk` information.

It is possible to download newer versions of the kernel to install in a running Linux system. You must have the kernel source code files, which are usually available for download from the Linux Kernel Archives at `http://www.kernel.org`. Compiling and installing a new kernel is not for the beginner. Numerous steps are involved in the process. If you decide to upgrade your Linux kernel, please read all the documentation that comes with the kernel source code and any tips provided by your specific Linux distribution support group.

CAUTION

Installing a new Linux kernel falls under the category of "if it ain't broke, don't fix it." If your Linux server is not experiencing any problems, don't attempt to install a new kernel just because it is newer. Many Linux distributions are fine-tuned to work with a specific kernel; changing only the kernel can bring unpredictable results.

The Linux Libraries

The Linux operating system also depends heavily on the C programming language. The kernel, many device drivers, and almost all the utilities were written using the C language. It is not surprising that most of the application programs written for the Linux platform were also written in C.

In Unix, the `lib` prefix denotes library files. A library table keeps track of all the shared libraries registered on the system. The file `/etc/ld.so.conf` contains the list of libraries that are inserted into the library table. You can display the current library table on your Linux system by using the `ldconfig` command. Listing 3.7 shows a sample partial output from the `ldconfig` command on a Mandrake 6.0 Linux system. This is only a partial listing because, as shown in line 2, 534 different libraries are registered on this Linux system.

LISTING 3.7 Sample `ldconfig` Partial Output

```
[rich@shadrach]$ /sbin/ldconfig -p
534 libs found in cache `/etc/ld.so.cache' (version 1.7.0)
        libzvt.so.2 (libc6) => /usr/lib/libzvt.so.2
        libzvt.so.2 (libc6) => /usr/lib/libzvt.so.2
        libz.so.1 (libc6) => /usr/lib/libz.so.1
        libz.so.1 (libc6) => /usr/lib/libz.so.1
        libx11amp.so.0 (libc6) => /usr/X11R6/lib/libx11amp.so.0
        libxml.so.0 (libc6) => /usr/lib/libxml.so.0
        libxml.so.0 (libc6) => /usr/lib/libxml.so.0
        libvgagl.so.1 (libc6) => /usr/lib/libvgagl.so.1
        libvgagl.so.1 (libc5) => /usr/i486-linux-libc5/lib/libvgagl.so.1
        libvgagl.so.1 (libc6) => /usr/lib/libvgagl.so.1
        libvgagl.so (libc6) => /usr/lib/libvgagl.so
        libvgagl.so (libc6) => /usr/lib/libvgagl.so
        libvga.so.1 (libc6) => /usr/lib/libvga.so.1
        libvga.so.1 (libc5) => /usr/i486-linux-libc5/lib/libvga.so.1
        libvga.so.1 (libc6) => /usr/lib/libvga.so.1
        libvga.so (libc6) => /usr/lib/libvga.so
        libvga.so (libc6) => /usr/lib/libvga.so
        libuulib.so.5 (libc6) => /usr/lib/libuulib.so.5
        libuulib.so.5 (libc6) => /usr/lib/libuulib.so.5
        libuulib.so (libc6) => /usr/lib/libuulib.so
        libuulib.so (libc6) => /usr/lib/libuulib.so
```

Each Linux implementation requires that a version of the standard C library be installed. The standard C library contains many of the commonly used functions for the system.

If you do not know which library your Linux distribution is using, you can find out by looking for the libraries in the `/lib` directory. Table 3.5 shows the different C libraries that might be present on a Linux system.

TABLE 3.5 List of Linux C Libraries

Library	*Description*
`libc.so`	`libc1` a.out library
`libc.so.2`	`libc2` a.out library
`libc.so.3`	`libc3` a.out library
`libc.so.4`	`libc4` a.out library
`libc.so.5`	`libc5` ELF library
`libc.so.6`	Symbolic link to a `glibc` library
`libc-2.0.x.so`	`glibc` 2.0 ELF library
`libc-2.1.x.so`	`glibc` 2.1 ELF library

The GNU Project

The GNU Project was created in 1984 to create a free Unix-like operating system. It is responsible for maintaining open source versions of many common Unix utilities. Without the GNU Project, the Linux operating system would not be very exciting. Most of the core pieces of the Linux operating system are products of the GNU Project. This section describes three programs that are crucial to the operation of the mail server: the bash shell, the `gcc` compiler, and the `make` utility.

GNU bash

The kernel requires some kind of macro processor to enable a user to execute commands (programs) on the system. In the Unix world, that macro processor is called the *shell*. The most common shell in the Unix environment is the Bourne shell, named after its creator, Stephen Bourne. The Bourne shell is a program that runs as a process on the system and has an interactive session that enables the user to enter commands at a command prompt. The commands can be executable programs, internal shell commands, or a program file that contains shell commands (called a *script file*). The shell launches executable programs by creating a new process and running the program within that new process. This allows every program that runs from the shell to have its own process on the system.

The GNU Project developers knew that it was crucial to have a good open source shell to use with an open source Unix-like operating system. The shell program they developed was called bash, for Bourne-Again SHell. The bash shell is compatible with the original Bourne shell (called sh). The bash shell also includes features from other shells that have been developed in the Unix environment: the C shell (csh) and the Korn shell (ksh). bash has become the default shell for Linux systems. The current version of bash at the time of this writing is version 2.03.

The shell a user utilizes after logging in to a Linux system is determined by the user's entry in the `/etc/passwd` file. A typical record in this file looks like this:

```
riley:x:504:506:Riley M.:/home/riley:/bin/bash
```

Colons are used to separate the fields in the record. The first field identifies the user login name. The second field is a placeholder for the user password since this particular Linux system uses shadow passwords. As a result, the real password is encrypted and placed in a separate file. The third and fourth fields are the user id and group id for the user. The fifth field is the text identifier for the user. The sixth field identifies the user's default, or home, directory when he logs in to the system. The last field identifies the default shell for the user. This points to the location of the bash shell executable file on the server.

The bash shell has several different configuration files that you can use to modify the features of the shell as a user logs in. When bash is invoked as a shell from a login process, any commands present in the `/etc/profile` file are executed. This occurs for all users who specify the bash shell as the default login shell in the password file. Listing 3.8 shows the default `/etc/profile` file from a Mandrake 6.0 Linux system.

LISTING 3.8 Sample /etc/profile File

```
# /etc/profile

# System wide environment and startup programs
# Functions and aliases go in /etc/bashrc

PATH="$PATH:/usr/X11R6/bin"
PS1="[\u@\h \W]\\$ "

# In bash2 we can't define a ulimit for user :-(
[ "$UID" = "0" ] && {
ulimit -c 1000000
}

if [ `id -gn` = `id -un` -a `id -u` -gt 14 ]; then
    umask 002
else
    umask 022
fi

USER=`id -un`
LOGNAME=$USER
MAIL="/var/spool/mail/$USER"

HOSTNAME=`/bin/hostname`
HISTSIZE=1000
HISTFILESIZE=1000
export PATH PS1 HOSTNAME HISTSIZE HISTFILESIZE USER LOGNAME MAIL

for i in /etc/profile.d/*.sh ; do
    if [ -x $i ]; then
        . $i
    fi
done

unset i
```

The main thing the `/etc/profile` file does is create new environment variables for the shell to identify special characteristics for the session that application programs running in the shell can use. The `MAIL` environment variable is of special interest to the mail administrator. It points the user's mail program to the proper mailbox for the user. If the Postfix server is configured to use mailbox files located in the user's `$HOME` directory, this environment variable must be changed.

After the common `/etc/profile` program executes, bash looks for three more configuration files in the user's default (home) directory. If they exist, the `.bash_profile`, `.bash_login`, and `.profile` files execute, in order. Each of these files should be located in the user's home directory, so these files can be specific for a particular user. One final configuration file is available for use: `.bash_logout`. This script file executes when the user logs out of the interactive session. By using a combination of script files, the system administrator can fine-tune the bash shell for each user on the system.

GNU gcc

If you plan to install software programs that are distributed in source code, you must be able to compile the code to create an executable file. To do this, you need the proper compiler. All the programs described in this book are written in the C programming language. This requires that a C compiler be installed on your Unix server. The most common C compiler package for Linux is the GNU Compiler Collection (gcc).

The gcc package has itself had quite an interesting past. The GNU Project team developed gcc and released version 1 in early 1990. Back then the gcc actually stood for GNU C Compiler, because it only supported the C language. The GNU Project continued development of gcc, creating version 2.0 and continuing with improvements until version 2.8 was released in 1997. At the same time, another group of developers was working on a C++ compiler called egcs (pronounced "eggs"). After gcc 2.8, both projects were combined into the egcs project and egcs 1.0 was released. egcs 1.0 combined both the C and C++ compilers into one package.

Unfortunately, the egcs project was short-lived (only getting up to version 1.1). Now both the gcc and egcs projects have been rolled into the gcc project again (thus the name change for gcc). At the time of this writing, the current version of gcc is version 2.95.2, although version 3.0 is rumored to be ready for release soon. This version supports C, C++, and Java compilers.

To determine the version of gcc that your Linux distribution uses, you can use the `--version` option as follows:

```
[rich@shadrach]$ gcc --version
2.95.2
```

The sample Mandrake 7.0 Linux system shown is using the current gcc version 2.95.2.

GNU make

Large C and C++ projects often become complicated. There are several different source code files, each with several different header files. Compiling individual source files creates multiple object files that must be linked together in specific combinations to create executable files.

Maintaining the source, object, and executable files is often a difficult job. To simplify this task, most C and C++ compilers utilize the `make` program. The job of the `make` program is to control the creation of executable files, based on changes made to the source code files or to variables in a standard `make` configuration file.

The GNU Project has a version of `make` that is compatible with the gcc compiler. At the time of this writing, the current version available is version 3.79.1.

The meat and potatoes of the `make` utility is the Makefile. The Makefile is a text file that specifies how the `make` utility should compile the source code to create the executable program(s). A sample Makefile is shown in Listing 3.9.

LISTING 3.9 Sample Makefile

```
# Makefile -- Make file for test program
#

# Edit the following for your installation

CC  =   gcc
#===================================

# Compiler and linker flags

CFLAGS  =   -O
LFLAGS  =   -O

# This program's object code files

OBJS    =   test.o

# File dependencies

all:    test

objs:   $(OBJS)

clean:
    rm -f $(OBJS)
    rm -f test

test: $(OBJS)
    $(CC) -o $@ $(LFLAGS) $(OBJS) $(LIBS)

test.o:  test.c
   $(CC) -c $(CFLAGS) -o $@ $<
```

The line numbers are not part of the original Makefile, but were added to aid in the discussion. Lines 6, 11, 12, and 16 show the use of variables within the Makefile. The user can change these values to the appropriate values for the system. Line 18 declares the `make` targets for the system. You can build each target individually by specifying the target name as a parameter on the `make` command line. For example, to run the `clean` target, which removes any old object and executable files, you can type

```
make clean
```

To create just the object files for the test program, you can type

```
make objs
```

If you type only `make` at the command line, the `all` target will be executed, which builds the executable file `test`.

Summary

The Postfix mail server package was written to run on a Unix platform. The Unix operating systems provide the file and process control that Postfix requires to handle multiple processes and files.

The core of the Unix operating system is the kernel. The kernel controls many facets of the operating system, including memory management, process management, device management, and filesystem management.

Postfix can run on many different Unix platforms. The Linux distributions are excellent Unix implementations that are available for minimal or no cost. The core of Linux is the Linux kernel. Along with the kernel, the Bourne-again shell (bash) and the Linux C libraries combine to make a complete system.

Linux uses many utilities developed by the GNU Project. It uses gcc to compile C programs. To aid in compiling complex programs (such as Postfix), the GNU `make` utility is often used to create scripts to allow all of the source code modules to be compiled in a single command. With Postfix, Linux, and the GNU utilities, you can easily turn a standard IBM-compatible computer into a full-featured e-mail server.

CHAPTER 4

DNS and Postfix

One of the most important yet misunderstood aspects of an e-mail system is the use of hostnames. It is crucial to ensure that hostnames are defined properly in order for mail systems to communicate. Postfix is no different.

The *domain name system (DNS)* was developed to allow systems to communicate using a hierarchy of hostnames instead of the native IP numbering scheme. DNS also identifies servers that provide special services for domains, such as e-mail. This is where DNS becomes crucial for e-mail servers.

Although knowledge of DNS isn't essential for installing and configuring Postfix, it certainly helps when you are trying to troubleshoot mail problems. At some point in your mail administration career, you will most likely meet a customer who is positive that he is sending his e-mail message to the right address, but it still bounces back as undeliverable. It will be your job to prove why the message bounced.

This chapter describes the history and design of DNS. It also presents some common applications that you can use on a Unix host to troubleshoot DNS problems.

History of Computer Names

Back in the old days when the Internet was small (just a few hundred computers), it wasn't too complicated to locate another computer. Each Internet computer maintained its own local database of hostnames and IP addresses. Internet hostnames could be anything the administrator desired: Fred, Barney, Acct1, anything. There was a central clearinghouse for keeping track of new computer names and addresses. Once a week or so, a system administrator would download a new copy of the current database.

Of course this system did have its drawbacks. When someone brought a new computer online, he needed to search the database to make sure that nobody had already taken the clever new hostname he wanted to use. It didn't take system administrators long to figure out that this method was on a collision course with progress. As the Internet grew, so did the database. As the database grew, so did the time it took to download and search it. It also became difficult to come up with a unique hostname. Something had to be changed, and it was.

Domain Names

The method agreed upon was DNS, which uses a hierarchical, distributed database to break up the hostname database. Now no one computer has to maintain the entire database of all Internet devices. The database is distributed over multiple computers, called *DNS servers*, on the Internet. For client computers to locate another computer on the Internet, they only need to find the nearest DNS server and query for the target's IP address. In order to implement this system, a new protocol was devised to pass DNS information from the DNS server to both clients and other servers. New software was also created to implement the new database system on local DNS servers.

DNS Structure

The structure of a hierarchical database is similar to an organization chart. It has nodes connected in a tree-like manner (the hierarchical part of the model). The top node is called the *root*. The root node does not explicitly show up in addresses, so it is called the nameless node.

Multiple categories were created under the root level to divide the database into large pieces called top-level domains. Each domain maintains its own DNS servers that are responsible for the database of local computer names (the distributed part of the model). Figure 4.1 shows a diagram of how the DNS domains are distributed in relation to one another.

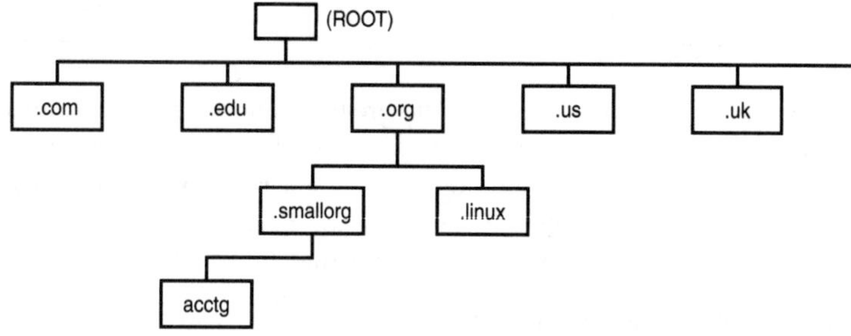

FIGURE 4.1

A diagram of the Internet domain name system.

The first (or top) level of distribution is divided into domains based on country codes. Additional top-level domains for specific types of U.S. organizations were created to prevent the `.us` domain from getting overcrowded. The domain name is appended to the end of the computer's local hostname to form the unique Internet hostname for that computer. This is the common hostname format that we are now familiar with. Table 4.1 shows how the top-level DNS domains are laid out.

TABLE 4.1 DNS Top-Level Domain Names

Name	*Description*
`.com`	U.S. commercial organizations
`.edu`	U.S. educational institutions
`.gov`	U.S. government organizations
`.mil`	U.S. military sites
`.net`	U.S. Internet providers
`.org`	U.S. nonprofit organizations

TABLE 4.1 Continued

Name	*Description*
`.us`	Other U.S. organizations
`.ca`	Canadian organizations
`.de`	German organizations
(other country codes)	Other countries' organizations

NOTE

Recently there have been a few more top-level domain names approved for use in the United States. It appears that top-level domains may soon explode much like the rest of the Internet has.

As the Internet grows, the top-level domains are each divided into subdomains, or *zones*. Each zone is an independent domain in its own right but relies on its parent domain for connectivity to the database. A parent zone must grant permission for a child zone to exist and is responsible for the child zone's behavior. Each zone must have at least two DNS servers that maintain the DNS database for the zone.

The original specifications stipulated that the DNS servers for a single zone must have separate connections to the Internet and be housed in separate locations for fault-tolerance purposes. Because of this stipulation, many organizations rely on other organizations to host their secondary and tertiary DNS servers.

Hosts within a zone add the zone's domain name to their local hostname to form their unique Internet name. Thus, computer "fred" in the `ispnet1.net` domain becomes `fred.ispnet1.net` when fully qualified. It becomes a little confusing because a domain can contain hosts as well as zones.

For example, the `ispnet1.net` domain can contain the host `fred.ispnet1.net`, as well as grant authority for the zone `acctg.ispnet1.net` to a subdomain, which in turn can contain another host, such as `barney.acctg.ispnet1.net`. Although this simplifies the database system, it makes finding hosts on the Internet more complicated. Figure 4.2 shows an example of a domain and a subdomain associated with it, along with the responsible DNS name servers (NS).

NOTE

In the past few years Internet domain names have become a hot topic. In the past, one single corporation controlled all U.S. domain names in the `.com`, `.net`, and `.org` domains: the Internic Corporation. Recently, a non-profit organization, the Internet Corporation for Assigned Names and Numbers (ICANN), was created to control this process. ICANN is now responsible for the management of all U.S. domain names. The purchase of a domain name can now be made from multiple vendors, not just one company. All U.S. domain names must be cleared by the ICANN.

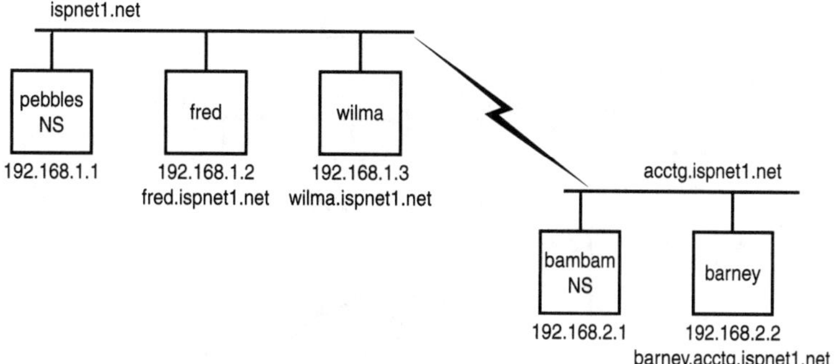

FIGURE 4.2

A sample domain and subdomain on the Internet.

Three different scenarios can occur in finding an IP address using DNS:

- A computer that wants to communicate with another computer in the same zone queries the local DNS server to find the address of the remote computer. The local DNS server should have the address of the remote computer in its local database and return the IP address.
- A computer that wants to communicate with a computer in another zone queries the DNS server local to its own zone. The local DNS server realizes the requested computer is in a different zone and queries a root-level DNS server for the answer. The root DNS server then "walks" the tree of DNS servers to find the DNS server responsible for the desired remote host's zone and requests its IP address. The root DNS server then passes the address to the local DNS server, which in turn passes the information to the requesting computer. Part of the information that is returned with the IP address of the remote computer is a time to live (TTL) value. This instructs the local DNS server that it can keep the IP address of the remote computer in a local name cache for the amount of time specified in the TTL value. This speeds up any subsequent name requests.
- A computer that wants to communicate with the remote computer from the previous example queries the DNS server in its local zone. The local DNS server checks its name cache, and if the TTL value has not expired, the server sends the IP address of the remote computer to the requesting client computer. This is considered a non-authoritative response, as the local DNS server is assuming that the remote computer's IP address has not changed since it was last checked.

In all three instances, the local computer needs to know only the IP address of its local DNS server to find the IP address of any computer on the Internet. It is the job of the local DNS server to find the proper IP address for the requested hostname. The local computer's life is now much simpler. Figure 4.3 shows a diagram of how these different functions operate.

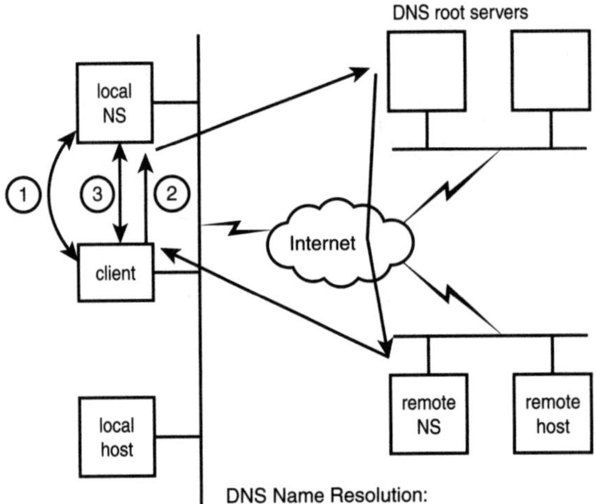

FIGURE 4.3

A diagram of different DNS resolution methods.

As the DNS tree grows, new demands are made on DNS servers. As mentioned, parent DNS servers are required to know the IP addresses of their children zone DNS servers to properly pass DNS queries on to them for resolution. The tricky part comes into play with the lower-level zone DNS servers. In order for them to properly process DNS queries, they have to be able to start their name searches somewhere in the DNS tree. When the Internet was in its infancy, most of the name searches were for local hostnames. The bulk of the DNS traffic was able to stay local to the zone DNS server or, at worst, its parent. However, with the increased popularity of the Internet and Web browsing, more DNS requests were made for remote hostnames. When a DNS server did not have the hostname in its local database, it would need to query a remote DNS server.

The most likely candidate for the remote DNS server is a top-level domain DNS server that has the knowledge to work its way down the tree until it finds the responsible zone DNS server for the remote host and returns the result to the local DNS server. This puts a great deal of stress on the root servers. Fortunately there are quite a few of them, and they do a good job of distributing the load. The local DNS servers communicate with the top-level domain DNS servers using the DNS protocol that is discussed later in this chapter.

DNS is a two-way street. Not only is it useful for finding the IP address of a computer based on its hostname, but it is also useful for finding the hostname of a computer based on its IP address (often called a *reverse lookup*). Many Internet Web and FTP sites restrict access based on a client computer's domain. When a connection request is received from a client, the host server passes the IP address of the client to the DNS server as a reverse

DNS query. If the client's DNS zone database is configured correctly, the client's hostname should be returned to the server, which in turn can decide whether to grant access to the client.

NOTE

If your organization uses Dynamic Host Configuration Protocol (DHCP) to dynamically assign IP addresses to workstations, you may have to create DNS records for all possible DHCP addresses that can be assigned by the server. Often a generic hostname can be assigned to each address, such as `station1.ispnet1.net`.

DNS Database Records

Each DNS server is responsible for keeping track of the hostnames in its zone. To accomplish this, the DNS server must have a method of storing host information in a database that remote machines can query. The DNS database is a collection of text files that consist of resource records (RRs) describing computers and functions in the zone. The Unix server must run a DNS server software package, usually `named` (part of the BIND package), to communicate the DNS information from the database to remote DNS servers and clients.

The DNS server's database first must declare the zone(s) that it is responsible for. Then, it must declare each host computer in its zone(s). Finally, the database can declare special information for the zone, such as e-mail and name servers. Resource record formats were created to track all the information required for the DNS server. RFC 1035 defines most of the common RRs that are used in a DNS zone definition.

Table 4.2 shows some of the basic RRs that a DNS database might contain. DNS database design has become a hot topic lately with researchers wanting to add more information to the database as well as increase the security of the information that is already there. New record types are constantly being added to the DNS database. The record types in Table 4.2 represent the core records needed to establish a zone in the DNS database.

TABLE 4.2 DNS Database Resource Record Types

Record Type	*Description*
`SOA`	Start of Authority
`A`	Internet Address
`NS`	Name Server
`CNAME`	Canonical Name (nickname)
`HINFO`	Host Information
`MX`	Mail Exchanger
`PTR`	Domain Name Pointer

Each domain DNS server should contain resource records for the hosts in the domain. There should be one SOA record for the domain listed at the top of the database. Any other resource records for the domain can be added in any order after that. Figure 4.4 demonstrates how the DNS database would look for the sample network that was shown previously in Figure 4.2. The next section describes the DNS records in more detail.

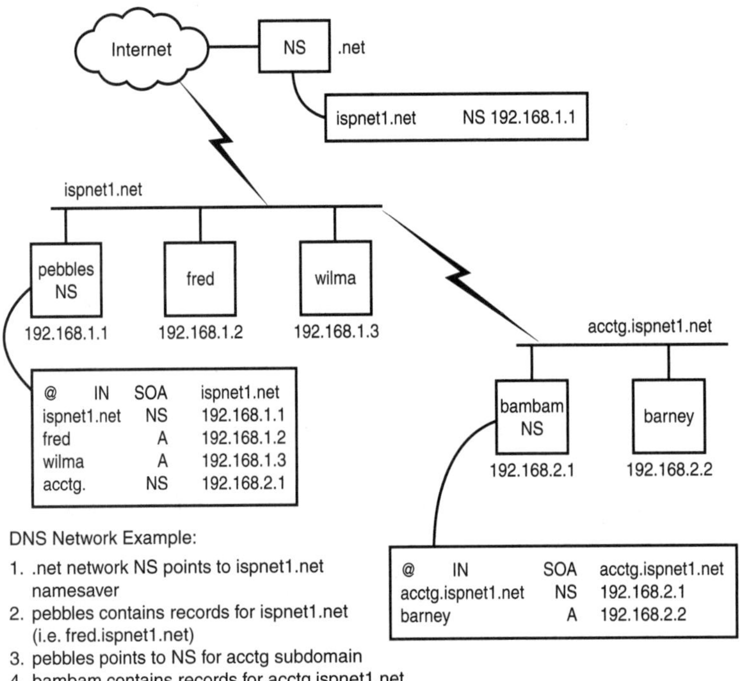

FIGURE 4.4

DNS records for the sample network.

Start of Authority Record (SOA)

Each database starts with an SOA record that defines the zone in which the database resides. The SOA record indicates that the file is authoritative for its particular zone. The format for the SOA record is

```
domain name     [TTL] [class] SOA origin person (
                        serial number
                        refresh
                        retry
                        expire
                        minimum)
```

- *domain name* is the name of the zone that is being defined (the `@` sign can be used as a placeholder to signify the computer's default domain).
- *TTL* is the time (in seconds) that a requesting computer is allowed to keep any DNS information from this zone in its local name cache. This value is optional.
- *class* is the protocol that is being used (which in our case is always class `IN` for Internet). This value is optional and defaults to `IN`.
- *origin* is the name of the computer where the master zone database is located. Be careful to include a trailing period (.) after the hostname, or your local domain name will be appended to the hostname (unless of course you want to use that feature). It is extremely important to use correct syntax when editing DNS zone files!
- *person* is the e-mail address of a person responsible for the zone. This is a little different than usual because the `@` sign is already used to signify the default domain name, so it can't be used in the mail address. Instead, use a period in place of the `@` sign. For example, instead of using `sysadm@ispnet1.net`, you would use `sysadm.ispnet1.net`. If there are any periods in the name part, they must be escaped by using a backslash `\`. An example of this would be the address `john.jones@ispnet1.net`. This address would translate to `john\.jones.ispnet1.net`.
- *serial number* is a unique number that identifies the version of the zone database file and acts as a sort of version-control code. Often the date created plus a version count is used (such as 200102051 for the first version created on February 5, 2001). This number should be incremented by one every time the file is edited.
- *refresh* is the frequency (in seconds) with which a secondary DNS server should query a primary DNS server to check the `SOA` serial number. If it has changed, the secondary requests an update to its database. Specifying one hour (3600 seconds) is common for this value.
- *retry* is the time (in seconds) that a secondary DNS server should wait before retrying after a failed refresh attempt.
- *expire* is the time (in seconds) that a secondary DNS server can use the data retrieved from the primary DNS server without getting refreshed. This value should usually be large, such as 3600000 (about 42 days).
- *minimum* is the time (in seconds) that should be used as the `TTL` in all RRs in this zone. Usually 86,400 (1 day) is a good value.

Internet Address Record (A)

Each host in the zone should have a valid `A` record to define its hostname to the Internet. The format for the `A` record is

```
host    [TTL]    [class]    A    address
```

- *host* is the fully qualified hostname for the computer (including the domain name).
- *address* is the IP address of the computer.

Canonical Name Record (CNAME)

Besides a normal hostname, many computers also have nicknames. This is useful if you want to identify particular services without having to rename computers in your domain, such as `www.ispnet1.net`. The `CNAME` record links nicknames with the real hostname. The format of the `CNAME` record is

```
nickname    [TTL]    [class]    CNAME    hostname
```

Name Server Record (NS)

Each zone should have at least two DNS servers. `NS` records are used to identify these servers to other DNS servers trying to resolve hostnames within the zone. The format of an `NS` record is

```
domain    [TTL]    [class]    NS    server
```

- *`domain`* is the domain name of the zone that the DNS server is responsible for. If it is blank, the `NS` record refers to the zone defined in the `SOA` record.
- *`server`* is the hostname of the DNS server. There should also be an associated `A` record to identify the IP address of the DNS server.

Host Information Record (HINFO)

Additional information about a computer can be made available to DNS servers by using the `HINFO` record. The format of the `HINFO` record is

```
host    [TTL]    [class]    HINFO    hardware    software
```

- *`host`* is the fully qualified hostname of the computer the information applies to.
- *`hardware`* is a text description of the type of hardware the computer is using.
- *`software`* is a text description of the OS type and version of the computer.

Pointer Record (PTR)

In addition to an `A` record, each computer in the zone should also have a `PTR` record. This allows the DNS server to perform reverse queries from the IP address of the computer. Without this information, remote servers could not determine the domain name where your computer is located. The format of a `PTR` record is

```
IN-ADDR name    [TTL]    [class]    PTR    name
```

- *`IN-ADDR name`* is literally the reversed DNS name of the IP address. This name allows the DNS server to work its way backward from the IP address of the computer. The `IN-ADDR.ARPA` address is a special domain to support gateway location and Internet address-to-host mapping. Inverse queries are not necessary because the IP address is mapped to a fictitious hostname. The `IN-ADDR` name of a computer with IP address `192.168.0.1` would be `1.0.168.192.IN-ADDR.ARPA`.

- *`name`* is the fully qualified hostname of the computer as found in the `A` record.

Mail Server Record (`MX`)

Most important (at least as far as we mail administrators are concerned) are the `MX` records. They instruct remote mail servers where to forward mail destined for your zone. The format of the `MX` record is

```
name     [TTL]     [class]     MX     preference     host
```

- *`name`* is the zone name (or the `SOA` zone if it is blank). This can also be a hostname if you want to redirect mail for a particular host in your network.
- *`preference`* is an integer signifying the order in which remote servers should try connecting if multiple mail servers are specified (0 being the highest preference with decreasing preference for increasing numbers). This is used to create primary and secondary mail servers for a zone. When a remote mail server queries the DNS server for a mail server responsible for the zone, the entire list of servers and preferences are sent. The remote mail server should attempt to connect to the highest priority mail server listed, and if that fails, continue down the list by preference.
- *`host`* is the fully qualified hostname of the mail server. There should also be an associated `A` record to identify the IP address of the mail server.

A Sample DNS Database for a Domain

If you allow your ISP to host your domain name and e-mail, it has records in its DNS database identifying your domain to the Internet. The `SOA` record identifies your domain name but points to the ISP's host as the authoritative host. The `NS` records for your domain point to your ISP's DNS servers, and your `MX` records point to your ISP's mail servers. As far as the rest of the Internet is concerned, these computers are part of your network, even though they do not really exist on "your" physical network. Listing 4.1 shows a sample of how your ISP might define your zone definitions in its DNS database. The line numbers shown are added to aid in the discussion of the database.

LISTING 4.1 DNS Zone Database Entry

```
1  ispnet1.net  IN  SOA   master.isp.net. postmaster.master.isp.net (
2                                2001020501    ;unique serial number
3                                8H          ; refresh rate
4                                2H          ;retry period
5                                1W          ; expiration period
6                                1D)          ; minimum
```

LISTING 4.1 Continued

```
7
8            NS     ns1.isp.net.    ;defines primary name server
9            NS     ns2.isp.net.    ; defines secondary name server
10
11           MX     10 mail1.isp.net.    ; defines primary mail server
12           MX     20 mail2.isp.net.    ; defines secondary mail server
13
14  www      CNAME    host1.isp.net.    ;defines your www server at the ISP
15  ftp      CNAME    host1.isp.net.    ; defines your FTP server at the ISP
16
17   host1.isp.net.   A    10.0.0.1
18
19  1.0.0.10.IN-ADDR.ARPA    PTR    host1.isp.net.    ; pointer address for
➥reverse DNS
```

Lines 1–6 show the `SOA` record for your new domain. Comments can be placed on each line after a semicolon. The ISP points service requests for your domain name `ispnet1.net` to the ISP server `master.isp.net`. Lines 8 and 9 define the primary and secondary DNS servers that are used to resolve your hostnames (again, belonging to the ISP), and lines 11 and 12 define the primary (`mail1.isp.net`) and secondary (`mail2.isp.net`) mail servers that receive and spool mail for your domain.

Lines 14 and 15 define nicknames for services in your domain. The hostname `www.ispnet1.net` is a nickname that points to the ISP server that hosts your Web pages. The address `ftp.ispnet1.net` is also a nickname that points to the same ISP server that also hosts your FTP site. This is a service that most ISPs provide to customers who cannot afford to have a dedicated connection to the Internet, but who want to provide Web and FTP services to their customers. Lines 17 and 19 provide the Internet IP address information so that remote clients can connect to this server.

NOTE

Often `PTR` records like the one shown in line 19 are placed in a separate database file on the server to help simplify the databases. In this example with just one `PTR` record, that is not a problem, but often there can be dozens or even hundreds of them.

CAUTION

One very important consideration for mail administrators is the way the `MX` record is defined. Many MTA packages do not work properly if the `MX` record points to a hostname defined as a `CNAME`. It is best to use only hostnames defined in `A` records to define `MX` mail hosts.

When a DNS server has a valid database installed, it must be able to communicate with other DNS servers to resolve hostname requests from clients and to respond to other DNS servers' queries about hosts in its zone. The DNS protocol was invented to accomplish that.

DNS and E-Mail

Computers must follow a set process to properly deliver e-mail, and knowing how that process works sometimes helps out when it comes time to troubleshoot e-mail problems. When a remote client tries to send an e-mail message to `prez@ispnet1.net`, several steps are taken before the message is sent:

1. The local DNS server for the client must first determine which computer in `ispnet1.net` to send the e-mail to. It does this by looking for an `MX` record for the `ispnet1.net` domain.
2. If the local DNS server does not contain any information in its local database or name cache, it must traverse the Internet searching for an answer. The first stop would be one of the top-level root DNS servers. That server would not have the requested `MX` record, but it would know how to get to a DNS server for the `.net` domain.
3. That server in turn would not have the needed information but would (or at least *should*) know the IP address of a DNS server for the `ispnet1.net` domain. The server then queries `ispnet1`'s DNS server for the appropriate `MX` record. If one or more `MX` records exist, they are sent back up the chain until they get to the requesting client computer. Along the way, the local DNS server caches the information for the next query attempt.
4. When the client has the address(es) in hand, it must then try to establish an SMTP connection (see Chapter 5, "SMTP and Postfix") to the primary mail server for the `ispnet1.net` domain.
5. If that connection fails, it then tries the secondary mail server address and so on until it either establishes a connection or runs out of servers to try. At this point, the client's mail program must determine what to do next. Most try the same process again a few hours later, up to a preconfigured point when they finally give up.

If your domain database is not configured correctly, the DNS search for your mail host fails, and the client cannot deliver the mail message. Remember that at no point in the DNS search process was the mail message sent anywhere. The purpose of this process is that the remote client must first find the IP address of a computer that would accept mail messages for the `ispnet1.net` domain. When it finds an address, it can then (hopefully) initiate an SMTP mail session.

Using DNS Client Programs

If you do not have a dedicated connection to the Internet, you should not use your Unix server as a DNS server for your domain. If someone tried sending e-mail to you at three o'clock in the morning and your DNS server was not up and connected to the Internet, she might not be able to resolve your domain name and send the message. Most ISPs provide their clients with a DNS server that is continually connected to the Internet. The ISP's DNS server directs the remote client to the proper e-mail server for your domain. Again, if your network is not directly connected to the Internet, most likely your ISP accepts and spools e-mail messages for your domain so your mail server can pick them up when it is convenient.

If you have a dedicated connection to the Internet but you still want the ISP to host your DNS domain records, you can configure your Unix server to use the ISP DNS server for resolving remote hostnames. The following sections describe how to configure your Unix server to do this.

Configuring DNS Client Files

Three files are needed to use your Unix server as a DNS client to resolve hostnames: `resolv.conf`, `hosts`, and `host.conf` (sometimes called the `nsswitch.conf` on some Unix implementations). All three files are normally located in the `/etc` directory.

Hostname Resolver File

The `/etc/resolv.conf` file is used to list the DNS server(s) you want to handle your DNS queries. You can list up to three DNS servers. The second and third entries are used as backups if no response is received from the first (primary) server. If you have a local DNS server in your network, you should use that as your primary, although it isn't required. If you access other computers in your local network by name, it would increase performance to specify the local DNS server because it would provide the name resolution quickly. If you just use DNS to access remote computers, there probably won't be much performance increase.

You can also specify a default domain name to use when looking up domain names. If your domain is `ispnet1.net`, you can specify that as the default domain to search in. That way if you need the IP address for hostname `fred.ispnet1.net`, you can just look up `fred`, and the lookup function automatically appends the `ispnet1.net` to it. Unfortunately, that can work against you. The DNS software automatically appends `ispnet1.net` to *everything* that it tries to resolve. If you try connecting to `www.freebsd.org`, it first attempts to find `www.freebsd.org.ispnet1.net`. When that fails, it tries `www.freebsd.org`. Listing 4.2 shows a sample `/etc/resolv.conf` file used on a Unix server.

LISTING 4.2 Sample `/etc/resolv.conf` File

```
search ispnet1.net
nameserver 10.0.0.1
nameserver 10.0.0.2
nameserver 10.0.0.3
```

The first line shows the search statement that defines the default domain to use in all DNS queries. Remember that this slows down queries for hosts not in your domain, as the search text is appended to all queries. The next three lines show the primary, secondary, and tertiary DNS servers that service this Unix machine. Most often they are the DNS servers assigned to you by your ISP, although you are free to try other DNS servers (unless of course your ISP filters out DNS requests).

Hosts File

Another method of resolving hostnames is to use a local host database, much like what was previously done on the Internet. The `/etc/hosts` file contains a list of hostnames and associated IP addresses. Listing 4.3 shows a sample `/etc/hosts` file for a Unix server.

At the minimum, this must contain your local hostname and IP address, as well as the common loopback address `127.0.0.1` for internal communications on the Unix machine. If there are remote hosts that you regularly access, you could find their IP addresses and manually enter them into the `/etc/hosts` file. Then every time you accessed those hostnames, the server would have the addresses on hand and not have to perform a DNS lookup (see the `host.conf` description in the following section). This greatly improves the connection time.

LISTING 4.3 Sample `/etc/hosts` File

```
127.0.0.1     localhost
192.168.0.1     shadrach.ispnet1.net shadrach.ispnet1 shadrach
10.0.0.1      mail1.isp.net
10.0.0.2      mail2.isp.net
10.10.0.3      fred.otherplace.com
```

The first two lines show the IP addresses used for the local Unix server. Note that the second line shows multiple names being assigned to the IP address. This way, if the user refers to the machine as just "shadrach.ispnet1" or even just "shadrach" the correct IP address will still be returned.

The subsequent lines show IP addresses for commonly used computers on this network. This allows the server to access these sites by name quicker than by using DNS.

NOTE

All Unix computers include a special hostname called *localhost*. This name always points to the special IP address 127.0.0.1, which is associated with a special network device called the loopback device. This name and address allows internal processes to communicate with other processes on the same system using network protocols. Many programs are configured to use the localhost address. Changing localhost to point to anything else could change the behavior of these programs and would harm the system's functionality.

DNS Resolution File

The `/etc/host.conf` file specifies the methods and order in which Linux can attempt to resolve hostnames. Some other Unix distributions use the same principle with the `nsswitch.conf` file. Unfortunately, different Unix distributions configure this file differently. Listing 4.4 shows a sample `/etc/host.conf` file for a Mandrake 7.0 Linux server.

LISTING 4.4 Sample `/etc/host.conf` File

```
order hosts,bind
multi on
```

The order in which the methods are listed is the order in which the server attempts to resolve the hostname. This shows that first the server looks up the hostname in its local `/etc/hosts` file and then attempts to use DNS (`bind`) if it is not found there. If the server is using an NIS database, that could also be added to the list.

DNS Utilities

Numerous utilities have been written for Unix systems that help system administrators find DNS information for remote hosts and networks. The Internet Software Consortium has created the Berkeley Internet Name Domain (BIND) package for Unix systems, which includes three of my favorite and most often used utilities: `host`, `nslookup`, and `dig`. On most Unix distributions, these programs come prebuilt in the software distribution.

These utilities often come in handy when trying to troubleshoot e-mail problems on the Internet. Often a customer copies an e-mail address incorrectly, and his e-mail is rejected. Of course he then indicates that he is 100% sure that he is using the proper address and can't understand why the message is getting rejected. With a little DNS work, you can determine whether the host part of the e-mail address is correct or contains a typo.

The `host` Program

The `host` program does basic DNS name resolution. There are several different versions of the `host` program. The format of the `host` command varies depending on the version. On a Mandrake 7.0 Linux system, the format of the `host` command is as follows:

```
host [-l] [-v] [-w] [-r] [-d] [-t querytype] [-a] host [server]
```

By default, `host` attempts to resolve the hostname *`host`* by using the default DNS server specified in the `/etc/resolv.conf` file. If *`server`* is added, `host` attempts to use that instead of the default DNS server. By adding additional parameters to the command line, you can modify the output and behavior of `host`. Table 4.3 shows these parameters.

TABLE 4.3 `host` Command Parameters

Parameter	*Description*
`-l`	Lists the complete domain info
`-v`	Uses verbose output format
`-w`	Makes `host` wait indefinitely for response
`-r`	Turns off recursion
`-d`	Turns on debugging
`-t` *`querytype`*	Specifies definite query type
`-a`	Retrieves all DNS records and types

You can use the `-l` option to find information about all the hosts listed in a domain. This is often used with the `-t` option to filter particular types of information (such as `-t MX`, which returns all the `MX` records for a domain). Unfortunately in this day of security awareness, it is often difficult to use the `-l` option because many DNS servers refuse attempts to access all the host information contained in the database.

If you are trying to get information from a slow DNS server (or a slow link to the network), you might want to try the `-w` parameter. This tells the `host` program to wait forever for a response to the query. Without the `-w` parameter, it times out after about one minute.

One useful parameter is `-r`, which tells the DNS server to return only information regarding the query that it has in its own local DNS database or cache. The DNS server does not attempt to contact a remote DNS server to find the information.

This is useful in determining whether your DNS server is properly caching DNS answers. First, try resolving a hostname using the `-r` parameter. If no one else has gone there, you should not get an answer back from your DNS. Then try it without the `-r` parameter. You should get the normal DNS information back, because the local DNS server was allowed to contact a remote DNS server to retrieve the information. Next, try the `host` command again with the `-r` parameter. You should now get the same information that you received from the previous attempt. This means that the DNS server did indeed cache the results from the previous DNS query in its local name cache. If you did not receive any information back, your local DNS server did not cache the previous response. You should have noticed a significant decrease in time that it took to respond with an answer from cache than when it responded after doing the DNS query on the network.

By default, `host` attempts to produce its output in human readable format. For example, Listing 4.5 shows a typical output. If you use the `-v` option, the output changes to resemble the normal RR format found in the DNS database. This can be useful in trying to debug a DNS problem with the configuration of the DNS server.

LISTING 4.5 Sample `host` Output

```
[rich@shadrach]$ host -t mx linux.org
linux.org mail is handled (pri=20) by router.invlogic.com
linux.org mail is handled (pri=10) by mail.linux.org
```

The first line shows the basic format for using the `host` command to find the mail servers for a domain. The result from the `host` command shows that the domain name has two different mail server (`MX`) records. Notice that `host` also lists the preference of each mail server. For this domain, the `mail.linux.org` host is the primary mail server. This is a good technique to use if you think your mail server is not behaving properly in delivering messages to a remote site.

The `nslookup` Program

The `nslookup` program is an extremely versatile tool that you can use in a variety of troubleshooting situations. `nslookup` can run under two modes. In non-interactive mode, it behaves much like the `host` command discussed previously. The interactive mode is where all the fun lies. It can give more detailed information about remote computers and domains because you can change options as you traverse the DNS database. The basic format of the `nslookup` command is

```
nslookup [-option ...] [host-to-find | -[server]]
```

If you enter the *`host-to-find`* parameter on the command line, `nslookup` operates in non-interactive mode and returns the result of the query similar to the `host` command. If no arguments are given or the first argument is a hyphen (-), `nslookup` enters into interactive mode. If you want to use a different DNS server, you can specify that using the *`-server`* argument, where *`server`* is the IP address of the DNS server to use. Otherwise `nslookup` uses the default DNS server as listed in the `/etc/resolv.conf` file.

You can change option settings in the `nslookup` program in three ways. One way is to list them as options in the `nslookup` command line. Another way is to specify them on the interactive command line after `nslookup` starts by using the `set` command. The third way is to create a file in your `$HOME` directory called `.nslookuprc` and enter one option per line. A list of available options is shown in Table 4.4.

TABLE 4.4 nslookup Options

Option	*Description*
`all`	Prints the current values of options
`class`	Sets the DNS class value (default=`IN`)
`[no]debug`	Turns debugging mode on (or off) (default = `nodebug`)
`[no]d2`	Turns exhaustive debugging mode on (or off) (default = `nod2`)
`domain=name`	Sets the default domain name to `name`
`srchlist=name1/name2...`	Changes the default domain name to `name1` and the search list to `name1`, `name2`, and so on, up to a maximum of 6 names
`[no]defname`	Appends the default domain name to a single component lookup request
`[no]search`	Appends the domain names in search list to the hostname (default = `search`)
`port=value`	Changes TCP/UDP port to `value` (default = `53`)
`querytype=value`	Changes type of information requested to type `value` (default = `A`)
`type=value`	Same as `querytype`
`[no]recurse`	Tells name server to query other servers to obtain an answer (default = `recurse`)
`retry=number`	Sets number of retries to `number` (default = `4`)
`root=host`	Changes name of root server to host (default = `ns.internic.net`)
`timeout=number`	Changes initial timeout interval to wait for a reply to `number` (default = 5 seconds)
`[no]vc`	Always uses a virtual circuit (default = `novc`)
`[no]ignoretc`	Ignores packet truncation errors (default = `noignoretc`)

Listing 4.6 shows a sample `nslookup` session used to get information for host `www.linux.org`. The default parameters return the IP address for the hostname. This example demonstrates changing the parameters to find the mail servers for the domain.

LISTING 4.6 Sample nslookup Session

```
[rich@shadrach]$ nslookup
Default Server:  dns1.ispnet1.net
Address:  192.168.1.10

> www.linux.org
Server:  dns1.ispnet1.net
Address:  192.168.1.10

Non-authoritative answer:
Name:    www.linux.org
```

LISTING 4.6 Continued

```
Address:  198.182.196.56

> set q=mx
> linux.org
Server:  dns1.ispnet1.net
Address:  192.168.1.10

Non-authoritative answer:
linux.org        preference = 10, mail exchanger = mail.linux.org
linux.org        preference = 20, mail exchanger = router.invlogic.com

Authoritative answers can be found from:
linux.org        nameserver = NS.invlogic.com
linux.org        nameserver = NS0.AITCOM.NET
mail.linux.org   internet address = 198.182.196.60
NS.invlogic.com internet address = 207.245.34.122
NS0.AITCOM.NET   internet address = 208.234.1.34
> exit
```

The first example shows the query for the hostname `www.linux.org`. The DNS server used to process the query is displayed, and the lines that follow show that the server contained a non-authoritative answer for the IP address. Obviously someone must have accessed this site before and its IP address was still in the DNS server's local name cache.

Next, the option is set to return information on the mail servers in the domain, and a query is made on the `linux.org` domain. The results show the answer section of the DNS packet, which again indicates that the answer is non-authoritative and lists the two mail servers responsible for the `linux.org` hostname. Following that, `nslookup` provides hostnames and IP addresses for nameservers that have authoritative answers for the domain.

If you want to extend this example, you could change the default DNS server to one of the authoritative DNS servers listed (by using the `server` command) and retry the `MX` query to see whether the information has changed at all from the information returned from the non-authoritative DNS server.

The `dig` Program

The `dig` program uses a simple command-line format to query DNS servers regarding domain information. The format for the `dig` command is as follows:

```
dig [@server] domain [query-type] [query-class] [+query-option]
➥ [-dig-option] [%comment]
```

- *server* is an optional DNS server that you can specify. By default, `dig` uses the DNS server defined in the `/etc/resolv.conf` file. You can specify the *server* option by using either an IP address or a hostname. If you use a hostname for the *server* option, `dig` uses the default DNS server to resolve the hostname, and then it uses that DNS server to find the information on the domain.
- *query-type* is the RR type of information that you are requesting, such as the `A`, `SOA`, `NS`, and `MX` records. You can use a query-type of `any` to return all information available about a domain.
- *query-class* is the network class of information that you are requesting. The default is Internet (`IN`), which is the type of information we are looking for.
- *+query-option* changes an option value in the DNS packet or changes the format of the `dig` output. Many of these options shadow options available in the `nslookup` program. Table 4.5 shows the query-options available to use.

TABLE 4.5 `dig` query-options

Option	*Description*
`[no]debug`	Turns on (off) debugging
`[no]d2`	Turns on (off) extra debugging
`[no]recurse`	(Doesn't) use recursive lookups
`retry=#`	Sets number of retries
`time=#`	Sets timeout length
`[no]ko`	Keeps open option (implies vc)
`[no]vc`	(Doesn't) use virtual circuit
`[no]defname`	(Doesn't) use default domain name
`[no]search`	(Doesn't) use domain search list
`domain=NAME`	Sets default domain name to `NAME`
`[no]ignore`	(Doesn't) ignore truncation errors
`[no]primary`	(Doesn't) use primary server
`[no]aaonly`	(Doesn't) set Authoritative query only flag
`[no]cmd`	(Doesn't) echo parsed arguments
`[no]stats`	(Doesn't) print query statistics
`[no]Header`	(Doesn't) print basic header
`[no]header`	(Doesn't) print header flags
`[no]ttlid`	(Doesn't) print TTLs
`[no]cl`	(Doesn't) print class info
`[no]qr`	(Doesn't) print outgoing query
`[no]reply`	(Doesn't) print reply
`[no]ques`	(Doesn't) print question section
`[no]answer`	(Doesn't) print answer section

TABLE 4.5 Continued

Option	*Description*
`[no]author`	(Doesn't) print authoritative section
`[no]addit`	(Doesn't) print additional section
`pfdef`	Sets to default print flags
`pfmin`	Sets to minimal print flags
`pfset=#`	Sets print flags to `#`
`pfand=#`	Bitwise AND prints flags with `#`
`pfor=#`	Bitwise OR prints flags with `#`

`-dig-option` specifies other options that affect the operation of `dig`. Table 4.6 shows some of the other options available to fine-tune the `dig` command and its output.

TABLE 4.6 `dig` Options

Option	*Description*
`-x`	Specifies inverse address mapping in normal dot notation
`-f`	Reads a file for batch mode processing
`-T`	Time in seconds between batch mode command processing
`-p`	Port number to use
`-P`	After a response, issues a `ping` command
`-t`	Specifies type of query
`-c`	Specifies class of query
`-envsav`	Specifies that the `dig` options should be saved to become the default `dig` environment

Listing 4.7 shows a sample `dig` session output.

LISTING 4.7 Sample `dig` Output

```
[rich@shadrach]$ dig www.linux.org

; <<>> DiG 8.2 <<>> www.linux.org
;; res options: init recurs defnam dnsrch
;; got answer:
;; ->>HEADER<<- opcode: QUERY, status: NOERROR, id: 4
;; flags: qr rd ra; QUERY: 1, ANSWER: 1, AUTHORITY: 2, ADDITIONAL: 2
;; QUERY SECTION:
;;      www.linux.org, type = A, class = IN
```

LISTING 4.7 Continued

```
;; ANSWER SECTION:
www.linux.org.          10h47m19s IN A  198.182.196.56

;; AUTHORITY SECTION:
linux.org.              1d22h45m35s IN NS  NS.INVLOGIC.COM.
linux.org.              1d22h45m35s IN NS  NS0.AITCOM.NET.

;; ADDITIONAL SECTION:
NS.INVLOGIC.COM.        1d23h37m51s IN A  207.245.34.122
NS0.AITCOM.NET.         20h2m29s IN A   208.234.1.34

;; Total query time: 13 msec
;; FROM: shadrach.ispnet1.net to SERVER: default -- 192.168.1.10
;; WHEN: Fri Feb  9 19:41:19 2001
;; MSG SIZE  sent: 31  rcvd: 145
```

As you can see, the `dig` program produces the same information as `host` and `nslookup`, but it shows more detail on how and where the answers came from.

Summary

This chapter discussed the domain name system (DNS) and how it relates to e-mail. Each computer connected to the Internet has a unique hostname and a unique IP address. The DNS database system matches the hostnames and IP addresses together. The database is distributed among many different servers on the Internet, so no one server has to maintain one massive list of all computers.

You can find a remote computer's IP address by its hostname by sending a DNS query to a DNS server. That server can "walk" the DNS tree to find the database record that relates the hostname to the IP address, or vice versa. Many domains use their domain name as a generic e-mail address. Your e-mail server must know how to use DNS to find a server responsible for receiving e-mail messages for a destination domain.

The mail administrator can determine whether the proper DNS mail entries have been made for a remote domain by using the `host`, `nslookup`, and `dig` programs. These programs manually query the DNS server to determine the necessary information regarding the remote domain.

CHAPTER 5

SMTP and Postfix

The Simple Mail Transfer Protocol (SMTP) has been used since 1982 to deliver e-mail messages and attachments to many different types of computer systems. Its ease of implementation and platform independence has made it the standard protocol used to transfer messages between computer systems on the Internet. To understand how e-mail works, you should get to know SMTP.

The Local Mail Transfer Protocol (LMTP) is a newer protocol that can streamline mail transfers without using message queues.

Postfix is one of a few MTAs that support communicating with Mail Delivery Agents (MDAs) using LMTP. This lets Postfix delegate the chore of delivering local messages to one or more MDA programs, thus freeing it up for other duties.

This chapter describes both SMTP and LMTP and shows how the Postfix software uses them to send mail messages.

SMTP Description

SMTP was designed to work on many different types of transport media. The most common transport is a TCP/IP connection on the Internet using port 25. A common troubleshooting technique for checking whether a remote server is running an SMTP server package is to telnet to TCP port 25 and see if you get a response. You can test this out on your own Unix server by telnetting to hostname `localhost` using port 25.

Listing 5.1 shows a sample telnet session to a Linux server running the Postfix package.

LISTING 5.1 Sample Telnet Session to Port 25

```
[rich@shadrach]$ telnet localhost 25
Trying 127.0.0.1...
Connected to localhost.
Escape character is '^]'.
220 shadrach.ispnet1.net ESMTP Postfix
QUIT
221 Bye
Connection closed by foreign host.
```

The first line shows the `telnet` command format using host `localhost` and TCP port 25. If the server is running an SMTP-based daemon, you should see a response similar to the one shown. The first number is a 3-digit response code. You can use this code for troubleshooting purposes if mail is not being transferred properly. Next, the hostname of the SMTP server and a description of the SMTP software package that the server is using are displayed. This server is using the Postfix SMTP software package using the `smtpd` program to accept incoming SMTP connections. Many mail administrators block the MTA package name in the greeting banner to help hide the software they are using. You can close the telnet connection by typing the word `QUIT` and pressing the Enter key. The SMTP server should send you a closing message and end the TCP connection.

As you can see in this example, SMTP accepts simple ASCII text commands and returns 3-digit reply codes with optional ASCII text messages. SMTP is defined in the Request For Comment (RFC) document number 821 maintained by the Internet Engineering Task Force (IETF) published on August 21, 1982. Several modifications and enhancements have been made to SMTP over the years, but the basic protocol commands still remain in use.

Basic SMTP Client Commands

When a TCP session has been established and the SMTP server acknowledges the client by sending a welcome banner (as shown in Listing 5.1), it is the client's responsibility to control the connection and transmit data to the server. The client accomplishes this by sending special commands to the server. The server responds according to each command it receives.

RFC 821 defines the basic client commands that an SMTP server should recognize and respond to. Since then, there have been several extensions to SMTP that not all servers have implemented. This section documents the basic SMTP keywords that are defined in RFC 821. The section "Extended SMTP" covers some of the new extensions that have been implemented by several SMTP software packages.

The basic format of an SMTP command is

```
command [parameters]
```

where *`command`* is a 4-character SMTP command, and *`parameters`* are optional qualifying data for the command. For SMTP connections, the command names are not case sensitive. Table 5.1 shows the basic SMTP commands that are available.

TABLE 5.1 SMTP Basic Commands

Command	*Description*
`HELO`	Opening greeting from client
`MAIL`	Identifies sender of message
`RCPT`	Identifies recipient(s)
`DATA`	Identifies start of message
`SEND`	Sends message to terminal(s)
`SOML`	Send-or-Mail; sends message to mailbox or terminal of recipient(s)
`SAML`	Send-and-Mail; sends message to mailbox *and* terminal of recipient(s)
`RSET`	Reset; aborts SMTP connection and discards information
`VRFY`	Verifies that username exists on server
`EXPN`	Verifies that mailing list exists on server

TABLE 5.1 Continued

Command	*Description*
`HELP`	Requests list of commands
`NOOP`	No operation; only elicits an "OK" from server
`QUIT`	Ends the SMTP session
`TURN`	Requests that the systems reverse their current SMTP roles

The following sections describe these commands in more detail.

`HELO` Command

This is not a typo. By definition, SMTP commands are four characters long, thus the opening greeting by the client to the server is the `HELO` command. The format for this command is

```
HELO hostname
```

The purpose of the `HELO` command is for the client to identify itself to the SMTP server. Unfortunately, this method was devised in the early days of the Internet before mass hacker break-in attempts. As you can see, the client can identify itself as whatever it wants to use in the text string. That being the case, most SMTP servers use this command just as a formality. If they really need to know the identity of the client, they try to use a reverse DNS lookup of the client's IP address to determine the client's DNS name. For security reasons, many SMTP servers refuse to talk to hosts whose IP address does not resolve to a proper DNS hostname.

By sending the `HELO` command, the client indicates that it wants to initialize a new SMTP session with the server. By responding to this command, the server acknowledges the new connection and should be ready to receive further commands from the client.

PEOPLE CLIENTS VERSUS HOST CLIENTS

In SMTP you must remember to differentiate between people and hosts. When creating a new mail message, the e-mail user is the client of his local host. Once the user sends his message, he is no longer the client in the SMTP process. His local host computer takes over the process of mailing the message and now becomes the client as far as SMTP is concerned. When the local host contacts the remote host to transfer the message using SMTP, it is now acting as the client in the SMTP process. The `HELO` command identifies the local hostname as the client, not the actual sender of the message. This terminology often gets confusing.

`MAIL` Command

The `MAIL` command initiates a mail session with the server after the initial `HELO` command is sent. It identifies from whom the message is being sent. The format of the `MAIL` command is

```
MAIL reverse-path
```

The `reverse-path` argument not only identifies the sender, but it also identifies how to reach the sender with a return message. If the sender were a user on the client computer that initiated the SMTP session, the format for the `MAIL` command would look something like this:

```
MAIL FROM:rich@shadrach.ispnet1.net
```

Notice how the `FROM` section denotes the proper e-mail address for the sender of the message, including the fully qualified hostname of the client computer. This information should appear in the text of the e-mail message in the `FROM` section (but more on that later). If the e-mail message has been routed through several different systems between the original sender and the desired recipient, each system adds its routing information to the `reverse-path` section. This documents the path that the e-mail message traversed to get to the server.

Often, mail from clients on private networks has to traverse several mail relay points before getting to the Internet. The `reverse-path` information is often useful in troubleshooting e-mail problems or in tracking down senders who are purposely trying to hide their identity by bouncing their e-mail messages off of several unknowing SMTP servers.

`RCPT` Command

The `RCPT` command identifies the intended recipient of the message. In order to deliver the same message to multiple recipients, each recipient must be listed in a separate `RCPT` command line. The format of the `RCPT` command is

```
RCPT forward-path
```

The `forward-path` argument defines where the e-mail is ultimately destined. This is usually a fully qualified e-mail address but could be just a username that is local to the SMTP server. For example, the following `RCPT` command

```
RCPT TO:haley
```

would send the message to user `haley` on the local SMTP server that is processing the message.

The protocol also allows messages to be relayed—sent to users on computer systems other than the server currently handling the SMTP connection.

For example, sending the following `RCPT` command

```
RCPT TO:riley@meshach.ispnet1.net
```

to the SMTP server on `shadrach.ispnet1.net` would cause `shadrach.ispnet1.net` to make a decision. Because the recipient is not local to `shadrach`, it must decide what to do with the message. `shadrach` could take three possible actions with the message:

- `shadrach` could accept the message for later forwarding to the specified destination and return an OK response to the client. In this scenario, `shadrach` would prepend its hostname to the message's `<reverse-path>`.
- `shadrach` could refuse to forward the message but could reply to the client that it would not deliver the message. The response could also verify that the address of `meshach.ispnet1.net` was a correct address for another server. Then the client could try to resend the message directly to `meshach.ispnet1.net`.
- `shadrach` could refuse to forward the message and could reply to the client that this operation (relaying) is not permitted from this server. It would be up to the system administrator at the client to figure out what happened and why.

In the early days of the Internet, it was common to run across computers that used the first scenario and blindly forwarded e-mail messages across the world. Unfortunately, that courteous behavior was exploited by e-mail *spammers*, people who do mass mailings across the Internet for either fun or profit. Spammers often use unsuspecting, unsecured SMTP servers that blindly forward e-mail messages in an attempt to disguise the origin of their mail messages. To combat this situation, most mail system administrators have either completely turned off mail relaying or have at least limited it to hosts within their domain. Many ISPs allow their customers to relay e-mail from their mail server but restrict outside computers from that privilege.

In the case of multiple recipients, it is up to the client how to handle situations in which some of the recipients are not allowed by the server. Some clients abort the entire message and return an error to the sending user. Some continue sending the message to the recipients that are acknowledged and list the recipients that aren't acknowledged in a return message.

`DATA` Command

The `DATA` command is the meat and potatoes of the SMTP operation. After the `MAIL` and `RCPT` commands are worked out, the `DATA` command initiates the actual message transfer. The format of the `DATA` command is

```
DATA
```

Anything that appears after the command is treated as part of the message being transferred. Usually the SMTP server adds a timestamp and `return-path` information to the head of the message. The client indicates the end of the message by sending a line with just a single period. The format for that line is

```
<CR><LF>.<CR><LF>
```

When the SMTP server receives this sequence, it knows that the message transmission is done and should return a response code to the client indicating whether the message has been accepted.

Much work has been done on the format of the actual DATA messages. Technically there is no wrong way to send a message, although work has been done to standardize a method (see the "Message Formats" section later in the chapter). Any combination of valid ASCII characters is transferred to the specified recipients. Listing 5.2 shows a sample session sending a short mail message to a local user on an SMTP server.

LISTING 5.2 Sample SMTP Session

```
$ telnet localhost 25
Trying 127.0.0.1...
Connected to localhost.ispnet1.net.
Escape character is '^]'.
220 shadrach.ispnet1.net ESMTP
HELO localhost
250 shadrach.ispnet1.net
MAIL FROM: rich@localhost
250 ok
RCPT TO:rich
250 ok
DATA
354 go ahead
This is a short test of the SMTP e-mail system.
.
250 ok 959876575 qp 40419
QUIT
221 shadrach.ispnet1.net
Connection closed by foreign host.

you have mail
$ mail
Mail version 8.1 6/6/93.  Type ? for help.
"/var/mail/rich": 1 message 1 new
>N  1 rich@localhost        Thu Jun  1 11:22   8/339
& 1
Message 1:
From rich@localhost Thu Jun  1 11:22:55 2000

This is a short test of the SMTP e-mail system.

& x
```

Listing 5.2 shows a typical SMTP exchange between two hosts. After entering the message header information, the client enters the `DATA` command, and the server responds. Next the client sends the text message. Following the completed message is the terminating period, indicating the end of the message to the server. As you can see, the SMTP server transferred the `DATA` portion of the message to the local user's mailbox account exactly as the server received it. Also note that the SMTP server prepended a timestamp and `return-path` information to the text of the e-mail message.

`SEND` Command

The `SEND` command sends a mail message directly to the terminal of a logged-in user. This command works only when the user is logged in and usually pops up as a message much like the Unix `write` command. This command does have a serious drawback. It is an easy way for an external user to determine who is logged in to a computer system at any given time without having to log in to the system. Hackers have exploited this "feature" by searching the Internet for unsuspecting victims' usernames and login patterns. Because it is such a security threat, most SMTP software packages do not implement this command anymore.

`SOML` Command

The `SOML` command stands for `SEND` or `MAIL`. If the recipients are logged on to the computer system, it behaves like the preceding `SEND` command. If not, it behaves like the `MAIL` command and sends the message to the recipients' mailboxes. The "exploit-ability" of this command has made it another victim of the Internet world, and it is often not implemented on newer SMTP server packages.

`SAML` Command

The `SAML` command stands for `SEND` and `MAIL`. This command tries to cover both bases by sending a message to the terminal of a logged-in user as well as placing the message in the user's mailbox. Again, the "exploit-ability" of this command has rendered it unsafe to implement.

`RSET` Command

The `RSET` command is short for *reset*. If the client somehow gets confused by the responses from the server or thinks that the SMTP connection has gotten out of sync, it can issue the `RSET` command to return the connection to the `HELO` command state. Of course, all `MAIL`, `RCPT`, and `DATA` information already entered is lost. Often this is used as a last-ditch effort when the client either has lost track of where it was in the command series or did not expect a particular response from the server.

`VRFY` Command

The `VRFY` command is short for *verify*. You can use the `VRFY` command to determine whether an SMTP server can deliver mail to a particular recipient before entering the `RCPT` command. The format of this command is

```
VRFY username
```

When received, the SMTP server determines whether the user is on the local server. If the user is local to the server, it returns the full e-mail address of the user. If the user is not local, the SMTP server can either return a negative response to the client or indicate that it is willing to forward any mail messages to the remote user, depending on whether the SMTP server forwards messages for the particular client.

The `VRFY` command can be a very valuable troubleshooting tool. Often users incorrectly type a username or hostname in an e-mail message and don't know why their mail messages did not get to where they wanted them to go. Of course the first thing they do is complain about the lousy mail system, and then contact you, the mail administrator. As the mail administrator, you can attempt to verify the e-mail address in two ways. First, use the DNS `host` command to determine whether the domain name is correct and has a mail server associated with it. Then, you can telnet to port 25 of the mail server and use the `VRFY` command to determine whether the username is correct. Listing 5.3 shows an example of using the `VRFY` command to check the validity of usernames.

LISTING 5.3 Example of the `VRFY` Command

```
[richard@shadrach]$ telnet localhost 25
Trying 127.0.0.1...
Connected to localhost.
Escape character is '^]'.
220 shadrach.ispnet1.net ESMTP Sendmail 8.9.3/8.9.3;
➥ Thu, 26 Aug 1999 19:20:16 -050
HELO localhost
250 shadrach.ispnet1.net Hello localhost [127.0.0.1], pleased to meet you
VRFY rich
250 <rich@shadrach.ispnet1.net>
VRFY prez@mechach.ispnet1.net
252 <prez@mechach.ispnet1.net>
VRFY jessica
550 jessica... User unknown
QUIT
221 shadrach.ispnet1.net closing connection
Connection closed by foreign host.
```

Note the difference between the return codes for the usernames `rich` and `prez`. The `VRFY` command for `rich` returns a 250 code, which indicates that the server accepts messages for `rich`, who is a local user. The result from the `prez` `VRFY` command is 252, which indicates that the user is not local, but the mail server is willing to forward the message for him. The result codes will be explained in more detail in the "Server Responses" section later in the chapter.

Much like some of the other useful commands, hackers can exploit the `VRFY` command. Because of this, many sites do not implement the `VRFY` command. While this will seriously impede your ability to troubleshoot bad e-mail addresses, it has become a must in this day of Internet security.

`EXPN` Command

The `EXPN` command is short for *expand*. This command queries the SMTP server for mailing lists and aliases. Mailing lists are handy ways of sending mass mailings to groups of people via just one address. Chapter 19, "Using Majordomo with Postfix," looks at the topic of mailing lists more in depth. The format of the `EXPN` command is

```
EXPN mail-list
```

where *`mail-list`* is the name of the mailing list or alias. The SMTP server returns either an error code if the client does not have privileges to see the list (or if the list does not exist) or the complete mailing list, one e-mail address per line. Again, often this command is disabled for security reasons.

`HELP` Command

The `HELP` command asks the server to return useful information to the client. `HELP` with no arguments returns a list of SMTP commands that the SMTP server understands. Listing 5.4 shows the output from a `HELP` command issued to a Linux server running the `sendmail` SMTP package version 8.9.3.

LISTING 5.4 SMTP `HELP` Command Output

```
[richard@shadrach]$ telnet localhost 25
Trying 127.0.0.1...
Connected to localhost.
Escape character is '^]'.
220 shadrach.ispnet1.net ESMTP Sendmail 8.9.3/8.9.3;
➥ Thu, 26 Aug 1999 19:50:57 -050
HELO localhost
250 shadrach.ispnet1.net Hello localhost [127.0.0.1], pleased to meet you
HELP
214-This is Sendmail version 8.9.3
214-Topics:
214-     HELO    EHLO    MAIL    RCPT    DATA
214-     RSET    NOOP    QUIT    HELP    VRFY
214-     EXPN    VERB    ETRN    DSN
214-For more info use "HELP <topic>".
214-To report bugs in the implementation send e-mail to
214-     sendmail-bugs@sendmail.org.
214-For local information send e-mail to Postmaster at your site.
```

LISTING 5.4 Continued

```
214 End of HELP info
HELP RCPT
214-RCPT TO: <recipient> [ <parameters> ]
214-    Specifies the recipient.  Can be used any number of times.
214-    Parameters are ESMTP extensions.  See "HELP DSN" for details.
214 End of HELP info
HELP VRFY
214-VRFY <recipient>
214-    Verify an address.  If you want to see what it aliases
214-    to, use EXPN instead.
214 End of HELP info
QUIT
221 shadrach.ispnet1.net closing connection
Connection closed by foreign host.
```

By sending the HELP command with an argument that is another SMTP command, the server returns a more detailed description of the command, including any parameters that are required.

NOOP Command

The NOOP command is short for *no operation.* This command has no effect on the SMTP server other than making it return a positive response code. This is often a useful command to send to test connectivity without actually starting the message transfer process.

QUIT Command

The QUIT command indicates that the client computer is finished with the current SMTP session and wants to close the connection. It is the responsibility of the SMTP server to respond to this command and to initiate the closing of the TCP connection. If the server receives a QUIT command in the middle of an e-mail transaction, any data previously transferred will be deleted and not sent to any recipients.

TURN Command

The TURN command is generally not implemented on SMTP servers today for security reasons. It is part of the RFC 821 standard because it was a great idea that, unfortunately, was exploited by hackers. The TURN idea was modified in the extended SMTP RFCs, and it is discussed in the section "Extended SMTP." It is described here as a background reference for the extended SMTP version ETRN.

The TURN command allows two-way mail transfer between two computers during one TCP connection. Normally, SMTP sends mail in only one direction for each connection. The client host is in control of the transmission session and directs the actions of the server by sending SMTP commands. Mail can only be sent from the client to the server.

It might be desirable for a computer to make contact with an SMTP server, and not only be able to send mail to the server, but also be able to receive any mail that the server is waiting to send to the client.

As discussed previously, the server uses the domain name indicated by the `HELO` command text string to identify the client it is talking to. The idea of the `TURN` command is to allow the SMTP server to switch roles with the client and send any mail destined for the client's domain name to the client. The problem with this idea is the assumption by the SMTP server that the client is actually who it claims to be. If a hacker connected to the SMTP server and identified himself as another computer domain name, then `TURN`ed the connection, the server would unknowingly send all the mail messages destined for the specified domain name to the hacker. Ouch!

Server Responses

For each command that the client sends to the SMTP server, the server must send a reply. As you can see from Listings 5.2 and 5.3, these response messages contain two parts. The first part is a 3-digit code that indicates to the client whether the command was successful, and if not, why. The second part is a text string that helps humans understand the reply. Often the text string is passed on by the SMTP-based software and displayed to the user as part of a response message.

Usually a space separates the code from the text string. In the case of multiline responses (such as the `HELP` and `EXPN` commands in Listing 5.4), a dash (-) separates the code from the text on all but the last line, which conforms to the normal pattern of using a space. This helps the client identify when to expect more lines from the server. There are four different groups, or categories, of reply codes. The following sections explain these codes.

SMTP Error Response Codes

Table 5.2 shows the response codes for error conditions that could occur from various problems in the SMTP transaction.

TABLE 5.2 SMTP Error Response Codes

Code	*Description*
500	Syntax error, command not recognized
501	Syntax error in parameters or arguments
502	Command not implemented
503	Bad sequence of commands
504	Command parameter not implemented

SMTP error responses are not overly descriptive. They just give a general idea of what might have gone wrong in the SMTP process. When troubleshooting mail problems, it is helpful to be able to watch the actual SMTP transactions and watch for command errors if you are communicating with an unfamiliar SMTP server. Often 500, 502, and 504 errors occur when trying to implement extended SMTP commands with older SMTP software servers.

SMTP Informational Response Codes

The next category of response codes is informational codes. Table 5.3 shows these codes.

TABLE 5.3 SMTP Informational Response Codes

Code	*Description*
211	System status, or system help reply
214	Help message

As shown in Listing 5.4, the 214 response code is used when displaying output from the `HELP` command. When you have multiple lines of output, a dash after the response code signifies that more lines are coming. The last line uses a space to separate the response code from the text.

SMTP Service Response Codes

Another response code category is the service codes, which denote the status of the SMTP service in the connection. Table 5.4 shows these codes.

TABLE 5.4 SMTP Service Response Codes

Code	*Description*
220	Service ready
221	Service closing transmission channel
421	Service not available, closing transmission channel

Each of these response codes includes the hostname of the SMTP server in the text string portion, as well as the text description. The 421 response code is a little misleading. Many mail administrators think that this response code is returned when there is no SMTP software available on the remote server. Although this can happen, usually this response code means that there is an SMTP server, but it is not accepting mail messages at the time. Sometimes a server locks its filesystem to perform nightly data backups. The SMTP server would be unable to store mail messages on the locked filesystem, so the SMTP server shuts down temporarily while the backup is running. Trying to connect to the same server a little later in the evening would result in a successful transaction.

SMTP Action Response Codes

The last response code category relates to replying to SMTP client actions. Table 5.5 shows the action codes used in an SMTP transaction.

TABLE 5.5 SMTP Action Response Codes

Code	*Description*
250	Requested mail action OK, completed
251	User not local; will forward to <forward-path>
354	Start mail input; end with <CRLF>.<CRLF>
450	Requested mail action not taken: mailbox unavailable
451	Requested action aborted: error in processing
452	Requested action not taken: insufficient system storage
550	Requested action not taken: mailbox unavailable
551	User not local; please try <forward-path>
552	Requested mail action aborted: exceeded storage allocation
553	Requested action not taken: mailbox name not allowed
554	Transaction failed

Action codes are a result of the SMTP server trying to perform a function requested by the client, such as `MAIL`, `RCPT`, and `DATA` commands. They return the status of the requested action so that the client knows what actions to take next in the SMTP process.

SMTP server response codes are often behind-the-scenes players in the SMTP world. Some e-mail client packages forward any error response codes that they receive back to the sender of the e-mail. When this happens, it is easy to check the response codes against the code lists to determine what went wrong. Sometimes it is difficult to determine what went wrong with an e-mail message that does not get processed properly. When a return e-mail message does not get routed back properly to the client, no error text is sent to the user. Often the mail administrator has to resort to using network analyzers to watch the actual TCP packets on the LAN to see the response codes that are coming from the SMTP server. Remember that the SMTP data packets are ASCII text, so they are easy to read and decode.

Extended SMTP

Since its invention in 1982, SMTP has performed well in transporting messages between computers across the Internet. As it aged, system administrators began to recognize its limitations. Instead of trying to replace a standard protocol that was in use all over the world, work was done to try and improve the basic SMTP protocol by keeping the original specifications and adding new features.

RFC 1869, "SMTP Service Extensions," was published in 1995 and defined a method of extending the capabilities of SMTP.

Extended SMTP (ESMTP) replaces the original SMTP greeting (`HELO`) with a new greeting command: `EHLO`. When an ESMTP server receives this command, it should realize that the client is capable of sending extended SMTP commands. Listing 5.5 shows a sample `EHLO` session and the commands that are available on the server.

LISTING 5.5 Extended SMTP Commands

```
[richard@shadrach]$ telnet localhost 25
Trying 127.0.0.1...
Connected to localhost.
Escape character is '^]'.
220 shadrach.ispnet1.net ESMTP Sendmail 8.9.3/8.9.3;
➥ Mon, 30 Aug 1999 16:36:48 -050
EHLO localhost
250-shadrach.ispnet1.net Hello localhost [127.0.0.1], pleased to meet you
250-EXPN
250-VERB
250-8BITMIME
250-SIZE
250-DSN
250-ONEX
250-ETRN
250-XUSR
250 HELP
HELP DSN
214-MAIL FROM: <sender> [ RET={ FULL | HDRS} ] [ ENVID=<envid> ]
214-RCPT TO: <recipient> [ NOTIFY={NEVER,SUCCESS,FAILURE,DELAY} ]
214-                     [ ORCPT=<recipient> ]
214-    SMTP Delivery Status Notifications.
214-Descriptions:
214-    RET     Return either the full message or only headers.
214-    ENVID   Sender's "envelope identifier" for tracking.
214-    NOTIFY  When to send a DSN. Multiple options are OK, comma-
214-            delimited. NEVER must appear by itself.
214-    ORCPT   Original recipient.
214 End of HELP info
HELP ETRN
214-ETRN [ <hostname> | @<domain> | #<queuename> ]
214-    Run the queue for the specified <hostname>, or
214-    all hosts within a given <domain>, or a specially-named
214-    <queuename> (implementation-specific).
214 End of HELP info
QUIT
221 shadrach.ispnet1.net closing connection
Connection closed by foreign host.
```

Notice that the server indicates that some additional commands are available now that it is in "extended" mode. One of the new groups of commands is the Delivery Status Notification options. These options can be used on the `MAIL` and `RCPT` commands to indicate the delivery status of a particular e-mail message for the client. One command that we are extremely interested in as mail administrators is the `ETRN` command.

The ETRN Command

I briefly mentioned the TURN SMTP command earlier. This command was extremely useful, but not very secure. To compensate for that, RFC 1985 defines a new method of implementing the TURN command that is more secure.

The ETRN command allows an SMTP client to issue a request for the SMTP server to initiate another SMTP connection with the client to transfer messages back to it. This differs from the original TURN command in that the ETRN command is just a request to start another SMTP session, not to reverse the data flow of the existing session. This way, the SMTP server can contact the client using the normal DNS hostname resolution methods. This does not rely on who the client says it is. If a hacker establishes an unauthorized SMTP connection and issues an ETRN command, the SMTP server just starts a new SMTP connection with the real client and sends any mail—no harm done.

The format for the ETRN command is

```
ETRN name
```

where *name* can be either an individual hostname or a domain name if you are requesting mail for an entire domain. The ETRN command is a valuable tool for the mail administrator. If you elect to have an ISP spool mail for your e-mail server, you might use this method to notify the ISP when you are ready to receive your spooled mail.

The AUTH Command

Another extended SMTP command gaining popularity is the AUTH command, which allows an SMTP client to identify itself to the SMTP server with a username and password pair or other agreed-upon authentication technique. Once the client is positively identified by the server, it may be allowed to perform special functions, such as using the server as a mail relay, which non-authenticated clients would not be allowed to do.

The Cyrus-SASL package is a popular software package that can be used to provide SMTP AUTH command support for many MTA packages, including Postfix. The mail administrator must maintain a separate username and password database that allows authentication of remote SMTP clients.

LMTP

SMTP and ESMTP are well-established protocols that are in widespread use on the Internet. However, they both have one drawback: Both were designed to work with mail servers that maintain a message queue.

This section describes the Local Mail Transfer Protocol (LMTP), which attempts to solve this problem.

Using LMTP

Even though the SMTP client can specify multiple `RCPT TO` addresses, when a message is sent with the `DATA` command, the SMTP server returns only a single response code. If an error is returned, the client has no way of knowing which (if any) recipients received the message. Thus, the client must queue the message for another delivery attempt.

When transferring messages to local MDAs, it is not always possible or feasible for the MTA to queue messages. Instead, the message sender might prefer a mechanism that sends notification of which messages were accepted and which were rejected. Then it can notify the original mail sender of the status of individual recipients. This allows both the MTA and MDA to avoid having to place messages in temporary delivery queues. In fact, you can configure a single MTA to use multiple MDA programs to deliver local mail more efficiently.

LMTP was designed to provide a mechanism for multiple return codes thereby minimizing the number of retransmissions for e-mail messages. This makes it an ideal protocol to use for communications between MTA and MDA packages.

LMTP Commands

LMTP uses the same command set as SMTP/ESMTP with two exceptions. First, the standard `HELO`/`EHLO` command is replaced with the LMTP `LHLO` command. This allows a client to introduce itself as an LMTP-enabled mail host.

Second, the normal single SMTP return code generated after the server accepts the message text from the client is broken into multiple LMTP return codes. One return code message is generated for each `RCPT TO` command received by the server. Listing 5.6 shows an LMTP example.

LISTING 5.6 LMTP Session

```
220 ispnet3.net LMTP server ready (smtpfeed 1.10, PID 13576)
LHLO ispnet1.net
220-meshach.ispnet3.net Hello ispnet1.net
220-8BITMIME
220-DSN
220 SIZE
MAIL FROM: <rich@ispnet1.net>
250 <rich@ispnet1.net> Sender ok
RCPT TO: <haley@ispnet3.net>
250 <haley@ispnet3.net> Recipient ok
RCPT TO: <riley@ispnet3.net>
250 <riley@ispnet3.net> Recipient ok
RCPT TO: <alex@ispnet3.net>
250 <alex@ispnet3.net> Recipient ok
DATA
```

LISTING 5.6 Continued

```
354 Enter mail, end with "." on a line by itself
From : rich@ispnet.net
To: haley@ispnet3.net, riley@ispnet3.net, alex@ispnet3.net
Date: February 14, 2001 19:20:00
Subject: Test LMTP message

This is a test LMTP message.
.
250 <haley@ispnet3.net>... OK (meshach.ispnet3.net [192.168.1.10])
250 <riley@ispnet3.net>... OK (meshach.ispnet3.net [192.168.1.10])
550 <alex@ispnet3.net>... User unable to accept messages
QUIT
221 meshach.ispnet3.net closing connection
```

As you can see from the listing, the first LMTP command is the `LHLO` command to introduce the remote host to the LMTP server. Next, a standard SMTP session is performed, identifying the mail sender and the multiple recipients. After the `DATA` command is entered and the message data is transferred, the LMTP server indicates three separate return codes (one for each recipient). In this example, two of the intended recipients received the message `OK`, while the third one was unable to receive the message. The LMTP client can now inform the original sender of the one failed delivery attempt.

Message Formats

Listing 5.2 shows a simple example of an SMTP session. The format of the message was extremely basic: just one line of text. As shown in the example, the resulting e-mail message was functional, but not too exciting. Today's e-mail messages are much more complex, and users are beginning to expect that level of complexity from their e-mail service. Niceties such as Subject:, CC:, and BCC: lines are now the norm in e-mail messages. RFC 822 describes a standard e-mail message format that most SMTP systems implement to somewhat "standardize" the look and feel of e-mail. Simple one-line text messages are now unacceptable in the business world.

Standard RFC 822 Header Fields

RFC 822 specifies splitting the message into two separate parts. The first part is called the *header*. Its job is to store information about the message. The second part is the *body* of the message. The header consists of data fields that can be used whenever additional information is needed in the message. The header fields should appear before the text body of the message and should be separated by one blank line. Header fields do not need to appear in any particular order, and the message can have multiple occurrences of any header field (though this is deprecated). Figure 5.1 shows how a basic RFC 822–compliant message would look.

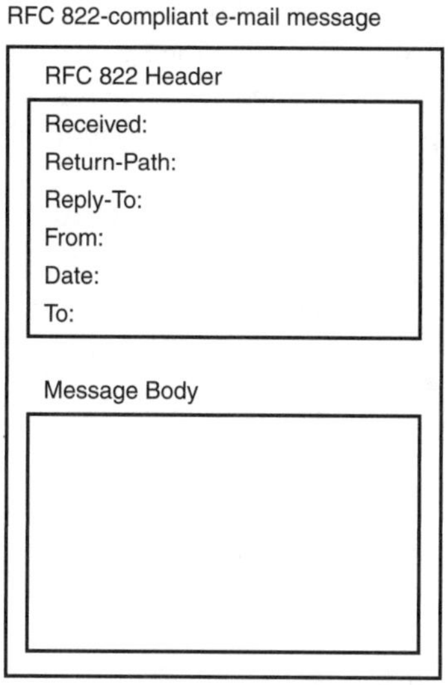

RFC 822-compliant e-mail message

RFC 822 Header

Received:
Return-Path:
Reply-To:
From:
Date:
To:

Message Body

FIGURE 5.1

The RFC 822 message format.

Received Header Field

The format for the received header field is as follows:

```
Received:
    from sending host
    by receiving host
    via physical path
    with link/mail protocol
    id receiver message-id
    for initial form
    ; date-time received
```

The received header field identifies the SMTP servers that were used to relay the e-mail message from the originating sender to the destination. Each server adds a new received field to the beginning of the e-mail message identifying specific details about itself. The subfields in the received header field further identify the paths, protocols, and computers that were used in transferring the e-mail message.

Return-Path Header Field

The return-path header field format is as follows:

```
Return-path: route-addr
```

The last SMTP server in the relay chain adds the return field to the message. Its purpose is to identify the route that was taken to pass the message to the destination server. If the message was sent directly to the destination server, only one address appears in this field. Otherwise, this lists the full path that was taken to transfer the message.

Originator Header Fields

The originator field shows the address from which the message originated and where the sender would like replies to be sent. This is extremely useful on messages that have been bounced around several times on private networks before making it to the Internet. The format of this field is

```
Reply-To: address
```

The originator field is a subset of the authentic header.

Resent Header Field

The resent header field identifies an e-mail message that for some reason had to be re-sent from the client. The format for this field is

```
Resent-Reply-To: address
```

Authentic Header Fields

The authentic header fields identify the sender of the e-mail message. The format of the authentic field is

```
From:    user-name
Sender:  user-name
```

The From: field identifies the author of the original message. Usually the from and sender fields are the same user, so only one is needed. If the situation should occur in which the sender of the e-mail is not the original author, both can be identified for return mail purposes.

Resent-Authentic Header Fields

The resent-authentic header identifies the sender of an e-mail message that for some reason had to be re-sent by the client. The format for this is

```
Resent-From:   user-name
Resent-Sender: user-name
```

The resent-from and resent-sender fields behave just like the from and sender authentic fields. They just signify that the e-mail message was re-sent from the client for some unknown reason.

Date Header Fields

The date header fields are used to timestamp the message as the client sends it to the server. The format for the date field is

```
Date:    date-time
Resent-Date:  date-time
```

The date header field passes the information in the message header exactly as it is entered in the original message. This is useful for tracking message times in responses, especially multiple responses.

Destination Header Fields

The destination header fields identify e-mail addresses that are the intended recipients of the mail message. These fields are purely informational. The SMTP server does not send a message to a user mailbox unless a `RCPT` command has been issued for that user (see the "Basic SMTP Client Commands" section earlier in the chapter). The formats for the destination fields are

```
To: address
Resent-To: address
cc: address
Resent-cc: address
bcc: address
Resent-bcc: address
```

The To:, CC:, and BCC: fields are now the standard way e-mail is presented. Most e-mail packages now use this terminology to classify the recipients of a message. The To: field is intended for the main recipient of the message. The CC: field, much like in a memo, lists recipients that should receive a "copy" of the message. One new item that e-mail has brought into the world is the term BCC:, or *blind carbon copy*. A blind carbon copy is a recipient who receives a copy of the message, but whose address won't show up on the message for other people to see (sneaky). Some debate has occurred in computer ethics circles over the ethics of such a tactic, but practically every e-mail package in use today implements this feature.

Optional Header Fields

Optional header fields are fields that further identify the message to the SMTP server but are not required for a message to be RFC 822 compatible. These fields include some of the niceties mentioned earlier that many e-mail customers have now come to expect. The formats of some of the optional header fields are

```
Message-ID:  message-id
Resent-Message-ID:  message-id
In-Reply-To: message-id
References: message-id
Keywords: text-list
```

```
Subject: text
Comments:  text
Encrypted: word
```

The most useful and most often used optional header field is the Subject field. Most e-mail packages allow the sender to include a one-line subject that identifies the e-mail message for the recipient. This text string is often used in the e-mail client package when listing multiple e-mail messages. Other optional header fields help further identify the e-mail message. The message-id fields give it a unique message ID that can be referred to in return messages. The Encrypted field indicates whether the e-mail message has been encrypted for security purposes, and the Keywords field offers keywords that can be used when searching for specific content in multiple messages.

Using the RFC 822 Format in an SMTP Mail Transaction

A sample SMTP mail transaction using full RFC 822 message formats is shown in Listing 5.7. Line numbers have been added to aid in the discussion following the listing.

LISTING 5.7 Sample SMTP RFC 822 Message Transaction

```
1  [rich@shadrach]$ telnet localhost 25
2  Trying 127.0.0.1...
3  Connected to localhost.
4  Escape character is '^]'.
5  250 shadrach.ispnet1.net Hello localhost [127.0.0.1], pleased to meet you
6  MAIL FROM:rich@localhost
7  250 rich@localhost... Sender ok
8  RCPT TO:rich
9  250 rich... Recipient ok
10 DATA
11 354 Enter mail, end with "." on a line by itself
12 Return-Path:rich@localhost
13 received: from localhost by localhost with TCP/IP id 1 for Richard Blum
14 Reply-to:rich@localhost
15 From:rich
16 Date:8/27/99
17 To:rich
18 cc:jessica
19 cc:katie
20 bcc:barbara
21 bcc:haley
22 Message-ID:1
23 Subject:Test RFC 822 message
24
25 This is a test message sent from the local host to rich.
```

LISTING 5.7 Continued

```
26 This message is a little larger, but in the right format.
27 .
28 250 PAA02866 Message accepted for delivery
29 QUIT
30 221 shadrach.ispnet1.net closing connection
31 Connection closed by foreign host.
32 You have new mail in /var/spool/mail/rich
33 [rich@shadrach]$ mail
34 Mail version 8.1 6/6/93.  Type ? for help.
35 "/var/spool/mail/rich": 1 message 1 new
36 >N  1 rich@shadrach.smallo  Fri Aug 27 18:50  18/622   "Test RFC 822 message"
37 &1
38 Message 1:
39 From rich@ispnet1.net  Fri Aug 27 18:50:21 1999
40 From: rich@shadrach.ispnet1.net
41 Reply-to: rich@shadrach.ispnet1.net
42 Date: 8/27/99
43 To: rich@shadrach.ispnet1.net
44 cc: jessica@shadrach.ispnet1.net
45 cc: katie@shadrach.ispnet1.net
46 Subject: Test RFC 822 message
47
48 This is a test message sent from the local host to rich.
49 This message is a little larger, but in the right format.
50
51 &x
```

This example is similar to the example in Listing 5.2, but notice the differences. Lines 12–23 show the RFC 822 header fields that were used for the message. Line 36 shows how the e-mail reader package has used the RFC 822 subject field as a short description of the e-mail message. Lines 39–46 show how the header fields were displayed by the e-mail reader package in the message. One thing that stands out is the missing BCC: field. It makes sense that the BCC: field does not show up in the e-mail reader.

Another obvious difference is the date line. Line 28 in Listing 5.2 shows a complete date that was automatically added by the e-mail package. Line 42 in Listing 5.5 shows the date as it was set by the RFC 822 message. This e-mail reader package allowed the RFC 822 field to override its automatic field insertion.

MIME and Binary Data

You might have noticed that the `DATA` command is the only way to transfer messages to the SMTP server. You might also have noticed that the `DATA` command allows for only

ASCII text lines to be entered. You are probably wondering how you can e-mail those great digital pictures to all of your relatives if SMTP mail only sends text messages. The answer is simple. The client's e-mail program must convert the binary data message into an ASCII text message before it passes it on to the SMTP program. Then of course the recipient's e-mail program must be able to convert the ASCII text message back into the binary data message that was originally sent. That is much easier said than done.

Several years before SMTP was invented, Unix system administrators were sending binary data using ASCII text mail programs. The method they used to convert binary data into ASCII text was called `uuencode` and `uudecode`. The `uu` stands for Unix-to-Unix, a protocol suite that was invented to help transfer data between Unix computers using modems. When SMTP became popular, it was natural for Unix system administrators to use these existing utilities for transferring binary data within an SMTP message across the Internet. Many older e-mail packages still use this method for encoding binary data to send via SMTP. Unfortunately, many newer e-mail packages don't include this capability.

NOTE

If you receive a binary file that was uuencoded and your e-mail software can't decode it, don't worry. You can save the entire message as a text file and run `uudecode` to extract the binary file. Most Unix distributions come with the `uudecode` utility, and many DOS and Windows versions of `uudecode` are available also.

The reason many newer e-mail packages don't use `uuencode` is because an Internet standard for encoding binary data has been created. RFCs 2045 and 2046 describe the *Multipurpose Internet Mail Extensions (MIME)* format. MIME is more versatile than `uuencode`.

It identifies the type of binary file that was attached to the e-mail message and passes additional information about the file to the decoder. MIME enables binary data to be directly incorporated into a standard RFC 822 message. Five new header fields were defined to identify binary data types embedded in the RFC 822 message. E-mail packages must be able to process these five new header types in order to properly handle MIME messages. Figure 5.2 demonstrates how this fits together in a standard e-mail message.

MIME-Version Header Field

The first additional header type identifies the version of MIME that the sender used to encode the message. Currently this value is always 1.0.

Content-Transfer–Encoding

The content-transfer–encoding header field identifies how the binary data embedded in the message is encoded. There are currently seven different ways to encode the binary data, but the most common is the `base64` type. This method encodes the binary data by mapping 6-bit blocks of data to 8-bit blocks of printable ASCII text.

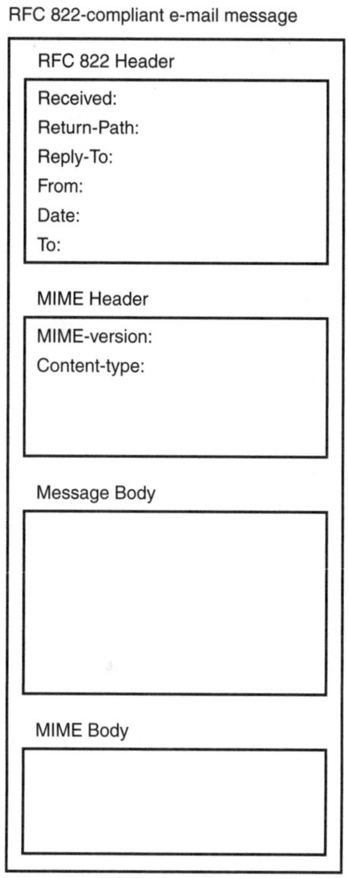

FIGURE 5.2

The MIME message header fields.

Content-ID

The content-ID header field identifies MIME sessions with some unique identification code when using multiple contents.

Content-Description

The content-description header field is an ASCII text description of the data to help identify it in the text of the e-mail message. This comes in handy when sending binary data such as word processing documents or graphic images that would otherwise be unidentifiable by their `base64` encoding.

Content-Type Header Field

The content-type header field is where the action is. This field identifies the type of data that is encapsulated in the MIME message so that the MUA can pick an appropriate program to present the data to the user. Currently MIME identifies seven basic classes of content-type. Each type has different subtypes that further define the type of data in the message.

The `text` content-type identifies data that is in ASCII format and should be readable as is. There are two subtypes: `plain`, which signifies unformatted ASCII text, and `enriched`, which signifies formatting features similar to a rich text format (RTF). Many newer e-mail packages can display messages in rich text format.

The `message` content-type allows the e-mail package to send RFC 822 messages within a single RFC 822 message. The subtypes for this content-type are `rfc822`, which specifies a normal embedded RFC 822 formatted message, `partial`, which allows for breaking up long e-mail messages into separate bodies, and `external-body`, which allows for a pointer that points to an object that is not within the e-mail message.

The `image` content-type defines embedded binary data streams that represent graphic images. Currently two subtypes are defined: `jpeg` and `gif`.

The `video` content-type defines embedded binary data streams that represent video data. The only subtype defined at this time is the `mpeg` format.

The `audio` content-type defines embedded binary data streams that represent audio data. Currently its only subtype is `basic`, which defines a single-channel ISDN mu-law encoding at an 8kHz sample rate.

The `application` content-type identifies embedded, uninterpreted binary data, such as spreadsheets, word processor documents, and other applications. Currently two formal subtypes are defined: `postscript` and `octet-stream`. Often the `octet-stream` subtype is used when embedding application-specific data, such as Microsoft Word documents and Microsoft Excel spreadsheets.

The `multipart` content-type identifies messages that contain different data content-types combined in one message. This type is supported by e-mail packages that can present a message in a variety of ways, such as ASCII text, HTML, and audio formats. A boundary identifier separates each section of content, each of which is identified with its own content-type header field. The `multipart` content-type has four subtypes. The `mixed` subtype specifies a generic mixed set of parts that are independent of one another and should be presented to the recipient in the order in which they were sent. The `parallel` subtype indicates that each of the parts are independent of one another but are intended to be viewed simultaneously. The `alternative` subtype indicates that the same data is being presented in multiple formats. The best method available for the recipient is used. The `digest` subtype indicates that there are multiple portions but that they are all in RFC 822 format.

Listing 5.8 demonstrates the use of content-type definitions in a multipart e-mail message. Line numbers have been added to aid in the discussion following the listing.

LISTING 5.8 Sample SMTP Multipart MIME Message Session

```
1  $ telnet localhost 25
2  Trying 127.0.0.1...
3  Connected to localhost.
4  Escape character is '^]'.
5  220 shadrach.ispnet1.net ESMTP
6  HELO localhost
7  250 shadrach.ispnet1.net
8  MAIL FROM:rich@localhost
9  250 ok
10 RCPT TO:rich
11 250 ok
12 DATA
13 354 go ahead
14 From:"Rich Blum" <rich@localhost>
15 To:"rich"<rich@localhost>
16 Subject:Formatted text message test
17 MIME-Version: 1.0
18 Content-Type: multipart/alternative; boundary=bounds1
19
20 --bounds1
21 Content-Type: text/plain; charset=us-ascii
22
23 This is the plain text part of the message that can be read by simple
24 e-mail readers.
25
26 --bounds1
27 Context-Type: text/enriched
28
29 This is the <bold>rich text</bold> version of the <bigger>SAME</bigger>
➥message.
30
31 --bounds1--
32 .
33 250 ok 959882500 qp 84053
34 QUIT
35 221 shadrach.ispnet1.net
36 Connection closed by foreign host.
```

The sample message shows a two-part MIME message. Line 18 shows the content-type definition for the entire message. The multipart/alternative type indicates that multiple content-types are included in this message and that they are separated by the boundary identifier `bounds1`. The first content-type starts at line 21 and is a simple plain ASCII text message that virtually any e-mail reader can read.

The second content-type starts at line 27 and is a fancier enriched text message that uses the standard rich text format for the message. Because the MIME content-type specified for the message was multipart/alternative, it is left to the discretion of the e-mail reader which content-type version of the message to present. Figure 5.3 shows a sample of how a Eudora reader would display the message. Notice how the plain ASCII text part of the message was discarded, and the enriched text part was presented to the reader. In a normal multipart/alternative type e-mail message, both parts would have the same message. I made them different here to show which version the e-mail reader would use.

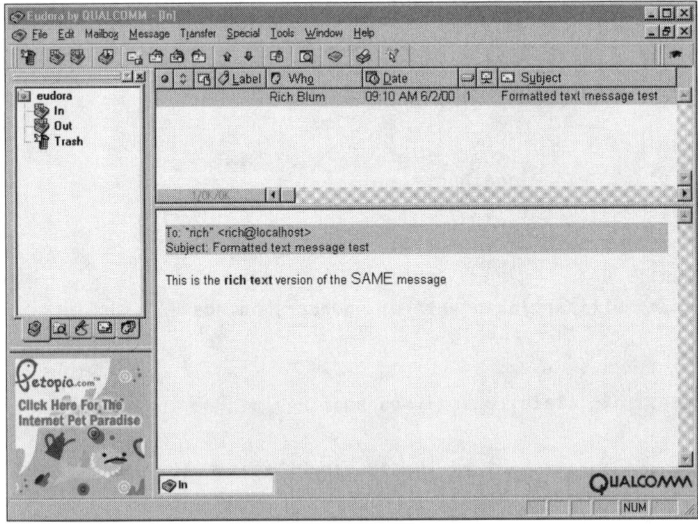

FIGURE 5.3

Using Eudora to read a MIME multipart message.

Summary

The Simple Mail Transfer Protocol (SMTP) allows computers to transfer messages from one user to another user (or multiple users), probably on another computer, using a standard method. SMTP is defined in RFC 821 and establishes a standard set of commands that identify the mail sender and recipients, and actually transfer the message.

SMTP has been extended with additional features in Extended SMTP (ESMTP). Two of the additional features used are the `ETRN` command, which allows a host to signal a remote mail server to forward messages back to the host, and the `AUTH` command, which allows clients to authenticate themselves to the SMTP server.

The Local Mail Transfer Protocol (LMTP) is a recent addition that allows mail servers to transfer messages to local MDAs without using message queues. Each individual recipient of a message is acknowledged, allowing the server to resend messages only for recipients that did not receive the message properly.

The actual message can be in any form, but a standard format has been set forth in RFC 822. This format provides for two different sections: the message header and the message body. The message header contains fields that identify important parts of the message such as the sender, recipients, subject, and comments. Binary data must be encoded into an ASCII text stream before it can be sent via SMTP/ESMTP. An Internet standard has been implemented for encoding and transferring binary data within a standard RFC 822 message. RFCs 2045 and 2046 describe new RFC 822 header fields that help identify the binary data encoding as well as its purpose.

PART II

Installing and Configuring Postfix

CHAPTER 6

Installing Postfix

The previous chapters provided background information describing how the e-mail process works and the general function of Postfix as an e-mail server. This chapter begins the specific Postfix installation instructions by describing how to obtain and install the main Postfix software.

Wietse Venema created and wrote the Postfix software package while working at IBM's T.J. Watson Research Center. IBM has released the Postfix package under a public license so that it can be available free of charge to any Unix e-mail administrator who wants to use it. Venema has continued to work on the Postfix project and continually releases new updates.

The Postfix software releases consist of a naming format that contains the year and date of the release. The current official release of Postfix is version 20010228. Thus the current production release is called release-20010228. The previous production release was called postfix-19991231. Also, various patches are released to correct bugs found in official release levels. Many Linux distributions included the postfix-19991231 version with different patch levels. The 19991231 release stopped at patch level 13. It used the name postfix-19991231-pl13.

There are also several experimental releases of Postfix. As with the official releases, experimental releases are named using the year and date of the release. The experimental releases are all named "snapshot" because they are basically snapshots of what the code looks like on a particular release date. Venema states that the experimental releases are production quality, but have not been as extensively tested as the official releases. You should take some care when downloading and installing experimental releases, although they have been proven to be relatively stable (even more so than some commercial e-mail packages).

At the time of this writing, the current experimental release of Postfix is snapshot-20010228. The experimental release changes frequently, so by the time you read this there will probably have been several new experimental releases, if not a new production release.

The following sections describe how to install Postfix from both the Mandrake RPM binary release and the source code experimental release. Following that, a description of the Postfix utilities installed is presented.

Installing Postfix from an RPM

Although Venema does not provide a binary distribution of Postfix, many Linux distributions create their own binary distribution that fits their particular system.

The Mandrake Linux distribution includes an RPM-formatted distribution of Postfix that includes compiled binary versions of the Postfix programs. Mandrake Linux 7.1 includes an RPM of the 19991231 patch 6 release of Postfix named `postfix-19991231-6mdk.i586.rpm`. For many mail servers, this release should work fine. If you would prefer to use the latest version of Postfix, you should skip to the source code installation section.

The RPM distribution packages the compiled core and utility programs, along with the documentation and man pages for Postfix. Sample configuration files are also provided to help the mail administrator get an MTA system running. This section describes the Postfix RPM package and how to install it on a Linux system.

The RPM Package Layout

If you are using the KDE desktop manager, you can use the `/usr/bin/kpackage` program to display the contents of the Postfix RPM file. Figure 6.1 shows an example of using the `kpackage` program to display the contents of the RPM file.

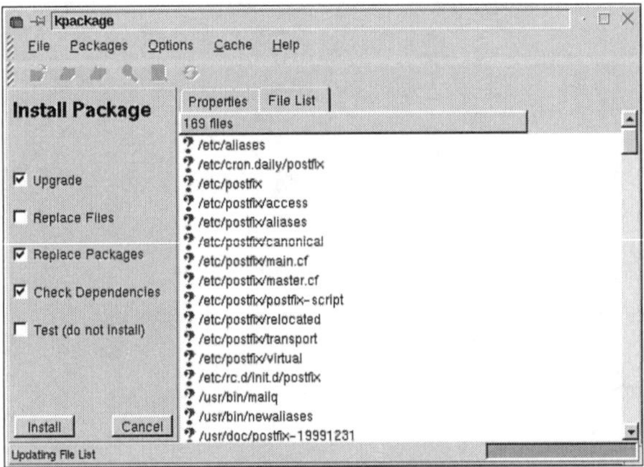

FIGURE 6.1

kpackage display of the `postfix-19991231-6mdk.i586.rpm` file.

As you can see, the RPM package will automatically install the Postfix files into the proper directories for operation.

Table 6.1 shows the file locations that are used in the RPM distribution.

TABLE 6.1 Postfix RPM Distribution Directories

Directory	*Description*
`/etc/postfix`	Postfix configuration files and lookup table
`/usr/bin`	Postfix administration programs
`/usr/doc/postfix-19991231/html`	Postfix documentation
`/usr/doc/postfix-19991231/sample`	Sample Postfix configurations
`/usr/lib/postfix`	Postfix core programs
`/usr/man`	Postfix man pages

TABLE 6.1 Continued

Directory	*Description*
`/usr/sbin`	Postfix administrator utility programs
`/var/spool/postfix`	Postfix message queues

The RPM file contains the compiled binary executables of all the Postfix programs. Listing 6.1 shows the locations of the various Postfix binary programs and configuration files as installed by the RPM package.

LISTING 6.1 Postfix File Locations

```
/etc/aliases
/etc/cron.daily/postfix
/etc/postfix
/etc/postfix/access
/etc/postfix/aliases
/etc/postfix/canonical
/etc/postfix/main.cf
/etc/postfix/master.cf
/etc/postfix/postfix-script
/etc/postfix/relocated
/etc/postfix/transport
/etc/postfix/virtual
/etc/rc.d/init.d/postfix

/usr/bin/mailq
/usr/bin/newaliases

/usr/lib/postfix/bounce
/usr/lib/postfix/cleanup
/usr/lib/postfix/error
/usr/lib/postfix/local
/usr/lib/postfix/master
/usr/lib/postfix/pickup
/usr/lib/postfix/pipe
/usr/lib/postfix/postalias
/usr/lib/postfix/postcat
/usr/lib/postfix/postconf
/usr/lib/postfix/postdrop
/usr/lib/postfix/postfix
/usr/lib/postfix/postkick
/usr/lib/postfix/postlock
```

LISTING 6.1 Continued

```
/usr/lib/postfix/postlog
/usr/lib/postfix/postmap
/usr/lib/postfix/postsuper
/usr/lib/postfix/qmgr
/usr/lib/postfix/sendmail
/usr/lib/postfix/showq
/usr/lib/postfix/smtp
/usr/lib/postfix/smtp-sink
/usr/lib/postfix/smtp-source
/usr/lib/postfix/smtpd
/usr/lib/postfix/trivial-rewrite
/usr/lib/sendmail

/usr/sbin/postalias
/usr/sbin/postcat
/usr/sbin/postconf
/usr/sbin/postdrop
/usr/sbin/postfix
/usr/sbin/postkick
/usr/sbin/postlock
/usr/sbin/postlog
/usr/sbin/postmap
/usr/sbin/postsuper
/usr/sbin/postconf
/usr/sbin/sendmail
```

Installing the RPM

To install the Postfix RPM package, you must be logged in as `root`. If you are using the KDE, you should have the `kpackage` program. Using the `kpackage` program you can install the RPM by clicking on the Install button on the display window (as shown in Figure 6.1). This automatically installs the RPM on the Linux system.

If KDE and `kpackage` are not available or if you are working remotely, you can also manually install the RPM package. Simply invoke the command line `/bin/rpm` with the update option, like so:

```
/bin/rpm -Uvh postfix19991231-6mdk.i586.rpm
```

This command either installs Postfix if it is not already on the system or upgrades an existing installation.

Both types of RPM installations automatically perform the following actions:

- Create a new system user named *postfix*
- Create a new system group named *postfix*
- Create the `/etc/postfix` and `/var/spool/postfix` directories
- Create all Postfix message queue directories
- Create a default Postfix configuration file
- Create a default Postfix aliases database

The Postfix RPM package automatically creates a default Postfix `main.cf` configuration file, but you should check it to make sure that it matches your mail environment before starting Postfix.

NOTE

Chapter 8, "The `main.cf` Configuration File," describes the different parts of the `main.cf` configuration file. You most likely will need to change some parameters for Postfix to work properly in your environment.

Once the RPM package is installed and configured, Postfix will be ready to go to work as the MTA server for your Linux server.

Downloading and Compiling the Postfix Source Code

If your Linux distribution does not include an RPM package or if you want to install the most current version of Postfix, you will have to use a source code distribution. The Postfix source code distributions can be found on many Postfix mirror sites described on the `www.postfix.org` main Web page.

At the time of this writing the most current experimental release is version 20010228, and can be downloaded from

```
ftp://ftp.porcupine.org/mirrors/postfix-release/experimental/
snapshot-20010228.tar.gz
```

Notice that experimental releases are denoted by the term "snapshot" instead of the normal "postfix" heading. Also, remember to use caution when installing an experimental Postfix release on a production mail server.

Download the distribution file to a temporary area using the FTP BINARY mode. This file is a GNU-zipped `tar` file, meaning the filename ends in `.tar.gz`. Before you can compile the source, you must uncompress and expand the file.

You should pick a common area to extract source code distributions so they don't clutter up your workspace. It has become a fairly common practice among Linux users to extract source code into the `/usr/local/src` directory.

CAUTION

Remember that you must be logged in as the `root` user to write to the `/usr/local/src` directory.

To extract the source code into a working directory, you can use the `tar` command with the `-C` parameter:

```
tar -zxvf snapshot-20010228.tar.gz -C /usr/local/src
```

This command creates the directory `/usr/local/src/snapshot-20010228` and places the source code in it. The Postfix source code distribution contains several subdirectories that contain documentation and scripts as well as source code for the release.

Creating the Postfix userid and groupid

For Postfix to work properly, you must create a specific user and group named `postfix`. The `postfix` user is required to own all Postfix message queue directories. The numeric user and group *ids* assigned by the Linux system are not important, but the user and group *names* must be `postfix`.

In Linux you can create a new user and group with the `useradd` command:

```
/usr/sbin/useradd -M postfix
```

This creates a user account with the next available `uid` on the system. The `postfix` user does not need a home directory or a login shell, so the `-M` option is used to avoid creating a home directory for `postfix`.

Determining Postfix `maildrop` Security

At this point in the installation, you must decide at what level of security you want your Postfix system to operate. The default installation of the Postfix source code distribution creates a `maildrop` message queue directory that is writable by all local users (see Chapter 2, "Postfix Services").

To increase security on your mail server, you can instead create a separate group to own the `maildrop` message queue. The `maildrop` message queue directory will only be writable by this special `maildrop` group. This prevents local users not in the group from inserting their own messages (or attempting any trickery with the `maildrop` message queue).

You can create a separate system group for `maildrop` by using the Linux `groupadd` command:

```
/usr/sbin/groupadd maildrop
```

This creates the group `maildrop` that Postfix uses to control the `maildrop` message queue. When the `maildrop` message queue is restricted, the Postfix `sendmail` program automatically notices and calls the `postdrop` program to insert new messages into the `maildrop` message queue.

The `maildrop` group name will be entered when running the Postfix install script later on in the install process.

Compiling Postfix

Once all the Postfix-related user and group names are created, you can compile the executable programs. The Postfix source code distribution includes a Makefile that will attempt to use the standard compiler for the Unix system being used. For Linux systems, this is the GNU C compiler, gcc.

CAUTION

You should ensure that you have the GNU C development programs and libraries loaded on your Linux system before attempting to compile from the source code distribution. As a quick test, you can try to use the command `gcc --version`. This should return the version of the GNU C compiler used on your system.

To compile the source code files, change directories to the top-level Postfix distribution directory (such as `/usr/local/src/snapshot-20010228`) and just type

```
make
```

This calls the GNU `make` program to process the Makefile and build the individual executable programs. As the `make` program runs, it produces messages indicating its progress. The `make` program traverses subdirectories for each Postfix executable program and compiles the programs. Depending on your C environment, some warning messages may appear. This is normal. When it finishes compiling the programs it will return to the command-line prompt.

Installing Postfix

Before you actually install the new binaries, you may have to do a little housekeeping.

Postfix uses copycat commands to replace all `sendmail` functionality. For instance, the Postfix `sendmail`, `mailq`, and `newaliases` commands are direct replacements for the same `sendmail` commands. If your system previously had `sendmail` installed, you may want to copy these files to an alternate location or filename in case you need to "fall back" to process mail messages in the `sendmail` mail queue (see Chapter 14, "Migrating from Sendmail to Postfix"). You can rename these programs for safekeeping using the Unix `mv` command (as `root`):

```
mv /usr/sbin/sendmail /usr/sbin/sendmail.OLD
mv /usr/bin/mailq /usr/bin/mailq.OLD
mv /usr/bin/newaliases /usr/bin/newaliases.OLD
```

Remember that the `sendmail` program uses the Unix setuid to grant its programs root privileges when they run. Thus, even though you have moved the programs, they may still be a security risk. To alleviate this problem, it is wise to change the permission settings on these files to remove the setuid privileges:

```
chmod 755 /usr/sbin/sendmail.OLD
chmod 755 /usr/bin/mailq.OLD
chmod 755 /usr/bin/newaliases.OLD
```

NOTE

Some `sendmail` installations create symbolic links for the `mailq` and `newaliases` programs. You should delete these links.

Now that you have created the Postfix executables and the housekeeping is done, you must run the `INSTALL.sh` script to install everything in its proper place. You can run the Postfix install script from the source code distribution directory as `root` like so:

```
/bin/sh INSTALL.sh
```

The install script allows you to specify where to place various types of executables, as well as determine what maildrop security level you want Postfix to use.

Listing 6.2 shows the file paths requested by the install script as well as Postfix's default values for each.

LISTING 6.2 Postfix Install Script Questions

```
install_root: [/]
tempdir: [/usr/local/src/snapshot-20010228]
config_directory: [/etc/postfix]
daemon_directory: [/usr/libexec/postfix]
command_directory: [/usr/sbin]
queue_directory: [/var/spool/postfix]
sendmail_path: [/usr/sbin/sendmail]
newaliases_path: [/usr/bin/newaliases]
mailq_path: [/usr/bin/mailq]
mail_owner: [postfix]
setgid: [no] maildrop
manpages: [/usr/local/man]
```

To use the default values suggested by Postfix, simply press the Enter key. To use custom values, enter them at the appropriate prompt.

Remember that by default Postfix will be installed using the less secure world-writable `maildrop` message queue. If you want to use a protected `maildrop` message queue instead, you must specify the group name that you created for write access to the `maildrop` message queue when the `setgid` option line is presented. In the preceding example, the `maildrop` group was specified.

The install options that were selected are written to the `/etc/postfix/install.cf` configuration file for future reference.

NOTE

You may notice that when you install using the source code distribution the Postfix message queue directories are not created. This will be remedied as soon as the Postfix `master` program is started. The `master` program scans the Postfix message queue directory (`/var/spool/postfix`) and determines what (if any) subdirectories are missing. The `master` program will create any missing message queue directories.

If you install Postfix using the `INSTALL.sh` script and after awhile decide you need to change something (such as making the maildrop directory protected), you can always rerun the `INSTALL.sh` script and enter the new information. The new values replace any existing configurations.

At this point Postfix should be installed using the default operating parameters. Of course it still needs to be configured to meet the requirements of your particular e-mail environment.

Installing Postfix in a `chroot` Environment

As an extra security precaution, the Postfix system can run in a restricted area on the mail server. This ensures that even if a mail program is compromised, the attacker will not be able to access files in the mail server system directories. Postfix uses the Unix `chroot` command to accomplish this.

The Unix `chroot` program forces a command to treat the specified directory as the filesystem root directory. After `chroot` has been run, the program can no longer access any files or executables above the specified directory. Files outside the specified directory structure can be considered "safe" from the particular `chroot`'d program. Since the program can't "get out," the specified directory is often referred to as a "`chroot`'d jail."

All of the Postfix core programs except `local` and `pipe` can run using the `chroot` environment. By default, the Postfix `chroot` script (discussed below) sets `/var/spool/postfix` as the root directory for Postfix programs.

To run the Postfix core programs in a chroot environment, two things must be configured. First, the /var/spool/postfix directory must be modified to accommodate being used as the root directory for Postfix, and second, the master.cf file must be modified to indicate which Postfix programs should be run in the chroot environment.

Postfix must be able to access certain system files in order to operate properly. When using /var/spool/postfix as the chroot directory, the normal system libraries and binaries are no longer accessible. To compensate for this, the e-mail administrator must copy these files under the /var/spool/postfix directory. It's also important to maintain proper directory structures. For instance, if a Postfix program normally requires a file in /usr/lib, the administrator must make a /var/spool/postfix/usr/lib directory and place the file there.

To make this task easier, the Postfix source code distribution includes sample script files for various operating systems. These script files are located in the examples/chroot-setup subdirectory under the source code directory. The script file used to set up a chroot environment on a Linux server is called LINUX2. The version included with the snapshot-20010228 version is shown in Listing 6.3.

LISTING 6.3 Sample Linux chroot Script

```
set -e
umask 022
POSTFIX_DIR=${POSTFIX_DIR-/var/spool/postfix}
cd ${POSTFIX_DIR}
mkdir etc
cp /etc/localtime /etc/services /etc/resolv.conf /etc/nsswitch.conf etc
mkdir -p usr/lib/zoneinfo
ln -s /etc/localtime usr/lib/zoneinfo
mkdir lib
cp /lib/libnss_* lib
```

The chroot-setup script for Linux creates the etc and lib subdirectories under the /var/spool/postfix directory. Files necessary for the Postfix core programs are copied from their standard locations on the system to the new chroot location.

After the chroot files have been copied to the Postfix directory, the master.cf configuration file must be modified to indicate which core programs should be run in the chroot environment. You can select any core programs except local and pipe to be run in the chroot environment. Programs that communicate with remote hosts, such as smtpd and smtp, are the most susceptible to attacks by outside hackers, so they are the best candidates for chroot. Chapter 7, "The master.cf Configuration File," describes the master.cf configuration file in detail, including how to set a program to run in the chroot environment.

The Postfix Utility Programs

Whichever method you use to install Postfix, all of the Postfix executable programs, message queue directories, and configuration files should now be installed and ready for use. Although the Postfix `master` program automatically runs the core programs it needs while processing mail messages, it is up to the e-mail administrator to use the Postfix utility programs as needed. This section describes the format of the Postfix utility programs as found in the snapshot-20010228 version of Postfix and how the administrator can use them within the Postfix system.

Checking Mail Queues

The `mailq` utility can display the current messages waiting in the various message queues in Postfix. It uses the `showq` core program to display the status of each message queue on the Postfix system. The format of the `mailq` command is simply

```
mailq
```

The `mailq` command emulates the functionality of the old `sendmail` command using the `-bp` parameters. Listing 6.4 shows a sample output from a `mailq` command.

LISTING 6.4 Sample `mailq` Output

```
[root@meshach postfix]# mailq
-Queue ID- --Size-- ----Arrival Time---- -Sender/Recipient-------
4AB61C365       717 Wed Oct 11 13:07:04  rich@shadrach.ispnet1.net
➥  rich@meshach.ispnet1.net
693ABC362       717 Wed Oct 11 13:07:03  rich@shadrach.ispnet1.net

➥   jessica@meshach.ispnet1.net

C39F7C364       717 Wed Oct 11 13:07:03  rich@shadrach.ispnet1.net
➥   katie@meshach.ispnet1.net

61F9AC366       717 Wed Oct 11 13:07:04  rich@shadrach.ispnet1.net
➥    barbara@meshach.ispnet1.net

6D922C352 *     717 Wed Oct 11 13:07:02  rich@shadrach.ispnet1.net
➥   haley@meshach.ispnet1.net

-- 4 Kbytes in 5 Requests.
```

The output from the `mailq` utility displays the vital statistics of all messages in the message queues. The e-mail administrator can use this information to determine whether there are any problems with mail delivery on the server.

Starting and Stopping Postfix

The `postfix` utility controls the overall operation of the Postfix software. It is the command used to start, stop, reload, and even check the Postfix system. The format of the `postfix` command is

```
postfix [-c config_dir] [-D] [-v] command
```

where *config_dir* is the location of an alternate `main.cf` configuration file, and *command* is the operation you want to perform. The `-D` option allows the `postfix` process to be run through the debugger defined in the `main.cf` configuration file. The `-v` option allows for verbose logging in the syslog files.

You can issue six different commands to the Postfix system using the `postfix` utility, as shown in Table 6.2.

TABLE 6.2 `postfix` Utility Commands

Command	*Description*
`abort`	Immediately stops the Postfix processes.
`check`	Checks the Postfix configuration for bad directory and file permissions and missing message queue directories.
`flush`	Attempts to immediately deliver all messages in the `deferred` message queue.
`reload`	Re-reads the configuration files. All running Postfix programs are terminated when they become available. This is the proper way to load updated configurations (rather than successive stop-start commands).
`start`	Performs the Postfix configuration check process and starts the Postfix `master` program.
`stop`	Performs an orderly shutdown of the Postfix systems. Programs that are in the process of delivering messages are allowed to complete their processes before being terminated.

The proper way to stop a running Postfix server is to use the `postfix stop` command. This allows any programs in the middle of processing messages to complete their tasks before shutting down.

Maintaining Postfix User Alias Names

The `postalias` utility allows the mail administrator to maintain and query the Postfix aliases binary database from a text-based command line. The format of the `postalias` utility is

```
postalias [-Ninrvw] [-c config_dir] [-d key] [-q key] [file_type:]file_name ..
```

NOTE

The Postfix aliases database is described in detail in Chapter 9, "Postfix Lookup Tables."

The parameters used in the `postalias` utility are shown in Table 6.3.

TABLE 6.3 The `postalias` Utility Parameters

Parameter	*Description*
`-N`	Include terminating null character to terminate lookup keys.
`-i`	Read entries from standard input and append them to the existing database.
`-n`	Don't include the terminating null character to terminate lookup keys.
`-r`	Do not warn about duplicate alias table entries.
`-w`	Warn about duplicate alias table entries.
`-c` *`config_dir`*	Use the `main.cf` configuration file from the location *`config_dir`*.
`-d` *`key`*	Delete one entry from the alias table that matches *`key`*.
`-q` *`key`*	Query the alias table and print the first entry that matches *`key`*.
`-v`	Toggle levels of verbosity in logs.
`file_type`	The database scheme to use for the alias table.
`file_name`	The name of the alias table to use.

The alias table can use several different database types. Table 6.4 shows the different types allowed.

TABLE 6.4 Postfix Alias Database Types

Type	*Description*
btree	A B-tree indexed database named *`file_name`*`.db` using the db database system.
dbm	A dbm formatted database that creates two files: *`file_name`*`.pag` and *`file_name`*`.dir`.
hash	A hashed database file named *`file_name`*`.db` using the db database system.

If no *`file_type`* parameter is used, the `postalias` utility uses the value listed in the `main.cf` configuration file for the *`database_type`* parameter. The default value used if the parameter does not exist depends on the Unix system that the Postfix system is installed on.

Listing 6.5 shows an example of using the `postalias` command to maintain an aliases database.

LISTING 6.5 Sample postalias Command Session

```
[root@shadrach]# postalias -q root /etc/postfix/aliases
rich
[root@shadrach]# echo fred: rich | postalias -i /etc/postfix/aliases
[root@shadrach ich]# postalias -q fred /etc/postfix/aliases
rich
[root@shadrach]# postalias -d fred /etc/postfix/aliases
[root@shadrach]# postalias -q fred /etc/postfix/aliases

[root@shadrach]#
```

You must perform this kind of update as `root`. The first example shows a key query looking to see whether the `root` user is included in the `aliases` lookup table. The response from the query indicates that the `root` user is pointing to the username `rich`. The second example shows using the `insert` command to insert an aliases record into the lookup table. By using the query command we see that the insert was successful. Finally, the delete command removes the inserted record from the `aliases` lookup table.

CAUTION

When using the `postalias` utility, be careful that the binary `aliases` lookup table does not get out of sync with the text aliases file. This is a great source of confusion for unsuspecting mail administrators.

Printing Mail Queue Messages

The `postcat` utility can display the contents of messages stored in the Postfix message queues. Each message is stored as a separate file using a special file format that incorporates the sending and receiving addresses, as well as the message header and body. The format of the `postcat` utility is

```
postcat [-v] filename
```

where *`filename`* is the name of the message file stored in the message queue. The `-v` option is used to produce verbose logging details in the system log. Listing 6.6 shows an example of using the `postcat` utility.

LISTING 6.6 Sample postcat Output

```
[root@shadrach]# postcat 2C3BFC352
*** ENVELOPE RECORDS 2C3BFC352 ***
message_size:           437          120          1
```

LISTING 6.6 Continued

```
arrival_time: Wed Oct 11 16:42:01 2000
sender: rich@shadrach.ispnet1.net
recipient: rblum@meshach.ispnet1.net
*** MESSAGE CONTENTS 2C3BFC352 ***
Received: by shadrach.ispnet1.net (Postfix, from userid 500)
        id 2C3BFC352; Wed, 11 Oct 2000 16:42:01 -0500 (EST)
To: rblum@meshach.ispnet1.net
Subject: Test message to bad site
Message-Id: <20001011214201.2C3BFC352@shadrach.ispnet1.net>
Date: Wed, 11 Oct 2000 16:42:01 -0500 (EST)
From: rich@shadrach.ispnet1.net (Rich Blum)

Hello, this is a test message sent to a bad site. This message
should stay in the deferred message queue for awhile.
*** HEADER EXTRACTED 2C3BFC352 ***
return_receipt:
errors_to: rich@shadrach.ispnet1.net
*** MESSAGE FILE END 2C3BFC352 ***
[root@shadrach deferred]#
```

Listing 6.6 shows a sample message that was stuck in the Postfix `deferred` message queue waiting for another attempt to be delivered. The first part of the message shows the Postfix envelope values for the message. These are all parameters that Postfix stores in the message for easy processing of the message. They indicate the size of the message, the time Postfix first received the message for processing, and the sender and recipient of the message.

The second part of the message, labeled Message Contents, includes the complete RFC822 header and body of the mail message. The last part of the message indicates whether any reply messages should be triggered when Postfix processes this message. These values show that no return receipts have been requested. And if any fatal errors occur, the message should be bounced back to `rich@shadrach.ispnet1.net`.

Maintaining the Configuration File

The `postconf` utility can query and modify parameters in the `main.cf` configuration file. There are two different formats for the `postconf` utility:

```
postconf [-dhmnv] [-c config_dir] [parameter ...]
postconf [-ev] [-c config_dir] [parameter=value ...]
```

The first format is used for querying the parameter values. Table 6.5 shows the options and parameters used.

TABLE 6.5 `postconf` Utility Query Options

Option	*Description*
`-d`	Shows the default parameter settings instead of the configured settings
`-h`	Shows parameter values only, not their labels
`-m`	Lists the names of the lookup table types supported
`-n`	Shows only the parameters that are set to non-default values
`-v`	Enables increasingly verbose output for logging to the system logger
`-c`	Uses the `main.cf` file located in the *`config_dir`* directory

If no parameters are listed on the command line, all current parameter values are displayed. Alternatively, you can enter a list of parameter names to minimize the output. Listing 6.7 shows a sample `postconf` query output.

LISTING 6.7 Sample `postconf` Query Output

```
[nicholas@shadrach nicholas]$ /usr/sbin/postconf -n
alias_database = hash:/etc/postfix/aliases
alias_maps = hash:/etc/postfix/aliases
command_directory = /usr/sbin
daemon_directory = /usr/libexec/postfix
debug_peer_level = 2
default_destination_concurrency_limit = 10
home_mailbox = Maildir/
local_destination_concurrency_limit = 2
mail_owner = postfix
queue_directory = /var/spool/postfix
```

The second format of the `postconf` utility is used for editing parameter values in the `main.cf` configuration file. Table 6.6 shows the options that can be used for this command.

TABLE 6.6 `postconf` Utility Edit Options

Option	*Description*
`-e`	Edits the `main.cf` file values
`-v`	Enables verbose output for logging to the system logger
`-c`	Uses the `main.cf` file located in the *`config_dir`* directory

This format of the `postconf` utility requires that a parameter name and value be on the command line. There should be no spaces between the parameter name, the = sign, and the parameter value. Also note that `root` needs to execute the editing.

Listing 6.8 shows an example of using the `postconf` edit command.

LISTING 6.8 Sample postconf Edit Output

```
[root@shadrach]# postconf -e command_directory=/usr/testing
[root@shadrach]# postconf -n
alias_database = hash:/etc/postfix/aliases
alias_maps = hash:/etc/postfix/aliases
command_directory = /usr/testing
daemon_directory = /usr/libexec/postfix
debug_peer_level = 2
default_destination_concurrency_limit = 10
home_mailbox = Maildir/
local_destination_concurrency_limit = 2
mail_owner = postfix
queue_directory = /var/spool/postfix
[root@shadrach rich]#
```

Notice in Listing 6.8 that the changed value appears in the `postconf` query command. Although this value now appears in the configuration file, it does not take effect until the Postfix system has been reloaded.

Sending Messages to Postfix Programs

The `postkick` utility sends messages to a running Postfix program. The Postfix system allows programs to communicate among themselves using Unix pipes. The `postkick` utility uses these pipes to force a message to the program.

The format of the `postkick` utility is

```
postkick [-c config_dir] [-v] class service request
```

where the `-c` and `-v` options are the standard Postfix options to define an alternative configuration directory and to enable verbose logging, respectively.

The *`class`* parameter identifies the class of transport channel to use to communicate with the program (either private or public). The *`service`* parameter is the name of the program to send the message to, and the *`request`* parameter is the message to send.

Postfix programs communicate among themselves using the Unix pipe and a Postfix proprietary protocol. For example, the Postfix `qmgr` program receives messages from other programs and determines what actions need to be performed next based on those messages. Each message is one character long. The messages are sent via the Unix pipe to the Postfix program.

Table 6.7 shows the messages that the `qmgr` program responds to.

TABLE 6.7 Postfix `qmgr` Message Actions

Message	*Action*
A	Ignore the deferred queue file time stamps.
D	Start a `deferred` messages queue scan.
F	Purge all information about dead transports and destinations.
I	Start an `incoming` message queue scan.
W	Wake up. This is normally sent by the master program to keep programs active. The `qmgr` begins an `incoming` message queue scan when it receives this message.

Locking Postfix Mailbox Files

The `postlock` utility locks a mailbox file for exclusive access while the specified action is being performed on it. The format of the `postlock` utility is

```
postlock [-c config_dir] [-v] mailbox command
```

where the `-c` and `-v` options are the standard Postfix options used to define an alternative configuration directory and to enable verbose logging.

Once the mailbox file is successfully locked, the *`command`* listed runs using the `fork()` process. The number of times that the `postlock` utility attempts to lock a mailbox file before giving up can be defined in the `main.cf` configuration file.

Logging Postfix Messages

The `postlog` utility forwards messages to the Unix logging facility running on the mail server. Each instance of the `postlog` utility creates one record in the system log. The format of the `postlog` utility is

```
postlog [-iv] [-c config_dir] [-p priority] [-t tag] [text...]
```

The options used for the `postlog` utility are shown in Table 6.8.

TABLE 6.8 The Postfix `postlog` Utility Options

Option	*Description*
`-c`	Uses the `main.cf` file located in the *`config_dir`* directory
`-i`	Includes the process ID in the logging tag
`-p`	Specifies the logging priority for the log record
`-t`	Specifies the logging tag used to identify the record
`-v`	Enables verbose logging to the logger

The record priority must be one of the five standard `syslogd` priorities: info, warn, error, fatal, and panic. If no priority is indicated, the record is logged at an info priority.

NOTE

Chapter 13, "Postfix Server Administration," describes the Unix `syslogd` program and how it logs records in more detail.

On most Linux systems, the system log is located in the `/var/log/message` file. As shown in Chapter 13, depending on how your particular Linux system is configured, it may send mail-related logs to a separate file for easier viewing. On Mandrake Linux systems, all mail-related log messages are, by default, stored in the `/var/log/maillog` file.

Listing 6.9 shows an example of using the `postlog` utility to force messages into the `maillog` log file.

LISTING 6.9 Sample `postlog` Session

```
[rich@shadrach]$ postlog This is a test
postlog: This is a test

[rich@shadrach]$ postlog -t test This is a test
test: This is a test

[rich@shadrach]$ postlog -p warn -t test This is a test
test: warning: This is a test

[rich@shadrach]$ postlog -i -p warn -t test This is a test
test: warning: This is a test

[rich@shadrach]$ su
Password:

[root@shadrach]# tail /var/log/maillog
Oct 12 13:23:51 shadrach postlog: This is a test
Oct 12 13:24:36 shadrach test: This is a test
Oct 12 13:24:45 shadrach test: warning: This is a test
Oct 12 13:24:54 shadrach test[23482]: warning: This is a test
```

Listing 6.9 shows an example of the different forms of using the `postlog` utility. Each time the `postlog` utility runs, it logs a message to the system `/var/log/maillog` log file. Each example in the listing demonstrates a different option available for the `postlog` utility.

Maintaining Postfix Lookup Tables

The postmap utility queries, updates, or creates the many lookup tables that Postfix uses. Each Postfix lookup table is converted from an ASCII text file to a binary database file using a standard Unix database utility. The postmap utility creates the binary database using the values defined on the command line. The format of the postmap utility is

```
postmap [-Ninrvw] [-c config_dir] [-d key] [-q key] [file_type:]file_name
```

Table 6.9 describes the command-line options that can be used with the postmap utility.

TABLE 6.9 The Postfix postmap Utility Options

Option	*Description*
-N	Includes terminating NULL characters in lookup keys and values
-i	Appends entries from standard input to the existing database
-n	Does not include terminating NULL characters in lookup keys and values
-r	Does not warn about duplicate keys when updating the database
-v	Enables verbose logging
-w	Warns about duplicate keys when updating the database
-c *config_dir*	Uses the main.cf file located in the *config_dir* directory
-d *key*	Removes the database record identified by the key *key*
-q *key*	Queries the database for the record identified by the key *key*

Previously, Table 6.4 listed the different types of databases that can be used for lookup tables in Postfix. In addition to these lookup table types, Postfix also supports tables on NIS, LDAP, and MySQL servers, as well as tables that contain regular expression mappings. The most common lookup table type used on Linux systems is the hash table type.

The postmap utility creates a lookup table from an ASCII text file. The format of the text file is

```
key value
```

where *key* is the item that Postfix searches for in the database and *value* is the value that is returned to Postfix from the database search.

NOTE

Chapter 9 describes the format and use of the Postfix lookup tables in more detail.

Listing 6.10 shows an example of using the postmap command to query and update the virtual Postfix lookup table.

LISTING 6.10 Sample postmap Session

```
[root@shadrach]# postmap -q katie virtual
katie@otherhost.net
[root@shadrach]# postmap -d katie virtual
[root@shadrach]# postmap -q katie virtual

[root@shadrach]# echo katie katie@otherhost.net | postmap -i  virtual
[root@shadrach]# postmap -q katie virtual
katie@otherhost.net
```

Listing 6.10 shows several `postmap` sessions for using the Postfix `virtual` lookup table. First, the lookup table is queried for a record for the user `katie`. A result is returned showing that the `katie` username is mapped to the address `katie@otherhost.net`. Next, the `postmap` delete command deletes the record for `katie` in the lookup table. Notice that the next query does not return an answer. The record for `katie` has been successfully deleted from the `virtual` lookup table. Finally, the record is replaced using the `postmap` append command. The record is then queried from the existing lookup table.

CAUTION

Much like the `postalias` utility, the `postmap` utility can also be dangerous. By manually manipulating the values within the binary databases, the text versions of the databases become outdated and could be misleading. Many a mail administrator has been fooled by assuming that the binary database matched the text file used to originally create it.

Maintaining Postfix Message Queues

The `postsuper` utility helps maintain the Postfix message queue directories. As its name suggests, only the system superuser (`root`) can use it. The format of the `postsuper` utility is

```
postsuper [-p] [-s] [-v] [directory ...]
```

By default the `postsuper` utility attempts to organize the Postfix message queue directories by moving files that may be in the wrong message queue, removing unused lower-level subdirectories, and removing any files stuck after a system crash. Remember that Postfix resumes delivery of any messages stuck in message queues after a system crash. Unfortunately, if any messages become corrupt during the crash, they will not be processed and must be cleaned up with the `postsuper` command.

The `-p` option can remove only stale files in the message queues. Likewise, the `-s` option can remove only unused subdirectories and move files to the proper areas. As always, `-v` increases the level of logging that `postsuper` will do.

Listing 6.11 shows an example of using the `postsuper` utility on the Postfix system.

LISTING 6.11 Sample Postfix `postsuper` Utility Session

```
[root@shadrach]# postsuper -v
postsuper: queue: maildrop
postsuper: queue: incoming
postsuper: queue: active
postsuper: queue: deferred
postsuper: queue: defer
postsuper: queue: bounce
postsuper: queue: flush

[root@shadrach]# tail /var/log/maillog
Oct 12 14:56:24 shadrach postfix/postsuper[23642]: queue: maildrop
Oct 12 14:56:24 shadrach postfix/postsuper[23642]: queue: incoming
Oct 12 14:56:24 shadrach postfix/postsuper[23642]: queue: active
Oct 12 14:56:24 shadrach postfix/postsuper[23642]: queue: deferred
Oct 12 14:56:24 shadrach postfix/postsuper[23642]: queue: defer
Oct 12 14:56:24 shadrach postfix/postsuper[23642]: queue: bounce
Oct 12 14:56:24 shadrach postfix/postsuper[23642]: queue: flush
[root@shadrach postfix]#
```

As you can see, the default action of the `postsuper` utility is to check all of the message queue directories for problems and clean them up. It is advisable to use the `postsuper` utility before starting the Postfix services on the mail server.

Summary

There are two different ways to install the Postfix software on a Unix system. If your Linux distribution supports the RPM binary package installation method, you can use the prepackaged RPM distribution. This automatically installs the Postfix executable and configuration files into the proper places. If you do not have an RPM distribution, you can install Postfix from the source code distribution.

The source code distribution is released as a GNU-zipped `tar` file. You must expand the distribution file into a working directory. After the source code is expanded, it can be compiled using the GNU `make` command. Once the source code is compiled, it can be installed into the proper locations by using the `INSTALL.sh` install script.

During the install you will be asked where to place different pieces of the Postfix distribution. One of the questions asked is whether or not you want to install Postfix using the setuid system. By creating a separate group for the `maildrop` message queue, you can protect the incoming messages from internal hacker attacks and misuse. After Postfix is installed, you must fix the configuration settings to reflect your e-mail environment.

CHAPTER 7

The master.cf Configuration File

Once the Postfix software is installed, the next step is to configure it to work properly in your particular e-mail environment. Postfix uses straightforward plain-text files to assign values to intuitive parameter names.

The Postfix `master` program controls when and how the Postfix core programs are started and stopped. The mail administrator can control how the `master` program performs these tasks by editing the `master.cf` configuration file.

This chapter describes the layout, format, and use of the Postfix `master.cf` configuration file.

The Postfix `master` Program

The Postfix `master` program continuously runs in background mode on the e-mail server. Its function is to receive signals from other core Postfix programs and start the appropriate Postfix program to handle incoming messages. Both command-line options and the configuration file values control the `master` program.

The command-line options for the `master` program are

```
master [-C config_dir] [-D] [-t] [-v]
```

The `-C` option allows the e-mail administrator to start the `master` program using an alternate configuration file. The `config_dir` parameter is the directory where the alternate `master.cf` and `main.cf` files are located. You can use this option to test out new configuration parameters *before* deploying them on a production server.

The `-D` option allows the e-mail administrator to enable advanced debugging to trace any Postfix-related problems that may be occurring. Chapter 23, "Common Postfix Problems," describes how to configure Postfix to automatically start a standard Unix debugger program while Postfix is running.

The `-t` option is handy when starting the `master` program from a shell script. It checks to see whether the `master` program is already running on the mail server by monitoring a file that the `master` program creates when it starts. Only one master program is allowed to run on the mail server at a time. By default the `master.pid` file is located in the `/var/spool/postfix/pid` directory, and contains the process id (PID) of the currently running `master` program.

The `-v` option allows the e-mail administrator to enable verbose logging. This increases the level of detail in the messages Postfix logs as it receives and delivers e-mail. In addition to the command-line options, the `master.cf` configuration file also controls the `master` program. The next section describes this file.

Configuring Process Behavior in Postfix

A single configuration file controls the behavior of the Postfix processes. The `master.cf` configuration file contains the information that the `master` program uses to run the core processes. The mail administrator can fine-tune how Postfix operates by editing the `master.cf` configuration file. It is located in the standard Postfix configuration file directory, normally set to `/etc/postfix`.

The `master.cf` file is a text file that maintains values used when Postfix calls the core programs to deliver messages. Each core program is listed as a separate record (line) in the text file. Each record contains fields that describe the operation of the core program. The format of the `master.cf` file is

```
service   type   private   unprivileged   chroot   wakeup   maxprocess  command
```

The `master.cf` configuration file is normally owned by the `root` user and is only editable by the `root` user. The mail administrator should take care when editing the `master.cf` file. An improper `master.cf` file may prevent individual Postfix programs or even the `master` program from running.

Table 7.1 describes the contents of the fields of the `master.cf` records.

TABLE 7.1 The `master.cf` Record Fields

Field	*Description*
`service`	Name of the service being configured
`type`	Communication transport type used by the service
`private`	External security restrictions for service
`unprivileged`	User privileges the service is allowed to run with
`chroot`	Flag indicating whether the service runs in a restricted directory structure
`wakeup`	Number of seconds between consecutive wake up signals sent to the service to keep it alive
`maxprocess`	The maximum number of processes that can use the service at one time
`command`	The Postfix core daemon invoked to run the service

After assembling records for the appropriate services and inserting related field values, you might get something like the sample `master.cf` configuration file shown in Listing 7.1.

LISTING 7.1 Sample `master.cf` Configuration File

```
#service  type  private unprivileged chroot  wakeup  maxprocess  command
smtp      inet  n       -            n       -       -           smtpd
pickup    fifo  n       n            n       60      1           pickup
cleanup   unix  -       -            n       -       0           cleanup
qmgr      fifo  n       -            n       300     1           qmgr
```

LISTING 7.1 Continued

```
rewrite   unix  -    -    n    -      -    trivial-rewrite
bounce    unix  -    -    n    -      0    bounce
defer     unix  -    -    n    -      0    bounce
flush     unix  -    -    n    1000?  0    flush
smtp      unix  -    -    n    -      -    smtp
showq     unix  n    -    n    -      -    showq
error     unix  -    -    n    -      -    error
local     unix  -    n    n    -      -    local
```

This sample `master.cf` file demonstrates a simple Postfix configuration that uses default values. None of the Postfix core programs run in a `chroot` environment and the `pickup`, `qmgr`, and `flush` programs are scheduled for periodic `wakeup` calls. The following sections describe the values in the sample record fields in more detail.

Service Name

The `service` name field in the `master.cf` file defines the Unix service that the record defines. Each Postfix service must have a record in the `master.cf` file describing its behavior.

The specific format of the `service` field depends on its associated transport type field (discussed in the next section).

Table 7.2 describes the allowable entries for the `service` field and their related Postfix functions.

TABLE 7.2 Postfix Service Names

Service	*Description*
`bounce`	Delivers bounced e-mail messages back to the original sender
`bsmtp`	Delivers e-mail messages using the `BSMTP` protocol
`cleanup`	Processes incoming e-mail, fixing any address problems
`cyrus`	Delivers e-mail messages using the `Cyrus` mail engine
`defer`	Delivers e-mail that failed a delivery attempt to the `deferred` message queue
`error`	Forces e-mail to bounce
`flush`	Maintains records of deferred e-mail messages
`ifmail`	Delivers e-mail messages using the `ifmail` mail engine
`lmtp`	Delivers e-mail messages using the LMTP protocol
`local`	Delivers e-mail messages to local users
`pickup`	Determines that new e-mail messages are waiting in the `incoming` message queue
`qmgr`	Processes incoming messages and determines the delivery method required
`rewrite`	Rewrites or resolves addresses to the fully qualified domain name (FQDN) format

TABLE 7.2 Continued

Service	*Description*
showq	Reports Postfix message queue status
smtp	Receives and delivers messages using the SMTP protocol
uucp	Receives and delivers messages using the UUCP protocol

You may notice that the services listed here and Postfix programs do not match up on a one-to-one basis. For example, in Listing 7.1, the `bounce` and `defer` services both point to the Postfix `bounce` program, whereas the Postfix `smtp` service points to both the `smtpd` and `smtp` programs.

You can identify services that use the Internet socket transport type (discussed in the next section) either by the socket name listed in the `/etc/services` file or by the numeric TCP port number they use. Besides the Postfix name, services that use the Internet sockets transport type can also specify an interface name along with the service name in the form

```
interface:servicename
```

Services that use Internet sockets can also be restricted based on the host and port number. For example, by starting the `smtpd` program record with the following `service` entry

```
localhost:smtp
```

only SMTP connection requests *from the local system* will be accepted.

In the following example, `shadrach` is the local host. Assume that its IP address is 192.168.1.1 and that its `master.cf` file has been configured as above. Listing 7.2 shows a sample SMTP session from this machine.

LISTING 7.2 Example of Restricting Services to an Address

```
[rich@shadrach]$ telnet localhost 25
Trying 127.0.0.1...
Connected to localhost.
Escape character is '^]'.
220 shadrach.ispnet1.net ESMTP Postfix
QUIT
221 Bye
Connection closed by foreign host.

[rich@shadrach]$ telnet 192.168.1.1 25
Trying 192.168.1.1...
telnet: Unable to connect to remote host: Connection refused
```

The first connection attempt was permitted since it was *from* the local host *to* the local host. The second connection attempt was denied even though it was generated locally because it was addressed to the machine's external IP address. The `master.cf` file was configured to reject any non-`localhost` attempts.

If you substitute `8025` for `smtp` in the `smtpd` record's service entry like so

```
localhost:8025
```

Postfix only accepts SMTP connections on TCP port 8025 (instead of the standard TCP port `25`).

Listing 7.3 shows a sample SMTP session using this configuration.

LISTING 7.3 Example of Using an Alternative TCP Port

```
[rich@shadrach]$ telnet localhost 25
Trying 127.0.0.1...
telnet: Unable to connect to remote host: Connection refused

[rich@shadrach]$ telnet localhost 8025
Trying 127.0.0.1...
Connected to localhost.
Escape character is '^]'.
220 shadrach.ispnet1.net ESMTP Postfix
QUIT
221 Bye
Connection closed by foreign host.
```

As shown in Listing 7.3, using the `8025` entry in the `master.cf` file for the service changes the behavior of Postfix. Now, instead of accepting SMTP connections on the normal TCP port 25, it only accepts connections on port 8025. This is true for both the network and local host interfaces on the mail server.

Transport Type Name

The Postfix system is written as a group of modular programs. As an e-mail message moves through the Postfix system, each module must be able to communicate with other modules. The transport type (simply called `type` in the record) identifies how the individual programs communicate with other modules. Postfix currently supports three different transport types:

- Internet sockets (inet)
- Unix sockets (unix)
- Unix named pipes (fifo)

Each transport method has its own underlying mechanisms for initiating and terminating connections. The Postfix software handles all of the low-level details required for these communications.

Private

The `private` field indicates whether the communications channel is available to processes outside the Postfix system. Placing an `n` in this field opens the Postfix service to any process running on the mail server. Leaving the default dash (-) character keeps the service private.

The Postfix system uses two subdirectories, `public` and `private`, to contain the named pipes needed by each service in the `master.cf` file. The `private` subdirectory contains the pipes for processes marked as private, while the `public` subdirectory contains the pipes for processes marked as public.

Listing 7.4 shows a sample directory listing from a default Postfix installation.

LISTING 7.4 Sample Postfix Directory Structure

```
[rich@shadrach]$ ls -l
total 17
drwx------   2 postfix  root          1024 Oct 16 15:24 private
drwxr-xr-x   2 postfix  root          1024 Oct 16 15:24 public

[rich@shadrach]$ ls -l private
total 2
srw-rw-rw-   1 postfix  postfix          0 Oct 16 15:24 bounce
srw-rw-rw-   1 postfix  postfix          0 Oct 16 15:24 bsmtp
srw-rw-rw-   1 postfix  postfix          0 Oct 16 15:24 cleanup
srw-rw-rw-   1 postfix  postfix          0 Oct 16 15:24 cyrus
srw-rw-rw-   1 postfix  postfix          0 Oct 16 15:24 defer
srw-rw-rw-   1 postfix  postfix          0 Oct 16 15:24 error
srw-rw-rw-   1 postfix  postfix          0 Oct 16 15:24 flush
srw-rw-rw-   1 postfix  postfix          0 Oct 16 15:24 ifmail
srw-rw-rw-   1 postfix  postfix          0 Oct 16 15:24 lmtp
srw-rw-rw-   1 postfix  postfix          0 Oct 16 15:24 local
srw-rw-rw-   1 postfix  postfix          0 Oct 16 15:24 rewrite
srw-rw-rw-   1 postfix  postfix          0 Oct 16 15:24 smtp
srw-rw-rw-   1 postfix  postfix          0 Oct 16 15:24 uucp

[rish@shadrach]$ ls -l public
total 0
prw--w--w-   1 postfix  postfix          0 Oct 16 15:24 pickup
prw--w--w-   1 postfix  postfix          0 Oct 16 15:24 qmgr
srw-rw-rw-   1 postfix  postfix          0 Oct 16 15:24 showq
```

Listing 7.4 shows the default installation setup for the Postfix system. The first `ls` command shows the permission setting for the `public` and `private` directories. Notice that the `public` directory allows read permission to the public services for anyone on the system. The `private` directory denies all access to the private services to everyone except the `postfix` user.

Unprivileged

The `unprivileged` field indicates what user privileges the Postfix service will have when it is running. When this field contains a `y` character, the service attempts to run with the user privilege indicated by the `mail_owner` parameter in the `main.cf` configuration file. By default this is the `postfix` user that was created on the system.

You can also run services with the `root` user privileges by placing an `n` character in this field. When the service starts, it automatically gains `root` privileges. This is not a safe method to use, especially if your mail server is susceptible to internal hackers. By keeping the Postfix services running at a lower user privilege, they will become useless if a hacker invades the service.

Chroot

The `chroot` field indicates which services run in the `chroot` environment (as described in Chapter 6, "Installing Postfix"). Forcing services to run in a `chroot` environment adds another layer of security to the Postfix system and may help prevent damage from hacker attacks. With a few exceptions, any services that have contact with untrusted users are good candidates for being run `chroot`.

The `chroot` root directory becomes the Postfix spool directory, normally `/var/spool/postfix`. As described in Chapter 6, extra library files need to be copied to this directory if the Postfix programs are run in the `chroot` environment.

To activate the `chroot` environment for a service, place a `y` character in the `chroot` field. Remember, though, that the `local` and `pipe` programs *cannot* be run in the `chroot` environment.

Wakeup

The `wakeup` field indicates whether and how often the `master` program should contact the running service. This is a handy way of keeping important processes running in background mode. You can also use it as a timer to schedule events within the programs.

The number entered in the `wakeup` field represents the number of seconds that `master` waits before sending successive `wakeup` events to the service. Setting this value to `0` indicates that the service should never be sent a `wakeup` event.

Currently only the `pickup`, `qmgr`, and `flush` services use this feature. By having the `master` program send `wakeup` events to the `qmgr` and `pickup` programs, they can be scheduled to check the mail queues at set intervals. The default `master.cf` file installed from the source code distribution is set to wake up the `pickup` program every 60 seconds, and the `qmgr` program every 300 seconds. This forces Postfix to check for new local messages every minute, and new deferred or remote messages every five minutes.

CAUTION

Be careful when selecting these values. Checking the message queues too frequently could unnecessarily consume system resources and affect other system processes.

Another feature of the `wakeup` field is the question mark (`?`). You can append it to the numeric `wakeup` interval to indicate that the `master` program should only attempt to send a `wakeup` event message to the service if it is running. Currently, the `flush` service is the only service that uses this feature.

Maxprocess

The `maxprocess` field helps throttle the amount of system resources the Postfix system will use. The `maxprocess` field controls the number of processes that may execute the service simultaneously.

You can configure the default value of this field with the `default_process_limit` parameter in the `main.cf` configuration file. If you do not specify this parameter, the default process limit is set to 50. This allows up to 50 processes to run the service simultaneously.

For e-mail servers running on smaller platforms (such as i486 computers), you would be wise to set this value considerably lower to conserve system resources.

CAUTION

Currently, Venema suggests setting the `bounce`, `cleanup`, and `defer` services' `maxprocess` to `0` to prevent Postfix from becoming stuck under heavy load. He also advises that the `qmgr` and `pickup` services' `maxprocess` always be set to `1` to prevent multiple processes from servicing the same message.

Commands

The `command` field specifies the Postfix program that will be used to handle the data from the service. The path of each command is relative to the Postfix command directory specified by the `program_directory` parameter in the `main.cf` configuration file. By default no pathnames should be required.

You can specify each Postfix program with one or both of the following options:

- `-v`—Enables verbose logging of events
- `-D`[debugger]—Enables debugging by the specified debugger

It is often useful to include the `-v` and `-D` options when trying to troubleshoot Postfix problems. By adding `-v` options (up to two), the amount of detail logged can be increased. You may increase the logging detail for one particular service if you feel that it may be causing problems.

Listing 7.5 shows a log fragment for a single e-mail message where `qmgr` had verbose logging set.

LISTING 7.5 Sample Verbose Log Output

```
Oct 20 16:30:16 shadrach postfix/qmgr[7694]: print string:
➥ rich@shadrach.ispnet1.net
Oct 20 16:30:16 shadrach postfix/qmgr[7694]: print string:
Oct 20 16:30:16 shadrach postfix/qmgr[7694]: print long: 972077415
Oct 20 16:30:16 shadrach postfix/qmgr[7694]: print long: 84
Oct 20 16:30:16 shadrach postfix/qmgr[7694]: print string:
➥ rich@shadrach.ispnet1.net
Oct 20 16:30:16 shadrach postfix/qmgr[7694]: print string: 0
Oct 20 16:30:16 shadrach postfix/qmgr[7694]: qmgr_deliver: site
➥ `shadrach.ispnet1.net'
Oct 20 16:30:16 shadrach postfix/qmgr[7694]: watchdog_start: 0x8069b60
Oct 20 16:30:16 shadrach postfix/local[7700]: 285F8C352: to=
➥ <rich@shadrach.ispnet1.net>, relay=local, delay=1,
➥ status=sent (mailbox)
Oct 20 16:30:16 shadrach postfix/qmgr[7694]: mail_scan_any: read string:
Oct 20 16:30:16 shadrach postfix/qmgr[7694]: mail_scan_any: read integer: 0
Oct 20 16:30:16 shadrach postfix/qmgr[7694]: qmgr_queue_unthrottle:
➥ queue shadrach.ispnet1.net
Oct 20 16:30:16 shadrach postfix/qmgr[7694]: qmgr_active_done: 285F8C352
Oct 20 16:30:16 shadrach postfix/qmgr[7694]: dir_forest: 285F8C352 -> 2/8/
Oct 20 16:30:16 shadrach postfix/qmgr[7694]: dir_forest: 285F8C352 -> 2/8/
Oct 20 16:30:16 shadrach postfix/qmgr[7694]: qmgr_active_done: remove 285F8C352
Oct 20 16:30:16 shadrach postfix/qmgr[7694]: watchdog_start: 0x8069b60
```

Listing 7.5 is just a partial listing of the complete verbose logging of a single e-mail message. This demonstrates the log produced by adding a single level of verbose logging to the `qmgr` service. Each major step of the `qmgr` process is logged as an event, as opposed to just logging the `qmgr` process as a single event. Adding a second `-v` option to the command line produces even more verbose output in the log file.

Summary

The Postfix master program controls the overall operation of the Postfix system by calling core programs as needed. The master.cf configuration file instructs the master program on how to handle the core programs. The master.cf configuration file is located in the /etc/postfix directory by default. It consists of text lines, each line representing the configuration for a single Postfix core program. Each configuration line specifies the settings that the master program uses to control the core program when it is called. The Unix service name and transport type are listed so the master program knows how to communicate with the core program.

The unprivileged, unprivileged, and chroot fields indicate how the core program runs when it is started. Unprivileged core programs can only be accessed by Postfix services, whereas any processes that are running on the mail server can access programs tagged as public. The unprivileged field indicates that the program will run as a normal system user account and not as the root user. This helps decrease the damage a hacker can do if he manages to break into the program. The chroot field indicates an even higher level of security. A program running in a chroot environment is not allowed to access files outside of the directory specified when it is run. This further limits the damage that a hacker can do if he manages to break into a running Postfix program. The wakeup field allows the master program to send wakeup messages to Postfix programs to ensure that they remain running in background mode on the server. The maxprocess field controls the amount of system resources Postfix will be allowed to consume by restricting the number of programs that can use the service at the same time. Finally, the Postfix command that manipulates data from the service is listed, along with any command-line options that are desired. Currently, the -v and -D options can be used to enable verbose logging and debug mode, respectively.

CHAPTER 8

The main.cf Configuration File

Similar to `sendmail`, Postfix uses a configuration file to define its operational behavior. What's different about the Postfix configuration file is that instead of using cryptic codes, or needing to be compiled, it uses plain text and common-sense descriptions for parameter names and values.

The global Postfix configuration file is called `main.cf`. It is located in the Postfix configuration directory, which by default is `/etc/postfix`. Many Postfix programs allow for utilizing an alternative configuration file by using the `-c` command-line option and specifying the different configuration directory.

This chapter describes the format and the most common parameters used in the `main.cf` configuration file. More than 200 different parameters can be used in the `main.cf` configuration file. Fortunately, most of them can use default values that will work perfectly fine on most e-mail servers.

The Postfix Configuration File Format

Each Postfix parameter is listed on a separate line in the configuration file along with its value, in the form

```
parameter = value
```

Both parameters and values are plain ASCII text strings that the mail administrator can easily read. The Postfix `master` program reads the parameter values in the `main.cf` file when Postfix is first started, and again whenever a `postfix reload` command is issued.

CAUTION

Any changes made to the `main.cf` configuration file do not take effect until either the Postfix system is shut down and restarted or the mail administrator issues a reload command using the `postfix` program. Remember that the text `main.cf` file may not necessarily reflect the actual parameter values that the current running Postfix system is using.

Note that within the `main.cf` file you can refer to other parameter names in the value portion of the parameter/value pair by placing a dollar sign in front of the parameter name:

```
mydestination = $myhostname
```

This makes it easy to refer to other previously set values later in the file. It also means fewer changes when updating the system.

Configuration Parameters

The following sections describe various Postfix configuration parameters by grouping them as they appear in the default `main.cf` file created by the Postfix source code distribution.

Local Pathname Information

The first parameters listed in the `main.cf` file define the locations of the Postfix files when they were installed. When the installation script ran, it queried the administrator for several different directory locations. These locations are automatically defined in a skeleton `main.cf` file. Three different file categories are used:

- Message queue directories
- Command files
- Daemon files

The parameter lines that are created from the install script are

```
queue_directory = /var/spool/postfix
command_directory = /usr/sbin
daemon_directory = /usr/libexec/postfix
```

The directories entered during the install process appear in the value portion of these pairs. If you decide later to move a Postfix program into an alternate directory, you must modify the appropriate value for the corresponding parameter.

Queue and Process Ownership

The next set of parameters defines usernames that are used in the Postfix process. Each username defined must be a valid system username created by the mail administrator.

The mail_owner

The `mail_owner` parameter defines the dedicated Unix username that was used to identify the owner of the mail directories:

```
mail_owner = postfix
```

This username should have been created during the Postfix installation process described in Chapter 6, "Installing Postfix." It is used as the owner of the Postfix queue directories. Listing 8.1 shows the directory layout and ownership of the Postfix directories.

LISTING 8.1 Postfix Queue Directory Ownership

```
[root@shadrach]# ls -al /var/spool/postfix
total 14
drwxr-xr-x   14 root     root          1024 Oct 23 11:09 .
drwxr-xr-x   15 root     root          1024 Oct 23 11:11 ..
drwx------    2 postfix  root          1024 Oct 23 11:09 active
drwx------    2 postfix  root          1024 Oct 23 11:09 bounce
drwx------    2 postfix  root          1024 Oct 23 11:09 corrupt
drwx------    2 postfix  root          1024 Oct 23 11:09 defer
drwx------    2 postfix  root          1024 Oct 23 11:09 deferred
drwx------    2 postfix  root          1024 Oct 23 11:09 flush
drwx------    2 postfix  root          1024 Oct 23 11:09 incoming
drwx-wx--T    2 postfix  maildrop      1024 Oct 23 11:08 maildrop
drwxr-xr-x    2 postfix  root          1024 Oct 23 11:09 pid
drwx------    2 postfix  root          1024 Oct 23 15:33 private
drwxr-xr-x    2 postfix  root          1024 Oct 23 15:33 public
drwx------    2 postfix  root          1024 Oct 23 11:09 saved
```

As shown in Listing 8.1, the Postfix directories are owned by the username `postfix` and the group name `root`. If you are using the protected `maildrop` queue option, the `maildrop` directory will have the special group name that you created for it.

default_privs

Another ownership parameter that Postfix uses is the `default_privs` parameter. This parameter defines the privileges that the Postfix local mail delivery agent uses when forwarding messages to files and external commands:

```
default_privs = nobody
```

By default this is set to the `nobody` system username. The `nobody` user is a special user that has no privileges on the Unix system. This is the safest way to operate Postfix. It will help prevent damage to your system should a hacker obtain control of the mail delivery system.

CAUTION

You should never assign `root` as the `default_privs` value. This would allow a hacker to use the Postfix system to replace system files on the server, thus totally compromising the system.

Internet Host and Domain Names

To ensure proper operation of the mail server, you must specify its host and domain name. This enables Postfix to know how to properly address e-mail messages.

myhostname and mydomain

The myhostname and mydomain parameters are used to specify the Internet address scheme of the mail server:

```
myhostname = host.domain.name
mydomain = domain.name
```

The myhostname parameter specifies the fully qualified domain name (FQDN) of the mail server. This address will be used as the default address for all local users, unless specified otherwise by the mail administrator.

The mydomain parameter uses the assigned DNS domain name of the mail server. You can use this parameter instead of the myhostname parameter when a mail server is configured to receive messages for an entire domain.

Both of these parameters can take default values from the system where the Postfix server is running. If the myhostname parameter is not defined in the configuration file, Postfix uses the gethostname() function call to obtain a default system name. It then attempts to determine the domain name part of the hostname and assign it to the mydomain parameter.

You can determine the configured hostname of your system by using the uname command with the -n option:

```
[root@shadrach]# uname -n
shadrach.ispnet1.net
```

In the preceding example, the myhostname parameter will default to the value shadrach.ispnet1.net, while the mydomain parameter will default to the value ispnet1.net.

The myhostname parameter must be used if the local mail system is not using an FQDN hostname. Often test machines that are not part of an Internet domain are just named with a short hostname with no domain added. In this case the myhostname and mydomain parameters can be defined as fictitious domain addresses.

Also, if the Postfix system is using a virtual interface for testing, the myhostname parameter must be specifically defined for the virtual interface. This technique is described in Chapter 10, "Using Postfix."

Sending Mail

When sending messages to remote hosts, the Postfix server must determine how to format the mail header addresses from the local mail server. Proper address formats are necessary to ensure that return messages will actually come back to the right place.

myorigin

The myorigin parameter defines the format of the origin address for all messages sent by the Postfix system:

```
myorigin = $mydomain
```

By default, the myorigin parameter will assume the value of the myhostname parameter. This adds the FQDN to local user addresses, as shown in Listing 8.2.

LISTING 8.2 Sample Message Demonstrating Default myorigin

```
[rich@shadrach]$ mail rich
Subject: Test message
This is a test message.
.

[rich@shadrach]$ mail
Mail version 8.1 6/6/93.  Type ? for help.
"/var/spool/mail/rich": 1 message 1 new
>N  1 rich@shadrach.ispne  Mon Oct 23 18:55  13/454   "Test message"
&1
Message 1:
From rich@shadrach.ispnet1.net  Mon Oct 23 18:55:38 2000
Delivered-To: rich@shadrach.ispnet1.net
To: rich@shadrach.ispnet1.net
Subject: Test message
Date: Mon, 23 Oct 2000 18:55:38 -0500 (EST)
From: rich@shadrach.ispnet1.net (Rich)

This is a test message.

&
```

As you can see, the message received by the user rich has the From: address set to the FQDN of the local host. This allows the recipient to reply to the sender with a correctly formatted e-mail address.

Some mail administrators prefer to use the domain name as the e-mail address. This requires that the return address contain only the domain name instead of the local hostname and the FQDN. The myorigin parameter can change the address format in messages sent from the Postfix server. By setting myorigin to the domain name value (or pointing it to the mydomain value) all messages sent from the server will use just the domain name in the return address. Listing 8.3 demonstrates this.

LISTING 8.3 Using the Domain Name in Return Addresses

```
[rich@shadrach]$ mail rich@shadrach.ispnet1.net
Subject: Second test message
This is the second test message.
.

[rich@shadrach]$ mail
Mail version 8.1 6/6/93.  Type ? for help.
"/var/spool/mail/rich": 1 message 1 new
>N  1 rich@ispnet1.net      Mon Oct 23 19:11  13/443  "Second test message"
&1
Message 1:
From rich@ispnet1.net  Mon Oct 23 19:11:11 2000
Delivered-To: rich@shadrach.ispnet1.net
To: rich@shadrach.ispnet1.net
Subject: Second test message
Date: Mon, 23 Oct 2000 19:11:11 -0500 (EST)
From: rich@ispnet1.net (Rich)

This is the second test message.

&
```

The `From:` header line now uses only the domain name instead of the FQDN of the local host. Of course this method assumes that there is a valid MX record defined for the domain name in the DNS database.

CAUTION

Care should be taken when changing the `myorigin` parameter to the `mydomain` value. When this occurs, any user addresses not containing a hostname will default to the domain name. If the MX record for your domain does not point to the local Postfix server, this creates a mail delivery problem for local users not using FQDN addresses.

Receiving Mail

Postfix also uses parameters to define how it will receive mail messages. Postfix can be configured to only receive messages from certain interfaces on the host system.

inet_interfaces

First, Postfix needs to know what interfaces it should monitor for incoming messages. This is defined in the `inet_interfaces` parameter.

The interfaces available on the Unix system can be determined by using the `ifconfig` command:

```
[root@shadrach]# ifconfig
eth0      Link encap:Ethernet  HWaddr 00:E0:7D:74:DF:C7
          inet addr:192.168.1.1  Bcast:192.168.1.255  Mask:255.255.255.0
          UP BROADCAST RUNNING MULTICAST  MTU:1500  Metric:1
          RX packets:1107 errors:0 dropped:0 overruns:0 frame:0
          TX packets:878 errors:0 dropped:0 overruns:0 carrier:0
          collisions:0 txqueuelen:100
          Interrupt:10 Base address:0x6400

lo        Link encap:Local Loopback
          inet addr:127.0.0.1  Mask:255.0.0.0
          UP LOOPBACK RUNNING  MTU:3924  Metric:1
          RX packets:5277 errors:0 dropped:0 overruns:0 frame:0
          TX packets:5277 errors:0 dropped:0 overruns:0 carrier:0
          collisions:0 txqueuelen:0
```

By default, Postfix monitors all interfaces for incoming messages:

```
inet_interfaces = all
```

You can specify a single interface to limit Postfix to receiving messages from just that interface and ignore messages on any other interfaces.

For example, if you specify only the `localhost` value

```
inet_interfaces = localhost
```

the Postfix `smtpd` program accepts only messages from the `localhost` interface and not from external hosts. Listing 8.4 demonstrates this.

LISTING 8.4 Limiting Postfix to the `localhost` Interface

```
[haley@shadrach haley]# telnet 192.168.1.1 25
Trying 192.168.1.1...
telnet: Unable to connect to remote host: Connection refused

[haley@shadrach haley]# telnet localhost 25
Trying 127.0.0.1...
Connected to localhost.
Escape character is '^]'.
220 shadrach.ispnet1.net ESMTP Postfix
QUIT
221 Bye
Connection closed by foreign host.
```

This is a handy feature to use for testing Postfix without making the mail server available on the network. As you will see in Chapter 10, you can create a virtual interface, and Postfix can be limited to receiving messages on just that interface. This is a great tool to use for testing and troubleshooting Postfix systems.

mydestination

The `mydestination` parameter defines what hostnames the Postfix server accepts messages for as the final destination. This parameter applies only to the main hostname and aliases for the local system and should not include virtual domains for other hosts. The format of the `mydestination` value portion is a comma-separated list:

```
mydestination = $myhostname, localhost.$mydomain
```

This allows Postfix to receive messages addressed to its normal FQDN as well as the special `localhost` hostname.

CAUTION

Remember not to list virtual domains for this parameter. Postfix uses the `virtual` lookup table (described in Chapter 9, "Postfix Lookup Tables") for this purpose.

The `mydestination` parameter often supports hosts that may have DNS names other than the normal hostname assigned to it. For example, suppose a Postfix server was also the company Web server. It is normal to assign a DNS alias name to Web machines such as `www.ispnet1.net`. The `mydestination` parameter can be configured as:

```
mydestination = $myhostname, localhost.$mydomain, $mydomain, www.$mydomain
```

This allows the Postfix server to accept messages for addresses in the following formats:

```
webmaster
webmaster@shadrach.ispnet1.net
webmaster@ispnet1.net
webmaster@www.ispnet1.net
```

Messages sent to any of the four addresses are accepted and delivered to the Webmaster user on the local Postfix server.

mynetworks

The `mynetworks` parameter is used to control which SMTP clients Postfix will relay mail for. By default, Postfix will relay mail from any client whose IP address matches the settings in the `mynetworks` parameter.

The mynetworks parameter contains a list of IP network addresses, along with subnet values, to specify alternative network restrictions on SMTP clients. The format of the mynetworks parameter is

```
mynetworks = ipaddress1, ipaddress2, ...
```

where *ipaddress1* and *ipaddress2* represent IP address network values. An example of this would be

```
mynetworks = 192.168.100.0/28, 127.0.0.1/8
```

This restricts clients that can use the Postfix server as an SMTP mail relay.

mynetworks_style

The mynetworks_style parameter is used to define how the IP network addresses are used to restrict the remote SMTP clients. There are two possible values for this parameter:

```
mynetworks_style = class
mynetworks_style = subnet
```

The class value indicates that the IP network specified in the mynetworks parameter defines a complete class A, B, or C subnet. The subnet value defines a partial subnet of the official class address for the network. The default value is subnet.

Connecting to Internet or Intranet Servers

The Postfix server software is versatile in that it can be used in a variety of e-mail server situations. Some situations require that the Postfix server forward all outbound mail to a central e-mail host for delivery.

One such situation is in an office intranet, which may have dozens of Unix workstations. Rather than have each workstation forward mail messages to all the other workstations, it is often easier to designate a central Unix server as the office mail server and configure the individual workstations to forward all messages to that central mail server for distribution.

Another situation in which this would be needed is when the e-mail server is not connected to the Internet full time. In this scenario, the Postfix server must be able to relay messages destined for external mail hosts to another e-mail server for delivery. This process is called using a relay host.

NOTE

Chapter 12, "Using Postfix as an Office Mail Server," discusses these scenarios in more detail.

relay_host

The relay_host parameter defines a relay host for the Postfix server. There are two formats of the relay_host parameter:

```
relay_host = gateway.my.domain
relay_host = [an.ip.add.ress]
```

The first format identifies a relay host mail server by its DNS name. Postfix forwards all outbound mail messages to this host. The second format identifies the relay host by its numeric IP address. You should use the second format for Postfix servers that use dial-up connections to the relay host. Since the Postfix server is not connected to the Internet full time to resolve the relay host DNS name, it is best to refer to it using the IP address. This prevents problems in mail delivery due to DNS errors.

Rejecting Unknown Local Users

By default, Postfix receives messages for any mail address. Once the message is placed in the incoming mail queue, it attempts to deliver the message. If it determines that the destination address is local but the user does not exist in either the password file or one of the local lookup tables, it attempts to bounce the message back to the sender.

This process can be shortened if the Postfix server can attempt to look up the destination address before it accepts the mail message. This is possible using the local_recipient_maps parameter.

local_recipient_maps

The local_recipient_maps parameter defines a list of places that Postfix can look to determine whether a local username is valid. The format of the value portion of local_recipient_maps is a comma- or whitespace-separated list:

```
local_recipient_maps = $alias_maps unix:passwd.byname
```

The values defined for the parameter instruct Postfix where to look on the system to validate the message recipient address. The preceding example instructs Postfix to first check the aliases lookup table and then to use the Unix system password file.

Listing 8.5 shows an example of an SMTP session where Postfix verifies the local username before accepting the message.

LISTING 8.5 Rejecting Messages for Unknown Users

```
[riley@shadrach riley]$ telnet localhost 25
Trying 127.0.0.1...
Connected to localhost.
Escape character is '^]'.
220 shadrach.blum.lan ESMTP Postfix
```

LISTING 8.5 Continued

```
HELO shadrach.ispnet1.net
250 shadrach.ispnet1.net
MAIL FROM: <rich@shadrach.ispnet1.net>
250 Ok
RCPT TO: <baduser@shadrach.ispnet1.net>
550 <baduser@shadrach.blum.lan>: User unknown
QUIT
221 Bye
Connection closed by foreign host.
```

As shown in Listing 8.5, the SMTP connection requests delivery of the message to user `baduser@shadrach.ispnet1.net`. The `local_recipient_maps` parameter instructs the Postfix server to check the aliases and password files for the user. Because the user is not found, the Postfix server returns an SMTP 550 error message, indicating the results to the requesting mail server. This prevents Postfix from having to process the entire mail message before determining that the user does not exist.

"User not found" Options

Postfix allows the mail administrator to define how some actions are performed. One of those actions is what happens when a mail message is received for a user who is not on the local system. As shown in Listing 8.5, the Postfix server returned an SMTP 550 error message when the user was not found.

Some Internet security experts consider this a security risk. A hacker could attempt to send mail messages to a host and watch the SMTP error codes. By evaluating the return codes, the hacker could determine valid usernames on the system.

The Postfix system allows for customizing SMTP return codes. The default values used for the various SMTP codes are

```
access_map_reject_code = 550
invalid_hostname_reject_code = 501
maps_rbl_reject_code = 550
reject_code = 550
relay_domains_reject_code = 550
unknown_address_reject_code = 450
unknown_client_reject_code = 450
unknown_hostname_reject_code = 450
```

The mail administrator can change these as deemed necessary.

CAUTION

Do not arbitrarily change the SMTP error codes. Some MTA packages will break if they receive an SMTP code they are not expecting. Make sure that you fully understand the SMTP error codes before changing these values. See Chapter 5, "SMTP and Postfix," for a description of the various SMTP error codes.

relocated_maps

If a local user has moved to a new mail host, you can configure Postfix to forward his mail. Often people leave companies and are in the middle of changing business cards. It is convenient to have the old e-mail address forward messages to the new e-mail address for some period of time.

Postfix allows for this by using a lookup table that maps the old e-mail address to the new address. The `relocated` lookup table is used for this purpose. You can specify the location of the `relocated` lookup table using the `relocated_maps` parameter:

```
relocated_maps = hash:/etc/postfix/relocated
```

Postfix looks up the old local mail address listed in the `relocated` table and forwards the message to the new address.

NOTE

Remember to add the `relocated_maps` value to the `local_recipient_maps` parameter list if you are verifying local addresses.

Address Rewriting

Often Postfix must rewrite sender and recipient addresses on messages. The `trivial-rewrite` program, as described in Chapter 2, "Postfix Services," serves this function. It uses several different parameters to define how to do the rewriting.

allow_percent_hack, append_at_myorigin, append_dot_mydomain

The first set of parameters used for address rewriting is

```
allow_percent_hack = yes
append_at_myorigin = yes
append_dot_mydomain = yes
```

These parameters instruct the `trivial-rewrite` program to rewrite an address in one format to another format. The function of these parameters is shown in Table 8.1.

TABLE 8.1 Address Rewriting Parameters

Parameter	*Original*	*Rewrite*
`allow_percent_hack`	`user%domain`	`user@domain`
`append_at_myorigin`	`user`	`user@$mydomain`
`append_dot_mydomain`	`user@host`	`user@host.$mydomain`

When the `trivial-rewrite` program detects an address with one of the "original" addresses shown in Table 8.1, it automatically replaces it with the address shown.

`empty_address_recipient`

The `empty_address_recipient` defines the mail address that bounce notifications should be returned to for messages that bounce but have no sender address defined. The format is

```
empty_address_recipient = MAILER-DAEMON
```

The `MAILER-DAEMON` address is a common e-mail catchall address for reporting errors to. If you use this address for your system, you must remember to create an alias in the Postfix `aliases` lookup table to point to a real user on the local system (usually the mail administrator).

`masquerade_domains, masquerade_exceptions`

The `masquerade` parameters deal with situations in which the Postfix server is "masquerading" as another mail server. Just as the name suggests, masquerading causes the mail server to pretend to be something that it is not. In most cases, the Postfix server will masquerade as a domain mail server.

So, the server `shadrach.ispnet1.net` may want to masquerade as the mail server `ispnet1.net`. This way, remote users can send mail to addresses using just the domain name instead of the full hostname. For masquerading to work properly, the `trivial-rewrite` program must know what addresses it should append the masqueraded address to. The following parameters define the masquerade environment:

```
masquerade_domains = $mydomain
masquerade_exceptions = root
```

Here, the `trivial-rewrite` program appends the value of the `mydomain` parameter to all messages leaving the mail server, except those from the `root` user. Often, it is best to leave `root`'s address unmodified because you want to ensure that messages sent to `root` are properly received.

NOTE

Don't confuse the `masquerade` parameters with the `myorigin` parameter. The `myorigin` parameter only changes message header values. The `masquerade` parameters are used to change message envelopes as well as headers, so that no mention of the original system is shown on the message.

swap_bangpath

The swap_bangpath parameter can be used when dealing with UUCP-style addresses. The UUCP protocol defines mail addresses as user!hostname. This format can confuse some DNS-based mailers, and is best changed to the standard DNS form user@hostname. The format for this parameter is

```
swap_bangpath = yes
```

canonical_maps

As a final catchall, the trivial-rewrite program can use a Postfix lookup table to change mail envelope and header addresses as needed. The canonical lookup table can create one-to-one mappings of addresses. There are three parameters that can be used to define canonical lookup tables:

```
canonical_maps
recipient_canonical_maps
sender_canonical_maps
```

The canonical_maps parameter defines a lookup table that is used to change both sender and recipient addresses in all mail messages. If the mail administrator wants to just change addresses for recipients or senders, he can use one of the other two parameters.

The canonical lookup table comes in handy when the mail administrator wants to use aliases for all of the e-mail users on the system. Unlike the aliases lookup table, the canonical lookup table can be applied to sender as well as recipient addresses. The most common use for this is for sites that want to use full names as e-mail addresses, such as richard.blum. Because these names cannot be used as system usernames, the canonical lookup table can be used to map an e-mail full name to a system username for each e-mail user. Thus, all mail sent by the user will properly show his full e-mail name instead of the Unix username.

NOTE

The canonical lookup table is described in more detail in Chapter 9.

Virtual Domains

One feature of MTAs is the capability to receive mail destined for other locations. Once the mail is received, it must be stored until the remote location connects to the mail server to retrieve it. This is called a *virtual domain*.

The Postfix software supports virtual domains by creating a lookup table that lists all of the domains for which the mail server should receive messages.

virtual_maps

The `virtual_maps` parameter defines the type and location of the `virtual` lookup table:

```
virtual_maps = hash:/etc/postfix/virtual
```

The `virtual` lookup table lists each address or domain to be redirected on a separate line.

Each line then points to a local address that holds the mail messages destined for that domain/address. At some later time, a mail server for the destination domain connects to the Postfix server and retrieves the messages.

Transport Map

By default, Postfix uses SMTP to transfer mail messages to remote hosts. However, the Postfix programs were built to be modular, so any other protocols can be added to the Postfix system.

transport_maps

The `transport` lookup table can define what protocol Postfix should use to send mail to particular remote hosts:

```
transport_maps = hash:/etc/postfix/transport
```

The `transport` lookup table lists each remote host and the protocol that Postfix can use to send messages to that host. The `qmgr` daemon can determine which Postfix program to use to send the messages based on the protocol listed in the table.

Alias Database

Postfix supports `sendmail`-type alias databases to be used by the `local` delivery program. Unlike `sendmail`, Postfix can support several alias databases, each using different database types. Two parameters inform Postfix to look in alias databases for usernames.

alias_maps

The `alias_maps` parameter specifies what alias databases Postfix can access. The format of `alias_maps` is

```
alias_maps = hash:/etc/postfix/aliases, nis:mail.aliases
```

The alias databases are listed in a comma- or space-separated list. Postfix searches the alias databases in the order in which they are entered as the parameter value. Thus, in the preceding example, Postfix checks the local `/etc/postfix/aliases.db` lookup table and then attempts to use the Network Information System (NIS) `mail.aliases` map to resolve the address.

alias_database

The alias_database parameter defines the list of alias databases that Postfix has direct control over. It differs from the alias_maps parameter in that the alias_maps parameter lists programs that local can access, but that Postfix does not necessarily control. The alias_database parameter can also specify external alias databases, such as those used by the Majordomo program. The format of the alias_database parameter is

```
alias_database = hash:/etc/postfix/aliases, hash:/etc/majordomo/aliases
```

Remember that alias databases controlled by programs other than Postfix need to be maintained by the administrator of the external program (although that is often the same person as the mail administrator).

NOTE

Majordomo is a program designed to simplify the administration of mail lists. It is described in Chapter 19, "Using Majordomo with Postfix."

allow_mail_to_commands, allow_mail_to_files

One of the features of the sendmail-style alias databases is the ability to forward messages both to external commands and to files. By default, Postfix does not allow these features (for reasons of system security). If you want to use either of these features, you must include the appropriate parameter in the main.cf file:

```
allow_mail_to_commands = alias, forward
allow_mail_to_files = alias, forward
```

By enabling these features, Postfix can be configured to deliver mail messages to an external program or archive messages to a file on the system. The format for using these features in the alias database file is

```
alias1: |command
alias2: /filename
```

When Postfix receives a message for alias1, it automatically forwards it to the program command, using the privileges of the default_privs parameter.

When Postfix receives a message for alias2, it appends it to the file /filename.

Address Extensions

Postfix can extend the normal system username by using a specified extension character. This enables local mail users to create extensions of their address for various purposes, usually filtering-related.

recipient_delimiter

The `recipient_delimiter` parameter defines the character that Postfix uses to separate the normal system username from the address extension defined by the user. The format and default separator is

```
recipient_delimiter = +
```

This feature allows users to create their own private mail lists on the Postfix system without the mail administrator having to intervene. Mail delivered to an address that is an extension of a normal system username is delivered based on directions in a forwarding file created by the user.

For example, the user `katie` can create a forwarding file called `.forward+cats` in her home directory. She needs to remember to use the delimiter specified in the `main.cf` file when naming the `.forward` file as well. In this file, she can place mail addresses of recipients in her mailing list as shown in Listing 8.6.

LISTING 8.6 Sample `.forward+cats` File

```
rich
barbara
jessica@meshach.ispnet2.net
riley@abednego.ispnet1.net
alex@othercompany.com
haley
```

This list can contain both local and remote mail addresses. Once the forward file is created, messages sent to the `katie+cats` mail address are forwarded to each user on the list. The user `katie` has just made an ad hoc mailing list, as shown in Listing 8.7.

LISTING 8.7 Sample Message Sent to Mail List

```
[rich@shadrach]$ mail katie+cats
Subject: Test message sent to the "cats" mail list
Hello all -

    This is a test message sent to the "cats" mailing list.
Everyone remember to be nice to your cats today.

                                Rich

.

[rich@shadrach]$ mail
Mail version 8.1 6/6/93.  Type ? for help.
"/var/spool/mail/rich": 1 message 1 new
```

LISTING 8.7 Continued

```
>N  1 rich@indytest.dfas.m  Thu Oct 26 11:01  21/739   "Test message sent to "
&1
Message 1:
From rich@shadrach.ispnet1.net  Thu Oct 26 11:01:18 2000
Delivered-To: rich@shadrach.ispnet1.net
Delivered-To: katie+cats@shadrach.ispnet1.net
To: katie+cats@shadrach.ispnet1.net
Subject: Test message sent to the "cats" mail list
Date: Thu, 26 Oct 2000 11:01:17 -0500 (EST)
From: rich@shadrach.ispnet1.net (Rich Blum)

Hello all -

    This is a test message sent to the "cats" mailing list.
Everyone remember to be nice to your cats today.

                                Rich

&
```

As shown in Listing 8.7, the message sent to the `katie+cats` mail address was forwarded to the appropriate addresses in the mail list specified by the `.forward+cats` file.

Mailbox Delivery

Postfix supports three different types of mail delivery on the local host. In addition to delivering mail to users on the local host, you can also configure Postfix to pass messages along to an external Mail Delivery Agent (MDA) program.

home_mailbox

The `home_mailbox` parameter can define where Postfix delivers messages to local mail users. Postfix can use three different delivery styles:

- `sendmail`-style `/var/spool/mail` mailboxes
- Individual `$HOME/Mailbox` files
- `qmail`-style `$HOME/Maildir` directories

By default, Postfix delivers messages to the standard system mailbox directory. On most Linux systems this is the `/var/spool/mail` directory. Normally Postfix determines the location of the mail directory by default. If it does not, you can assign a value to the `mail_spool_directory` parameter:

```
mail_spool_directory = /var/spool/mail
```

Each system user has an individual file in this directory that receives all of the new mail messages for that user. The permissions are set so that users only have write access to their own mail files.

Some administrators do not like grouping all of the user mailboxes under one directory. An alternative method is to create a user mailbox in the `$HOME` directory of each user. This can be configured in Postfix using the `home_mailbox` parameter:

```
home_mailbox = Mailbox
```

This instructs Postfix to deliver messages to the file `$HOME/Mailbox` for each user. The mail administrator can change the mailbox name to anything he wants. Remember, though, that the `home_mailbox` parameter specifies the pathname *relative* to the user's `$HOME` directory.

Dan Bernstein created an alternative to the one-file-per-user mailbox system. He created the `qmail` mail system as another alternative to the `sendmail` MTA program. Within this system, he designed a system where each user has an individual directory for messages, and each message is stored as a separate file within the mailbox directory. This is called the Maildir method, for the name of the directory that is normally created:

```
home_mailbox = Maildir/
```

It is important to note the trailing `/` character at the end of the `Maildir` name. This denotes the use of Maildir-type directories instead of Mailbox files. While the mail administrator is free to use any name for this directory, `Maildir` is the most common name used.

mailbox_command

Alternatively, instead of Postfix having to worry about delivering the local mail messages, it can pass them off to an external MDA. This can be specified using the `mailbox_command` parameter. The format for this is

```
mailbox_command = /some/where/procmail -a "$EXTENSION"
```

The value associated with this parameter must point to the full pathname of the MDA program, along with any command-line options and parameters needed for it to deliver the message. The command-line parameters can be created by Postfix-supplied variables.

Table 8.2 shows the variables that Postfix can forward to the command.

TABLE 8.2 Postfix Environment Variables for `mailbox_command`

Variable	*Description*
`$HOME`	The user's home directory
`$SHELL`	The user's Unix shell
`$LOGNAME`	The user's Unix username

TABLE 8.2 Continued

Variable	*Description*
$USER	The recipient's username
$EXTENSION	The address extension
$DOMAIN	The domain part of the address
$LOCAL	The local part of the address

mailbox_transport, fallback_transport

The `mailbox_transport` parameter specifies the mail transport defined in the `master.cf` configuration file to be used for delivering local mail messages. The format of this parameter is

```
mailbox_transport = cyrus
```

This parameter allows the mail administrator to use an external MTA mailer program such as cyrus to deliver the local mail.

The `fallback_transport` parameter specifies the mail transport defined in the `master.cf` file to be used when a local user is not found in the Unix password database. The format of this parameter is

```
fallback_transport = uucp
```

This parameter allows the mail administrator to use an alternative mail transport for forwarding messages to users on other systems.

luser_relay

The `luser_relay` parameter specifies a catchall destination address to use when a local mail address is not found on the local system. Instead of the undeliverable messages bouncing, they are forwarded to the `luser_relay` value. This parameter can use environment variables similar to the `mailbox_command` parameter to define remote addresses. The format of this parameter is

```
luser_relay = $user@other.host
```

This example demonstrates forwarding mail sent to a nonexistent user on the local system to the same username on the mail system `other.host`.

UCE Controls

Unsolicited Commercial E-mail (UCE), otherwise known as *spam*, has become the scourge of the Internet. Everyone cringes when they check their e-mail and see lots of messages explaining how they can make $1,000 a day at home mailing envelopes. Postfix attempts to help control UCE by enforcing the parameters discussed in the following section.

header_checks

The simplest form of UCE control is rejecting mail from known spammers. The `header_checks` parameter is used as a starting point for this process. The `header_checks` parameter specifies a regular expression lookup table that can compare known spam headers and reject messages containing them. The format of this parameter is

```
header_checks = regexp:/etc/postfix/filename
```

The filename specified as the value must be a regular expression lookup table (described in Chapter 9) matching known spam headers along with the final word REJECT.

NOTE

Configuring the `header_check` lookup table for UCE filtering is discussed in more detail in Chapter 13, "Postfix Server Administration."

Fast ETRN Service

As described in Chapter 2, newer versions of Postfix use the `flush` program to quickly find messages queued for a remote host when it receives an SMTP `ETRN` command. The action of the `flush` program is controlled by a parameter in the `main.cf` file.

fast_flush_policy

The `fast_flush_policy` parameter allows the mail administrator to specify what remote hosts will use the fast flush ETRN feature. The format of this parameter is

```
fast_flush_policy = all
```

The possible values for this parameter are the default "relay," which uses fast flush only for hosts defined as relay sites; "all" for all remote host sites; and "none" for not using the fast flush feature at all.

SMTP Greeting Banner

As seen in Listing 8.5, when Postfix receives an SMTP connection request, it begins the session with a greeting banner. The mail administrator can configure the format of this banner.

smtpd_banner

The `smtpd_banner` parameter specifies the greeting banner that will be used for SMTP connections. For security reasons, many e-mail administrators do not want to provide too much information in the greeting banner. Others want to provide as much information as possible to assist remote hosts connecting to the site. The format of the parameter is

```
smtpd_banner = $myhostname ESMTP $mail_name ($mail_version)
```

where `$myhostname` uses the `myhostname` parameter value, `$mail_name` specifies the Postfix name, and `$mail_version` specifies the version of Postfix running on the mail server. The banner produced by this example would look like this:

```
220 shadrach.ispnet1.net ESMTP Postfix (Snapshot-20001005)
```

NOTE

Be careful when creating the SMTP greeting banner. Many MTA packages (including Postfix) use the hostname part of the banner to prevent *message loops*: connecting to themselves to transfer messages.

Parallel Delivery to the Same Destination

As a means to help politely speed up mail delivery, Postfix supports parallel delivery of mail messages. This technique allows Postfix to establish more than one connection with a mail host when there is more than one message for that host. Several parameters are used to control this feature.

initial_destination_concurrency

The `initial_destination_concurrency` parameter was added to the newer Postfix experimental releases and establishes a starting point in determining how many parallel messages to send to a remote site. By setting this value low, Postfix can determine the capabilities of the remote system by slowly increasing the value while messages are sent.

The format for this parameter is

```
initial_destination_concurrency = 3
```

The default value for this parameter is 2. If you feel that the hosts you normally send mail to can handle more, you can increase this value.

default_destination_concurrency_limit

The default_destination_concurrency_limit parameter places an upper limit on the number of parallel messages sent to a remote site. The format for this parameter is

```
default_destination_concurrency_limit = 10
```

It is a good idea not to make this value too high or your Internet neighbors might start complaining. You can easily bog down a smaller mail server with multiple message transactions occurring simultaneously.

local_destination_concurrency_limit

The local_destination_concurrency_limit parameter is the partner to the preceding parameter. It controls the number of parallel messages sent to the same recipient on the *local* mail server for processing. The format of this parameter is

```
local_destination_concurrency_limit = 2
```

Remember that each local user has a separate mailbox on the system and that messages are delivered sequentially. Thus, each message that must be delivered to the same user must be delivered to the same place, causing contention for the files and directories. Each process must wait its turn to obtain the mailbox file, thus defeating any benefits gained from parallel transmission.

default_destination_recipient_limit

The default_destination_recipient_limit parameter controls the number of recipients per message that Postfix will send to a remote host. The format of this parameter is

```
default_destination_recipient_limit = 10
```

This parameter helps break up large lists of recipients for a single remote host by creating multiple messages instead of one message with a large list of recipients. Each message will contain no more than the limit of recipients specified by this parameter.

Debugging Control

Postfix provides facilities to enable the mail administrator to debug the Postfix server when problems arise. This group of parameters controls how Postfix handles debugging situations.

debug_peer_list, debug_peer_level

The debug_peer_list parameter contains a set of remote hosts listed by either IP address or hostname. When Postfix interacts with a remote system in that set, Postfix is instructed to increase its debugging level. The amount by which the debugging level is increased is specified by the debug_peer_level. The format of these parameters is

```
debug_peer_level = 2
debug_peer_list = some.domain
```

This example sets Postfix to increase the verbose logging level by 2 anytime it interacts with the mail server for some.domain. If you are having problems sending or receiving mail with a particular remote site, these parameters allow you to increase the logging levels for this site without having to pore over verbose logs for all of the other remote sites with which you may interact.

debug_command

The debug_command parameter specifies the program that Postfix calls when the administrator uses the -D option with a Postfix program. As shown in Chapter 7, "The master.cf Configuration File," the administrator can specify the -D option for individual Postfix core programs in the master.cf file.

The format of this parameter is

```
debugger_command =
        PATH=/usr/bin:/usr/X11R6/bin
        xxgdb $daemon_directory/$process_name $process_id & sleep 5
```

The mail administrator may use any debugger, but the most common are the GNU gdb and xxgdb debugger programs.

NOTE

Chapter 23, "Common Postfix Problems," describes how to use a debugger with Postfix in more detail.

Placing Limits on Objects

In order to conserve scarce resources, the e-mail administrator can place restrictions on the size of several kinds of mail message attributes.

message_size_limit

The message_size_limit parameter allows the mail administrator to configure Postfix to refuse incoming messages that are larger than a predetermined size. The format of this parameter is

```
message_size_limit = 500000
```

The value is the maximum size of the message in bytes, including the message header information. Messages larger than this limit are rejected by the Postfix server before they are stored in a message queue. The default value for this parameter is 10,240,000 bytes.

line_length_limit

The `line_length_limit` parameter limits the length of an incoming SMTP response line. The format of this parameter is

```
line_length_limit = 1000
```

The value is the maximum size of a single line of text in bytes. One well-known hacker technique is to attempt to overflow buffers using extra long text lines as input. This parameter prevents this from being possible. The default value for this parameter is 2,048 bytes.

header_size_limit

The `header_size_limit` parameter limits the amount of data present in a message header. The format of this parameter is

```
header_size_limit = 1000
```

The value is the maximum size of the header allowed in bytes. Any part of the header that is larger than the specified amount is placed in the body of the message. The default value for this parameter is 102,400 bytes.

Displaying and Modifying Configuration Parameters

As mentioned earlier, you should never assume that the parameter values present in the `main.cf` configuration file reflect the actual values that are being used by Postfix. To display the actual parameter values used by Postfix, you should use the `postconf` command. Several different options can be used to produce different types of output. The general formats of the `postconf` command are

```
postconf [-dhmnv] [-c config_dir] [parameter ...]
postconf [-ev] [-c config_dir] [parameter=value ...]
```

Using the `postconf` command by itself produces a list of all the possible Postfix parameters and their current values as defined in the `main.cf` configuration file. Using the 20001005 snapshot of Postfix, my listing produced 190 different parameters that could be set to control the operation of Postfix. If this sounds like a lot of parameters to configure, it is. But don't be alarmed. All parameters have default values that are usable by most mail configurations. All the mail administrator needs to define in the `main.cf` configuration file are the specific parameters that need to be *changed*.

To display all parameter values defined in the `main.cf` file, the mail administrator can use the `postconf` program with the `-n` option.

Listing 8.8 shows the output from a `postconf -n` command.

LISTING 8.8 Sample postconf Output

```
[rich@shadrach]$ /usr/sbin/postconf -n
alias_maps = hash:/etc/postfix/aliases
command_directory = /usr/sbin
daemon_directory = /usr/libexec/postfix
debug_peer_level = 2
default_destination_concurrency_limit = 10
local_destination_concurrency_limit = 2
mail_owner = postfix
queue_directory = /var/spool/postfix
virtual_maps = hash:/etc/postfix/virtual
```

This particular Postfix configuration sets nine parameters in the `main.cf` file. All of the other parameters are using default values. Always use this feature when trying to determine the parameters that are used in the running Postfix system.

Summary

Postfix uses the `master` program to start individual core programs to process incoming and outgoing messages. Postfix must be configured to properly handle the messages between the core programs.

The `main.cf` configuration file defines parameters that affect the operation of the Postfix programs. There are more than 200 different parameters that can be configured on the Postfix system. Fortunately, most of them can revert to default values that will work fine in most mail situations.

The parameters that must be changed are defined as text entries in the `main.cf` configuration file. Each entry represents the value of one parameter. When the Postfix system is started, the `main.cf` file is read by the `master` program and the parameters are stored for use by the other core programs.

After Postfix is started, the `main.cf` file may be changed without restarting the Postfix system. In this situation, the `main.cf` file does not properly represent the parameter values that are being used by the running Postfix system.

To determine the parameter values currently used by a running Postfix system, use the Postfix `postconf` utility with the `-n` option.

CHAPTER 9

Postfix Lookup Tables

In the preceding chapter, I explained the Postfix `main.cf` configuration file. One of the features described in the configuration file is the use of lookup tables to map information in a database type format. This chapter describes the different types of lookup tables Postfix can use and how they help speed up the access of mail information.

Postfix Lookup Table Support

Many of the Postfix core programs match information contained in mail messages with lists of addresses in lookup tables to determine how and where to deliver e-mail messages.

Table 9.1 lists all supported Postfix lookup tables.

TABLE 9.1 Postfix Lookup Tables

Table	*Description*
`access`	Allows Postfix to selectively accept or reject messages based on the originating sender name/host/network, and so on
`aliases`	Allows Postfix to redirect mail coming in for local recipients
`canonical`	Provides local and non-local address mappings
`relocated`	Provides information used in "user has moved to *new_location*" bounce messages
`transport`	Provides mappings of domain names to delivery methods and/or relay hosts
`virtual`	Provides redirections for local and non-local recipients or domains

Each lookup table plays a particular role in the mail delivery process. Core programs use information stored in lookup tables specific to their functions.

Table 9.2 lists the lookup tables again, this time showing the core programs that use them.

TABLE 9.2 Postfix Lookup Tables and Core Programs

Table	*Program*
`access`	`smtpd`
`aliases`	`local`
`canonical`	`cleanup`
`relocated`	`qmgr`
`transport`	`trivial-rewrite`
`virtual`	`cleanup`

Not only are there several types of lookup tables, each lookup table can also use three different database formats:

- Indexed binary database files (for example, btree, hash, dbm)
- Regular expression text files (for example, regexp)
- External database systems (for example, nis, ldap, mysql)

Any lookup table can be stored in any of the three different types of databases. A simple way to determine which database formats your particular Postfix system can use is to run the `postconf` program with the `-m` option:

```
[rich@shadrach]$ /usr/sbin/postconf -m
nis
regexp
environ
btree
unix
hash
```

This particular Postfix installation can use several different types of databases for lookup tables. The following section describes the different database types and how they are created.

Indexed Binary Database Files

To help improve response time in delivering messages, Postfix can use indexed database files for the lookup tables. This method requires a Unix database utility to convert an ASCII text file into an indexed file based on a specific key value.

Unfortunately, this makes *creating* lookup tables a little more difficult. There is a two-step process for creating indexed database type lookup tables, as shown in Figure 9.1.

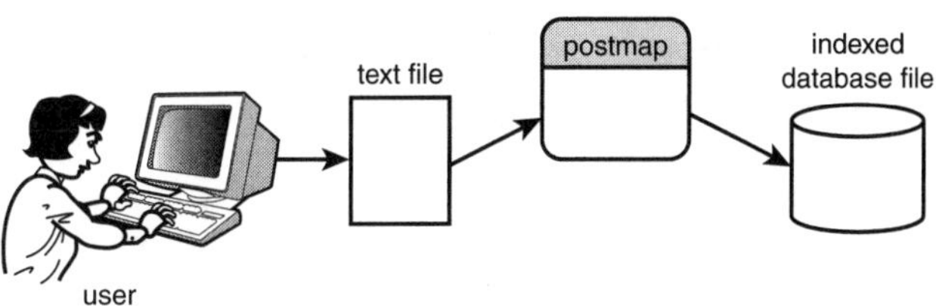

FIGURE 9.1

Creating Postfix lookup tables.

Using a two-step system can be confusing at times. There are many instances of novice e-mail administrators changing the text file but forgetting to re-create the binary database file. The mail administrator must also ensure that the text version of the configuration file properly reflects the current database.

Creating the Text File

The first step in building a lookup table is to create a text version of the table containing the information that needs to be mapped. This allows the mail administrator to easily enter the information for the table without requiring any special tools other than a standard text editor.

On most Unix systems, the notorious `vi` program is used as the standard text editor. Once you master the basics, `vi` is a handy tool to use for creating text files. Alternatively, you can use any other text editing programs available on your Unix system to create the text lookup table.

The text lookup table consists of one or more records of information mapping one text string (called the `pattern`) to another text string (called the `result`). Each record is placed on a single line. Comments can be added to the text lookup table by starting the line with a pound sign (#).

The record format for most of the lookup tables is

```
pattern value
```

I mentioned the word "most" because the Postfix `aliases` table requires a slightly different format:

```
pattern: value
```

This format makes the table compatible with the `sendmail` MTA `aliases` table format.

A sample text Postfix lookup table is shown in Listing 9.1.

LISTING 9.1 Sample Postfix Text Lookup Table

```
#Create canonical mappings so messages sent out map to
#users' full names instead of system usernames
#
#Engineering
rich Rich.Blum
katie Katie.Blum
jessica Jessica.Blum
#Finance
riley Riley.Mullen
haley Haley.Snell
frank Frank.Williams
#Sales
melanie Melanie.Williams
nicholas Nicholas.Williams
#
```

LISTING 9.1 Continued

```
#Don't forget the company president
alex Alex.Pierce
```

Listing 9.1 is an example of a `canonical` table, which allows mapping of nonexistent usernames to valid system usernames. This is often used when creating aliases for full usernames as e-mail addresses. For example, although an e-mail address of `Rich.Blum@ispnet1.net` may be easy to remember, "Rich.Blum" is not a valid system login name. Thus, the e-mail administrator can use a mapping to make things easier for everyone.

The text in the listing also includes comment lines, which Postfix ignores when the binary database is created. This enables the mail administrator to make comments to help break up the monotony of a long lookup table, as well as document entries in the file.

After the text lookup table is created, the mail administrator must convert it into an indexed database file for Postfix to use.

Creating the Indexed Database File

Postfix supports three different types of local indexed database files. The text data entered by the mail administrator runs through one of the three types of Unix database utilities to create the actual indexed database file. Most Unix systems do not support all three types, but almost all support at least one type. The three types of indexed database files are

- btree databases
- hash databases
- dbm databases

Most Unix systems use the hash database type, whereas most BSD-based systems (such as FreeBSD) use the dbm method. Most Linux systems support both the btree and hash methods, although the hash method is the most commonly used.

The `postmap` and `postalias` programs convert the text lookup table to an indexed database file.

postmap

As discussed in Chapter 6, "Installing Postfix," the `postmap` program creates, queries, and updates the Postfix binary indexed database files (except for `aliases`). The format of the `postmap` command is

```
postmap [-Ninrvw] [-c config_dir] [-d key] [-q key] [file_type:]file_name ...
```

You can use several options with the `postmap` command. Table 9.3 shows these options.

TABLE 9.3 The Postfix `postmap` Utility Options

Option	*Description*
`-N`	Include terminating NULL characters in lookup keys and values.
`-i`	Append entries from standard input to the existing database.
`-n`	Do not include terminating NULL characters in lookup keys and values.
`-r`	Do not warn about duplicate keys when updating the database.
`-v`	Enable verbose logging.
`-w`	Warn about duplicate keys when updating the database.
`-c` *`config_dir`*	Use the `main.cf` file located in the *`config_dir`* directory.
`-d` *`key`*	Remove the database record identified by the key *`key`*.
`-q` *`key`*	Query the database for the record identified by the key *`key`*.

The *`file_type:filename`* parameter specifies the type of indexed database file to create, along with the filename of the text file used. If you want to use the default database type defined in the `main.cf` file (using the `default_type` parameter), you can omit the *`file_type`* parameter from the string.

Assume that the example in Listing 9.1 is stored as the file `/etc/postfix/canonical`. To create an indexed database from this file, you would use the following command:

```
postmap /etc/postfix/canonical
```

This creates an indexed database file using the database type defined in the parameter `default_type` in the `main.cf` file. If the `default_type` parameter is not defined, Postfix attempts to use the system default.

For Linux systems, the hash database type is the default. By using no options, the `postmap` command creates a hashed index database file and calls it `canonical.db`.

NOTE

Always remember to include the appropriate maps parameter in the `main.cf` file to point to the new lookup table. For this example, the entry would be

```
canonical_maps = hash:/etc/postfix/caconical
```

Note that although the actual database filename uses a `.db` extension, it is not included in the parameter value field.

postalias

The postalias program creates the aliases table from the text aliases file. Remember from Chapter 6 that the format of the postalias command is

```
postalias [-Ninrvw] [-c config_dir] [-d key] [-q key] [file_type:]file_name ..
```

The postalias command uses the exact same options and parameters as the postmap command. In fact, it operates much the same way.

The difference is that postalias must be used to create the aliases table because the alias text file uses the : character to separate the pattern and result values.

Regular Expression Lookup Tables

The second type of lookup table is the regular expression lookup table, which uses a standard Unix regular expression as the key value. This method allows for multiple matches for each key value.

The term "regular expression" comes from the old days of the Unix sed editor. The sed editor is a command-oriented line editor that uses command characters and wildcard characters to define an expression. Items matching the expression are edited, and items not matching the expression are ignored.

Postfix supports two different types of regular expression tables: the POSIX Regular Expression form (regexp) and the Perl Compatible Regular Expression form (PCRE). Both forms are described in the following sections.

regexp

POSIX regular expression tables support the standard Unix regular expressions commonly used on Unix systems. Much like the text lookup tables described in the preceding section, they match a pattern with a result value, one per line. There are two formats of a regular expression pattern:

```
pattern value
pattern1!pattern2 value
```

The first format is exactly like the text version of the lookup tables. The difference is that the pattern may contain special characters along with expression commands.

The second format allows the mail administrator to further restrict pattern matches. This format returns the result value if the expression matches pattern1, but not pattern2.

A common starting and ending character delimits regular expression patterns. The characters must be the same and may not be any special characters used by the regular expression. The most commonly used character is the forward slash (/).

Characters within the delimiters are used to match against the input string. You may append a command character to the terminating delimiter to define an action to take with the pattern. The possible actions are

- i—Do not ignore case
- x—Do not use extended expressions
- m—Use multi-line mode

The following section describes the format of the pattern that is used between the delimiters.

Regular Expression Formats

There is much confusion over the format of regular expressions. Regular expressions consist of zero or more branches separated by pipes (|) containing zero or more concatenated pieces. Each piece consists of zero or more atoms, which may be followed by a control character. The control character defines the matches for the atom:

- *—A sequence of zero or more matches
- +—A sequence of 1 or more matches
- ?—A match of the atom or the null string

Each atom consists of the pattern to match enclosed in parentheses, a range enclosed in square brackets ([ ]), and a special character:

- .—Matches any one character
- ^—Matches beginning null character
- $—Matches terminating null character

The easiest way to understand a POSIX regular expression is to see some examples. The regular expression examples used in the Postfix `regexp_table` man pages are from a standard access table:

```
/[%!@].*[%!@]/ 550 Sender-specified routing rejected
/^postmaster@.*$/ OK
/^(.*)-outgoing@(.*)$/!/^owner-.*/ 550 Use ${1}@${2} instead
```

The first example demonstrates using a range within the regular expression. If either the username or hostname part of the e-mail address contains a transport character (the %, !, and @ symbols), the header matches the expression and the message is rejected.

The second example demonstrates the use of the beginning and terminating null characters to look for a complete string. This expression looks for pattern strings with the exact username `postmaster`. Note that this would *not* match the usernames `web-postmaster`, `postmaster-local`, or even `postmasters`. Although it doesn't matter what host or domain is specified, the username is very clearly defined. Thus, any mail message sent from the `postmaster` username received from any host is allowed.

The last example demonstrates a two-part regular expression. The first part checks to match any username ending with the text `-outgoing`. This is generally used for Majordomo mail lists. However, the second part of the expression checks to ensure that the text does not contain the `owner-` prefix. Messages from the `owner-` Majordomo addresses are allowed. However, messages sent to `-outgoing` accounts are blocked.

PCRE

On some older Unix systems, the POSIX regular expression format is not available. To compensate for this, Postfix provides its own expression format, the Perl Compatible Regular Expression (PCRE) format.

You can load the PCRE format on any Unix system that is running the Perl scripting language. Once loaded, Postfix can use lookup tables formatted in the PCRE format.

You can obtain the `pcre` program from the standard Postfix download sites. At the time of this writing, one location is

```
ftp://ftp.porcupine.org/mirrors/postfix-release/official/pcre-2.08.tar.gz
```

As you can see from the filename, the most recent version of PCRE at the time of this writing is version 2.08.

Once downloaded, the file can be expanded into a working directory using the following command:

```
tar -zxvf pore-2.08.tar.gz -C /usr/local/src
```

This command creates the directory `/usr/local/src/pcre-2.08` and expands the source code into it. The Makefile should be modified to suit your particular Unix environment, but the default values are suitable for most Linux installations. Once the Makefile is modified, you can compile and install the source code using the following commands:

```
make
make install
```

This creates two library files that are installed in the standard Unix library directory on the system. These libraries enable Postfix to use the PCRE database format for lookup tables.

The PCRE database format uses the same expression formats as POSIX regular expressions. You can now create database tables using regular expressions on systems that do not normally support POSIX regular expressions.

Using External Databases

Postfix can also accept information stored in external databases. This allows the mail administrator great flexibility in how data can be stored and retrieved.

Currently Postfix can retrieve messages from the following types of external databases:

- Network Information System (NIS) queries
- Lightweight Directory Access Protocol (LDAP) queries
- MySQL database table queries

The following sections describe these databases and how Postfix can be configured to use them.

NIS

The Network Information System (NIS) protocol often enables multiple hosts to share the same Unix password file and other information using the NIS protocol. Postfix can use the NIS protocol to obtain information from NIS servers by specifying the `nis` database type.

The name of the NIS server must be included on the parameter line:

```
alias_maps = hash:/etc/postfix/alias, nis:neshach.ispnet1.net
```

This example shows a common use of the NIS database lookup tables. The Postfix server first searches the local alias database for user alias names. If the alias is not found, Postfix attempts to contact the NIS server at `meshach.ispnet1.net` to resolve the alias.

MySQL

The MySQL database product has become a very popular SQL database implementation on Unix systems. Postfix supports retrieving information from tables in a MySQL database located on any server. Figure 9.2 demonstrates how this works.

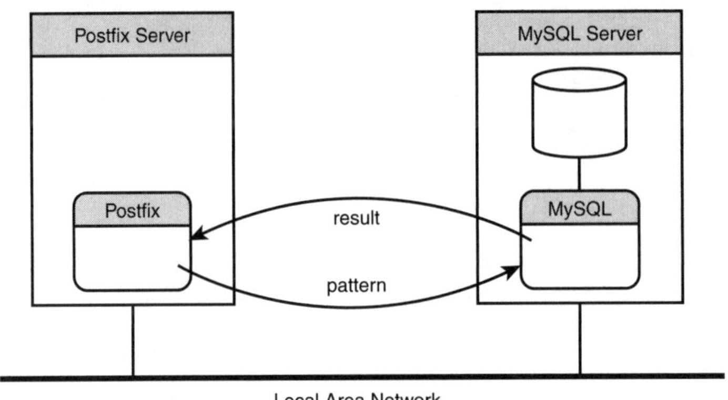

FIGURE 9.2

Using a MySQL database as a lookup table.

Using a MySQL database as a lookup table requires a few additional parameter entries. The MySQL parameter entry in the `main.cf` file points to an additional configuration file that contains the necessary MySQL parameters:

```
alias_maps = mysql:/etc/postfix/mysql-alias.cf
```

The `mysql-alias.cf` file defined must contain the information necessary for Postfix to connect to the MySQL database and retrieve the information. A basic parameter file of this type is shown in Listing 9.2.

LISTING 9.2 A Basic MySQL Parameter File

```
user = rich
password = guitar
dbname = aliases
table = Postfix_aliases

select_field = real_address
where_field = alias_address
additional_conditions = and status = 'current'

hosts = meshach.ispnet1.net
```

The information shown in Listing 9.2 allows Postfix to connect to the MySQL database located on `meshach.ispnet1.net`, log in as the user `rich`, connect to the aliases database, and perform the following SQL query:

```
SELECT real_address from Postfix_aliases where alias_address = '$lookup' and
➥ status = 'current'
```

The `$lookup` value is replaced with the pattern value supplied by Postfix. The SQL result is returned as the result value back to Postfix.

NOTE

Using MySQL with Postfix is described in more detail in Chapter 17, "Using MySQL with Postfix."

LDAP

The Lightweight Directory Access Protocol (LDAP) is quickly becoming a standard method for sharing information on large Unix networks. Similar in plan to Novell's NetWare Directory Service (NDS) or Microsoft's Active Directory (AD), LDAP works as a hierarchical database that maintains network information.

The most common implementation of LDAP for the Unix environment is the OpenLDAP software package. OpenLDAP is open source software that is freely available for download and installation. Postfix can use an OpenLDAP directory database as a lookup table. Figure 9.3 demonstrates this process.

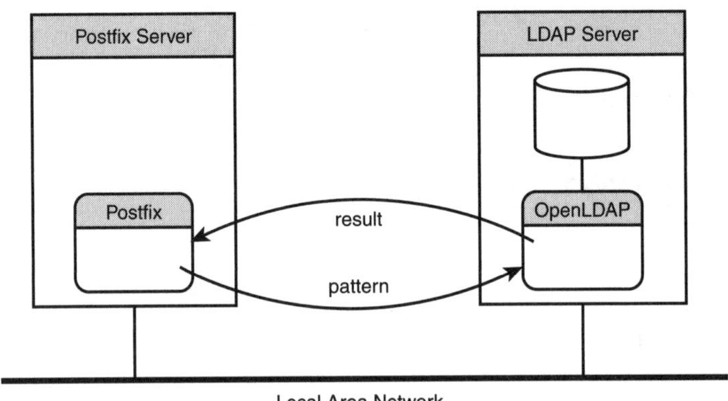

FIGURE 9.3

Using an OpenLDAP database as a lookup table.

Much like the MySQL database access method, Postfix requires several parameters to be defined for connection to the LDAP server. Unlike the MySQL example, all of the LDAP parameters are included in the `main.cf` file.

The LDAP server must be identified to Postfix by a name tag defined in the maps parameter line:

```
alias_maps = hash:/etc/postfix/aliases, ldap:ldaptag
```

Postfix supports using multiple LDAP databases as lookup tables. Therefore, each LDAP database must be identified with a unique "tag" name. In this example, the e-mail administrator chose to refer to the LDAP database as `ldaptag`. The unique LDAP tag for that database must precede each of the LDAP configuration parameters used to connect to the database.

Several parameters define the LDAP connection. Note that the first part of all these parameters is a direct reference to the "tag" chosen previously. The variable portions of the parameters listed in Table 9.4 are in italics.

TABLE 9.4 Postfix LDAP Parameters

Parameter	*Description*
`ldaptag_server_host`	The address of the LDAP server.
`ldaptag_server_port`	The TCP port number to connect to (default is 389).
`ldaptag_search_base`	The LDAP base in which to begin the search.
`ldaptag_timeout`	The timeout value to use when waiting for a response. Default = 10 (seconds).
`ldaptag_query_filter`	The LDAP database value to query. Default is `mailacceptinggeneralid`.
`ldaptag_result_attribute`	The LDAP attribute that will be returned. Default is `maildrop`.
`ldaptag_bind`	Whether to bind to the LDAP server. Older servers require the client server to bind a connection.

By default, Postfix will query the LDAP server for the `maildrop` LDAP attribute. If your LDAP server uses a different attribute to contain mail address information, you must specify it using the `ldaptag_result_attribute` parameter.

A simple LDAP configuration might look something like this:

```
alias_map = hash:/etc/postfix/aliases, ldap:myldap
myldap_server_host = meshach.ispnet1.net
myldap_search_base = dc = ispnet1, dc = net
myldap_result_attribute = mailbox
```

After reloading the `postfix` configuration, the Postfix server uses the LDAP server to resolve alias addresses not found in the alias database. In this example, it contacts LDAP server `meshach.ispnet1.net`, logs in using an anonymous login, searches the `mailacceptgeneralid` attribute for the pattern supplied, and returns the `mailbox` attribute value as the result to Postfix.

NOTE

Chapter 18, "Using OpenLDAP with Postfix," describes using an LDAP server as a lookup table in more detail.

The Postfix Lookup Tables

The previous sections discussed the different database formats Postfix can use in lookup tables. This section describes the different lookup tables and their functions in the Postfix system.

The access Table

As seen in Table 9.2, the Postfix smtpd program uses the access table. The smtpd program is responsible for accepting SMTP connections from remote hosts and receiving mail messages for local users. In this day of constant unsolicited commercial e-mail (UCE), it has become common to disallow access by specific sites known to produce UCE messages. This is the function of the access table.

You can use the access table to restrict an individual e-mail address, a host address, or an entire domain. The mail administrator can also configure the smtpd program to deny SMTP connections from all hosts except for specified hosts. This can result in super-tight security, allowing mail only from known hosts. Figure 9.4 demonstrates this process.

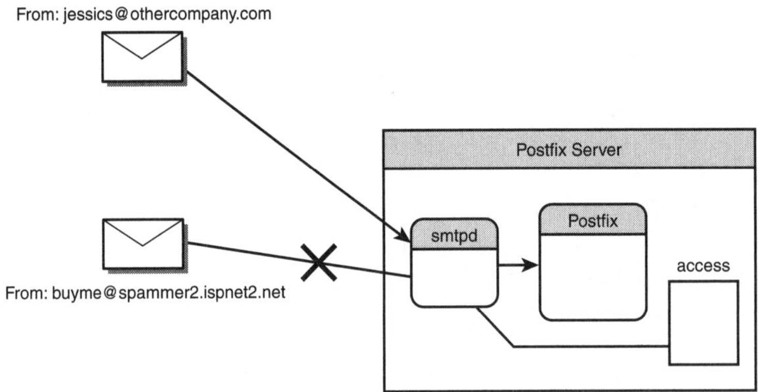

FIGURE 9.4

Using the access table to restrict mail access.

The access table defines a pattern and an action when a match is found. The pattern is matched against an e-mail address used in the SMTP connection.

Table 9.5 shows the formats used to specify the patterns.

TABLE 9.5 access Table Pattern Formats

Pattern	*Description*
user@domain	A specific e-mail address
hostname.domain	All users from a specific mail host
domain	All users from all mail servers on a specific domain
user@	All users from all hosts with a specific username
aaa.bbb.ccc.ddd	All users from a specific mail server using IP address aaa.bbb.ccc.ddd
aaa.bbb.cc	All users from all mail servers with an IP address beginning with aaa.bbb.ccc

TABLE 9.5 Continued

Pattern	Description
`aaa.bbb`	All users from all mail servers with an IP address beginning with `aaa.bbb`
`aaa`	All users from all mail servers with an IP address beginning with `aaa`

Once the pattern is defined, the mail administrator must specify the desired result to return to the remote SMTP server.

Table 9.6 shows the different actions that the mail administrator can take.

TABLE 9.6 `access` Table Result Formats

Result	Description
OK	Allow the SMTP session
REJECT	Deny the SMTP session
XXX text	Refuse the SMTP session with the specified SMTP reject code (XXX) and the specified text
text	Allow the SMTP session and return the specified text

Using the `access` table can be a complicated matter. The Postfix `smtpd` program can use `access` tables for a number of different parameters in the `main.cf` file. Each parameter can point to a separate lookup table, providing different levels of access restrictions. Table 9.7 shows a list of the different parameters that can use an access map.

TABLE 9.7 Postfix `smtpd` Parameters That Use `access` Tables

Parameter	Description
`smtpd_client_restrictions`	Restricts which clients may send messages
`smtpd_helo_restrictions`	Restricts which specific hostnames are allowed in SMTP `HELO` and `EHLO` commands
`smtpd_sender_restrictions`	Restricts who may send e-mail with the SMTP `MAIL FROM` command
`smtpd_recipient_restrictions`	Restricts who may receive mail with the SMTP `RCPT TO` command

Each parameter in Table 9.7 defines an `access` table that the `smtpd` program uses to restrict or allow mail transfer. The Postfix configuration can use one or all of the preceding parameters, each with its own `access` table. Of course when one or more `access` tables are used, they need to be named using a unique filename.

As an example, here's a simple sample access table that can refuse mail messages from two particular e-mail addresses known to send UCE mail:

```
rich@spammer.ispnet1.net REJECT
buyme@spammer2.ispnet2.net 550 Take that, spammer!
```

Of course, once you save the text file as `/etc/postfix/access`, you must be convert it to an indexed database file with the following command:

```
postmap /etc/postfix/access
```

Once the `access` table is created, you must modify the `main.cf` file to use the new `access` table with the following line:

```
smtpd_sender_restrictions = hash:/etc/postfix/access
```

Now, after issuing a `postfix reload` command, the `smtpd` program should be prepared to stop messages from these known troublemakers. Listing 9.3 shows a sample SMTP session.

LISTING 9.3 Sample SMTP Session Using the access Table

```
[rich@shadrach]$ telnet localhost 25
Trying 127.0.0.1...
Connected to localhost.
Escape character is '^]'.
220 shadrach.ispnet1.net ESMTP Postfix
HELO fake.host.name
250 shadrach.ispnet1.net
MAIL FROM: <rich@spammer.ispnet1.net>
250 Ok
RCPT TO: <rich@shadrach.ispnet1.net>
554 <rich@spammer.ispnet1.net>: Sender address rejected: Access denied
QUIT
221 Bye
Connection closed by foreign host.

[rich@shadrach]$ telnet localhost 25
Trying 127.0.0.1...
Connected to localhost.
Escape character is '^]'.
220 shadrach.ispnet1.net ESMTP Postfix
HELO fake.host.name
250 shadrach.ispnet1.net
MAIL FROM: <buyme@spammer2.ispnet2.net>
250 Ok
```

LISTING 9.3 Continued

```
RCPT TO: <rich@shadrach.ispnet1.net>
550 <buyme@spammer2.ispnet2.net>: Sender address rejected: Take that, spammer!
QUIT
221 Bye
Connection closed by foreign host.
```

As shown in Listing 9.3, both spammers were successfully prevented from sending messages to the local users. This is an effective way of blocking known spammers.

The `aliases` Table

You can use the `aliases` table to map "fake" e-mail addresses to actual system users, commands, or filenames on the system. This is directly compatible with the `sendmail` program's system of `aliases` tables.

The `aliases` table differs from most of Postfix's other lookup tables in that it has a slightly different format:

```
pattern: result
```

The colon is added to the pattern to make the Postfix alias file compatible with `sendmail` alias files. This allows for easily converting `sendmail` mail servers to Postfix.

The alias file allows three different types of message redirection:

- Delivering to an alternative e-mail address
- Piping to a command
- Appending to a file
- Delivering to a list of addresses in an external text file

All Postfix aliases used on the mail server should be entered in a common file. The `aliases` file is normally located at `/etc/postfix/aliases`, but you can change it in the `main.cf` file using the `alias_maps` parameter.

The format of an aliases line that delivers the message to an alternative address (or multiple addresses) is

```
name:    name_1, name_2, name_3, ...
```

where `name` is the alias and `name_1`, `name_2`, and so on are the addresses where the message will be sent next. One or more different addresses can be associated with each alias.

Each valid address listed receives a copy of the message. Aliases are always considered local to the mail server on which they are configured.

The format of an aliases line that pipes the message into a system command is

```
name:     |program
```

where `program` is the full pathname to a program that can process the message. To use this feature, you must have the `allow_mail_to_commands` parameter value set to `yes`.

The format of an aliases line that appends the message to a file is

```
name:     file
```

where `file` is a full pathname pointing to a text file. Any messages sent to the alias address name are spooled to the text file given. For this feature to work properly, you must set the correct read/write system permissions on both the text file and the directory where the text file is located. Also, the `main.cf` file must contain the `allow_mail_to_files` parameter set to the value `yes`.

The format of an aliases line that delivers the message to a mailing list is

```
name:     :include:filelist
```

where `filelist` is the full pathname to a file that contains a list of e-mail addresses. This has the same effect as listing each of the e-mail addresses on the aliases line separated by commas as in the first format. A file may be easier to manipulate if you have a large mail list that changes membership frequently.

Listing 9.4 shows a sample `aliases` file. The line numbers in this listing are only for later reference and should not be included in your actual `aliases` file.

LISTING 9.4 Sample `/etc/postfix/aliases` File

```
#
#   @(#)aliases 8.2 (Berkeley) 3/5/94
#
#  Aliases in this file will NOT be expanded in the header from
#  Mail, but WILL be visible over networks or from /bin/mail.
#
#   >>>>>>>>>>  The program "newaliases" must be run after
#   >> NOTE >>  this file is updated for any changes to
#   >>>>>>>>>>  show through to sendmail.
#

# Basic system aliases -- these MUST be present.
MAILER-DAEMON:  postmaster
postmaster: root

# General redirections for pseudo accounts.
```

LISTING 9.4 Continued

```
17 bin:         root
18 daemon:      root
19 games:       root
20 ingres:      root
21 nobody:      root
22 system:      root
23 toor:        root
24 uucp:        root
25
26 # Well-known aliases.
27 manager:     root
28 dumper:      root
29 operator:    root
30
31 # trap decode to catch security attacks
32 decode:      root
33
34 # Person who should get root's mail
35 root:        rich
36
37 # Program used to auto-reply to messages
38 auto-test:     |/home/rich/auto-test
39
40 # Send all messages to a text file
41 saveme:    /home/rich/test.txt
42
43 # Send all messages to remote site
44 rich:         rich@othercompany.com
45
46 #Create a simple multi-user mail list
47 officenews:         :include:/home/rich/office.txt
```

Lines 13–32 redirect mail messages for various standard Linux system usernames to the `root` user. This is usually a good idea to ensure that no one is trying to hack into the system using one of the default system usernames. If these names are not aliased to `root`, any mail messages generated to them are lost.

Line 35 is also a good idea. It redirects any mail for the `root` user to a regular username that should log in to the system on a frequent basis.

NOTE

Remember, a good system administrator should not be logging in as the `root` user very frequently.

Line 38 illustrates redirecting messages to a program. The program must be shown with its full pathname so that the shell can find it.

Line 41 demonstrates using a text file to store any messages sent to an address. Remember to be careful about read/write permissions for the file.

Line 44 demonstrates that although the alias name must be local to the mail server, the names that it aliases do not have to be. The aliases file allows you to redirect a mail message for a user to another e-mail account on a completely different system.

Line 47 demonstrates calling a mail list text file from the aliases file. The file `/home/rich/office.txt` is a plaintext file that lists e-mail addresses. When a message is received for the `officenews` alias, the `office.txt` file is checked and the message is sent to all e-mail addresses present in that file.

The `canonical` Table

The `cleanup` program uses the `canonical` table to rewrite message addresses contained in the message header. The mail administrator can use one `canonical` lookup table for both received messages and sent messages or separate tables for each.

The `canonical` table is often used in conjunction with the alias file to provide address header rewriting of *outgoing* mail messages. Many sites want their e-mail addresses to appear in the following format:

```
Firstname.Lastname
```

Unfortunately, these cannot be entered as normal Unix system usernames. Instead, the mail administrator can use the `aliases` table to map e-mail addresses in this format to individual system usernames:

```
Richard.Blum: rich
Barbara.Blum: barbara
Katie.Blum: katie
Jessica.Blum: jessica
```

This method works fine for receiving messages destined to the new e-mail addresses, but there is one drawback. Messages that these users send out still show the real Unix system username as the sending address. This defeats the purpose of using the aliases.

To compensate for this, the `cleanup` program can use a `canonical` table to replace the normal Unix system username with the alias name for all outbound messages. The `canonical` table will look like this:

```
rich Richard.Blum
barbara Barbara.Blum
katie Katie.Blum
jessica Jessica.Blum
```

Once the `canonical` table is created, it can replace the e-mail addresses in all outbound messages using the `canonical_maps` parameter. This parameter enables all outbound messages to use the alias name for the sender. Listing 9.5 shows an example of this.

LISTING 9.5 Sample E-Mail Message Using Canonical Mapping

```
[jessica@shadrach]$ mail
Mail version 8.1 6/6/93.  Type ? for help.
"/var/spool/mail/jessica": 1 message 1 new
N  1 Richard.Blum@shadrac  Tue Oct 31 15:01  13/552   "This is a test of the"
& 1
Message 2:
From Richard.Blum@shadrach.ispnet1.net  Tue Oct 31 15:01:13 2000
Delivered-To: jessica@meshach.ispnet1.net
To: jessica@meshach.ispnet1.net
Subject: This is a test of the canonical lookup table
Date: Tue, 31 Oct 2000 15:01:13 -0500 (EST)
From: Richard.Blum@shadrach.ispnet1.net (Rich Blum)

This is a test message using the canonical lookup table.

&
```

As you can see in Listing 9.5, the `From:` header address of the mail message has been replaced with the canonical map value from the username. This allows for proper behavior when the recipient uses the "reply" feature of the MUA program.

By default, the canonical map changes both sender and recipient addresses. Alternatively, the mail administrator can use the `canonical` table to replace just the sender or recipient address using the following parameters:

```
sender_canonical_maps = hash:/etc/postfix/canonical
recipient_canonical_maps = hash:/etc/postfix/canonical
```

The `relocated` Table

The `relocated` table provides information to remote hosts that send messages to users that are no longer on your e-mail server. The information contained in the `relocated` table is inserted into the bounce message and returned to the sender.

The result text of the `relocated` table can be any text value, including the user's new e-mail address, new street address, new phone number, or all three. The information is provided in the text of the bounce message. The heading for the text will be

```
user has moved to
```

The text you enter is appended to that phrase. A sample relocated table entry would be

```
barbara barbara@newcompany.com. Please change your addressbook.
```

Once the relocated text file is created, you can create the indexed database file using the postmap command:

```
postmap hash:/etc/postfix/relocated
```

The parameter that identifies the relocated lookup table in the main.cf file is the relocated_map parameter. It must point to the table location and the database type:

```
relocated_maps = hash:/etc/postfix/relocated
```

After you make the entry in the main.cf file, you must reload the Postfix server using the postfix reload command.

Listing 9.6 shows the heading text of a sample message sent to the relocated address in the previous example.

LISTING 9.6 Sample Bounced Message with Relocated Text

```
[rich@shadrach]$ mail
Mail version 8.1 6/6/93.  Type ? for help.
"/var/spool/mail/rich": 1 message 1 new
>N  1 MAILER-DAEMON@shadra  Tue Oct 31 15:26  64/2100  "Undelivered Mail Returned"
&1
Message 1:
From MAILER-DAEMON  Tue Oct 31 15:26:10 2000
Delivered-To: rich@shadrach.ispnet1.net
Date: Tue, 31 Oct 2000 15:26:10 -0500 (EST)
From: MAILER-DAEMON@shadrach.ispnet1.net (Mail Delivery System)
Subject: Undelivered Mail Returned to Sender
To: Richard.Blum@shadrach.ispnet1.net
MIME-Version: 1.0
Content-Type: multipart/report; report-type=delivery-status;
        boundary="D7BF7C352.973023970/shadrach.ispnet1.net"

This is a MIME-encapsulated message.

--D7BF7C352.973023970/shadrach.ispnet1.net
Content-Description: Notification
Content-Type: text/plain

This is the Postfix program at host shadrach.ispnet1.net.
```

LISTING 9.6 Continued

```
I'm sorry to have to inform you that the message returned
below could not be delivered to one or more destinations.

For further assistance, please send mail to <postmaster>

If you do so, please include this problem report. You can
delete your own text from the message returned below.

                        The Postfix program

<barbara@shadrach.ispnet1.net>: user has moved to barbara@newcompany.com. Please
    change your addressbook.

--D7BF7C352.973023970/shadrach.ispnet1.net
Content-Description: Delivery error report
Content-Type: message/delivery-status

Reporting-MTA: dns; shadrach.ispnet1.net
Arrival-Date: Tue, 31 Oct 2000 15:26:09 -0500 (EST)

Final-Recipient: rfc822; barbara@shadrach.ispnet1.net
Action: failed
Status: 5.0.0
Diagnostic-Code: X-Postfix; user has moved to barbara@newcompany.com. Please
    change your addressbook.

--D7BF7C352.973023970/shadrach.ispnet1.net
Content-Description: Undelivered Message
Content-Type: message/rfc822

Received: by shadrach.ispnet1.net (Postfix, from userid 500)
        id D7BF7C352; Tue, 31 Oct 2000 15:26:09 -0500 (EST)
To: barbara@shadrach.ispnet1.net
Subject: Test message to relocated user
Message-Id: <20001031202609.D7BF7C352@shadrach.ispnet1.net>
Date: Tue, 31 Oct 2000 15:26:09 -0500 (EST)
From: Richard.Blum@shadrach.ispnet1.net (Rich Blum)

This is a test message.

--D7BF7C352.973023970/shadrach.ispnet1.net--

&
```

Note that the relocated text is appended to the standard Postfix bounce message. It is up to the original sender to forward the message to the new address.

CAUTION

Remember, the `relocated` table does not forward messages to the new address. If you want this functionality, you must use the `aliases` table instead.

The `transport` Table

The `transport` table determines the default method of forwarding messages to a remote host. Each record in the `transport` table identifies a remote host or domain and the Postfix transport method used to send messages to it.

Postfix can use different types of transports to send messages to remote hosts. Figure 9.5 shows a block diagram of this feature.

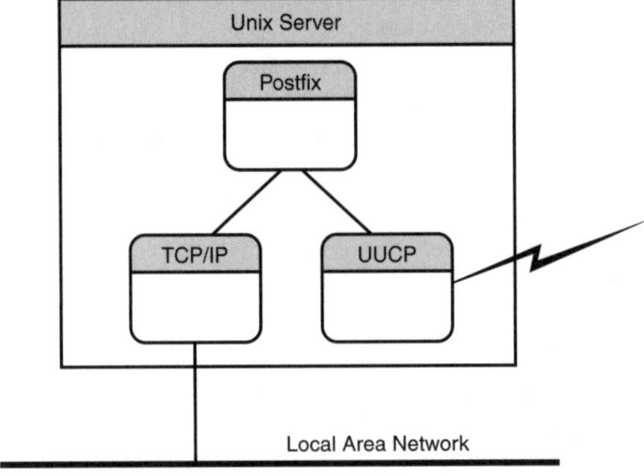

FIGURE 9.5

Postfix transport communication.

The most commonly used transport these days is the SMTP transport, which is what Postfix uses by default when establishing a session with a remote mail server.

The Unix-to-Unix Copy Protocol (UUCP) was popular in the days of 1,200-baud dial-up modems. It created a way to transfer files and mail messages between Unix systems over normal phone lines. Although the Internet has replaced the demand for UUCP, many sites still use UUCP for security and cost reasons. Not having a dedicated connection to the Internet makes it more difficult to get hacked.

If the Postfix server is running on a mail server that is only on a UUCP network, you can change the default transport by using the `default_transport` parameter:

```
default_transport = uucp
```

This ensures that all communications with remote mail servers are done using the UUCP protocol. If you are in a mixed environment where some remote hosts are contacted via SMTP on the Internet and some are using a UUCP network, the `transport` lookup table is required.

As with other lookup tables, the `transport` table maps patterns to values. The patterns for the `transport` table are mail addresses or domains. The result value is the transport method that Postfix should use to forward messages to the domain.

With UUCP networks, it is common to forward a message to a host that in turn forwards it to another host. This continues until the message reaches the destination host. By using the "nexthop" method, the Postfix server may only be connected to a single UUCP server in a larger UUCP network.

To support this environment, the result may include the hostname of the next hop:

```
destination transport:[nexthop]
```

An example of a `transport` table is shown in Listing 9.7.

LISTING 9.7 Sample `transport` Table

```
shadrach.ispnet1.net local:
localhost.ispnet1.net local:
ispnet2.net uucp:ispnet2
remotecompany.com smtp:
othercompany.com smtp:isphost.net
lastcompany.com smtp:isphost2.net:8025
```

As shown in Listing 9.7, each destination is recorded on a separate line with the transport method required to forward messages to that site. The first two entries are required to ensure that Postfix delivers mail destined for local users to the local machine using the local mail delivery process. Since it is possible for a Unix system to establish an SMTP connection to itself, Postfix may just in fact attempt that. The last entry demonstrates using an alternative TCP port for the SMTP connection.

The `main.cf` file parameter used for defining the transport map is of course the `transport_maps` parameter. This parameter defines the database type and location of the transport map:

```
transport_maps = hash:/etc/postfix/transport
```

CAUTION

Remember that for each transport, an associated service record must be in the `master.cf` configuration file defining how Postfix can access that transport.

The `virtual` Table

Internet service providers (ISPs) that want to receive messages for client domains most often use the `virtual` table. Once the messages are received, they are stored on the mail server until the real domain mail server retrieves them. Figure 9.6 demonstrates this process.

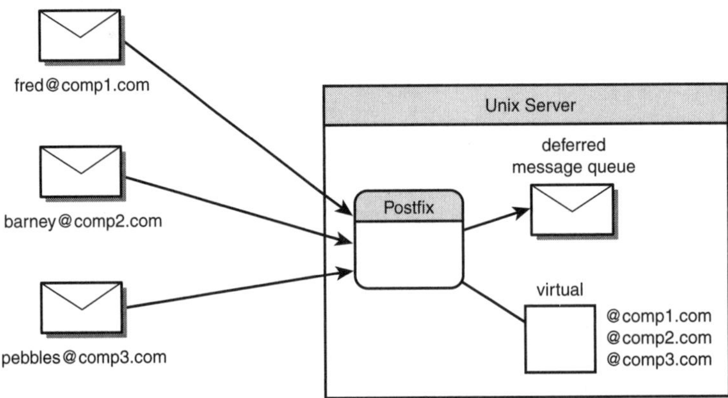

FIGURE 9.6

Receiving messages for virtual domains.

There are four different record types in the `virtual` lookup table. Each one defines a different type of virtual domain. Table 9.8 lists the different record types.

TABLE 9.8 Virtual Domain Record Types

Record	*Description*
`domain.name <anything>`	Allows Postfix to receive messages for `domain.name` and place them in the message queue.
`user@domain address1, address2, ...`	Receives messages for `user@domain` and forwards them to addresses listed. This redirection has the highest priority.
`user address1, address2, ...`	Receives messages for `user` on the local host and forwards them to the addresses listed.
`@domain address1, address2, ...`	Receives messages for all users in `domain` and forwards them to the addresses listed.

The first form of record is the most common one used by mail administrators who want to receive messages for virtual domains. The value text is unimportant. When Postfix receives messages destined for the listed domain, it places them in the deferred message queue (assuming that it cannot forward them directly to the real domain mail server). The real domain mail server must then connect to the Postfix server using the SMTP protocol and issue an `ETRN` command to tell Postfix it is available to receive its messages.

NOTE

This method of storing mail for virtual domains is discussed in detail in Chapter 11, "Using Postfix as an ISP Mail Server."

A simpler form of supporting virtual domains is putting mail in individual mailboxes. This allows either the individual mail recipients or the real domain mail server to use common MUA programs to retrieve the messages.

For example, if you want to support the virtual domain for a small company whose domain name is `testcompany.com`, you can create a `virtual` table that looks like this:

```
testcompany.com virtual
prez@testcompany.com prez
rich@testcompany.com rich
jim@testcompany.com jim
alecia@testcompany.com alecia
riley@testcompany.com alecia
haley@testcompany.com haley
```

This method assumes that the Postfix server has system usernames created for each user in the virtual domain. The individual users do not necessarily need home directories on the Postfix server. But if they are using an MUA program that supports the IMAP protocol, they will need somewhere to store their mail folders, so a home directory is often used anyway.

After any new system usernames are created, the `virtual` table must be converted to an indexed database file:

```
postmap hash:/etc/postfix/virtual
```

And of course the `virtual` table must be defined in the `main.cf` file:

```
virtual_maps = hash:/etc/postfix/virtual
```

After the mail administrator issues a `postfix reload` command, the Postfix server should be able to receive messages for all of the defined users in the `virtual` table. The users then only need to establish a POP3 or IMAP connection to the server to retrieve their mail messages.

NOTE

Supporting a POP3 or IMAP server is described in detail in Chapter 20, "Using POP3 and IMAP with Postfix."

Summary

The Postfix system uses several lookup tables to map information in a database format. Each lookup table can be created using one of several different database techniques.

The most common method uses a standard Unix indexed binary database file. These files use the Unix hash, btree, or dbm database libraries. By creating an indexed binary database file, Postfix can access information faster, thus improving response time for mail delivery.

An alternative method is to use a regular expression database file. Regular expression databases can match multiple patterns to a single result. This is often handy in tables that require general definitions, such as the `access` table. By using a regular expression, a single record may match against several possible results. Unix systems that do not have support for regular expression files can use the Postfix Perl Compatible Regular Expression (PCRE) package. This package uses the Perl language to manipulate regular expressions.

Finally, Postfix can use external databases for lookup table information. Postfix supports retrieving data from NIS, LDAP, and MySQL databases.

Postfix uses six lookup tables to deliver messages. The `access` table defines rules for allowing particular hosts to transfer messages to the server. The `aliases` table maps false mail usernames to valid system users, commands, or files. The `canonical` table allows the mail administrator to change addresses within mail headers and envelopes to preserve alias names. The `relocated` table allows a method for administrators to notify remote users when a local user no longer resides on the mail server. The `transport` table specifies a specific communications transport to use when forwarding messages to a remote host. And finally, the `virtual` table defines virtual addresses for which Postfix can receive messages.

CHAPTER 10

Using Postfix

The previous chapters discussed the individual parts of the Postfix system. This chapter puts the pieces together and gets a simple Postfix server running on a Unix server. The commands and files discussed individually in the previous chapters are laid out as they are bundled together in building the mail server. You may notice some repetition in the commands and file descriptions. The purpose for this is to help tie together the individual pieces into the total Postfix server picture.

If you have been following along in the previous chapters, Postfix should be installed and ready to run. Here's a last-minute checklist to help you determine whether all of the Postfix pieces are installed and ready to go:

1. The Postfix username and groupname(s) should be configured (`postfix` username, `postfix` group, `maildrop` group).
2. The `/var/spool/postfix` directory should be created (if you installed Postfix from the source code it may be empty).
3. The Postfix core programs and utilities should be installed in the `/usr/sbin` and `/usr/libexec/postfix directories`.
4. The `/etc/postfix` directory should be created, along with skeleton `master.cf` and `main.cf` files.

If you have completed all of these steps, you are ready to test the Postfix installation and use it as the MTA on your mail server. This chapter goes through a step-by-step basic Postfix server setup and configuration. Later chapters will describe more detailed configurations for more specific Postfix installations.

Several steps are necessary to configure the Postfix server. The basic steps involved in this process are

1. Edit the `master.cf` file.
2. Determine local mail delivery method.
3. Edit the `main.cf` file.
4. Create an `aliases` table.
5. Start and test Postfix.
6. Create a boot script to start Postfix.
7. Create any user-defined files.

Editing the `master.cf` File

The `master.cf` file controls the operational behavior of the core Postfix programs. You must determine how your Postfix server will operate to configure the `master.cf` file.

A skeleton `master.cf` file should be located in the `/etc/postfix` directory. You can edit this file and make any changes necessary for your site.

Listing 10.1 shows a sample skeleton `master.cf` file installed by the `snapshot-20001217` Postfix source code installation.

LISTING 10.1 Sample `master.cf` Configuration File

```
smtp       inet  n    -    n    -    -    smtpd
pickup     fifo  n    n    n    60   1    pickup
cleanup    unix  -    -    n    -    0    cleanup
qmgr       fifo  n    -    n    300  1    qmgr
#qmgr      fifo  n    -    n    300  1    nqmgr
rewrite    unix  -    -    n    -    -    trivial-rewrite
bounce     unix  -    -    n    -    0    bounce
defer      unix  -    -    n    -    0    bounce
flush      unix  -    -    n    1000?     0    flush
smtp       unix  -    -    n    -    -    smtp
showq      unix  n    -    n    -    -    showq
error      unix  -    -    n    -    -    error
local      unix  -    n    n    -    -    local
lmtp       unix  -    -    n    -    -    lmtp
cyrus      unix  -    n    n    -    -    pipe
   flags=R user=cyrus argv=/cyrus/bin/deliver -e -m ${extension} ${user}
uucp       unix  -    n    n    -    -    pipe
   flags=F user=uucp argv=uux -r -n -z -a$sender - $nexthop!rmail ($recipient)
ifmail     unix  -        n        n        -        -        pipe
   flags=F user=ftn argv=/usr/lib/ifmail/ifmail -r $nexthop ($recipient)
bsmtp      unix  -        n        n        -        -        pipe
   flags=F. user=foo argv=/usr/local/sbin/bsmtp -f $sender $nexthop $recipient
```

The skeleton file values should be fine for a simple Postfix server. As mentioned in Chapter 7, "The `master.cf` Configuration File," you may also choose to run Postfix in a `chroot` environment for security purposes. You can accomplish this by editing the `master.cf` file and changing the values in the fifth field to `y`. Remember it is recommended that sites connected to the Internet have at *least* the `smtp` and `smtpd` programs set to run in the `chroot` environment.

If you do decide to run any programs in the `chroot` environment, remember to also run the included Postfix `chroot` setup script for your Unix system. It creates the appropriate directories in the `/var/spool/postfix` directory and copies in the necessary system files. If this is not done, the programs set to run in the `chroot` environment will fail. This was also discussed in Chapter 7.

Determining Local Mail Delivery

Postfix can use four different methods of local mail delivery. Before you start Postfix, you must decide which one of the methods will work in your e-mail environment. As outlined in Chapter 2, "Postfix Services," the four delivery methods are

- Writing to `sendmail`-style mailboxes located in `/var/spool/mail`
- Writing to `sendmail`-style mailboxes located in the users' `$HOME` directories
- Writing to `qmail`-style `Maildir` mailboxes located in the users' `$HOME` directories
- Invoking a separate mail delivery program such as `procmail` or `binmail`

The following sections describe these four types and will help you decide which method may be right for your environment.

Using `sendmail`-Style Mailboxes

The most basic form of local mail delivery is to let Postfix deliver messages directly to `sendmail`-style mailboxes. The `sendmail`-style mailboxes place all messages for a user in a single text file located in a common mailbox directory. Each user has a separate mailbox file that only that user can access.

`sendmail`-Style Mailboxes

`sendmail`-style mailboxes are located in a common mail directory, usually `/var/spool/mail` on Linux systems, or `/var/mail` on BSD systems. This delivery method is 100% compatible with the `sendmail` MTA system and can be used by both Postfix and `sendmail` servers running on the same system. New e-mail messages for users are simply appended to any existing messages in their mailbox. If the mailbox doesn't already exist, it is created.

Listing 10.2 shows a sample mailbox file for a user.

LISTING 10.2 Sample Mailbox File

```
[rich@shadrach]$ cat /var/spool/mail/rich
From jessica@shadrach.ispnet1.net  Wed Nov  1 15:28:22 2000
Return-Path: <jessica@shadrach.ispnet1.net>
Delivered-To: rich@shadrach.ispnet1.net
Received: by shadrach.ispnet1.net (Postfix, from userid 501)
        id BD2A0C352; Wed,  1 Nov 2000 15:28:21 -0500 (EST)
To: Richard.Blum@shadrach.ispnet1.net
Subject: First test message
Message-Id: <20001101202821.BD2A0C352@shadrach.ispnet1.net>
Date: Wed,  1 Nov 2000 15:28:21 -0500 (EST)
From: jessica@shadrach.ispnet1.net
Status: O
```

LISTING 10.2 Continued

```
This is the first test message.

From jessica@shadrach.ispnet1.net  Wed Nov  1 15:28:34 2000
Return-Path: <jessica@shadrach.ispnet1.net>
Delivered-To: rich@shadrach.ispnet1.net
Received: by shadrach.ispnet1.net (Postfix, from userid 501)
        id D92C1C352; Wed,  1 Nov 2000 15:28:33 -0500 (EST)
To: Richard.Blum@shadrach.ispnet1.net
Subject: Second test message
Message-Id: <20001101202833.D92C1C352@shadrach.ispnet1.net>
Date: Wed,  1 Nov 2000 15:28:33 -0500 (EST)
From: jessica@shadrach.ispnet1.net
Status: O

This is the second test message.
```

As you can see in Listing 10.2, each message is just appended to the preceding message. It is up to the MUA software to determine the start of a new message in the mailbox.

Configuring Postfix to Use `sendmail`-Style Mailboxes

Configuring Postfix for using `sendmail`-style mailboxes is simple. No configuration parameters are required. Postfix delivers mail for local users to `sendmail`-style mailboxes by default. If your Unix system is using a nonstandard mailbox directory, you can specify the location using the `mail_spool_directory` parameter in the `main.cf` file:

```
mail_spool_directory = /var/spool/testing/mail
```

`$HOME/Mailbox` Delivery

A few problems have been identified with the `sendmail`-style mailbox system. By placing all of the user mailboxes in a single directory, the mail system is vulnerable to both security and disk access speed problems.

By creating a common mail directory that every user must have access to, the `sendmail`-style mailbox system opens a security can of worms. Because the mailbox must be user writable, the mailbox directory must be writable by everyone, which creates a possible security problem.

With one mailbox file for every user, systems that support thousands of users have lots of mailbox files. This creates quite a large mailbox directory. It has been proven that large directories slow down disk access speeds. It is much better to have many directories with one file than one directory with a lot of files.

`$HOME/Mailbox` Mailboxes

To solve the problems identified with the `sendmail`-style mailbox system, Postfix can use two alternative mailbox systems. The first moves the users' `sendmail`-style mailboxes to their home directory. Figure 10.1 demonstrates how this system works.

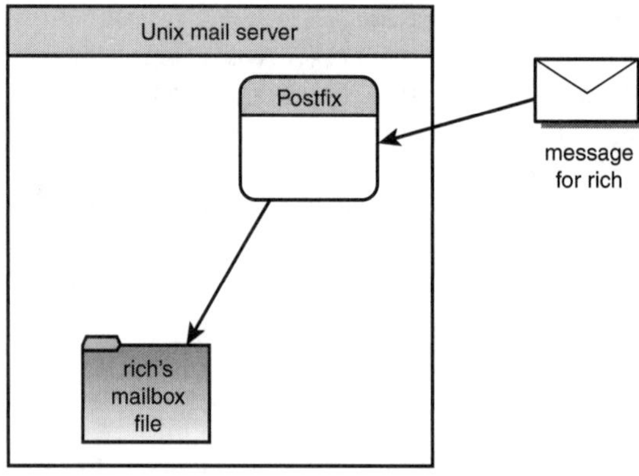

FIGURE 10.1

The Postfix `$HOME/Mailbox` mailbox format.

When user mailboxes are moved to their respective home directories, both the security and disk access problems are greatly decreased. Each user's mailbox is created as a file in his or her home directory. While this solves some problems, it creates a new problem.

Most MUA software has been written to use the `sendmail`-style mailbox format. By moving the users' mailboxes to their home directories, Postfix creates a problem for many MUA programs: The MUA programs do not know that the mailboxes have been moved.

To solve this problem, some mail administrators have written patches for some of the more common MUA programs to allow them to access the relocated user mailboxes. Another solution is to create symbolic links from the new user mailboxes to the location where the normal `sendmail`-style mailboxes would be located. This solution works for most of the common MUA programs and is easy to implement.

To ensure that no mail is lost in the conversion process, you should perform the following steps with the MTA program disabled and with no users logged in to the system:

1. As `root`, move each user mailbox found in the `sendmail`-style mailbox area to the user's `$HOME` directory, renaming it to `Mailbox`:

   ```
   mv /var/spool/mail/barbara /home/barbara/Mailbox
   ```

2. Create a link from the `sendmail`-style mailbox location to the new mailbox location:

   ```
   ln -s /home/barbara/Mailbox /var/spool/mail/barbara
   ```

This allows Postfix to store mail messages in users' `$HOME/Mailbox` files, while still allowing MUA programs to access those files via the link to the old `sendmail`-style mailbox locations.

CAUTION

Some Unix systems use the Network File System (NFS) to mount user `$HOME` directories from remote systems. This practice is dangerous, and you should not use it if you are using `$HOME/Mailbox` mailboxes. The NFS protocol has been known to use unreliable file locking techniques, which can make the mailbox file corrupt and unusable.

Configuring Postfix to Use `$HOME/Mailbox`

For Postfix to deliver messages for local users to their `$HOME/Mailbox` files, you must set one parameter in the `main.cf` file:

```
home_mailbox = Mailbox
```

Now Postfix will use the `$HOME/Mailbox` method to deliver messages. The mail administrator can use any mailbox name as the value. Whatever text is used becomes the name of the mailbox located in the users' `$HOME` directories where Postfix will store messages.

CAUTION

Be very careful not to include a trailing `/` at the end of the mailbox name. You will find out why in the next section.

`$HOME/Maildir` Delivery

The second alternative mailbox system that Postfix can use is the Maildir system. The Maildir system takes the `$HOME/Mailbox` method one step further. Not only is each user's mailbox moved to his or her home directory, the `sendmail`-style mailbox format is changed.

Maildir Mailboxes

Dan Bernstein, the creator of the `qmail` MTA package, designed the Maildir mailbox method. One problem identified with the `sendmail`-style mailbox system is that it is highly vulnerable to data corruption. Because the mailbox contains all of the user's mail messages, corrupting the mailbox could have catastrophic results. The Maildir system changes the method used for storing user messages.

User messages are stored as separate files within a specially formatted user mailbox directory. This ensures that even if one message becomes corrupt, the rest of the messages are safe within the mailbox directory.

Figure 10.2 shows how the Maildir mailbox format works. The Maildir system is described in more detail in Chapter 15, "Using the Maildir Mailbox Format."

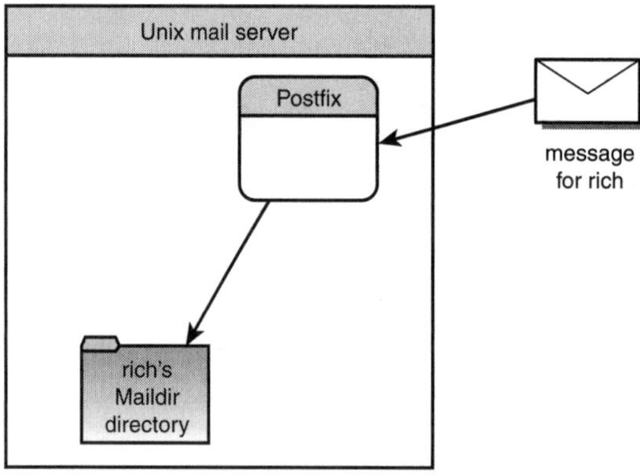

FIGURE 10.2

The Maildir mailbox system.

Configuring Postfix for Maildir Mailboxes

For Postfix to deliver messages to the local users' Maildir directories, the `main.cf` configuration file must include the following parameter:

```
home_mailbox = Maildir/
```

Note the trailing slash (`/`) at the end of the mailbox name. This is required to indicate a `qmail`-type Mailbox directory. The directory name can be anything the mail administrator wants, but the trailing slash must be present.

External MDA Delivery

The last method of mail delivery that Postfix supports is the use of external Mail Delivery Agents (MDAs). Postfix passes the message to the MDA program for actual delivery. Once the message is passed to the MDA program, Postfix assumes that it will be delivered and is no longer involved.

Figure 10.3 shows a diagram of how Postfix interacts with an MDA program.

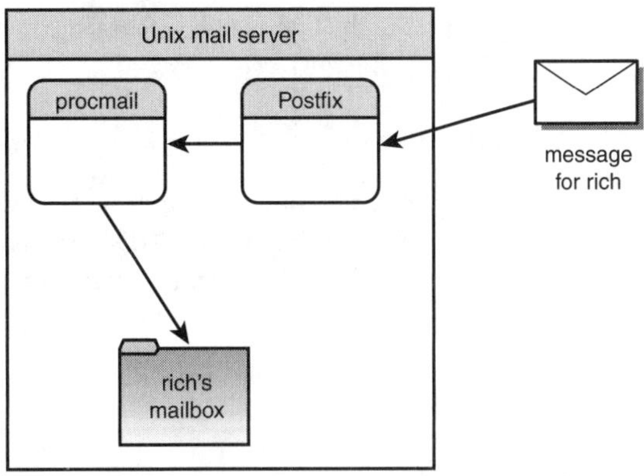

FIGURE 10.3

Using an MDA program with Postfix.

Many different local mail delivery programs can be used on Unix platforms. You must know the local mailer that your Unix system is using to select the right values for Postfix.

Using MDA Programs

Postfix can use any of the MDA programs available on Unix systems. The most common programs in use are

- `binmail` (which is called `mail`). There are two different versions of the `binmail` program: for both V7 and SRV4 systems. Linux systems use the V7 version of `binmail`.
- `mail.local`, which is used by BSD 4.4 Unix systems such as FreeBSD.
- `procmail`, which can be installed as an additional option on all Unix systems.

Although the `procmail` program must be installed as a separate package, it is a commonly used local MDA program that has been known to work well on most Unix systems. Many Linux distributions now install it on the system by default.

NOTE

Chapter 16, "Using MDA Programs with Postfix," discusses the different Unix MDA programs and how to use them with Postfix in more detail.

Configuring Postfix to Use an MDA Program

For Postfix to use an external MDA program to deliver local mail, the `main.cf` configuration file must be set accordingly. The `mailbox_command` parameter defines the MDA program:

```
mailbox_command = /usr/sbin/procmail
```

You should use the full pathname so that Postfix can find the MDA program on the system. Postfix can also pass environment variables to the MDA program as command-line parameters. This enables Postfix to call the MDA program with information regarding the message to deliver.

Table 10.1 lists the different environment variables that Postfix can pass along.

TABLE 10.1 Postfix MDA Environment Variables

Variable	*Description*
`$HOME`	The user's home directory
`$SHELL`	The user's Unix shell
`$LOGNAME`	The user's Unix username
`$USER`	The recipient's username
`$EXTENSION`	The recipient's address extension
`$DOMAIN`	The domain part of the address
`$LOCAL`	The local part of the address

The `procmail` program can use command-line options to indicate how to deliver the message, thus the `main.cf` parameter for using `procmail` could be

```
mailbox_command = /usr/sbin/procmail -a "$EXTENSION" -d "$USER"
```

Editing the `main.cf` File

The next step in getting Postfix up and running is to determine what parameters are needed in the `main.cf` configuration file. For a basic configuration, it is possible that no parameters are necessary. However, it is a good idea to go over the basic parameters before starting the Postfix server. The following sections describe the basic parameters that should be checked to ensure proper mail delivery on the mail server.

Determining Interfaces

The Postfix server can receive messages on any or all interfaces running on the mail server. You may elect to receive messages on just a single interface if you are in a multiple-network environment.

To determine the interfaces available on your system, you can use the Unix `ifconfig` command:

```
[haley@shadrach]$ /sbin/ifconfig
eth0      Link encap:Ethernet  HWaddr 00:E0:7D:74:DF:C7
          inet addr:192.168.1.1  Bcast:192.168.1.255  Mask:255.255.255.0
          UP BROADCAST RUNNING MULTICAST  MTU:1500  Metric:1
          RX packets:681 errors:0 dropped:0 overruns:0 frame:0
          TX packets:604 errors:0 dropped:0 overruns:0 carrier:0
          collisions:0 txqueuelen:100
          Interrupt:10 Base address:0x6400

lo        Link encap:Local Loopback
          inet addr:127.0.0.1  Mask:255.0.0.0
          UP LOOPBACK RUNNING  MTU:3924  Metric:1
          RX packets:37193 errors:0 dropped:0 overruns:0 frame:0
          TX packets:37193 errors:0 dropped:0 overruns:0 carrier:0
          collisions:0 txqueuelen:0
```

Each interface is listed along with the IP address and interface statistics. If you are using a dial-up connection to the Internet, remember that the PPP interface will not be present unless you are currently dialed in to the ISP.

By default, Postfix receives messages on all the interfaces available on the mail server. You can specify an individual interface using the `inet_interfaces` parameter:

```
inet_interfaces = localhost.$mydomain
```

This restricts Postfix to receiving messages only on the `localhost` loopback interface, `lo`. This means that no external mail traffic can get into the system.

Determining Recipient Addresses

You must determine what hostnames Postfix will use to receive messages for the local mail server. You need to set the `mydestination` parameter in the `main.cf` file to define the various hostnames that Postfix will accept messages for.

By default, Postfix receives messages addressed to the hostname of the local mail server, as well as messages sent to the special host name `localhost`. This is represented by the `mydestination` parameter:

```
mydestination = $myhostname, localhost.$mydomain
```

These values assume that the mail server hostname and domain names are properly set on the system.

Alternatively, you may want the Postfix server to receive mail messages sent to alias hostnames of the mail server, such as `www.ispnet1.net`. You can accomplish this by adding the alias name value to the `mydestination` parameter:

```
mydestination = $myhostname, localhost.$mydomain, www.$mydomain
```

This assumes that the DNS entries for your domain include a CNAME entry for the www address (See Chapter 4, "DNS and Postfix").

Finally, you may want the Postfix server to receive mail messages sent to your domain. This has become a popular method for companies that just want to use their company name in the e-mail address, such as `prez@mycompany.com`. The format for the `mydestination` parameter would then be:

```
mydestination = $myhostname, localhost.$mydomain, $mydomain
```

CAUTION

Be careful not to include any virtual domains in the `mydestination` parameter because this is not where they belong. The `virtual` table stores addresses for virtual domains that Postfix will receive messages for. See Chapter 11, "Using Postfix as an ISP Mail Server," for more details.

Determining the Origin Address

The last basic item to configure in the configuration file is `myorigin`: the address Postfix will advertise as your origin address. This affects the format in which your address appears in messages sent to users on remote mail servers.

By default, the `myorigin` parameter is set to the hostname of the local mail server:

```
myorigin = $myhostname
```

If you are using an alias hostname, such as a `www` address, you may want your messages to be sent out as `webmaster@www.ispnet1.net` so remote users will have your alias hostname to use as the return address. You can do this using the parameter

```
myorigin = www.$mydomain
```

Alternatively, you may decide to use just your domain name in your mail messages. This requires that Postfix use just the domain name in all header addresses sent out. You can do this using the parameter

```
myorigin = $mydomain
```

Creating the `aliases` Table

Once the `main.cf` configuration file is completed, you should check the `aliases` lookup table to ensure that all of the system usernames are configured, and that the `root` username points to a normal user who logs into the system on a daily basis.

Most Unix systems contain several usernames that are configured in the `/etc/passwd` file, but are not necessarily used as logins. These can include addresses for the ftp server, uucp server, and for shutting down the system. Although these usernames are normally set to not allow logins, it is a good idea to forward their mail messages to a common place to watch for hacker attempts via the mail system. The best place to forward these usernames to is `root`.

Listing 10.3 shows a listing of the default system usernames on a Mandrake Linux system.

LISTING 10.3 System Usernames Found on a Mandrake System

```
root:x:0:0:root:/root:/bin/bash
bin:x:1:1:bin:/bin:
daemon:x:2:2:daemon:/sbin:
adm:x:3:4:adm:/var/adm:
lp:x:4:7:lp:/var/spool/lpd:
sync:x:5:0:sync:/sbin:/bin/sync
shutdown:x:6:0:shutdown:/sbin:/sbin/shutdown
halt:x:7:0:halt:/sbin:/sbin/halt
mail:x:8:12:mail:/var/spool/mail:
news:x:9:13:news:/var/spool/news:
uucp:x:10:14:uucp:/var/spool/uucp:
operator:x:11:0:operator:/root:
games:x:12:100:games:/usr/games:
gopher:x:13:30:gopher:/usr/lib/gopher-data:
ftp:x:14:50:FTP User:/home/ftp:
nobody:x:99:99:Nobody:/:
lists:x:500:500:BeroList:/dev/null:/dev/null
xfs:x:100:238:X Font Server:/etc/X11/fs:/bin/false
```

In addition to these usernames, there are several other well-known mail addresses that are used on the Internet:

- The MAILER-DAEMON generic account
- The postmaster generic account
- The webmaster generic account

It is a good idea to ensure that these addresses are included in the aliases file and point to a real address of the responsible administrator.

Finally, it is always a good idea to redirect messages sent to the `root` user to a normal user account. For one thing, it is never a good idea to regularly log in to the mail server using the `root` account, and for another, some MDA programs (such as `procmail`) refuse to deliver messages to the `root` account for security reasons.

The Postfix source code distribution attempts to create a skeleton aliases file in the `/etc/postfix` directory. You can edit this file using any Unix text editor to add your specific changes. A completed aliases file might look similar to the example shown in Listing 10.4.

LISTING 10.4 Sample Aliases File

```
# Basic system aliases -- these MUST be present
MAILER-DAEMON:  postmaster
postmaster: root
webmaster: root

# General redirections for pseudo accounts
bin:         root
daemon:      root
named:       root
nobody:      root
uucp:        root
www:         root
ftp-bugs:    root
postfix:     root

# Put your local aliases here.
Rich.Blum rich
Richard.Blum rich

# Well-known aliases
manager:     root
dumper:      root
operator:    root
abuse:       postmaster

# trap decode to catch security attacks
decode:      root

# Person who should get root's mail
#root:       you
root:   rich
```

Once the text aliases file is created, you must convert it to an indexed binary database file using the `postalias` command:

```
postalias /etc/postfix/alias
```

This creates either the `aliases.db` or `aliases.dbm` file that is used by Postfix, depending on the database type your system uses. You should ensure that the `main.cf` file contains the proper pointer to the new `aliases` table using the `alias_maps` parameter:

```
alias_maps = hash:/etc/postfix/aliases
```

Testing Postfix

With all of the pieces in place, it's time to start up Postfix and watch what happens. This section describes three different methods that can be used to test Postfix on your mail server.

Sending Mail Only

If you are installing Postfix on a high-volume mail server and are concerned about losing incoming mail messages, you can install Postfix to only *send* mail. This will allow you to test your basic Postfix configuration while allowing the existing MTA to receive incoming mail messages.

This method requires that Postfix ignore messages coming from the SMTP daemons on the Postfix server. You can do this by commenting out the `smtpd` line in the `master.cf` configuration file. Any SMTP messages received by the mail server will be handled by the legacy mail system.

To start the Postfix software, you must be logged in as the `root` user and use the following command:

```
postfix start
```

The first time Postfix is started, it will check the `/var/spool/postfix` directory and create any message queue directories as needed:

```
postfix-script: warning: creating missing Postfix pid directory
postfix-script: warning: creating missing Postfix incoming directory
postfix-script: warning: creating missing Postfix active directory
postfix-script: warning: creating missing Postfix bounce directory
postfix-script: warning: creating missing Postfix defer directory
postfix-script: warning: creating missing Postfix deferred directory
postfix-script: warning: creating missing Postfix flush directory
postfix-script: warning: creating missing Postfix saved directory
postfix-script: warning: creating missing Postfix corrupt directory
```

```
postfix-script: warning: creating missing Postfix public directory
postfix-script: warning: creating missing Postfix private directory
```

You should be able to check the log where your mail logs are kept (often the `/var/log/maillog` file) to see whether Postfix started properly:

```
Nov  2 05:49:56 shadrach postfix-script: starting the Postfix mail system
Nov  2 05:49:56 shadrach postfix/master[864]: daemon started
```

You should not see any warning or error messages (other than the ones for creating the missing directories). If you do, compare the messages with your configurations to determine what might possibly be wrong.

NOTE

Chapter 13, "Postfix Server Administration," gives more information on how to read mail logs. Also, Chapter 23, "Common Postfix Problems," describes some of the common problems found when running Postfix.

If Postfix started properly, you should see three new processes running in background mode on the mail server. You can list all of the processes running on the server using the `ps` command. Different Unix systems use different options for the `ps` command. Most Linux systems can use the `ax` command to display all processes running:

```
[rich@shadrach]$ ps ax
864 ?        S      0:00 /usr/libexec/postfix/master
865 ?        S      0:00 pickup -l -t fifo
866 ?        S      0:00 qmgr -l -t fifo -u
```

The first field is the process id of the running program. The programs are shown in the last field. The `master` program should run at all times. The `pickup` and `qmgr` programs should be configured in the `master.cf` configuration file to wake up at predetermined intervals, so they should also remain running.

The Postfix install method outlined in Chapter 6, "Installing Postfix," replaces the `/usr/sbin/sendmail` file with the Postfix version of the same name. If this has been done, all new e-mail messages should be sent using the Postfix system. You can test this by sending a test message to a remote user and watching the Postfix processes:

```
[rich@shadrach]$ ps ax
864 ?        S      0:00 /usr/libexec/postfix/master
865 ?        S      0:00 pickup -l -t fifo
866 ?        S      0:00 qmgr -l -t fifo -u
885 ?        S      0:00 cleanup -t unix -u
886 ?        S      0:00 trivial-rewrite -n rewrite -t unix -u
896 ?        S      0:00 smtp -t unix -u -c
```

If Postfix is installed properly, it should call the `cleanup`, `trivial-rewrite`, and `smtp` programs to help it deliver the message to the final destination. These programs stay active in background mode until they reach their timeout limit set in the `master.cf` file, then they quietly go away. Of course, the best way to determine whether Postfix worked is to see if the message actually made it to the remote user.

Virtual Interfaces

You can configure Postfix to use a virtual interface on the local mail server. This allows Postfix to both send and receive messages without affecting any other running MTA programs.

For Postfix to use a virtual interface, one must first be configured. You can do this using the Unix `ifconfig` and `route` commands. The Postfix source code distribution supplies examples for different Unix systems. Three steps are required to configure a virtual interface:

1. Create an alias for an existing interface using a bogus IP address.
2. Add a new route to the bogus IP address from the existing system address.
3. Add a hostname to the system host table to assign a bogus hostname to the new bogus IP address.

For a Linux system, the commands for the first two steps would be

```
ifconfig add eth0:1 10.0.0.1
route add 10.0.0.1 dev eth0:1
```

You can select any IP address to use, although using one of the well-known "test" IP networks (10.0.0.0 or 192.168.0.0) might cause less confusion later. After performing the preceding commands as `root`, edit the `/etc/hosts` table to add the new virtual host entry:

```
10.0.0.1     bogushost.test.lan
```

To test the virtual setup, you can `telnet` to the newly created host:

```
[rich@shadrach]$ telnet bogushost.test.lan
Trying 10.0.0.1...
Connected to bogushost.test.lan.
Escape character is '^]'.
Welcome to shadrach.ispnet1.net
Linux Mandrake release 7.0 (Air) - i486
Kernel 2.2.14-24mdk_i486 on an i486
login:
```

If the test was successful, you should get a login prompt from your system. Next, you must configure Postfix to only accept messages from the new interface. You do this with three parameters in the `main.cf` file:

```
myhostname = bogushost.test.lan
mydestination = $myhostname
inet_interfaces = $myhostname
```

Next, either use the `postfix reload` command or start Postfix if it wasn't already running by using the `postfix start` command:

```
postfix start
```

Postfix should start as normal. Check the mail log to make sure it did. To test the virtual host setup, try establishing an SMTP connection to the virtual host address on port 25:

```
[rich@shadrach]$ telnet bogushost.test.lan 25
Trying 192.168.1.1...
Connected to bogushost.test.lan.
Escape character is '^]'.
220 bogushost.test.lan ESMTP Postfix
```

As expected, Postfix allowed the SMTP connection to the virtual address. You can continue the SMTP session and manually send a message to a local user (see Chapter 5, "SMTP and Postfix," for details). To remove the virtual interface, simply reboot the mail server. It will be gone when the server comes back up.

Sending and Receiving Mail

If you are adventurous, you may decide to test Postfix as the sole MTA software for the mail server. First, you must ensure that no other MTA software is currently running on the server (and taken out of any startup scripts) and that the Postfix software is configured correctly as shown in the previous sections.

Start the Postfix server by using the following command:

```
postfix start
```

As in the other tests, you should be able to check the mail log file to determine whether Postfix started correctly and check the running processes to ensure that the `master`, `pickup`, and `qmgr` programs are running. Once you start Postfix, you can test several different mail scenarios.

Sending Mail to a Local User

You can use the local system MUA program (usually called `mail`) to test Postfix mail delivery. First, try sending a message to yourself:

```
[rich@shadrach]$ mail rich
Subject: test message
This is a test message.
.
```

```
[rich@shadrach]$ mail
Mail version 8.1 6/6/93.  Type ? for help.
"/var/spool/mail/rich": 1 message 1 new
>N  1 rich@shadrach.blum.l  Thu Nov  2 06:55  13/454   "test message"
& 1
Message 1:
From rich@shadrach.blum.lan  Thu Nov  2 06:55:27 2000
Delivered-To: rich@shadrach.blum.lan
To: rich@shadrach.blum.lan
Subject: test message
Date: Thu,  2 Nov 2000 06:55:27 -0500 (EST)
From: rich@shadrach.blum.lan (Rich)

This is a test message.

&
```

The `mail` command is a simple method of sending text messages. Don't forget the single period on the line by itself. That's what tells the `mail` program that your message is finished. Depending on the mail delivery system you selected, the message should be delivered to your system mailbox. You can see the Postfix programs that were used by using the `ps` command:

```
1278 ?        S      0:00 /usr/libexec/postfix/master
1345 ?        S      0:00 pickup -l -t fifo
1346 ?        S      0:00 qmgr -l -t fifo -u
1351 ?        S      0:00 cleanup -t unix -u
1352 ?        S      0:00 trivial-rewrite -n rewrite -t unix -u
1353 ?        S      0:00 local -t unix
```

Notice that the `local` program is called to deliver the message to the local user.

Sending Mail to a Remote User

The next step is to test delivering a message to a user on a remote mail server. Again, you can use the `mail` program. By examining the log file, you can determine whether the delivery was successful:

```
Nov  2 09:41:41 shadrach postfix/pickup[18446]: BA693C352: uid=500 from=<rich>
Nov  2 09:41:41 shadrach postfix/cleanup[18450]: BA693C352:
➥ message-id=<20001102144141.BA693C352@shadrach.ispnet1.net>
Nov  2 09:41:41 shadrach postfix/qmgr[17799]: BA693C352:
➥ from=<rich@shadrach.ispnet1.net>, size=370, nrcpt=1 (queue active)
Nov  2 09:41:42 shadrach postfix/smtp[18452]: BA693C352:
➥ to=<rich@meshach.ispnet1.net>, relay=meshach.ispnet1.net[192.168.1.10]
➥ ,delay=1, status=sent (250 ok 973176071 qp 87116)
```

As you can see in the last line of the log listing, the status of the message received from the remote host is recorded. For this message the status is OK. The remote user should have successfully received the test message.

Sending Mail to a Nonexistent User

As a final test, try sending a message to a nonexistent user. This message should bounce back to you as a bounce message:

```
[rich@shadrach]$ mail fred
Subject: Test bounce message
This message should bounce back.
.

[rich@shadrach rich]$ mail
Mail version 8.1 6/6/93.  Type ? for help.
"/var/spool/mail/rich": 1 message 1 new
>N  1 MAILER-DAEMON@shadra  Thu Nov  2 09:48  62/1975  "Undelivered Mail Retu"
&1
Message 1:
From MAILER-DAEMON  Thu Nov  2 09:48:23 2000
Delivered-To: rich@shadrach.ispnet1.net
Date: Thu,  2 Nov 2000 09:48:23 -0500 (EST)
From: MAILER-DAEMON@shadrach.ispnet1.net (Mail Delivery System)
Subject: Undelivered Mail Returned to Sender
To: Richard.Blum@shadrach.ispnet1.net
MIME-Version: 1.0
Content-Type: multipart/report; report-type=delivery-status;
        boundary="8958DC352.973176503/shadrach.ispnet1.net"

This is a MIME-encapsulated message.

--8958DC352.973176503/shadrach.ispnet1.net
Content-Description: Notification
Content-Type: text/plain

This is the Postfix program at host shadrach.ispnet1.net.

I'm sorry to have to inform you that the message returned
below could not be delivered to one or more destinations.

For further assistance, please send mail to <postmaster>
```

```
If you do so, please include this problem report. You can
delete your own text from the message returned below.

                        The Postfix program

<fred@shadrach.ispnet1.net>: unknown user: "fred"

--8958DC352.973176503/shadrach.ispnet1.net
Content-Description: Delivery error report
Content-Type: message/delivery-status

Reporting-MTA: dns; shadrach.ispnet1.net
Arrival-Date: Thu,  2 Nov 2000 09:48:22 -0500 (EST)

Final-Recipient: rfc822; fred@shadrach.ispnet1.net
Action: failed
Status: 5.0.0
Diagnostic-Code: X-Postfix; unknown user: "fred"

--8958DC352.973176503/shadrach.ispnet1.net
Content-Description: Undelivered Message
Content-Type: message/rfc822

Received: by shadrach.ispnet1.net (Postfix, from userid 500)
        id 8958DC352; Thu,  2 Nov 2000 09:48:22 -0500 (EST)
To: fred@shadrach.ispnet1.net
Subject: Test bounce message
Message-Id: <20001102144822.8958DC352@shadrach.ispnet1.net>
Date: Thu,  2 Nov 2000 09:48:22 -0500 (EST)
From: Richard.Blum@shadrach.ispnet1.net (Rich Blum)

This message should bounce back.

--8958DC352.973176503/shadrach.ispnet1.net--

&
```

As you can see, the message did indeed bounce back to the sender. You can watch the Postfix programs that were loaded by using the `ps` command:

```
15785 ?        S      0:01 /usr/libexec/postfix/master
17799 ?        S      0:00 qmgr -l -t fifo -u
18446 ?        S      0:00 pickup -l -t fifo
18480 ?        S      0:00 cleanup -t unix -u
18481 ?        S      0:00 trivial-rewrite -n rewrite -t unix -u
18482 ?        S      0:00 local -t unix
```

```
18483 ?        S      0:00 bounce -t unix -u
18484 ?        S      0:00 bounce -t unix -u
```

The Postfix program used the `bounce` program to send the original message and the bounce message back to the sender.

Starting Postfix from a Boot Script

Once you are sure that Postfix can run properly in your mail environment, you should establish a method for it to be loaded automatically when the mail server boots. Different Unix implementations do this using different methods.

On BSD Systems

If you are using a BSD version of Unix, processes are loaded at boot time from the `/etc/rc` script. One of the items in the `/etc/rc` script is to include scripts located in the `/usr/local/etc/rc.d` directory. By placing a simple script in this directory, the system will attempt to run it at boot time. A simple startup script for Postfix could be:

```
#!/bin/sh
postfix start
```

You should create the script as `root`, with execute permissions only for `root`. Also remember to remove any scripts from the old mail server software that may be present. The next time the mail server is booted, the Postfix software should start automatically. You can determine this by displaying the running processes after bootup.

On System V Systems

System V–based Unix systems such as Linux use a more complicated method of controlling scripts used for starting and stopping processes at boot and shutdown times. As described in Chapter 3, "Server Requirements for Postfix," the Linux system uses six different run levels. Each run level uses a different set of startup scripts located in directories `/etc/rc.d/rcx.d`, where `x` is the run level. This allows Linux to start different programs depending on the run level at which the system is started.

The startup scripts located in the `rcx.d` directories are links to the actual script files located in a central script directory `/etc/rc.d/init.d`. The mail administrator must create a simple startup script and link it to the appropriate init directories.

First, a startup script must be created. The Mandrake Linux distribution includes a Postfix RPM package that includes a sample startup script. Listing 10.5 shows the sample Postfix startup script.

LISTING 10.5 Sample Postfix Startup Script

```
#!/bin/sh
#
# postfix       This shell script takes care of starting and stopping
#               postfix.
#
# chkconfig: 2345 80 30
#
# description: Postfix is a Mail Transport Agent, which is the program
#              that moves mail from one machine to another.

# Source function library.
. /etc/rc.d/init.d/functions

# Source networking configuration.
. /etc/sysconfig/network

# Check that networking is up.
[ ${NETWORKING} = "no" ] && exit 0

[ -f /usr/sbin/postfix ] || exit 0

# See how we were called.
case "$1" in
  start)
        # Start daemons.
        echo -n "Starting postfix: "
        newaliases
        for I in access canonical relocated transport virtual
        do
        if [ -f /etc/postfix/$I ] ; then
           /usr/sbin/postmap hash:/etc/postfix/$I < /etc/postfix/$I
        fi
        done
        /usr/sbin/postfix start 2>/dev/null
        echo postfix
        touch /var/lock/subsys/postfix
        ;;
  stop)
        # Stop daemons.
        echo -n "Shutting down postfix: "
        /usr/sbin/postfix stop 2>/dev/null
        echo postfix
        rm -f /var/lock/subsys/postfix
```

LISTING 10.5 Continued

```
        ;;
  restart)
        $0 stop
        $0 start
        ;;
  reload)
        /usr/sbin/postfix reload
        ;;
  status)
        status master
        ;;
  *)
        echo "Usage: $0 {start|stop|restart|reload|status}"
        exit 1
esac

exit 0
```

The Mandrake Postfix startup script does a few auxiliary things in addition to starting Postfix. As you can see from the `start` section, the script first runs the `newaliases` command to rebuild the aliases database. Next, it cycles through each of the other possible lookup tables and rebuilds those lookup tables as well (if they exist). After all this is done, the Postfix system is finally started using the standard `postfix start` command.

You can place the startup script shown in Listing 10.5 in the `/etc/rc.d/init.d` directory as the file `postfix`. This file can then be linked into the appropriate `rc.d` subdirectories for the run levels at which Postfix should be started:

```
ln -s /etc/rc.d/init.d/postfix /etc/rc.d/rc3.d/S80postfix
ln -s /etc/rc.d/init.d/postfix /etc/rc.d/rc5.d/S80postfix
```

The example shown places the Postfix startup scripts in the run level 3 and 5 directories and assigns them start names where the original `sendmail` startup scripts would normally load.

User Controlled Files

Once Postfix is running smoothly on the mail server, you can turn your attention to the mail users. Postfix allows local users to create a configuration file themselves to alter their mail delivery. This section describes these files.

The `.forward` File

Postfix allows users to change the way their own mail is delivered. Any user can create the `.forward` file and place it in her `$HOME` directory to change where her mail is delivered.

The format of the `.forward` file is exactly the same as used in the right side of the `aliases` lookup table. Users can forward messages to other users, commands, files, or a list of users contained in a separate file. Multiple actions can be used, with each action listed on a separate line.

As an example, if user `jessica` created a `.forward` file

```
rich
katie
/home/jessica/mail
```

any messages sent to the username `jessica` would be forwarded to both `rich` and `katie`, and would be stored in a text file mail in Jessica's `$HOME` directory.

Address Extensions

A very powerful feature of Postfix is the capability for users to create their own mailing lists. This is done using address extensions defined in the `main.cf` configuration file.

The `recipient_delimiter` parameter defines whether address extensions are used. If this parameter is not defined, address extensions are not allowed. If it is, any user address can be extended using the `recipient_delimiter` character and additional text. The normal character used as the recipient delimiter is the plus sign (+):

```
recipient_delimiter = +
```

For example, user `chris` can create a new mailing list called `chris+football` by creating a `.forward` file called

```
.forward+football
```

in his home directory. Inside the `.forward+football` file, Chris can place the list of all of the e-mail addresses that should be part of the mailing list (or point to an external file that contains the list). Each recipient in the list receives a copy of any messages sent to the `chris+football` mail name on the host. This is an easy way to provide simple mail lists for your users.

NOTE

Chapter 19, "Using Majordomo with Postfix," describes how to set up a full-feature mail list server on a Postfix server.

Summary

Once the Postfix system is installed, you can configure it for your particular e-mail environment and start it. The first file that you should check is the `master.cf` configuration file. The `master.cf` file installed by default by the Postfix source code distribution contains values that should be fine for most mail setups. If you want, you can select certain Postfix programs to run in a `chroot` environment.

After configuring the `master.cf` file, you must decide which method of local mail delivery your Postfix server will use. Postfix can deliver mail to local users directly to their mailboxes in three different formats: using `sendmail`-style mailboxes, using a `$HOME/Mailbox` mailbox, and using the `qmail`-style `$HOME/Maildir` directory. Alternatively, you can configure Postfix to forward messages to an external MDA program that will be responsible for delivering the message to the local user.

The next step is to configure the `main.cf` configuration file. You can set several parameters in this file depending on your particular e-mail environment. You should check the `myhostname`, `mydestination`, `inet_interfaces`, and `myorigin` parameters to ensure that they are set to the proper values. You should also modify the Postfix `aliases` lookup table to reflect the usernames on your system. You should always create a mail alias for the `root` user so messages are forwarded to a normal user who logs in on a regular basis.

After the configuration is complete, you can test the Postfix installation using three different methods. By removing the `smtpd` program from the `master.cf` file, you can disable Postfix's receiving capability and use the existing MTA software while you test Postfix. Alternatively, you can create a virtual interface on an existing interface and set the `inet_interfaces` parameter to the new interface while leaving the existing MTA program alone. Finally, you can disable existing MTA software and test Postfix on the full e-mail server. Once you test Postfix, you can create a startup script to start Postfix at system boot time. Different Unix implementations use different methods for storing startup scripts.

Finally, once users are using the Postfix server, they can create their own `.forward` files to redirect messages to other users, commands, or files. Also, they can create their own simple mailing lists if the Postfix server is configured to support address extensions.

CHAPTER 11

Using Postfix as an ISP Mail Server

With the increasing popularity of the Internet, providing e-mail accounts has become a large industry. Home users are requesting new e-mail accounts at an astounding rate. Some homes have separate e-mail accounts for every member of the family (yes, even the pets). Although most big businesses have already jumped onto the Internet bandwagon, still hundreds of small businesses and organizations are waiting to take the plunge into the Internet world. With all of the demand for e-mail accounts, it's no wonder that the demand on Internet service providers (ISPs) has increased. Many new ISPs are appearing every week. ISPs can provide simple e-mail services for people and businesses that can't afford direct connections to the Internet.

This chapter describes how to use Postfix to set up a commercial-quality ISP mail server on a Unix platform. This mail server can service both individual customers who dial in to a single e-mail account, as well as small-to-medium-sized corporate customers who have their own local mail servers that dial in to the ISP and retrieve mail for their entire corporate domain.

Features of an ISP E-Mail Server

Before describing the specifics of creating an ISP mail server, it may be helpful to understand the features and functions required. ISP e-mail servers have more demands placed on them than a standard office mail server has, and are often more complicated to configure.

Many small- and medium-sized offices do not have dedicated connections to the Internet, so they rely on a remote host to accept and store incoming e-mail messages for their domains. The local mail server for the office can then contact the Internet host via a dial-up modem at regular intervals and check whether there are any incoming messages to download.

The ISP mail servers must be able to accept mail for these "dial-up" domains. In fact, if the ISP is servicing more than one customer, it must be able to accept messages for several dial-up domains. The mail must somehow be kept separate so that individual domain mail servers can contact the ISP mail server to retrieve the correct mail. Servicing multiple domains on a single mail server is called hosting *virtual domains*.

Another requirement for an ISP mail server is *mail relaying*. Most customers who dial up to an ISP cannot send outgoing e-mail messages directly to their intended Internet destination. Instead, the customers' mail clients must rely on a "smart" mail server where they can send all their outgoing messages for delivery to the Internet. This smart mail server is most often the ISP mail server. To accomplish this, the ISP mail server must allow relaying messages.

Relaying was once a commonly offered service. The SMTP protocol has a built-in method for clients to send messages ultimately destined for remote Internet users to a common e-mail server, which in turn resends the message via SMTP to the appropriate destination mail server. When a mail server accepts any such service request, regardless of who the requestor is, it is called *open relaying*.

But with the increase of unsolicited commercial e-mail (UCE), open relaying has become an ugly subject. It is not politically correct on the Internet to recklessly forward e-mail from any user to another mail server. Instead, some degree of intelligence is required to filter for appropriate e-mail senders. This is called *selective relaying*.

The following sections describe virtual domains and relaying in more detail and how they relate to Postfix.

Virtual Domains

Using virtual domains on an e-mail server is becoming a common practice for ISPs. Many ISPs support e-mail for small- and medium-sized organizations and businesses using this technique. Figure 11.1 shows a diagram of a virtual domain on the ISP accepting an incoming e-mail message for the user `prez` in the virtual domain. The local office mail server can retrieve the message to store in `prez`'s mailbox. Once stored there, `prez` can retrieve it using any common MUA program.

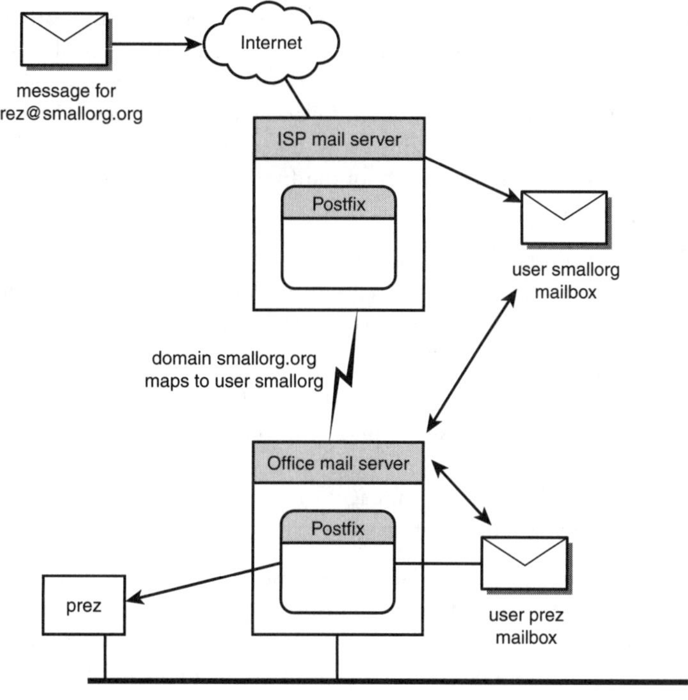

FIGURE 11.1

Using virtual domains for e-mail.

The main idea behind virtual domains is the capability to store mail messages for another mail server locally on the ISP server. When the remote mail server is available to retrieve the messages, the ISP mail server must be able to queue the messages and send them to the remote mail server.

For virtual domain mail service to work, the ISP must first be able to accept messages destined for the offsite domain and place them where they can be retrieved later. This usually involves forwarding all messages for a particular domain either to a special spool area or to a designated user account on the Unix system.

Secondly, the office mail server responsible for the offsite domain must be able to connect to the ISP mail server and retrieve the messages. Once the messages are retrieved from the ISP, the office mail server must be able to parse the message header fields to determine the correct recipient and deliver the message to that user's mailbox. Many software packages can accomplish this function.

Selective Relaying

Mail relaying has become a complicated issue on the Internet. In the early days of the Internet, mail relaying was a common courtesy extended to other mail servers on the network. If a mail server attempted to deliver a mail message to your mail server destined to a user on a different mail server, you gladly accepted the message. Once your mail server accepted the message it forwarded it to the appropriate remote mail server for the user. Unfortunately, with the popularity of the Internet came abuse of the Internet and e-mail systems.

Mass marketers are constantly looking for ways to send out massive quantities of advertisements to unsuspecting users via e-mail servers. A key to the successful mass marketer is the ability to hide the message's originating e-mail address. (Otherwise, people might be able to track them down and complain to their service providers.)

Enter mail relaying. By using some basic SMTP trickery, a user can bounce e-mail messages off an Internet mail relay using a phony originating mail address. The original SMTP protocol did not allow for validating the mail address of incoming messages, so the mail relay happily forwards the messages to the recipients using the phony originating e-mail address. Figure 11.2 demonstrates this principle.

A message originating from some clandestine host on the Internet is sent to the `ispnet1.net` mail server destined for an unsuspecting user on the `ispnet2.net` domain. The `ispnet1.net` mail server accepts the message and forwards it to the mail server for the `ispnet2.net` domain. When the message is received, it contains the originating address from the `shadrach.ispnet1.net` server.

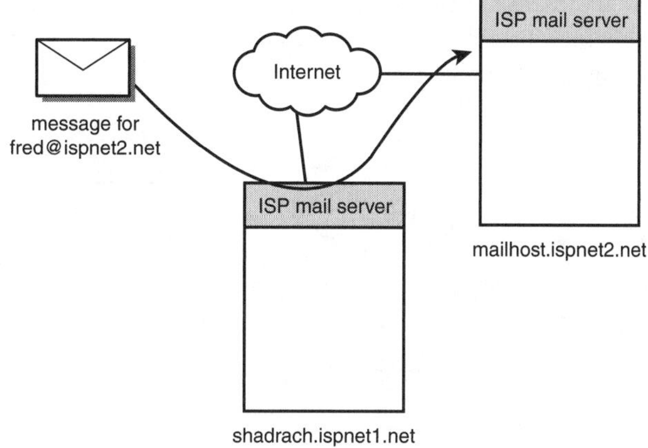

FIGURE 11.2

Using an open mail relay for UCE.

There has been much discussion on how to control UCE on the Internet. The most obvious methods involve modifying the SMTP protocol to validate information sent in the `MAIL FROM` headers. This would ensure that users could not falsify the mail addresses in their messages.

New SMTP extensions have made many improvements to the security of Internet e-mail. However, many (if not most) Internet mail servers either don't use software that takes advantage of the new SMTP extensions, or haven't configured their software properly to use the new features.

To compensate for this, most e-mail software packages have their own methods of screening SMTP connection requests. There are basically two approaches to responsible relaying on the Internet. The first and most obvious solution is for the MTA to refuse all relayed messages and only accept messages that are destined for users on the local mail server. This is the safest and easiest solution.

Unfortunately, most ISPs have users who dial in to the ISP and use some type of MUA program on their PCs to receive mail. These programs must also be able to send messages to remote users on the Internet. The method that almost all MUA programs use to send messages is forwarding the messages via SMTP to a smart host. The smart host is assumed to be able to relay the message to the appropriate destination mail server. This is where the problem is.

If you are a conscientious mail administrator and have disabled relaying on your mail server, none of your remote customers will be able to use your mail server to relay messages to the Internet. That would not be good for business. To compensate for this, Postfix implements a method called *selective relaying* and gets the best of both worlds.

Figure 11.3 demonstrates the principle of selective relaying. By allowing the MTA mail program to check a local database, it can determine on a case-by-case basis what messages to relay and what messages to refuse.

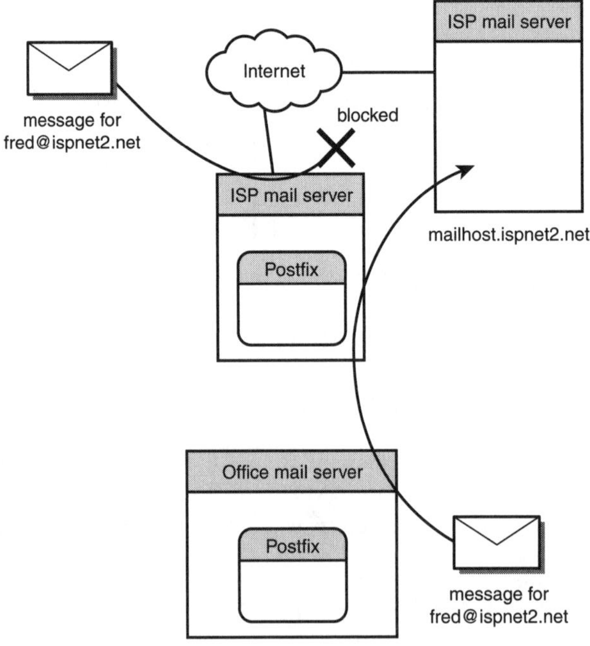

FIGURE 11.3

Using selective relaying on a mail server.

By placing all of the local IP addresses that are assigned to your customers in a relaying database, the MTA program can allow those addresses to use it as a smart host and forward any messages destined for remote Internet users. However, any message coming from an IP address not in the database and destined for a remote user will be refused.

Configuring Virtual Domains

The Postfix e-mail package allows for hosting multiple virtual domains on the ISP mail server. You can use three methods to host a virtual domain using the Postfix mail server.

The first method involves placing all mail destined for a particular domain in a special mail account. It is then the responsibility of the real domain mail server to connect to the Postfix server and retrieve the messages from the account. The real domain mail server must then be able to parse the messages and deliver them to the appropriate users. This method is best to use when the Postfix server must host a virtual domain for many users.

The second method that you can use involves Postfix selectively mapping individual user accounts in the virtual domain to a normal system user account. The individual user must be able to connect to the account and download the messages using a standard MUA Program. This method is best to use when the Postfix server is hosting a virtual domain consisting of just a few users who do not want to purchase a separate domain mail server.

The final method that you can use to map virtual domains employs a little bit of Postfix trickery. Instead of using the Postfix `virtual` lookup table, you can use the Postfix `transport` table. You can configure the `transport` table to accept messages for several different domains and send them to the local mail server. This method is handy to use when the Postfix server is supporting several large virtual domains where the individual users still connect to the server to retrieve their messages. By using the `transport` table, the individual user accounts do not need to be created twice: once on the system and once in the `virtual` lookup table. Instead, the `transport` table automatically maps the virtual domain user to the same local user.

The following sections describe the configurations required to support virtual domains on the Postfix server in each of the mentioned scenarios.

Configuring DNS Records for Virtual Domains

Before you can do anything with the Postfix software, you must add the proper DNS records to inform remote Internet hosts where to send messages for the virtual domain.

The first step for hosting a virtual domain is to obtain a domain name. As mentioned in Chapter 4, "DNS and Postfix," you must register each Internet domain with the Internet Corporation for Assigned Names and Numbers (ICANN). This enables Internet hosts to uniquely associate an organization with IP address(es). For the purposes of this example, we will use the fictitious domain `othercompany.com`. Figure 11.4 shows a diagram of how the domain will interact with the Internet.

When you register the `othercompany.com` domain, you must specify two DNS servers that will support this domain. If the ISP site also offers DNS service to domains that it hosts, you may want to include them as one or both of the DNS servers for your domain. Once the DNS server is identified as being an authoritative server for the `othercompany.com` domain, you must configure the DNS server with the appropriate DNS records. You must set up the DNS MX records to point to the ISP mail server. Then all mail destined for `othercompany.com` will be directed to their ISP's mail server.

As shown in Chapter 4, you must configure several records on the DNS server for the domain to be defined on the Internet. Listing 11.1 shows an example of what the DNS records for the `othercompany.com` domain might look like. Line numbers have been added to help in the description. The actual DNS records will not have the line numbers included.

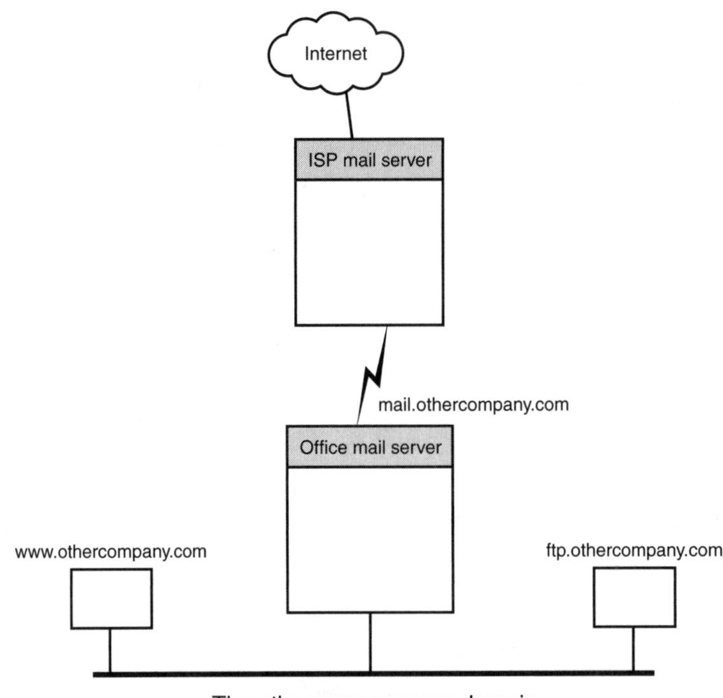

FIGURE 11.4

Sample domain `othercompany.com` connected to the ISP.

LISTING 11.1 Sample `othercompany.com` DNS Definition

```
othercompany.com IN SOA   host1.ispnet1.net. postmaster.host1.ispnet1.net (
                   20001105001      ;unique serial number
                   8H                ; refresh rate
                   2H              ;retry period
                   1W              ; expiration period
                   1D)             ; minimum
            NS     host1.ispnet1.net.     ;defines primary name server
            NS     ns1.ispnet2.net.       ; defines secondary name server
            MX     10 host1.ispnet1.net.  ; defines primary mail server
host1.isp.net.    A        10.0.0.1
1.0.0.10.IN-ADDR.ARPA  PTR  host1.isp.net ; pointer address for reverse DNS
```

As shown in Listing 11.1, lines 1–6 define the Start of Authority (SOA) record for the `othercompany.com` domain. The origin part of the SOA record points to the master DNS server for the domain, which for a virtual domain will be the ISP's DNS server. Lines 8 and 9 define the primary and secondary DNS servers for the domain.

Line 11 is important. It defines who will accept mail messages for the domain. You must ensure that the proper MX record for the domain is used or messages from remote Internet users will not get delivered properly. The MX record for the domain must point to the ISP mail server. This ensures that any messages destined for the domain will be sent to the ISP mail server (which later on will be configured to accept them).

Lines 13 and 15 define the Internet address of the ISP host that is being used to host the virtual domain. This allows other Internet mail servers to be able to connect to the ISP mail server to transfer messages.

Once the DNS MX record properly points to the ISP mail server hosting the virtual domain, it is up to the mail administrator to configure the Postfix server to accept the incoming messages.

Configuring Postfix for Virtual Domains

As mentioned, you can use three different methods to create virtual domain addresses in Postfix:

- Receive mail for an entire virtual domain
- Receive mail for individual users in a virtual domain
- Use the `transport` lookup table for virtual domains

Each method has its own particular function and uses. The following sections describe these methods and help you decide which would work best for your particular user groups.

An Entire Domain

The most common virtual domain scenario is when the ISP handles messages for an entire domain. The messages must be kept on the mail server until a mail server in the remote domain can connect and download them. Figure 11.5 demonstrates this.

To allow Postfix to receive messages for a virtual domain, the mail administrator must first configure the `virtual` lookup table. Each virtual domain that the mail server will receive messages for must be entered in a separate line, like:

```
othercompany.com anytext
othercompany2.com anytext
anothercompany.com anytext
```

The right-hand values in the table are not important. They can be any text value that you want, although the text "virtual" is becoming a popular default.

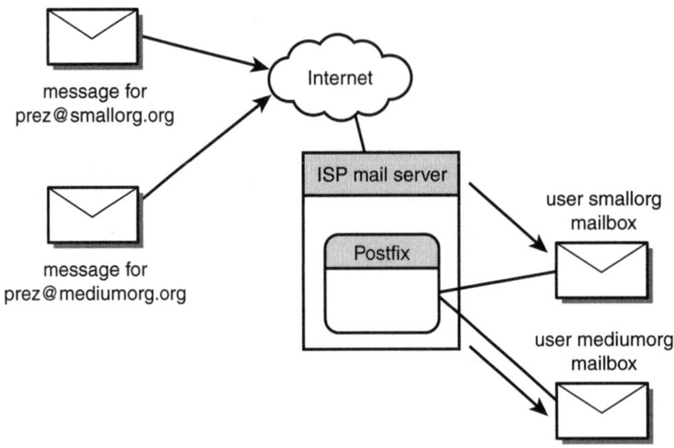

FIGURE 11.5

Storing messages for virtual domains.

Once the virtual domains are identified, the location to which their messages will go must be defined in the `virtual` table:

```
@othercompany.com local_user1
@othercompany2.com local_user2
@anothercompany.com local_user3
```

These entries map any e-mail address in the virtual domain to a specific local username. The addresses that are used to receive the mail messages should exist on the Postfix system and have a normal system mailbox using the default mailbox method of the Postfix server.

CAUTION

Be careful when entering information into the `virtual` lookup table. Remember that any leading whitespace on a line means that the whole line is a continuation of the previous line. Many mail administrators try to "pretty-up" the `virtual` table by indenting the `@company` line, only to find out that their virtual domains don't work.

Once the `virtual` lookup table is created, it must be converted to the indexed database type of your choice using the `postmap` command:

```
postmap hash:/etc/postfix/virtual
```

After the lookup table is created, it must be referenced in the `main.cf` configuration file using the `virtual_maps` parameter:

```
virtual_maps = hash:/etc/postfix/virtual
```

After the change the administrator must issue the `postfix reload` command for the change to take effect.

Messages sent to any user at the virtual domain will now be forwarded to the Postfix user account specified in the `virtual` table. Listing 11.2 shows an example of this.

LISTING 11.2 Sample Message Sent to a Virtual Domain User

```
$ whoami
local_user1
$ mail jessica@othercompany.com
Subject: First test to virtual domain
This is the first message sent to a virtual domain account.
.
EOT

$ mail katie@othercompany.com
Subject: Second test to virtual domain
This is the second message sent to a virtual domain account.
.
EOT


you have mail

$ mail
Mail version 8.1 6/6/93.  Type ? for help.
"/var/mail/local_user1": 2 messages 2 new
>N  1 local_user1@shadrach.ispnet1  Wed Nov  8 11:41  13/525   "First test to
➥virtual"
 N  2 local_user1@shadrach.ispnet1  Wed Nov  8 11:42  13/525   "Second test to
➥virtua"
& 1
Message 1:
From local_user1@shadrach.ispnet1.net  Wed Nov  8 11:41:39 2000
Delivered-To: local_user1@shadrach.ispnet1.net
To: jessica@othercompany.com
Subject: First test to virtual domain
Date: Wed,  8 Nov 2000 11:41:39 -0500 (EST)
From: local_user1@shadrach.ispnet1.net (User Local_user1)

This is the first message sent to a virtual domain account.

& 2
```

LISTING 11.2 Continued

```
Message 2:
From local_user1@shadrach.ispnet1.net  Wed Nov  8 11:42:01 2000
Delivered-To: local_user1@shadrach.ispnet1.net
To: katie@othercompany.com
Subject: Second test to virtual domain
Date: Wed,  8 Nov 2000 11:42:00 -0500 (EST)
From: local_user1@shadrach.ispnet1.net (User Local_user1)

This is the second message sent to a virtual domain account.

&
```

The example shown in Listing 11.2 is somewhat trivial, but it does show what happens with mail for virtual domain users. The `local_user1` user was used to send messages to two separate users in the `othercompany.com` domain. Both messages were delivered to the `local_user1` username as specified in the sample `virtual` lookup table.

Note that in both instances, the message `To:` header still points to the proper virtual domain recipient. This is important for the real domain mail server to be able to parse the messages out to the proper recipient (as explained in Chapter 12, "Using Postfix as an Office Mail Server").

Individual Users on a Domain

Often, an ISP cannot place the e-mail messages for an entire virtual domain in one local mailbox. The users may be individuals who want to have a novelty domain name but still log in to the ISP server to retrieve their messages. Postfix can accommodate this situation as well, allowing the mail administrator to create individual virtual domain accounts and pointing them to unique local usernames.

As with an entire domain, first you must define the virtual domain name to Postfix in the `virtual` lookup table:

```
othercompany.com virtual
```

In this situation, instead of specifying only one local username to map the domain to, the mail administrator must map every valid user in the domain to a valid local user on the Postfix system:

```
mike@othercompany.com mike
evonne@othercompany.com evonne
dave@othercompany.com sales_team
alex@othercompany.com sales_team
```

This mapping ensures that the Postfix server will only accept messages for the defined users in the virtual domain. Those messages will be forwarded to the local users specified in the lookup table. Note that the last two entries in the `virtual` lookup table both point to the same system username. This allows for a single user account to have multiple virtual addresses. Listing 11.3 shows an example of using this `virtual` lookup table.

LISTING 11.3 Sample SMTP Session Using Virtual Domains

```
$ telnet localhost 25
Trying 127.0.0.1...
Connected to localhost.ispnet1.net.
Escape character is '^]'.
220 shadrach.ispnet1.net ESMTP Postfix
HELO shadrach.ispnet1.net
250 shadrach.ispnet1.net
MAIL FROM: <rich@shadrach.ispnet1.net>
250 Ok
RCPT TO: <fred@othercompany.com>
550 <fred@othercompany.com>: User unknown
RCPT TO: <mike@othercompany.com>
250 Ok
DATA
354 End data with <CR><LF>.<CR><LF>
From: rich@shadrach.ispnet1.net
To: mike@othercompany.com
Date: 11 Nov 2000 12:10:00
Subject: Virtual Domain test

This is a test of the virtual domain settings.
.
250 Ok: queued as 07E7131FB
QUIT
221 Bye
Connection closed by foreign host.
$
```

As you can see in Listing 11.3, Postfix did not accept the attempted message for the nonexistent user `fred` but gladly accepted the message for the configured user `mike`. The message was delivered to the mailbox for the system username `mike`. That user can now connect to the mail server and retrieve his messages using a standard MUA program.

Using the Transport Table for Virtual Domains

One downside to the previous method is that the mail administrator must create two sets of user files. The virtual domain user must be added to the `virtual` lookup table, and the real username must be added to the normal system password file. For systems supporting thousands of users, that could mean a lot of work!

To help solve this problem, some administrators use a trick with the `transport` lookup table instead of using the `virtual` table. The `transport` lookup table enables the mail administrator to define how to deliver mail for a particular host or domain. By specifying the local mail transport as the delivery method, the administrator can automatically map any username in the virtual domain to the local host.

To accomplish this, first you must enter the virtual domain in the `transport` table listing the local delivery transport as the transport method:

```
othercompany.com local:
othercompany2.com local:
anothercompany.com local:
```

Don't forget the colon at the end of the transport name. Once the table is created, you must convert it to an indexed database type:

```
postmap hash:/etc/postfix/transport
```

Once created, you must reference the new `transport` lookup table in the `main.cf` configuration file using the `transport_maps` parameter:

```
transport_maps = hash:/etc/postfix/transport
```

After all this is done, you can issue the `postfix reload` command and test the new configuration.

CAUTION

Use extreme caution when creating multiple virtual domains using the `transport` table method. Remember that all virtual domains are sharing the same system username pool. Duplicate usernames are harder to detect when they are not listed in a single handy `virtual` table.

Using this configuration, any messages sent to users in the `othercompany.com`, `othercompany2.com`, and `anothercompany.com` domains will automatically be forwarded to the system user with the same username. Again, those users can connect to the Postfix server using a standard MUA mail package to retrieve the messages in their mailboxes. As with the `virtual` lookup table, any mail messages sent to virtual domain users that do not map to local system users are rejected.

Configuring Selective Relaying

Another important feature that the ISP must support is the ability for customers to use the ISP mail server to forward outbound messages to the Internet. The standard small office mail server does not have a full-time connection to the Internet, so it cannot send messages to remote users.

Instead, the small office mail server must place any outgoing messages in a message queue to send to the ISP mail server the next time a connection is made. It is the responsibility of the ISP mail server to be able to forward those messages to the appropriate remote mail servers.

While forwarding messages from customers is required, at the same time the ISP needs to block forwarding attempts by other Internet hosts. This is where it gets tricky. The mail administrator must configure the mail system to reject e-mail relaying requests from some clients while allowing other clients to relay messages. This section describes the methods that you can use to implement selective relaying on an ISP Postfix server.

Setting Relaying Parameters

Postfix provides several parameters that the mail administrator can use to control how mail is delivered on the mail server. The most common and easiest method of restricting mail relaying is to control how Postfix delivers (or refuses to deliver) messages received from external hosts. The parameter best suited for this job is the `smtpd_recipient_restrictions` parameter.

Postfix uses the `smtpd_recipient_restrictions` parameter to restrict the recipients that the Postfix smtpd server will accept messages for. By carefully setting this parameter, the administrator can successfully block mail relaying attempts from unknown remote hosts while allowing customers to continue using the Postfix server as a mail relay.

The format of the `smtpd_recipient_restrictions` parameter is just like any other parameter in the `main.cf` configuration file:

```
smtpd_recipient_restrictions = value
```

Multiple values can be added to the parameter by separating them with either a comma or whitespace. Restrictions are added in the value list and are applied from left to right in the list.

One thing that does make this parameter different from most other Postfix parameters is that if the parameter is used, it must have at least one of three essential values listed in the value list. The three essential values are

- `check_relay_domains` Checks whether the message is intended for a recipient address in the `$mydestination`, `$inet_interfaces`, `$virtual_maps`, or `$relay_domains` parameter values.
- `reject` Refuses all messages, even local ones.
- `reject_unauth_destination` Refuses all messages unless they meet the `check_relay_domains` criteria.

This section defines the values that you can use with the `smtpd_recipient_restrictions` parameter and how you can combine them to prevent mail relay abuse on your Postfix server.

Default Values

The default behavior of the parameter assumes that the `permit_mynetworks` and `check_relay_domains` values are set.

The `permit_mynetworks` value accepts messages for any recipient from any client that is a member of the `$mynetworks` group in the `main.cf` file (generally, those hosts with an IP address on your local subnet). If you assign addresses to your customers based on a set subnetwork number that the Postfix server is in, this is a good choice. This allows any client on your subnet to use the Postfix server as a mail relay, while blocking any external mail servers.

If you assign IP addresses other than from the subnetwork that the Postfix server is in to your clients, then you must use an additional value to specify the allowed network clients. This will require one of the database-check values described later.

The `check_relay_domains` value allows additional clients to use the mail relay based on other configured Postfix parameters. They are

- Any client listed in the `$relay_domains` parameter, which by default includes the `$mydestination` parameter.
- Any destination address in the `$relay_domains` parameter list.
- Any destination address listed in the `$inet_interfaces` parameter.
- Any destination address listed in a `virtual` lookup table.

You may notice that by default Postfix allows relaying from any client as long as the message is destined for a recipient host that the Postfix server is configured to accept messages for. Although you may not consider this relaying, technically it is (the Postfix server is relaying the message to itself).

Rejection Values

You can also prevent remote sites from using the Postfix server as a mail relay by including several different reject values to the `smtp_recipient_restrictions` parameter. Reject values deny relaying to hosts or clients that match certain defined criteria. Table 11.1 lists the reject values and their descriptions.

TABLE 11.1 Reject Values

Value	*Requests Restricted*
`reject`	All requests, even local.
`reject_invalid_hostname`	Invalid HELO hostnames.
`reject_maps_rbl`	If client is listed in `$maps_rbl_domains`.

TABLE 11.1 Continued

Value	*Requests Restricted*
`reject_non_fqdn_hostname`	Non-FQDN HELO hostnames.
`reject_non_fqdn_recipient`	Non-FQDN recipient addresses.
`reject_non_fqdn_sender`	Non-FQDN sender addresses.
`reject_unauth_destination`	Mail not intended for destinations that match `$mydestination`, `$inet_interfaces`, `$virtual_maps`, or `$relay_domains`.
`reject_unauth_pipelining`	Mail sent from SMTP pipelining software.
`reject_unknown_client`	Client hostname is not known.
`reject_unknown_hostname`	HELO hostname that does not have a DNS A or MX entry.
`reject_unknown_recipient_domain`	Mail sent to domains without a DNS A or MX record.
`reject_unknown_sender_domain`	Mail sent from domains without a DNS A or MX record.

By specifying particular reject values, the Postfix server can prevent relaying either from or to particular domains. You can enter multiple values separated by either commas or spaces for the parameter.

As an example, you can add the following parameter line in the `main.cf` file:

```
smtpd_recipient_restrictions = reject_non_fqdn_hostname,
➥ reject_unauth_destination
```

After issuing the `postfix reload` command, the Postfix server should now reject mail from hosts that do not properly identify themselves in the HELO statement:

```
shadrach# telnet localhost 25
Trying 127.0.0.1...
Connected to localhost.ispnet1.net.
Escape character is '^]'.
220 shadrach.ispnet1.net ESMTP Postfix
HELO dude
250 shadrach.ispnet1.net
MAIL FROM: <rich@shadrach.ispnet1.net>
250 Ok
RCPT TO: <rich@shadrach.ispnet1.net>
504 <dude>: Helo command rejected: need fully-qualified hostname
QUIT
221 Bye
Connection closed by foreign host.
shadrach#
```

As shown, the attempt to send a message to a remote host through the Postfix server is blocked after the `SMTP RCPT TO:` command is issued. Any attempts from would-be spammers or relayers to send mail using a phony `HELO SMTP` command (as they often will try to do) will be rejected.

Permit Values

Alternately, the mail administrator can create scenarios where remote users are permitted to relay mail messages through the Postfix server. There are three values that explicitly permit mail relaying:

- `permit`
- `permit_auth_destination`
- `permit_mx_backup`

The `permit` value works similarly to its cousin, `reject`. It will permit any client to send mail to any host (open relaying). It is usually used as a final action in a list of restrictive values, where by default the mail server will permit mail relaying.

The `permit_auth_destination` value is used to allow Postfix to accept mail for any of the local host designations (`$mydestination`, `$inet_interfaces`, `$virtual_maps`, and `$relay_domains`). This value can be used in combination with a list of reject values to ensure that local mail will be accepted.

The `permit_mx_backup` value is a handy value to use if you must be the backup mail server for a domain. When the Postfix server is a backup mail server, it is given a lower MX value for the DNS record:

```
othercompany.com  IN SOA      host1.ispnet1.net. postmaster.host1.ispnet1.net (
                     20001105001      ;unique serial number
                     8H                ; refresh rate
                     2H               ;retry period
                     1W               ; expiration period
                     1D)              ; minimum

               MX      10 host1.ispnet1.net. ; defines primary mail server
               MX      20 host2.ispnet1.net. ; defines secondary mail server
```

All mail messages for the `othercompany.com` domain will be sent to the `host1.ispnet1.net` mail server. If that server is down, then the `host2.ispnet1.net` mail server must be able to accept mail messages for the domain. The `permit_mx_backup` value allows Postfix to accept messages for the domains defined in DNS records that point to the Postfix server.

Database Checks

Possibly the most versatile feature of Postfix is its ability to read data from lookup tables. This feature can be used in mail relaying by incorporating lookup tables in what is restricted by the `smtpd` server program. There are four values that can be used to define lookup tables to restrict mail relay behavior:

- `check_client_access`
- `check_helo_access`

- `check_recipient_access`
- `check_sender_access`

Each of the four values points to a database type and name used for the lookup table, such as

```
check_client_access hash:/etc/postfix/clients
```

The lookup table must be created using the database type listed in the value. The format of the database records is

```
address value
```

The *address* field can be an individual hostname, IP address, domain name, or IP network range. It will be matched against the object represented in the *value* name (client, HELO, recipient, or sender). The right-hand *value* field describes the action Postfix will take when a message is received that matches the address. The word REJECT is used to force Postfix to refuse messages that match the address field.

Alternately, the mail administrator can place an SMTP error code (4XX or 5XX) along with descriptive text in the action field. This code and text will be returned to the remote host in the SMTP reply statement.

Any other text used for *value* will allow the host address that matches the address field to relay messages through the Postfix server.

An example of building a very tight mail relay domain would be to use the `check_helo_access` value along with a very specific lookup table:

```
ispnet1.net OK
ispnet2.net OK
ispnet3.net OK
```

By constructing the `smtpd_recipient_restrictions` parameter to reject by default, only domains listed in the `check_helo_access` value will be permitted to send messages to the Postfix server.

The `main.cf` configuration parameter line should look like this:

```
smtpd_recipient_restrictions = check_helo_access hash:/etc/postfix/helo, reject
```

After running the `postmap` utility on the `helo` lookup table, and running the `postfix reload` command, the Postfix server should now only accept mail messages from hosts that identify themselves as being in one of the three domains listed in the `helo` lookup table. Listing 11.4 shows some sample SMTP sessions using this configuration.

LISTING 11.4 Sample SMTP sessions using check_helo_access

```
[rich@shadrach]$ telnet localhost 25
Trying 127.0.0.1...
Connected to localhost.
Escape character is '^]'.
220 shadrach.ispnet1.net ESMTP Postfix
HELO dude
250 shadrach.ispnet1.net
MAIL FROM: <spammer>
250 Ok
RCPT TO: <rich@shadrach.ispnet1.net>
554 <rich@shadrach.ispnet1.net>: Recipient address rejected: Access denied
QUIT
221 Bye
Connection closed by foreign host.

[rich@shadrach]$ telnet localhost 25
Trying 127.0.0.1...
Connected to localhost.
Escape character is '^]'.
220 shadrach.ispnet1.net ESMTP Postfix
HELO ispnet3.net
250 shadrach.ispnet1.net
MAIL FROM: <rich@ispnet3.net>
250 Ok
RCPT TO: <rich@othercompany.com>
250 Ok
DATA
354 End data with <CR><LF>.<CR><LF>
From: <rich@ispnet3.net>
To: <rich@othercompany.com>
Date: 11 Nov 2000 10:50
Subject: Mail Relay blocking
Rich -

    This is a test of mail blocking using the SMTP HELO value.
.
250 Ok: queued as 4C3533B11A
QUIT
221 Bye
Connection closed by foreign host.
[rich@shadrach]#
```

As you can see in the first example in Listing 11.4, the remote SMTP server did not identify itself properly in the SMTP `HELO` command. When it tried to send a message through the Postfix server, it was blocked. In the second example, the remote SMTP server did identify itself correctly, and its domain was listed in the lookup table configured for the `check_helo_access` value. It was allowed to send a message to a recipient on a third host. The Postfix server accepted the message, and will now try to forward that message to the appropriate mail server.

Summary

Using Postfix as an ISP mail server to provide e-mail access to remote users is a simple task. Postfix can be configured to support three different types of virtual domain hosting.

First, Postfix can be configured to support an entire virtual domain by forwarding all messages to any user in the domain to a single system user account on the Postfix server. The remote domain server can then connect to the Postfix server at its leisure and download the messages for its users.

Postfix can also support hosting individual virtual domain users on the local mail server by pointing individual accounts to local usernames. The individual users can then connect to the Postfix mail server using a standard MUA program and retrieve their mail messages.

Finally, the mail administrator can utilize the Postfix `transport` table to trick Postfix into thinking the virtual domain name mail should be sent to itself (the local mailer). This enables the mail administrator to enter virtual usernames as system users one time without having to maintain a separate `virtual` table.

Another feature of an ISP mail server is the ability to relay mail for customers, but block mail relaying for others. You can do this in Postfix using the `smtpd_recipient_restrictions` parameter. The mail administrator can use several combinations of values to restrict mail relaying to local networks or individual customers anywhere on the network. At the same time, it can block attempts by spammers to use the Postfix server as an open relay to forward spam mail through.

CHAPTER 12

Using Postfix as an Office Mail Server

The previous chapter described how a Postfix mail server could be configured as an ISP mail server. Postfix can also be configured to support several other types of mail server environments. The most common types of mail servers found in offices are

- Workstation mail servers
- Company Intranet mail servers
- Full-time Internet mail servers
- Dial-up Internet mail servers
- Firewall Internet mail servers

Each mail server environment requires a different configuration for Postfix. This chapter describes how to modify Postfix to meet the requirements of each of these environments.

Internal Office Mail Servers

Often small organizations do not require (or want) Internet mail service. However, they would like some kind of in-house messaging system to allow users within the organization to send messages to one another. You can usually accomplish this with a single internal mail server acting as a mail hub. All mail messages are routed through the mail hub. Figure 12.1 shows a diagram of a simple office mail hub.

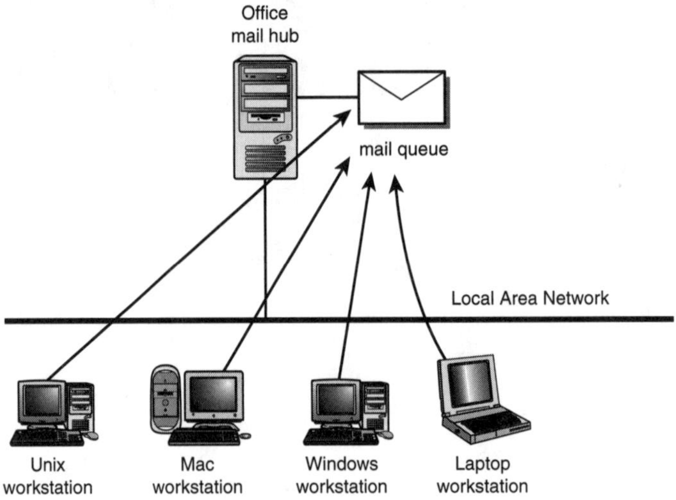

FIGURE 12.1

Simple office mail hub.

All of the organization's users are configured on the central hub, so no mail routing is required. Although individual workstations may or may not have an MTA program running on them, all mail is still forwarded to the central mail hub for routing.

Unix workstations in this mail environment must be configured using a `nullcient` configuration. This requires that the Postfix software running on the workstation routes all messages to the central hub rather than to individual workstations. This enables any user to log in to any workstation and retrieve his or her messages from the central hub.

This section describes the Postfix configurations that can be used to configure a `nullclient` workstation as well as the central mail hub.

Workstations

Many organizations such as programming and engineering shops contain Unix-type workstations used by employees. Although having lots of high-powered workstations on the network is great for some applications, mail is not necessarily one of them.

If each Unix workstation were configured to act as an individual mail server, sending mail messages on the network could become confusing. Each user's e-mail address would consist of the user's unique workstation name and the user's system username. Figure 12.2 shows an example of what this could be like.

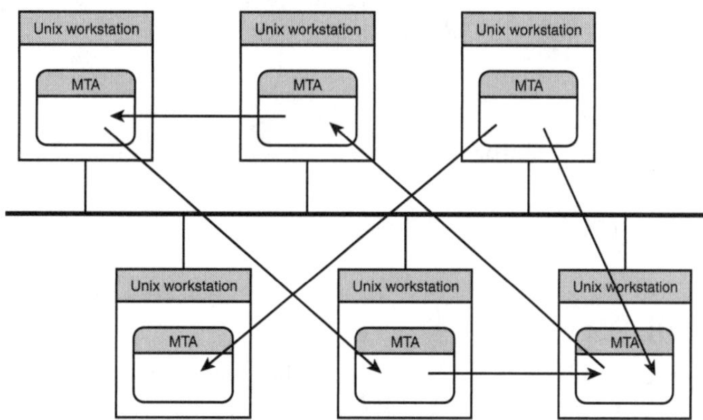

FIGURE 12.2

A fully routed workstation mail network.

As shown in Figure 12.2, each workstation MTA program would have to send each message to the appropriate workstation on the network. Each time a workstation was removed from the network (or a new one added), the mail addresses would change. Of course, this environment would not be good for sharing or changing workstations. Each time a user switched workstations, his e-mail address would change! This would get very confusing, very fast.

To compensate for this environment, a server dedicated as a central mail hub is established. This server maintains a user account for everyone in the organization. The mail for each user can either be forwarded directly to his or her workstation, or the users can connect to the central hub to retrieve their messages, whichever the mail administrator prefers.

The Postfix configuration for each Unix workstation in the network will be exactly the same.

Each Postfix `nullclient` configuration will utilize the `relayhost` parameter in the `main.cf` file to point to the central mail hub:

```
relayhost = mailhub.ispnet1.net
```

Assuming that the organization is using a fictitious domain name (as it is not on the Internet), it may or may not choose to support the fictitious domain with a DNS server (see Chapter 4, "DNS and Postfix"). If it does, you can specify the mail hub by name in the `relayhost` parameter; otherwise, you must use the numeric IP address of the mail hub:

```
relayhost = 192.168.1.1
```

Although messages are originally sent from a specific workstation, they should all use a common return address. You can ensure that all messages are sent with the proper return address on them by setting the `myorigin` parameter in `main.cf`:

```
myorigin = $mydomain
```

This will replace individual machine names with your fictitious domain name on all outgoing mail messages.

The next section describes how a central mail hub should be configured.

Intranet Mail Servers

While the latest trend is to be connected to the Internet, some small organizations either cannot afford full-time Internet connectivity or for security reasons do not want to be connected with the Internet. However, many do want internal e-mail messaging systems to allow employees to communicate within the organization.

You can accomplish this by creating a central mail hub. The central hub handles all messages within the organization. Each user on the network can connect to the central mail hub using an MUA program to read his or her messages (see Chapter 20, "Using POP3 and IMAP with Postfix").

The Postfix configuration on the central hub is fairly straightforward. If the local intranet is configured with a DNS server, you can configure the Postfix mail hub to use the designated domain name as the origin address, as well as a destination address in the `main.cf` configuration file:

```
mydestination = $myhostname, $mydomain
myorigin = $mydomain
```

If the local intranet is not using a DNS server, you should enter these addresses as numeric IP addresses, and you should set the parameter

```
disable_dns_lookups = yes
```

as well. This configuration allows the central mail hub to receive messages from workstations without using the DNS system. Remember, though, that you will need to specify all addresses in numeric IP address format.

External Office Mail Servers

Office mail servers that are used to pass e-mail to and from the Internet require special considerations. The type of connection to the Internet determines how Postfix will be configured to hold and pass messages between remote Internet hosts.

To be able to pass e-mail messages outside the organization, the external office mail server must be able to establish a TCP/IP connection with the ISP server. This section describes both the TCP/IP software requirements and the Postfix configuration requirements to allow the mail administrator to connect an office mail server to the Internet.

Full-time Internet Mail Server

With Internet communications improving, small and medium-sized organizations can now afford a full-time connection to the Internet. Often this is via an ISDN or DSL modem connection, although now many cable TV systems are offering cable modem connectivity to the Internet. Figure 12.3 demonstrates one configuration for using a full-time connection to the ISP for the office mail server.

There are many pros and cons regarding full-time connectivity to the Internet. Each corporate situation is unique, so it is impossible to recommend a generic solution. The network administrator must weigh the pros and cons for the organization to determine which (if any) full-time connectivity solution is best.

CAUTION

Remember that if your mail server is connected full time to the Internet, it may be susceptible to hacker attacks. Exercise extra caution for mail servers that are directly connected to the Internet. Although networks can utilize firewalls to deter intruders, nothing is perfect. Always closely monitor system logs for improper activity.

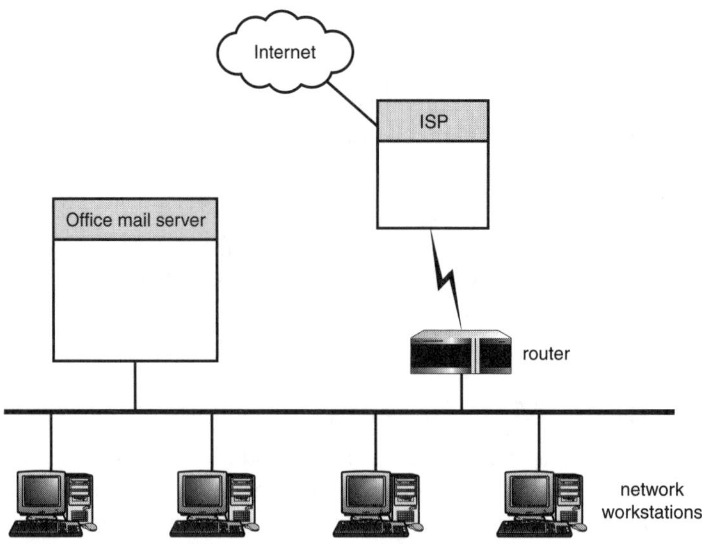

FIGURE 12.3

Full-time Internet connectivity to the ISP.

Connectivity

For cable and DSL systems, the remote network connection is usually a standard network router. The mail server will contain a network card and connect to the remote router network. Postfix will use the IP address assigned to the mail server's network card to send and receive mail messages.

ISDN connectivity requires a slightly different approach. Linux supports direct ISDN connectivity using both plug-in PC ISDN cards and external ISDN terminal adapters (modems). A primary rate ISDN connection in the United States supports two B channels. Each B channel can handle 64kbp/s of data. If two-channel service is purchased, the organization can use 128kbp/s of full-time connectivity to the ISP. This is usually more than enough bandwidth to support e-mail and simple web browsing for small and even medium-sized organizations.

The `isdn4linux` program is designed to configure and run ISDN modems from the Linux system. It makes connecting the mail server to the Internet via ISDN simple.

Once the mail server is connected to the Internet, it can be configured to support the entire organization's e-mail.

Postfix Configuration

The Postfix configuration for a mail server directly connected to the Internet is another fairly straightforward process. If the mail server is supporting mail for the entire domain, you must configure the `myorigin` and `mydestination` parameters in `main.cf` appropriately:

```
mydestination = $myhostname, localhost.$mydomain, $mydomain
myorigin = $mydomain
```

This mail server now accepts all messages sent to the domain. Each domain user must have a username configured on the mail server. Once the messages are received on the mail server, the individual users must connect to the mail server using an MUA program to retrieve their messages.

NOTE

Chapter 22, "Performance Tuning Postfix," describes other configuration options that can be modified for the Internet mail server. Chapter 20 describes how to install and configure MUA software on the mail server to allow remote users to read messages in their mailboxes.

Dial-Up Internet Mail Server

Organizations that do not want a full-time Internet connection can dial in to the ISP to retrieve mail messages. The ISP mail server is configured to receive mail messages destined for the office domain. Once received, the messages are stored in either a mail spool area or a single user account.

The office mail server must connect to the ISP mail server to retrieve any messages waiting in the mail spool for the domain, as well as to transfer any outgoing messages to the ISP for the Internet. In order for the office mail server to transfer messages with the ISP mail server, it must be able to establish a TCP/IP connection. The office mail server can use the Point-to-Point Protocol (PPP) to transfer IP packets with the ISP mail server. This service is often considerably cheaper than a full-time connection, and for simple e-mail service is more than adequate. Figure 12.4 demonstrates a dial-up connection to the ISP.

Linux supports PPP as a kernel function. The `pppd` program supplements the kernel PPP functionality to provide PPP support.

All Linux distributions include the `pppd` program as a binary distribution. Once the `pppd` program is installed, you can configure it to connect to the ISP mail server via a dial-up modem at predetermined intervals. The following sections describe configuring the `pppd` program to connect with the ISP mail server.

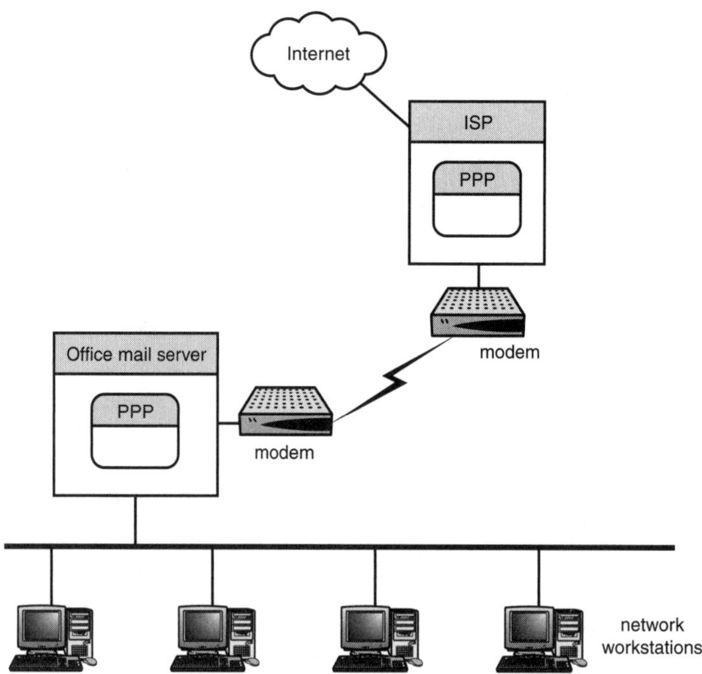

FIGURE 12.4

Dial-up connectivity to the ISP.

Connectivity

The `pppd` program uses a standard modem to connect with the remote ISP mail server. The format of the `pppd` program is

```
pppd <tty line> <speed> [options]
```

where *<tty line>* is the COM port where your modem is connected, and *<speed>* is the speed at which you want to connect to the modem. The art of using the `pppd` program comes in choosing the proper options for the client and server commands. Here are some of the options available to use `pppd` as a client:

- The `connect` option allows the `pppd` program to use an executable or shell script to set up the serial link before the `pppd` program will attempt to connect.
- The `crtscts` option uses RTS/CTS hardware flow control on the serial line.
- The `defaultroute` option adds a default route to the kernel routing table pointing to the remote IP address of the PPP server. The route table entry is deleted when the PPP session is terminated. This allows the server to know to send IP traffic destined for other network devices out the PPP connection.

- The `lock` option creates a UUCP-style lock file to indicate that the modem is in use.
- The `mru` and `mtu` options allow the client to attempt to set the Maximum Receive Unit (mru) and Maximum Transmit Unit (mtu) sizes during the PPP negotiation phase. It is still up to the PPP server to agree to the new sizes. Often this is used on slower modem connections to reduce the PPP packet size.
- The `modem` option allows the Unix system to use the modem control lines. With this option, the `pppd` program will wait for the CD (carrier detect) modem signal when opening the modem line, and will drop DTR (data terminal ready) briefly when the PPP connection is terminated.

The `pppd` program uses the `connect` option to establish the modem connection with the remote ISP. Usually this option utilizes the `chat` program to dial the modem to establish the connection.

The `chat` program is a part of the `pppd` distribution and simplifies the connect string for `pppd`. The chat program can use a simple script file and communicate with the modem to initiate the connection with the PPP server. The chat script uses text strings that it can send to the remote server in response to text strings received. It tries to match the text strings in a "chat" session, one response for each string received. Listing 12.1 shows an example of a sample chat script used for `pppd`. Line numbers have been added to clarify the description. They are not part of the actual script file.

LISTING 12.1 Sample Chat Script `isp.chat`

```
1  ""
2  ATDT5551234
3  CONNECT
4  ""
5  "ogin:"
6  rich
7  "word:"
8  guitar
9  "$"
10 "exec /usr/sbin/pppd silent modem crtscts proxyarp 10.0.0.100:10.0.0.2"
```

Line 2 shows the command that `pppd` will send to the modem to dial the ISP phone number. Line 3 shows what text string `pppd` should wait for to establish that a connection has been made to the PPP server. Line 4 indicates that, when the chat program receives a connection notice from the modem, it should send a single carriage return. Line 5 shows what text string to wait for from the server. If the server is allowing terminal logins from this modem line, it should issue a welcome banner with a login prompt. In line 6, `pppd` sends the userid to the PPP server, and in line 8 it sends the password. When `pppd` gets a command prompt from the PPP server (as shown in line 9), it then issues the host `pppd` command on the PPP server. The correct program and parameters used in this command line are unique to your ISP and should be provided by the ISP. Most ISPs provide simple batch files for clients to use.

Once you have created a successful chat script, you can use it in the `pppd` configuration to dial the ISP mail server when the `pppd` program executes. The `connect pppd` option calls the chat script using the following format:

```
pppd ttyS1 38400 connect '/usr/sbin/chat -v -f /home/rich/isp.chat' modem
➥ crtscts defaultroute
```

The `connect` option uses the chat program in its script to connect to the PPP server. The preceding command line will automatically call the PPP server and start the `pppd` program on the remote server. The `-v` option used in the chat program allows for extremely verbose output to the `/var/log/messages` file. Use this for testing purposes and then remove it when you have all the bugs worked out. Listing 12.2 shows the lines that the `pppd` and `chat` programs place in the message log during a client PPP session.

LISTING 12.2 Lines from `/var/log/messsage` for `pppd` and `chat`

```
Sep 22 06:56:56 shadrach pppd[663]: pppd 2.3.5 started by root, uid 0
Sep 22 06:56:56 shadrach kernel: registered device ppp0
Sep 22 06:56:57 shadrach chat[664]: send (ATZS7=100^M)
Sep 22 06:56:57 shadrach chat[664]: expect (OK)
Sep 22 06:56:57 shadrach chat[664]: ATZS7=100^M^M
Sep 22 06:56:57 shadrach chat[664]: OK
Sep 22 06:56:57 shadrach chat[664]:  -- got it
Sep 22 06:56:57 shadrach chat[664]: send (ATDT5551234^M)
Sep 22 06:56:58 shadrach chat[664]: expect (CONNECT)
Sep 22 06:56:58 shadrach chat[664]: ^M
Sep 22 06:57:18 shadrach chat[664]: ATDT5551234^M^M
Sep 22 06:57:18 shadrach chat[664]: CONNECT
Sep 22 06:57:18 shadrach chat[664]:  -- got it
Sep 22 06:57:18 shadrach chat[664]: send (^M)
Sep 22 06:57:18 shadrach chat[664]: expect (ogin:)
Sep 22 06:57:18 shadrach chat[664]:  28800/V42BIS^M
Sep 22 06:57:19 shadrach chat[664]: ^M
Sep 22 06:57:19 shadrach chat[664]: ^MRed Hat Linux release 5.2 (Apollo)
Sep 22 06:57:19 shadrach chat[664]: ^MKernel 2.0.36 on an i486
Sep 22 06:57:19 shadrach chat[664]: ^M
Sep 22 06:57:19 shadrach chat[664]: ^M^M
Sep 22 06:57:19 shadrach chat[664]: mail1.isp.net login:
Sep 22 06:57:19 shadrach chat[664]:  -- got it
Sep 22 06:57:19 shadrach chat[664]: send (rich^M)
Sep 22 06:57:19 shadrach chat[664]: expect (word:)
Sep 22 06:57:19 shadrach chat[664]:  rich^M
Sep 22 06:57:19 shadrach chat[664]: Password:
```

LISTING 12.2 Continued

```
Sep 22 06:57:19 shadrach chat[664]:  -- got it
Sep 22 06:57:19 shadrach chat[664]: send (guitar^M)
Sep 22 06:57:20 shadrach chat[664]: expect (rich]$)
Sep 22 06:57:20 shadrach chat[664]:  ^M
Sep 22 06:57:20 shadrach chat[664]: Last login: Tue Sep 21 20:45:47^M
Sep 22 06:57:21 shadrach chat[664]: [rich@mail1 rich]$
Sep 22 06:57:21 shadrach chat[664]:  -- got it
Sep 22 06:57:21 shadrach chat[664]: send (exec /usr/sbin/pppd
➥ passive silent modem crtscts^M)
Sep 22 06:57:22 shadrach pppd[663]: Serial connection established.
Sep 22 06:57:23 shadrach pppd[663]: Using interface ppp0
Sep 22 06:57:23 shadrach pppd[663]: Connect: ppp0 <--> /dev/ttyS1
Sep 22 06:57:27 shadrach pppd[663]: local  IP address 10.0.0.100
Sep 22 06:57:27 shadrach pppd[663]: remote IP address 10.0.0.2
```

Using the `chat` script and the `pppd` client commands establishes a PPP session with the ISP mail server. The next step is to create a method to establish the connection with the ISP on a regular basis. The Unix `cron` program is just the answer.

Paul Vixie developed the `cron` program that most Linux systems use. It reads a configuration file that contains commands and times that the commands should be executed. When the specified times are reached, the commands are executed.

You can use the `crontab` program to access the `cron` configuration file. To list the contents of your crontab, use the `-l` parameter. To edit the contents, use the `-e` parameter. This brings the crontab up using the vi editor.

Crontab entries use the following format:

```
min hour daym month dayw program
```

The first five placeholders represent the time(s) that the `program` parameter should be run. Table 12.1 shows the time values represented by the placeholders.

TABLE 12.1 Crontab Time Placeholders

Placeholder	*Description*
`min`	The minute of the day
`hour`	The hour of the day
`daym`	The day of the month
`month`	The month
`dayw`	The day of the week

Wildcards and ranges are allowed in defining the times the program should run. For example, using the * wildcard character defines all values for the placeholder. Ranges such as 1–5 or 1,4,5 define specific times the program should be run. For example, the entry

```
0,15,30,45 * * * * /home/rich/dialup
```

runs the script /home/rich/dialup every 15 minutes of every hour of every day of every month. This is exactly what you need for the pppd program to dial the ISP on a regular basis.

Due to the large command-line entry for the pppd program, it is often beneficial to create a script with the pppd program and its parameters, and use the script for the crontab entry.

CAUTION

Be careful with permissions of the script file as well as the pppd program. Remember to set the executable permissions of the script to allow the userid that runs the crontab to execute the script file.

You may have to experiment with the frequency of running the pppd program to balance efficient mail transfer with needless phone calls. Often it is best to have several different crontab entries covering different times of the day and week. Although dialing the ISP every 15 minutes is good during business hours, it is wasteful at 1 o'clock in the morning. Here's an example of a multi-entry crontab:

```
0,15,30,45 8-17 * * 1-5 /home/rich/dialup
0,30 0-7,18-23 * * 1-5 /home/rich/dialup
0,30 * * * 6,7 /home/rich/dialup
```

The first entry starts the pppd connection every 15 minutes between 8 a.m. and 5 p.m. every Monday through Friday. The second entry starts pppd every half hour between midnight and 7 a.m., and 6 p.m. through midnight every Monday through Friday. The last entry starts pppd every half hour on Saturdays and Sundays.

Postfix Configuration

Once you have configured the office e-mail server to dial up the ISP mail server at regular intervals, you must configure the Postfix system to act accordingly. In this scenario, Postfix will forward all outbound messages to the ISP mail server for forwarding to the Internet. Because the connection to the ISP is not available at all times, Postfix must be able to queue the outbound messages in a message queue and then transfer them when the connectivity is present.

As with other Postfix configurations, you must define the destination and origin parameters for the mail server in the main.cf file:

```
mydestination = $myhostname, localhost.$mydomain, $mydomain
myorigin = $mydomain
```

This example demonstrates using the mail server to service all mail for the company domain. Also, you must enter the ISP mail server address as the relay host address to forward all outbound messages to:

```
relayhost = 10.0.0.1
```

Remember that since the mail server is not connected to the ISP full time, it will most likely not have DNS service, thus you must enter the `relayhost` parameter address as a numeric IP address and not as a DNS hostname.

The last two parameters required specify the unique situation for the office e-mail server. By default, Postfix attempts to deliver all messages as they are received. By not being connected to the ISP mail server full time, you must configure the office mail server to defer all outbound messages, placing them in the message queue to wait for the PPP connection. Also, as mentioned in the previous paragraph, the mail server should not use DNS name lookups. So, in the `main.cf` file, set the following parameters:

```
defer_transports = smtp
disable_dns_lookups = yes
```

When the Postfix server is started, you will notice that all messages waiting to be delivered remain in the deferred message queue. You can see this in the Postfix mail log:

```
Nov 13 18:41:22 shadrach postfix/qmgr[8396]: E1C9031FB:
➥ from=<rich@shadrach.ispnet1.net>, size=318, nrcpt=1 (queue active)
Nov 13 18:41:22 shadrach postfix/qmgr[8396]: E1C9031FB:
➥ to=<richard.blum@meshach.ispnet3.net>, relay=none, delay=1,
➥ status=deferred (deferred transport)
```

The Postfix log notes that the message was sent using a deferred transport, and the message is placed in the deferred message queue. Once the PPP session with the ISP is established, Postfix must know to empty the deferred queue.

You can do this using the Postfix `sendmail` program. Normally this is installed in the `/usr/sbin` directory. To empty the deferred message queue, you must invoke the `sendmail` program with the `-q` option:

```
/usr/sbin/sendmail -q
```

All messages in the deferred message queue are processed for delivery. You would not want to enter this command every time the PPP link is established. You can add the `sendmail` command to the script that starts the PPP session to automatically flush the deferred message queue when the PPP session is established.

Retrieving Inbound Messages

Messages waiting on the ISP server to be sent to the office mail server can be retrieved using one of several different e-mail packages. One very good package to use is `fetchmail`.

NOTE

Most Linux distributions include the `fetchmail` package. You can download it from the `fetchmail` Web site at `http://www.tuxedo.org/~esr/fetchmail/index.html`.

The `fetchmail` program is extremely versatile in being able to retrieve mail messages from remote mail servers. For this scenario, the `fetchmail` program will be configured to retrieve messages from a single mailbox on the ISP mail server using POP3.

Once `fetchmail` retrieves the mail messages from the ISP mail server, it must be able to parse the RFC822 header fields to determine the local user for which the message is intended. This feature can be configured in the `fetchmail` configuration file.

Each user on the Postfix mail server has a unique `fetchmail` configuration file. The location of the file is `$HOME/.fetchmailrc`. In this scenario, the root user will use a `fetchmail` configuration file that will be set up to log in to the ISP mail server using POP3 with the ISP-assigned userid and password. Also, each local user that will receive mail from the Internet must be defined in the root user's `.fetchmailrc` file. Any mail that is retrieved by `fetchmail` that is not destined for a defined local user will be stored in the mailbox of the userid running the `fetchmail` program (in this case the root user). Listing 12.3 shows a sample `.fetchmailrc` file that can be used for this scenario. Line numbers have been added to help in the explanation of the file. You should not use them in the actual `.fetchmailrc` file.

LISTING 12.3 Sample `$HOME/.fetchmailrc` Configuration File

```
poll mail.isp.net with proto POP3
 localdomains othercompany.com
 no envelope
 no dns
 user "rich" with password "guitar" is
    rich
    barbara
    katie
    jessica
    haley
    riley
    chris
    matthew
 here
```

In Listing 12.3, line 1 defines the ISP mail server that `fetchmail` will connect with to retrieve the domain mail. Line 1 also indicates to use the POP3 protocol for the connection. Lines 2–4 define options that will be used for the connection. Line 2 indicates what domain `fetchmail` will look for as the local domain address in message headers. Thus it will recognize the address `rich@othercompany.com` as the local mail server user `rich`. Line 3 indicates not to use the `X-Envelope-To:` header field to parse the recipient address. These header fields are often added by MTAs as the mail passes from one site to another. They can be confusing to `fetchmail`. Line 4 indicates not to use DNS to confirm the identity of the sending host. Line 5 identifies the ISP mailbox userid and password that `fetchmail` will use to connect to the ISP mail server. These should be provided by your ISP.

Lines 6–13 list all of the local users on the Postfix mail server that can receive mail. `fetchmail` will parse the RFC822 message header fields and look for these usernames. If one is found, `fetchmail` forwards the message to that local user. If the destination user does not match any of the local usernames listed, `fetchmail` delivers the message to the userid that ran `fetchmail` (the root user in this scenario). It is the job of the mail administrator to add new local users to the list. Line 14 indicates that the local usernames are located on the local host on which `fetchmail` is running.

Once you have created the `.fetchmailrc` file and stored it in the `$HOME` directory of the userid that will run `fetchmail` (for this example the root user), you can run the program. By typing *`fetchmail`* on the command line, `fetchmail` should automatically connect to the ISP mail server and download any mail messages waiting in the common ISP mailbox. If this is successful, the next step is to add the `fetchmail` command to the `pppd` startup script to automate the mail retrieval process.

Firewall Internet Mail Server

In this office mail server scenario, the Postfix server runs on the organization's firewall. With the increased concern for security, many organizations are setting up Linux servers as firewalls between their direct connections to the Internet and their internal machines. It is possible to run the Postfix mail server software on the firewall server and configure it to pass mail in and out of the secured network. The firewall mail server must be able to hide the identity of any internal mail servers for which it receives messages. This section describes this process.

Connectivity

The firewall mail server should be connected to the Internet router for the organization and then to the Local Area Network (LAN) of the organization. Figure 12.5 shows a diagram of how a firewall is placed on an office network.

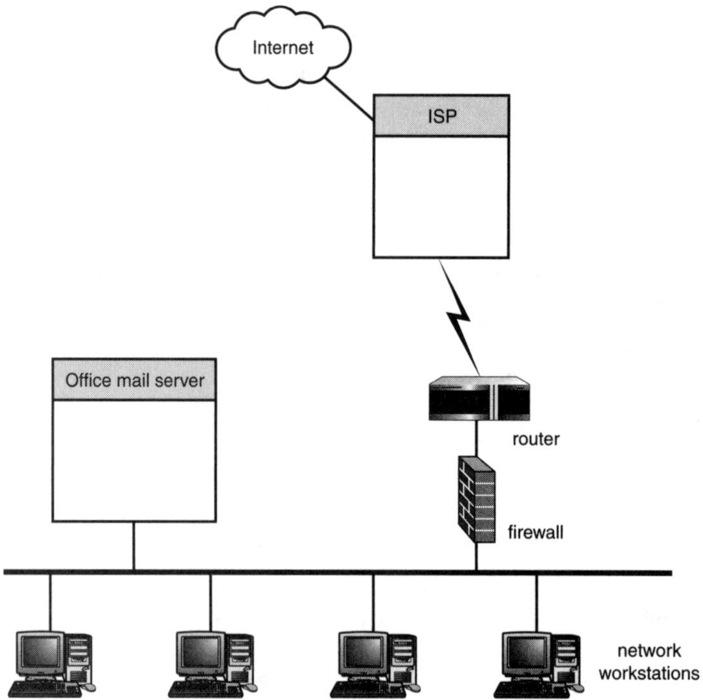

FIGURE 12.5

Using a firewall on a full-time Internet connection.

The firewall should use some kind of packet-filtering software to help prevent external hosts from establishing network connections with internal network hosts. The Linux system uses the `ipchains` software developed and maintained by Rusty Russell. While the main `ipchains` Web site is normally located at

```
http://www.rustcorp.com/linux/ipchains
```

at the time of this writing it is experiencing difficulties. The `ipchains` documentation can be found at several mirror sites, one of which is

```
http://netfilter.filewatcher.org/ipchains/
```

Most Linux distributions that use a version 2.2 or higher kernel include a binary distribution of `ipchains`. The most current version of `ipchains` at the time of this writing is version 1.3.10. It can also be downloaded from the mirror site:

```
http://netfilter.filewatcher.org/ipchains/ipchains-1.3.10.tar.gz
```

Once downloaded it can be unpacked and compiled to create the binary executable file `ipchains`.

The `ipchains` program uses the concept of chaining rules together to filter packets as they pass through the Linux server. Figure 12.6 is an illustration of how the chains are configured.

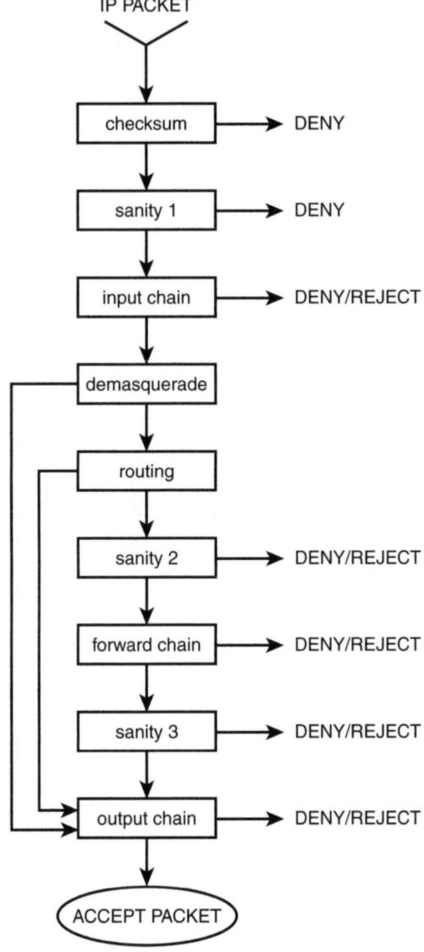

FIGURE 12.6

`ipchains` rule processing.

The processes shown in Figure 12.6 control how packets are processed in the Linux server. Table 12.2 describes these processes.

TABLE 12.2 `ipchains` Packet Filtering Processes

Process	*Description*
checksum	Checks for corrupted packets
sanity 1	Checks for malformed packets
input chain	Firewall input chain check
demasquerade	If reply to a masqueraded packet, must be converted back to original packet address
routing	Destination checked to see if it is local or needs to be forwarded
sanity 2	Checks for malformed packets
forward chain	Firewall forward chain check
sanity 3	Checks for malformed packets
output chain	Firewall output chain check

The packet must successfully pass each of the appropriate processes listed in Table 12.2 before it is accepted to be either processed on the local host or forwarded to a remote host.

The input, forward, and output chains use rules that are set in the NAT table by the `ipchains` program. The format of the `ipchains` command varies depending on the category that is used. The formats that ipchains can use are

```
ipchains -[ADC] chain rule-specification [options]
ipchains -[RI] chain rulenum rule-specification [options]
ipchains -D chain rulenum [options]
ipchains -[LFZNX] [chain] [options]
ipchains -P chain target [options]
ipchains -M [ -L | -S ] [options]
```

The first parameter is the command that controls the function that `ipchains` performs. Table 12.3 lists the commands available to use.

TABLE 12.3 `ipchains` Command Types

Command	*Description*
`-A`	Appends one or more rules
`-D`	Deletes one or more rules
`-C`	Checks the packet against selected chain
`-R`	Replaces a rule in the selected chain
`-I`	Inserts one or more rules as the given rule number
`-L`	Lists all rules in selected chain
`-F`	Flushes the selected chain
`-Z`	Zeros the counters for all chains
`-N`	Creates a new user-defined chain
`-X`	Deletes selected user-defined chain

TABLE 12.3 Continued

Command	*Description*
`-P`	Sets the policy for the chain
`-M`	Views the current masqueraded connections

The next parameter is the chain name. This can be either one of the system chains (input, output, or forward) or a user-defined chain name that was created using the `-N` command. User-defined chains are often used to help simplify complex rules.

The rule specification consists of parameters that specify the actions taken in the rule. Table 12.4 lists the parameters that are available.

TABLE 12.4 `ipchains` Parameter Types

Parameter	*Description*
`-p protocol`	The protocol to check
`-s address[/mask]`	Source address to check
`--source-port port`	Source port to check
`-d address[/mask]`	Destination address to check
`--destination-port`	Destination port to check
`--icmp-type`	ICMP type to check
`-j target`	Target to jump to if packet matches
`-i name`	Interface name
`-f`	Rule refers to fragment packets

The `-j` option can jump to six special targets when a packet matches the rule. Table 12.5 lists the targets that are available.

TABLE 12.5 `ipchains` Target Types

Target	*Description*
`ACCEPT`	Allows packet to pass
`DENY`	Prevents packet from passing
`REJECT`	Prevents packet from passing and returns ICMP error to sender
`MASQ`	Masquerades forward packets
`REDIRECT`	Sends packet to local port instead of destination
`RETURN`	Drops out of chain immediately

Besides parameters, you can use additional options to further define the rule. Table 12.6 lists the options that are available.

TABLE 12.6 ipchains Option Types

Option	*Description*
`-b`	Bidirectional mode
`-v`	Verbose output
`-n`	Numeric output
`-l`	Turn on logging
`-o [maxsize]`	Copy matching packets to userspace device
`-m markvalue`	Mark matching packets
`-t andmask xormask`	Masks used to modify the TOS field
`-x`	Expand numbers
`-y`	Only match TCP packets with SYN set and ACK and FIN cleared

As you enter each `ipchains` command, the NAT table is modified accordingly. When the server is rebooted, the NAT table resets and any changes made previously are lost. To solve this problem, `ipchains` uses two script files to save the NAT table in a file that can be read back into the NAT table at boot time.

Use the `ipchains-save` script to save the existing NAT table configuration into a file specified. The format of the `ipchains-save` command is

```
ipchains-save > filename
```

where *`filename`* is the name of the file where you want to save the NAT table configuration. You must be logged in as the `root` user to execute this command. To restore the NAT table, you can create an initialization script that uses the `ipchains-restore` script. The format of the `ipchains-restore` command is

```
ipchains-restore < filename
```

where *`filename`* is the full pathname of the location where the original NAT table configuration was stored. Again, you should run this command as the `root` user, preferably during the server initialization scripts.

Listing 12.4 shows an example of `ipchains` commands that you can use to enable masquerading and basic firewalling on a Linux server.

LISTING 12.4 Sample `ipchains` Commands for a Firewall

```
/sbin/ipchains -P forward DENY
/sbin/ipchains -A forward -i ppp0 -j MASQ
/sbin/ipchains -A input -I ppp0 --destination-port 25 -y -j ACCEPT
/sbin/ipchains -A input -i ppp0 -l -y -j DENY
```

In Listing 12.4, the first line sets the default policy for the forward chain to deny. The second line appends a rule to the forward chain. Any packets forwarded to the `ppp0` interface are passed to the masquerading target first. The masquerading feature allows internal hosts to connect with external hosts using the firewall's IP address. This assumes that the `ppp0` line is the connection to the ISP. The third and fourth lines add the firewall features.

The third line allows connection requests on port 25 for external hosts. This enables hosts to send mail messages to the firewall mail server.

The last command denies any remaining TCP SYN packet coming into the input chain on the `ppp0` interface. Assuming that the `ppp0` interface is the Linux server's connection to the ISP, this prevents Internet hosts from establishing connections with hosts on the office network. The use of the `-l` option allows any connection attempt to be logged in the kernel log file. By carefully monitoring the log files, the system administrator can detect unauthorized attempts by hackers to connect to internal workstations and hosts.

CAUTION

The `ipchains` scenario shown here is just an example. Firewalls and network security are complex topics that this section does not fully explore. If you are implementing a firewall solution for your network, please consult appropriate network security documents to ensure your network has the highest possible security protection.

Postfix Configuration

The Postfix configuration for the firewall mail server is similar to a domain mail server, except that all messages received by the firewall-based mail server must be forwarded to an internal mail gateway server for delivery. For security reasons, no users should be allowed to connect to the firewall mail server to retrieve messages, nor should the firewall mail server accept any messages for itself.

For this configuration, the standard `main.cf` parameters, `mydestination` and `myhostname`, are set to the normal mail server name. To configure Postfix not to accept any messages, you must trick it a little. Normally the `relay_domains` parameter informs Postfix what hosts it will receive messages for. By explicitly setting this value to nothing, Postfix refuses to accept messages for any host, including itself. Thus, the parameter in the `main.cf` file would look like this:

```
relay_domains =
```

Note that there is only a carriage return after the `=` sign. Now that the Postfix server does not accept mail messages for local delivery, you must configure it to pass along messages to the internal mail gateway server. You can do this using a `transport` table with a single line:

```
othercompany.com smtp:internal.othercompany.com
```

This line configures the Postfix transport to receive messages for the domain `othercompany.com`. When messages are received, they are immediately sent using the SMTP transport to the `internal.othercompany.com` mail server inside the firewall.

Once the transport table is created an indexed binary database file must be created using the `postmap` utility

```
postmap hash:/etc/postfix/transport
```

and the `main.cf` configuration file must be modified to point to the new transport lookup table:

```
transport_maps = hash:/etc/postfix/transport
```

After issuing the Postfix `reload` command, the new firewall mail server should accept messages for the `othercompany.com` domain and forward them to the internal mail server. The mail administrator can then configure the `internal.othercompany.com` mail server to receive and deliver messages for the `othercompany.com` domain.

Special Mail Situations

Supporting mail in an office environment is not a simple task. Often, special circumstances require special configurations. This section describes two "special" situations that some office mail administrators run into: host address masquerading and using special mail address names.

Address Masquerading

In larger offices, it is sometimes beneficial to split the mail server functions into several small servers rather than having one large server. The idea behind the multiple mail-server network is that one server still acts as the central e-mail hub, while other servers can support clients connecting in to read and send mail messages. The role of the central e-mail hub is to gather all incoming and outgoing messages and ensure they get to the right address.

This does take some load off of the main mail server, but unless you are dealing with thousands of users, it is usually more of a hassle than a benefit. Of course there are times when multiple e-mail servers are a result of political reasons rather than technical reasons. Figure 12.7 shows an example of a multi-server e-mail network. The mail hub receives all messages from the Internet via the ISP mail server and forwards them to the appropriate mail spoke server. Conversely, each mail spoke server must forward any Internet mail to the mail hub.

The main mail server will still use a standard Postfix configuration to connect to the ISP to transfer mail destined for the Internet.

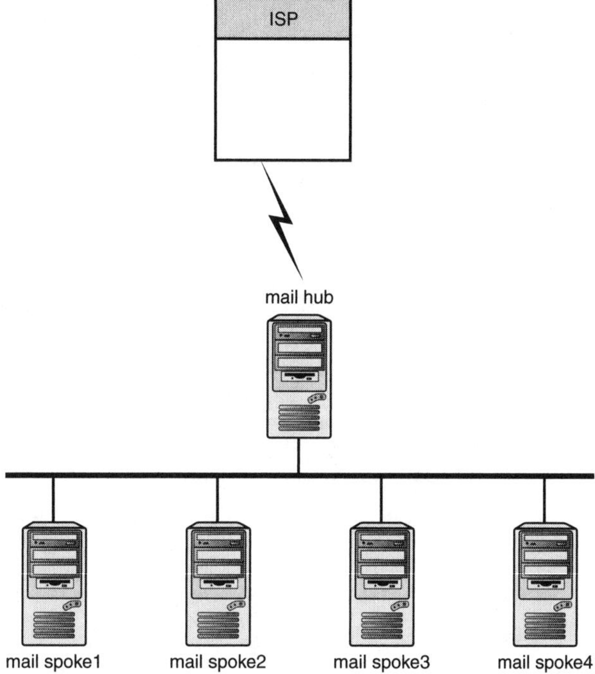

FIGURE 12.7

Multi-server e-mail network.

Each of the individual "spoke" mail servers should be configured in the `main.cf` configuration file to use the main hub mail server as its smart host, as well as use the normal `myorigin` parameter to change the return address of users to match the domain name:

```
relay_host = hub.smallorg.org
myorigin = smallorg.org
```

Using this configuration simplifies outbound messages in that no matter which spoke server the user is located on, the return e-mail address will always be the same (assuming that no two spoke servers have the same username). However, in this scenario inbound messages become a problem.

For example, suppose that a spoke mail server called `spoke1.smallorg.org` has a user called `fred` on it. All outbound messages from `spoke1.smallorg.org` have been configured to go through the hub mail server (and then on to the ISP for delivery). By using the domain name for the `myorigin` parameter, the return address for `fred` will be `fred@smallorg.org`, no matter from which spoke the mail originates. Figure 12.8 demonstrates this example.

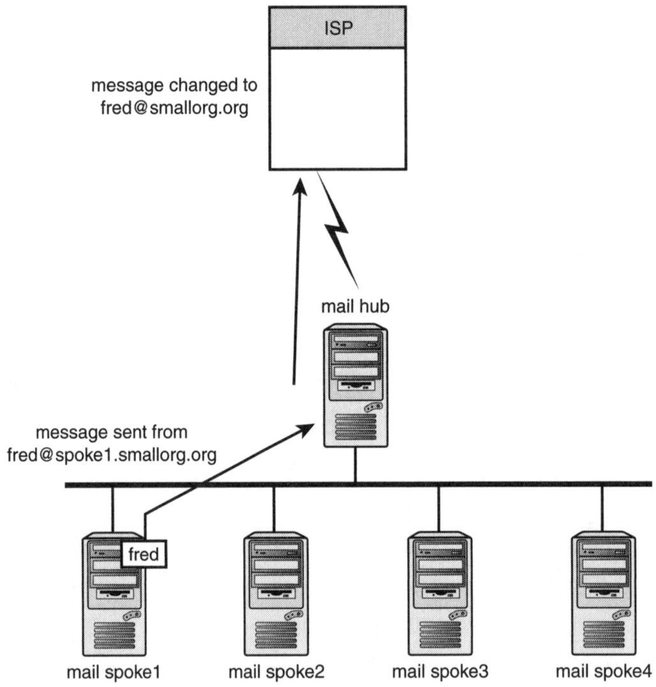

FIGURE 12.8

Example of outbound messages from a spoke mail server.

So far, so good. The outbound message is passed from the spoke server to the main hub server, to the ISP, out to the Internet. Now, what about the return inbound message? Assume for this scenario that the DNS mail record for the domain points to the main hub mail server. Once the main hub mail server receives the message, it must determine which spoke mail server it should be forwarded to. If the main hub cannot determine on which spoke mail server the user is located, it must bounce the message back to the sender. Figure 12.9 demonstrates this scenario.

If the incoming reply message were addressed to `fred@spoke1.smallorg.org`, the main hub's job would be easy: just forward the message to the `spoke1.smallorg.org` server where the user `fred` is located.

However, in this example (and in real life), the return message is addressed to `fred@smallorg.org`. The main hub (`hub.smallorg.org`) is set to receive messages for `smallorg.org`. Because it thinks that it is the `smallorg.org` domain, it assumes that `frank` must be a local user on `hub.smallorg.org`. Of course this is not the case, so the message will be returned as being undeliverable. Ouch.

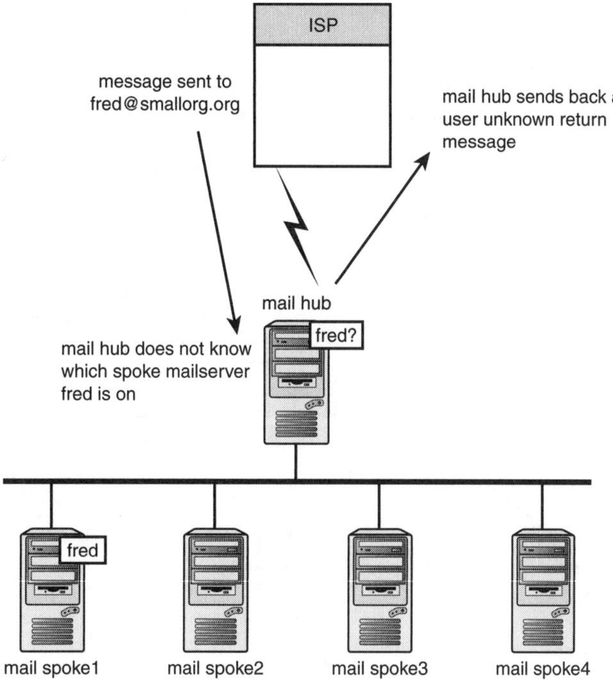

FIGURE 12.9

Example of inbound messages for a spoke mail server user.

One way to solve this problem is to use the `aliases` file on `hub.smallorg.org`. By entering an alias for `fred` and pointing it to `fred@spoke1.smallorg.org`, the return message will get to the proper mail server for `fred` to be able to read it. Although this method works, it tends to be a little clunky. By utilizing another feature of Postfix called *virtual hosting*, we can get `fred`'s mail forwarded to the proper spoke mail server, and then hopefully to `fred`'s mailbox.

Virtual Hosting

The `virtual` table is a lookup table that allows Postfix to redirect inbound mail messages. This table is similar to the `aliases` file, but is more robust in its options. Figure 12.10 demonstrates how the `virtual` user table operates.

First, you must add a new parameter in the `main.cf` configuration file for the main hub mail server. To use virtual hosting you need to add the `virtual` lookup table parameter. It should look like this:

```
virtual_maps = hash:/etc/postfix/virtual
```

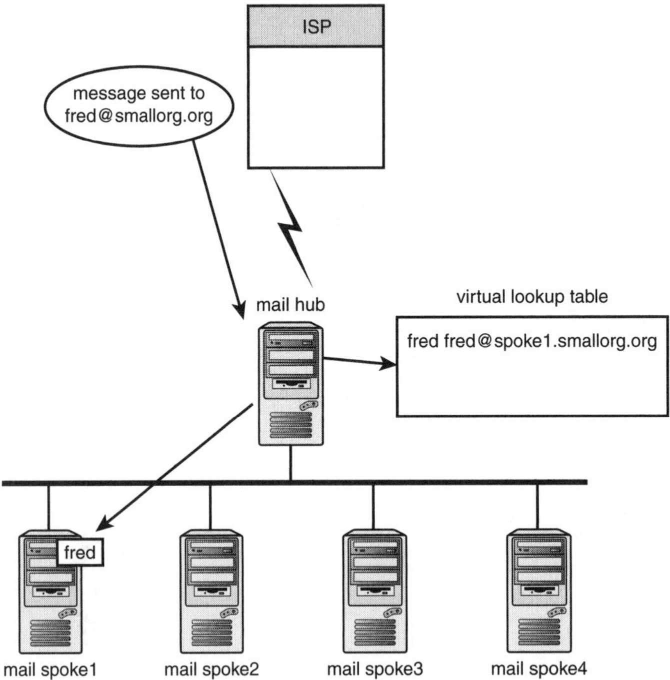

FIGURE 12.10

Mail forwarding using the `virtual` user table.

The next step is to create the `virtual` lookup table that will direct Postfix how to forward messages. Again, much like the `aliases` file, the virtual users file is a text file that must be converted into an indexed binary database file.

You can create the text version of the file at

```
/etc/postfix/virtual
```

Each mail user should be listed on a separate line. The format of the `virtual` lookup table is

```
virtaddress realaddress
```

where *`virtaddress`* is the virtual user address that Postfix will receive messages for, and *`realaddress`* is the actual address that it will forward the message to. Listing 12.5 shows an example of a virtual user lookup table.

LISTING 12.5 Sample `/etc/postfix/virtual` File

```
fred@smallorg.org fred@spoke1.smallorg.org
melanie@smallorg.org melanie@spoke1.smallorg.org
haley@smallorg.org haley@spoke2.smallorg.org
riley@smallorg.org riley@spoke2.smallorg.org
katie@smallorg.org katie@spoke3.smallorg.org
jessica@smallorg.org jessica@spoke3.smallorg.org
rich@smallorg.org rich
barbara@smallorg.org barbara
```

In Listing 12.5, lines 1 and 2 demonstrate users who are on the `spoke1.smallorg.org` mail server. When the main hub mail server receives a message destined for `fred@smallorg.org`, it is automatically forwarded to `fred@spoke1.smallorg.org`.

Similarly, in lines 3 and 4 users on the `spoke2.smallorg.org` server also receive their Internet mail via the hub mail server. This continues for all of the spoke servers in the local network. Each time a new user is added to a spoke server, a new user entry must be added to the `virtual` lookup table. Also remember that no two spokes can use the same username.

Lines 7 and 8 are a little different. They demonstrate deliberately defining local users on the `hub.smallorg.org` mail server. By default, if a username does not appear in the `virtual` lookup table, Postfix assumes that it is a local user. Lines 7 and 8 are therefore unnecessary, but sometimes it helps to include obvious things for documentation purposes.

After the `/etc/postfix/virtual` file is created, it must be converted into the indexed binary database format that Postfix uses. The `postmap` program is used for this:

```
postmap hash:/etc/postfix/virtual
```

Each time the `virtual` user table is changed, the `postmap` program must be rerun to re-create the binary database file. Using this technique, the mail administrator can distribute users in the organization across several small mail servers, each feeding into one central mail server.

Fancy Mail Addresses

One limitation to using Unix mail servers is the system usernames. Unfortunately, most Unix systems limit the format of a system username to eight characters. While this is fine for most applications, sometimes customers want to use fancier e-mail addresses. One common format is to use the user's full name, such as

```
Firstname.Lastname@othercompany.com.
```

Postfix can accommodate fancy e-mail addresses by mapping them back to a specified system username. By mapping the fancy e-mail address to the username, Postfix can still utilize the normal mailbox methods on the Unix system. You can use several methods to accomplish this.

The simplest method is to use the Postfix aliases and canonical lookup tables. The aliases lookup table maps the fancy e-mail address to a normal system username. The canonical table allows the cleanup program to change all occurrences of the normal system username to the fancy e-mail address.

First, the mail administrator must create the text aliases lookup table that maps fancy e-mail addresses to system usernames:

```
Richard.Blum: rich
Barbara.Blum: barbara
Katie.Blum: katie
Jessica.Blum: jessica
```

After the aliases lookup table is created, it must be converted to the indexed binary database file using postalias:

```
postalias hash:/etc/postfix/aliases
```

Then the main.cf configuration file must be modified to point to the aliases file:

```
aliases_maps = hash:/etc/postfix/aliases
```

Next, the mail administrator must create the text canonical file that contains the fancy e-mail addresses:

```
rich Richard.Blum
barbara Barbara.Blum
katie Katie.Blum
jessica Jessica.Blum
```

After the text file is created, it must be converted to an indexed binary database file using the postmap utility:

```
postmap hash:/etc/postfix/canonical
```

After the indexed binary database file is created, the main.cf configuration file must be modified to point to the new canonical lookup table:

```
canonical_maps = hash:/etc/postfix/canonical
```

After issuing the postfix reload command, the new e-mail address mappings should take effect:

```
$ mail Richard.Blum
Subject: fancy email address test
This is a test message.
```

```
.
EOT

$ mail
Mail version 8.1 6/6/93.  Type ? for help.
"/var/mail/rich": 1 message 1 new
>N  1 Richard.Blum@shadrac  Wed Nov 15 12:47  13/523   "fancy email address t"
&1
Message 1:
From Richard.Blum@shadrach.ispnet1.net  Wed Nov 15 12:47:28 2000
To: Richard.Blum@shadrach.ispnet1.net
Subject: fancy email address test
Date: Wed, 15 Nov 2000 12:47:28 -0500 (EST)
From: Richard.Blum@shadrach.ispnet1.net (Rich Blum)

This is a test message.

&
```

As you can see, the Postfix server recognized the mail user `Richard.Blum`, and forwarded the message to the standard user `rich` as set in the `aliases` lookup table. Notice in the mail header that both the sender and recipient addresses have been changed by the `canonical` lookup table entry. This enables the normal system user `rich` to send messages using his fancy e-mail address.

Summary

Postfix can use several different configurations to meet the requirements of different e-mail environments. You can configure Postfix to work as a `nullclient` workstation mail server, forwarding all messages to a central mail hub. You can also configure Postfix as the central mail hub for an intranet.

If you want to connect the office mail server to the Internet, you can use Postfix in several different configurations. Offices with full-time connections to the Internet can use Postfix to receive all messages for the domain name. Offices with dial-up connectivity to an ISP can use Postfix to connect to the ISP and transfer outbound messages for the domain, and retrieve any inbound messages.

You can also use Postfix as a firewall mail server by allowing it to forward all inbound messages to a mail server inside the firewalled network. Finally, you can use Postfix to accommodate special mail situations, such as using Postfix as a central hub for several server spokes within the organization and using fancy e-mail addresses.

CHAPTER 13

Postfix Server Administration

Once the Postfix software is installed and configured you should have a fully operational e-mail server. Now your job is done...wrong. There are many tasks that the mail administrator must do to ensure that the mail server is operating properly, and that no attempts are being made to compromise the system.

This chapter outlines two duties that are essential for mail administrators: monitoring system logs and controlling unsolicited commercial e-mail (UCE). Both of these functions are necessary to keep the mail server running smoothly.

The Unix `syslogd` Program

A Unix system has the capability to track events that occur on the system and log messages for each event in system log files. The program that handles this is the `syslogd` program. As the mail administrator you should be able to locate the log files and track any problems that may appear in the log files. You should get in the habit of scanning through the log files at least once a day to watch for possible system or security problems.

This section describes the `syslogd` program and how to configure it to log events in log files.

`syslogd` Parameters

The command syntax of `syslogd` varies on different Unix systems. For Linux systems, the command syntax is

```
syslogd [  -a socket ] [ -d ] [ -f config ] [ -h ] [ -l hostlist ]
➥ [ -m interval ] [ -n ] [ -p socket ] [ -r  ] [ -s domainlist ] [ -v ]
```

Table 13.1 describes the options available for the Linux version of `syslogd`.

TABLE 13.1 `syslogd` Options

Option	*Description*
`-a socket`	Specifies additional sockets to listen to for remote connections.
`-d`	Turns on debugging mode.
`-f config`	Uses the configuration file specified by `config`.
`-h`	Forwards any remote messages to forwarding hosts.
`-l hostlist`	Specifies a list of hosts that are logged only by hostname.
`-m interval`	Sets the MARK timestamp interval in the log file. Setting to 0 disables the timestamp.
`-n`	Avoids auto-backgrounding.
`-p socket`	Specifies an alternative socket on which to listen for remote syslog connections.
`-r`	Enables receiving remote syslog connections.
`-s domainlist`	Specifies a list of domain names that will be stripped off before logging.
`-v`	Prints syslogd version and exits.

The syslogd program is normally started at boot time by an init script and quietly runs in background mode. Most Unix distributions start syslogd by default. You can check to see whether syslogd is running on your Unix system by using the command

```
ps ax | grep syslogd
```

The syslogd program should show up in the list of processes running on your system. When syslogd starts, it reads a configuration file to determine what types of messages to log and how to log them. The next section describes the format of the syslogd configuration file.

syslogd Configuration File

The syslogd configuration file is located by default at /etc/syslog.conf. It contains directives that instruct the syslogd program on what types of events to log and how (and where) to log them. syslogd can log many types of events, as shown in Table 13.2.

TABLE 13.2 syslogd Event Types

Event	*Description*
auth	Security/authorization events
authpriv	Private security/authorization events
cron	Cron daemon events
daemon	System daemon events
kern	System kernel events
lpr	Line printer events
mail	Mail program events
mark	Internal check
news	Network News program events
syslog	Internal syslogd events
user	User-level events
uucp	UUCP program events
local*n*	Locally defined events (*n* = 0–7)

Each event type has a hierarchy of message priorities. Lower priorities mean smaller problems. Higher priorities mean bigger problems. Table 13.3 shows the event priorities that are available.

TABLE 13.3 `syslogd` Message Priorities

Priority	*Description*
`debug`	Debugging events
`info`	Informational events
`notice`	Normal notices
`warning`	Warning messages
`err`	Error condition events
`crit`	Critical system conditions
`alert`	System alerts
`emerg`	Fatal system conditions

In Table 13.3, the events are prioritized from `debug` having the lowest priority to `emerg` having the highest priority.

The format of the `/etc/syslog.conf` file is

```
event.priority        action
```

Each line in the `/etc/syslog.conf` file represents different actions. There are three actions that can be taken for events:

- Displaying the event message to the system console
- Logging the event message to a log file
- Sending the event message to a remote log host

The `syslogd` configuration file consists of combinations of events and actions that define the characteristics of the `syslogd` program. This is best explained by an example. Listing 13.1 shows a sample `/etc/syslog.conf` file from a Mandrake Linux server. Line numbers have been added to the normal file for explanation purposes.

LISTING 13.1 Sample `/etc/syslog.conf` File

```
# Log all kernel messages to the console.
# Logging much else clutters up the screen.
kern.*                          /dev/console

# Log anything(except mail) of level info or higher.
# Don't log private authentication messages!
*.info;mail.none;authpriv.none              /var/log/messages

# The authpriv file has restricted access.
authpriv.*                      /var/log/secure

```

LISTING 13.1 Continued

```
12 # Log all the mail messages in one place.
13 mail.*                          /var/log/maillog
14
15 # Everybody gets emergency messages, plus log them on another
16 # machine.
17 *.emerg                         *
18 *.emerg                         @meshach.ispnet1.net
19
20 # Save mail and news errors of level err and higher in a
21 # special file.
22 uucp,news.crit                           /var/log/spooler
```

Listing 13.1 shows a typical `/etc/syslog.conf` file from a Linux system. Lines 1 and 2 start off by showing how to use comments within the configuration file. These lines are not processed by `syslogd`.

Line 3 is an example of using wildcard characters in the configuration. This indicates that all kernel event messages of any priority will be sent to the system console.

Line 7 is a good example of a complex configuration. Multiple events can be configured for a single action line. A semicolon is used to separate event and priority pairs. The first pair is `*.info`. This defines all events of priority informational and higher. It is important to remember that specifying a particular priority also includes the priorities higher in the list.

The second pair, `mail.none`, may look confusing. You might be wondering why a "none" priority is absent from the priorities table. This event pair is excluding all mail events of any priority from the previous definition. The next pair, `authpriv.none`, does the same. This statement in effect logs all events except `mail` and `authpriv` events, of priority informational and higher to the log file `/var/log/messages`.

Lines 10 and 13 define what is happening to the `authpriv` and `mail` events. Line 10 defines that all `authpriv` events of any priority get logged to a separate file, `/var/log/secure`. Similarly, line 13 defines that all mail events of any priority get logged to a separate file named `/var/log/maillog`. This is an extremely handy way of parsing event messages by separating them into their own log files. As the mail administrator, it is a good idea to define a separate place to put all mail-related event messages to make it easier to spot mail problems on the system.

Line 18 shows an example of using a remote syslog server to log messages. Any emergency priority messages are sent to the remote host `meshach.ispnet1.net`. If there is a serious error on the host, you may not get a chance to see the log file on it, so it is often a good idea to send these messages elsewhere (assuming that the serious error does not prevent the system from sending the messages).

NOTE

Besides emergency use, remote host logging is also a good way to log all server activity to help notice log tampering by hackers.

Postfix Logging Formats

Postfix logs messages to the `mail` event types. Most mail administrators prefer to configure `mail` events to a separate log file than other system events. You can do this using the `syslogf.conf` line:

```
mail.*        /var/log/maillog
```

Once this is entered in the `syslogd.conf` file, the `syslogd` program can be restarted using the `SIGHUP` command. On Linux systems you can use the `killall` command:

```
killall -HUP syslogd
```

CAUTION

Do not use the `killall` program on Solaris systems! On Solaris it does what it says—kills all of the running processes. Often it is safer to use the long method of determining the PID of the `syslogd` program (using `ps`) and using the `kill` program on just the single PID.

Postfix Starting Log Entries

When Postfix is started, you will see an entry generated in the log file:

```
Nov 16 12:12:54 shadrach postfix-script: starting the Postfix mail system
Nov 16 12:12:54 shadrach postfix/master[7308]: daemon started
```

If Postfix starts properly, it will indicate so in the log file. Notice that there are three parts of a standard Postfix daemon log entry:

```
program[pid]: text
```

The program that generates the log entry is identified both by name and by process ID (pid). The text part of the log entry describes the action that was taken. In the example, the Postfix `master` program reports that it was properly started using PID 7308.

Postfix Message Entries

Each time Postfix receives or sends a message it is logged in the system log. The mail administrator can watch the log entries to determine whether there is a mail delivery problem.

Under normal conditions, Postfix logs each step of the mail delivery process. Listing 13.2 shows an example of a locally generated and delivered mail message.

LISTING 13.2 Sample Local Mail Message

```
Nov 16 19:30:53 shadrach postfix/pickup[7831]: 1AE24C352: uid=500 from=<rich>

Nov 16 19:30:53 shadrach postfix/cleanup[7836]: 1AE24C352:
➥ message-id=<20001116193052.1AE24C352@shadrach.ispnet1.net>

Nov 16 19:30:53 shadrach postfix/qmgr[7832]: 1AE24C352:
➥ from=<rich@shadrach.ispnet1.net>, size=317, nrcpt=1 (queue active)

Nov 16 19:30:53 shadrach postfix/local[7838]: 1AE24C352:
➥ to=<rich@shadrach.ispnet1.net>, relay=local, delay=1,
➥ status=sent ("|/usr/bin/procmail -a "$EXTENSION"")
```

In the example shown in Listing 13.2, a simple mail message is sent from the local user `rich` to himself. The log entry shows the Postfix `pickup` program recognizing that a new message has been placed in the `maildrop` message queue. The second log entry is from the `cleanup` program, indicating that the message has been processed. Next, the `qmgr` program indicates the specifics of the message (who it is from, the message size, and the number of recipients). Finally, the Postfix `local` program logs the detail of the delivery attempt to the local user. It completes with a status code, `sent`, and the method used to deliver the message (`/usr/bin/procmail`).

When Postfix receives a message from an external host, it logs details about the SMTP connection in the log file. Listing 13.3 shows a sample SMTP session log.

LISTING 13.3 Sample SMTP Session Log

```
Nov 16 19:35:03 shadrach postfix/smtpd[12336]: connect from
➥ meshach.ispnet1.net[192.168.1.10]

Nov 16 19:35:24 shadrach postfix/smtpd[12336]: 4CACE320B:
➥ client=meshach.ispnet1.net[192.168.1.10]

Nov 16 19:36:13 shadrach postfix/cleanup[12337]: 4CACE320B:
➥ message-id=<20001116193524.4CACE320B@shadrach.ispnet1.net>
```

LISTING 13.3 Continued

```
Nov 16 19:36:13 shadrach postfix/qmgr[10900]: 4CACE320B:
➥ from=<rich@meshach.ispnet1.net>, size=417, nrcpt=1 (queue active)

Nov 16 19:36:13 shadrach postfix/local[12339]: 4CACE320B:
➥ to=<rich@shadrach.ispnet1.net>, relay=local, delay=49,
➥ status=sent (mailbox)

Nov 16 19:36:15 shadrach postfix/smtpd[12336]: disconnect from
➥ meshach.ispnet1.net[192.168.1.10]
```

Notice in Listing 13.3 that there are two events logged by Postfix. The `smtpd` program logs the SMTP connection from the remote host. When the host transfers a mail message, it is logged as it passes through standard Postfix processes. Finally, when the remote host disconnects the SMTP session, the `smtpd` program logs the disconnection.

Postfix Error Entries

The Postfix log entries are not only good for seeing what is happening during mail deliveries; they also come in handy when things don't work as planned. Postfix programs generate many good error messages that help the mail administrator determine when things aren't right.

One example of an error condition is when Postfix is looking for a defined lookup table that doesn't exist. Listing 13.4 shows an example of this situation.

LISTING 13.4 Sample Postfix Error Messages

```
Nov 16 19:50:49 shadrach postfix/pickup[12267]: CC85C320B:
➥ uid=1001 from=<rich>
Nov 16 19:50:49 shadrach postfix/cleanup[12374]: CC85C320B:
➥ message-id=<20001116195049.CC85C320B@shadrach.ispnet1.net>
Nov 16 19:50:50 shadrach postfix/qmgr[10900]: CC85C320B:
➥ from=<rich@shadrach.ispnet1.net>, size=338, nrcpt=1 (queue active)
Nov 16 19:50:50 shadrach postfix/local[12376]: fatal: open database
➥ /etc/postfix/aliases.db: No such file or directory
Nov 16 19:50:51 shadrach postfix/qmgr[10900]: warning:
➥ mail_scan_any: got EOF; expected: string
Nov 16 19:50:51 shadrach postfix/master[1776]: warning:
➥ process /usr/libexec/postfix/local pid 12376 exit status 1
Nov 16 19:50:51 shadrach postfix/master[1776]: warning:
➥ /usr/libexec/postfix/local: bad command startup -- throttling
Nov 16 19:50:51 shadrach postfix/qmgr[10900]: warning:
➥ private/local: malformed response
```

Listing 13.4 shows an example of when things go bad. The first few lines start off just fine: the Postfix `pickup`, `cleanup`, and `qmgr` programs are able to do their jobs. The first indication of trouble appears when the Postfix `local` program attempts to deliver the message (shown in bold).

In order for the `local` program to deliver the message, it must check the `aliases` lookup table that was defined in the `main.cf` configuration file. Unfortunately for this mail administrator, the `aliases.db` file does not exist (or at least not where Postfix is looking for it). Once the local program determines there is a problem, it generates an error that is detected by the `qmgr` program, which called the `local` program. The `qmgr` program in turn generates another error log entry, and sends an error to the `master` program. The Postfix `master` program also produces an error log entry for the `qmgr` failure.

In this scenario, five error log entries are generated, although there is only one real problem: the `aliases.db` file was not created. Don't be alarmed when you see multiple error entries in the log file, just calmly walk your way through the messages until you get to the main message that describes the true problem.

NOTE

Chapter 23, "Common Postfix Problems," describes the use of error messages in troubleshooting Postfix in more detail.

Postfix Mail Delivery Problems

In addition to internal Postfix problems, you can use the log entries to watch the status of remotely delivered mail messages. The Postfix `smtp` program logs all remote delivery attempts. If a remote delivery attempt fails, the response code from the remote server is recorded in the log file.

Listing 13.5 shows a successful SMTP session with a remote mail server on the Internet.

LISTING 13.5 Sample Log Entries for SMTP Delivery

```
Nov 16 19:38:07 shadrach postfix/pickup[7831]: 321A6C352: uid=500 from=<rich>

Nov 16 19:38:07 shadrach postfix/cleanup[7965]: 321A6C352:
➥ message-id=<20001116203807.321A6C352@shadrach.ispnet1.net>


Nov 16 19:38:07 shadrach postfix/qmgr[7832]: 321A6C352:
➥ from=<rich@shadrach.ispnet1.net>, size=306, nrcpt=1 (queue active)
```

LISTING 13.5 Continued

```
Nov 16 19:38:07 shadrach postfix/smtp[7967]: 321A6C352:
➥ to=<rich@[192.168.1.1]>, relay=192.168.1.1[192.168.1.1], delay=0,
➥ status=sent (250 Ok: queued as 1C064320A)
```

In Listing 13.5, the final log entry by the `smtp` program shows the status of the remote message. In addition to the status, the SMTP result received from the remote mail server is also recorded. If the message is not delivered, you can contact the mail administrator for the remote system and use the queue number assigned from the SMTP message to track the message on the system.

Often delivery attempts to remote mail servers fail due to network or server problems. Postfix places a failed message in the `deferred` message queue and re-attempts the delivery later. After a specified number of failed delivery attempts, Postfix finally stops attempting to deliver the message. Listing 13.6 shows a failed remote message delivery.

LISTING 13.6 Failed SMTP Delivery Log Entries

```
Nov 16 16:00:27 shadrach postfix/pickup[7831]: 40C94C352: uid=500 from=<rich>

Nov 16 16:00:27 shadrach postfix/cleanup[8069]: 40C94C352:
➥ message-id=<20001116210027.40C94C352@shadrach.ispnet1.net>

Nov 16 16:00:27 shadrach postfix/qmgr[7832]: 40C94C352:
➥ from=<rich@shadrach.ispnet1.net>, size=314, nrcpt=1 (queue active)

Nov 16 16:00:37 shadrach postfix/smtp[8070]: 40C94C352:
➥ to=<fred@meshach.ispnet1.net>, relay=meshach.ispnet1.net[192.168.1.1],
➥ delay=10, status=bounced (host meshach.ispnet1.net[192.168.1.1]
➥ said: 550 <fred@meshach.ispnet1.net>: User unknown)

Nov 16 16:00:37 shadrach postfix/cleanup[8069]: EA9E7C357:
➥ message-id=<20001116210037.EA9E7C357@shadrach.ispnet1.net>

Nov 16 16:00:38 shadrach postfix/qmgr[7832]: EA9E7C357:
➥ from=<>, size=1998, nrcpt=1 (queue active)

Nov 16 16:00:38 shadrach postfix/local[8075]: EA9E7C357:
➥ to=<rich@shadrach.ispnet1.net>, relay=local, delay=1,
➥ status=sent ("|/usr/bin/procmail -a "$EXTENSION"")
```

In Listing 13.6, the log entry from the `smtp` program (shown in bold) reveals what happened to the message sent to the remote user. The status indicates that the remote server did not know the user, so the message bounced. The exact SMTP reply message from the remote server is shown in the log entry. Once Postfix receives the error response, it automatically creates a bounced message and sends it back to the original sender.

Postfix Verbose Entries

Postfix also allows the mail administrator to increase the amount of text placed in the log file from the programs. By increasing the verbose level of a program, it places increasingly more descriptive text in the log.

The configuration file used to define the Postfix program behavior is the `master.cf` file, usually located in the `/etc/postfix` directory. Each program used by Postfix is listed on a separate line in the `master.cf` file.

To increase the descriptive text used in the log file, you can add one or two `-v` options to the program entry in the `master.cf` file:

```
smtp      inet  n   -   n   -   -   smtpd -v
```

It is not advisable to set too many Postfix programs to verbose mode at the same time because adding verbose logging generates lots of additional log entries. Listing 13.7 shows a partial listing of the log entries from the `smtpd` program with one level of verbose logging.

LISTING 13.7 Sample Verbose Logging

```
postfix/smtpd[8172]: watchdog_create: 0x80700c8 18000
postfix/smtpd[8172]: watchdog_stop: 0x80700c8
postfix/smtpd[8172]: watchdog_start: 0x80700c8
postfix/smtpd[8172]: connection established
postfix/smtpd[8172]: master_notify: status 0
postfix/smtpd[8172]: name_mask: resource
postfix/smtpd[8172]: name_mask: software
postfix/smtpd[8172]: > localhost[127.0.0.1]:
➥ 220 shadrach.ispnet1.net ESMTP Postfix
postfix/smtpd[8172]: connect from localhost[127.0.0.1]
postfix/smtpd[8172]: watchdog_pat: 0x80700c8
postfix/smtpd[8172]: < localhost[127.0.0.1]: HELO meshach.ispnet1.net
postfix/smtpd[8172]: > localhost[127.0.0.1]: 250 shadrach.ispnet1.net
postfix/smtpd[8172]: connect from localhost[127.0.0.1]
postfix/smtpd[8172]: watchdog_pat: 0x80700c8
postfix/smtpd[8172]: < localhost[127.0.0.1]: HELO meshach.ispnet1.net
postfix/smtpd[8172]: > localhost[127.0.0.1]: 250 shadrach.ispnet1.net
postfix/smtpd[8172]: watchdog_pat: 0x80700c8
postfix/smtpd[8172]: < localhost[127.0.0.1]: MAIL FROM:
➥ <rich@meshach.ispnet1.net>
```

LISTING 13.7 Continued

```
postfix/smtpd[8172]: extract_addr: input: <rich@meshach.ispnet1.net>
postfix/smtpd[8172]: extract_addr: result: rich@meshach.ispnet1.net
postfix/smtpd[8172]: > localhost[127.0.0.1]: 250 Ok
postfix/smtpd[8172]: watchdog_pat: 0x80700c8
postfix/smtpd[8172]: < localhost[127.0.0.1]: DATA
postfix/smtpd[8172]: > localhost[127.0.0.1]: 354 End data with <CR><LF>.<CR><LF>
postfix/cleanup[8173]: 34869C352:
➥ message-id=<20001116211711.34869C352@shadrach.ispnet1.net>
postfix/smtpd[8172]: mail_scan_any: read integer: 0
postfix/smtpd[8172]: > localhost[127.0.0.1]: 250 Ok: queued as 34869C352
postfix/smtpd[8172]: watchdog_pat: 0x80700c8
postfix/qmgr[8167]: 34869C352:
➥ from=<rich@meshach.ispnet1.net>, size=377, nrcpt=1 (queue active)
postfix/local[8175]: 34869C352:
➥ to=<rich@shadrach.ispnet1.net>, relay=local, delay=21,
➥ status=sent ("|/usr/bin/procmail -a "$EXTENSION"")
postfix/smtpd[8172]: < localhost[127.0.0.1]: QUIT
postfix/smtpd[8172]: > localhost[127.0.0.1]: 221 Bye
postfix/smtpd[8172]: disconnect from localhost[127.0.0.1]
postfix/smtpd[8172]: master_notify: status 1
postfix/smtpd[8172]: connection closed
postfix/smtpd[8172]: watchdog_stop: 0x80700c8
postfix/smtpd[8172]: watchdog_start: 0x80700c8
postfix/smtpd[8172]: rewrite stream disconnect
postfix/smtpd[8172]: watchdog_stop: 0x80700c8
postfix/smtpd[8172]: watchdog_start: 0x80700c8
postfix/smtpd[8172]: idle timeout -- exiting
```

As you can see, the `smtpd` program produces lots of detailed information that is logged into the mail log file, including the complete SMTP session text. This information can be invaluable when trying to troubleshoot a problem with the Postfix server.

Postfix UCE Parameters

The e-mail administrator should also try to protect customers from unsolicited commercial e-mail (UCE). The rise in UCE has become a nuisance to many e-mail users. The mail administrator should attempt to implement controls to minimize the amount of UCE that is delivered to local users. This section describes several methods that Postfix provides for the mail administrator to filter known UCE sites and messages.

Blocking UCE Sites

One technique used by UCE senders to hide their identity is to use phony addresses in the From: mail header lines. This is possible due to a security limitation in the standard SMTP protocol.

During a normal SMTP session, both the `HELO` and the `MAIL FROM:` commands identify the sender (see Chapter 5, "SMTP and Postfix"). The remote host can enter any value for these commands. The receiving host must decide whether to verify this information before passing the received message to the local mail handler.

Postfix provides several methods to verify the identity of remote hosts. This section describes the techniques that can be used to block messages from remote hosts that are trying to hide their identities.

Verifying `HELO` Addresses

The SMTP `HELO` command identifies the sending mail server to the receiving mail server. Although the SMTP creators intended for mail servers to be honest when using this command, the remote host does not specifically have to enter the proper mail server name for this value. UCE servers exploit this to help hide their identity.

Postfix allows the mail administrator to restrict remote hosts that do not properly identify themselves in the `HELO` command. You can do this using the `smtpd_helo_restrictions` parameter in the `main.cf` configuration file.

By default, Postfix does not do any checking of the value submitted by the `HELO` command. The e-mail administrator can configure Postfix to check this value in several different ways. Table 13.4 shows the `HELO` restrictions that can be configured for Postfix.

TABLE 13.4 Postfix `HELO` Restriction Values

Value	*Description*
`check_helo_access maptype:mapname`	Checks for the `HELO` hostname in specified lookup table
`check_client_access maptype:mapname`	Checks client network address in specified lookup table
`permit`	Allows any `HELO` hostname
`permit_mynetworks`	Allows if client network address is included in the `mynetworks` parameter
`permit_naked_ip_address`	Allows if `HELO` address is an IP address without enclosing brackets
`reject`	Rejects all `HELO` hostnames
`reject_unknown_client`	Rejects if client address has no DNS PTR record
`reject_maps_rbl`	Rejects if the client address is included in the `$maps_rbl_domain` value
`reject_invalid_hostname`	Rejects if `HELO` hostname is malformed
`reject_unauth_pipelining`	Rejects hosts using SMTP command pipelining

TABLE 13.4 Continued

`reject_unknown_hostname`	Rejects `HELO` hostnames without a DNS A or MX record
`reject_non_fqdn_hostname`	Rejects `HELO` hostnames not in FQDN format

You may select multiple values for the parameter to be as specific as needed when trying to block remote UCE servers. The format of the parameter is

```
smtpd_helo_restrictions = reject_unknown_hostname, permit_mynetworks
```

You can list multiple values for the parameter, separated by either a comma or a space. Postfix checks the values in the order they are entered in the list. Listing 13.8 shows an example using the preceding values.

LISTING 13.8 Sample SMTP Session with Bad `HELO` Hostname

```
[rich@shadrach]$ telnet localhost 25
Trying 127.0.0.1...
Connected to localhost.
Escape character is '^]'.
220 shadrach.ispnet1.net ESMTP Postfix
HELO dude
250 shadrach.ispnet1.net
MAIL FROM: <spammer@badguy.com>
250 Ok
RCPT TO: <rich@shadrach.ispnet1.net>
450 <dude>: Helo command rejected: Host not found
QUIT
221 Bye
Connection closed by foreign host.
```

In Listing 13.8, the remote host failed to identify itself properly in the `HELO` command. Although Postfix did not complain about it then, it did refuse to accept a message destined to a local user from the remote host.

The mail administrator can also create a lookup table of known UCE sites for the `check_client_access` value. Each time a user complains about receiving a UCE message from a site, the mail administrator can add the site to the lookup table. Postfix will refuse to accept mail messages from sites in the lookup table.

First, the mail administrator must create the text version of the lookup table. The format of the table is

```
pattern action
```

The *pattern* is a UCE site listed by hostname, IP address, or an individual user address specified as `user@hostname`. This allows the mail administrator great flexibility in specifying entire domains, single hosts, or individual users.

The *action* listed in the lookup table describes how Postfix will react when it sees the pattern. Three possible actions can be taken:

- `OK`—Allow the host to transfer messages.
- `REJECT`—Block the host from transferring messages.
- `4XX` or `5XX`—Block the host from transferring messages and return the result code listed.

A sample lookup table would look like this:

```
spammer.org REJECT
nuisance@badguy.com 550 You have been rejected
10.5. REJECT
freemoney@ REJECT
```

The sample lookup table lists different e-mail addresses to block. The last one, `freemoney@`, blocks any messages from any host using the user name `freemoney`. Once the text lookup table is created, it must be converted to an indexed binary database file using the `postmap` utility:

```
postmap hash:/etc/postfix/spammers
```

The table can then be referenced in the `main.cf` configuration file using the `smtpd_helo_restrictions` parameter:

```
smtpd_helo_restrictions = check_helo_access hash:/etc/postfix/spammers
```

After saving the new configuration file and issuing the `postfix reload` command, you can test the restrictions. Listing 13.9 shows an example of the new restrictions.

LISTING 13.9 Sample HELO Access Restrictions

```
[rich@shadrach]$ telnet localhost 25
Trying 127.0.0.1...
Connected to localhost.
Escape character is '^]'.
220 shadrach.ispnet1.net ESMTP Postfix
HELO spammer.org
250 shadrach.ispnet1.net
MAIL FROM: <rich@spammer.org>
250 Ok
RCPT TO: <rich@shadrach.ispnet1.net>
554 <spammer.org>: Helo command rejected: Access denied
```

LISTING 13.9 Continued

```
QUIT
221 Bye
Connection closed by foreign host.
```

As you can see in Listing 13.9, Postfix refused to allow the remote host listed in the lookup table to send messages to local users or relay messages to other hosts.

Verifying `MAIL FROM:` Addresses

Another useful technique for blocking UCE is to verify the sender used in the `MAIL FROM:` command. By default, Postfix allows any user and hostname to be used in this command. No attempt is made to verify the information provided by the remote mail server.

This is prime ground for UCE. Many UCE mail servers purposely use false information in the `MAIL FROM:` command to hide where the actual message came from. To prevent this, the mail administrator can use the `smtpd_sender_restrictions` parameter.

The `smtpd_sender_restrictions` parameter defines restrictions that can be placed in the information accepted by the Postfix server in the `MAIL FROM:` command. Table 13.5 shows the possible values that can be used for this parameter.

TABLE 13.5 Postfix `MAIL FROM:` Restriction Values

Value	*Description*
`check_client_access <maptype:mapname>`	Checks client address in specified lookup table
`check_helo_access <maptype:mapname>`	Checks `HELO` address in specified lookup table
`check_sender_access <maptype:mapname>`	Checks sender address in specified lookup table
`permit`	Allows any sender hostname
`permit_mynetworks`	Allows any sender address listed in the `mynetworks` parameter
`permit_naked_ip_address`	Allows if `HELO` address is an IP address without enclosing brackets
`reject`	Rejects all sender hostnames
`reject_invalid_hostname`	Rejects if `HELO` hostname is malformed
`reject_maps_rbl`	Rejects if client is listed in the `$maps_rbl_domains` parameter
`reject_non_fqdn_hostname`	Rejects `HELO` hostname if not in FQDN format
`reject_non_fqdn_sender`	Rejects sender hostname if not in FQDN format
`reject_unauth_pipelining`	Rejects hosts using SMTP command pipelining
`reject_unknown_client`	Rejects if the client has no DNS PTR record

TABLE 13.5 Continued

Value	*Description*
`reject_unknown_hostname`	Rejects `HELO` hostnames without a DNS A or MX record
`reject_unknown_sender_domain`	Rejects sender hostnames without a DNS A or MX record

As with the `HELO` restrictions, you may list multiple values for the parameter to specifically define how you want Postfix to examine the incoming messages. An example of this would be

```
smtpd_sender_restrictions = reject_unknown_sender_domain, permit_mynetworks
```

Listing 13.10 shows an example of using these restrictions.

LISTING 13.10 Bad `MAIL FROM:` Example

```
$ telnet localhost 25
Trying 127.0.0.1...
Connected to localhost.ispnet1.net.
Escape character is '^]'.
220 shadrach.ispnet1.net ESMTP Postfix
HELO dude
250 shadrach.ispnet1.net
MAIL FROM: <badguy@spammer.com>
250 Ok
RCPT TO: <rich@shadrach.ispnet1.net>
450 <badguy@spammer.com>: Sender address rejected: Domain not found
QUIT
221 Bye
Connection closed by foreign host.
```

As you can see in Listing 13.10, the Postfix server rejected the attempt from the UCE mail server to use a fictitious address in the `MAIL FROM:` command.

Getting Outside Help

You may have noticed that each of the previous two examples used to block UCE messages contained the `reject_maps_rbl` value. This value points Postfix to another parameter, `maps_rbl_domains`.

This parameter lets Postfix enlist help from an outside source. The Realtime Blackhole List (RBL) is a network database used to keep a list of known UCE mail servers in the world. It is maintained by the Mail Abuse Prevention System LLC (MAPS). Mail administrators can submit addresses of known UCE mail servers to MAPS to be added to the RBL when verified. The Web site for MAPS is located at `http://www.mail-abuse.org`.

Postfix can utilize the RBL database to determine whether a hostname is listed as participating in UCE messages. The `maps_rbl_domains` parameter points to an RBL server. When another parameter specifies to use the RBL, Postfix can connect to the RBL server and determine whether the site is on the list. The format of the `maps_rbl_domains` parameter is

```
maps_rbl_domains = blackholes.mail-abuse.org, dialups.mail-abuse.org
```

The sites used to connect to the RBL database do change occasionally. You should always consult the `www.mail-abuse.org` Web site to verify the current values. Once you set the `maps_rbl_domains` parameter to the appropriate RBL servers, you can add the RBL feature to the specific parameter used to block UCE:

```
smtpd_helo_restrictions = reject_maps_rbl
smtpd_sender_restrictions = reject_maps_rbl
```

The parameter entries shown allow Postfix to check the `HELO` and `MAIL FROM:` command values against the current RBL database. Any UCE mail site currently listed on the RBL site is prevented from sending messages to your mail server.

CAUTION

A few companies always complain that their mail servers are erroneously listed in the RBL database. The MAPS team is very responsive to posting ongoing litigation with listed sites. If you decide to implement RBL support on your Postfix server, you should regularly check the MAPS Web site for the current status of sites. If your users complain about not receiving messages from a listed site, you should be prepared to explain your reasons for using the RBL database and fully support the MAPS team decisions as to which servers are listed and why.

Blocking Known UCE Messages

While the previous examples blocked UCE messages based on e-mail addresses, this is not always possible. Given the increase of UCE blocking software, UCE mail servers now often use perfectly legitimate mail server addresses (at least until enough people complain to get them shut down, then they just switch to a new address). Postfix provides another method for trying to block UCE messages that does not rely on mail addresses.

You can use the `header_checks` parameter to scan message headers, looking for particular phrases contained in the message. Messages that include the phrase are blocked from delivery. The format of the `header_checks` parameter is

```
header_checks = regexp:/etc/postfix/spammers
```

The `header_checks` parameter uses either a regular expression lookup table or a pcre lookup table to use wildcard text matching for the defined phrase. The text lookup table is created in the form

```
pattern action
```

where *pattern* is a regular expression to match in the header fields, and *action* is the action to take if the pattern is matched. There are three possible actions that can be taken:

- `REJECT`—Rejects the message.
- `OK`—Accepts the message.
- `IGNORE`—The header line is discarded from the message.

Each line in the lookup table is compared against the message header fields until a matching line is found and the message is rejected. If no lines match, the message is accepted. A sample `header_check` lookup table looks like this:

```
/^subject: more money$/ REJECT
/^subject: I LOVE YOU$/ REJECT
/^to: our valued customer$/ REJECT
/^from: your friend$/ REJECT
```

Each line in the lookup table contains a different regular expression that is matched against the text in the message header lines. Listing 13.11 shows an example of how Postfix rejects a message that matches a pattern in the lookup table.

LISTING 13.11 Sample `header_check` Session

```
$ telnet localhost 25
Trying 127.0.0.1...
Connected to localhost.ispnet1.net.
Escape character is '^]'.
220 shadrach.ispnet1.net ESMTP Postfix
HELO goodguy.com
250 shadrach.ispnet1.net
MAIL FROM: <spammer@goodguy.com>
250 Ok
RCPT TO: <rich@shadrach.ispnet1.net>
250 Ok
DATA
354 End data with <CR><LF>.<CR><LF>
From: spammer@goodguy.com
To: rich@shadrach.ispnet1.net
Date: 20 Nov 2000 19:40
Subject: more money
```

LISTING 13.11 Continued

```
How would you like to make more money?
Just call us to find out our secret method.
.
552 Error: content rejected
QUIT
221 Bye
Connection closed by foreign host.
$
```

As you can see in Listing 13.11, Postfix allows the remote mailer to enter the message body because it did not meet any of the other anti-UCE methods. However, once the message is completed, Postfix applies the `header_checks` lookup table to the values received in the message header. One line in the lookup table matches the contents in the `Subject:` header field, and the message is rejected. Postfix then notifies the remote mailer that the message was rejected.

Although this method is primarily intended to stop UCE mail servers, you can also use it as a preliminary method to stop mail viruses that are known to use a common subject field, such as the notorious Melissa virus.

Summary

Once the Postfix software is installed, configured, and running, the mail administrator can turn his attention to maintenance. Several things need to be monitored on a running Postfix server.

It is always good practice to check the system log files on a daily basis. These can give clues to when things are going wrong (or are about to go wrong). You can configure the Postfix `master.cf` configuration file to enable verbose logging on a particular Postfix program when you suspect that something is not working properly. The added detail in the verbose logging allows for easier troubleshooting of internal Postfix problems.

The mail administrator must also monitor the constant bombardment of unsolicited commercial e-mails. These e-mails can become bothersome to users and can be blocked. Postfix supports several different methods of blocking UCE messages. Two methods force Postfix to verify the sending hostname supplied in either the `HELO` or the `MAIL FROM:` commands during the SMTP session. If the hostname fails the verification process, messages from that host are rejected.

Another method of blocking UCE messages is using message header filtering. By scanning the RFC822 header fields of incoming messages, Postfix can block known UCE mail servers as well as messages sent with common UCE mail subjects. This gives the mail administrator a tool to use to help stop UCE messages.

CHAPTER 14

Migrating from Sendmail to Postfix

The preceding chapters described the process of installing and configuring a Postfix mail server. Unfortunately, many mail server sites have been running other mail server software prior to the installation of the Postfix software. This creates a problem for the mail administrator: how to migrate an existing mail server to the Postfix environment. This process requires more planning and coordination than just creating a new mail server. Care must be taken that no messages are lost from the old mail server package, and that the mail server switch is transparent to the mail server users (except, of course, for the better performance that Postfix offers).

This chapter describes one of the most common MTA software packages used on the Unix platform, the Sendmail package, and the steps necessary to migrate an existing Sendmail mail server to a Postfix mail server.

What Is Sendmail?

The Sendmail software package was designed to be a complete MTA package for Unix platforms. The Sendmail package has been developed under the guidance of the Sendmail Consortium (`http://www.sendmail.org`). Also, Sendmail, Inc. (`http://www.sendmail.com`) provides commercial support as well as a commercial version of the Sendmail mail package. A Sendmail user's group has formed and also operates a Web site at `http://www.sendmail.net`.

The `sendmail` program is one of the most robust and versatile MTA programs available. Because of its versatility it is also one of the most complicated to configure. `sendmail` gets most of its configuration settings from a single configuration file (`sendmail.cf`). This file can often run a few hundred lines in length. Within the configuration file are parameters that control how `sendmail` handles incoming messages and routes outgoing messages.

Incoming messages run through a complicated series of rules that can be used to filter messages from the system. The rules used for filtering are also stored in the configuration file (hence the large file size). Messages can be checked for header content and handled according to either the source or destination information available.

Outgoing messages must be routed to the proper location for delivery. `sendmail` must be configured according to the method used to connect the mail server to the Internet. Often a mail server for a small office is configured to pass all outgoing messages to the ISP, which in turn can relay the messages to the proper destination. As in Postfix, this method is called using a "smart host."

The following sections describe the functionality that `sendmail` provides.

`sendmail` Files and Directories

The `sendmail` program does not work alone. It requires a host of files and directories to properly do its job. To properly migrate the `sendmail` server the mail administrator should know and understand what pieces are being replaced. This section lists and describes the files and directories used in a default installation of `sendmail`.

The `sendmail` Executable Program

Unlike Postfix, Sendmail uses a single program as the mail engine. The `sendmail` program normally runs as a daemon waiting for connections for incoming mail, and checks the mail queue at set intervals for outgoing mail. Alternatively, you can configure the inetd TCP wrapper program to run `sendmail`. This saves some server memory by not having the `sendmail` program in the background all the time, but it does decrease performance because `sendmail` must read its configuration file every time it starts. The `sendmail` program is run as the `root` user, so it can access directories owned by `root`. Non-`root` users can run `sendmail`, but will not have access to many of the default file locations, such as the default mail queue.

The `sendmail` Configuration File

For `sendmail` to operate properly, it must be configured for the specific mail server implementation. The main configuration file for `sendmail` is `sendmail.cf`. All definitions of how `sendmail` processes mail are stored in this configuration file. These definitions are called *rule sets*. `sendmail` uses the rule sets to parse the sender and recipient addresses in messages, and determines how to deliver the messages to intended recipients.

In addition to the rule sets, the `sendmail.cf` configuration file also includes definitions for how `sendmail` will handle incoming and outgoing mail messages. Like Postfix, `sendmail` utilizes several lookup tables that contain information for various mail functions such as virtual domains and allowed relaying hosts. These tables are defined in the `sendmail.cf` configuration file using cryptic two-character tags. Reading through the `sendmail.cf` file is not nearly as pleasant as reading the Postfix `main.cf` configuration file.

`sendmail` reads the configuration file when it starts up. Unlike Postfix, the `sendmail` daemon must be halted and restarted before any changes made to the configuration file can take effect.

The `sendmail` Message Queue

The `mqueue` directory contains the queued e-mail messages waiting to be processed. Unlike Postfix, which utilizes a series of subdirectories to parse messages in the queue (`maildrop`, `incoming`, `active`, and `bounce`), `sendmail` places all queued messages in the same `mqueue` directory. The owner of this directory should be the `root` user. `sendmail` ensures that all queue files stored here are set with the proper permissions to prevent users from reading messages in the mail queues.

The default location of the `sendmail` message queue is `/var/spool/mqueue`. The mail administrator can change the location of the mail queue directory by either adding an entry to the `sendmail.cf` file or invoking `sendmail` from the command line with the appropriate option.

Querying the Message Queue

The `mailq` executable is a symbolic link to the `sendmail` program. When executed as `mailq`, `sendmail` prints a summary of the current contents of the mail queue. Since all messages are stored in the `mqueue` directory, only one message queue needs to be searched by `mailq`.

Creating Mail Aliases

The `newaliases` executable is also a link to the `sendmail` program. When `sendmail` runs as the `newaliases` program, it reads the `/etc/aliases` plaintext file and creates an aliases database using an installed Unix database package. It is common to create a binary indexed database file using the hash function as the aliases database.

Aliases Database

One nice feature of the `sendmail` program is the ability to create e-mail aliases for usernames. With aliases, you don't have to create a separate mailbox for the new username. You can assign an alias name and point it to an existing e-mail user. Any messages sent to the alias e-mail address are automatically redirected by `sendmail` to the user that the alias points to.

All `sendmail` aliases used on the mail server are listed in a common file. The `aliases` file is normally located at `/etc/aliases`, but can be changed in the `sendmail` configuration file. The `aliases` file can be used to point alias e-mail names to real addresses, programs, or files. As a result of these different mappings, an entry in the plaintext `aliases` file can have one of four different formats. One format of the `aliases` file is

```
name:    name1, name2, name3, ...
```

where *`name`* is the alias name, and *`name1`*, *`name2`*, and so on are the address names of where the message will be sent instead of the original name. You can use one or more different addresses for each alias. Each e-mail address listed receives a copy of the message. Aliases are always considered local to the mail server on which they are configured.

Another use of an alias line can be

```
name:    |program
```

where *`program`* is the full pathname of a program that can process the message. Often this feature is used for mail list programs such as Majordomo.

Still another use of an alias line can be

```
name:    file
```

where *`file`* is a full pathname pointing to a text file. Any messages sent to the e-mail address name will be spooled to the text file given. For this feature to work properly, the proper read/write system permissions must be set on both the text file and the directory in which the text file is located.

The last format that the alias line can assume is

```
name:     :include:filelist
```

where *filelist* is the full pathname of a file that can contain a list of e-mail addresses. This has the same effect as listing each of the e-mail addresses on the aliases line separated by commas as in the first format. This format may be easier to manipulate if you have a large mail list that changes frequently.

Listing 14.1 shows a sample sendmail aliases file. Line numbers have been added to aid in the discussion of the file

LISTING 14.1 Sample /etc/aliases File

```
#
#   @(#)aliases 8.2 (Berkeley) 3/5/94
#
#  Aliases in this file will NOT be expanded in the header from
#  Mail, but WILL be visible over networks or from /bin/mail.
#
#   >>>>>>>>>>  The program "newaliases" must be run after
#   >> NOTE >>  this file is updated for any changes to
#   >>>>>>>>>>  show through to sendmail.
#

# Basic system aliases -- these MUST be present.
MAILER-DAEMON:  postmaster
postmaster: root

# General redirections for pseudo accounts.
bin:        root
daemon:     root
games:      root
ingres:     root
nobody:     root
system:     root
toor:       root
uucp:       root

# Well-known aliases.
manager:    root
dumper:     root
operator:   root

# trap decode to catch security attacks
decode:     root
```

LISTING 14.1 Continued

```
33
34 # Person who should get root's mail
35 root:          rich
36
37 # Program used to auto-reply to messages
38 auto-test:            |/home/rich/auto-test
39
40 # Send all messages to a text file
41 saveme:         /home/rich/test.txt
42
43 # Send all messages to remote site
44 rich:          richard@othercompany.com
45
46 #Create a simple multi-user mail list
47 officenews:          :include:/home/rich/office.txt
```

In Listing 14.1, lines 13–32 redirect any mail messages received for various standard system usernames to the `root` user. This is usually a good idea to ensure that no one is trying to hack into the system by sending bogus mail messages to one of the default system usernames. If these usernames are not aliased to `root`, any mail messages sent to them are lost in the mail queue. Line 35 is also a good idea. It redirects any mail for the `root` user to a common username that should log in to the system on a regular basis. Remember, if you are a good system administrator, you should not be logging in as the `root` user very frequently.

Line 38 demonstrates redirecting messages to a program. The program must be invoked with its full pathname so the shell can find it. Line 41 demonstrates using a text file to store any messages sent to an address. Remember to be careful about read/write permissions for the file.

Line 44 demonstrates that although the alias name itself must be local to the mail server, the names that it aliases *to* do not have to be. You can redirect a mail message for a user to another e-mail account on a completely different system. This is a handy feature to use when users move to different e-mail machines within the organization, or if they leave the organization for another company.

Line 47 demonstrates the use of a mail list text file in the aliases file. The file `/home/rich/office.txt` is a plaintext file that lists e-mail addresses. When a message is received for the `officenews` alias, the `office.txt` file is checked and the message is sent to all e-mail addresses present in that file. This is sometimes used as a simple method to create mailing lists.

Once created, the text `aliases` file must be converted to a binary indexed database file using the `newaliases` command described previously. The `sendmail` program uses the binary version of the file to quickly search the aliases database as new messages are received.

Getting Mail Statistics

The `hoststat` executable is another link to the `sendmail` program. When executed as `hoststat`, `sendmail` attempts to read a host statistics file and display the status of the last mail transaction to all of the remote hosts to which it has sent mail.

Resetting Mail Statistics

The `purgestat` executable is also a link to the `sendmail` program. When executed as `purgestat`, `sendmail` deletes all of the information in the host statistics file.

Storing Mail Statistics

The `/var/spool/mqueue/.hoststat` directory contains files that contain statistics for each accessed remote host. The `hoststat` program uses these files to display the status of remote host transactions.

Setting `sendmail` to Record Mail Statistics

The presence of the `sendmail.st` file indicates that the mail administrator wants to collect statistics about the outgoing mail traffic. If this file is not present, `sendmail` will not collect any statistics about transferred messages. This file is initially created as a null file (0 bytes). Although the `/etc` directory is the default location, many Unix distributions, including most Linux distributions, change the location of the `sendmail.st` file to `/var/log/sendmail.st`.

The `sendmail` Help File

The `sendmail.hf` file is used to produce a help file for the SMTP `HELP` command. The help file is in a special format that `sendmail` can parse as remote SMTP hosts request information using the SMTP `HELP` command. As shown in Chapter 5, "SMTP and Postfix," remote clients can issue either a general SMTP `HELP` command, or specific `HELP` commands along with the command for which they want help. To parse the information in the help file, `sendmail` uses tags at the start of each line. Listing 14.2 shows a partial `sendmail.hf` file.

LISTING 14.2 Partial `/usr/lib/sendmail.hf` File

```
cpyr
cpyr    Copyright (c) 1998 Sendmail, Inc.  All rights reserved.
cpyr    Copyright (c) 1983, 1995-1997 Eric P. Allman.  All rights reserved.
cpyr    Copyright (c) 1988, 1993
cpyr     The Regents of the University of California.  All rights reserved.
cpyr
cpyr
```

LISTING 14.2 Continued

```
cpyr    By using this file, you agree to the terms and conditions set
cpyr    forth in the LICENSE file which can be found at the top level of
cpyr    the sendmail distribution.
cpyr
cpyr    @(#)sendmail.hf 8.18 (Berkeley) 11/19/1998
cpyr
smtp    Topics:
smtp        HELO    EHLO    MAIL    RCPT    DATA
smtp        RSET    NOOP    QUIT    HELP    VRFY
smtp        EXPN    VERB    ETRN    DSN
smtp    For more info use "HELP <topic>".
smtp    To report bugs in the implementation send e-mail to
smtp        sendmail-bugs@sendmail.org.
smtp    For local information send e-mail to Postmaster at your site.
help    HELP [ <topic> ]
help        The HELP command gives help info.
helo    HELO <hostname>
helo        Introduce yourself.
ehlo    EHLO <hostname>
ehlo        Introduce yourself, and request extended SMTP mode.
ehlo    Possible replies include:
ehlo        SEND        Send as mail            [RFC821]
ehlo        SOML        Send as mail or terminal    [RFC821]
ehlo        SAML        Send as mail and terminal   [RFC821]
ehlo        EXPN        Expand the mailing list     [RFC821]
ehlo        HELP        Supply helpful information  [RFC821]
ehlo        TURN        Turn the operation around   [RFC821]
ehlo        8BITMIME    Use 8-bit data          [RFC1652]
ehlo        SIZE        Message size declaration    [RFC1870]
ehlo        VERB        Verbose             [Allman]
ehlo        ONEX        One message transaction only    [Allman]
ehlo        CHUNKING    Chunking            [RFC1830]
ehlo        BINARYMIME  Binary MIME         [RFC1830]
ehlo        PIPELINING  Command Pipelining      [RFC1854]
ehlo        DSN     Delivery Status Notification    [RFC1891]
ehlo        ETRN        Remote Message Queue Starting   [RFC1985]
ehlo        XUSR        Initial (user) submission   [Allman]
mail    MAIL FROM: <sender> [ <parameters> ]
mail        Specifies the sender.  Parameters are ESMTP extensions.
mail        See "HELP DSN" for details.
rcpt    RCPT TO: <recipient> [ <parameters> ]
rcpt        Specifies the recipient.  Can be used any number of times.
```

LISTING 14.2 Continued

```
50 rcpt         Parameters are ESMTP extensions.  See "HELP DSN" for details.
51 data     DATA
52 data         Following text is collected as the message.
53 data         End with a single dot.
54 rset     RSET
55 rset         Resets the system.
56 quit     QUIT
57 quit         Exit sendmail (SMTP).
```

In Listing 14.2, lines 14–21 show the standard help message that will be returned in response to an SMTP `HELP` command. After that, each individual command is listed with the command on the left side and the help message displayed. For example, the SMTP command `HELP MAIL` would result in lines 45, 46, and 47 being sent to the client. To test this you can log in to the `sendmail` TCP port and issue the SMTP command manually, as demonstrated in Chapter 5 and shown in Listing 14.3.

LISTING 14.3 Sample SMTP `HELP` Command

```
[rich@shadrach]$ telnet localhost 25
Trying 127.0.0.1...
Connected to localhost.
Escape character is '^]'.
220 shadrach.smallorg.org ESMTP Sendmail 8.9.3/8.9.3; Tue, 5 Oct 1999
➥ 19:19:39 -0500
HELP MAIL
214-MAIL FROM: <sender> [ <parameters> ]
214-    Specifies the sender.  Parameters are ESMTP extensions.
214-    See "HELP DSN" for details.
214 End of HELP info
QUIT
221 shadrach.smallorg.org closing connection
Connection closed by foreign host.
```

User-Controlled Mail Forwarding

Each local user on the mail server can create a `.forward` file in his or her `$HOME` directory. Before `sendmail` attempts to pass mail for the local user to the local mail processor, it will check for this file.

The `.forward` file contains information used to forward messages received for the user. The messages can be forwarded to several different types of recipients:

- Another mail user address
- A filename on the mail server
- A program on the mail server
- A list of mail addresses contained in a text file

Multiple destinations can be included in the `.forward` file. Each destination is placed in a separate line in the file. `sendmail` will attempt to forward a copy of the message to each destination listed in the `.forward` file. Listing 14.4 shows a sample `.forward` file.

LISTING 14.4 Sample `.forward` File

```
jessica
katie
barbara@othercompany.com
/home/rich/messages
```

The example shown in Listing 14.4 will forward any messages sent to the user to local users `jessica` and `katie`, as well as to remote user `barbara@othercompany.com`. Finally, it will append a copy of the message to the file `/home/rich/messages`.

NOTE

`sendmail` forwards the message to all recipients listed in the `.forward` file. If the original recipient of the message is not listed in the `.forward` file, he will not receive a copy of the message. If you want the original recipient of the message to receive the message as well, ensure that he is listed in the `.forward` file.

Configuring Postfix to Use Sendmail Files

The Postfix package was designed to work well in Sendmail environments. This includes making it as easy as possible to drop the Postfix software onto a server that was previously running Sendmail. The following sections describe the steps necessary to convert an existing Sendmail mail server to a Postfix server.

Replacing the Sendmail Program Files

As described in Chapter 6, "Installing Postfix," the Postfix package directly replaces some of the program files installed by Sendmail. It is always wise to move the Sendmail program files to a safe location before Postfix overwrites them. This may be helpful if you must "fall back" to the original Sendmail system for any reason. The Sendmail program files that Postfix replaces are

- `sendmail`
- `mailq`
- `newaliases`

You should move these files to an alternate location before installing Postfix. To do this, issue the following commands as `root`:

```
mv /usr/sbin/sendmail /usr/sbin/sendmail.OLD
mv /usr/bin/mailq /usr/bin/mailq.OLD
mv /usr/bin/newaliases /usr/bin/newaliases.OLD
```

Now Postfix can install its version of these programs without deleting the Sendmail versions. Because the Sendmail programs were installed using the Unix setuid to grant `root` privileges when they run, you may want to remove these permissions using the `chmod` program:

```
chmod 755 /usr/sbin/sendmail.old
```

NOTE

Some Unix installations of the `sendmail` program place these programs in different locations. You can use the Unix `find` command to determine the locations of these programs on your particular mail server.

Using Sendmail Mailboxes

An existing Sendmail installation should already contain mailboxes for the users on the local mail server. Different Unix implementations tend to use different locations for these mailboxes—usually `/var/spool/mail` on Linux systems and `/var/mail` on BSD systems. Again, the Unix `find` command may be helpful in locating this directory.

Within the base mail directory each user should have a separate mailbox file using the system username as the filename:

```
[rich@shadrach]$ ls -al
total 5
drwxrwxr-x   2 root     mail        1024 Nov 19 04:02 .
drwxr-xr-x  11 root     root        1024 Oct 10 12:15 ..
-rw-------   1 chris    mail           0 Oct 15 11:43 chris
-rw-------   1 haley    mail           0 Nov 25 08:40 haley
-rw-------   1 jessica  mail         437 Nov 27 15:09 jessica
-rw-------   1 katie    mail           0 Oct 26 10:57 katie
-rw-------   1 matt     mail         261 Nov 18 15:28 matt
-rw-------   1 rich     mail           0 Nov 20 10:02 rich
-rw-------   1 riley    mail          35 Nov 24 09:32 riley
[rich@shadrach mail]$
```

Don't be alarmed if you do not see a mailbox entry for each user configured on the system. When userids are created, the corresponding mailboxes are not created. By default, the mailbox files are only created after a message has been sent to the user. Once the mailbox file is created, it does not get deleted even if there are no messages in it (thus the 0-byte file sizes).

Normal Mailbox Delivery

By default, Postfix will automatically send messages for local users to the standard `sendmail`-style mailboxes in the `/var/spool/mail` directory. No parameters need to be set in the Postfix `main.cf` configuration file for this to happen.

If your Unix system is using a non-standard location for the mailboxes, you must specify the different location using the `mail_spool_directory` parameter in `main.cf`:

```
mail_spool_directory = /usr/alt/mail
```

Postfix will then deliver messages to the `sendmail`-style mailboxes located in that directory. Postfix will also create mailboxes as necessary as it delivers messages to the local users.

Postfix `$HOME/Mailbox` Delivery

One alternative mail delivery method that Postfix can use is writing to a `Mailbox` file in the user `$HOME` directory. When using this method of local mail delivery, Postfix uses the standard mailbox format for each mailbox, but locates the user's mailbox in her `$HOME` directory instead of the standard `/var/spool/mail` directory.

NOTE

Chapter 10, "Using Postfix," discusses the Postfix `Mailbox` mail delivery method in more detail.

If the previous Sendmail system was using standard mailboxes, but you want to use the `$HOME/Mailbox` method, you will need to move any messages in the users' current mailboxes to the new Postfix mailbox location. It is best to perform this with no users logged on to the mail server, and without *any* MTA programs running (to prevent message loss during the mailbox transfer).

The following command can be used to move user `rich`'s standard mailbox to a new `Mailbox` file in his home directory:

```
mv /var/spool/mail/rich /home/rich/Mailbox
```

This command must be entered as the `root` user. The user must own the new `Mailbox` in order to access it. This requires an additional step for the mail administrator:

```
chown rich.rich /home/rich/Mailbox
```

This command changes the ownership of the `Mailbox` to the user. The exact process of changing file ownership varies on different Unix systems. If the mail server will be using MUA programs that need to access messages in the old mailbox location, you can create a link from the new `$HOME/Mailbox` location to the old mailbox location:

```
ln -s /home/rich/Mailbox /var/spool/mail/rich
```

This will allow Postfix to store new messages using the `$HOME/Mailbox` format, while allowing older MUA programs to access those messages in the old standard mailbox location.

Postfix `$HOME/Maildir` Delivery

Another alternative Postfix mailbox format is the `$HOME/Maildir` format. This format utilizes a separate mail directory to contain messages for each user. Each user's mail directory stores messages as separate files within the directory.

> **NOTE**
>
> Chapter 15, "Using the Maildir Mailbox Format," describes using Maildir mailboxes in detail.

Because this mailbox method is completely different from the standard mailbox format, the two are incompatible. An external program must be run to convert messages in the standard mailbox to messages in the Maildir mailbox. At the time of this writing, the current version of Postfix does not include a utility to do this.

If you decide that it is imperative to move messages in the user's old mailbox format to the new Maildir format, you can use the `mutt` MUA program. The `mutt` program can access both mailbox-and Maildir-type mailboxes, and transfer messages from one mailbox to another. Although this might be fine for moving messages for an individual user, it could become cumbersome for moving thousands of users' mailboxes.

If you must move mail for thousands of users, there are some utilities written by Postfix users that can do this without using the `mutt` program. One such utility was written by Ollivier Robert using the Perl programming language, and can be found in the Postfix mail list archives:

```
http://archives.neohapsis.com/archives/postfix
```

The article is posted in the December 1999 archive. Remember that these utilities are not part of the normal Postfix distribution, and should be used with caution.

Postfix MDA Program Delivery

If the Postfix `main.cf` configuration file defines an external local mail delivery agent (MDA) to use to deliver local mail with the `mailbox_command` parameter, no changes need to be made to either the Postfix configuration or the mailboxes. The local MDA will continue to deliver messages for local users just as when it was under the `sendmail` program.

NOTE

Chapter 16, "Using MDA Programs with Postfix," describes in more detail how to utilize external MDA programs for local mail delivery.

Using the Sendmail `aliases` File

One nice feature of the Sendmail package is the aliases database, which allows the mail administrator to point e-mail names to

- Another mail user address
- A filename on the local mail server
- A program on the mail server
- A list of mail addresses contained in a text file

The mail administrator creates a text version of the `aliases` file, then uses the `newaliases` Sendmail command to convert it to an indexed binary database file. This section describes how to migrate an existing Sendmail aliases database to Postfix.

The `aliases` Database File

The mail administrator creates the `aliases` database file as a text file. This text file is converted to an indexed binary database file for `sendmail` to parse quickly as mail is being delivered. This allows `sendmail` to deliver messages more quickly than if it had to read through the text database file.

Postfix fully supports the use of the aliases database function of Sendmail. Postfix uses two separate parameters in the `main.cf` configuration file to identify alias databases:

```
alias_maps = hash:/etc/postfix/aliases
alias_database = hash:/etc/postfix/aliases
```

There has been much confusion as to why there are two alias parameter entries. Wietse Venema has explained the two parameters as follows:

- `alias_maps` specifies the list of alias databases used by the local delivery agent (not necessarily under Postfix's control).
- `alias_database` specifies the alias database(s) that are built with the Postfix `newaliases` command and are controlled by Postfix.

The difference may be easier to see in a specific example. Often large network administrators run Network Information System (NIS) servers to control usernames and passwords on multiple systems on the network. Postfix can interface with the NIS server to map aliases with real usernames on the network.

Postfix must know about the NIS aliases database, as well as any locally created `aliases` database files. However, Postfix is not responsible for creating or maintaining the NIS database file, it just reads data from it. If the mail administrator uses the `newaliases` command, it must know about the locally created `aliases` database file, but it shouldn't mess with the NIS alias database. Thus, the alias parameters for the `main.cf` file would be

```
alias_maps = hash:/etc/postfix/aliases, nis:nishost.ispnet1.net
alias_database = hash:/etc/postfix/aliases
```

The `alias_maps` parameter points to all the possible aliases databases that Postfix will check: the local `aliases` file as well as the NIS aliases database. The `alias_database` parameter tells Postfix which aliases databases should be converted when using the `newaliases` command. This example would create a new aliases database from the `/etc/postfix/aliases` file, but ignore the NIS server database. When Postfix checks for alias names when delivering messages, it checks both the local `/etc/postfix/aliases` database file and the remote NIS server `nishost.ispnet1.net`.

The `newaliases` Program

As mentioned in the previous section, Postfix supports the `sendmail`-style `newaliases` command to create indexed binary database files from text `aliases` files. Under the default install of `sendmail`, the `newaliases` command is itself an alias for the `sendmail` command, using the `-bi` option.

The `newaliases` command attempts to create an indexed binary database file from the `aliases` text files specified by the configuration parameter `alias_database`. Each database listed in this parameter is converted to an indexed binary database. If this parameter is not present, `newaliases` assumes a default database location of `/etc/aliases`.

Different Unix systems utilize different default database types. The aliases database type is controlled by the `database_type` parameter. For Linux systems the default database type is the hash database.

The indexed aliases database can also be created using the Postfix `postalias` command. The format of the `postalias` command is

```
postalias [-Ninrvw] [-c config] [-d key] [-q key] [file_type:]file_name ...
```

Table 14.1 lists the options that are available for the `postalias` command.

TABLE 14.1 postalias Command Options

Option	*Description*
-N	Includes terminating null character to terminate lookup keys
-i	Reads entries from standard input and appends them to the existing database
-n	Doesn't include the terminating null character to terminate lookup keys
-r	Does not warn about duplicate aliases table entries
-w	Warns about duplicate aliases table entries
-c *config*	Uses the main.cf configuration file from the location *config*
-d *key*	Deletes one entry from the aliases table that matches *key*
-q *key*	Queries the aliases table and prints the first entry that matches *key*
-v	Toggles levels of verbosity in logs
file_type	The database scheme to use for the aliases table
file_name	The name of the aliases table to use

Unlike the newaliases command, the name of the aliases database to (re)build must be included in the postalias command line. If the default database type is used, the mail administrator can omit that value when specifying the database name:

```
postalias /etc/postfix/aliases
```

The postalias command is most useful when creating separate alias database files using a non-default database type:

```
postalias dbm:/etc/postfix/otheraliases
```

Supporting Files and Commands

Two options in the sendmail aliases file, forwarding messages to commands and to files, are controlled by main.cf parameter settings in Postfix. This feature often confuses mail administrators, especially when Postfix has changed this behavior between releases.

The parameters used for these functions are

```
allow_mail_to_commands = alias, forward, include
allow_mail_to_files = alias, forward, include
```

Each value listed for the parameter defines under what circumstances forwarding e-mail to commands or files is allowed. The mail administrator can determine which parameters and values are necessary based on the features used in the aliases in the aliases database file.

Older versions of Postfix had these features turned off in all circumstances by default. This confused many mail administrators expecting to migrate Sendmail alias files with no problems. In Postfix release version 19980809, Venema changed the default behavior of the two parameters to allow commands and files as destinations in the alias and .forward files. To allow commands and files in include files, the mail administrator must add the parameters with the include value in the main.cf configuration file.

Using `.forward` Files in Postfix

The `sendmail` program allows users to forward messages sent to their own e-mail accounts to other users as well as to commands and files. Each user can create a `.forward` file in his or her `$HOME` directory, placing forwarding information in the file. Postfix fully supports this capability without any modifications or configuration changes.

As with the `aliases` file, Postfix uses the `allow_mail_to_commands` and `allow_mail_to_files` parameters in `main.cf` to restrict these features from the `.forward` function. In newer versions of Postfix the commands and files features are enabled by default for `.forward` files. If you want to restrict users from using either of these features you can remove the "forward" value from these parameters accordingly.

Using the Sendmail `virtusertable` and `sendmail.cw` Files

If the previous Sendmail server was implementing virtual domains, they should be defined in the `virtusertable` file. This file is normally located in `/etc/virtusertable` by default.

The `virtusertable` file maps user and domain addresses to local (or even remote) addresses for `sendmail` to send all messages to. Listing 14.5 shows a sample `/etc/virtusertable` file.

LISTING 14.5 Sample Sendmail `/etc/virtusertable` file

```
prez@smallorg.org      fred
@smallorg.org          smallorg
@mediumorg.org         mediumorg
riley@ispnet1.net      alecia
```

In Listing 14.5, line 1 shows `sendmail` mapping an individual e-mail address to a local system username. Lines 2 and 3 show examples of mapping an entire domain name to local usernames. Any messages received for the `smallorg.org` domain (except for the `prez` username) are delivered to the local system username `smallorg`.

These `virtusertable` entries must be replicated in the Postfix `virtual` lookup table. Chapter 9, "Postfix Lookup Tables," describes the format of the `virtual` lookup table. To create a `virtual` lookup table to duplicate the functionality shown in Listing 14.5, you must use the `virtual` lookup table shown in Listing 14.6.

LISTING 14.6 Sample Postfix `virtual` Lookup Table

```
smallorg.org virtual
mediumorg.org virtual
ispnet1.org virtual
```

LISTING 14.6 Continued

```
prez@smallorg.org fred
@smallorg.org smallorg
@mediumorg.org mediumorg
riley@ispnet1.net alecia
```

The first three lines define the virtual domains that Postfix will accept messages for. Without these lines Postfix will not accept messages for the virtual domains. The following lines define the individual mappings for usernames and domain names.

Besides the `virtusertable`, Sendmail also utilizes the `/etc/sendmail.cw` file to define what domain- and hostnames it should receive mail for. This is different from the `virtusertable` file in that domains or hosts listed in the `sendmail.cw` file must map directly to local users. Each domain is listed on a separate line in the `sendmail.cw` file. The mail administrator is responsible for coordinating this file with the DNS MX records for the domains (see Chapter 4, "DNS and Postfix").

Postfix duplicates this functionality with the `mydestination` parameter, which instructs Postfix under what domains and hostnames to receive messages destined for local users. Messages received for those domains and hostnames are mapped to local users on the mail server.

The format of the `mydestination` parameter is

```
mydestination = $myhostname, localhost.$mydomain, ispnet2.net, mail.ispnet3.net
```

Each entry in the original `sendmail.cw` file should be included in the `mydestination` parameter values.

CAUTION

Remember that virtual domains are listed in the `virtual` lookup table, not using the `mydestination` parameter. Only domain names that the Postfix server will directly receive messages for are listed in the `mydestination` parameter.

Checking the Sendmail Mail Queue

After Postfix has been successfully installed on the mail server, you should check the old Sendmail message queue to ensure that no messages have been left over from the Sendmail installation. Any messages left over should be processed.

By default, the Sendmail mail queue is located in the `/var/spool/mqueue` directory. A setting in the `sendmail.cf` configuration file can change this location though, so make sure you are checking the right mail queue.

Hopefully this queue will be empty. If it is not, messages are still waiting to be delivered on the old Sendmail system. As the mail administrator you must make an executive decision: either delete the "leftover" messages or attempt to deliver them. Although deleting the messages may sound like the easier way, depending how you uninstalled Sendmail, delivering them to the proper destination is usually not too much trouble. The extra effort may make the difference between happy and not-so-happy customers.

If when installing Postfix you copied the old `/usr/bin/sendmail` program to an alternative location (such as `/usr/bin/sendmail.OLD`), you can perform a one-time run of the `sendmail` program to check the Sendmail mail queue and attempt to deliver any messages waiting for delivery. The format for this command is

```
/usr/bin/sendmail.OLD -q
```

By not specifying a time parameter with the `-q` option, `sendmail` will immediately process any messages in the message queue and exit. If all of the delivery attempts are successful the Sendmail mail queue directory should be empty, and you can continue with your Postfix installation.

CAUTION

Of course this also assumes that the original Sendmail configuration files have not been deleted from the mail server. It is often the best practice to leave things alone on the system until you are sure that you no longer need them. This definitely applies when migrating to a new mail system.

Summary

This chapter described the steps necessary when migrating an existing Sendmail mail server to the Postfix environment. Postfix was designed with this in mind, so the process is not too difficult.

First, the `sendmail` application programs should be moved so that they are available after the Postfix installation.

Next, any user mailboxes used on the Sendmail system should be migrated to the Postfix environment. Depending on the mailbox style chosen for the Postfix installation, this can be either an easy or a difficult job.

Next, any existing `aliases` database files should be converted using the Postfix `newaliases` or `postalias` commands. Postfix can convert the original text `aliases` file that was used with Sendmail.

Postfix supports the use of individual `.forward` files located in users' `$HOME` directories without any modifications. If the old Sendmail mail server supported any virtual domains, the mail administrator should migrate them from the Sendmail `virtusertable` to the Postfix `virtual` lookup table. Any hostnames or domains listed in the `sendmail.cw` file should be added to the Postfix `mydestination` parameter in the `main.cf` file.

Finally, the mail administrator should check the old Sendmail message queue to determine whether any undelivered messages are stuck there. If so, the old `sendmail` program can be run to attempt to clear out the message queue. Any really undeliverable messages should be deleted.

CHAPTER 15

Using the Maildir Mailbox Format

Previous chapters described how to install and configure a basic Postfix mail server. When configuring the Postfix server, one of the options available to the mail administrator is the method Postfix uses to store messages for local users. Of the four methods available, the Maildir method is the most unique and possibly most confusing. This chapter describes the Maildir mailbox format in more detail, and also demonstrates how to use it on a production mail server.

Standard Unix Mailboxes

Unix systems have been using e-mail for a long time. All Unix systems include a local mail delivery program to transfer simple text messages between users on the local machine (see Chapter 1, "E-Mail Services"). The first local mail delivery program was called `binmail` because of its normal location on the system: `/bin/mail`. BSD Unix systems use a similar program called `mail.local`.

The `binmail` and `mail.local` programs use a specific format for storing messages destined for local users on the mail server. This format is often referred to as the *mbox mailbox format*. Over the years there has been much discussion and research on the reliability and efficiency of the mbox mailbox format.

Dan Bernstein, the creator of the qmail MTA system, designed the Maildir mail directory format. The Maildir mailbox format provides a reliable and efficient replacement for the mbox mailbox format. To understand why the Maildir format was created, you must first understand the original mbox mailbox format and its pitfalls. This section describes the mbox mailbox format.

Local Message Storage

Any kind of mail messaging system requires a standard formatting method to store messages for users. Early Unix platforms commonly used the `sendmail` program to provide MTA support. `sendmail` used a centralized common mail directory. This directory contained individual user files that were the concatenation of all the messages destined for each respective local user. Figure 15.1 demonstrates this method.

Mailbox Message Format

Within a user's mbox mail file, messages are saved following a strict format. The start of each message needs to be identified for the MUA, so a message header line is created. The message header line uses the format

```
From sender date
```

where *sender* is the complete e-mail address of the sender of the message, and *date* is the complete date and timestamp of when the message was received. Timestamps are shown in the Unix `ctime()` format (the same format used by the Unix `date` command).

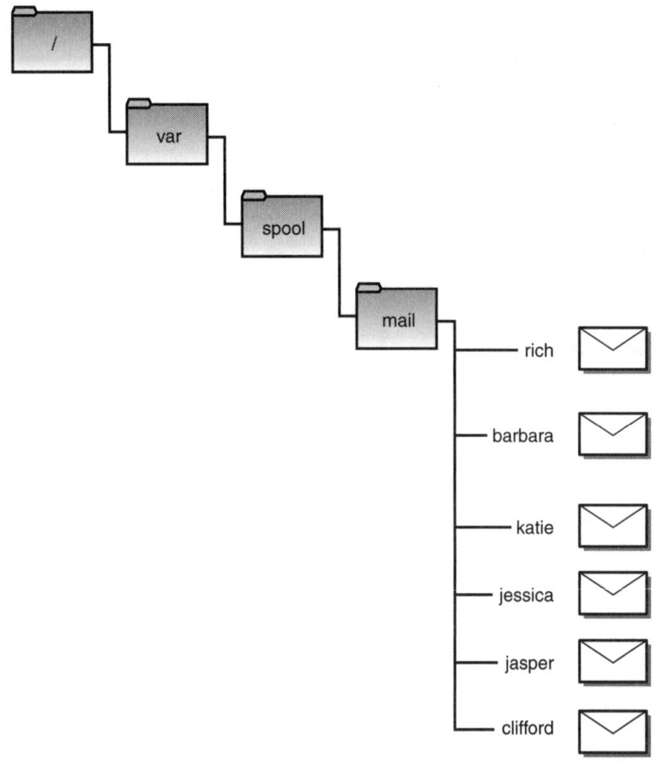

FIGURE 15.1

The standard Unix mailbox layout.

After the message header line the complete text of the message is stored. To assure proper MUA translation, the message should be in RFC822 format (see Chapter 5, "SMTP and Postfix"). A blank line is appended to the end of the normal message text. A blank line followed by a `From` header line signifies the start of another message in the mailbox. Thus new messages are appended to previous messages in the mailbox without any confusion as to where one ends and the next begins.

The `local` mail delivery program creates the `From` message header line before appending the message to the destination mailbox. It is important to remember that this header line does *not* have a colon after the word *From*. This differentiates it from the normal RFC822 mail `FROM:` header field in the message. Listing 15.1 shows a sample user mailbox containing two messages.

LISTING 15.1 Sample Unix User Mailbox

```
$ cat /var/spool/mail/rich
From rich  Fri Mar 10 17:15:08 2000
Return-Path: <rich>
Received: (from rich@localhost)
        by shadrach.ispnet1.net (8.8.7/8.8.7) id RAA07208
        for rich; Fri, 10 Mar 2000 17:15:07 -0500
Date: Fri, 10 Mar 2000 17:15:07 -0500
From: rich@shadrach.ispnet1.net
Message-Id: <200003102215.RAA07208@shadrach.ispnet1.net>
To: rich@shadrach.ispnet1.net
Subject: Test message 1

This is the first test message.

From rich  Fri Mar 10 17:15:20 2000
Return-Path: <rich>
Received: (from rich@localhost)
        by shadrach.ispnet1.net (8.8.7/8.8.7) id RAA07213
        for rich; Fri, 10 Mar 2000 17:15:20 -0500
Date: Fri, 10 Mar 2000 17:15:20 -0500
From: rich@shadrach.ispnet1.net
Message-Id: <200003102215.RAA07213@shadrach.ispnet1.net>
To: rich@shadrach.ispnet1.net
Subject: Test message 2

This is the second test message.
```

As shown in Listing 15.1, each message is identified by a separate `From` line identifying the sender and date of the message. The full RFC822 header and body of the message are stored in the mailbox file after the message header line.

Problems with the mbox Mailbox Format

Much has been researched and debated on the mbox mailbox format. For mail servers with lots (thousands) of users, file access speeds begin to deteriorate because it takes longer for the Unix operating system to access files within a directory with lots of other files.

Along with disk access speeds, some experts have questioned the reliability of the mbox mailbox format. By using a system in which new messages are appended to a file containing old messages, errors could have catastrophic effects.

If the mail server crashes while a message is being written to the user mailbox, the entire mailbox is at risk of becoming corrupted. If the `local` mail delivery program fails to create the `From` header line properly, MUA programs will not recognize the message as a new message, and they will instead read it as part of the preceding message. This not only corrupts the new message, but also corrupts the previous message. If a fatal error occurs when a message is being written to the user's mailbox, the entire mailbox file could be corrupted, thus causing all of the user's messages to be lost.

Local Message Retrieval

Using the mbox mailbox format also requires MUA programs to use a standard method to extract messages from the mailbox. Any MUA program required to display messages from the user mailbox must be able to interpret the mbox mailbox format to differentiate messages stored for the user.

If the MUA program displays a list of all the messages along with the `Subject:` header fields, it must parse through the contents of the entire mailbox when it starts up. Figure 15.2 demonstrates an MUA program reading messages contained in a user's mailbox.

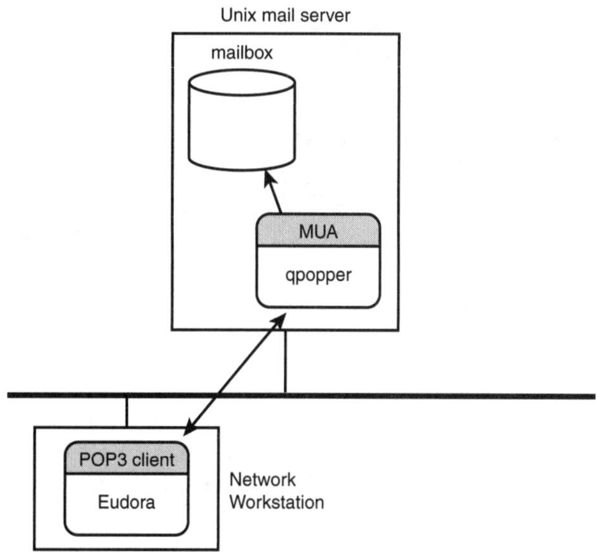

FIGURE 15.2

Using an MUA program to read mail messages.

When the POP3 client on the workstation (such as Eudora) requests a mail message from the MUA program (such as `qpopper`), the MUA program must directly access the individual user's mailbox file to retrieve the appropriate message. Each message must be parsed properly to separate the individual messages for the user. Listing 15.2 shows a sample output from the standard Unix `mail` program reading the mailbox messages shown in Listing 15.1.

LISTING 15.2 Sample `mail` Program Output

```
$ mail
Mail version 8.1 6/6/93.  Type ? for help.
"/var/spool/mail/rich": 2 messages 2 new
>N  1 rich@shadrach.ispnet  Fri Mar 10 17:15  13/385   "Test message 1"
 N  2 rich@shadrach.ispnet  Fri Mar 10 17:15  13/386   "Test message 2"

& 1
Message 1:
From rich  Fri Mar 10 17:15:08 2000
Date: Fri, 10 Mar 2000 17:15:07 -0500
From: rich@shadrach.ispnet1.net
To: rich@shadrach.ispnet1.net
Subject: Test message 1

This is the first test message.

& 2
Message 2:
From rich  Fri Mar 10 17:15:20 2000
Date: Fri, 10 Mar 2000 17:15:20 -0500
From: rich@shadrach.ispnet1.net
To: rich@shadrach.ispnet1.net
Subject: Test message 2

This is the second test message.

&
```

As you can see in the first part of Listing 15.2, the `mail` program lists the messages and the beginning of the `Subject:` header fields for each message. After the messages are listed, the user is presented with a command-line prompt from which he can manipulate the messages individually. Notice how the first line of each message contains the mailbox header line. It has become a part of the message, even though neither the sender nor the sending MTA program generated it.

Another disadvantage of the mbox mailbox format is that if a user is using an MUA program to read messages at the same time the `local` mail delivery program is storing new messages, file access could possibly become an issue. This might prevent new messages from being written, or worse, corrupt the entire mailbox file.

The Maildir Format

To compensate for the possible problems with the mbox mailbox format, Dan Bernstein designed a new mail storage system that could be more reliable. The new mailbox system stores messages individually in a separate mailbox directory for each user. This solves the file access speed, locking, and incomplete message problems possible with standard Unix mailboxes.

Normally each user's mailbox directory is located in his or her home directory to simplify security issues. Figure 15.3 demonstrates the normal Maildir directory format.

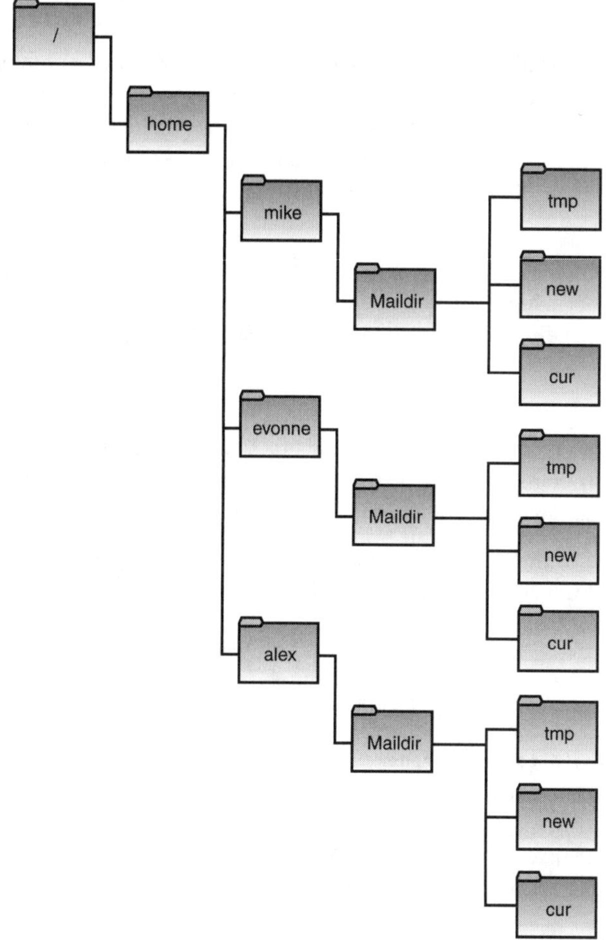

FIGURE 15.3

The Maildir mailbox format.

As you can see in Figure 15.3, Maildir is a directory divided into three separate subdirectories: `tmp`, `new`, and `cur`. Each individual message is stored as a separate file within one of the three `Maildir` subdirectories.

Postfix can be configured to store messages using the Maildir system. As discussed in Chapter 8, "The `main.cf` Configuration File," the `home_mailbox` parameter in the `main.cf` configuration file can be set to specify the Maildir mailbox format.

The following sections describe storing messages in and retrieving messages from a Maildir mailbox.

Local Message Storage

Unlike the mbox mailbox message storage method, Maildir uses a complicated system to ensure that any messages received by Postfix are properly created and stored in the Maildir mail directory. The three subdirectories in the Maildir directory manipulate the messages so Postfix knows exactly what state the messages are in. The following sections describe the Maildir directories and how messages are manipulated in them.

The Maildir `new` Directory

The `new` directory is used for storing new messages that the user has not read. Each message stored in this directory is given a unique filename using the naming convention

```
time.pid.host
```

where *`time`* is the number of seconds since 00:00 January 1, 1970, *`pid`* is the process ID of the receiving program, and *`host`* is the complete hostname of the receiving mail server. This ensures a unique filename for each message received.

Messages stored in the `new` subdirectory are stored exactly as they were received by Postfix. No additional header lines are added to the message. Listing 15.3 demonstrates a sample user's `new` Maildir subdirectory.

LISTING 15.3 Sample Maildir new Subdirectory and Messages

```
[rich@meshach rich]$ cd Maildir/new
[rich@meshach Maildir/new]$ ls -l
total 8
-rw-------   1 rich rich 412 Nov 21 09:31 974817093.14252_0.meshach.ispnet1.net
-rw-------   1 rich  rich  413 Nov 21 09:31 976517093.14252_1.meshach.ispnet1.net

[rich@meshach Maildir/new]$ cat 974817093.14252_0.meshach.ispnet1.net
Return-Path: <rich@meshach.ispnet1.net>
Delivered-To: rich@meshach.ispnet1.net
```

LISTING 15.3 Continued

```
Received: by meshach.ispnet1.net (Postfix, from userid 500)
        id 1BECDC352; Tue, 21 Nov 2000 09:31:32 -0500 (EST)
To: rich@meshach.ispnet1.net
Subject: Test message 1
Message-Id: <20001121143132.1BECDC352@meshach.ispnet1.net>
Date: Tue, 21 Nov 2000 09:31:32 -0500 (EST)
From: rich@meshach.ispnet1.net (Rich Blum)

This is the first test message.
[rich@meshach new]$
```

As you can see in Listing 15.3, this user's `new` mailbox contains two messages. Each message is shown as a separate file, each with a unique filename based on the `time` and `pid` numbers. By using the Unix `cat` command, the message that is contained in the message file can be displayed. As you can see, the message is stored in standard RFC822 format, complete with the message header and body. No additional header fields or lines have been added by Postfix to store the message.

The Maildir `cur` Directory

The `cur` directory is used for storing messages that have been read by the user using some type of MUA program. Once the user has read the message it is moved to the `cur` directory and given a new filename. The format of the new filename is

```
time.pid.host:info
```

The *`time`*, *`pid`*, and *`host`* parameters are exactly the same values as those used for the message in the `new` directory. The additional `info` parameter helps identify the status of the message for MUA programs.

The `info` parameter consists of flags that are used by most Maildir-enabled mail readers. Each flag identifies the status of the message. The flag consists of two parts, each part separated by a comma. The first part is a number, which identifies the type of flags used:

- `1` for experimental message flags
- `2` for standard message flags

For the purposes of a production Postfix server, the standard flags should always be used.

Table 15.1 shows the flags that can be used for standard messages stored in the `cur` directory.

TABLE 15.1 Standard Message Flags Used for `info`

Flag	*Description*
`R`	Replied
`S`	Seen
`F`	User-defined flag

Each message can have any number of flags set, including none. Multiple flags should be listed in alphabetical order. Listing 15.4 shows an example of a `cur` directory with multiple messages.

LISTING 15.4 Sample `Maildir/cur` Subdirectory

```
$ cd /home/rich/Maildir/cur
$ ls -l
total 2
-rw-----  1 rich rich 347 Nov 15 09:32 953130728.64111.meshach.ispnet1.net:2,S
-rw-----  1 rich rich 348 Nov 15 09:32 953130741.64117.meshach.ispnet1.net:2,S
$ cat 953130728.64111.meshach.ispnet1.net:2,S
Return-Path: <rich@meshach.ispnet1.net>
Delivered-To: rich@meshach.ispnet1.net
Received: by meshach.ispnet1.net (Postfix, from userid 500)
        id 1BECDC221; Wed, 15 Nov 2000 09:31:32 -0500 (EST)
To: rich@meshach.ispnet1.net
Subject: Test message 1
Message-ID: <20000315143207.64107@meshach.ispnet1.net>
Date: 15 Nov 2000 14:32:07 -0000
From: rich@meshach.ispnet1.net

This is the first test message.
$
```

As you can see from Listing 15.4, two messages are stored in this user's mailbox. They are both identified as having been seen (presumably the user read them). As seen from the Unix `ls` command, both messages retained the same filenames from when they were in the `new` subdirectory (as shown in Listing 15.3) except for the additional `info` section. Both messages are tagged as being type 2 messages (as expected), and having been seen by the user. It is the responsibility of the MUA program to properly set the message flags.

The Maildir `tmp` Directory

The `tmp` directory is used for creating new messages in the user's mailbox. Postfix uses the `tmp` directory to create the initial file that holds the incoming new message to ensure that the message is safely written. Once the message is written, it is moved to the Maildir `new` directory.

When Postfix receives a message destined for a local user, it follows six steps to safely store the message in the user's mailbox. These steps are

1. Change to the user's Maildir directory.
2. Use the Unix `stat()` command to determine whether the file `tmp/time.pid.host` exists.
3. If the filename exists, wait two seconds and try again using the updated time parameter. After a set number of attempts, `local` gives up and returns an error.
4. The file `tmp/time.pid.host` is created.
5. The received message is written to the newly created file.
6. The file is linked to the file `new/time.pid.host`. This links the message to a file in the `new` directory with the same filename. Before creating the link, a 24-hour timer is set. If the timer expires before the link is created, Postfix returns an error, or if there is a successful link, the `tmp/time.pid.host` file is deleted.

These six steps ensure that each message is safely written to the user's Maildir directory.

Local Message Retrieval

Since the Maildir method uses a special format to store messages, any MUA programs used to retrieve messages from the Maildir directory must understand the Maildir message format. Unfortunately, only a limited number of MUA programs can read messages stored in the Maildir format.

The Maildir message reader must be able to distinguish between messages in the `new` directory and messages in the `cur` directory. Any message read from the `new` directory must be transferred to the `cur` directory. Also, as mentioned in the previous section, when the message is transferred its name must also be appended with the status flags for the message.

The messages stored will be in the same format as the original RFC822 formatted message. No additional text will be present. Listing 15.5 shows a sample POP3 session using a POP3 MUA program that reads a message from a Maildir-formatted mailbox.

LISTING 15.5 Sample Message from a Maildir Mailbox

```
$ telnet localhost 110
Trying 127.0.0.1...
Connected to localhost.
Escape character is '^]'.
+OK <64454.953155453@meshach.ispnet1.net>
USER rich
+OK
PASS guitar
```

LISTING 15.5 Continued

```
9  +OK
10 LIST
11 +OK
12 1 347
13 2 348
14 .
15 RETR 1
16 +OK
17 Return-Path: <rich@meshach.ispnet1.net>
18 Delivered-To: rich@meshach.ispnet1.net
19 Received: by meshach.ispnet1.net (Postfix, from userid 500)
20         id 1BECDC221; Wed, 15 Nov 2000 09:31:32 -0500 (EST)
21 To: rich@meshach.ispnet1.net
22 Subject: Test message 1
23 Message-ID: <20000315143207.64107@meshach.ispnet1.net>
24 Date: 15 Nov 2000 14:32:07 -0000
25 From: rich@meshach.ispnet1.net
26
27 This is the first test message.
28 .
29 QUIT
30 +OK
31 Connection closed by foreign host.
32 $
```

In Listing 15.5, line 1 shows an example of how to use the `telnet` program to manually connect to the POP3 server software running on the local mail server. Line 5 shows the greeting banner displayed by the POP3 server. In lines 6–9 the user is authenticated using a plaintext username and password. Line 10 shows the POP3 command used to list all of the messages that are in the user's mailbox. Lines 12–14 are the response from the server. There are two messages in the user's mailbox. In line 15 the user requests the first message. The message is then displayed in lines 17–28. Notice that this differs from the message that was stored in the standard Unix mailbox as shown in Listing 15.2. The standard `From` header line is not inserted into the message by the `local` mail program.

In addition to reading messages in the `new` and `cur` directories, the MUA is also expected to scan the contents of the `tmp` directory. Any messages left in the `tmp` directory for more than 36 hours are considered delivery failures, and should be deleted by the MUA program.

Configuring Postfix to Use Maildir Mailboxes

Postfix uses the `home_mailbox` parameter to determine where it places local user messages. By specifying a directory, Postfix assumes that the Maildir mailbox format should be used. The format for this is

```
home_mailbox = Maildir/
```

Note the trailing slash on the mailbox name. This indicates that the mailbox is a directory, and that Postfix should use the Maildir format when creating it. The mail administrator can use any text he wants for the actual directory name:

```
home_mailbox = postoffice/
```

Remember that whatever text is specified will be used for all users on the local mail server. In this case, if a directory named `postoffice` exists in a user's `$HOME` directory, Postfix will create the normal Maildir subdirectories beneath the currently existing directory. This may get confusing, so it is best to choose a standard directory name, and inform the local users not to create a directory with that name.

CAUTION

Be careful when creating exotic Maildir directory names. Many MUA packages that can utilize Maildir-formatted mailboxes expect the mail directory to be named Maildir. You may need to manually configure the MUA program to use any other directory names.

By default, Postfix will not create users' Maildir directories when Postfix is started. When an individual user receives a new message, Postfix will determine whether the pertinent Maildir directory exists. If it does not, Postfix will create it along with the appropriate subdirectories.

Some MUA packages that utilize Maildir-formatted mailboxes may have a problem with this. If a Maildir-formatted directory is not present when the MUA program is run, it produces an error. A simple solution to this problem is to send each new user an initial welcoming e-mail message. This forces Postfix to create the Maildir directory for each user.

Using a Maildir-Aware MUA Program

There are several different MUA programs that can be used to allow users to read messages stored in Maildir-formatted mailboxes. The courier-imap software package is one such popular MUA package. It allows users to connect to the Postfix mail server using the IMAP protocol to read their mail messages. Many popular client mail packages such as Microsoft Outlook Express and Netscape Communicator can be used by remote Windows workstation clients to read their mail messages.

This section describes how to install, configure, and use the courier-imap software package to allow users to read their mail in Maildir-formatted mailboxes.

Installing courier-imap

The courier-imap software was developed and is maintained by Double Precision, Inc. It is released under the terms of the GNU General Public License. The Web site for the courier-imap package is located at `http://www.inter7.com/courierimap`.

The courier-imap package is one piece of a complete e-mail server implementation developed by Double Precision called Courier. The courier-imap package can be downloaded as an individual source code package at

```
ftp://download.sourceforge.net/pub/sourceforge/courier/courier-imap-1.3.1.tar.gz
```

At the time of this writing, the current version of courier-imap is version 1.3.1. Once the source code distribution is downloaded it can be extracted into a working directory.

```
tar -zxvf courier-imap-1.3.1.tar.gz
```

CAUTION

Be careful when extracting the source code distribution. Unlike most other packages, the courier-imap distribution must be extracted into a directory owned by a normal user, not the `root` user. Thus, you cannot use the standard `/usr/local/src` directory.

Once the source code is extracted, you can change to the newly created directory to begin the building and installation process:

```
cd courier-imap-1.3.1
```

The first part of the installation is to run the `configure` utility to set any special pre-compilation configuration options. Table 15.2 lists common configuration options that can be used.

TABLE 15.2 courier-imap Configuration Options

Option	*Description*
`--prefix=`*`pathname`*	Changes the default installation directory
`--without-ipv6`	Does not include IPv6 support
`--enable-unicode`	Includes support for unicode characters in messages
`--enable-unicode=`*`charset`*	Includes unicode support for the specified character set
`--without-`*`module`*	Does not include support for the specified authentication module

TABLE 15.2 Continued

Option	*Description*
`--bindir=pathname`	Changes the default binary directory location
`--mandir=pathname`	Changes the default man pages directory location
`--with-db=db`	Includes support for the DB database library instead of the GDBM database library
`--with-piddir=dir`	Changes the default location of the `imapd.pid` file
`--with-userdb=file`	Changes the default location of the virtual users database file
`--enable-workarounds-for-imap-client-bugs`	Adds support for known IMAP client problems

The format of the `configure` command is

```
configure [options]
```

where *`options`* is a space-separated list of the desired options to use for compiling. A sample `configure` command would be

```
./configure --without-ipv6 --enable-workarounds-for-imap-client-bugs
```

This command runs the `configure` command (the `./` ensures that the `configure` command in the `courier-imap-1.3.1` directory is run) using options to not include support for IPv6 (most Linux kernels do not have this included by default), and to include support for known IMAP client bugs (the Netscape Communicator 4.7 mail browser is known to not work without this option).

CAUTION

The courier-imap package recommends using the GDBM database package if possible. Most Linux distributions include this as a binary package, although not all load it by default. Make sure this package is loaded on your Linux system before compiling the courier-imap package. If your Unix distribution does not include the GDBM package, you must have the Berkeley db database package libraries installed.

The `configure` command checks the system for installed compilers, libraries, and authentication modules. Because courier-imap is a modular program, the `configure` command loops through each individual module to set the proper options. A Makefile is created with the necessary parameters for compiling the source code on the server.

NOTE

Because many of the courier-imap modules use similar code, the `configure` command may seem to repeat the same commands. The process is not stuck in a loop, it's just going through the modules. Don't stop the configure process, just let it finish on its own.

After the `configure` command has finished, the source code should be ready to be compiled. You must use the GNU `make` command to compile the source code based on the Makefile generated by the `configure` command. The format of the `make` command is simple:

```
make
```

After the `make` command has finished compiling the program, you can check the new executable files to ensure that they are okay by using the `check` option on the `make` command:

```
make check
```

Several tests are performed on the created executables to ensure that they have been compiled properly. If the `make` command exits without an error, the executable code has passed the checks and is ready for installation.

NOTE

With some older versions of courier-imap, if you run the `configure` program with the `--enable-workarounds-for-imap-client-bugs` option, the `make check` process will fail. This is a normal result, and has been fixed since the 1.3.0 version.

To install the courier-imap programs to their normal locations, you must be logged in as the `root` user. Once logged in as the `root` user, you can use the `install` option on the `make` command:

```
make install
```

The `install` option places the courier-imap programs and man pages into the directories specified in the configure step. The default location for all courier-imap files is the `/usr/lib/courier-imap` directory. The directory should look something like this:

```
[nicholas@shadrach nicholas]$ cd /usr/lib/courier-imap
[nicholas@shadrach /usr/lib/courier-imap]$ ls -al
total 44
drwxr-xr-x   9 root     root         4096 Nov 20 16:44 .
drwxr-xr-x  43 root     root        12288 Nov 20 16:44 ..
drwxr-xr-x   2 root     root         4096 Nov 21 13:29 bin
drwxr-xr-x   2 root     root         4096 Nov 21 13:30 etc
drwxr-xr-x   3 root     root         4096 Nov 21 13:29 libexec
drwxr-xr-x   4 root     root         4096 Nov 20 16:44 man
drwxr-xr-x   2 root     root         4096 Nov 21 13:29 sbin
drwxr-xr-x   2 root     root         4096 Nov 21 13:29 share
drwxr-xr-x   3 root     root         4096 Nov 20 16:44 var
```

To install the configuration files, you must run the `make` command again, this time with the `install-configure` option:

```
make install-configure
```

This installs the courier-imap configuration files. Now courier-imap is ready to be configured to work in your particular e-mail environment.

Configuring courier-imap

The newly installed courier-imap package uses a generic configuration file that should be suitable for your specific server installation. The main pieces of the configuration that are required are the different authentication modules.

courier-imap can use several different methods to authenticate user login requests. Each method uses a different module that plugs into the courier-imap software. Table 15.3 lists the different authentication modules that can be used.

TABLE 15.3 courier-imap Authentication Modules

Module	*Description*
`authpwd`	Uses standard `/etc/passwd` files
`authshadow`	Uses shadow password files
`authpam`	Uses the PAM authentication library
`authuserdb`	Uses a courier-imap–specific user database file
`authcram`	Uses a specific user database file with CRAM-MD5 authentication
`authvchkpw`	Uses vpopmail password files
`authldap`	Uses an LDAP server
`authmysql`	Uses a MySQL database
`authdaemon`	Uses a background authentication proxy
`authcustom`	Uses a custom-built authentication program

courier-imap can use multiple authentication modules to authenticate a login attempt. Each module listed by the administrator is used in sequence to verify the login username. When one module reports a valid username, the session is authenticated and the user is allowed access to the mailbox.

The configuration file used is the `imapd.config` file located in the `/usr/lib/courier-imap/etc` directory by default. It contains the primary configuration parameters used by courier-imap.

The `AUTHMODULES` parameter defines the different authentication modules that are compiled into the existing courier-imap software. On the test system used, the `AUTHMODULES` parameter is

```
AUTHMODULES="authcustom authcram authuserdb authpam"
```

This allows for using a custom user database, a CRAM-MD5 user database, a DB user database, and using the PAM authentication library on the local system. The easiest to configure is the PAM authentication library.

The PAM authentication library allows the courier-imap package to use existing system usernames and home directories for IMAP access. Only one additional item needs to be configured for this authentication method to work. The PAM system must be configured to allow the IMAP server access to the library. The courier-imap package automatically adds a PAM configuration file to the system during the installation phase. The location of this configuration file by default is

```
/etc/pam.d/imap
```

Each application that wants to use the PAM authentication library to authenticate logins must be registered with the library. To register, a file must be created in the `/etc/pam.d` directory. The file specifies the appropriate library files that are required to communicate with the PAM database.

The configuration file automatically created by the courier-imap installation program looks like this:

```
#%PAM-1.0
#
# $Id: imapd.authpam,v 1.1 1999/10/12 16:43:17 mrsam Exp $
#

auth       required /lib/security/pam_pwdb.so shadow nullok
account    required /lib/security/pam_pwdb.so
session    required      /lib/security/pam_pwdb.so
```

The configuration file defines the library locations used for the different authentication methods. Under most circumstances, the courier-imap installation program uses the proper library definitions for the configuration file. If these definitions do not work for your server, you can look at other PAM application configuration files and use the same library filenames.

Using courier-imap

Once the authentication modules are configured, you can start the courier-imap server. Before starting the server, you should ensure that no other IMAP server is running on the system. Most other IMAP servers use the `inetd` program to monitor the network for IMAP connection requests. To ensure that no other IMAP server is running, check the `/etc/inetd.conf` file and make sure that the imap configuration line is commented out:

```
#imap    stream  tcp     nowait  root    /usr/sbin/tcpd imapd
```

The pound symbol (#) is used to comment out the line so that it is not processed by the `inetd` daemon.

To start the courier-imap server, you must run a startup script with the `start` parameter:

```
/usr/lib/courier-imap/libexec/imapd.rc start
```

You should see several courier-imap sessions running in background mode, waiting for new IMAP connections:

```
26032 ?    S       0:00 /usr/lib/courier-imap/libexec/authlib/authdaemond start
26036 ?    S       0:00 /usr/lib/courier-imap/libexec/authlib/authdaemond start
26037 ?    S       0:00 /usr/lib/courier-imap/libexec/authlib/authdaemond start
26038 ?    S       0:00 /usr/lib/courier-imap/libexec/authlib/authdaemond start
26039 ?    S       0:00 /usr/lib/courier-imap/libexec/authlib/authdaemond start
26040 ?    S       0:00 /usr/lib/courier-imap/libexec/authlib/authdaemond start
26841 ?    S       0:00 /usr/lib/courier-imap/libexec/couriertcpd -address=0
26843 ?    S       0:00 /usr/lib/courier-imap/libexec/logger imaplogin
```

You can easily test to see whether the IMAP server is accepting connections by telnetting to the IMAP port (143). Listing 15.6 shows a sample IMAP test session.

LISTING 15.6 Sample IMAP Session

```
[rich@shadrach]$ telnet localhost 143
Trying 127.0.0.1...
Connected to localhost.
Escape character is '^]'.
* OK Courier-IMAP ready. Copyright 1998-2000 Double Precision, Inc.
➥ See COPYING for distribution information.
a001 LOGIN rich guitar
a001 OK LOGIN Ok.
a002 SELECT INBOX
* FLAGS (\Answered \Flagged \Deleted \Seen \Recent)
* OK [PERMANENTFLAGS (\Answered \Flagged \Deleted \Seen)] Limited
* 27 EXISTS
* 0 RECENT
* OK [UIDVALIDITY 974757506]
a002 OK [READ-WRITE] Ok
a003 LOGOUT
* BYE Courier-IMAP server shutting down
a003 OK LOGOUT completed
Connection closed by foreign host.
```

Listing 15.6 shows a successful IMAP session. After connecting to TCP port 143, the courier-imap server issues a welcome banner. The client can then enter IMAP commands to log in to the server and connect to his INBOX mailbox.

Using Shared Folders

One very nice feature of the courier-imap server software is the use of shared folders. Shared folders allow users on the mail server to access common mail folders to read and store messages. This feature is great for announcing system problems (or improvements) as well as offering a place for users to share information.

The `maildirmake` utility is used to create shared folders. Any user can create a shared folder using the `maildirmake` utility, or alternatively, the mail administrator can control shared folders.

The format of the `maildirmake` utility is

```
maildirmake [ options ] maildir
```

where *`maildir`* is the pathname of the shared folder. There are lots of options that can be used with `maildirmake`. The options determine the behavior of the `maildirmake` utility. Table 15.4 lists the options available to use.

TABLE 15.4 `maildirmake` Options

Option	*Description*
`-S`	Creates a shared Maildir-formatted directory
`-f`	Creates a shared folder within a shared Maildir directory
`-s mode`	Sets the sharing mode of a shared folder
`--add`	Adds a shared directory to a user's `Maildir` directory
`--del`	Deletes a shared directory from a user's `Maildir` directory

Creating shared folders is a three-step process:

1. A shared Maildir-formatted directory is created.
2. One or more shared folders are created in the shared Maildir-formatted directory.
3. Users link to the shared Maildir-formatted directory from their own `Maildir` directories.

The owner of the shared folders performs the first two steps. The mail administrator can choose to perform these functions himself, or can allow individual users to create shared folders. Of course for individual users to do this, they must have shell access to the mail server.

As an example, the mail administrator will create a shared Maildir for everyone in the organization called `OfficeNews`. Within the shared Maildir will be three shared folders: `officechat`, `productinfo`, and `pcsupport`.

First, the mail administrator must create the shared Maildir-formatted directory that will contain the shared folders:

```
maildirmake -S /usr/local/share/OfficeNews
```

The `maildirmake` command uses the `-S` option to create the Maildir directory `OfficeNews`. When placing a shared Maildir-formatted directory on the mail server, you should make sure that the location is accessible to all users who need to access the shared folders. The courier-imap program will control access at the `OfficeNews` directory level, but the mail administrator must ensure that users have access to the `/usr/local/share` directory. If individual users create their own shared Maildir-formatted directories, the administrator must ensure that they create them in areas where other users can access the created Maildir. Often this is not in their `$HOME` directory.

Once the shared Maildir-formatted directory is created, the shared folders can be created within it. To do this the mail administrator must again use the `maildirmake` command, along with the `-s` and `-f` options.

The `-s` option allows the mail administrator to control access to the shared folder. There are four different sharing options that can be selected. Table 15.5 lists the different sharing options.

TABLE 15.5 courier-imap Shared Folder Sharing Options

Option	*Description*
`-s read`	Allows only read access to other users, and read/write access to the folder owner
`-s write`	Allows read and write access to all users on the mail server
`-s read,group`	Allows read access only to users in the same system group as the folder owner
`-s write,group`	Allows read and write access only to users in the same system group as the folder owner

Both the mail administrator and system users can use any of the four sharing options when creating shared folders. When a system user creates a shared folder using the group option, only other system users in the same group as the user will have access to the folder.

For this example, the mail administrator will create the shared folders with the following access rights:

- `officechat`—Write access to all users.
- `productinfo`—Write access to all users in the mail administrator's group.
- `pcsupport`—Read access to all users, but write access for the mail administrator.

The commands used to create these folders would be

```
maildirmake -s write -f officechat /usr/local/share/OfficeNews
maildirmake -s write,group -f productinfo /usr/local/share/OfficeNews
maildirmake -s read -f pcsupport /usr/local/share/OfficeNews
```

After the shared folders are created, each user, including the mail administrator, must use the `maildirmake` command to add the shared folders to their Maildir directory. This is done using the `--add` option of the `maildirmake` command. Instead of having to add each individual shared folder, the `--add` option links the shared Maildir-formatted directory to the user's Maildir.

If users do not have shell access to the mail server, the mail administrator must do this step for them. This can become a tedious process. The command used to create the shared folders link is

```
maildirmake --add OfficeNews=/usr/local/share/OfficeNews $HOME/Maildir
```

As mentioned, this command must be run for each user. Also, it must be run `su` as the individual user so that the directory permissions are set correctly.

Once the link to the shared folders Maildir-formatted directory is created, users can subscribe to the shared folders using their MUA program. This is often done in the configuration options of the MUA program.

As an example, in Netscape Communicator, clicking on the File menu option and selecting Subscribe does this. Figure 15.4 shows the resulting dialog box.

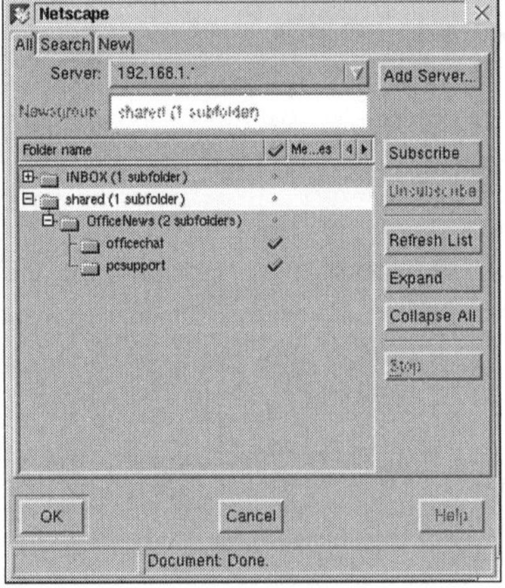

FIGURE 15.4

Netscape Communicator folder subscription dialog box.

When you click on the shared folder, the `OfficeNews` folder appears. When you click on that, the individual shared folders appear. Highlight the individual folders and click the Subscribe button to subscribe to the shared folder.

After subscribing to the shared folders, the user can see messages posted in the folder from the main mail window as shown in Figure 15.5.

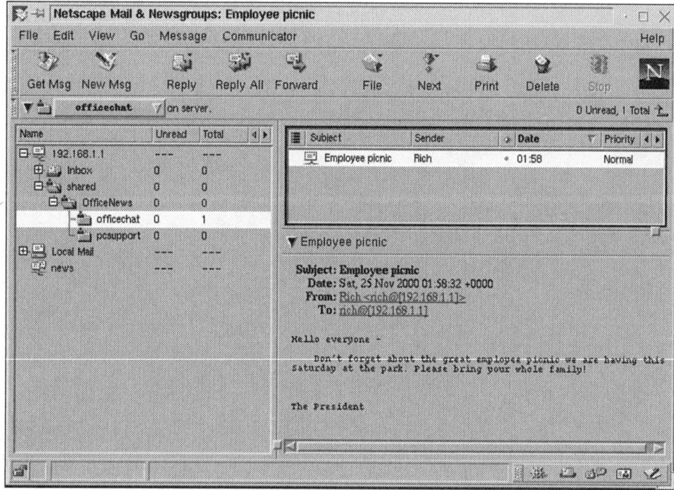

FIGURE 15.5

Netscape Communicator main message window.

The users should be able to move messages from their `Inbox` folder to the `officechat` folder, but should only be able to read messages posted in the `pcsupport` folder. Users in the same group as the mail administrator have write access to the `productinfo` folder, but users not in the same group will only have read access.

Summary

The Postfix program supports alternative mailbox types. One of these types is the Maildir mailbox format created by Dan Bernstein. The Maildir mailbox format uses a directory structure in which each message is stored in the mailbox directory as a separate file. This decreases the opportunity for message corruption and increases the access speed for reading messages.

The Maildir mailbox format utilizes three subdirectories for holding messages. The `tmp` directory is used for temporarily creating new messages. Once the message has been successfully created, it is moved to the `new` directory. Users read new messages from the `new` directory. Once a message has been read, it is moved to the `cur` directory for storage.

Special MUA programs must be used with the Maildir mailbox format. Not all MUA programs can read messages stored in Maildir-style mailboxes.

The courier-imap package provides a stable IMAP server that uses Maildir mailboxes to store messages. The courier-imap package also provides shared folders that can be used to share messages between users on the mail server.

CHAPTER 16

Using MDA Programs with Postfix

Postfix can deliver messages destined for users on the local mail server using its own mail delivery method. In fact, it supports three different methods of delivering mail to local users:

- Using `sendmail`-style mailbox files
- Using a separate file located in the user's `$HOME` directory
- Using Maildir-style mailbox directories in the user's `$HOME` directory

In addition to doing its own mail delivery, Postfix can use a fourth method of delivering mail: enlisting the support of an external MDA program. This chapter describes how MDA programs work and why you might want to use a separate MDA program when delivering messages to users on the local mail server. Following that, a popular MDA program, procmail, is described.

What Is a Local Mail Delivery Agent?

Often, MTA programs rely on separate MDA programs to deliver messages to local users. Because these MDAs concentrate only on delivering mail to local users, they can add additional bells and whistles that aren't available in MTAs. This enables the e-mail administrator to offer additional features to e-mail users.

The MDA receives messages from the MTA and must determine how those messages are to be delivered. Figure 16.1 demonstrates how the MDA program interacts with the MTA program.

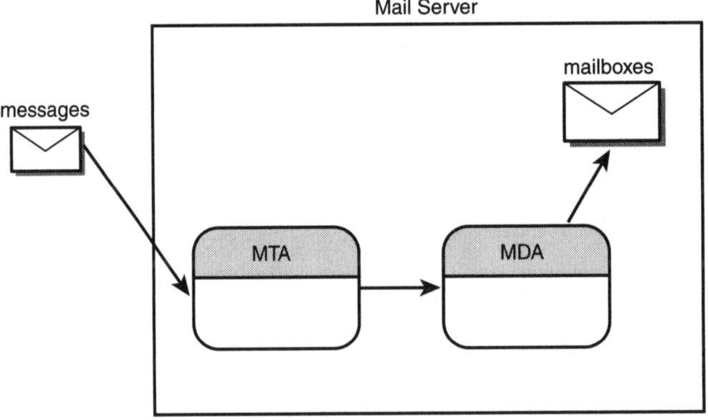

FIGURE 16.1

Using an MDA program on a mail server.

Many MDAs allow users to customize delivery of messages to their mailboxes. Often, advanced MDAs can provide special features such as

- Automatic filtering of messages
- Automatic replying to messages
- Automatic archiving of messages

These are features that the individual mail users can customize themselves without the mail administrator having to do any work. This section describes these features and how they can be used in a mail system.

Automatic Mail Filtering

Possibly the nicest and most used feature of MDA programs is the ability to filter incoming mail messages. For users who get lots of e-mail messages, this can be a lifesaver. Messages can be automatically sorted into separate folders based on text pattern matching, such as a subject header value or even just one word within a subject header field. Figure 16.2 demonstrates this process.

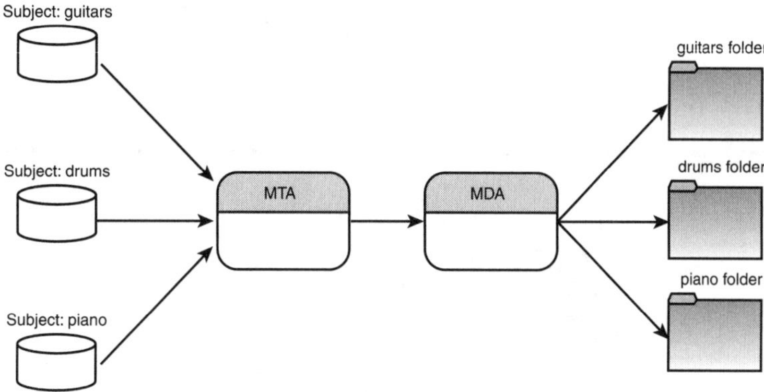

FIGURE 16.2

Sorting incoming mail messages into separate folders.

The MDA utilizes a configuration file that allows a user to specify regular expressions to search fields in the incoming message header. As expressions are matched, the message can be saved in a predetermined folder in the user's mail area.

An alternative feature similar to this is the ability to filter out and throw away undesirable messages. This feature can help reduce unwanted unsolicited commercial e-mail (UCE), but must be used with caution. *Any* message filtered out as UCE to be thrown away will be lost permanently—even if it is actually a legitimate e-mail!

Automatic Mail Replying

Another feature used in MDA programs is the ability for the mail user to configure an auto-reply for selected e-mail messages. Much like message filtering, many MDA programs also allow the mail user to send reply messages to senders based on values defined in the message header fields. Mail users can customize the auto-reply function to support many different types of responses to received messages. Figure 16.3 demonstrates the use of the auto-reply feature.

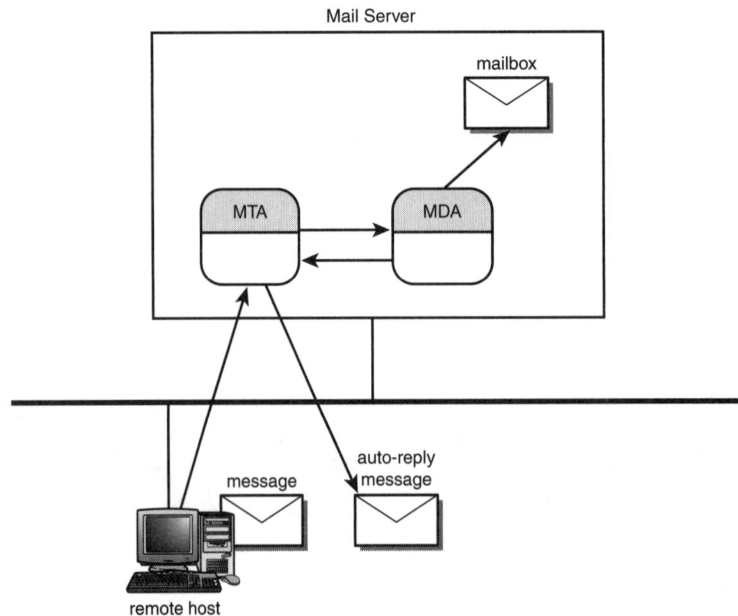

FIGURE 16.3

Using an auto-reply MDA feature to respond to e-mail messages.

The mail user can configure the MDA program to send mail responses to the original message sender based on predetermined values in the configuration file. Different values can elicit different text messages in the reply message. Many MDAs allow users to auto-reply to all messages. This is often used in situations where users know they will be away from their e-mail for awhile. The mail user can also determine whether the original message is stored in a mail folder or is discarded after responding to it.

Automatic Program Initialization by Mail

Still another common feature of MDAs is the ability for the mail user to run a program based on receiving a certain kind of message. The MDA program can also start different programs based on different text in the message body itself. Figure 16.4 demonstrates this process.

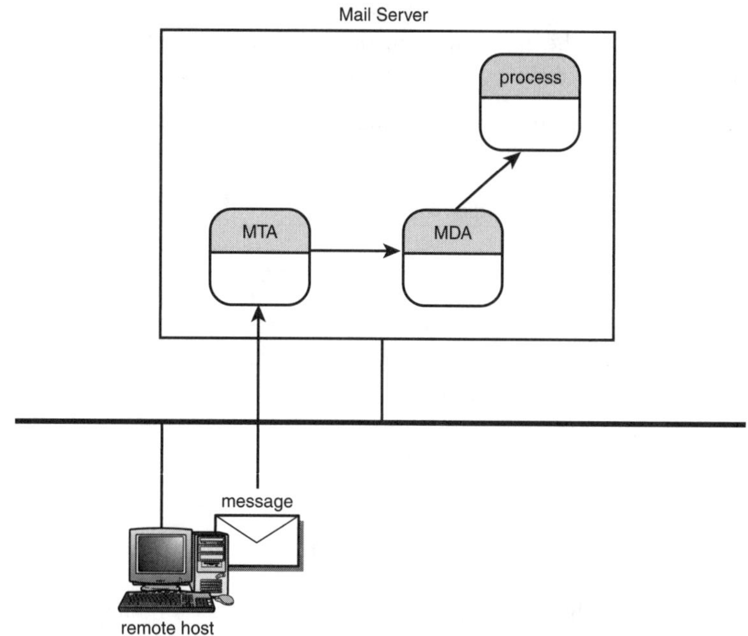

FIGURE 16.4

Starting a program from a mail message.

Many MDA programs allow the mail user to create a configuration in which programs are started based on values within the mail message, such as subject header values. This can allow such exotic functions as producing different workstation sounds based on a new message with a particular subject heading.

Using an External MDA Program with Postfix

Postfix can be configured to utilize external MDAs to deliver messages to local users. This section describes how to configure Postfix to utilize external MDAs, and how to monitor the log files to ensure that messages are being properly delivered to the MDA.

Configuring the `main.cf` File

The `mailbox_command` parameter in the `main.cf` configuration file defines the MDA program that Postfix will use. The format of the `mailbox_command` parameter is

```
mailbox_command = program [options]
```

where *program* is the full pathname of the MDA program to pass local messages to, and *options* is optional command-line parameters that can be passed to the program. Postfix allows the mail administrator to pass values from the mail message to the MDA program in the command line using environment variables. Any characters that are special shell metacharacters (such as the exclamation mark and spaces) are replaced by the underscore character to prevent any malicious attempts by renegade users.

Table 16.1 lists the environment variables that Postfix can pass to the MDA program.

TABLE 16.1 Postfix Environment Variables

Variable	*Description*
DOMAIN	The recipient's address domain (everything to the right of the @ symbol)
EXTENSION	The recipient's optional address extension
HOME	The recipient's home directory
LOCAL	The recipient's local address (everything to the left of the @ symbol)
LOGNAME	The recipient's name
RECIPIENT	The recipient's entire address
SHELL	The recipient's Unix login shell
USER	The recipient's name

The environment variables can be used in the MDA program options to define how the MDA program should deliver the message:

```
mailbox_command = /usr/bin/procmail -a "$EXTENSION"
```

This example passes the message recipient's address extension to the procmail MDA. When passing environment variables to the MDA program, quotes should be used to avoid any problems with special characters used in the variable.

CAUTION

When the `mailbox_command` parameter is set, any values used in the `home_mailbox` parameter are ignored. Often mail administrators experiment with external MDA programs and set the `mailbox_command`, then forget to comment it out and try setting a mail delivery method using the `home_mailbox` parameter. This can cause several hours of frustrating troubleshooting.

Watching MDA Programs in the Postfix Log

Postfix will log all messages that are passed to external MDA programs. The mail administrator can monitor the mail log to determine whether messages are being properly delivered to the MDA. Listing 16.1 shows a sample log entry of a message delivered to a local user using an MDA program.

LISTING 16.1 Sample Postfix Log Entry for an MDA Program

```
Dec  3 16:22:25 shadrach postfix/pickup[671]: C65423B1D4: uid=501 from=<rich>
Dec  3 16:22:26 shadrach postfix/cleanup[693]: C65423B1D4:
➥ message-id=<20001203212225.C65423B1D4@shadrach.ispnet1.net>
Dec  3 16:22:26 shadrach postfix/qmgr[672]: C65423B1D4:
➥ from=<rich@shadrach.ispnet1.net>, size=335, nrcpt=1 (queue active)
Dec  3 16:22:26 shadrach postfix/local[695]: C65423B1D4:
➥ to=<jessica@shadrach.ispnet1.net>, relay=local, delay=1, status=sent
➥ ("|/usr/bin/procmail -a "$EXTENSION"")
```

The log entry shown in Listing 16.1 documents a message as it is received from a local user (`rich`) and sent to another local user (`jessica`) on the mail server using the MDA program. The last entry in the listing shows the delivery to the procmail program (along with the `mailbox_command` definition as shown in the `main.cf` file example in the preceding section). The status indicates that the message was successfully sent to the MDA program.

If there is a problem with the MDA program, often you can troubleshoot the problem by watching the mail log file. Listing 16.2 shows an example of an MDA problem in the log.

LISTING 16.2 Sample MDA Program Problem Log Entries

```
Dec  4 19:40:44 shadrach postfix/pickup[40224]: 12B73211: uid=1001 from=<rich>
Dec  4 19:40:44 shadrach postfix/cleanup[40229]: 12B73211: message-id=
➥ <20001204214043.122B73211@shadrach.ispnet1.net>
Dec  4 19:40:44 shadrach postfix/qmgr[40225]: 12B73211:
➥ from=<rich@shadrach.ispnet1.net>, size=364, nrcpt=1 (queue active)
Dec  4 19:40:44 shadrach mail.local: usage:
➥ mail.local [-b] [-l] [-f from] [-s] user ...
Dec  4 19:40:44 shadrach postfix/local[40231]: 122B73211:
➥ to=<rich@shadrach.ispnet1.net>, relay=local, delay=1, status=bounced
➥ (service unavailable. Command output: mail.local:
➥ illegal option -- x mail.local: usage: mail.local [-b] [-l]
➥ [-f from] [-s] user ... )
```

As shown in Listing 16.2, a message sent from the local user `rich` was rejected by the MDA program. The error message received from the MDA program (`mail.local`) is returned to the Postfix local program and stored in the mail log. This particular error indicates that the mail administrator placed an invalid command-line option on the `mailbox_command` parameter line when he defined the `mail.local` command (oops). Note that the full text of the error message returned by the MDA program is reproduced in the mail log.

The mail log file can come in very handy when trying to troubleshoot problems when using external MDA programs. Note that in this situation, even the bounced message bounces because the local mailer is broken. The result is that no mail is delivered to any local users, including the mail administrator. Without seeing any output, it would be nearly impossible to troubleshoot this problem without the help of the mail log file.

NOTE

Chapter 23, "Common Postfix Problems," describes in greater detail how to use the mail log file for troubleshooting mail server problems.

The procmail MDA Program

One of the more popular MDA programs in use is the procmail program written by Stephen R. van den Berg. It has become so popular that many Linux distributions now install it by default, and many MTA programs include it in default configurations.

The popularity of the procmail program comes from its versatility in creating user-configured "recipes" that can allow a user to direct how received mail is processed. A user can create his own `$HOME/.procmailrc` file to direct messages based on regular expressions to separate mailbox files, to alternative e-mail addresses, or even to the `/dev/null` file to automatically trash (delete) unwanted mail.

This section describes how to install and use procmail on the Postfix mail server.

Installing procmail

Most Linux distributions include a binary distribution of the procmail package. The Mandrake 7.2 Linux distribution includes the RPM package

```
procmail-3.14-3mdk.i586.rpm
```

This package installs the 3.14 version of procmail. This package includes the procmail binary programs, the procmail man pages, and some procmail configuration file examples. Listing 16.3 shows the files that are included with this standard binary distribution.

LISTING 16.3 procmail-3.14 RPM Distribution Files

```
[rich@shadrach RPMS]$ rpm -qlp procmail-3.14-3mdk.i586.rpm | more
/usr/bin/formail
/usr/bin/lockfile
/usr/bin/mailstat
/usr/bin/procmail
/usr/share/doc/procmail-3.14
```

LISTING 16.3 Continued

```
/usr/share/doc/procmail-3.14/FAQ
/usr/share/doc/procmail-3.14/FEATURES
/usr/share/doc/procmail-3.14/HISTORY
/usr/share/doc/procmail-3.14/KNOWN_BUGS
/usr/share/doc/procmail-3.14/README
/usr/share/doc/procmail-3.14/examples
/usr/share/doc/procmail-3.14/examples/1procmailrc
/usr/share/doc/procmail-3.14/examples/1rmail
/usr/share/doc/procmail-3.14/examples/2procmailrc
/usr/share/doc/procmail-3.14/examples/2rmail
/usr/share/doc/procmail-3.14/examples/3procmailrc
/usr/share/doc/procmail-3.14/examples/3rmail
/usr/share/doc/procmail-3.14/examples/advanced
/usr/share/doc/procmail-3.14/examples/dirname
/usr/share/doc/procmail-3.14/examples/forward
/usr/share/doc/procmail-3.14/examples/mailstat
/usr/share/man/man1/formail.1.bz2
/usr/share/man/man1/lockfile.1.bz2
/usr/share/man/man1/procmail.1.bz2
/usr/share/man/man5/procmailex.5.bz2
/usr/share/man/man5/procmailrc.5.bz2
/usr/share/man/man5/procmailsc.5.bz2
```

To install an RPM package distribution, you can use the rpm package manager with the Linux system:

```
rpm -Uvh procmail-3.14-3mdk.i586.rpm
```

The command line shown installs the procmail package in the locations shown in Listing 16.3.

If your Linux distribution does not include a binary distribution package for procmail, or more likely, you would like to install the latest version, you can download a source code distribution package from the procmail Web site.

The main procmail Web site is located at `http://www.procmail.org`. From that page there are links to the current source code distribution file to download. At the time of this writing, there are two links for downloading the source code:

```
http://www.procmail.org/procmail.tar.gz
ftp://ftp.procmail.org/pub/procmail/procmail.tar.gz
```

Either link downloads the current version of procmail. At the time of this writing this is version 3.15.

The source code distribution is downloaded as a tarred GNUzipped file that must be expanded and extracted into a working directory. This can be accomplished using the command

```
tar -zxvf procmail.tar.gz -C /usr/local/src
```

When you use this command, the procmail source code is placed in the `/usr/local/src/procmail-3.15` directory. Once the source code distribution has been extracted into the working directory, you should check the Makefile to ensure that any installation variables are set to work on your particular Unix installation. Listing 16.4 shows a partial listing of the important Makefile variables that should be checked.

LISTING 16.4 Partial procmail Makefile File

```
#$Id: Makefile,v 1.73.4.1 2000/01/20 16:59:15 guenther Exp $

BASENAME     = /usr
VISIBLE_BASENAME= $(BASENAME)

ARCHITECTURE    =

BINDIR_TAIL = bin$(ARCHITECTURE)
MANDIR      = $(BASENAME)/man
BINDIR      = $(BASENAME)/$(BINDIR_TAIL)
VISIBLE_BINDIR  = $(VISIBLE_BASENAME)/$(BINDIR_TAIL)
MAN1SUFFIX  =1
MAN5SUFFIX  =5
MAN1DIR     = $(MANDIR)/man$(MAN1SUFFIX)
MAN5DIR     = $(MANDIR)/man$(MAN5SUFFIX)

#MANCOMPRESS = compress
LOCKINGTEST=__defaults__

SEARCHLIBS = -lm -ldir -lx -lsocket -lnet -linet -lnsl_s -lnsl_i -lnsl -lsun \
 -lgen -lsockdns -ldl
LIBPATHS=/lib /usr/lib /usr/local/lib

GCC_WARNINGS = -O2 -pedantic -Wreturn-type -Wunused -Wformat -Wtraditional \
 -Wpointer-arith -Wconversion -Waggregate-return \

CFLAGS0 = -O #$(GCC_WARNINGS)
LDFLAGS0= -s
LIBS=
```

LISTING 16.4 Continued

```
CFLAGS1 = $(CFLAGS0) #-posix -Xp
LDFLAGS1= $(LDFLAGS0) $(LIBS) #-lcposix

####CC  = cc # gcc
O    = o
RM   = /bin/rm -f
MV   = mv -f
LN   = ln
BSHELL  = /bin/sh
INSTALL = cp
DEVNULL = /dev/null
STRIP   = strip

SUBDIRS = src man
BINSS   = procmail lockfile formail mailstat
MANS1S  = procmail formail lockfile
MANS5S  = procmailrc procmailsc procmailex
```

Most Unix installations can use the default settings without any problems. The next file to check is the `config.h` file. This file contains many of the procmail parameters that define how procmail behaves on the installed system. This file defines lots and lots of parameters that can be set to fine-tune procmail for a specific installation. Listing 16.5 shows a few of the parameters that can be changed by the mail administrator.

LISTING 16.5 Partial Listing of the procmail `config.h` File

```
#define KEEPENV      {"TZ",0}
/*#define DEFSPATH   "PATH=/bin:/usr/bin"              /* */
/*#define DEFPATH    "PATH=$HOME/bin:/bin:/usr/bin"        /* */
#define PRESTENV     {"IFS","ENV","PWD",0}

/*#define GROUP_PER_USER
#define TRUSTED_IDS {"root","daemon","uucp","mail","x400","network",\
             "list","slist","lists","news",0}

/*#define NO_fcntl_LOCK     /* uncomment any of these three if you       */
/*#define NO_lockf_LOCK     /* definitely do not want procmail to make   */
/*#define NO_flock_LOCK     /* use of those kernel-locking methods       */

/*#define RESTRICT_EXEC 100 */
#define PROCMAILRC   "$HOME/.procmailrc" /* default rcfile for every
                              recipient;  if this file
```

LISTING 16.5 Continued

```
    is not found, mail delivery will proceed as normal to the default
    system mailbox.  This must be an absolute path or bad things will
    happen. */

#define ETCRC    "/etc/procmailrc"    /* optional global procmailrc startup
                          file (will only be read if procmail
    is started with no rcfile on the command line). */

#define ETCRCS  "/etc/procmailrcs/"
/*#define console    "/dev/console"
```

Because the `config.h` file is a normal C program header file, comments are not necessarily just one line and they use the standard C comment symbols:

- `/*` to start a comment block
- `*/` to end a comment block

CAUTION

Do not remove the pound symbols at the beginning of the define lines. These are not comment symbols, they are part of the `#define` C statement.

The `config.h` file allows the mail administrator to customize the procmail installation for a specific Unix server. You should skim over each of the possible `#define` lines and determine whether you need to change anything for your particular installation. The default values provided should work fine in most Unix installations.

Once the Makefile and `config.h` files have been modified as necessary, it is time to compile the programs. As the `root` user, execute the GNU `make` command with the `install` option:

```
make install
```

This performs five steps:

1. Checks the Unix system functions for compatibility and creates a new Makefile as necessary.
2. Executes the shell script `autoconf` to check the C compiler features and creates the `autoconf.h` header file accordingly.
3. Creates the procmail binary files, shell scripts, and man pages in the new directory.
4. Copies the binary files to `$(BINDIR)`.
5. Copies the man pages to `$(MAN1DIR)` and `$(MAN5DIR)`.

After the procmail installation process has completed, procmail should almost be ready for use. I say "almost" because there is still one problem: The normal system users will not be able to access and run it.

To allow normal system users to use the procmail programs, you must run one more `make` script:

```
make install-suid
```

This sets the procmail programs to setuid as the `root` user to allow normal system users to utilize procmail's features. The following sections describe how to use procmail.

The procmail Command Line

The procmail command line supports different options that affect the behavior of procmail. The different command-line options can be included when using the `mailbox_command` parameter from within the `main.cf` file in Postfix.

There are four separate formats that the procmail command line can have:

```
procmail -v
procmail [-ptoY] [-f fromwhom] [parameter=value | rcfile] ...
procmail [-toY] [-f fromwhom] [-a argument] -d recipient ...
procmail [-ptY] -m [parameter=value] ...  rcfile  [argument] ...
```

The first format is used to print its version number and some compile information. Listing 16.6 shows an example of using the `-v` option.

LISTING 16.6 Using the procmail -v Option

```
[rich@shadrach rich]$ procmail -v
procmail v3.13.1 1999/04/05, Copyright (c) 1999, Stephen R. van den Berg
                                                      <srb@cuci.nl>

Submit questions/answers to the procmail-related mailinglist by sending to:
        <procmail-users@procmail.org>

And of course, subscription and information requests for this list to:
        <procmail-users-request@procmail.org>

Locking strategies:      dotlocking, fcntl()
Default rcfile:          $HOME/.procmailrc
Your system mailbox:     /var/spool/mail/rich
[rich@shadrach rich]$
```

As shown in Listing 16.6, not only is the version of the procmail program shown, but some other useful information is also presented to the user. Most importantly, the location of the `.procmailrc` file and the default mailbox used by procmail are listed.

Although the `-v` option is informative, it is not normally used from within the Postfix program when transferring messages to local users.

The other three formats of the procmail command line are used to deliver messages to local users. Table 16.2 lists the command-line options that are available to use with `procmail`.

TABLE 16.2 procmail Command-Line Options

Option	*Description*
`-a arg`	Sets `$1` equal to the value of `arg` when running procmail.
`-d recip`	Uses explicit delivery mode to deliver messages as the `recip` user.
`-f from`	Generates a leading `From` line on the message using `from` as the sender.
`-m`	Turns procmail into a general-purpose mail filter. At least one `rc` file must be listed on the command line.
`-o`	Does not allow normal users to use the `-f` option to generate fake `From` lines.
`-p`	Preserves any existing environment variables.
`-t`	Causes procmail to return a message to the message queue if procmail fails to deliver it.
`-Y`	Assumes the standard Berkeley mailbox format, and ignores `Content-Length:` message header fields.
`param=value`	Sets the procmail parameter `param` equal to the value `value`.
`rcfile`	Lists alternative procmail `rc` files that will be used to process recipes.

The most common command-line option used when invoking procmail from Postfix is the `-a` option, which allows Postfix to pass the recipient environment information along to procmail:

```
mailbox_command = /usr/bin/procmail -a "$EXTENSION"
```

In this example, Postfix passes the address extension information to procmail as the `$1` argument. procmail will use this information to deliver the mail message to the local user.

As another example, you can use the following `mailbox_command` parameter in the `main.cf` file:

```
mailbox_command = /usr/bin/procmail -m /etc/procmailrc
```

This example allows the mail administrator to create a common `procmailrc` file that applies to all users. By default, procmail applies the recipes in the `/etc/procmailrc` file to all users, but using the `root` username. This means that the `root` user will own any folders created by this recipe. By specifying the -m option in the command line, procmail will run the recipes as the recipient username. This comes in handy when writing global recipes that store messages in separate folders.

A simple example recipe is to copy all messages to a folder in the recipient's $HOME directory. Create a /etc/promailrc file containing the following recipe:

```
:0 c
$HOME/messages
```

This recipe places a copy of all incoming mail messages into the user's $HOME/messages mailbox folder. Without the -m command-line option, procmail would create the message folder in the user's $HOME directory, but it would be owned by the root user. This would be impractical, since the user would not be able to access messages in that folder. Listing 16.7 demonstrates how this example would work.

LISTING 16.7 Simple procmailrc Recipe Example

```
[rich@shadrach]$ ls -al messages
ls: messages: No such file or directory

[rich@shadrach]$ mail rich
Subject: Test message
This is a test message
.

[rich@shadrach]$ ls -al messages*
-rw-------    1 rich     rich          453 Dec  4 05:51 messages

[rich@shadrach]$ cat messages
From rich@shadrach.ispnet1.net  Mon Dec  4 05:51:02 2000
Return-Path: <rich@shadrach.ispnet1.net>
Delivered-To: rich@shadrach.ispnet1.net
Received: by shadrach.ispnet1.net (Postfix, from userid 501)
        id 5AA913B1D4; Mon,  4 Dec 2000 05:51:02 -0500 (EST)
To: rich@shadrach.ispnet1.net
Subject: Test message
Message-Id: <20001204105102.5AA913B1D4@shadrach.ispnet1.net>
Date: Mon,  4 Dec 2000 05:51:02 -0500 (EST)
From: rich@shadrach.ispnet1.net (Rich)

This is a test message

You have mail in /var/spool/mail/rich
```

LISTING 16.7 Continued

```
[rich@shadrach]$ mail
Mail version 8.1 6/6/93.  Type ? for help.
"/var/spool/mail/rich": 1 message 1 new
>N  1 rich@shadrach.ispnet  Mon Dec  4 05:51  13/453   "Test message"
&1
Message 1:
From rich@shadrach.ispnet1.net  Mon Dec  4 05:51:02 2000
Delivered-To: rich@shadrach.ispnet1.net
To: rich@shadrach.ispnet1.net
Subject: Test message
Date: Mon,  4 Dec 2000 05:51:02 -0500 (EST)
From: rich@shadrach.ispnet1.net (Rich)

This is a test message

&
```

In Listing 16.7, first the file `/home/rich/messages` is queried to make sure that it does not exist. Next, a normal message is sent to a local user using the standard `mail` program. The message is successfully sent to the local user.

The `/home/rich/messages` file is again queried, and this time it exists. The file contents are then listed. As you can see, the complete message header and body were stored in the messages folder, just as in a normal mailbox.

To make sure that this is just a copy of the message, the mail program is again called to check the contents of the normal mail inbox. Indeed, the message was also delivered to the normal mail inbox of the local user, thus the copy recipe did work successfully.

The next section describes the format of recipes, and shows some examples of more complicated recipes that can be used by system users to augment their normal mail delivery.

User-Defined procmail Actions

The `.procmailrc` file located in each user's `$HOME` directory can control the delivery of mail messages from the `procmail` program. Individual users can create their own `.procmailrc` files to specify how they want their messages to be handled.

Mail delivery is defined by recipes in the `.procmailrc` file. Each recipe defines a pattern-matching expression value and an action for procmail to take when a message matches the expression. The format of a procmail recipe is

```
recipe header line
condition line(s)
action line
```

The recipe header line defines the basic action of the recipe. All recipe lines start with the heading

```
:0 [flags] [: locallockfile]
```

The flags identify the basic function that the recipe will perform. Table 16.3 lists the flags that are available.

TABLE 16.3 Recipe Flags

Flag	*Description*
`A`	This recipe will not be executed unless the conditions of the preceding recipe are met.
`a`	Same as `A` but with the additional restriction that the preceding recipe must have *successfully* completed.
`B`	`egrep` the body of the message.
`b`	Feeds the body of the message to the destination (default).
`c`	Generates a carbon copy of this message.
`D`	Distinguish between upper- and lowercase (default is to ignore case).
`E`	This recipe will not be executed unless the conditions of the preceding recipe were *not* met.
`e`	Same as `E` but with the additional restriction that the preceding recipe must have *failed* to complete.
`f`	Considers the pipe as a filter.
`H`	`egrep` the message header (default).
`h`	Feeds the header of the message to the destination (default).
`i`	Ignores any write errors on this recipe.
`r`	Does not ensure that messages end with an empty line (raw mode).
`W`	Waits for the filter or program to finish and checks the exit code. Suppresses any "Program failure" messages.
`w`	Waits for the filter or program to finish and check the exit code. Does not suppress any error messages.

The flags are listed in the recipe header line after the `:0` header (and a space character). More than one flag can be entered consecutively on the recipe header line.

After the flags, if a lock file is required, the mail administrator can specify either a specific lock file by name, or omit the lock file name to allow procmail to use a default lock file. For example, the recipe header line

```
:0:
```

implicitly directs procmail to use the default flags (`Hhb`), and to engage the default lock file when processing the message. Alternatively, the mail administrator can specify a lock file to use:

```
:0 Whc: msgid.lock
```

After the header line, one or more recipe condition lines must be defined. Each condition line must start with an asterisk (*). After the asterisk, a normal regular expression is used as the pattern-matching condition. In addition to normal regular expressions, procmail defines seven special conditions. Table 16.4 lists the special conditions.

TABLE 16.4 procmail Special Conditions

Condition	*Description*
`!`	Inverts the condition.
`$`	Evaluates the condition according to shell substitution rules inside double quotes.
`?`	Uses the exit code of the specified program.
`<`	Checks whether the total message length is less than the specified number of bytes (in decimal).
`>`	Checks whether the total message length is greater than the specified number of bytes (in decimal).
`variable ??`	Matches the remainder of the condition against the environment variable specified.
`\`	Quotes any of the special characters to use as a normal character. (Also used to split wrapping action lines.)

The easiest way to learn how to write condition lines is to see a few examples. This condition line checks whether the message subject header field contains the word *guitars*:

```
^Subject:.*guitars
```

Any `Subject` line with the word *guitars* in it would match this condition. The asterisk character before `guitars` is a standard regexp character that matches any number of characters.

This condition line checks whether the message subject header field contains both the words *guitars* and *bass*:

```
^Subject:.*guitars.*bass
```

Received messages with both *guitars* and *bass* in the message subject header field would match this condition line.

Finally, this condition line checks the entire message—body and headers—for the word *meeting*:

```
* meeting
```

Any received message with the word *meeting* anywhere in the message would match this condition line.

After the condition lines are defined, the procmail action line must be defined. The action line defines the action that procmail will take if the condition line is matched with a message.

Much like the condition line, the action line can start with a special character that describes the basic action that will be taken. Table 16.5 describes the action line special characters.

TABLE 16.5 procmail Action Line Special Characters

Character	*Description*
`! <e-mail address>`	Forwards message to the specified addresses
`| </path/to/program>`	Starts the specified program
`{`	Starts a block of recipes checked if the condition is matched
`}`	Ends a block of recipes checked if the condition is matched
`text`	Forwards message to the mailbox defined by `text`

Each recipe can only have one action line. The action line defines what procmail will do with any messages that match the condition lines. Again, the easiest way to explain this is to show some examples.

Listing 16.8 is an example of a `.procmailrc` file for a sample user on the mail server.

LISTING 16.8 Sample .procmailrc File

```
:0 c
messages

:0
* ^From.*guitar-list
{
    :0 c
    ! rich@ispnet3.net

    :0
    guitars
}
```

LISTING 16.8 Continued

```
:0 hc
* !^FROM_DAEMON
* !^X-Loop: rich@ispnet1.net
| (formail -r -I"Precedence: junk" \
-A"X-Loop: rich@ispnet1.net" ; \
echo "Thanks for your message, but I will be out of the office until 1/4") \
| $SENDMAIL -t

:0
* ^Subject.*network
/dev/null
```

The `.procmailrc` file shown in Listing 16.8 contains four separate recipes that are processed by procmail:

1. The first recipe places a copy of all received messages in the mail folder `messages`.
2. The second recipe demonstrates the use of recipes within a recipe. The main recipe first checks if the received message is from a sender with the word `guitar-list` in his or her address. If it is, both of the internal recipes are checked. First a copy of all matching messages is forwarded to the e-mail address `rich@ispnet3.net`. Next, the messages are delivered to the mail folder `guitars`.
3. The third recipe demonstrates using an external program as well as creating an auto-reply. All messages that are not sent from either a local daemon process (that uses the send name `DAEMON`) or from the original user `rich` are forwarded to the `formail` program.

   This program is included with the procmail distribution and is used to help filter header information from messages. Two header fields are added: a `Precedence:` line and an `X-Loop:` line to help prevent message loops. After that, the reply message is generated and sent to the local MTA process (Postfix, hopefully). Note that the second pipe is part of the `formail` call and not a second (illegal) procmail action call.
4. The last recipe demonstrates filtering messages based on a `Subject` header line. Any message with a `Subject` line that contains the word `network` anywhere in it is apparently placed in a mail folder called `/dev/null`. System administrators will recognize that this is actually a special system file: it maintains a 0-byte file size. Any information copied there is lost forever. Thus, this recipe deletes any messages that it matches. A recipe to be used with caution!

Each incoming e-mail message is processed against each recipe. Any recipes whose condition line matches the message are executed. Recipes that match a message but are not given the `c` header option simply redirect the message away from the normal inbox. For example, the fourth example in Listing 16.8 redirects messages with the `Subject` line containing the word `network` to `/dev/null`. These messages will not appear in the normal inbox mail folder.

The third example shown in Listing 16.8, creating auto-reply messages, is a great feature to use when you know you will be away from your e-mail for an extended period of time. Any message sent to your e-mail account will generate an automatic reply message to the sender with any text that you specify. Listing 16.9 shows an example of this feature using the recipe from Listing 16.8.

LISTING 16.9 Sample Auto-Reply Session

```
[jessica@shadrach]$ mail rich
Subject: Test message
Hi -

    This is a test message sent while you were out.
.
Cc:
[jessica@shadrach ]$ mail
Mail version 8.1 6/6/93.  Type ? for help.
"/var/spool/mail/jessica": 1 message 1 new
>N  1 rich@shadrach.ispnet1.n  Tue Dec  5 18:01  17/673   "Re: Test message"
&1
Message 1:
From rich@shadrach.ispnet1.net  Tue Dec  5 18:01:22 2000
Delivered-To: jessica@shadrach.ispnet1.net
To: jessica@shadrach.ispnet1.net
Subject: Re: Test message
References: <20001205160122.10428C352@shadrach.ispnet1.net>
In-Reply-To: <20001205160122.10428C352@shadrach.ispnet1.net>
X-Loop: rich@shadrach.ispnet1.net
Precedence: junk
Date: Tue,  5 Dec 2000 18:01:22 -0500 (EST)
From: rich@shadrach.ispnet1.net (Rich Blum)

Thanks for your message, but I will be out of the office until 1/4


&
```

Note that the recipe created for the auto-reply function uses the `c` flag. Thus, only a copy of the message is used for the auto-reply. The original message should be safely stored in the normal mailbox for when the user returns to read his mail.

There are many other recipes that are useful for local mail users. There are links on the procmail Web site (`http://www.procmail.org`) to posted recipe examples. These examples can help users create their own procmail delivery masterpieces.

Summary

The Postfix program can utilize external Mail Delivery Agent (MDA) programs to assist it in delivering messages to local users. There are several benefits to using this approach, including allowing users to individually customize their mail delivery.

Many MDAs allow users to write their own delivery configuration file to specify how to handle incoming messages. Messages can be automatically placed in special folders, sent to other mail addresses, or can even generate a reply message to the sender. These features help users manage their mailboxes more efficiently.

The procmail package is a popular MDA package that is utilized on most Unix systems. It allows mail users to create "recipes" that define message delivery options based on predefined control scripts. The user places the recipes in a configuration file in his `$HOME` directory. Each time a message is received for the user, Postfix passes the message to the procmail program, which in turn processes the user's configuration file to determine how to deliver the mail message.

PART III

Advanced Postfix Server Topics

CHAPTER 17

Using MySQL with Postfix

Postfix can utilize different types of databases as lookup tables. In addition to using indexed binary databases, Postfix can utilize external database packages. One such package is the MySQL database server.

The MySQL database package has become one of the most popular free database packages available for the Unix platform. It includes features that compete with many commercial database packages.

This chapter describes how to install and configure a MySQL database and how to configure Postfix to utilize information stored in the MySQL database as lookup tables.

What Is MySQL?

The MySQL database package was originally developed as a free database package to support large relational databases. It has grown from a simple data management package to a full-featured database system. The MySQL Corporation has been formed to support the ongoing development of MySQL (`http://www.mysql.com`), and the MySQL package is now offered for use under the terms of the GNU public license (GPL).

The MySQL package contains many features that database administrators expect from commercial packages:

- Support for relational databases
- Support for indexed databases
- Command-line SQL processing
- Support for remote clients
- Database export/import functions
- User id management
- ODBC and JDBC database support

The internal user id management feature is a nice attribute of MySQL. The database administrator can create MySQL internal usernames with passwords and grant access to database tables based on those usernames. This feature can be used to restrict access to the Postfix lookup table to a user id created exclusively for the Postfix user.

Another feature that Postfix utilizes is the ability for database clients to log in to the database remotely to access tables. This allows the MySQL database to be run on a separate Unix system from the Postfix mail server. The MySQL database can be maintained on a separate server, often incorporated with other databases, such as customer databases that include e-mail addresses. The Postfix mail administrator can configure Postfix to access the remote database system and extract the e-mail address based on additional values, such as whether or not the customer's account has been paid. Figure 17.1 demonstrates how this works.

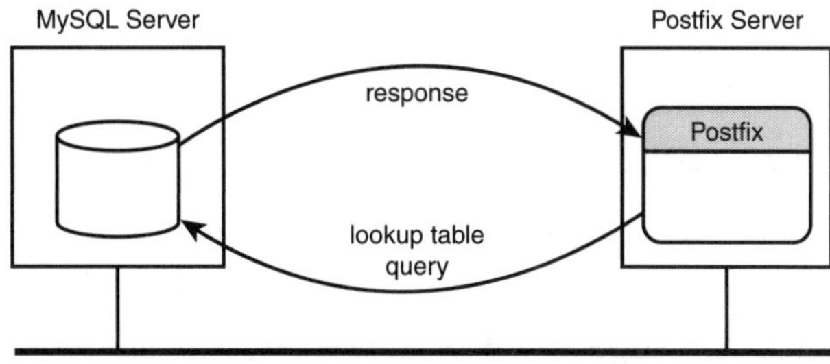

FIGURE 17.1

Using a remote MySQL database.

The following section describes how to install the MySQL software.

Installing MySQL

Before Postfix can utilize a MySQL database, the MySQL software must be installed and configured on the system. The MySQL software will operate on any Unix platform, including Linux distributions.

The MySQL database package is available in both binary and source code distributions. Many Linux distributions include a binary distribution for MySQL. This section describes how to install MySQL from either the binary or source code distributions.

Using a Binary Distribution

One type of binary distribution available is the RPM distribution. Both Red Hat and Mandrake Linux use RPM distribution files. The MySQL installation is divided among several different RPM packages, each one installing a different part of the MySQL distribution. The Mandrake 7.2 Linux distribution includes the following MySQL RPM files:

```
MySQL-3.23.23-1mdk.i586.rpm
MySQL-bench-3.23.23-1mdk.i586.rpm
MySQL-client-3.23.23-1mdk.i586.rpm
MySQL-devel-3.23.23-1mdk.i586.rpm
MySQL-shared-3.23.23-1mdk.i586.rpm
```

The base MySQL package contains the core files and programs needed to run the MySQL server. Listing 17.1 shows the core programs that are installed by this RPM package.

LISTING 17.1 MySQL-3.23.23 Core Program Files

```
/usr/bin/isamchk
/usr/bin/isamlog
/usr/bin/my_print_defaults
/usr/bin/myisamchk
/usr/bin/myisamlog
/usr/bin/myisampack
/usr/bin/mysql_config
/usr/bin/mysql_convert_table_format
/usr/bin/mysql_fix_privilege_tables
/usr/bin/mysql_install_db
/usr/bin/mysql_setpermission
/usr/bin/mysql_zap
/usr/bin/mysqlbug
/usr/bin/mysqlhotcopy
/usr/bin/pack_isam
/usr/bin/perror
/usr/bin/replace
/usr/bin/resolveip
/usr/bin/safe_mysqld
/usr/sbin/mysqld
```

In addition to the core RPM package, you should also install the MySQL-client package, which enables the database administrator to use the MySQL command-line interface to create tables and user ids. To get Postfix to work with the MySQL database server, you must also install the MySQL-devel and MySQL-shared packages. These packages provide the C libraries and header files necessary to compile Postfix for MySQL support, as well as to interact with the database.

The only RPM file that is optional is the MySQL-bench RPM file, which installs some benchmark scripts and data that can be used to test the particular MySQL installation.

To install an RPM file, you must be logged in as `root` and use the `rpm` command:

```
rpm -Uvh MySQL-3.23-1mdk.i586.rpm
rpm -Uvh MySQL-client-3.23.23-1mdk.i586.rpm
rpm -Uvh MySQL-devel-3.23.23-1mdk.i586.rpm
rpm -Uvh MySQL-shared-3.23.23-1mdk.i586.rpm
```

These commands install the MySQL database packages onto the server using the default directories specified in the RPM distribution.

NOTE

If your Linux distribution includes a MySQL binary distribution, I recommend that you use it rather than a newer source code distribution. Often Linux distributions tweak the MySQL installation for the peculiarities of the individual Linux installation to make it run faster or better. Any features gained by installing a newer release of MySQL may be lost in slower performance of the database system.

Using a Source Code Distribution

If your Linux distribution does not include a binary distribution of the MySQL database package or you want to try the latest version, you can download the source code distribution from the MySQL Web site (`http://www.mysql.com`) and compile it yourself.

The MySQL software source code is distributed in several different versions. The most recent version is usually the latest release of the development code. Much like Postfix distributions, the latest MySQL development code is usually stable and usable for most installations. If you are not willing to use a development release, there is also a stable release available for download.

At the time of this writing, the latest stable release is version 3.23.32. The URL for downloading this distribution is

```
http://www.mysql.com/Downloads/MySQL-3.23/mysql-3.23.32.tar.gz
```

After downloading the distribution, it must be extracted into a working directory:

```
tar -zxvf mysql-3.23.32.tar.gz -C /usr/local/src
```

Once you do this, you can begin the steps necessary to compile and install the source code. The following sections describe these steps.

Create the MySQL User Id and Group Id

The MySQL database system must have a dedicated user and group id that it can run under. This helps prevent security problems with the MySQL server software as it runs in the background. Most database administrators create a group and user id called "mysql." On Linux systems this can be accomplished using the following commands:

```
groupadd mysql
useradd -g mysql mysql
```

These commands create a new group and user using the next available user id and group id on the system.

Compile and Install MySQL

Once the MySQL user and group ids have been created, you can begin compiling. The source code should already be extracted into a working directory. All of the compiling commands should be performed from this directory. The directory used for this example is

```
/usr/local/src/mysql-3.23.32
```

There are two steps required to compile the MySQL source code into the executable programs used for the database system. First, you must use the `configure` program to configure the MySQL Makefile with any options necessary for your particular installation. There are lots of options that can be set. You can display a list of configurable options by using the following command:

```
./configure --help
```

Table 17.1 lists a few of the options that can be used with the `configure` command.

TABLE 17.1 MySQL Configure Options

Option	*Description*
`--prefix=PREFIX`	Installs architecture-independent files in `PREFIX`
`--exec-prefix=EPREFIX`	Installs architecture-dependent files in `EPREFIX`
`--bindir=DIR`	Installs user executables in `DIR`
`--sbindir=DIR`	Installs system admin executables in `DIR`
`--libexecdir=DIR`	Installs program executables in `DIR`
`--enable-shared`	Builds shared libraries (default)
`--enable-static`	Builds static libraries (default)
`--with-raid`	Enables RAID support
`--with-mysqld-user=USER`	Runs the mysqld daemon as `USER`
`--with-low-memory`	Compiles using less memory
`--without-server`	Compiles only the client programs
`--without-docs`	Does not install documentation
`--without-bench`	Does not install MySQL benchmark tests
`--with-berkeley-db[=DIR]`	Uses BerkeleyDB located in `DIR`

Any option not explicitly set assumes the default value for that option. After deciding which (if any) configure options are required for your MySQL installation, you can use the `configure` command to create the new Makefile:

```
./configure --without-bench --with-low-memory
```

The `configure` program performs various checks on the Unix system and creates the Makefile that directs the C compiler on how to properly compile the source code on your system.

After the `configure` program is run, the source code must be compiled using the GNU `make` command. This step is simple to accomplish with the following command:

```
make
```

The `make` command compiles all of the executable programs required by MySQL. Depending on the speed of your server, this may take quite a while. After the `make` program finishes, you can install the newly created executable programs. To do this, you must be logged in as `root` or perform the `su` command to change to `root`. To install the executable programs you can invoke the `make` command with the install option:

```
make install
```

The various program files required for MySQL are installed in either the default directories or the directories you specified when running the `configure` command. At this point, the MySQL server should be ready to be started and configured.

Start the MySQL Server

After the MySQL software has been installed, you must start the MySQL server before you can access the MySQL databases. Before the MySQL server can be started, though, there are two items that must be taken care of. First, you must run a MySQL script that creates the system tables. Then the database directory permissions must be changed to allow the newly created `mysql` system user to access the system database tables.

The system tables control both the database user id table and the access control list (ACL) that sets internal access rights to databases and tables within the MySQL server. A script is provided to perform this task. The `mysql_install_db` script should be located in the executable directory defined by either the RPM distribution or the `configure` command. You must run this script as `root`:

```
mysql_install_db
```

The script produces output as it creates the necessary system tables. The output from the script is as follows:

```
Creating db table
Creating host table
Creating user table
Creating func table
Creating tables_priv table
Creating columns_priv table

To start mysqld at boot time you have to copy support-files/mysql.server
to the right place for your system
```

```
PLEASE REMEMBER TO SET A PASSWORD FOR THE MySQL root USER !
This is done with:
/usr/local/bin/mysqladmin -u root -p password 'new-password'
/usr/local/bin/mysqladmin -u root -h shadrach.ispnet1.net -p password
'new-password'
See the manual for more instructions.

Please report any problems with the /usr/local/bin/mysqlbug script!

The latest information about MySQL is available on the web at
http://www.mysql.com
Support MySQL by buying support/licenses at https://order.mysql.com
```

Note that there are six tables created for the MySQL system database. These tables are used by MySQL to keep track of databases, user-created tables, and user ids within the MySQL system.

Following the table creations, the script reminds the administrator to change the default password for the MySQL `root` user. The MySQL `root` user has all privileges to all databases and tables within the MySQL server. It is imperative that you change the default password or you risk your database being compromised by a hacker. This cannot be done, though, until after the server is started.

Another step to perform before the server can be started is to ensure that the `mysql` user is the owner of the MySQL data directories. This allows the MySQL server to run under the `mysql` user id and helps prevent problems with hackers breaking into the server and obtaining `root` privileges. To change the ownership of the directories, you must use the Unix `chown` and `chgrp` commands:

```
chown -R mysql /usr/local/var
chgrp -R mysql /usr/local/var
```

The MySQL installation creates the `/usr/local/var` directory by default if it doesn't already exist. It contains all of the files necessary to support the MySQL databases on the system. The directory used as the data directory may vary depending on your system and whether you made any changes to the default values used in the `configure` command.

After the directory permissions are set, you can start the MySQL server software using a simple canned script file and command-line option:

```
/usr/local/bin/safe_mysqld --user=mysql &
```

This uses the `--user` option to allow the MySQL server programs to run as the created `mysql` user. The `&` symbol is used to place the MySQL server software in background mode. To check whether the MySQL server is running, you can use the Unix `ps` command:

```
[root@shadrach]# ps ax | grep mysqld
21147 pts/0    S     0:00 sh /usr/local/bin/safe_mysqld --user=mysql
21163 pts/0    S     0:00 /usr/local/libexec/mysqld --basedir=/usr/local --data
21166 pts/0    S     0:00 /usr/local/libexec/mysqld --basedir=/usr/local --data
21167 pts/0    S     0:00 /usr/local/libexec/mysqld --basedir=/usr/local --data
```

Note that the original `safe_mysqld` script runs continually in background mode, as well as the `mysqld` program. The presence of the `mysqld` program indicates that the server is running and waiting for connections.

Server Housekeeping Tasks

MySQL tracks users by both internal MySQL username and location. To ensure that no one can use the default MySQL `root` password, you must change the MySQL `root` password for two different locations: the localhost address and the DNS address of your system (as shown in the script output). You can do this with the following two commands:

```
/usr/local/bin/mysqladmin -u root -p password 'guitar'
/usr/local/bin/mysqladmin -u root -h shadrach.ispnet1.net -p password 'guitar'
```

When entering these commands, MySQL will prompt you for its `root` password. By default the MySQL `root` password is a null password. Just press the Enter key to enter a null password. Of course, after these commands are entered the password will be changed to what was entered.

As a final test of the installation, you can use the `mysqladmin` command to display the version of the running MySQL server:

```
[root@shadrach]# /usr/local/bin/mysqladmin -p version
Enter password:
/usr/local/bin/mysqladmin  Ver 8.12 Distrib 3.23.28-gamma, for
➥pc-linux-gnu on i686
Copyright (C) 2000 MySQL AB & MySQL Finland AB & TCX DataKonsult AB
This software comes with ABSOLUTELY NO WARRANTY. This is free software,
and you are welcome to modify and redistribute it under the GPL license

Server version          3.23.28-gamma
Protocol version        10
Connection              Localhost via UNIX socket
UNIX socket             /tmp/mysql.sock
Uptime:                 3 min 53 sec

Threads: 1  Questions: 7  Slow queries: 0  Opens: 7  Flush tables: 1
➥Open tables: 1 Queries per second avg: 0.030
```

Remember to use the new password that you entered in the previous step when MySQL queries you for the password.

Configuring MySQL for Postfix

Now that the MySQL server is successfully running, you must create a database environment that Postfix can use to store and access lookup table information. The following sections describe the steps necessary to perform these functions.

Creating a MySQL User

Postfix must have a MySQL username to access the MySQL database. It is not a good idea to use the MySQL `root` username for normal database activity. You should create a new username that *only* Postfix will use when accessing the lookup table. This ensures that if the Postfix username becomes compromised, the entire MySQL database will not be compromised as well.

There are several methods that you can use to create usernames in MySQL. The simplest method is to directly insert a new record in the MySQL user table in the `mysql` system database. To do this, you must first connect to the `mysql` system database as the MySQL `root` user:

```
[rich@shadrach]$ mysql -u root -p mysql
Enter password:
Reading table information for completion of table and column names
You can turn off this feature to get a quicker startup with -A

Welcome to the MySQL monitor.  Commands end with ; or \g.
Your MySQL connection id is 6 to server version: 3.23.28-gamma

Type 'help;' or '\h' for help. Type '\c' to clear the buffer

mysql>
```

The `mysql` command provides a command-line method of sending SQL statements to the MySQL server. You can specify command-line options indicating which MySQL username you want to connect to the server as (`-u root`), that you want to enter a password for that user (`-p`), and the name of the database you want to connect to (`mysql`). Once connected to the database, you can enter the following `SQL INSERT` statement to create a new MySQL user named `postfix`:

```
mysql> INSERT INTO user (host,user,password) VALUES('localhost','postfix','');

Query OK, 1 row affected (0.00 sec)

mysql>
```

The result of this SQL statement is the creation of a username `postfix` that can only connect from the `localhost`, with a null password. This command assumes that the Postfix server will operate on the same server as the MySQL server. If this is not the case, you can use the fully qualified DNS name of the Postfix server in place of the `localhost` name.

After the Postfix username is created you should assign it a password. You can do this using the following SQL `UPDATE` statement:

```
mysql> UPDATE user set password=PASSWORD('guitar') WHERE user='postfix';
Query OK, 1 row affected (0.00 sec)
Rows matched: 1  Changed: 1  Warnings: 0

mysql> FLUSH PRIVILEGES;
Query OK, 0 rows affected (0.01 sec)

mysql>
```

The `FLUSH PRIVILEGES` statement is required to update the system privileges in the MySQL tables so the new password will take effect immediately without reloading the server. The `UPDATE` statement changes the `postfix` user's password to *guitar*. The MySQL `PASSWORD()` function creates an encrypted version of the text password for the database. Displaying the MySQL user table can demonstrate this:

```
mysql> SELECT host, user, password FROM user;
+---------------------+---------+------------------+
| host                | user    | password         |
+---------------------+---------+------------------+
| localhost           | root    | 2098df6314ba5555 |
| shadrach.ispnet1.net | root    | 2098df6314ba5555 |
| localhost           |         |                  |
| shadrach.ispnet1.net |         |                  |
| localhost           | postfix | 02a3a952231c3910 |
+---------------------+---------+------------------+
5 rows in set (0.00 sec)
mysql>
```

CAUTION

When using the `UPDATE SQL` command to change a password, remember to include the `WHERE` clause to define the username. Without it, all users on the system will have their passwords changed. Depending on your system, that could be a problem.

Creating a New Database and Table

Now that the MySQL server is running and the `postfix` user id is created, you can create the database and table that Postfix will use to contain the lookup table information. It is best to create the database and table as the MySQL `root` user and grant permission to the MySQL `postfix` user to query the database.

The SQL CREATE DATABASE command can be used to create the new database, and the CREATE TABLE command can be used to create the new table. Listing 17.2 shows these commands and their output.

LISTING 17.2 Creating a New Database and Table

```
mysql> CREATE DATABASE maillist;
Query OK, 1 row affected (0.00 sec)

mysql> CREATE TABLE maillist.customers(
    -> alias_name varchar(30) primary key,
    -> system_name varchar(8),
    -> status varchar(15),
    -> address1 varchar(50),
    -> address2 varchar(50),
    -> city varchar(30),
    -> state varchar(2),
    -> zip varchar(10));
Query OK, 0 rows affected (0.00 sec)

mysql>
```

As shown in Listing 17.2, after creating the new database you can create the new table in the database by using the MySQL reference syntax:

```
database.table
```

Thus, to create a table called customers in the maillist database, you can use the syntax maillist.customers. The fields in the table can be created to meet whatever needs are required in your environment. There must be at least two fields in the table that Postfix can use to map the lookup table values. It also helps to create an index key on the field that Postfix will use as the lookup value to help speed up queries.

After creating the database and table, you must grant privileges to the MySQL postfix user to access the table:

```
mysql> GRANT select,insert,update ON maillist.customers TO postfix;
Query OK, 0 rows affected (0.00 sec)
```

This allows the MySQL postfix user to query the table, insert new records into the table, and change the values of existing records. Alternatively, you can choose to allow the MySQL postfix user to just query the table but not insert or update the records.

Using MySQL

After the database and table have been created, the chore of inputting and maintaining data begins. This section describes the processes required to input, display, change, and back up data contained in the MySQL database.

Adding Lookup Table Records

The `INSERT SQL` statement can be used to add new records to the database table. Each record must be added individually using this method. The format of the `INSERT` statement is

```
INSERT INTO table (field1, field2,...) VALUES (value1, value2, ...)
```

where *table* is the name of the table to insert the values into, *field1* and *field2* are field names that the values will be inserted into, and *value1* and *value2* are the values that will be placed in the corresponding fields. An example of this would be

```
INSERT INTO customers (alias_name,system_name) VALUES ('Richard.Blum','rich');
```

Note that not all fields in the records have to be included in the `INSERT` statement. Any fields not included are given a null value for the record. Also note that text strings must be enclosed by single quotes.

To insert new records you can connect to the database using the `mysql` command. Listing 17.3 shows an example of adding records to the customers table.

LISTING 17.3 Adding Records to the Customers Table

```
mysql> INSERT INTO customers (alias_name, system_name, status)
➥ VALUES ('Richard.Blum', 'rich', 'paid');
Query OK, 1 row affected (0.00 sec)

mysql> INSERT INTO customers (alias_name, system_name, status)
➥ VALUES ('Jessica.Blum','jessica', 'paid');
Query OK, 1 row affected (0.00 sec)

mysql> INSERT INTO customers (alias_name, system_name, status)
➥ VALUES ('Katie.Blum', 'katie', 'paid');
Query OK, 1 row affected (0.01 sec)

Mysql> INSERT INTO customers (alias_name, system_name, status)
➥ VALUES ('Dead.Beat', 'dead', 'unpaid');
Query OK, 1 row affected (0.00 sec)

mysql>
```

As each `INSERT` statement is executed, the MySQL server adds the new information to the database table. The next section describes how to query data from the table.

Displaying Lookup Table Records

To display information contained in the database table, you can use the SQL `SELECT` statement. The `SELECT` statement is one of the more complicated SQL statements, with many different options and formats. One format that will work for simple queries is

```
SELECT field1, field2 FROM table [WHERE field3=value1]
```

Where *`field1`* and *`field2`* are the record fields that you want displayed in the result, *`table`* is the table name to query, and *`field3=value1`* is an optional parameter to narrow the records returned in the result. Only records where *`field3`* is equal to *`value1`* are returned. Listing 17.4 demonstrates displaying records from the database table.

LISTING 17.4 Displaying Records from the Database Table

```
mysql> SELECT alias_name, system_name FROM customers WHERE status='paid';
+--------------+-------------+
| alias_name   | system_name |
+--------------+-------------+
| Richard.Blum | rich        |
| Jessica.Blum | jessica     |
| Katie.Blum   | katie       |
| Barbara.Blum | barbara     |
+--------------+-------------+
4 rows in set (0.00 sec)

mysql> SELECT alias_name, system_name FROM customers WHERE status='unpaid';
+------------+-------------+
| alias_name | system_name |
+------------+-------------+
| Dead.Beat  | dead        |
+------------+-------------+
1 row in set (0.01 sec)
mysql>
```

As shown in Listing 17.4, MySQL displays only the records that match the `WHERE` clause in the `SELECT` statement. This feature can be used by Postfix to add extra constraints to the normal lookup table function.

Changing Lookup Table Records

Once data is entered into the table you can change information using the SQL UPDATE statement. The format of the UPDATE statement is

```
UPDATE table SET field1=value1 [WHERE field2=value2]
```

where *table* is the table name to update, *field1* is the record field to update, and *value1* is the value to update it to. Optionally, a WHERE clause can be added to the UPDATE statement to limit the records that the update is applied to. By default, the update is applied to all records in the table. This is probably not what you would want to have happen. Usually you will want to update an individual record.

The WHERE clause can be used to narrow the update to records that match the *field2=value2* expression. Listing 17.5 shows an example of using the SQL UPDATE statement to change the value of a record field.

LISTING 17.5 Using the UPDATE Statement

```
mysql> UPDATE customers SET status='unpaid' WHERE alias_name='Richard.Blum';
Query OK, 1 row affected (0.00 sec)
Rows matched: 1  Changed: 1  Warnings: 0

mysql> SELECT alias_name, system_name FROM customers WHERE status='unpaid';
+--------------+-------------+
| alias_name   | system_name |
+--------------+-------------+
| Richard.Blum | rich        |
| Dead.Beat    | dead        |
+--------------+-------------+
2 rows in set (0.00 sec)

mysql>
```

As you can see in Listing 17.5, after issuing the UPDATE statement, MySQL returns the status of the query by showing how many rows (records) were affected by the update. You can issue a SELECT statement to ensure that the proper record has been updated.

Backing Up the Database

One often-overlooked function of the database administrator is backing up the database. This is a vital function and is necessary to protect the database from unforeseen damage.

If the database is fairly static and does not change very often, it may not be necessary to create a backup copy very often. However, if the database is dynamic and has lots of changes throughout the day, it is wise to perform a database backup on a daily basis.

The MySQL package contains a program that assists the database administrator in creating database backups. The `mysqldump` program can be used to create a backup file from a complete database. The `mysqldump` program creates a text script file that can be used to completely rebuild the database from scratch.

The format of the `mysqldump` command is

```
mysqldump [options] database [tables]
```

By default the `mysqldump` command will dump the entire database—table definitions as well as data—to the standard output. This output should be redirected to a file that can be stored outside of the server. To restore the database, the script file can be used with the `mysql` command to recreate the database and repopulate the tables with the data. Listing 17.6 shows an example of creating the backup script file.

LISTING 17.6 Creating a Backup Script

```
[rich@shadrach]$ mysqldump -u postfix -p maillist > backup
Enter password:
[rich@shadrach]$ cat backup
# MySQL dump 8.11
#
# Host: localhost    Database: maillist
#--------------------------------------------------------
# Server version        3.23.28-gamma

#
# Table structure for table 'customers'
#

CREATE TABLE customers (
  alias_name varchar(30) DEFAULT '' NOT NULL,
  system_name varchar(8),
  status varchar(15),
  address1 varchar(50),
  address2 varchar(50),
  city varchar(30),
  state char(2),
  zip varchar(10),
  PRIMARY KEY (alias_name)
);

# Dumping data for table 'customers'
```

LISTING 17.6 Continued

```
INSERT INTO customers VALUES ('Richard.Blum','rich','unpaid',NULL,
➥ NULL,NULL,NULL,NULL);
INSERT INTO customers VALUES ('Jessica.Blum','jessica','paid',NULL,
➥ NULL,NULL,NULL,NULL);
INSERT INTO customers VALUES ('Katie.Blum','katie','paid',NULL,
➥ NULL,NULL,NULL,NULL);
INSERT INTO customers VALUES ('Dead.Beat','dead','unpaid',NULL,
➥ NULL,NULL,NULL,NULL);
INSERT INTO customers VALUES ('Barbara.Blum','barbara','paid',NULL,
➥ NULL,NULL,NULL,NULL);
```

As you can see in Listing 17.6, the `mysqldump` program outputs the SQL statements necessary to re-create the tables for the database from scratch, including all of the data records.

The command in this example only backs up the data in the Postfix lookup table database. If the MySQL server should crash and you need to re-create the entire server database, this would not be sufficient. To perform a total database backup you can use the `-all-databases` option:

```
mysqldump -u root -p -all-databases > complete
```

The `complete` file should now contain the SQL to re-create the entire MySQL server database system, complete with internal usernames and table permissions.

The `mysql` command can be used to restore the database from the backup script file. Listing 17.7 shows an example of this.

LISTING 17.7 Restoring a Database

```
[rich@shadrach]$ mysql -u root -p maillist < backup
Enter password:
[rich@shadrach]$ mysql -u postfix -p maillist
Enter password:
Reading table information for completion of table and column names
You can turn off this feature to get a quicker startup with -A

Welcome to the MySQL monitor.  Commands end with ; or \g.
Your MySQL connection id is 36 to server version: 3.23.28-gamma

Type 'help;' or '\h' for help. Type '\c' to clear the buffer
```

LISTING 17.7 Continued

```
mysql> SELECT alias_name, system_name, status FROM customers;
+--------------+-------------+--------+
| alias_name   | system_name | status |
+--------------+-------------+--------+
| Richard.Blum | rich        | unpaid |
| Jessica.Blum | jessica     | paid   |
| Katie.Blum   | katie       | paid   |
| Dead.Beat    | dead        | unpaid |
| Barbara.Blum | barbara     | paid   |
+--------------+-------------+--------+
5 rows in set (0.00 sec)

mysql>
```

Configuring Postfix for MySQL

After the MySQL server and database have been configured, Postfix must be configured to be able to access data stored in the databases. This section describes how to configure Postfix to access MySQL databases and utilize them as lookup tables.

Compiling Postfix for MySQL Support

For Postfix to support accessing MySQL databases, it must be specifically compiled with MySQL support. Unfortunately, at the time of this writing, the most current version of Postfix does not support adding features after it is initially compiled. If you have already compiled Postfix without adding MySQL support, you must repeat the compile process.

If you are not sure whether the Postfix server you are currently running has MySQL support compiled in, you can use the `postconf` command with the `-m` option to list the available lookup table types:

```
[root@shadrach]$ postconf -m
nis
regexp
environ
btree
unix
hash
```

In this example the `mysql` lookup table type is not listed as being supported. This Postfix installation needs to be recompiled if you want to use MySQL.

Before you recompile, you should clean out the working source code directories. There are most likely object files left over from the previous compile that could cause problems for the new compile. Fortunately, Postfix includes a Makefile option that helps in this process. Change into the compile directory and give the command

```
make tidy
```

This removes all working files from any previous compiles. Once the working directories are clean, you can begin a fresh compile.

Before compiling, you must also configure the Postfix Makefile for MySQL support. You can do this using the `make` command using special parameters. The syntax for this command is

```
make -f Makefile.init makefiles \
    'CCARGS=-DHAS_MYSQL -I/usr/local/include/mysql' \
    'AUXLIBS=/usr/local/lib/mysql/libmysqlclient.a -lm'
```

You must add arguments to the compiler commands to ensure that the C compiler can find the MySQL include header files and the library file that contains the MySQL function calls. The `CCARGS` and `AUXLIBS` arguments must point to the locations of your MySQL installed libraries. The values shown in the example are valid if you installed MySQL from the source code distribution and used the default installation values. The backslash (\) characters allow you to continue a command line on separate lines.

CAUTION

If you installed MySQL from an RPM package, the `libmysqlclient.a` library file was most likely created using the zlib program. In order for Postfix to be able to use this library, you must also have the zlib and zlib-devel RPM packages installed and include the `-lz` option in the `AUXLIBS` arguments.

After the Makefile is re-created you can then create the normal Postfix installation files by using the following command:

```
make
```

After the new files are created, you should stop any running Postfix server and install the new files:

```
postfix stop
sh INSTALL.sh
```

After you install the files, the Postfix server can be restarted. You can use the `postconf` command to check that MySQL support has been added:

```
[root@shadrach]# postfix start
postfix-script: starting the Postfix mail system
[root@shadrach]# postconf -m
nis
regexp
environ
mysql
btree
unix
hash
```

Pointing Postfix to the MySQL Table

Now that Postfix is capable of connecting to a MySQL database, you must configure it to do so. There are two steps required to get Postfix to connect to the database.

The first step is to define the MySQL `alias_maps` entry in the `main.cf` configuration file as a reference to a second configuration file. The second configuration file defines the details necessary for Postfix to connect to the MySQL database. The `main.cf` configuration uses the `mysql` tag to reference the second configuration file:

```
alias_maps = hash:/etc/postfix/aliases, mysql:/etc/postfix/mysql-aliases.cf
```

The configuration file `mysql-aliases.cf` defines the parameters necessary for Postfix to connect to the MySQL database and send an SQL query to retrieve the result of the lookup. There are several parameters that must be defined. Table 17.2 shows these parameters.

TABLE 17.2 Postfix MySQL Parameters

Parameter	*Description*
`user`	MySQL username
`password`	MySQL user password
`dbname`	MySQL database name
`table`	MySQL database table
`select_field`	Field to return to Postfix
`where_field`	Field to match lookup value to
`additional_conditions`	Additional SQL parameters
`hosts`	MySQL database hosts to connect to

Postfix uses the values defined in the configuration file to create the SQL query to send to the MySQL database. The SQL query uses the form

```
SELECT select_field FROM dbname.table WHERE where_field= value
➥ additional_conditions
```

The `value` parameter is the value that Postfix uses to search the lookup table. The `additional_conditions` parameter allows the mail administrator to use other fields within the database to help define the query. The next section shows an example of this feature.

Using a MySQL Alias Lookup Table

Listing 17.8 shows a sample configuration file that can be used to connect to a MySQL database as an alias lookup table in Postfix.

LISTING 17.8 Sample MySQL Configuration File (`mysql-alias.cf`)

```
user=postfix
password = guitar

dbname = maillist
table = customers
hosts = localhost

select_field = system_name
where_field = alias_name

additional_conditions = and status = 'paid'
```

The parameters defined in Listing 17.8 can be saved in a file named `/etc/postfix/mysql-aliases.cf`. This file should be set so that only `root` can modify it. This will prevent any unauthorized tampering. However, you must also ensure that it is readable by all users. You can do this using the `chmod` command:

```
chmod 644 /etc/postfix/mysql-aliases.cf
```

After the configuration file is saved, you must define it in the `main.cf` configuration file. Since this is an alias lookup table, you must add it to any values present in the `alias_maps` parameter:

```
alias_maps = hash:/etc/postfix/aliases, mysql:/etc/postfix/mysql-aliases.cf
```

Remember that Postfix will search the alias databases in the order in which they are entered on the `alias_maps` line.

NOTE

Also remember that if you have an `alias_databases` parameter defined, the MySQL `aliases` file should not be included as a value. Postfix does not maintain this as a binary database.

After you perform a `postfix reload` command, the new database should be accessible by Postfix. Any alias mappings defined in the database should work for e-mail delivery. Listing 17.9 shows an example of this.

LISTING 17.9 Sample Delivery to a Postfix Alias

```
[jessica@shadrach]$ mail Jessica.Blum
Subject: Test message

This is a test message sent to an alias account.
.
Cc:
[jessica@shadrach]$ mail
Mail version 8.1 6/6/93.  Type ? for help.
"/var/spool/mail/jessica": 1 message 1 new
>N  1 jessica@shadrach.ispnet  Thu Dec 14 13:26  14/496   "Test message"
& 1
Message 1:
From jessica@shadrach.ispnet1.net  Thu Dec 14 13:26:25 2000
Delivered-To: jessica.blum@shadrach.ispnet1.net
To: Jessica.Blum@shadrach.ispnet1.net
Subject: Test message
Date: Thu, 14 Dec 2000 13:26:24 -0500 (EST)
From: jessica@shadrach.ispnet1.net (Jessica)


This is a test message sent to an alias account.

&
```

As shown in Listing 17.9, Postfix used the MySQL database to map the Jessica.Blum alias name to the system username `jessica`.

If a message is sent to an alias that is in the database but the `additional_conditions` parameter is not met, Postfix will bounce the message back to the sender with an error stating that the alias username does not exist. In this example, had the status field for the Jessica.Blum record been set to `unpaid`, the message would not have been delivered, and the sender would have received a bounce message indicating that the username does not exist on the server.

Summary

Postfix can use the MySQL database as lookup tables. The MySQL package is a popular relational database package that can run on the Unix platform. After installing MySQL, you must create a database and table for Postfix to use as the lookup table.

Once the MySQL database and table is defined, the Postfix configuration file must be modified to point to the database. The `mysql` tag can be used to point to a second configuration file that contains the parameters necessary to allow Postfix to log in to and query the database. Postfix can also create complex queries to use additional fields to alter the database result.

CHAPTER 18

Using OpenLDAP with Postfix

The previous chapter described how to use MySQL databases as lookup tables in Postfix. In a similar manner, Postfix also has the ability to utilize LDAP databases as lookup tables. With the increasing popularity of LDAP, this can be a very useful feature for mail administrators.

This chapter describes what LDAP is and how to utilize an LDAP database with Postfix. The popular OpenLDAP package is used to demonstrate how to install and use a free LDAP database.

What Is LDAP?

Network directory services has become one of the biggest crazes for computer networks. It allows multiple hosts on a network to share information regarding applications, resources, and users from a common database on the network. Novell's popular NetWare Directory Service and Microsoft's Active Directory are two examples of proprietary network directory services. Each uses its own protocol to communicate database queries from clients to database servers and return the results.

There are a number of standard network directory service protocols that can be utilized by any host or client on a TCP/IP network. One of the most recent is the *Lightweight Directory Access Protocol (LDAP)*. It is defined by several Internet Request for Comments (RFCs) posted to the public domain.

This section describes LDAP and how it can be used on a network to control information regarding network resources.

The LDAP System

Network directory services allow administrators to create a database to store information regarding network objects. These objects can be servers, applications, and even users. Any device on the network with the proper permissions can access the database and retrieve information regarding the objects. This has become a handy way to store usernames and passwords where any server in the network can verify a user password from the database and grant (or deny) access based on properties found in the database.

An LDAP database is based on a hierarchical database design, similar to how the DNS protocol stores domain names. Hierarchical databases are best known for fast read times but slow write times. This method assumes that once an object is written into the database it will be accessed many times. This works for most network situations where a user id is created once, and servers read the record each time the user attempts to log in. Objects in the LDAP database are connected to one another in a tree-like fashion. Each LDAP tree must have a root object, with other objects connected in sequence. Objects connect to other objects by reference, similar to the DNS naming system. Figure 18.1 shows a sample LDAP database structure.

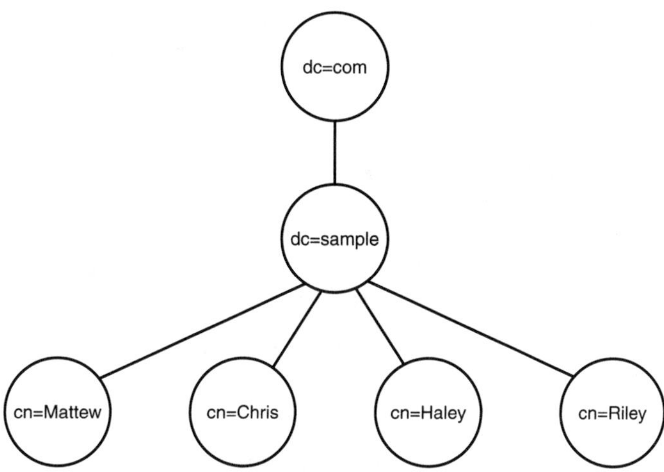

FIGURE 18.1

A sample LDAP directory tree.

An LDAP tree references objects using a *type* and one or more *values*. The LDAP type describes what type of object the object is. Different types have been defined for LDAP database objects. Most are derived from the standard X.500 naming convention:

- C—Country
- O—Organization
- OU—Organizational Unit
- CN—Common Name
- DC—Directory Context

Each type references different types of values. The directory context (dc) object values are standard names used for referencing different tree nodes.

Each object is uniquely referenced by its distinguished name (dn). The dn incorporates all LDAP tree nodes used from the object back to the root of the LDAP tree. For example, the dn

```
o="Sample, Inc.", c="US"
```

refers to the object containing the Sample, Inc. corporation located in the United States. To simplify names, many (if not most) companies have incorporated their registered domain name into their LDAP tree. This method is often implemented using the parts of the domain name for each directory context:

```
dc="sample", dc="com"
```

Once the base objects are defined for the corporation, more objects can be created underneath the corporation tree. Individual objects must be defined using unique distinguished names in the database.

The LDAP tree can "branch out" by having dc objects that are created to serve no other purpose but to contain other objects. This helps make the database more manageable than having all of the objects at one level. Figure 18.2 demonstrates a more complicated LDAP tree structure that utilizes objects as containers for other objects.

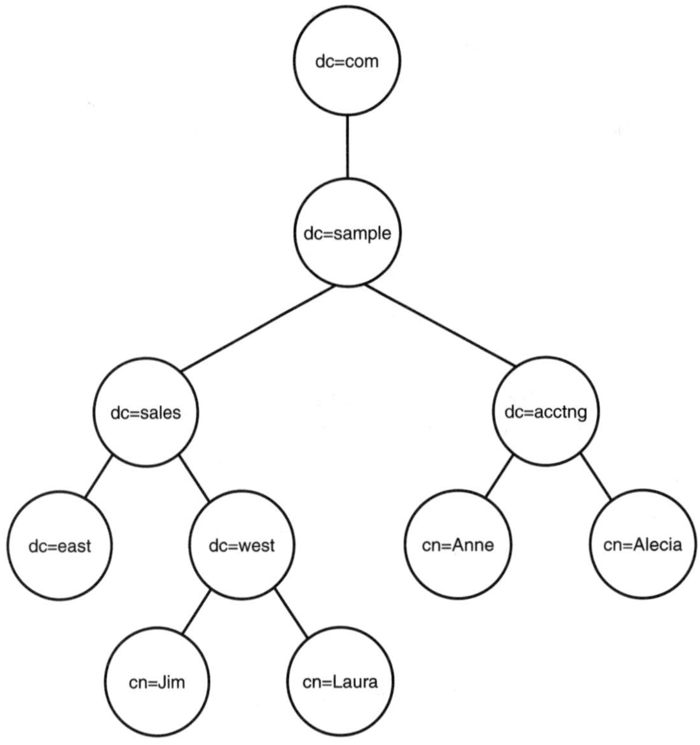

FIGURE 18.2

Complicated LDAP tree structure.

In this example, directory contexts (dc) are used to divide the LDAP directory not only by divisions within the organization, but also by parts within the divisions. Each individual user is referenced by a distinguished name (dn) that incorporates his or her division. For example, the user `jim` is referenced by the dn cn=jim, dc=west, dc=sales, dc=sample, dc=com.

LDAP Database Options

The LDAP database contains all of the objects defined in the tree. The LDAP database can be stored on one or more servers on the network. There are three different methods that you can use to store the LDAP database:

- The entire database on a single server (standalone)
- The entire database on multiple servers (replicated)
- Parts of the database on multiple servers (distributed)

Each method has its own unique way of storing information and operating on the network. The following sections describe these three methods and their differences.

Standalone

An LDAP server that is operating in *standalone mode* stores all of the objects contained in the defined LDAP database. Any requests for information from the LDAP database must be directed to the single LDAP server. The standalone server is responsible for responding to queries for data in the local LDAP database. Any requests for data outside of the defined LDAP database are not processed.

However, the single LDAP server for a network may also contain information about external LDAP servers responsible for other LDAP database trees. Any requests made by local clients regarding information outside of the local LDAP database can be forwarded to another LDAP server. This is called *referral mode*. The standalone LDAP server can be configured to operate in referral mode without affecting the local LDAP database.

Depending on the size of the network, having a single LDAP server can result in a large amount of traffic going to the LDAP server. The single server must be able to handle all requests for network information. On large networks this can require quite a large server for the LDAP database. With one single LDAP server there is also the potential problem of server crashes. If the single LDAP server crashes, no information can be retrieved from the LDAP database. To help alleviate these possible problems, the LDAP replicated mode was designed.

Replicated

In *replicated mode* there is more than one LDAP server, each holding the entire LDAP database. Because each server contains the entire database, any request for network information can be handled by any of the LDAP servers. This method works well for organizations that may have WAN links between sites. Network clients can be configured to query the LDAP server that is local to their WAN segment without having to obtain information from a remote LDAP server.

Since there are multiple servers, they must be in constant communication with each other. Any changes made to the LDAP database on one server must quickly be replicated to the other servers. This can become a tricky chore. The simplest method used to accomplish this is to have one LDAP server become the master server, while all other servers are designated as slaves. Changes can only be made on the master server. The master server is then responsible for keeping track of any database changes and replicating them to the slave servers.

Distributed

The last method used is the *distributed mode*. This can be the most complicated method to implement. In distributed mode, each server is only responsible for part of the LDAP database. No one server contains the entire LDAP database. For a client to resolve a query, it must connect to the LDAP server responsible for the section of the database that contains the information being queried. Figure 18.3 shows a simple distributed LDAP network.

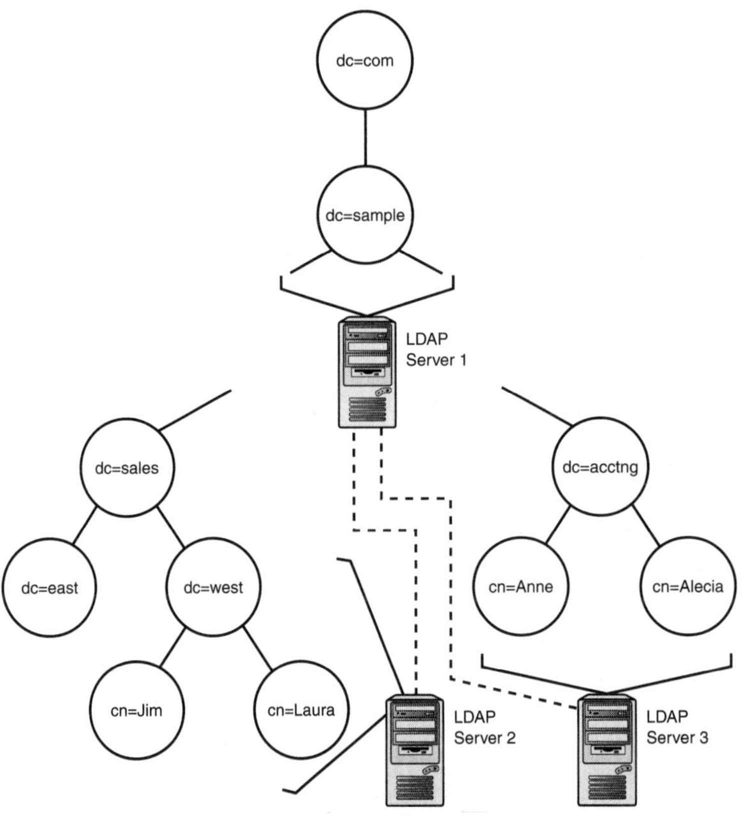

FIGURE 18.3

Simple distributed LDAP server network.

Clients wanting to retrieve information in the "dc=sales, dc=sample, dc=com" tree must connect to LDAP Server 2 to resolve their objects. This method works well for organizations that divide their LDAP database into geographical pieces, where each location can contain objects related to the local area.

Remember that the distributed mode does not provide for redundancy. If any of the LDAP servers crashes, information contained in that section of the LDAP database tree will become unavailable. Some LDAP implementations now allow for replicated distributed LDAP servers to combine the best of both the replicated and distributed modes.

Installing the OpenLDAP Package

The most popular LDAP implementation for the Unix platform has been the OpenLDAP package. This package allows a Unix server to host standalone, replicated, or distributed LDAP databases. It also includes client software to allow the Unix server to access an LDAP database on the network. The OpenLDAP software Web site is located at

```
http://www.openldap.org.
```

This section describes how to install the OpenLDAP software package on a Unix server. Once this has been done, you can configure Postfix to use the OpenLDAP database as a normal lookup table.

Binary Distribution

Many Linux distributions include a binary distribution of the OpenLDAP software. The Mandrake 7.2 distribution includes version 1.2.9 of the OpenLDAP software, which is divided into two separate RPM packages:

```
openldap-1.2.9-7mdk.i586.rpm
openldap-devel-1.2.9-7mdk.i586.rpm
```

The first package contains all of the OpenLDAP executable programs, configuration files, and documentation. The second package contains the libraries and header files necessary to compile OpenLDAP support into other software packages. This is required to rebuild the Postfix software to recognize OpenLDAP. Listing 18.1 lists the header and library files contained in this package.

LISTING 18.1 openldap-devel-1.2.9 RPM Package Files

```
/usr/include/disptmpl.h
/usr/include/lber.h
/usr/include/ldap.h
/usr/include/ldap_cdefs.h
/usr/include/srchpref.h
/usr/lib/liblber.a
```

LISTING 18.1 Continued

```
/usr/lib/liblber.la
/usr/lib/liblber.so
/usr/lib/libldap.a
/usr/lib/libldap.la
/usr/lib/libldap.so
```

You can install this package by using the RPM package installer program. You must be logged in as `root` to issue this command:

```
rpm -Uvh openldap-1.2.9-7mdk.i586.rpm
rpm -Uvh openldap-devel-1.2.9-7mdk.i586.rpm
```

The `-Uvh` options will install the software or update an existing OpenLDAP installation on the server.

Source Code Distribution

If your Unix platform does not include a binary distribution of OpenLDAP or you want to use the most current version of the software, you can download it from the OpenLDAP Web site.

There are two distribution paths that are available to use. The stable path is software that is known to work properly in most Unix environments. At the time of this writing, the stable version is 1.2.11.

The other distribution path available for download is the release path. This path offers the latest features and patches for the OpenLDAP software. Much like Postfix, the release versions are considered stable software, but they have not been extensively tested across all Unix platforms. At the time of this writing, the release version is 2.0.7.

NOTE

There have been significant features added to the 2.x versions of OpenLDAP, the most important being support for the new LDAP version 3 protocol (which allows for secure LDAP connections) and support for strict database schema definitions. I would strongly suggest using a 2.x version of OpenLDAP if at all possible for your LDAP server.

You can download the most current release version of OpenLDAP using the URL

```
ftp://ftp.openldap.org/pub/OpenLDAP/openldap-release.tgz
```

This is a link that always points to the most current release version of the software. Once downloaded, you must extract the source code into a working directory:

```
tar -zxvf openldap-release.tgz -C /usr/local/src
```

Remember that you must be `root` to perform this command. This command creates a working directory `/usr/local/src/openldap-2.0.7`. After moving to the working directory, there are three commands that you must run to compile OpenLDAP:

```
./configure
make depend
make
```

After the executable programs have been created you can test them by using the command

```
make test
```

This command starts performing tests on the OpenLDAP binaries. Each test reports on a different piece of the OpenLDAP software. If all of the tests are successful, you can install the OpenLDAP software with the command

```
make install
```

This places all of the executable program files into the proper directories and creates the `/etc/openldap` directory that contains skeleton configuration files.

OpenLDAP Programs

The OpenLDAP package consists of several executable programs that are used to maintain the LDAP database and to respond to network queries to the database. Two programs implement the LDAP server: `slapd` and `slurpd`. This section describes these two programs.

slapd

The `slapd` program is the heart of the OpenLDAP server. It runs as a background process to listen for LDAP requests from the network. Once an LDAP request is received, `slapd` attempts to process the request based on the configured LDAP database that it is using and returns any results to the client. `slapd` stands for Standalone LDAP Daemon.

The format of the `slapd` command line is

```
slapd [-f slapd-config-file] [-h URLs] [-d debug-level] [-n service-name]
➥ [-s syslog-level] [-l syslog-local-user] [-r directory]
➥ [-u user] [-g group]
```

As you can see, there are lots of command-line options that can be included with the `slapd` program, although all of them are optional. Invoking the `slapd` command without any options starts the LDAP server with default values for each of the options. Table 18.1 describes the different command-line options that can be used.

TABLE 18.1 slapd Command-Line Options

Option	*Description*
-f *slapd-config-file*	Specifies an alternative configuration file.
-h *URLs*	Specifies the URL(s) that the LDAP server will bind to for servicing LDAP requests. By default it uses the local host IP address and port 389.
-d *debug-level*	Turns on debugging at debug level *debug-level*.
-n *service-name*	Specifies an alternate service name for logging purposes. By default the service name is "slapd."
-s *syslog-level*	Specifies the debug level to log statements into the logging facility.
-l *syslog-local-user*	Selects the user-specified local name for the syslog facility. By default this is LOCAL4.
-r *directory*	Specifies a run-time chroot directory for `slapd` to operate in.
-u *user*	Specifies an alternate username to run `slapd` with.
-g *group*	Specifies an alternate group name to run `slapd` with.

Note that the `slapd.conf` configuration file controls the overall operation of `slapd`. This file is located in `/usr/local/etc/openldap` by default, although some Linux binary distributions have moved this to just `/etc/openldap`.

slurpd

The `slurpd` program, used when operating OpenLDAP in a replicated server environment, connects with `slapd` programs running on remote LDAP slave servers and propagates any LDAP database changes. The format of the `slurpd` command line is

```
slurpd [-d debug-level] [-f slapd-config-file] [-r slapd-replog-file]
➥ [-t temp-dir] [-o] [-k srvtab-file]
```

Much like the `slapd` program, all of the options for the `slurpd` program are optional. If no options are included in the command line, `slurpd` uses default values for each of the options. Table 18.2 describes the options available.

TABLE 18.2 slurpd Command-Line Options

Option	*Description*
-d *debug-level*	Turns on debugging at level *debug-level*
-f *slapd-config-file*	Specifies an alternate *slapd.conf* configuration file
-r *slapd-replog-file*	Specifies an alternate replication log file
-t *temp-dir*	Specifies an alternate location to copy the replication log file while processing it
-o	Runs once and exits
-k *srvtab-file*	Specifies an alternate location of the Kerberos `srvtab` file that contains keys for the replica LDAP servers

The `slurpd` program reads the replication log file, which identifies LDAP database changes, and connects to remote LDAP servers to submit the changes to the remote replica databases. After contacting all replicas, `slurpd` goes to sleep for a set period. When it wakes up, it rereads the replication log file. If it is empty, `slurpd` goes back to sleep. If it contains new database updates, `slurpd` again connects to the remote replica databases and sends the new database updates.

Configuring OpenLDAP for Postfix

After compiling and installing OpenLDAP, you must modify the configuration files to create an LDAP database for your organization. After the configuration file is modified, you can start OpenLDAP and begin entering individual objects into the database.

This section describes how to create a basic LDAP database for your organization and how to configure OpenLDAP to support that database. Once this is completed, you will be ready to configure Postfix to use this database as a lookup table.

Designing an Organizational LDAP Directory

After installing OpenLDAP, you should spend a few minutes (or hours) designing the LDAP database tree that will be used for your organization. As mentioned, you can take several approaches in designing the database.

Most organizations that implement LDAP databases use their registered domain names as the top-level directory contexts for the database. After that, additional dc's can be created to hold employee objects. By creating additional directory contexts, it will be easier for the LDAP administrator to manage the database, especially if there are lots of employees in your organization. Figure 18.4 demonstrates a simple LDAP database layout.

By using this layout, employee distinguished names would look like the following:

```
cn=bblum, dc=engineering, dc=ispnet1, dc=net
cn=nwilliams, dc=sales, dc=ispnet1, dc=net
cn=cwoenker, dc=marketing, dc=ispnet1, dc=net
cn=rmullen, dc=accounting, dc=ispnet1, dc=net
cn=hsnell, dc=tech, dc=ispnet1, dc=net
```

Once you have designed a suitable LDAP database for your organization, you must define it in OpenLDAP. The next section describes how to configure OpenLDAP to accommodate the LDAP database. The following sections then show how to enter information into the newly created LDAP database.

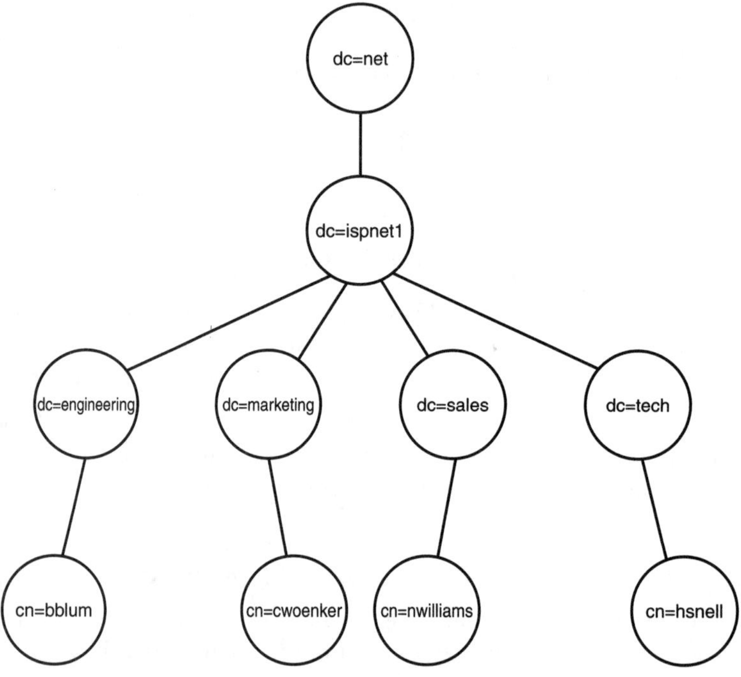

FIGURE 18.4

Sample LDAP database layout.

Creating the `slapd.conf` File

After you have designed your LDAP database, you can begin configuring OpenLDAP. The `slapd.conf` configuration file defines how the OpenLDAP server will work. It must be modified to represent your LDAP database design before the **`slapd`** program can be started.

You can use several parameters in the configuration file. Each parameter defines a particular aspect of the LDAP server. Table 18.3 describes a partial list of the parameters that can be used in an OpenLDAP version 2.x configuration file. You can see the entire list of parameters in the `slapd.conf` man pages.

TABLE 18.3 `slapd.conf` Configuration Parameters

Parameter	*Description*
`access`	Sets access control privileges for the database.
`attributetype`	Defines database object attributes that can be used.
`backend`	Defines the backend database that will be used.

TABLE 18.3 Continued

Parameter	*Description*
`cachesize`	Defines the number of entries the backend database can keep in cache memory.
`database`	Defines the start and type of a new database.
`dbcachesize`	Defines the number of bytes that can be used for database memory cache.
`dbnolocking`	Disables database locking.
`dbnosync`	Disables immediate syncing of memory cache to the database.
`defaultaccess`	Defines the default access level that will be granted when no access parameters are defined.
`directory`	Defines the directory used to contain the backend database files.
`idletimeout`	Defines the number of seconds to wait before closing an idle client session.
`include`	Defines a filename to read to include additional configuration information.
`index`	Defines the LDAP object to index in the database.
`loglevel`	Defines the logging level that `slapd` should use.
`mode`	Defines the Unix file mode that the database files should use.
`objectclass`	Defines database objects that can be used in the database.
`readonly`	Sets the database to read-only mode if set to *on*.
`referral`	Defines an alternate LDAP database server to pass the client to if the request cannot be resolved by the local database.
`replica`	Defines an LDAP replica server for this database.
`replogfile`	Defines the location of the replication log file used for updating replica servers.
`rootdn`	Specifies the dn that is not subject to access control restrictions. This object is considered the administrator of the database.
`rootpw`	Defines the password used for the `rootdn` object.
`sizelimit`	Defines the maximum number of entries to return from a search operation.
`suffix`	Defines the dn suffix that this database will respond to.
`timelimit`	Defines the maximum number of seconds `slapd` will spend answering a search request.
`updatedn`	Defines the dn allowed to make changes to a replica server.
`updateref`	Defines the URL sent to clients that submit update requests to a replica server.

The OpenLDAP installation automatically creates a skeleton `slapd.conf` file in the default configuration directory. If you installed OpenLDAP from the source code distribution, by default the configuration files are located in the `/usr/local/etc/openldap` directory. Again, some binary distributions (such as the ones for Mandrake) install the configuration files into the `/etc/openldap` directory.

The skeleton file contains default values that are appropriate for most simple LDAP installations. The `include` parameter is important in that it points to the standard OpenLDAP database schema that will be used to define all objects in the database. As you will see later, this becomes important when defining the Postfix attributes for user objects.

The only parameters that should need to be modified in the skeleton configuration file are

```
suffix      "dc=ispnet1, dc=net"
rootdn      "cn=Administrator, dc=ispnet1, dc=net"
rootpw      guitar
```

It is important that you change the `suffix` parameter to point to your LDAP tree definitions because you will want this database to accept objects for your tree. It is also important to change the `rootdn` and `rootpw` parameters to define an administrator for your LDAP database. The administrator object has the ability to make changes to the LDAP database. After making these changes, you should be ready to start the LDAP server.

Starting OpenLDAP

The system's `root` user should start the `slapd` program. To use the default `slapd.conf` configuration file and begin listening for LDAP requests, type the following command:

```
/usr/local/libexec/slapd
```

This is the default location of the `slapd` program, but this location may be different on your distribution. Once started, `slapd` becomes a background process and releases the terminal that started it.

To test `slapd`, you can send a simple LDAP search query to the LDAP database using the `ldapsearch` command. The `ldapsearch` options must specify the desired query to send to the LDAP database. With an empty database there's not too much to search for, but you can at least see if you get a response from the server. Listing 18.2 shows an example of the `ldapsearch` command on an empty database.

LISTING 18.2 Sample `ldapsearch` Command Session

```
$ ldapsearch -b '' -s base namingContexts
version: 2

#
# filter: (objectclass=*)
# requesting: namingContexts
#

#
dn:
namingContexts: dc=ispnet1,dc=net
```

LISTING 18.2 Continued

```
# search result
search: 2
result: 0 Success

# numResponses: 2
# numEntries: 1
```

The simple search shown in Listing 18.2 verifies that the LDAP server is working and that the database context is indeed set to your desired tree layout.

Now that the server is configured and running, the next step is to create the database's `organization` and `administrator` objects and start adding `user` objects to store the information that Postfix will use for the lookup table.

Creating the Database Organization and Administrator Objects

The objects defined in the `suffix` and `rootdn` parameter in the `slapd.conf` configuration file must be added to the LDAP database to start the database definition. The `suffix` parameter should define the organization directory contexts of the database, while the `rootdn` parameter object represents a common name object that has special privileges on the LDAP database: it can enter new data.

You can enter data into the LDAP database with the `ldapadd` command. The `ldapadd` command accepts data formatted in the LDAP Data Interchange Format (LDIF) and attempts to add the data to the LDAP database. The data can be entered from the standard input or read from a file.

The easiest method to use for this purpose is to create a file defining the LDAP information for the administrator object in LDIF format. Listing 18.3 shows a sample LDIF file that can be used to create the administrator account using the values defined in the sample `slapd.conf` file created earlier.

LISTING 18.3 Sample LDIF File

```
dn: dc=ispnet1, dc=net
objectclass: organization
o: ISP test network

dn: cn=Administrator, dc=ispnet1, dc=net
objectclass: organizationalRole
cn: Administrator
```

This LDIF file defines two separate objects for the database. Each object is defined by its distinguished name. Also, each distinguished name must have an `objectclass` that it is derived from. The `objectclass` defines the object type to the LDAP database. Each `objectclass` requires different attributes to further define the object in the database. Each attribute helps define values for the object.

The first entry defines the `organization` object for the LDAP database (since it has the `objectclass` of the same name). The organization object requires that the `o` attribute be defined, which is a text description of the organization. The second entry defines the `Administrator` object for the LDAP database. This was the `rootdn` object defined in the `slapd.conf` configuration file. The distinguished name for the `Administrator` object is defined using the `dn` attribute. The administrator is defined as using the `organizationalRole objectclass`. This object requires the `cn` attribute, which defines the common name associated with the object.

After creating the LDIF file, the data it holds can be entered into the database using the `ldapadd` command, which can use lots of command-line options to modify its behavior. Fortunately, for simple databases you can ignore most of them. The command that should work in this situation is

```
ldapadd -D 'cn=Administrator, dc=ispnet1, dc=net' -W -f ldif1.txt
```

This `ldapadd` example uses the `rootdn` object defined in the configuration file to enter the LDIF information stored in the file `ldif1.txt`. The `-D` option indicates the user object to use to enter the new data. Remember that this object has special privileges in the LDAP database. The `-W` option produces a password prompt where you must enter the `rootpw` value defined in the `slapd.conf` file:

```
$ ldapadd -D 'cn=Administrator, dc=ispnet1, dc=net' -W -f ldif1.txt
Enter LDAP Password:
adding new entry "dc=ispnet1, dc=net"

adding new entry "cn=Administrator, dc=ispnet1, dc=net"
```

As you can see in the sample session, after entering the proper `rootpw` value, the `ldapadd` command returns messages indicating the successful addition of the two new objects. To verify that the objects were indeed entered into the database you can use the `ldapsearch` command, this time searching for all `objectclasses` in the new organization. Listing 18.4 demonstrates this.

LISTING 18.4 Searching for LDAP Objects

```
$ ldapsearch -b 'dc=ispnet1, dc=net' '(objectclass=*)'
version: 2

#
```

LISTING 18.4 Continued

```
# filter: (objectclass=*)
# requesting: ALL
#

# ispnet1, dc=net
dn: dc=ispnet1, dc=net
objectClass: organization
o: "ISP test network"

# Administrator, dc=ispnet1, dc=net
dn: cn=Administrator, dc=ispnet1, dc=net
objectClass: organizationalRole
cn: Administrator

# search result
search: 2
result: 0 Success

# numResponses: 3
# numEntries: 2
```

The output from the `ldapsearch` command shows that, indeed, the two objects have been successfully entered into the LDAP database.

Adding User Objects

Now to make the LDAP database useful, you must create the remainder of the designed database using LDIF files. First, you would create any organization dc objects that you designed into the database. For the example database, you would create organization objects for each of the defined departments in the database:

```
dn: dc=accounting, dc=ispnet1, dc=net
objectclass: organization
o: Accounting Department

dn: dc=engineering, dc=ispnet1, dc=net
objectclass: organization
o: Engineering Department

dn: dc=sales, dc=ispnet1, dc=net
objectclass: organization
o: Sales Department
```

```
dn: dc=hq, dc=ispnet1, dc=net
objectclass: organization
o: Front Office
```

After creating an LDIF file, you can enter the information into the database using the `ldapadd` command:

```
$ ldapadd -D 'cn=Administrator, dc=ispnet1, dc=net' -W -f ldif2.txt
Enter LDAP Password:
adding new entry "dc=accounting, dc=ispnet1, dc=net"

adding new entry "dc=engineering, dc=ispnet1, dc=net"

adding new entry "dc=sales, dc=ispnet1, dc=net"

adding new entry "dc=hq, dc=ispnet1, dc=net"
```

After these department objects are created, you can begin creating objects for the users. Unfortunately, this can be a tricky task.

When Postfix queries the LDAP database, by default it uses two attributes:

- `mailacceptinggeneralid`
- `maildrop`

The `mailacceptinggeneralid` attribute defines the alias name that Postfix will accept mail for and use to query the LDAP database. The corresponding `maildrop` attribute defines the system name that Postfix will retrieve from the LDAP database and deliver the mail to.

The method that can be used to include these attributes in the LDAP database differs depending on the version of OpenLDAP you are using. The following sections describe the differences in this process.

OpenLDAP Versions Earlier Than 2.0

In OpenLDAP versions earlier than 2.0, the administrator is allowed to assign any `attributetype` to any object, whether the `attributetype` has been defined in the database schema or not. The administrator can define users as `person` objects and then add on the two Postfix attributes. This can be done in an LDIF file like so:

```
dn: cn=bblum, dc=engineering, dc=ispnet1, dc=net
objectclass: person
sn:Blum
mailacceptinggeneralid: Barbara.Blum
maildrop: barbara
cn: bblum
```

```
dn: cn=nwilliams, dc=sales, dc=ispnet1, dc=net
objectclass: person
sn:Williams
mailacceptinggeneralid: Nicholas.Williams
mailacceptinggeneralid: Nick.Williams
maildrop: nicholas
cn: nwilliams
```

Notice that the second object demonstrates using multiple occurrences of an attribute for an object (two `mailacceptinggeneralids`). This is allowed and often used with Postfix aliases.

After using the `ldapadd` command to enter the LDIF file data into the LDAP database, Postfix can begin using the LDAP server to map alias names to the system username (as shown in the "Configuring Postfix for LDAP" section).

OpenLDAP Version 2.0 and Later

Unfortunately for Postfix administrators, OpenLDAP began enforcing strict database schema requirements with version 2.0. No objects or attributes can be entered into the database without first being defined in the database schema. The problem is that the `mailacceptinggeneralid` and `maildrop` attributes are not defined in the default OpenLDAP schema. There are two methods that can be used to overcome this obstacle:

- Define new object and attribute types for Postfix
- Be creative with existing object and attribute types

Each of these methods is examined in this section.

Defining New Object and Attribute Types

Defining new object and attribute types is quite a challenge. Each object and attribute is registered with a globally unique Object Identifier (OID). OID values are based on the ASN.1 numbering system that is controlled by the Internet Assigned Numbers Authority (IANA).

This system may be familiar to you if you have used the Simple Network Management Protocol (SNMP). Each value is assigned a unique number string. Organizations must apply for assigned numbers in the 1.3.6.1.4.1 enterprise tree. Thus, if you are assigned an organization number 1123, you can assign OID numbers under the 1.3.6.1.4.1.1123 tree.

If you are just implementing a local LDAP server for your organization, you can use generic OID numbers to extend the default schema database with the object and attribute types necessary for Postfix. You can create a new schema file in the `/usr/local/etc/openldap/schema` directory and call it `myPostfix.schema`. Listing 18.5 shows a sample schema file that can be used to define the new object and attribute types.

LISTING 18.5 Sample Extended Schema File

```
attributetype (1.1.2.1.1 NAME 'mailacceptinggeneralid'
        DESC 'Postfix alias attribute'
        EQUALITY caseIgnoreIA5Match
        SYNTAX 1.3.6.1.4.1.1466.115.121.1.26)

attributetype (1.1.2.1.2 NAME 'maildrop'
        DESC 'Postfix system user attribute'
        EQUALITY caseIgnoreIA5Match
        SYNTAX 1.3.6.1.4.1.1466.115.121.1.26)

objectclass (1.1.2.2.1 NAME 'myPostfixPerson'
        DESC 'Postfix Object'
        SUP person
        MUST (mailacceptinggeneralid $ maildrop))
```

This extended schema file first defines the two new attribute types needed by Postfix objects. The `attributetype` parameter defines the OID value assigned to the attribute, its name, its description, how it will be matched in queries, and a syntax. The syntax is itself another OID value that describes the type of data the attribute can assume. The OID value shown defines an ASCII text string.

Next, the schema defines a new object type that uses the `person` object type as its superior object, thus inheriting all of its attributes. The new object is assigned an OID value, a name, a description, and a listing of what attributes must be defined for the object. The definition in this example requires that all objects of type `myPostfixPerson` include the `mailacceptinggeneralid` and `maildrop` attributes.

Once the schema file is defined it must be included in the `slapd.conf` configuration file using the `include` parameter:

```
include /usr/local/etc/openldap/schema/myPostfix.schema
```

When the `slapd` program is (re)started, it will read the new schema values and allow the administrator to add objects of the `myPostfixPerson` type:

```
dn: cn=bblum, dc=engineering, dc=ispnet1, dc=net
objectclass: myPostfixPerson
sn:Blum
mailacceptinggeneralid: Barbara.Blum
maildrop: barbara
cn: bblum
```

After entering the new values into LDAP, Postfix can query the database using the `mailacceptinggeneralid` query value and retrieve information using the standard `maildrop` value.

Using Existing Object and Attribute Types

If you are not able or willing to obtain a unique assigned OID value from the IANA, you can be creative and utilize existing objects and attributes from the default OpenLDAP schema for Postfix.

In addition to the core database schema file, OpenLDAP also includes several other schema files. One of these is the `misc.schema` file, also located in the `/usr/local/etc/openldap/schema` directory. This schema contains one `objectclass` and three attribute types for e-mail use.

The `inetLocalMailRecipient objectclass` can be used to create user objects. Each object can contain the `mailLocalAddress` and `mailRoutingAddress` attributes that are included in the schema.

You must also include this schema file in the `slapd.conf` configuration file using the `include` parameter:

```
include /usr/local/etc/openldap/schema/misc.schema
```

After entering the new schema definition you must stop and restart the `slapd` program. To enter database objects using the new object and attribute definition, you must create an LDIF file:

```
dn: cn=bblum, dc=engineering, dc=ispnet1, dc=net
objectclass: inetLocalMailRecipient
sn:Blum
mailLocalAddress: Barbara.Blum
mailRoutingAddress: barbara
cn: bblum

dn: cn=nwilliams, dc=sales, dc=ispnet1, dc=net
objectclass: inetLocalMailRecipient
sn:Williams
mailLocalAddress: Nicholas.Williams
mailRoutingAddress: nicholas
cn: nwilliams
```

Again, you can use the `ldapadd` command to insert the LDIF file values into the LDAP database. After the objects have been created, you must configure Postfix to use the alternative attribute names. The next section discusses how to do this.

Configuring Postfix for LDAP

Similar to the MySQL support, LDAP support must be compiled into the Postfix executable code. This requires rebuilding the source code and recompiling. After LDAP support is compiled into the executables, Postfix can be configured to use the LDAP database server and search for specified objects as lookup tables. This section describes the processes required to accomplish this.

Compiling LDAP Support into Postfix

Unfortunately, at the time of this writing, the current version of Postfix does not support adding LDAP support without recompiling the source code. You can check whether your current Postfix installation includes LDAP support by using the `postconf` command:

```
[rich@shadrach]$ postconf -m
nis
regexp
environ
ldap
btree
unix
hash
```

This example shows that the installed Postfix supports LDAP database searches. If this is not the case, you must recompile.

Before you recompile, it is wise to clean out the working source code directories. There are most likely object files left over from the previous compile that could cause problems for the new compile. Fortunately, Postfix includes a Makefile option that helps in this process. The command

```
make tidy
```

removes all working files from any previous compiles. Once the working directories are clean, you can begin a fresh compile.

Before compiling, you must first configure the Postfix Makefile for LDAP support. This can also be done by invoking the `make` command with special parameters. The syntax for this command is

```
make -f Makefile.init makefiles \
    'CCARGS=-DHAS_LDAP -I/usr/local/include' \
    'AUXLIBS=/usr/local/lib/libldap.a /usr/local/lib/liblber.a'
```

You must add arguments to the compiler commands to ensure that the C compiler can find the OpenLDAP include header files and the library file that contains the OpenLDAP function calls. The `CCARGS` and `AUXLIBS` arguments must point to the locations of your OpenLDAP installed libraries. The values shown in the example are valid if you installed OpenLDAP from the source code distribution and used the default installation values.

CAUTION

If you installed OpenLDAP from an RPM package, the `libldap.a` and `liblber.a` library files were most likely created using the zlib program. In order for Postfix to be able to use this library, you must also have the zlib and zlib-devel RPM packages installed and include `-lz` in the `AUXLIBS` arguments.

NOTE

You may have noticed that the LDAP recompile `make` command uses the same format as the MySQL recompile `make` command. If you require both MySQL and OpenLDAP support in your Postfix installation, you can combine both sets of parameters in one `make` command.

After the Makefile is re-created you can then create the normal Postfix installation files by using the command

```
make
```

After the new files are created, you should stop any running Postfix server before installing the new files:

```
postfix stop
sh INSTALL.sh
```

After installing the files, the Postfix server can be restarted. You can run the `postconf` command to check that OpenLDAP support has been added.

LDAP Parameters

Once OpenLDAP support has been added to the Postfix installation, you can modify the `main.cf` configuration file to add OpenLDAP lookup tables. Unlike the method used to define remote MySQL lookup tables, Postfix uses multiple `main.cf` configuration parameters to define the OpenLDAP lookup tables.

Each OpenLDAP lookup table definition starts with a pointer to a unique tag that is used to identify the LDAP database:

```
alias_maps = hash:/etc/postfix/aliases, ldap:myldaptag
```

This parameter entry in the `main.cf` configuration file defines a second aliases database located on an LDAP database server. At this point, only the unique tag name (`myldaptag`) is defined in the parameter. All definition parameters for this LDAP server will start with this unique tag name.

Postfix uses additional parameters to define the values required to connect to the LDAP database and query for the required result. Table 18.4 describes the additional parameters that can be used.

TABLE 18.4 Postfix LDAP Parameters

Parameter	*Description*
`server_host`	The IP address or hostname of the LDAP server.
`server_port`	The TCP port used to connect to the LDAP database server.
`search_base`	The LDAP distinguished name used as the starting base for searches.
`timeout`	The amount of time to wait for a search to complete.
`query_filter`	The LDAP attribute used to search on.
`domain`	A list of domains to restrict LDAP searches to.
`result_attribute`	The LDAP attribute Postfix wants returned as a result of the query.
`special_result_attribute`	The attribute of objects that can contain distinguished names. This value is used to perform recursive searches.
`scope`	The LDAP search scope. Can be one of `sub`, `base`, or `one`.
`bind`	Defines whether or not to bind to the LDAP server.
`bind_dn`	The distinguished name to use to bind to the LDAP server.
`cache`	Defines whether or not to use a cache for the LDAP connection.
`cache_expiry`	Defines the time in seconds that any cache entries will expire.
`cache_size`	Defines the size in bytes that the cache should be.
`dereference`	Defines when to dereference LDAP aliases.

As mentioned, each of the LDAP parameters listed in Table 18.4 must be preceded by the tag name defined in the table definition. For most simple LDAP connections the default values can be used for the majority of the parameters. A simple example of using an LDAP database as an `aliases` lookup table would be

```
alias_maps = hash:/etc/postfix/aliases, ldap:myldaptag
alias_database = hash:/etc/postfix/aliases

myldaptag_server_host = localhost
myldaptag_search_base = dc=ispnet1, dc=net
myldaptag_query_filter = (mailLocalAddress=%s)
myldaptag_result_attribute = mailRoutingAddress
```

This example shows several different features of the LDAP parameter definitions:

- The LDAP database definition is not included in the `alias_database` parameter.
- The LDAP database can be located on the same host as the Postfix server.
- Do not use any quotes when defining distinguished names.
- Postfix can use alternate attributes for querying the database and returning results.

Of all the features, the capability to change the attribute types for queries is the most versatile. As mentioned in the previous section, by default Postfix uses the query attribute

```
mailacceptinggeneralid
```

This is the attribute that Postfix will try to match the query value to in the LDAP database. You can modify the default query by using the `query_filter` parameter. Not only can you change the default attribute, you can also add additional query matches:

```
myldaptag_query_filter =  (&(mailLocalAddress=%s)(status='paid'))
```

This example utilizes two attributes for the query: the attribute `title`, which matches the value queried; and the attribute `status`, which is equal to the text string `'paid'`. Both attribute matches must be met for LDAP to return a result to Postfix.

Similarly, you can modify the LDAP result attribute that will retrieve data from the database. By default Postfix uses the result attribute:

```
maildrop
```

This is the attribute that Postfix will request to be returned by the LDAP database server if the query matches a database value. If your LDAP database does not use this attribute type, you can modify Postfix to request an alternate attribute:

```
myldaptag_result_attribute = mailRoutingAddress, mailbox
```

Notice that the result attribute can be set to return multiple attribute values if they exist in the LDAP database.

NOTE

The example shown utilized an LDAP database as an `aliases` lookup table. You can also create LDAP databases for any of the other lookup table types used in Postfix. Remember to use a unique tag name for each LDAP database used for each lookup table.

Summary

Postfix can use a network LDAP database as a lookup table. Lightweight Directory Access Protocol (LDAP) databases are becoming a popular way to store user information on networks. The LDAP database uses a hierarchical database topology that can be replicated as well as broken up and distributed among multiple servers. Individual LDAP servers can be configured to run in standalone, replicated, or distributed mode.

The OpenLDAP package is a popular LDAP server implementation for the Unix platform. Postfix can be configured to work with OpenLDAP. It must be recompiled pointing to the LDAP libraries. Once Postfix is reconfigured, new parameters can be added to the configuration file to define the LDAP server and what lookup table it can be used for. Each LDAP user object must have attributes defined that can be used to represent the alias and system name for the user. Postfix will accept messages sent to the alias name and deliver them to the defined system name for the user.

CHAPTER 19

Using Majordomo with Postfix

Mailing list servers allow users to post messages for large audiences of people to see. They have become popular as a means of communication for people involved with supporting and using many open source software packages. Postfix itself has multiple mailing lists that you can subscribe to if you want to keep current with new Postfix developments and ask questions about Postfix installations.

A popular mailing list server package is Majordomo, originally written by Brent Chapman. It consists of a set of Perl programs that manipulate messages using an `aliases` lookup table and a system of configuration files and directories for the different mail lists that it handles.

This chapter describes the features of mailing lists and how to install and use the Majordomo mailing list program on a Postfix mail server.

Features of a Full Service Mailing List

You may already be familiar with mailing list servers as a subscriber. If you have ever sent a message to a mailing list with the word "subscribe" in the body of the message, you probably have interacted with a large mailing list system. The ability of remote users to request a subscription is just one feature of real mailing list servers. This section describes some of the common features found in various mailing list servers.

Open and Closed Mailing Lists

When you want to become a member of a mailing list, you must first send a message asking to subscribe. There are several different options that the mailing list server can use to handle new subscription requests.

In an open mailing list, anyone is allowed to subscribe. No checks are made to authenticate the e-mail address that is requesting the subscription. This is the simplest type of mailing list to administer because there are almost no functions that need administering. There is one drawback to this feature: You have to assume that the e-mail address specified in the subscription request actually belongs to the person who initiated the request. Sometimes this assumption can be dangerous. Just like pranksters who send in magazine subscription cards with other people's names on them, pranksters can subscribe other people's e-mail addresses to the mail list without the owners knowing.

To combat this situation, most mailing list server programs allow open mailing lists, but confirm the actual subscription. When a request to subscribe to a mailing list is received, the server sends a message back to the e-mail address requesting the subscription, asking that they reply with a confirmation message. Often a special id code is used so that it would be difficult to fake the return confirmation message. When a proper return confirmation message is received, the e-mail address is added to the subscription list.

In a closed mailing list, all subscription requests are sent to the list owner (an individual responsible for deciding who may join a particular mailing list). New e-mail addresses are not added to the mailing list unless the list owner sends the server a special message allowing the addition. This gives the mailing list owner complete control over who is allowed access to the mailing list.

Moderated and Unmoderated Mail Lists

Once a mailing list is created and e-mail addresses are added to its subscription list, users can begin sending messages to the list. In an unmoderated mail list, no checking of messages is done. Any member of the list can send any message to the list and it will be automatically forwarded to every member of the list.

Some mailing list owners get a little scared with this feature. For various reasons, list owners may want or need to control the content that is sent to the list members. A moderated mailing list allows the list owner to screen all messages sent to the list before they are sent to the list members. If the list owner does not want a particular message forwarded to the list, he or she can stop the message. If the message is okay, it can be sent to the list as normal. This feature creates a large amount of work for the list owner. Depending on the scope of the mail list, it may be a necessary job.

Remote Administration of Mailing Lists

An extremely nice feature of sophisticated mailing list server software packages is the ability to remotely administer mailing lists. Most packages allow list owners to create special passwords to gain access to administration functions on their particular mailing lists. Once the owner has access, she can then change the configuration of her mailing list via specially formatted e-mail messages. Because the configuration is done via e-mail, the list owner can be anywhere in the world, as long as she can still send e-mail messages to the server. This is a nice feature to have if the mailing list server is located remotely from a mailing list owner.

Each mailing list has a separate configuration file that can be maintained by the mailing list owner. Features such as whether the list is open or closed and moderated or unmoderated can be configured and changed remotely without any work having to be done on the mailing list server itself.

Digests of Mailing Lists

Another nice feature of full-service mailing list servers is the capability to compact messages sent over time to a particular mailing list into digests. You can configure a mailing list server to create digests of messages sent to lists on a daily, weekly, or monthly basis. A user can then request to receive the digests rather than receiving the individual messages. If there are mailing lists that generate lots of messages a day, this can be a nice feature to add. Sometimes it is better to receive just one large message at the end of the day rather than lots of small messages scattered throughout the day. Mailing lists that are time sensitive (where responses are generated often) may not be good candidates for digests.

Archives of Mail Lists

Archives are files that contain all the messages sent to a mailing list over a certain period of time. The list owner can select an archive period to use: daily, weekly, monthly, or yearly. All messages sent to the list in the archive period are saved to an archive file as well as sent to each mailing list member. New members of the list can request archives of past messages. The mailing list server can produce lists of available archive files, and members can select which files to receive via e-mail.

Installing Majordomo

This section describes the steps necessary to install Majordomo on a Postfix server. Several functions that must be performed during this process are outlined in this section. This section also includes the steps necessary to configure Postfix to accommodate the Majordomo installation.

Downloading Majordomo

Most Linux distributions do not include a binary package for Majordomo. If your version of Linux does not include a binary distribution of Majordomo or you want to get the latest version, you can download the source code distribution from the Internet. Many different Unix and Linux sites have Majordomo source code distributions available for download. At the time of this writing, Great Circle Associates has offered to host the official Majordomo Web and FTP sites. The Web site is located at

```
http://www.greatcircle.com/majordomo/
```

while the software can be downloaded at its FTP site `ftp.greatcircle.com` in the `/pub/majordomo` directory. The most current version available at the time of this writing is version 1.94.5. The file `majordomo-1.94.5.tar.gz` is a link that points to the most current version of Majordomo. Remember to change to the BINARY FTP mode before downloading the file to your server.

Creating a Majordomo System Username

First, Majordomo must be installed with its own unique username. This is used for security purposes, so the Perl programs will not be run as `root` and create possible vulnerabilities.

You should use your standard Unix `useradd` command to add the new username. In this case, you can allow the system to create a default `$HOME` directory because you must compile and install the Majordomo programs as this new user. You can use an existing group name, or you can create a new one if you want. For most Linux systems, you can add a new user with the `useradd` command:

```
useradd -g daemon majordom
```

For this example, the username `majordom` and group `daemon` were chosen to use as the Majordomo installation account. Also, remember to set a password for the `majordom` username to prevent unauthorized access to this account.

The Majordomo distribution file can then be copied to the `majordom $HOME` directory. The rest of the installation process should be done as the `majordom` user. To extract the software from the file, type

```
tar -zxvf majordomo-1.94.5.tar.gz
```

This creates the subdirectory `majordomo-1.94.5` and installs the Majordomo source code files. Next, you must modify the Makefile to reflect your particular installation of Majordomo.

Edit the Majordomo Makefile

The Makefile directs what features the Majordomo program will have when it is compiled. Listing 19.1 is a partial listing of the Makefile. The line numbers have been added to help in the description of the listing.

LISTING 19.1 Partial Listing of Majordomo Makefile

```
#$Modified: Wed Aug 27 17:52:25 1997 by cwilson $
#
# $Source: /sources/cvsrepos/majordomo/Makefile,v $
# $Revision: 1.63 $
# $Date: 1997/08/27 15:56:21 $
# $Header: /sources/cvsrepos/majordomo/Makefile,v 1.63 1997/08/27 15:56:21
# cwilson Exp $
#


#  This is the Makefile for Majordomo.
#
#------------  Configure these items ---------------#
#


# Put the location of your Perl binary here:
PERL = /usr/bin/perl


# What do you call your C compiler?
CC = gcc


# Where do you want Majordomo to be installed?  This CANNOT be the
# current directory (where you unpacked the distribution)
```

LISTING 19.1 Continued

```
W_HOME = /usr/local/majordomo

# Where do you want man pages to be installed?
MAN = $(W_HOME)/man

# You need to have or create a user and group which majordomo will run as.
# Enter the numeric UID and GID (not their names!) here:
W_USER = 507
W_GROUP = 2

# These set the permissions for all installed files and executables (except
# the wrapper), respectively.  Some sites may wish to make these more
# lenient, or more restrictive.
FILE_MODE = 644
EXEC_MODE = 755
HOME_MODE = 751
# If your system is POSIX (e.g. Sun Solaris, SGI Irix 5 and 6, Dec Ultrix
# MIPS, BSDI or other 4.4-based BSD, Linux) use the following four lines.
# Do not change these values!
WRAPPER_OWNER = root
WRAPPER_GROUP = $(W_GROUP)
WRAPPER_MODE = 4755
POSIX = -DPOSIX_UID=$(W_USER) -DPOSIX_GID=$(W_GROUP)
# Otherwise, if your system is NOT POSIX (e.g. SunOS 4.x, SGI Irix 4,
# HP DomainOS) then comment out the above four lines and uncomment
# the following four lines.
# WRAPPER_OWNER = $(W_USER)
# WRAPPER_GROUP = $(W_GROUP)
# WRAPPER_MODE = 6755
# POSIX =

# Define this if the majordomo programs should *also* be run in the same
# group as your MTA, usually sendmail.  This is rarely needed, but some
# MTAs require certain group memberships before allowing the message sender
# to be set arbitrarily.
# MAIL_GID =    numeric_gid_of_MTA

# This is the environment that (along with LOGNAME and USER inherited from
# the parent process, and without the leading "W_" in the variable names)
# gets passed to processes run by "wrapper"
W_SHELL = /bin/sh
W_PATH = /bin:/usr/bin:/usr/ucb
```

LISTING 19.1 Continued

```
65 W_MAJORDOMO_CF = $(W_HOME)/majordomo.cf
66
67 # A directory for temp files..
68 TMPDIR = /usr/tmp
```

Several lines in the Makefile shown in Listing 19.1 need to be modified to suit your particular Unix environment. Line 16 defines where Majordomo can find the `perl` program. Because the Majordomo scripts are written in Perl, you must have Perl installed on your Unix system, and Majordomo must know how to find it. Perl is a popular scripting program language developed by Larry Wall. It is included with almost all Linux distributions and usually is installed by default. Also, line 19 defines the C compiler used on the system. For most Linux distributions, the GNU C compiler, gcc, is included.

In addition to the compilers, you must specify the location where Majordomo will be installed. Line 23 defines the base directory for the Majordomo program. Don't get this confused with the home directory for the `majordom` user. They are not the same. They can be the same, but it is easier if you select another location that can be used for the scripts and configuration files. This example shows using the `/usr/local/majordomo` location. You will have to create this directory as the `root` user, and change the owner to the `majordom` user with these commands:

```
mkdir /usr/local/majordomo
chmod 755 /usr/local/majordomo
chown majordom.daemon /usr/local/majordomo
```

You will have to replace the `majordom.daemon` with the username and group name that you chose to install Majordomo as. Another item that needs to be changed in the Makefile is the `majordom` user id and group id. Lines 30 and 31 specify these values to the `majordomo` program. The Makefile is looking for the numerical values, not the text names. You can log in as the `majordom` user and type the command `id` to determine the user id and group id numbers. On the example system the `majordom` user id was 507, and the daemon group id was 2.

Creating and Editing the `majordomo.cf` File

The `majordomo.cf` file is the main configuration file that controls the behavior of the Majordomo installation. To create a new configuration file, you can copy the template file `sample.cf` located in the `majordomo-1.94.5` directory to `majordomo.cf` in the same directory. Listing 19.2 shows a sample `majordomo.cf` file created for a test mailing list server. Again, line numbers have been added to help in the discussion of the listing.

LISTING 19.2 Sample majordomo.cf File

```
#
# A sample configuration file for majordomo.  You must read through this and
# edit it accordingly!
#

# $whereami -- What machine am I running on?
#
$whereami = "ispnet1.net";

# $whoami -- Who do users send requests to me as?
#
$whoami = "Majordomo\@$whereami";

# $whoami_owner -- Who is the owner of the above, in case of problems?
#
$whoami_owner = "Majordomo-Owner\@$whereami";

# $homedir -- Where can I find my extra .pl files, like majordomo.pl?
# the environment variable HOME is set by the wrapper
#
if ( defined $ENV{"HOME"}) {
     $homedir = $ENV{"HOME"};
} else {
     $homedir = "/usr/local/majordomo";
}

# $listdir -- Where are the mailing lists?
#
$listdir = "$homedir/lists";

# $digest_work_dir -- the parent directory for digest's queue area
# Each list must have a subdirectory under this directory in order for
# digest to work. E.G. The bblisa list would use:
#     /usr/local/mail/digest/bblisa
# as its directory.
#
$digest_work_dir = "/usr/local/mail/digest";

# $log -- Where do I write my log?
#
$log = "$homedir/Log";
# $sendmail_command -- Pathname to the sendmail program
#                        usually /usr/lib/sendmail, but some newer BSD systems
```

LISTING 19.2 Continued

```
44 #                       seem to prefer /usr/sbin/sendmail
45 #
46 # $sendmail_command = "/usr/lib/sendmail";
47 $sendmail_command = "/usr/sbin/sendmail";
```

Several variables must be set in the `majordomo.cf` file. Line 8 defines the `$whereami` variable that is the address used for return messages. If Postfix is configured to use the domain name as the `$mydestination` parameter, the return address will be the domain name as shown in line 8. If not, the return address will be the fully qualified hostname. Lines 12 and 16 define the `$whoami` and `$whoami_owner` variables based on the `$whereami` variable. You should not need to change these values.

The `$homedir` variable shown on line 24 is important. It must point to the Majordomo program home directory that you configured in the Makefile. This is where Majordomo will look for the Perl scripts as it processes list messages. Line 29 defines the `$listdir` variable. This indicates where Majordomo will store the information for the mailing lists. The default location is a subdirectory called `lists` that is located in the Majordomo home directory.

In line 37 the `$digest_work_dir` variable defines where the mailing list digest files will be kept. If you are planning on using the digest feature of Majordomo, you may need to change this value and create a new subdirectory. Remember that digest files contain the full text of all messages sent during a given time period. You may need to use an area that has a fairly large amount of disk space, depending on the amount of mailing list messages you expect will be generated.

The `$log` variable described in line 41 defines the location of the Majordomo log file. Majordomo logs all transactions that it processes to this log file. You can change the location of this file to match your Unix distribution's current log file directory, such as `/var/log/majordomo.log`. By default, Majordomo creates a log file named `Log` in the base Majordomo directory.

Finally, line 47 defines the proper location for the system's `sendmail` program (whether it is provided by Postfix or not). By default, the location is set to `/usr/lib/sendmail`. This will need to be changed to reflect the location set by the Postfix installation, which by default is set to `/usr/sbin/sendmail`.

Compiling Majordomo

After the Makefile and `majordomo.cf` files are configured, you can use the GNU `make` utility to build the Majordomo executable files. This requires three steps:

- Run `make wrapper` to verify that the wrapper program will compile cleanly.
- Run `make install` as `majordom` to install the Majordomo scripts and executables in the Majordomo home directory.
- Run `make install-wrapper` as `root` to install the wrapper program setuid `root`.

At this point, Majordomo should be fully installed and ready to test. Log in as a user without any special rights and change to the Majordomo program's home directory (`/usr/local/majordomo` for this example). From there, type

```
./wrapper config-test
```

This runs the wrapper program and tests the configuration. Listing 19.3 shows the partial output generated by the wrapper program.

LISTING 19.3 Output from `wrapper config-test`

```
---------------------- end of tests ----------------------


Nothing bad found!  Majordomo _should_ work correctly.

If it doesn't, check your configuration file
(/usr/local/majordomo/majordomo.cf)
closely, and if it still looks okay, consider asking the majordomo-users
mailing list at "majordomo-users@greatcircle.com" for assistance.  Be sure
and fully specify what your problems are, and what type of machine (and
operating system) you are using.

Enjoy!
```

The final few lines of the long output that the `config-test` generates inform you whether the installation was successful. As you can tell, this Majordomo configuration passed the tests.

Creating Postfix Aliases for Majordomo

After successfully installing the Majordomo software, you must configure Postfix to recognize the mail lists. Majordomo processes mail lists using a set group of aliases for each mail list. These aliases must be placed in a Postfix `aliases` lookup table (see Chapter 9, "Postfix Lookup Tables").

Instead of placing all of the Majordomo aliases in the standard Postfix `aliases` table, most administrators find it easier to create a separate aliases file for Majordomo. For the default Majordomo configuration, add the lines shown in Listing 19.4 to a new file (call it `major-aliases`) created in the `/etc/postfix` directory.

LISTING 19.4 Majordomo Alias Lines

```
#  Majordomo aliases
majordomo:   "|/usr/local/majordomo/wrapper majordomo"
```

LISTING 19.4 Continued

```
3 owner-majordomo:    rich,
4 majordomo-owner:    rich
```

In Listing 19.4, line 2 shows the alias `majordomo` being redirected to the wrapper program with the command-line parameter of `majordomo`. This tells Postfix to run the wrapper program when it receives a message for the `majordomo` alias. Lines 3 and 4 are support aliases. If a list member is having difficulties with the mail list, he can send mail to the mail list owner asking for help, advice, and so on. These addresses should point to the real e-mail address of the mail list server administrator.

After new entries are made to the aliases file, you must run the `postalias` program for Postfix to recognize them:

```
postalias /etc/postfix/major-aliases
```

After the indexed binary database file is created, you must add its path to the `alias_maps` parameter in the `main.cf` configuration file:

```
alias_maps: hash:/etc/postfix/aliases, hash:/etc/postfix/major-aliases
```

There is one trick to using Postfix aliases to run the Majordomo wrapper program. Some Postfix installations use the `allow_mail_to_commands` parameter in `main.cf` to restrict piping messages to commands. By default, this parameter allows command piping in alias entries. If this parameter is present in your `main.cf` file, ensure that it includes the value `alias`.

Testing the Majordomo Installation

You can easily create a test mailing list to see whether the Majordomo installation is correct. First, you must create a dummy list file in the Majordomo lists directory as specified in the `majordomo.cf` file. In this example, the location is `/usr/local/majordomo/lists`. You can create the test file as the `majordom` user using the following command:

```
touch /usr/local/majordomo/lists/test
```

Once the file is created, you can send the Majordomo `lists` command to the `majordomo` alias to receive a listing of the available mail lists. Listing 19.5 shows an example of this.

LISTING 19.5 Sample Test of Majordomo Installation

```
[rich@shadrach]$ echo 'lists' | mail majordomo
[rich@shadrach]$ mail
Mail version 8.1 6/6/93.  Type ? for help.
"/var/spool/mail/rich": 1 message 1 new
>N  1 Majordomo@ispnet1.n    Tue Dec 26 12:23  22/623   "Majordomo results"
&1
```

LISTING 19.5 Continued

```
Message 1:
From Majordomo-Owner@ispnet1.net  Tue Dec 26 12:23:07 2000
Delivered-To: rich@ispnet1.net
To: rich@ispnet1.net
From: Majordomo@ispnet1.net
Subject: Majordomo results
Reply-To: Majordomo@ispnet1.net
Date: Tue, 26 Dec 2000 12:23:07 -0500 (EST)

--

>>>> lists
Majordomo@ispnet1.net serves the following lists:

  test

Use the 'info <list>' command to get more information
about a specific list.
```

Majordomo responds to the `lists` command by sending a list of all mailing lists supported on the mailing list server. The list includes the phony test mail list created.

As a final check of the Majordomo system, the command that you sent to Majordomo should have been logged in the Majordomo log file. Check the log to see whether it appears. The following line appeared in the `/usr/local/majordomo/Log` file of the example server:

```
Dec 26 18:23:07 ispnet1.net majordomo[1716] {rich@ispnet1.net (Rich Blum)} lists
```

The log file indicates the time, the e-mail address, and the command received. Frequent checking of the Majordomo log file helps in spotting any unauthorized activity with the mailing list server.

Configuring a Majordomo Mailing List

With the Majordomo program successfully installed, the next step is to configure actual mailing lists. To create a new list, first you must create an empty file that will be used to hold the e-mail addresses in the list. The name of the file must match the name of the mailing list.

This example will use the mailing list name "officenews." After the file is created, you must ensure that it has the proper access modes set. The commands to create the file and change the permissions are

```
touch /usr/local/majordomo/lists/officenews
chmod 644 /usr/local/majordomo/lists/officenews
```

After the mailing list file is created, you can create an information file for it. Majordomo will use the mailing list information file when someone requests information on the mailing list and also as the first message sent to users who subscribe to the mailing list. The filename of the information file should be in the form `<listname>.info`, where `<listname>` is the mailing list name. For this example the information file will be

```
/usr/local/majordomo/lists/officenews.info
```

This file should contain a simple text description of the mailing list:

```
This mailing list is used to help keep you informed about general information
that is happening in the organization.  Please post any announcements to
this mailing list.  Unauthorized use of this mailing list is prohibited.
```

Each mailing list requires several entries in the Postfix aliases file, depending on what features you want the mailing list to offer. Table 19.1 shows the aliases that may be used for a mailing list named officenews.

TABLE 19.1 Postfix Aliases used for a Majordomo Mail List

Alias	*Description*
`officenews`	The mailing list name/alias
`officenews-outgoing`	Actual list of subscribers
`owner-officenews`	Administrator/owner of the mailing list
`officenews-request`	Address for Majordomo requests about the officenews list
`officenews-approval`	E-mail address of the person who approves postings if officenews is a moderated list
`officenews-digest`	Address used if officenews is a digest list
`officenews-digest-request`	Address for digest requests

Listing 19.6 shows the necessary entries in the `/etc/postfix/major-aliases` file for the officenews mailing list. This list will be a simple no-frills mailing list. It will be open to the public, and no digests or archives will be created.

LISTING 19.6 Sample Mail List Alias Entries

```
#officenews mailing list entries
officenews:      "|/usr/local/majordomo/wrapper resend -l officenews
➥ officenews-list"
officenews-list:        :include:/usr/local/majordomo/lists/officenews
owner-officenews:       rich,
officenews-owner:       rich
officenews-approval:    officenews-owner
officenews-request:     "|/usr/local/majordomo/wrapper majordomo -l
➥ officenews"
```

As usual, remember to run the `postalias` program as `root` after adding the new aliases. At this point, the mailing list should be operational but not configured. The list owner can create a configuration file by e-mailing the mailing list with the `config` mailing list command. Majordomo will automatically create a default configuration file for the mailing list and mail it back. Listing 19.7 shows an example of this operation, plus a partial listing of the return message.

LISTING 19.7 Partial Sample Mail List Configuration Request

```
[rich@shadrach]$ mail officenews-request
Subject:
config officenews officenews.admin
.
Cc:
[rich@shadrach]$ mail
Mail version 8.1 6/6/93.  Type ? for help.
"/var/spool/mail/rich": 1 message 1 new
>N  1 Majordomo@ispnet1.net    Tue Dec 26 13:06 406/17066 "Majordomo results"
&1
Message 1:
From Majordomo-Owner@ispnet1.net  Tue Dec 26 13:06:35 2000
Delivered-To: rich@ispnet1.net
To: rich@ispnet1.net
From: Majordomo@ispnet1.net
Subject: Majordomo results
Reply-To: Majordomo@ispnet1.net
Date: Tue, 26 Dec 2000 13:06:34 -0500 (EST)

--

>>>> config officenews officenews.admin
admin_passwd         =   officenews.admin
administrivia        =   yes
advertise            <<  END
announcements        =   yes
approve_passwd       =   officenews.pass
archive_dir          =
comments             <<  END
date_info            =   yes
date_intro           =   yes
debug                =   no
description          =
digest_archive       =
digest_issue         =   1
```

LISTING 19.7 Continued

```
digest_maxdays      =
digest_maxlines     =
digest_name         =   officenews
digest_rm_footer    =
digest_rm_fronter   =
digest_volume       =   1
digest_work_dir     =
get_access          =   list
index_access        =   open
info_access         =   open
intro_access        =   list
maxlength           =   40000
message_footer      <<  END
message_fronter     <<  END
message_headers     <<  END
moderate            =   no
moderator           =
mungedomain         =   no
noadvertise         <<  END
precedence          =   bulk
purge_received      =   no
reply_to            =
resend_host         =
restrict_post       =
sender              =   owner-officenews
strip               =   yes
subject_prefix      =
subscribe_policy    =   open+confirm
taboo_body          <<  END
taboo_headers       <<  END
unsubscribe_policy  =   open
welcome             =   yes
which_access        =   open
who_access          =   open

#[Last updated Tue Dec 26 13:06:34 2000]
```

In Listing 19.7, the first line shows the mailing list owner sending an e-mail message to the officenews-request address. All mailing list commands should be sent to the `-request` version of the list name. Normally, any message sent to the list name will be automatically forwarded to everyone on the list. Majordomo contains a program called `resend` that can be used to screen incoming messages and bounce any messages that appear to be Majordomo commands sent to the list name by mistake. This greatly reduces the annoyance of seeing prospective members' `subscribe` commands forwarded to everyone on the list.

The body of the e-mail message shows the format that is used to request a configuration file for the mailing list. The third parameter on the line is the default mailing list administrative password. The default password for any Majordomo mailing list is `<listname>.admin`, where `<listname>` is the mailing list name. After sending the message, you receive a return message from Majordomo. The return address includes the complete configuration file that is created by Majordomo. The configuration file is stored in the `lists` directory as `<listname>.config`, where `<listname>` is the mailing list name.

The returned message from Majordomo shows the current configuration variable settings in the configuration file. Along with the variables are lengthy comments describing them. The explanatory comments have been removed from the original message. You can read the actual return message to get an idea of what each of the configuration parameters control.

To change the configuration, you can save the message, change the configuration parameters, and e-mail the new configuration file back to the mailing list using the `newconfig` command. The first line of the e-mail message should have the format

```
newconfig    <listname>    adminpasswd
```

where `<listname>` is the list name and ***adminpasswd*** is the administrative password for the mailing list. After the `newconfig` line, the normal configuration file with your changes should start.

Listing 19.8 shows some common variables (and settings for this example list) that should be changed from the default configuration file.

LISTING 19.8 Configuration File Changes for a Mail List

```
admin_passwd = newpassword
approve_passwd = newpassword2
description = A mailing list used to distribute general office news
subscribe_policy = open
who_access = list
```

This is a list of changes to make to the original configuration, not the complete configuration file. Most of the default values will work fine in a general mailing list. Please remember to change the administrator password for the new mailing list. In Listing 19.8, the fourth line changes the default subscription policy. The default policy is `open+confirm`, which allows an open mailing list, but requires that members confirm their subscription requests by responding to a message sent by Majordomo. This example changes this to a simple open policy, which allows anyone to subscribe to the list and doesn't verify e-mail addresses. If this mailing list contained sensitive company information, you might want to use a closed subscription policy where the mailing list owner must confirm each subscription request for the mailing list. The fifth line restricts who can issue the `who` command and receive a listing of mailing list members. Now the list will only return the current members of the list. Listing 19.9 shows the results of using this parameter when a non-member sends a "who" request.

LISTING 19.9 Sample who Command

```
[matthew@shadrach]$ echo 'who' | mail officenews-request
[matthew@shadrach]$ mail
Mail version 8.1 6/6/93.  Type ? for help.
"/var/spool/mail/matthew": 1 message 1 new
>N  1 Majordomo@ispnet1.net    Tue Dec 26 13:25  19/642   "Majordomo results"
&1
Message 1:
From Majordomo-Owner@ispnet1.net  Tue Dec 26 13:25:20 2000
Delivered-To: matthew@ispnet1.net
To: matthew@ispnet1.net
From: Majordomo@ispnet1.net
Subject: Majordomo results
Reply-To: Majordomo@ispnet1.net
Date: Tue, 26 Dec 2000 13:25:20 -0500 (EST)

--

>>>> who
**** List 'officenews' is a private list.
**** Only members of the list can do a 'who'.
**** You [ matthew@ispnet1.net (Matthew Woenker) ] aren't a member of list
➥ 'officenews'.
```

In Listing 19.9, the first line shows the user `matthew` sending a `who` command to the mailing list officenews to retrieve a list of mailing list members. The response received from the Majordomo server is then shown. Since the `who` command was configured as private to list members only, `matthew` is restricted from viewing the mailing list until he becomes a member.

That completes the basic installation and configuration of the Majordomo mailing list server. The next section describes how e-mail clients can use the new mailing list server.

Using Majordomo

Majordomo makes the tasks for general mailing list users simple. Subscribing, posting new messages, and unsubscribing are very straightforward. However, there are more complicated commands for advanced features, such as retrieving digests and archive files, as well as remotely managing the mailing list.

The first step to becoming a mailing list member is to request a subscription. Subscription requests are sent to the `-request` form of the mailing list name. Majordomo ignores the subject line, so it can be left blank. The body of the message should contain a single line with the word "subscribe" in it. Depending on the list mode, you should receive one of three possible messages: a subscription confirmation, a request for subscription request validation, or a message telling you to wait for the list owner to add you to a closed list. Listing 19.10 shows a sample subscription session.

LISTING 19.10 Sample Mail List Subscription Session

```
[rich@shadrach]$ mail officenews-request
Subject:
subscribe
.

[rich@shadrach]$ mail
Mail version 8.1 6/6/93.  Type ? for help.
"/var/spool/mail/rich": 3 messages 3 new
>N  1 Majordomo@ispnet1.net Fri Nov 19 04:42 44/162 "Welcome to officenews"
 N  2 Majordomo@ispnet1.net Fri Nov 19 04:42 18/696 "SUBSCRIBE officenews "
 N  3 Majordomo@ispnet1.net  Fri Nov 19 04:42  18/613   "Majordomo results"
&
Message 1:
From owner-officenews@ispnet1.net  Fri Nov 19 04:42:56 1999
Date: Fri, 19 Nov 1999 04:42:56 -0500
X-Authentication-Warning: shadrach majordomo set sender to owner-
officenews@ispnet1.net using -f
To: rich@ispnet1.net
From: Majordomo@ispnet1.net
Subject: Welcome to officenews
Reply-To: Majordomo@ispnet1.net

--

Welcome to the officenews mailing list!

Please save this message for future reference.  Thank you.

If you ever want to remove yourself from this mailing list,
you can send mail to <Majordomo@ispnet1.net> with the following
command in the body of your e-mail message:
```

LISTING 19.10 Continued

```
32
33     unsubscribe officenews
34
35 or from another account, besides rich@ispnet1.net:
36
37     unsubscribe officenews rich@ispnet1.net
38
39 If you ever need to get in contact with the owner of the list,
40 (if you have trouble unsubscribing, or have questions about the
41 list itself) send e-mail to <owner-officenews@ispnet1.net>.
42 This is the general rule for most mailing lists when you need
43 to contact a human.
44
45  Here's the general information for the list you've subscribed to,
46  in case you don't already have it:
47
48 Welcome to the ispnet1.net officenews mail list.
49
50 This mailing list is used to help keep you informed about general information
51 that is happening in the organization.  Please post any announcements to
52 this mailing list.  Unauthorized use of this mailing list is prohibited.
53
54 &
```

In Listing 19.10, lines 1–5 show the user `rich` sending a message to the `officenews-request` mail alias to subscribe to the mailing list. Users can also send requests to the `majordomo` alias, but the desired list name must follow the command so that Majordomo knows which mailing list you are requesting membership to. Lines 6–11 show the e-mail messages that are returned in response to the command. Line 11 shows the message that is returned confirming that Majordomo received the subscription request. Line 10 is a message that is sent to the mailing list owner (who also happens to be `rich`) saying that a new member has subscribed to the mailing list. Line 9 is the message returned by Majordomo confirming that the user is now a member of the mailing list.

Lines 13–54 show the text of the return message. Notice that Majordomo gives full instructions on how to unsubscribe from the mailing list in lines 29–37. Lines 48–52 reproduce the `officenews.info` file that was created for the mailing list.

There are several commands that can be sent to the `-request` mail alias requesting actions from the mailing list server. The following commands are available to users.

subscribe

As shown in Listing 19.10, the subscribe command is for new members to request subscriptions to the mail list. The format of the command is

```
subscribe <listname> [<address>]
```

where *<listname>* is the list name and *<address>* is the e-mail address that you want to add to the mail list. If you are sending the message to the *<listname>*-request version of the alias, you can omit the *<listname>* parameter. Also, if you want to subscribe the e-mail address that you are sending the message from, you can omit the *<address>* parameter. You are allowed to subscribe a different e-mail address. The results depend on the subscription policy configuration of the mailing list.

unsubscribe

The opposite of the subscribe command is unsubscribe. This is used to remove an e-mail address from the mailing list. The format of this command is

```
unsubscribe <listname> [<address>]
```

where again the *<listname>* and *<address>* parameters are optional.

get

The get command is used to retrieve an archived file from the mailing list. The format of this command is

```
get <list> filename
```

where *filename* refers to a file that is stored by the mailing list. This command is used when a mailing list is archived. A mailing list member can retrieve an archive file by issuing the get command with the desired archive name.

index

The index command is used to return a list of the archived files that are available from the mailing list. The format of this command is

```
index <listname>
```

The index command is used in conjunction with the get command when using mailing list archives.

which

The which command is used to determine which mailing lists on the Majordomo server an e-mail address is a member of. The format of the which command is

```
which [<address>]
```

If you want information regarding the e-mail address you are sending the request from, you can omit the <address> parameter.

who

The who command can be used to retrieve a listing of the members who are currently subscribed to a mailing list. The format of the who command is

```
who <listname>
```

As shown in Listing 19.9, the who command can be restricted to only subscribed members of the list.

info

The info command is used to retrieve the information file that is available for a mailing list. The format of the command is

```
info <listname>
```

The information retrieved is the text from the file list.info located in the Majordomo lists directory.

intro

The intro command is used to retrieve the introduction text message that is sent to new users. The format for this command is

```
intro <listname>
```

lists

The lists command is used to retrieve a listing of all the mailing lists available on the Majordomo server. The format of this command is

```
lists
```

help

The `help` command returns a message that lists all of the user commands available in Majordomo. No list-specific information is returned in the `help` command.

end

The `end` command is used to tell Majordomo to stop processing commands in the message. This command is used mainly when extra text may appear at the end of an e-mail message, such as when users have an e-mail client package that includes an automatic signature block at the bottom of the message. The `end` command should appear on a line by itself at the end of the command section of the message.

Mailing List Owner Commands

The designated owner of the mailing list has more commands available that can be used to control the operation of the mailing list. All of the commands are sent as normal e-mail messages to the `-request` form of the mailing list. This feature greatly simplifies the administration of a mailing list. Anyone from anywhere can functionally become the owner of a mailing list. They are not restricted to having physical contact with the mailing list server. Also, the mailing list owner does not need a login username for the system that the mailing list is running on. This section describes these commands in more detail.

approve

The `approve` command is used in closed mailing lists so the list owner can approve the subscription of a new member. The command format is

```
approve password subscribe/unsubscribe <listname> <address>
```

where *`password`* is the administrative password for the list, `subscribe/unsubscribe` is the action to approve, *`<listname>`* is the mailing list name, and *`<address>`* is the e-mail address to approve.

config

The `config` command is used to retrieve a copy of the mailing list configuration file `list.config`. The format of this command is

```
config <listname> <list password>
```

mkdigest

The `mkdigest` command is used to create a new digest on mailing lists that are using the digest feature. Digests can be created as frequently as necessary. The command format is

```
mkdigest <listname> <list password>
```

If there is a lot of traffic in the mailing list, sometimes it is desirable to create digests more frequently than configured in the list's base settings. The `mkdigest` command is used to force Majordomo to create a new digest.

newconfig

The `newconfig` command is used to create a new configuration file using the parameters sent. The command format is

```
newconfig <listname> <list password>
```

Following the command should be the text of the new configuration file. Majordomo will replace the existing configuration file with the new one and automatically follow the new configuration guidelines. This feature allows the mailing list owner to completely change the configuration of the mailing list with a single e-mail message. This is extremely handy when administering a mailing list from a remote location.

newinfo

The `newinfo` command is used to change the text in the `list.info` file via e-mail. The format for this command is

```
newinfo <listname> <list password>
```

The text immediately following the `newinfo` command should be the desired text of the new information file. Majordomo will replace the `list.info` file with the text sent. This is another handy remote administration feature.

passwd

The `passwd` command is used to change the mailing list password. The format of the `passwd` command is

```
passwd <listname> old-passwd new-passwd
```

This command may cause some confusion. Normally, the mailing list password is stored in the `list.config` file, which can be modified using the `newconfig` command. Alternatively, if you do not want to mess with sending a whole new configuration file, you can use the `passwd` command to just change the password. However, this command does not replace the password present in the configuration file. It creates a new file—

`list.passwd`—that indicates the new password. If the password in the configuration file does not match the password in the `list.passwd` file, both passwords become active.

CAUTION

If you feel that the admin password has been compromised, don't change it using the `passwd` command, because the old password will still be usable. Use the `newconfig` command to change the password.

---

writeconfig

The `writeconfig` command is used to reformat the existing configuration file with all current or new keywords. If there is no config file yet, default values are added in. The command format is

```
writeconfig <listname> <list password>
```

This command can be used when the configuration file is hopelessly scrambled, possibly due to errors when using the `newconfig` command. Because you can only retrieve the existing configuration file, you might not be able to fix the errors using `newconfig`. The `writeconfig` command attempts to reformat the existing configuration file back to the original format.

Summary

One nice feature of Postfix servers is the capability to support sophisticated mailing list programs. Majordomo is a popular mail list program that offers many features for both the mailing list administrator and the mailing list user. Majordomo can manage multiple mailing lists on a single server. The are many different types of mailing lists that range from publicly open, unmoderated mailing lists to closed, restricted mailing lists. Mailing list digests and archives can be created to help simplify message retrieval. Majordomo also allows remote administration of mailing lists, so the mailing list owner does not require physical access to the mailing list server. User commands are kept simple to make subscribing, posting, and unsubscribing to the mailing lists easy for non-technical list members.

CHAPTER 20

Using POP3 and IMAP with Postfix

After successfully installing the Postfix software, your mail server should be receiving e-mail messages from both local users and remote users on other mail hosts. However, this only gets the messages to the user mailboxes on the mail server. It is still up to the individual e-mail clients on the mail server to retrieve their own mail from their mailboxes.

Users who have physical access to the mail host can log in to an interactive session such as a console screen or an X Window session. Once logged in to the mail server, users can use a Mail User Agent (MUA) program such as `pine`, `elm`, or `kmail` to access the local mailbox and manage their messages. These types of programs allow users to view and delete mail messages from an interactive session on the local mail server. Chapter 1, "E-Mail Services" describes MUA programs in more detail.

But many users do not have physical access to the mail server host. In fact, in most cases it is impossible for all users on the network to have physical access to read e-mail messages on the same mail server. The next possible solution for remote clients is to utilize the telnet, ssh, or X terminal programs to establish a connection with the remote mail server. Although this works, it can be extremely inefficient for reading mail messages. Both telnet and X terminal sessions create a large network overhead for just reading a few lines of text messages.

The best solution mail administrators have available is remote MUAs. Remote MUAs offer a method for remote users to access their mailboxes on the local mail server without a large network overhead. The MUA can access a remote mailbox and download just the information necessary for the client computer to present the message to the user. Figure 20.1 shows remote clients accessing mail messages residing on the mail server using a remote MUA.

Two protocols that allow remote access of mailboxes are the Post Office Protocol (POP3) and the Interactive Mail Access Protocol (IMAP). POP3 and IMAP allow remote users to view and delete mail messages on the mail server from a remote workstation using an e-mail client program. The Unix mail server must run server software that supports either POP3 or IMAP to allow remote users this kind of access to their mailboxes.

This chapter describes two server software packages that allow a Unix mail server to support the POP3 and IMAP retrieval of e-mail messages. The University of Washington IMAP program supports both POP3 and IMAP. Qualcomm's `qpopper` program can be used to support POP3 access of normal Postfix `sendmail`-style mailboxes from remote e-mail clients. But first, a short discussion about MUA protocols is presented.

E-Mail MUA Protocols

Although POP3 and IMAP programs perform similar functions, the methods they use to access mailboxes are totally different. This section compares and contrasts the two most common e-mail client MUA protocols to help the mail administrator decide which protocol(s) to implement and for what reasons.

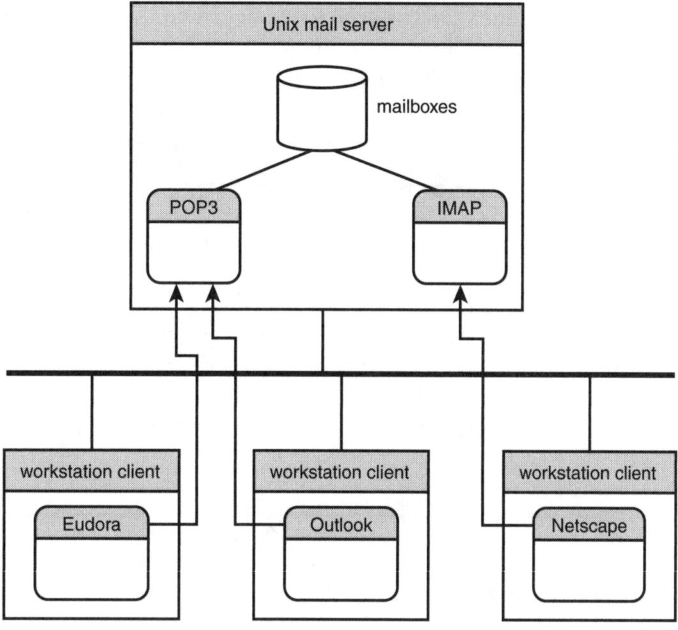

FIGURE 20.1

Remote network clients retrieving mail messages from a server.

POP3

POP has become an extremely popular protocol. Currently it is on its third official release version (thus the name POP3). Figure 20.2 demonstrates how POP3 can be used to retrieve mail from a mail server.

The user's client computer can use POP3 to download messages from the user's mailbox on the mail server. The POP3 client must be configured beforehand to either delete messages from the main server after download or to leave them intact there. By default, most POP3 MUAs delete messages from the main server after download. In either situation, the message is downloaded in its entirety so that the user can view it locally.

POP3 is popular with ISPs who must maintain hundreds of e-mail mailboxes on their servers. POP3 allows the ISP to force the messages to be deleted from the server as they are downloaded, thus saving on server disk space. One potentially unfortunate consequence of this scenario is that the user's mail is kept on the computer where he or she happened to check the mail. If this is always the same computer, there is not a problem. However, in today's world many people must be able to check e-mail messages from home as well as from the office. This is where POP3 can become a problem. If the user checks for e-mail at home and downloads 20 new messages, those downloaded messages remain on the home PC. If POP3 has been set to delete on download, when the user gets into work the messages will not be on the e-mail server, and thus unobtainable. This is why IMAP (discussed in the following section) is a popular alternative to POP3.

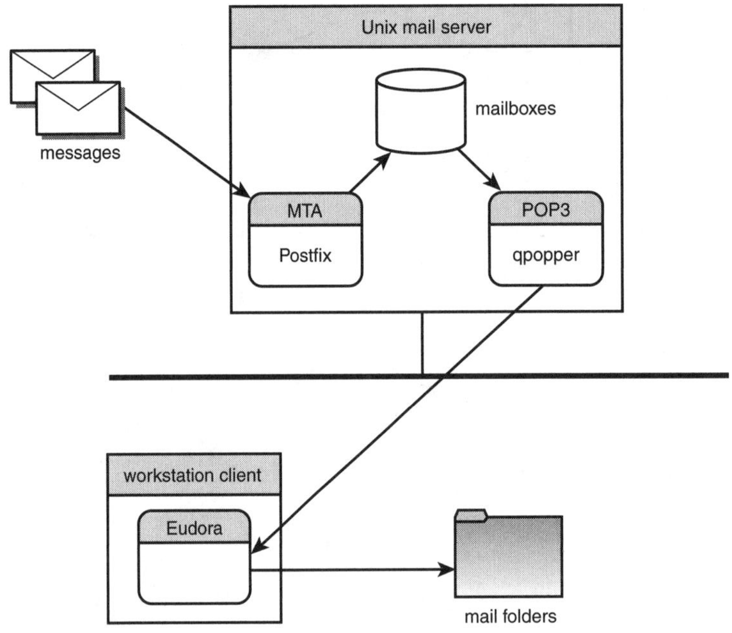

FIGURE 20.2

Overview of POP3.

POP3 is a text-based protocol that relies on the client sending a text command to the server. The server responds to the command with either the results of the command or an error message. Table 20.1 shows the POP3 commands the client can send.

TABLE 20.1 POP3 Commands

Command	*Description*
`USER` *`name`*	Sends a username to the POP3 server
`PASS` *`password`*	Sends a user password to the POP3 server
`APOP` *`name digest`*	Sends a username and an encrypted value to authenticate the user
`AUTH` *`method`*	Negotiates the authentication method used with the POP3 server
`STAT`	Retrieves a short summary of the user's mailbox
`LIST` *`num`*	Retrieves a short listing of the messages (or message number *`num`*) in the mailbox

TABLE 20.1 Continued

Command	*Description*
`RETR` *`num`*	Retrieves the entire text of message number *`num`*
`DELE` *`num`*	Removes message number *`num`* from the mailbox
`NOOP`	Solicits a response from the server (no operation is performed)
`RSET`	Resets the POP3 connection state
`TOP` *`msg num`*	Retrieves the first *`num`* lines from message number *`msg`*
`UIDL`	Displays the unique message identification number for each message
`QUIT`	Terminates the POP3 session with the server

POP3 is very simple in the way the client interacts with the remote mail server. The POP3 server listens for TCP connections on port 110. You can test your POP3 server software by telneting to port 110 on the local mail server. Listing 20.1 demonstrates a sample POP3 session with the local mail server. Line numbers have been added to aid in the discussion of the listing.

LISTING 20.1 Sample POP3 Session

```
1  $ telnet localhost 110
2  Trying 127.0.0.1...
3  Connected to localhost.ispnet1.net.
4  Escape character is '^]'.
5  +OK QPOP (version 3.0) at shadrach.ispnet1.net starting.
6  user rich
7  +OK Password required for rich.
8  pass guitar
9  +OK rich has 4 visible messages (0 hidden) in 1637 octets.
10 stat
11 +OK 4 1637
12 list
13 +OK 4 visible messages (1637 octets)
14 1 408
15 2 409
16 3 410
17 4 410
18 .
19 retr 1
20 +OK 408 octets
21 Return-Path: <rich@shadrach.ispnet1.net>
22 Delivered-To: rich@shadrach.ispnet1.net
23 Received: (Postfix 25364 invoked by uid 1001); 3 May 2000 14:39:52 -0000
24 Date: 3 May 2000 14:39:52 -0000
```

LISTING 20.1 Continued

```
Message-ID: <20000503143952.25363@shadrach.ispnet1.net>
From: rich@shadrach.ispnet1.net
To: rich@shadrach.ispnet1.net
Subject: Test message one
X-UIDL: JOJ22435FF

This is the first test message

.
dele 1
+OK Message 1 has been deleted.
list
+OK 3 visible messages (1229 octets)
2 409
3 410
4 410
.
uidl
+OK uidl command accepted.
2 3a1ec71700000001
3 3a1ec71700000002
4 3a1ec71700000003
.
top 3 5
+OK Message follows
Return-Path: <rich@shadrach.ispnet1.net>
Delivered-To: rich@shadrach.ispnet1.net
Received: (Postfix 25388 invoked by uid 1001); 3 May 2000 14:40:14 -0000
Date: 3 May 2000 14:40:14 -0000
Message-ID: <20000503144014.25387@shadrach.ispnet1.net>
From: rich@shadrach.ispnet1.net
To: rich@shadrach.ispnet1.net
Subject: Test message three
X-UIDL: ALW22009GGJ

This is the third test message

.
quit
+OK Pop server at shadrach.ispnet1.net signing off.
Connection closed by foreign host.
you have mail
```

Line 1 shows the command to telnet to the POP3 port on the local mail server. After receiving the welcome banner from the POP3 software, you can enter the `USER` and `PASS` commands to log in to the POP3 server as a local user (shown in lines 6–9). Line 9 shows a banner provided by the POP3 server giving a synopsis of the user's mailbox. In line 10 the user sent the `stat` command, which provides the same synopsis of the mailbox contents.

Line 12 shows the POP3 `list` command being sent to the mail server to obtain an individual account of each mail message. Lines 13–18 show the results returned by the `list` command. Each message is listed with a message number and the number of bytes that are required to store the message. In line 19 the user sent the `retr` command requesting to download the first mail message. The complete mail message including the RFC 822 headers is downloaded, as shown in lines 20–33.

Line 34 shows the user sending the `dele` command to remove the first mail message from the mailbox. In line 36 a `list` command is sent to verify that the message has been removed.

Each message is numbered sequentially for the POP3 session. As shown in lines 37–41, when message 1 was removed, messages 2, 3, and 4 remain with the same message numbers. However, if this POP3 session was terminated and a new one started, the messages would be renumbered for the new session starting with message number 1.

This could be disastrous if you do not pay attention to which message is which number. To solve this problem, POP3 provides a system for uniquely identifying each message. You can use the `uidl` command to display the unique message number for each message. Line 42 shows an example of using the `uidl` command to display the unique message numbers for each message. These numbers do not change between POP3 sessions.

Finally, line 48 shows the use of the POP3 `top` command. This allows clients to request a subset of the message text instead of having to download the entire message. This comes in handy for client MUA programs that want to display the message subject headers without having to download the entire message.

IMAP

IMAP has been a lesser-known protocol in the e-mail world, but it is quickly gaining popularity. Currently it is at release version 4 revision 1 (commonly called IMAP4rev1). Figure 20.3 demonstrates how IMAP works.

IMAP also uses a series of text commands that can be sent from the network client to the mail server. Each command instructs the mail server to perform a particular function. Table 20.2 shows the IMAP commands that can be used by the network client.

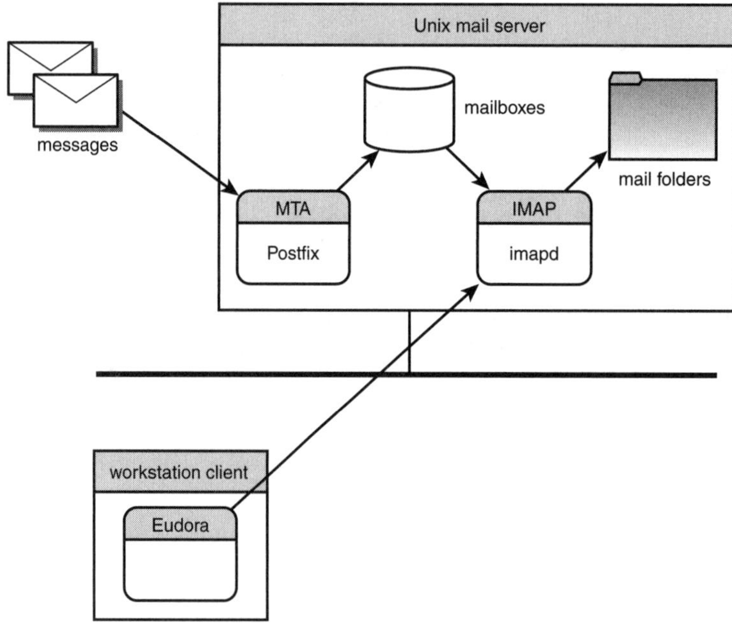

FIGURE 20.3

Overview of IMAP.

TABLE 20.2 IMAP Commands

Command	*Description*
`LOGIN`	Uses plaintext userid and password to log in to the IMAP server
`AUTHENTICATE`	Negotiates an alternative login authentication method with the server
`SELECT`	Opens a specific mailbox folder on the server
`EXAMINE`	Opens a specific mailbox folder for read-only
`CREATE`	Creates a new mailbox folder
`DELETE`	Deletes an existing mailbox folder
`RENAME`	Renames an existing mailbox folder to a new name
`SUBSCRIBE`	Adds a specific mailbox folder to a user's active list
`UNSUBSCRIBE`	Removes a specific mailbox folder from a user's active list
`LIST`	Lists all mailbox folders available for the user on the server
`LSUB`	Lists all mailbox folders that the user has subscribed to
`STATUS`	Displays the current status of a mailbox
`APPEND`	Places a message at the end of a specific mailbox file
`CHECK`	Marks a checkpoint for mailbox operations; forces the IMAP server to delete any messages marked for deletion

TABLE 20.2 Continued

Command	*Description*
CLOSE	Closes an open mailbox folder
EXPUNGE	Removes all messages marked for deletion from a folder without closing the folder
SEARCH	Searches for a message in a mailbox folder based on specified criteria
FETCH	Displays the message header, body, or both for a specific mailbox message
STORE	Alters flag information for a mailbox message
COPY	Copies messages from one mailbox folder to another
UID	Displays the internal unique identification number for the mailbox messages
CAPABILITY	Displays a list of IMAP capabilities that the IMAP server supports
NOOP	Tests the connectivity of the IMAP server (no operation is performed)
LOGOUT	Terminates the current session from the IMAP server

Most IMAP commands use parameters indicating the mailbox folder or message that needs to be processed. Also, the IMAP protocol requires that each command line sent to the server be identified with a unique tag. This enables the client to send multiple commands to the server and identify which responses are associated with which commands. The format of an IMAP command is

```
tag command parameters
```

where `tag` is the unique identifier for the command line. Tags usually follow a sequential order throughout the IMAP session to simplify identification for the client and server. A sample command line with a tag would be

```
a001 LOGIN rich guitar
```

This command line uses the `LOGIN` IMAP command with its required parameters, along with a tag to identify it.

To test the IMAP server, you can telnet directly to the IMAP TCP port (143) on the local mail server and issue IMAP commands. Listing 20.2 shows a sample IMAP session with the local mail server.

LISTING 20.2 Sample IMAP Session

```
$ telnet localhost 143
Trying 127.0.0.1...
Connected to localhost.ispnet1.net.
Escape character is '^]'.
* OK localhost.ispnet1.net IMAP4rev1 v12.250 server ready
a1 login rich guitar
```

LISTING 20.2 Continued

```
a1 OK LOGIN completed
a3 lsub "" *
a3 OK LSUB completed
a4 create newbox
a4 OK CREATE completed
a5 subscribe newbox
a5 OK SUBSCRIBE completed
a6 create stuff/junk
a6 OK CREATE completed
a7 subscribe stuff/junk
a7 OK SUBSCRIBE completed
a8 lsub "" *
* LSUB () "/" newbox
* LSUB () "/" stuff/junk
a8 OK LSUB completed
a9 select inbox
* 4 EXISTS
* 0 RECENT
* OK [UIDVALIDITY 957373049] UID validity status
* OK [UIDNEXT 5] Predicted next UID
* FLAGS (\Answered \Flagged \Deleted \Draft \Seen)
* OK [PERMANENTFLAGS (\* \Answered \Flagged \Deleted \Draft \Seen)]
➥ Permanent flags
a9 OK [READ-WRITE] SELECT completed
a11 fetch 2:3 body[header.fields (date from subject)]
* 2 FETCH (BODY[HEADER.FIELDS ("DATE" "FROM" "SUBJECT")] {98}
Date: 3 May 2000 16:56:42 -0000
From: rich@shadrach.ispnet1.net
Subject: Second test message

)
* 3 FETCH (BODY[HEADER.FIELDS ("DATE" "FROM" "SUBJECT")] {97}
Date: 3 May 2000 16:56:56 -0000
From: rich@shadrach.ispnet1.net
Subject: Third test message

)
a11 OK FETCH completed
a12 copy 2:3 stuff/junk
a12 OK COPY completed
a13 select stuff/junk
* 2 EXISTS
```

LISTING 20.2 Continued

```
48 * 0 RECENT
49 * OK [UIDVALIDITY 957373506] UID validity status
50 * OK [UIDNEXT 3] Predicted next UID
51 * FLAGS (\Answered \Flagged \Deleted \Draft \Seen)
52 * OK [PERMANENTFLAGS (\* \Answered \Flagged \Deleted \Draft \Seen)]
➥ Permanent flags
53 a13 OK [READ-WRITE] SELECT completed
54 a14 fetch 1:2 body[header.fields (date from subject)]
55 * 1 FETCH (BODY[HEADER.FIELDS ("DATE" "FROM" "SUBJECT")] {98}
56 Date: 3 May 2000 16:56:42 -0000
57 From: rich@shadrach.ispnet1.net
58 Subject: Second test message
59
60 )
61 * 2 FETCH (BODY[HEADER.FIELDS ("DATE" "FROM" "SUBJECT")] {97}
62 Date: 3 May 2000 16:56:56 -0000
63 From: rich@shadrach.ispnet1.net
64 Subject: Third test message
65
66 )
67 a14 OK FETCH completed
68 a15 capability
69 * CAPABILITY IMAP4 IMAP4REV1 NAMESPACE IDLE SCAN SORT MAILBOX-REFERRALS
➥ LOGIN-REFERRALS AUTH=LOGIN THREAD=ORDEREDSUBJECT
70 a15 OK CAPABILITY completed
71 a16 logout
72 * BYE shadrach.ispnet1.net IMAP4rev1 server terminating connection
73 a16 OK LOGOUT completed
74 Connection closed by foreign host.
```

Line 1 demonstrates the command used to initiate an IMAP session with the local mail server. If the IMAP server software is running, you should get a welcome banner, as shown in line 5. Line 6 shows a sample `login` command sent to the IMAP server. Note that the IMAP commands can be entered using either upper- or lowercase letters. Line 7 indicates that the login attempt was successful. Line 8 shows an example of using the `lsub` command to check for subscribed mailbox folders. Line 9 indicates that none exist. In lines 10 and 14 two new mailbox folders are created on the IMAP server, and in lines 12 and 16 they are subscribed to. The next `lsub` command issued in line 18 indicates that now both of the new mailboxes are subscribed (as shown in lines 19–21).

Line 22 shows the client using `select` to open the standard INBOX mailbox where all new messages are stored. The response from the IMAP server, shown in lines 23–29, indicates that there are 4 messages in the INBOX.

Line 30 shows an example of using the `fetch` command to retrieve the header information from a subset of messages in the INBOX. The IMAP server responds by sending the requested information from the messages in lines 31–43. In line 44, the client requests that the second and third messages in the INBOX be copied to the `stuff/junk` mailbox folder on the server. This represents a subfolder named "junk" that is contained in a folder named "stuff." To verify this operation, the client selects the new mailbox (in line 46) and fetches the header information (in line 54). Notice that now both messages have been relocated to the `stuff/junk` folder.

Line 68 shows an example of using the `capability` command. The IMAP server responds with the current capabilities of the server.

The main difference between IMAP and POP3 is where retrieved mail is located. For POP3, the mail messages are spooled on the mail server but downloaded to the client for further manipulation. Often the messages on the server are deleted as soon as the client downloads them.

In contrast, IMAP maintains all of the messages, stored in folders, on the server. Each user has a default folder named INBOX. New messages are placed in the INBOX to be read. Each time the client connects to the IMAP server, the user can obtain a listing of the INBOX messages and can retrieve any or all of the messages, even from different client computers. As you can see in Listing 20.2, the user can even create separate mail folders on the IMAP server to manipulate messages on the server.

The use of folders on the IMAP server is a great advantage to users who must check mail from multiple workstations throughout the day. No matter which workstation is used, the mail messages and folders always remain constant.

University of Washington IMAP

The most common POP3 and IMAP package used on the Unix platform was developed at the University of Washington. Although the software package is called IMAP, it includes a POP3 server as well as an IMAP4rev1 server. This section describes how to install and configure the UW IMAP software to support remote POP3 and IMAP clients from your Unix mail server.

Downloading and Installing UW IMAP

Many Linux distributions already come with a UW IMAP binary package. You can choose to install UW IMAP from the distribution that came with your Unix system, or you can download the current source code file and build it yourself.

The University of Washington currently supports a Web site for the IMAP software project:

```
http://www.washington.edu/imap/
```

This site contains information about the UW IMAP project at the university, as well as links to the current release of UW IMAP. The current release at the time of this writing is version 2000b.

NOTE

This is the first UW IMAP release that uses the year as part of the version name. The version that preceded the 2000 series was version 4.0.7.

You can download the source code distribution of this version by the link provided using the Web site. Alternatively, you can also connect directly to the FTP site at `ftp.cac.washington.edu` and check the `/imap` directory for the current release version. A link named `imap.tar.Z` always points to the current release version. The source code distribution comes as a compressed `tar` file, `imap-2000.tar.Z`. Remember to use BINARY mode when retrieving the file.

Once the source code distribution file is downloaded, it can be extracted into a working directory using the command

```
tar -zxvf imap-2000.tar.Z -C /usr/local/src
```

This produces a subdirectory named `imap-2000b` and places the source code in subdirectories underneath it.

The UW IMAP program does not have any feature options that are necessary to add at compile time with the `configure` program. The main requirement for building the IMAP distribution executables is to know what type of system you are compiling the source code on and use the appropriate Makefile section. Table 20.3 shows common IMAP `make` options for various Unix implementations.

TABLE 20.3 UW IMAP `make` Options

Option	*Description*
`bsf`	BSD-based systems
`lnx`	Traditional Linux systems
`lnp`	Linux with Pluggable Authentication Modules (PAM)
`sl4`	Linux using `-lshadow` for passwords
`sl5`	Linux using shadow passwords
`slx`	Linux using `-lcrypt` for passwords

There are different Makefile sections for Linux depending on the type of user authentication method your system uses. For Mandrake 7.1 Linux systems you can use the `slx` option:

```
make slx
```

This compiles the source code and produces the IMAP executables located in the `imapd` and `ipopd` subdirectories in the distribution. The next step is to install and configure the individual pieces of IMAP.

Configuring UW POP3

For the UW POP3 server software to work properly, you must set it up and configure it after compiling it. The first step is to copy the executables into a common system directory. Because the `ipop3d` and `imapd` programs were written to be used by the `tcpd` wrapper program, it is best to locate them in the same directory: `/usr/sbin` on a Linux system. The `ipop3d` program is located in the `ipopd` subdirectory under the `imap-2000a` directory. Also included in this directory is a POP2 server, `ipop2d`. This is mainly for compatibility with older e-mail clients that do not support POP3. If you are establishing a new e-mail system, you should stick with the POP3 implementation. Plenty of new clients are available that use POP3.

CAUTION

Make sure you are `root` when copying the `ipop3d` file to the `/usr/sbin` directory or the copy will fail.

Once you place the executable in the proper directory, you must modify the `inetd`-related configuration files. The first file to modify is `/etc/services`. You must make sure that the standard POP3 TCP port is defined. The POP3 line should look like this:

```
pop-3        110/tcp              # POP version 3
```

This indicates that any connection received on TCP port 110 will be passed to the program defined by the `pop-3` tag in the `/etc/inetd.conf` file.

The `/etc/inetd.conf` configuration file indicates, among other things, where the relevant executables are located when a connection is passed off to it. The necessary POP3 line in the `/etc/inetd.conf` file is

```
pop-3   stream  tcp     nowait  root    /usr/sbin/tcpd  ipop3d
```

The `pop-3` tag in the `inetd.conf` file relates the `ipop3d` program to the `pop-3` TCP port tag in the `/etc/services` file. The controlling program points to the `tcpd` program. The `tcpd` wrapper program is utilized to help control and log network connections to the server. Once `tcpd` approves the connection request, it will invoke `ipop3d` itself.

To activate the new `inetd.conf` settings, you must restart the currently running `inetd` daemon by sending a `SIGHUP` signal to it. You can use the following command on a Linux system for this:

```
[root@shadrach]# killall -HUP inetd
```

With the `inetd` daemon restarted, you can now test the UW IMAP installation. Listing 20.3 shows an example of testing the POP3 server.

LISTING 20.3 Testing the POP3 Server

```
[rich@shadrach]$ telnet localhost 110
Trying 127.0.0.1...
Connected to localhost.
Escape character is '^]'.
+OK POP3 localhost v2000.69 server ready
USER rich
+OK User name accepted, password please
PASS guitar
+OK Mailbox open, 2 messages
QUIT
+OK Sayonara
Connection closed by foreign host.
```

Listing 20.3 shows a telnet session to the POP3 server on TCP port 110. As you can see, a greeting banner is received from the UW POP3 server, indicating that it is indeed running.

One optional feature available for the UW POP3 server is the capability to use APOP user authentication. The APOP authentication method allows the client to send a username in clear text and then submit a password that is an encryption of the password and a known secret value. If the UW POP3 server detects that the file `/etc/cram-md5.pwd` exists, it will support both the APOP protocol and an alternative authentication protocol, CRAM-MD5. Both methods use the same technique of hashing a seed value with a secret word to create the encrypted password used for authentication. The APOP seed value is displayed on the POP3 greeting banner. Both the server and the client must already know the secret word that will be hashed with the seed value.

In the case of UW POP3, the secret words are stored in the `/etc/cram-md5.pwd` file. Each line of the file contains the username and the secret word that the user will use. Listing 20.4 shows a sample `/etc/cram-md5.pwd` file.

LISTING 20.4 Sample `/etc/cram-md5.pwd` File

```
rich        newpasswd
barbara     reading
riley       firetruck
haley       starwars
katie       boxcar
jessica     sharks
```

As you can see in Listing 20.4, `cram-md5.pwd` is a plaintext file. To protect the passwords, you should ensure that the file is set to mode 600 so normal users cannot view it. This means that the mail administrator must have `root` access to modify passwords. Also, this means that users cannot modify their own passwords.

To check whether the APOP feature is available, after creating the `/etc/cram-md5.pwd` file telnet to the POP3 port. The new greeting banner should be present showing the seed value. Listing 20.5 shows an example of an APOP-enabled POP3 server.

LISTING 20.5 Sample APOP Enabled POP3 Server Greeting Banner

```
[rich@shadrach]$ telnet localhost 110
Trying 127.0.0.1...
Connected to localhost.
Escape character is '^]'.
+OK POP3 v2000.69 server ready <2c29.3a4b427d@localhost>
USER rich
+OK User name accepted, password please
PASS newpasswd
+OK Mailbox open, 2 messages
QUIT
+OK Sayonara
Connection closed by foreign host.
```

Listing 20.5 again shows a sample telnet session to the POP3 server port. This time the IMAP server produces a different greeting banner than the example in Listing 20.3. Included in the greeting banner is the APOP seed value (the value enclosed in the less-than and greater-than signs). The POP3 client can encrypt the user password sent for authentication using this seed value. UW POP3 allows a user to connect using either the APOP or user/password methods. This is especially good for users who may connect to the mail server using different PCs and different e-mail client software packages.

CAUTION

If the POP3 server is configured for APOP authentication and the client authenticates using the user/password method, his password will be whatever is set in the `/etc/cram-md5.pwd` file, not the system password file.

Configuring UW IMAP

Much like the POP3 server software, the UW IMAP software utilizes the `inetd` program. This requires additional information to be included in the `inetd` configuration files. The first line required is in the `/etc/services` file:

```
imap        143/tcp     imap4        # Interactive Mail Access Protocol
```

The standard IMAP server uses TCP port 143 to listen for incoming network connections. The UW IMAP program uses the IMAP version 4, revision 1 protocol, which still uses port 143.

You should also modify the `/etc/inetd.conf` file to contain the information necessary for the IMAP server. This is an example of what the configuration line should look like:

```
imap    stream  tcp     nowait  root    /usr/sbin/tcpd  imapd
```

This example assumes that the `tcpd` wrapper program is located in the `/usr/sbin` subdirectory. You must change this to the proper location on your Unix system. Also, if you prefer not to use the `tcpd` wrapper program you can reference the location of the `imapd` program directly.

To activate the new `inetd.conf` settings, you must restart the currently running `inetd` daemon by sending a `SIGHUP` signal to it.

Once you have restarted the `inetd` daemon, you can test the installation of the IMAP server by telneting to the IMAP port, number 143. Listing 20.6 shows an example of this.

LISTING 20.6 Testing the IMAP Server

```
[rich@shadrach]$ telnet localhost 143
Trying 127.0.0.1...
Connected to localhost.
Escape character is '^]'.
* OK localhost IMAP4rev1 v12.264 server ready
a1 LOGIN rich guitar
a1 OK LOGIN completed
a2 SELECT INBOX
* 2 EXISTS
* 0 RECENT
* OK [UIDVALIDITY 975095575] UID validity status
* OK [UIDNEXT 3] Predicted next UID
* FLAGS (\Answered \Flagged \Deleted \Draft \Seen)
* OK [PERMANENTFLAGS (\* \Answered \Flagged \Deleted \Draft \Seen)]
➥ Permanent flags
a2 OK [READ-WRITE] SELECT completed
a3 LOGOUT
* BYE shadrach.ispnet1.net IMAP4rev1 server terminating connection
a3 OK LOGOUT completed
Connection closed by foreign host.
```

The qpopper Program

The qpopper program is another MUA package that is frequently used on Unix servers. It differs from the UW package in that it only supports POP3 connections. However, its POP3 server has some extra features that make it attractive to mail administrators.

qpopper is freeware originally released by the University of California at Berkeley, but now maintained by the Qualcomm corporation. It was written to provide POP3 server software for most types of Unix servers. It works just great on Linux mail servers.

qpopper supports both the normal user/password POP3 logins and a special APOP POP3 encrypted authentication. By default, the user/password login method sends usernames and passwords across the network in clear text format.

The user/password login feature supports using the standard Linux password files, as well as a special feature for Linux shadow password files. The APOP feature supports encrypted passwords using a separate password database file that the mail administrator must maintain separately.

You can find information about qpopper on its Web site at

```
http://www.eudora.com/qpopper/index.html
```

The current release version of qpopper at the time of this writing is version 3.1.2.

CAUTION

If you happen to come across a version of qpopper earlier than version 2.41, don't use it. The earlier versions had some serious buffer overflow problems that could allow a hacker to gain root access to your mail server.

Downloading qpopper

The Qualcomm FTP site (ftp.qualcomm.com) hosts the most current version of qpopper. The directory where qpopper is located is

```
/eudora/servers/unix/popper
```

Make sure you are using the FTP BINARY mode and download the version that you want to use. For this example, the file qpopper3.1.2.tar.gz will be used:

```
ftp://ftp.qualcomm.com/eudora/servers/unix/popper/qpopper3.1.2.tar.gz
```

Once you have downloaded the file, you can extract the source code files into a working directory:

```
tar -zxvf qpopper3.1.2.tar.gz -C /usr/local/src
```

The Unix `tar` utility creates a subdirectory `/usr/local/qpopper3.1.2` and places the source code files in subdirectories beneath it.

Configuring qpopper

The `qpopper` program utilizes the `configure` program to examine the operating environment and create a Makefile that references the specific locations of the C compiler, libraries, and include files. The `configure` program also uses command-line parameters to change specific features that you may want to include in your implementation of the `qpopper` server. I will describe these later.

The default `qpopper` configure environment uses no extra command-line parameters and can be built by using the commands

```
./configure
make
```

This creates a default POP3 server that does not recognize the APOP authentication method or the shadow password database on Linux systems.

The `qpopper` executable program is called `popper` and is located in the `popper` subdirectory beneath the `qpopper3.1.2` directory. You will need to copy this program to a common system location as `root`. The `qpopper` documentation recommends using the `/usr/local/lib` directory.

The `popper` program can use command-line parameters to modify the behavior of the POP3 server. Table 20.4 shows the available command-line parameters.

TABLE 20.4 popper Command-Line Parameters

Parameter	*Description*
`-b`	Turns on bulletins and sets the default directory for bulletins
`-c`	Changes all usernames to lowercase
`-d`	Enables debugging
`-D <drac-host>`	Enables DRAC
`-e <x=value>`	Sets POP3 extensions
`-f <config-file>`	Reads additional runtime options from the specified file
`-k`	Enables Kerberos support
`-p <0|1|2|3>`	Sets plaintext password handling options
`-s`	Enables statistics logging
`-t <trace-file>`	Defines an alternate debug and log file
`-K <service>`	Uses the specified Kerberos service (instead of the compiled-in value)
`-S`	Enables server mode
`-T <timeout>`	Changes the default timeout waiting for reads
`-R`	Disables reverse client address lookups

The popper program is invoked by inetd. The inetd program listens for network connections and passes those connections to the appropriate program depending on the TCP or UDP port number on which the connection is established.

The pertinent line in /etc/services should look like the following:

```
pop-3        110/tcp              # POP version 3
```

After ensuring that the /etc/services file supports POP3, the next step is to configure the inetd configuration file to support POP3. The inetd configuration file is /etc/inetd.conf. You should add a line to the configuration file that corresponds to the tag in the /etc/services line (pop-3) and identifies the program to start when a connection is established. The new line should look like the following:

```
pop-3  stream  tcp nowait  root    /usr/local/lib/popper   popper -s
```

This inetd.conf entry assumes that the popper program is located in the /usr/local/lib directory and turns on statistics logging with the -s option. By default, statistics will be logged in the Unix default mail syslog file (usually /var/log/maillog for Linux systems). Unlike the UW IMAP package, qpopper does not recommend using the tcpd wrapper program. You can still utilize this method by pointing the controlling program to the tcpd program with the popper -s option.

To activate the new inetd.conf settings, you must restart the currently running inetd daemon by sending a SIGHUP signal to it.

You can test the qpopper installation by using the telnet program to connect to port 110 on the mail server as shown in Listing 20.7.

LISTING 20.7 Testing the qpopper POP3 Server

```
[rich@shadrach]$ telnet localhost 110
Trying 127.0.0.1...
Connected to localhost.
Escape character is '^]'.
+OK QPOP (version 3.1.2) at shadrach.ispnet1.net starting.
QUIT
+OK Pop server at shadrach.ispnet1.net signing off.
Connection closed by foreign host.
[rich@shadrachch]$
```

In Listing 20.7, the first line shows the user telneting to port 110 of the localhost. The fifth line shows the greeting banner produced by the qpopper program.

The default qpopper configuration will work fine in some simple POP3 implementations running on basic Unix mail servers. However, you can implement other features to make qpopper more versatile.

Shadow Password Support

Many modern Unix systems make use of shadow passwords. Shadow passwords remove the actual encrypted password from the world-readable `/etc/passwd` file and place them in a separate file readable only by the `root` user. This helps prevent unauthorized users from accessing the encrypted password file to try brute-force attacks. FreeBSD supports shadow passwords using the `/etc/master.passwd` file. By default, `qpopper` recognizes the FreeBSD shadow password file without any modifications.

However, many Linux distributions have incorporated the use of a different shadow password file system. When a shadow password file is used, programs that verify username/password pairs must be aware of its existence.

For `qpopper` to work with Linux shadow password files, you must include additional parameters on the configure command line. The `specialauth` parameter instructs `qpopper` to look for the alternate shadow password file.

If you have previously compiled a version of `qpopper`, you must clean the object and executable files from the build directory. You can accomplish this by using the following command from the `qpopper3.1.2` directory:

```
make clean
```

This command removes files that have been added or modified by the install script. The next step is to run the `configure` script with the parameter that includes shadow password support. The format of this command is

```
./configure --enable-specialauth
```

This re-creates the Makefile using parameters necessary for the GNU gcc compiler to add support for shadow password files. After the `configure` program finishes building the Makefile, you can then run the GNU `make` against it to create a new `popper` executable program in the `popper` subdirectory. Again, you must copy this file as `root` to the location specified in the `inetd.conf` file. There is no need to restart the `inetd` daemon because the configuration file `/etc/inetd.conf` was not modified.

After copying the new executable `popper` file to the appropriate directory, you can test the configuration by telneting to port 110 and attempting to log in as a system user. An example of this is demonstrated in Listing 20.8.

LISTING 20.8 Sample POP3 Login Session

```
[riley@shadrach]# telnet localhost 110
Trying 127.0.0.1...
Connected to localhost.
Escape character is '^]'.
+OK QPOP (version 3.1.2) at shadrach.ispnet1.net starting.
```

LISTING 20.8 Continued

```
USER riley
+OK Password required for riley.
PASS firetruck
+OK riley has 3 visible messages (0 hidden) in 1261 octets.
QUIT
+OK Pop server at shadrach.ispnet1.net signing off.
Connection closed by foreign host.
```

Again, the fifth line shows the greeting banner produced by `qpopper`, indicating that it is indeed up and running. Next the user enters his username and password using the `USER` and `PASS` commands. After authenticating the login, `qpopper` informs the user that he has 3 messages waiting to be downloaded.

APOP Authentication Support

As shown in Listing 20.8, our poor MUA user had to send his username and password in clear text to the `qpopper` server. Had Riley been checking his mail from across the Internet, a hacker could have captured this information and used it for illicit purposes. However, POP3 provides a solution for this problem.

POP3 can use alternative methods to authenticate a user. The `qpopper` program supports the APOP method of authenticating a user. This method uses encrypted passwords, which greatly reduces the risk of being compromised. To accommodate the different passwords, the APOP method requires that the mail administrator create a separate user password database.

It is often best to create a new system user (often called `pop`) to control the `qpopper` access database. This reduces the risk of logging in as `root` to add new users.

To add this capability to the `popper` executable program, you must recompile the program. First you must remove the object and executable files that were created from any previous builds using the following command:

```
make clean
```

Next, you must run the `configure` script again including parameters to define the location of the APOP password database and the userid of the APOP administrator:

```
./configure --enable-apop=/etc/pop.auth --with-popuid=pop
```

This creates a new Makefile using the values `/etc/pop.auth` for the authentication database location, and the user `pop` being the database administrator. You can then create the new executables by using the GNU `make` command as before. With the APOP option, two executable files are created: `popper` and `popauth`.

As before, copy the `popper` executable file to the location specified in the `inetd.conf` file (such as `/usr/local/lib`). The `popauth` file created allows the APOP administrator to add users to the APOP authentication database specified in the configure command line.

To test the new `qpopper` configuration, you can telnet to port 110 and observe the new greeting banner. Listing 20.9 shows an example of a `qpopper` server using APOP authentication.

LISTING 20.9 Sample qpopper Greeting Banner Using APOP

```
1  [rich@shadrach]$ telnet localhost 110
2  Trying 127.0.0.1...
3  Connected to localhost.
4  Escape character is '^]'.
5  +OK QPOP (version 3.0b18) at shadrach.smallorg.org starting.
➥ <17166.940368317@shadrach.smallorg.org>
6  QUIT
7  +OK Pop server at shadrach.smallorg.org signing off.
8  Connection closed by foreign host.
```

The fifth line shows the new greeting banner that is generated by `qpopper`. It differs from the greeting banner shown in Listing 20.8 in that it includes the APOP seed information (again, the information within the less-than and greater-than signs). The POP3 server supplies this seed value on the greeting banner for the client to use in the encryption of the password. Both sides of the POP3 connection must know the secret word so the hashed value can be matched. The `qpopper` server stores the secret words in the authentication database.

To create the APOP authentication database, enter the following command as `root`:

```
./popauth -init
```

This creates a new authentication database in the location specified (`/etc/pop.auth` in the example). The username specified in the `-with-popuid` parameter is now the APOP administrator and can add users to the authentication database. One strange characteristic about `qpopper` is that once a username is added to the authentication database, that user *must* use APOP authentication to connect to the POP3 server.

To add a new user to the authentication database, the APOP administrator can type the command

```
popauth -user user1
```

where *`user1`* is the Unix system username of the user. The `popauth` program queries the administrator for a password for the user to be used for APOP authentication. This password can be different from the normal Unix system login password. To remove a user from the authentication database, the administrator can type

```
popauth -delete user
```

where *user* is the Unix system username of the user to be removed. If users have shell access to the mail server, they can change their APOP passwords by using the `popauth` command without any parameters.

`qpopper` Bulletins

Another feature that you can add to `qpopper` is the use of bulletins. Bulletins give users the ability to send messages to all POP3 users. When a user connects via POP3 to the mail server, `qpopper` checks the bulletin directory and determines which bulletins the user has not read. Any unread bulletins are added to the normal mail messages for the user. The mail administrator can restrict who can send bulletins by setting appropriate permissions on the `bulletins` directory.

First, as before, if you have already compiled a version of `qpopper`, you must delete any existing object and executable files:

```
make clean
```

Next you must run the `configure` program with the `--enable-bulletins` parameter added. You can run the `configure` program with multiple parameters if you also need shadow password and/or APOP support as well as bulletins. The format for using bulletins with shadow password support would look like this:

```
./configure --enable-bulletins=/var/spool/bulls --enable-specialauth
```

where the `--enable-bulletins` parameter points to the directory where you want the bulletins to reside. Also, remember to include any other parameters required for your mail server, such as the `specialauth` parameter. After the `configure` program completes you must run the GNU `make` utility to create the `popper` executable. When this completes you must again copy the `popper` executable to the directory pointed to by the `inetd.conf` configuration file.

To use the bulletins feature, you must create a separate file for each bulletin, and place them in the `bulletins` directory. The filenames should be in the format

```
nnnnn.string
```

where *nnnnn* is a five-digit number to identify the bulletin number, and `string` is text used to identify the bulletin. An example would be `00001.Test_Bulletin`. Bulletins must be numbered sequentially for `qpopper` to keep track of which bulletins each user has seen. Once a POP3 client has downloaded a given bulletin, it will not appear in the user's mailbox again. The text of the bulletin file must follow strict RFC 822 message formats. Listing 20.10 shows a sample bulletin.

LISTING 20.10 Sample qpopper Bulletin Text

```
From pop Wed Oct 20 18:25:00 1999
Date: Wed, 20 Oct 1999 18:25:00 (EST)
From: "Mail Administrator" <postmaster@shadrach.smallorg.org>
Subject: Test bulletin

This is a test of the Qpopper mail bulletin system.  This is only a test
Had this been a real bulletin you would have been instructed to do
something important, like log off of the system.
This is the end of the bulletin test.
```

The bulletin is checked for download as long as it is in the `bulletins` directory. If you remove the bulletin file, new POP3 clients will not see the bulletin in their mail.

Summary

Once Postfix delivers incoming mail messages to users' mailboxes, its job is done. The mail administrator must determine how users can retrieve their mail messages from their mailboxes. Because most mail users are located remotely from the mail server, some method of retrieving their mail across the network is required. Remote Mail User Agents can be utilized to help minimize network traffic for this process.

The Post Office Protocol (POP3) and Interactive Mail Access Protocol (IMAP) are two MUA protocols that are utilized to help remote clients retrieve their mail. POP3 is a simple protocol that allows users to download their messages to their workstations from the mail server. IMAP allows users to create mail folders on the mail server and keep their mail messages on the mail server.

Two popular MUA server packages that will work on Postfix hosts are the University of Washington IMAP package and the Qualcomm `qpopper` package. Both packages provide POP3 server programs that can read messages in standard `sendmail`-style mailboxes. The UW package also includes IMAP server software that can be used by clients to place their mail messages in folders on the mail server.

CHAPTER 21

Using SqWebMail with Postfix

Installing Postfix is just half of the e-mail server battle. E-mail customers expect other mail services from mail servers. With the increasing popularity of Web-based e-mail services such as Yahoo Mail and Microsoft's Hotmail, a Web interface to users' mailboxes is almost a necessity.

If you decide to support Web-based mailbox access, you must install a separate package. At the time of this writing Postfix does not include software that allows users to access their mailboxes from the Web. One of the most popular Web-based MUA programs available for the Unix platform is the SqWebMail package. This chapter describes how to install SqWebMail on the Postfix server to allow users to read messages in their Maildir-formatted Postfix mailboxes.

Web-Based Mail Clients

The increase in popularity of the World Wide Web has spawned new lines of software products in many areas. Programmers are finding that using a Web-based interface for their programs increases the usability of their programs. Most users already know how to navigate around Web pages, so little if any user training is required when programmers use standard Web page controls such as hot links, drop-down lists, and control buttons.

E-mail client software is no different. Many companies have realized that by using Web-based e-mail client software, users can access their mail messages with little training and can access their mailboxes from a wider variety of computers. Figure 21.1 shows how the Web-based e-mail client software interacts with the standard mail server.

Clients can use any standard Web browser to access messages stored in their mailboxes. Additionally, most Web-based e-mail packages allow users to create folders and store messages on the mail server in separate folders.

Several popular Web-based e-mail client packages are available for the Unix platform. Most of these packages require that both an MTA package and a Web server package be installed on the same server (see Figure 21.1). This section compares some of the Web-based e-mail packages available to mail administrators.

SqWebMail

One of the most popular Web-based e-mail client packages is SqWebMail, which is part of a complete MTA package called Courier. The Courier mail server package contains a complete MTA, IMAP server, and Web-based e-mail client solution. The Courier IMAP server package was discussed in detail in Chapter 15, "Using the Maildir Mailbox Format."

The Courier package is written modularly, so each piece can be used independently from the others. The SqWebMail Web interface to Maildir-formatted mailboxes is extremely popular with both Postfix and qmail MTA administrators. The SqWebMail program directly interfaces with Maildir mailboxes without the help of any other MUA servers (no POP3 or IMAP servers need to be running on the mail server).

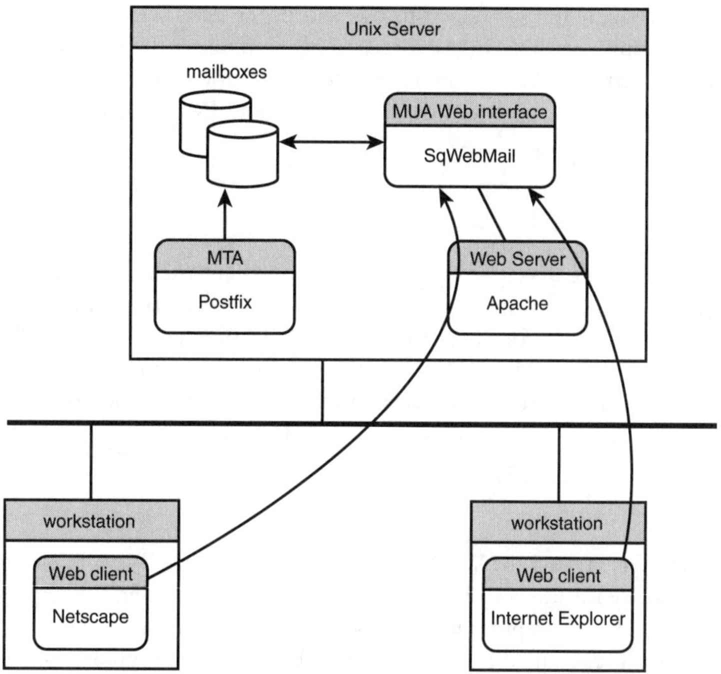

FIGURE 21.1

Using Web-based e-mail client software.

One of the features that makes SqWebMail unique is its support for several different methods of user id authentication. By using separate authentication modules, SqWebMail can support user authentication by standard `/etc/passwd` files, shadow password files, Pluggable Authentication Modules (PAM), MySQL, LDAP, its own binary indexed hash database, or any combination of these.

SqWebMail is implemented as a CGI program that any Web browser using any Unix Web server can run. The most popular Web server in the Unix environment is the Apache Web server. SqWebMail is fully supported by the Apache server.

IMHO

The IMHO Web-based e-mail client package was developed by the Roxen Internet Software corporation. It is based on the Roxen Unix Web server software and will only work on that platform. IMHO was written using the Pike programming language that is only supported by the Roxen server.

Unlike SqWebMail, IMHO connects to user mailboxes using a standard IMAP connection, thus requiring a separate IMAP server to be running on the mail server. Of course this also means that the Web server and mail server do not necessarily have to be on the same server. The IMHO server can connect to a remote IMAP mail server to retrieve mailbox messages for users.

TWIG

Christopher Heschong developed the TWIG e-mail client package, which was originally released under the name Muppet. It is written using the PHP programming language and can be used with any Web browser that supports PHP programs. It uses the PHP IMAP programming interfaces so, like IMHO, it must connect to a running IMAP server to read mailbox messages. It also supports features other than e-mail access such as scheduling, contact manager, newsgroups, to do lists, and bookmarks.

WebMail

Sebastian Schaffert created the WebMail package as a Web-based Java interface to standard mailboxes. Although it utilizes Java scripts within the Web browser, Java support is not required on the client computer browser. WebMail uses standard HTTP 1.1 Java support or it can be run as a standard Java Servlet on Web servers that support Servlets. Sebastian claims that using a Java-based program is much faster than the normal CGI-based Web-based e-mail clients such as SqWebMail.

Installing SqWebMail

At the time of this writing, no Linux distributions include a binary package for SqWebMail. You must download the SqWebMail source code and compile it on your mail server. The official Web site for SqWebMail is located at `http://www.inter7.com/sqwebmail/`. From there you can click on the hot link to the download page. SqWebMail can be downloaded in either HTTP or FTP form:

```
http://download.sourceforge.net/courier/sqwebmail-1.2.4.tar.gz
ftp://download.sourceforge.net/pub/sourceforge/courier/sqwebmail-1.2.4.tar.gz
```

At the time of this writing, the most current version of SqWebMail is 1.2.4. After downloading the source code distribution you must uncompress and expand it into a working directory:

```
tar -zxvf sqwebmail-1.2.4.tar.gz -C /usr/local/src
```

This command places all of the source code under the working directory `/usr/local/src/sqwebmail-1.2.4`.

CAUTION

Remember you must be `root` to place files in the `/usr/local/src` directory.

The following sections describe the steps necessary to compile and install the SqWebMail software on the Postfix server.

Before You Compile

You have many options when using the SqWebMail software. Before compiling the executable programs, you must know the available options and decide how you want SqWebMail to operate. This section describes the things that you must consider before compiling the software package.

Authentication Modules

The most important and confusing part of SqWebMail is the user authentication method. As mentioned, SqWebMail supports several different methods of authenticating users. You must decide which authentication method you need to use on your mail server.

SqWebMail uses authentication modules. Each authentication method is contained in a module that SqWebMail calls to authenticate users. A SqWebMail server can use multiple modules to try and authenticate users. Figure 21.2 shows how SqWebMail interacts with the authentication modules to authenticate a user.

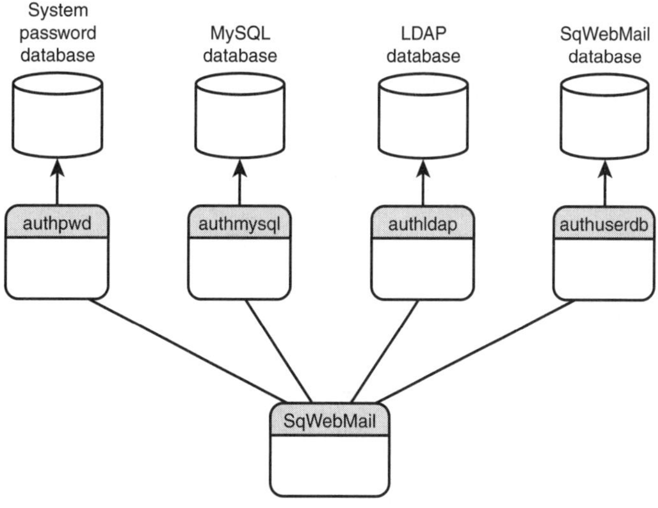

FIGURE 21.2

SqWebMail authentication modules.

Alternatively, the administrator can configure SqWebMail to use a separate authentication program to do the user authenticating for it. The separate program can interface with the various authentication modules. This feature is handy when using authentication modules that have a high connection overhead, such as MySQL and LDAP databases. The authentication program can maintain a pool of connections to the database and handle incoming authentication requests from SqWebMail in a more efficient manner.

SqWebMail attempts to autodetect your mail server environment and compile the appropriate authentication modules into the executable program. However, it is often best to decide which module(s) apply to your mail server and specify only those in the configure step to help reduce executable code size and to simplify the SqWebMail configuration.

The following sections describe the different authentication modules that can be used with SqWebMail.

Normal Password Support

The simplest method of user authentication uses the standard Unix `/etc/passwd` file. The `authpwd` authentication module assumes that all usernames in the `/etc/passwd` file are also valid e-mail usernames and compares the password entered by the user to the password stored in the matching `/etc/passwd` entry.

Most Unix systems now offer the ability to use shadow password files. The `authshadow` authentication module uses the system standard shadow password file to locate valid e-mail users and their passwords.

PAM Support

Some Unix systems utilize Pluggable Authentication Modules (PAM) to authenticate username/password pairs. SqWebMail supports this authentication method with the `authpam` authentication module. Some extra work is required to use this authentication method.

Each PAM implementation has its own method of identifying applications that are allowed to authenticate usernames. You must add the SqWebMail service to the list of allowed applications.

Most Linux systems (including Red Hat and Mandrake) use the `/etc/pam.d` directory to contain configuration files for applications allowed to authenticate usernames. Each application has its own individual file that defines what library will be used.

To allow SqWebMail to authenticate users, you must create a file called `webmail` in the `/etc/pam.d` directory. In it must be the following two lines:

```
auth        required    /lib/security/pam_pwdb.so shadow nullok
account     required    /lib/security/pam_pwdb.so
```

The name and location of the PAM libraries specified in the `webmail` file may be different on your particular Linux distribution. Some Linux distributions use the library name `pam_unix.so` instead of `pam_pwdb.so` as well.

Another format of the PAM configuration uses a single configuration file that contains all of the allowed applications. The `/etc/pam.conf` file contains separate lines that define each individual application. You must edit this file to insert two lines for the `webmail` application:

```
webmail auth    required pam_pwdb.so shadow nullok
webmail account required pam_pwdb.so shadow nullok
```

The `/etc/pam.conf` method is used on BSD-based systems such as FreeBSD, although on FreeBSD the PAM library is located in the `pam_unix.so` file.

CAUTION

If your system uses the `/etc/pam.conf` file, use extreme caution when editing it. If you accidentally remove the entries for the `login` program, you will not be able to log back in to the system. That would be bad, very bad.

SqWebMail User Database

An alternative authentication method that can be used with SqWebMail is `authuserdb`. This method utilizes an indexed binary database to maintain a SqWebMail user database separate from the system user database. This method lets the administrator create virtual e-mail users without creating corresponding system users.

The new user database operates similarly to the Postfix `aliases` file. You must maintain a plaintext user database file (usually located at `/etc/userdb`) and run a SqWebMail program to convert it into indexed binary database files (usually located at `/etc/userdb.dat` and `/etc/userdbshadow.dat`). Note that the SqWebMail password database scheme uses the shadow password technique to store passwords.

SqWebMail includes several Perl scripts to assist the administrator in maintaining the user database.

`vpopmail` User Database

The `vpopmail` program is a popular POP3 server implementation for Unix mail servers. It can maintain its own user database, like SqWebMail. SqWebMail includes the `authvchkpw` module that allows SqWebMail to use the `vpopmail` user database to authenticate users. At the time of this writing, the SqWebMail documentation strongly encourages administrators to convert `vpopmail` users into SqWebMail users in the `/etc/userdb.dat` database file.

MySQL User Database

At the time of this writing, SqWebMail does not yet support using MySQL databases for usernames, but support is on the way. The `authmysql` authentication module will be used to look up usernames in MySQL tables defined for SqWebMail. Again, this can be used to provide virtual user support for SqWebMail, allowing multiple SqWebMail users to share a single system user account.

LDAP User Database

The authldap authentication module lets the administrator use LDAP databases to authenticate SqWebMail users. Although it is still regarded as unstable, you can use the authldap module on the current version on SqWebMail to connect to an LDAP database. As with the authuserdb module, you can use the authldap module to maintain a database of virtual SqWebMail users that can share a common system user account.

Standalone Program

With all of the different authentication modules available for SqWebMail, authenticating users can get confusing and resource intensive. In an attempt to help consolidate these functions, the SqWebMail package includes its own authentication server program that can continually run in background mode and wait for SqWebMail to ask for user authentication. The authdaemon module interacts with a separate program, authdaemond, that authenticates the user using one of the SqWebMail authentication methods.

The authdaemond program must be configured to know which authentication modules are being used on the server. As a separate authentication program, authdaemond can establish connections to remote databases (such as MySQL and LDAP databases) before SqWebMail requests an authentication. This decreases the authentication time for SqWebMail.

Spell Checking

The SqWebMail user interface can include a spell-checking feature when creating e-mail messages. This is a handy feature to include for users. SqWebMail can use two different spell-check programs: aspell or ispell. Both programs are used as generic spell-check programs on most Unix platforms.

If you want SqWebMail to include spell checking, you must ensure that one of the two spell-checking programs is installed on your server. For Mandrake 7.2 Linux servers, both the aspell and ispell programs come as included RPM binary packages. You must also install the locales RPM package for these packages to work properly. To install the ispell program, you can use the following commands:

```
rpm -Uvh locales-2.3-10mdk.noarch.rpm
rpm -Uvh locales-en-2.3-10mdk.noarch.rpm
rpm -Uvh ispell-3.1.20-13mdk.i586.rpm
rpm -Uvh ispell-en-3.1.20-13mdk.i586.rpm
```

These commands install the English dictionary for the ispell program. If you require a different dictionary, install the appropriate locales and ispell dictionary RPM packages.

Web Server

For SqWebMail to operate on the mail server, you must have a Web server package installed and operational. The most popular Web server for the Unix platform is the Apache Web server package. Most Linux distributions include a binary package for

Apache. In fact, many Linux distributions either install it by default or offer the option to install it during the setup program.

On the Mandrake 7.2 Linux distribution, you can install the Apache Web server using the following commands:

```
rpm -Uvh apache-1.3.14-2mdk.i586.rpm
rpm -Uvh apache-common-1.3.14-2mdk.i586.rpm
```

These commands install the Apache Web server into the default directory locations for the Mandrake 7.2 Linux distribution. Alternatively, you can download the Apache source code distribution from the Apache Web site at `http://www.apache.org` and install it yourself.

Once you have installed the Apache Web server, you must make one modification to the standard configuration file for Apache. SqWebMail uses MIME encoding to process file attachments to messages. Unfortunately, the Microsoft Internet Explorer (MSIE) browsers (both versions 4.x and 5.x) have bugs in their code for handling MIME data in HTTP version 1.1 Web pages. To compensate for this, you must force the Web server to use the HTTP version 1.0 protocol when talking with MSIE clients.

These modifications must be made to the standard `httpd.conf` Apache configuration file. For the Mandrake Linux distribution, it is located in the `/etc/httpd/conf` directory. The `BrowserMatch` tag identifies special instructions for particular clients. You may notice that the default `httpd.conf` file already has several `BrowserMatch` tags defined for other known bugs. There should already be a tag for the MSIE 4.0b2 browser to force it to use the HTTP version 1.0 protocol. You can replace this line to make it apply to all 4.x and 5.x MSIE browsers. The new line should look like this:

```
BrowserMatch "MSIE" nokeepalive downgrade-1.0 force-response-1.0
```

After adding this entry, you can start the Apache Web server using either the `apachectl` command or the http startup script used for your server.

Compiling SqWebMail

After completing the necessary pre-compiler actions, you can begin compiling the SqWebMail program. Several steps are required to compile the executable files. Like other applications, SqWebMail uses the `configure` program to modify the Makefile environment to reflect the options you want added to the program. After the `configure` program is completed, you must use the GNU `make` program to compile the executable code. The following sections describe these steps in more detail.

Configuring the Installation

As mentioned, you must run the `configure` program from the source code directory to specify the various options that can be used with SqWebMail. You must list each option on the `configure` command line. Table 21.1 lists the `configure` options that you can use.

TABLE 21.1 SqWebMail `configure` Options

Option	*Description*
`--with-`*`mod`*	Adds authentication module *`mod`*.
`--without-`*`mod`*	Specifically omits authentication module *`mod`*.
`--with-cachedir=`*`dir`*	Creates a cache directory *`dir`* for caching login information; if *`dir`* is not specified `/var/run/sqwebmail` is used.
`--with-cacheowner=`*`owner`*	Specifies the owner of the cache directory; if *`owner`* is not specified `bin` is used.
`--without-gzip`	Does not compress Web pages. By default some Web pages are compressed before sending them to Web browsers that support compression.
`--with-db=`*`db`*	Specifies that the SqWebMail user database be created using the *`db`* database library. By default SqWebMail uses whichever one is installed, or GDBM if more than one is installed.
`--disable-utf7-folder-encoding`	Does not use modified UTF-7 to encode 8-bit characters in names of folders.
`--enable-unicode=`*`chset`*	Includes the *`chset`* Unicode character set.
`--enable-https`	Generates secure https Web pages instead of the standard http pages.
`--enable-https=login`	Generates secure https Web pages for the login pages only; all other pages will use http.
`--enable-webpass=no`	Does not allow SqWebMail-specific usernames and passwords. Only system username/password pairs can be used.
`--enable-webpass=vpopmail`	Uses the `vpopmail` authentication database to change passwords.
`--enable-hardtimeout=`*`sec`*	Disconnects any session that lasts longer than *`sec`* seconds.
`--enable-softtimeout=`*`sec`*	Disconnects any session that is inactive longer than *`sec`* seconds.
`--enable-autopurge=`*`days`*	Automatically purges deleted messages older than *`days`* days.
`--enable-maxpurge=`*`days`*	Limits the number of days users can specify to purge deleted files to *`days`* days.
`--with-htmllibdir=`*`dir`*	Directory where SqWebMail stores its html template files. The http server does not access these.
`--with-defaultlang=en`	Specifies an alternate language for Web pages. Currently only English is used.
`--enable-cgibindir=`*`dir`*	Specifies the location of the Web server CGI-BIN directory for script files.
`--enable-imagedir=`*`dir`*	Specifies the location of the Web server directory in which to place the SqWebMail image icons.

TABLE 21.1 Continued

Option	*Description*
`--enable-imageurl=`*`URL`*	Specifies the URL of the location of the Web server directory where the image icons are.
`--enable-mimetypes=`*`list`*	Specifies a colon-separated list of MIME types supported by the installed Web server.
`--enable-mimecharset=`*`charset`*	The default MIME character set to use for RFC 822 Content-Type: headers.
`--enable-lang=`*`lang`*	Specifies an alternate language for Web pages. Currently not used.
`--enable-bannerprog=`*`program`*	Specifies a program that SqWebMail will use to create banners in the Web pages. Used to customize Web pages.
`--with-maxargsize=`*`n`*	Sets the maximum size of an HTTP post that SqWebMail will accept.
`--with-maxformargsize=`*`n`*	Sets the maximum size of an HTTP multipart form that SqWebMail will accept. Often used to restrict the size of attachments in messages, although this includes the MIME encoding overhead of about 25%.
`--with-maxmsgsize=`*`n`*	Sets the maximum size of the total message, text, and any attachments. The default value is 2,097,152 bytes.
`--with-ispell=`*`dir`*	Specifies the location of the `ispell` program for spell checking.
`--without-ispell`	Disables spell-checking feature even if `ispell` is defined.
`--with-fcgi`	Enables fast CGI support.

With such a long list of configuration options, you might be scared to run the `configure` program. Fortunately, SqWebMail uses sensible default values for all of the options that should work for most installations. The `configure` program attempts to determine appropriate values for the directory locations and authentication modules.

By default, the `configure` program detects any installed authentication libraries, such as OpenLDAP or MySQL, and configures its own authentication modules accordingly. If you have these packages installed on the Unix server but do not want to use them with SqWebMail, you can specify the `--without` option to skip them.

A sample `configure` command line would look like this:

```
./configure --without-authldap --without-authmysql
```

By default if you use either the `authmysql` or `authldap` modules, SqWebMail attempts to use the `authdaemond` program to manage authentication. If you do not want to use the `authdaemond` program, you can also skip that in the `configure` command line:

```
./configure --without-authldap --without-authmysql --without-authdaemon
```

Much like Postfix, SqWebMail uses modular programming. You may notice that while the `configure` program runs, it repeats many of the same messages. This is normal because it is just performing the same tasks for each SqWebMail module. After the `configure` program finishes, you can test the new configuration using the `make` command. The output from this command shows where SqWebMail will install its various pieces:

```
[root@shadrach]# make configure-check
SqWebMail CGI will be installed in /home/httpd/cgi-bin
Images will be installed in /home/httpd/html/webmail
make[1]: Entering directory `/usr/local/src/sqwebmail-1.2.4/sqwebmail'
URL to the image directory is /webmail/
make[1]: Leaving directory `/usr/local/src/sqwebmail-1.2.4/sqwebmail'
```

If the configure check reports no errors, you are ready to compile the SqWebMail program.

Running the Compiler

After the `configure` program finishes, you can compile the source code modules to create the executable files. The GNU `make` command is used with no options to compile all of the modules:

```
make
```

SqWebMail includes a `make` option that can test the compiled program and configuration files. You can use the command

```
make check
```

to check the files. If it exits without any errors, the programs have been compiled successfully.

After using the `make check` command, you should have the executable `sqwebmail` program and the necessary configuration files, but they won't be installed into their proper directories yet. To install them, you must use the `make` command again using one of the understood `install` options. You can choose either the `install` or `install-strip` option for the executable:

```
make install-strip
```

The `install-strip` option is preferred because it removes debugging information from the executable program to make it smaller. Unfortunately, some Unix platforms do not support this feature, and you must use the `install` option and live with a bloated executable program.

After the executable is installed, you must install the configuration files. Again, you do this with the `make` command with a different install option:

```
make install-configure
```

This command places the SqWebMail configuration files into the proper locations. The next section describes the configuration files and how to modify them for your Unix environment.

Configuring SqWebMail

The SqWebMail install process places default configuration files into the SqWebMail configuration directory. These files are located in the `/usr/local/share/sqwebmail` directory by default. Depending on the authentication method you selected, the configuration files used will vary.

`authdaemond` Configuration Files

If you selected to use the `authdaemond` program for authentication, a set of configuration files should be created to control the operation of `authdaemond`. The `authdaemonrc` configuration file lists the parameters that `authdaemond` uses. Listing 21.1 shows the default `authdaemonrc` file created by the SqWebMail installation (minus extensive comments).

LISTING 21.1 Default authdaemonrc File

```
authmodulelist="authcustom authuserdb authldap authpam"
daemons=5
version=""
authdaemonvar=/usr/local/share/sqwebmail/authdaemon
```

Notice that the first parameter in the `authdaemonrc` file is the `authmodulelist`. This parameter defines all of the authentication modules that the `authdaemond` program should attempt to use. The original `authmodulelist` configuration file should now point to the `authdaemon` authentication module.

To help decrease login times, you should place your primary authentication method first in the `authmodulelist` parameter. The `daemons` parameter specifies the number of `authdaemond` programs that can run in the background at the same time. The more programs running, the better service users will get under heavy load. Be careful though, because too high a number may overload your Unix server.

After modifying the `authdaemonrc` configuration file, you must start the `authdaemond` program. You can do this either manually or by creating a boot script for your Unix installation. The command line you should use is

```
/usr/local/libexec/authlib/authdaemond start
```

The corresponding method to use to stop the `authdaemond` program is

```
/usr/local/libexec/authlib/authdaemond stop
```

Once the `authdaemond` program is running, you should be able to log in to the SqWebMail server.

Standard Configuration Files

If you opted not to use the `authdaemond` program for authentication, you must configure the `authmodulelist` file located in the `/usr/local/share/sqwebmail` directory. This file is a plaintext list of all the authentication methods that were compiled into your SqWebMail program. You must select the methods that you are using for authentication and delete the other module names. It is best to place the authentication methods in the order in which you want to authenticate users. A sample `authmodulelist` entry might be

```
authpam authldap authuserdb
```

Using this entry, SqWebMail attempts to look up the username in the standard system user PAM database. If the username is not found, it contacts the LDAP server configured in the `authldaprc` configuration file. If the username is still not found, it attempts to find it in its own user database.

When using this method of authentication, no other programs are required for user authentication. The clients simply connect to the Web server, SqWebMail authenticates them, and their e-mail session begins.

Shared Folders

One nice feature of the SqWebMail server is the capability to create shared mail folders where all users can place and view messages. You can configure two types of shared folders:

- Global shared folders
- User shared folders

Global shared folders are created by the administrator and appear in every user's folder list by default. Individual users must subscribe to the global folder to be able to view and place messages in the folder. User shared folders are created by individual users. Other users who want to view and place messages in the shared folder must manually create a link to the shared folder.

The command used to create and link shared folders is `maildirmake`, which is supplied with SqWebMail. To create a new shared folder, you must use the command

```
/usr/local/libexec/sqwebmail/maildirmake -S dirpath
```

where *`dirpath`* is the full pathname to a directory to contain the shared folders. You must have write permission to the shared folder directory. The `maildirmake` command takes care of all other user privileges required. Once the shared folder directory is created, you must create the actual shared folder

```
maildirmake -s access -f folder dirpath
```

where *access* is the access type granted to other users, *folder* is the name of the shared folder, and *dirpath* is the full pathname to the shared folder directory. The shared folder creator can grant either read or write access to other users.

A sample of creating a shared folder and granting write access to all other users would be

```
/usr/local/libexec/sqwebmail/maildirmake -S /home/rich/folders
/usr/local/libexec/sqwebmail/maildirmake -s write -f OfficeNews /home/rich/folders
```

After you create the shared folder, you must decide whether it will be made into a global folder. For the system to support global folders, the admin must create the file `/usr/local/share/sqwebmail/maildirshared`. This file contains the names and pathnames for all global folders. The name and pathname are separated with a tab character on the line. For the preceding example, the entry to make OfficeNews global would be

```
OfficeNews     /home/rich/folders
```

That is all that is required to create the global shared folder.

For user shared folders, each individual user who wants to subscribe to the folder must also execute the `maildirmake` command

```
/usr/local/libexec/sqwebmail/maildirmake --add folder=dirpath
```

where *folder* is the folder name and *dirpath* is the full pathname of the shared folder directory. For this example, the command would be

```
/usr/local/libexec/sqwebmail/maildirmake --add OfficeNews=/home/rich/folders
```

Configuring Postfix for SqWebMail

Now that SqWebMail has been configured and is operational, you must configure Postfix. This turns out to be a simple job. The only feature of Postfix that is required for SqWebMail is the use of Maildir-style mailboxes.

Chapter 15 described Maildir-style mailboxes and how to configure Postfix to use them. Simply, you need to add one line to the Postfix `main.cf` configuration file:

```
home_mailbox = Maildir/
```

It is crucial that you use the original Maildir mailbox name rather than your own creation, as this is the mailbox that SqWebMail uses. Also, remember that if you were previously using the `mailbox_command` parameter it must be commented out of `main.cf` again.

One quirk of SqWebMail is that it requires each user who logs in to the Web server to have an existing mailbox. Unfortunately, Postfix only creates mailboxes for users when they first receive mail messages. Thus, new users who have not received any mail messages will receive an error message when they try to use SqWebMail. A simple solution to this dilemma is to send an administrative message to the user when her account is first created. This automatically creates her Maildir mailbox and makes SqWebMail happy. An alternative solution would be to create a template Maildir directory in the skeleton directory used by the `useradd` command to create new user directories.

NOTE

Remember to restart the Postfix program using the `postfix reload` command after changing the parameters in the `main.cf` configuration file.

Using SqWebMail

If you have installed and configured all the parts of SqWebMail and Postfix properly, it is time to test the new system. You can use any standard Web browser from a network client and connect to the `sqwebmail` CGI program on the Web server:

```
http://www.ispnet1.net/cgi-bin/sqwebmail
```

Note that there is no trailing slash at the end of the URL. You may also configure an alias on your Web server to hide the ugly default URL that SqWebMail uses.

If SqWebMail is working, you should get the default login screen shown in Figure 21.3.

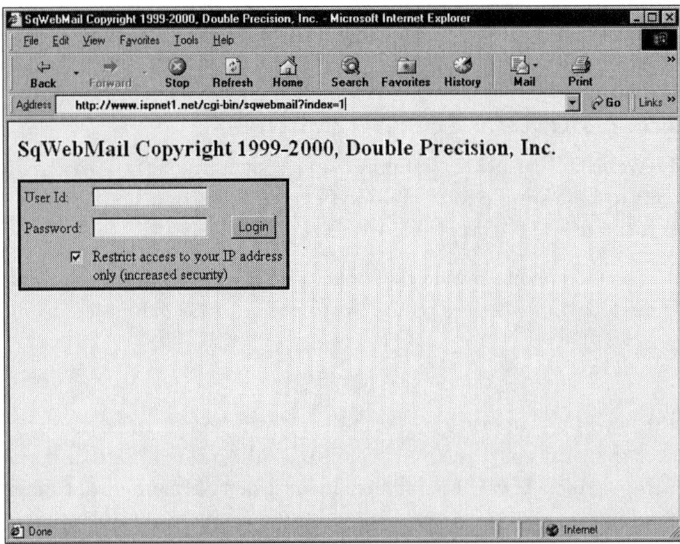

FIGURE 21.3

Default SqWebMail login screen.

The login screen consists of the user and password text fields, a Login button, and a security checkbox. The checkbox allows for an additional level of security if desired. SqWebMail records the IP address of your workstation and allows only requests from this same IP address during the e-mail session. This helps prevent another workstation from hijacking the IP connection.

The Folders Web Page

After entering a valid username and password, you should see the SqWebMail Folders Web page. The Folders Web page shows the folders available to store messages. By default you should see the following folders:

- INBOX
- Draft
- Sent
- Trash

All new messages should appear in the INBOX folder. SqWebMail indicates how many messages in the folder have not been read. All deleted messages are stored in the Trash folder. You may manually empty the Trash folder to save disk space, or the automatic purge function will clean it out for you at the time it is configured. All sent mail is saved in the Sent folder, and you can save draft messages in the Draft folder. Figure 21.4 shows the Folders Web page.

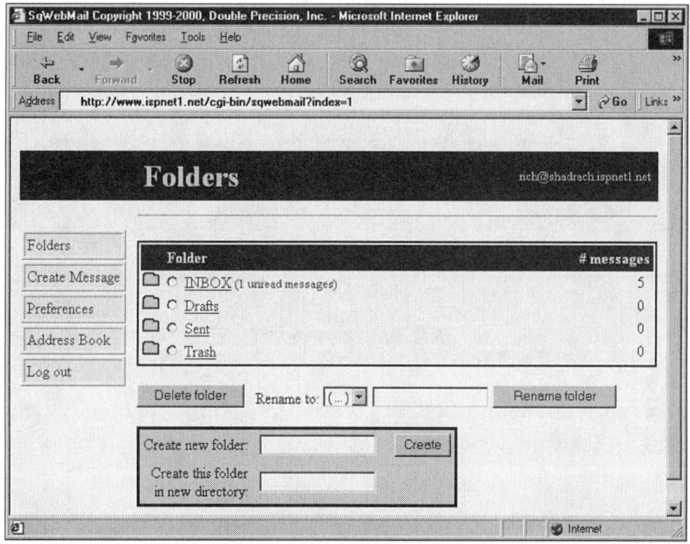

FIGURE 21.4

The SqWebMail Folders Web page.

You can also create your own folders. Once folders are created, you can move messages into them for storage.

CAUTION

Remember that all messages placed in the folders are stored on the mail server. On high volume servers, disk space can become a problem.

Reading Mail Messages

Clicking on one of the folders listed in the Folders Web page produces a list of mail messages stored in the folder. Figure 21.5 shows an example of this.

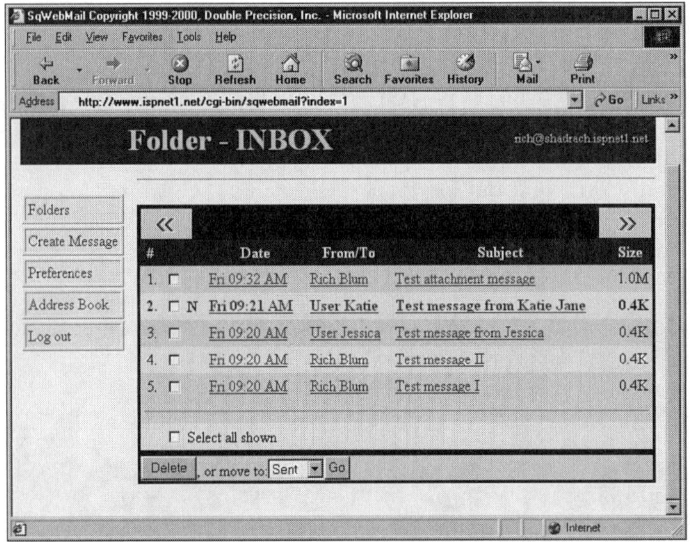

FIGURE 21.5

INBOX message list.

Clicking on any part of the message list produces a Web page showing the mail message. If the message includes any attachments, they are shown at the bottom of the message. You can click on the Download Attachment link to download the attached file to your workstation.

At the top of the message is a toolbar that contains buttons for various actions you can take with the message. Table 21.2 describes the toolbar buttons and their functions.

TABLE 21.2 Message Toolbar Button Functions

Button	*Function*
Previous Message	Displays the previous message in the current mailbox.
Next Message	Displays the next message in the current mailbox.
Delete Message	Sends the current message to the Trash folder.
Folder	Returns to the Folder Web page.
Reply	Starts the Create Message Web page using the sender of the message as the To: address.
Reply To All	Starts the Create Message Web page using the sender of the message as the To: address and any other recipients as the Cc: address.
Reply To List	Starts the Create Message Web page using the list of all recipients in the To: address.
Forward Message	Starts the Create Message Web page using the body of the message in the text area.
Forward As Attachment	Starts the Create Message Web page using the entire message as a text attachment.
Full Headers	Displays the complete RFC 822 mail headers included in the message.
Show For Printing	Creates a new Web window containing just the header and body of the message. This allows for printing the message without the SqWebMail banners and buttons.

You can return to the Folders Web page by clicking on the Folders link.

Sending Mail Messages

The Create Message link on the Folders and Messages Web pages takes you to the Create Message Web page shown in Figure 21.6.

From this page you can select e-mail addresses for the message and compose the text body of the message. If you have included the `ispell` program you can spell check the message body.

You can add file attachments to the message by clicking the Attachments button at the bottom of the page. When you have completed the message you can send it by clicking on the Send button.

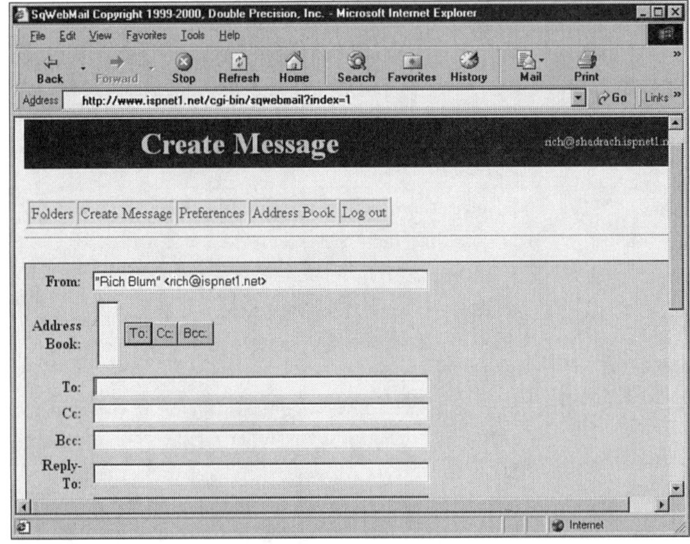

FIGURE 21.6

Create Message Web page.

Changing Preferences

You can set some of your personal preferences for SqWebMail by clicking the Preferences link. Table 21.3 shows the preferences that you can modify.

TABLE 21.3 SqWebMail Preferences Settings

Setting	*Description*
Display full message headers	Always displays the complete RFC 822 message header when reading messages.
Display HTML e-mail	Displays message sent in HTML format on the Web browser.
Purge deleted messages	Sets the number of days that messages will stay in the Trash folder before being deleted.
Sort messages by	Sets the field in which messages in the folder are displayed.
Messages per page	Sets the number of messages shown on one page of message listings.
Show oldest message first	The opposite of sorting messages by date. The oldest message appears first in the list.
Your signature	A short text message that will be added to the bottom of all messages sent from SqWebMail.
Mailing lists	A list of all mailing lists you are subscribed to.

Mail users can modify any of these preferences at any time. Values are stored in the individual user's `Maildir` directory.

The final preference the user can modify is his SqWebMail password. This feature is somewhat complicated in that if the mail user changes his password here, it is placed in his Maildir directory. This option does not update any existing authentication databases such as the PAM library, MySQL database, or LDAP database. Although this is a handy method to allow users to change their own passwords, it can get confusing for the mail administrator. You should use caution when allowing users to change their own passwords.

NOTE

To disable the change password feature, you can compile SqWebMail with the `--enable-webpass=no` option in the `configure` command.

Summary

Accessing e-mail mailboxes using a Web browser has almost become a network necessity. There are several packages you can use on the Postfix server to provide this service for mail users. If you are using Maildir-style mailboxes with Postfix, you can use the SqWebMail Web e-mail client.

The SqWebMail package is part of the Courier MTA e-mail package. You can install it as a separate module without installing the complete Courier package. The SqWebMail program operates as a CGI program in a standard Web server running on the mail server.

Once you have installed SqWebMail, you must decide how it will authenticate users. Several methods of authenticating users can be configured into the SqWebMail system. It can use standard `/etc/passwd` files, shadow password files, Pluggable Authentication Modules (PAM), a MySQL database, an LDAP database, or its own indexed binary database of users.

After creating the executable programs and necessary Web pages, you must install them in the standard Web server directories. Remote users can then connect to the Web server using a standard Web browser. Once connected, they must log in to the system using a user id/password pair that is authenticated using the specified authentication modules. After the user id is authenticated, the user has complete access to his e-mail mailbox, as well as additional folders that can be created for storing messages on the mail server. New messages can also be created and sent to users using the SqWebMail Web server interface.

CHAPTER 22

Performance Tuning Postfix

If you only have a hundred or so users on your e-mail system, you may never have to worry about how quickly Postfix processes incoming and outgoing mail messages. Using the default Postfix installation, most e-mail servers should be able to adequately handle normal traffic load.

However, many mail administrators are responsible for thousands of e-mail users on their servers. For them, every microsecond of performance is crucial. The default settings for Postfix may not be the most efficient way for their mail server to operate.

This chapter is for those mail administrators who have to worry about e-mail server performance. It describes some techniques that can help improve performance on large e-mail servers. These techniques range from altering default Postfix parameters to tweaking the Unix system to increase system performance.

Tuning Postfix Parameters

As mentioned, by default Postfix selects common values for most of the parameters used to control its behavior. To increase the performance of Postfix, you should look at the default values and decide which should be changed for your particular e-mail environment.

This section describes some of the various parameters used in configuration files that you can alter from their default values to improve the performance of the Postfix server.

The `master.cf` Configuration File

The `master.cf` configuration file controls the behavior of the Postfix processes. As discussed in Chapter 2, "Postfix Services," Postfix uses several modular programs to support MTA functionality. These processes are controlled by individual settings in the `master.cf` file.

Listing 22.1 shows the default `master.cf` configuration file as installed by the `snapshot-20001217` version of Postfix.

LISTING 22.1 Default `master.cf` Configuration File

```
# ==========================================================================
# service type  private unpriv  chroot  wakeup  maxproc command + args
#               (yes)   (yes)   (yes)   (never) (50)
# ==========================================================================
smtp      inet  n       -       n       -       -       smtpd
pickup    fifo  n       n       n       60      1       pickup
cleanup   unix  -       -       n       -       0       cleanup
qmgr      fifo  n       -       n       300     1       qmgr
#qmgr     fifo  n       -       n       300     1       nqmgr
```

LISTING 22.1 Continued

```
rewrite   unix  -   -   n   -     -   trivial-rewrite
bounce    unix  -   -   n   -     0   bounce
defer     unix  -   -   n   -     0   bounce
flush     unix  -   -   n   1000? 0   flush
smtp      unix  -   -   n   -     -   smtp
showq     unix  n   -   n   -     -   showq
error     unix  -   -   n   -     -   error
local     unix  -   n   n   -     -   local
lmtp      unix  -   -   n   -     -   lmtp
cyrus     unix  -   n   n   -     -   pipe
    flags=R user=cyrus argv=/cyrus/bin/deliver -e -m ${extension} ${user}
uucp      unix  -   n   n   -     -   pipe
    flags=F user=uucp argv=uux -r -n -z -a$sender - $nexthop!rmail ($recipient)
ifmail    unix  -   n   n   -     -   pipe
    flags=F user=ftn argv=/usr/lib/ifmail/ifmail -r $nexthop ($recipient)
bsmtp     unix  -   n   n   -     -   pipe
    flags=F. user=foo argv=/usr/local/sbin/bsmtp -f $sender $nexthop $recipient
```

The seventh field used in the `master.cf` configuration file defines the maximum number of processes that can be running at any one time for the listed program. If the value listed is a dash (-), the default value of 50 is used. This allows up to 50 different processes to be running at any one time for that program.

For most servers, this should not be a problem; however, for large volume e-mail environments, you may want to modify this number.

Configuring for Low-End Servers

Often mail administrators are constrained by the equipment available for their use. For smaller organizations, sometimes the equipment used can even become quite comical. It is still not unheard of today to find small organizations using discarded 486-class machines as network e-mail servers. One of the reasons for the recent Linux boom is that administrators can recycle old equipment into fairly productive Linux servers.

If you are using a low-end machine as an e-mail server, you will have to constantly monitor its performance and watch for problems. To ensure that Postfix doesn't go wild and swamp the server, you should place limits on what resources it is allowed to allocate.

One way to do this is to modify the `master.cf` configuration file. Just because the default Postfix configuration allows up to 50 concurrent processes for each program doesn't mean that you have to. For some e-mail servers, having 50 active SMTP sessions would bring the server to its knees, or even crash it. You can limit the number of Postfix processes to a reasonable level by placing specific values in the `maxprocess` field in the `master.cf` configuration file.

Wietse Venema recommends starting things off by specifying a `maxprocess` value of 10 for the `smtp` and `smtpd` processes. This allows up to 10 inbound and 10 outbound SMTP processes for the Postfix server. This should be adequate to handle most normal e-mail server traffic for the typical small office. You should always monitor the system load on the server to ensure that the Postfix server is not crippling it. You may even have to use values less than 10 to keep things running smoothly.

One command you can use to monitor the load of a Unix server is the `uptime` command. The `uptime` command displays the following:

- The current time
- How long the system has been running since the last reboot
- How many users are currently logged on
- System load averages for the last 1, 5, and 15 minutes

An example of using the `uptime` command is

```
[rich@shadrach]$ uptime
 10:05am  up 35 days, 23:13,  1 user,  load average: 3.02, 2.04, 1.60
```

The larger the average load number, the busier the server is. As you can see from the example, often the server will show high 1-minute load averages, but the 5- and 15-minute averages remain low. This represents a short burst of activity from the server and is normal. On heavily loaded machines, the 5- and 15-minute averages begin to increase as well. This indicates a more constantly overloaded server. In this case, you should consider reducing the number of processes allowed to run simultaneously.

Configuring for Sending-Intensive Servers

Many mail servers are utilized as mailing list servers (see Chapter 19, "Using Majordomo with Postfix"). While the servers receive only a limited number of postings for each mailing list, they must send each mail message out to potentially thousands of list subscribers. Limiting the server to just 50 SMTP client sessions may severely restrict how fast messages get delivered to mailing list users. It would be nice to increase the number of simultaneous SMTP sessions the mail server could establish. However, this can be a tricky decision.

While changing the `smtp maxprocess` value to a large number might sound like a good solution, you should do this with caution. Remember that there is more to the equation than just the number of processes Postfix spawns. First, there is the limitation of the network bandwidth the server is connected to. If the server is only connected via an ISDN or DSL line to the Internet, that line will quickly become saturated.

Other factors to consider when increasing the number of `smtp` processes are the server's memory, swap size, and CPU capacity. Just because you can increase the number of `smtp` processes doesn't necessarily mean that the server can handle the new load. You should always monitor server load and performance when increasing the `maxprocess` values for processes.

As discussed earlier, you can use the `uptime` command to determine server load. Once you determine that the server is experiencing an overload condition, you may want to determine what is causing the overload.

The `ps` command reports on individual server processes and displays information about the load that they are placing on the server. You can use many different options with the `ps` command to display different characteristics of the running processes. Unfortunately several different versions of the `ps` command are used on different Unix systems, so generalizing the different options is difficult.

On Linux systems, the version of `ps` used was originally written by Branko Lankester, and is currently maintained by Michael K. Johnson. It uses the Linux `proc` filesystem to gather information about the running processes. One format you can use to display running processes and their system load is `ps` *`axu`*.

The `a` option displays all processes to the terminal, including those of other users. The *`x`* option displays processes that have no controlling terminal, such as Postfix processes, and the *`u`* option displays the percent of CPU and memory usage of each running process.

In the output of the `ps` command, the `%CPU` field shows the CPU time of the process divided by the time the process is running. You can use this figure as a relative indication of which processes are hogging the CPU on the server.

Listing 22.2 shows a sample `ps` command output. For brevity, the listing shows only the running Postfix processes.

LISTING 22.2 Sample ps Command Output

```
[rich@shadrach]$ ps axu
USER       PID %CPU %MEM   VSZ  RSS TTY      STAT START   TIME COMMAND
root      2152  0.0  2.2  1532  704 ?        S    Jan12   0:08 master
postfix  14413  0.3  2.7  1668  828 ?        D    10:33   0:12 qmgr -l -t fifo -
postfix  14873  0.4  2.4  1616  756 ?        S    11:27   0:00 trivial-rewrite -
postfix  14879  0.9  2.7  1672  844 ?        S    11:27   0:01 smtp -t unix -u
postfix  14884  0.8  2.7  1672  844 ?        S    11:27   0:01 smtp -t unix -u
postfix  14891  0.8  2.7  1672  844 ?        S    11:27   0:01 smtp -t unix -u
postfix  15618  1.9  2.6  1660  812 ?        S    11:29   0:00 cleanup -t unix -
postfix  16162  5.6  2.3  1552  708 ?        S    11:30   0:00 pickup -l -t fifo
```

As you can see, on an e-mail server that is constantly sending outbound messages (such as a mailing list server), multiple `smtp` processes are running, each one handling an outbound message and placing a certain load on the server CPU. As you can also see, there are also other processes that are called in relation to the `smtp` process. In this particular example, the `cleanup` and `pickup` processes used to prepare the outbound messages take up more CPU time than the actual `smtp` processes used to deliver the messages.

The main.cf Configuration File

The main source of configuration parameters used by Postfix is the main.cf configuration file. Many parameters can alter the characteristics of how Postfix sends and receives messages. This section describes parameters that are used to affect the inbound and outbound message processing of Postfix and how you can modify them to suit your particular e-mail server environment.

Inbound Message Controls

One of the less-used features of Postfix is the capability to control the rate of inbound messages received from remote hosts via SMTP. The smtpd process is responsible for accepting and managing SMTP connections from remote hosts. You can modify several parameters to change how the smtpd process operates. This can greatly affect the performance of the server.

Chapter 13, "Postfix Server Administration" discussed using smtpd parameters to control Unsolicited Commercial E-mail (UCE). You can use additional parameters to further control the SMTP sessions. These parameters can help decrease the load of simultaneous inbound messages to the server. This section describes these parameters.

The smtpd_recipient_limit Parameter

The smtpd_recipient_limit parameter can limit the number of recipients allowed in a single incoming message. Some MTA software packages attempt to consolidate multiple users for a single message at a single mail host. While this technique does decrease network traffic, it increases the server load, because the individual recipients must be parsed out from the message. Usually this is a good thing, but sometimes gets out of hand.

For some mailing lists, it is possible to have hundreds of users on a single mail host receiving the same message. When there is a very large recipient list, Postfix must do extra work parsing the recipients and delivering the message. It is often easier to create multiple copies of the same message with fewer recipients per message. The maximum number of recipients can be specified using the smtpd_recipient_limit parameter:

```
smtpd_recipient_limit = 100
```

This entry would limit the maximum number of recipients to 100. The default value for this parameter is 1000.

If the remote host attempts to specify more recipients than the number allowed by the parameter, Postfix returns an error message. This means that the remote mail host must resend the message in batches using fewer recipients in each batch. Listing 22.3 shows an example of what happens if the smtpd_recipient_limit parameter is set to 2.

LISTING 22.3 Sample `smtpd_recipient_limit` Session

```
[rich@shadrach]$ telnet localhost 25
Trying 127.0.0.1...
Connected to localhost.
Escape character is '^]'.
220 shadrach.ispnet1.net ESMTP Postfix
helo meshach.ispnet1.net
250 shadrach.ispnet1.net
mail from: <rich@meshach.ispnet1.net>
250 Ok
rcpt to: <rich@shadrach.ispnet1.net>
250 Ok
rcpt to: <jessica@shadrach.ispnet1.net>
250 Ok
rcpt to: <katie@shadrach.ispnet1.net>
452 Error: too many recipients
data
354 End data with <CR><LF>.<CR><LF>
From: rich@meshach.ispnet1.net
To: rich@shadrach.ispnet1.net
To: jessica@shadrach.ispnet1.net
Subject: Test message
testing
.
250 Ok: queued as 26298C352
quit
221 Bye
Connection closed by foreign host.
You have new mail in /var/spool/mail/rich
[
```

Notice that after the third `RCPT TO:` command, Postfix returns an SMTP error message informing the remote host that too many recipients have been specified. Depending on the SMTP software used on the remote host, either the entire SMTP connection is terminated, or the remote host continues sending the message for the accepted recipients. Afterward, additional messages are sent for the remaining recipients.

CAUTION

Remember that when you limit recipients, you force more SMTP connections to occur. This may shift the load to another process on the server, thus not really saving any resources. Often you can determine the ideal number by extensive experimentation in your particular e-mail environment.

The smtpd_timeout Parameter

The `smtpd_timeout` parameter limits the amount of time Postfix waits for an SMTP client request after sending a response. This allows the Postfix administrator to quickly disconnect SMTP servers that "camp out" on the SMTP connection, utilizing system resources for the SMTP connection without actually sending a message.

The format of the `smtpd_timeout` parameter is

```
smtpd_timeout = value
```

The *value* can be specified in one of five time units. By default, Postfix will assume the value is in seconds. If you are specifying any other time unit, you must include a one-character abbreviation along with the value:

- `m`—Minutes
- `h`—Hours
- `d`—Days
- `w`—Weeks

Listing 22.4 shows a sample SMTP session using the `smtpd_timeout` parameter.

LISTING 22.4 Sample smtpd_timeout Session

```
[rich@shadrach]$ telnet localhost 25
Trying 127.0.0.1...
Connected to localhost.
Escape character is '^]'.
220 shadrach.ispnet1.net ESMTP Postfix
helo meshach.ispnet1.net
250 shadrach.ispnet1.net
421 Error: timeout exceeded
Connection closed by foreign host.
```

As you can see in the listing, after the `smtpd_timeout` value has been reached, Postfix terminates the SMTP connection with the remote host. Each session that is timed-out appears as an entry in the `maillog` log file:

```
Jan 16 14:29:06 shadrach postfix/smtpd[17040]: timeout after HELO from
➥ localhost[127.0.0.1]
```

CAUTION

Be careful not to set this value too low. Many Internet connections experience normal delays in transmission. If you see lots of timeout entries in the mail log, it is a good indication that the `smtpd_timeout` value is too low.

The smtpd_error_sleep_time Parameter

The smtpd_error_sleep_time parameter inserts an artificial delay when responding to SMTP errors from remote hosts. You may be wondering how inserting an artificial delay in an SMTP session increases performance.

Sometimes remote hosts use MTA software that easily becomes confused during an SMTP session. If that MTA receives an SMTP error message that it was not anticipating (such as the timeout error shown in the previous section), it may immediately disconnect the session, only to start up an identical SMTP session and generate the same error. This situation creates a constant loop of connecting and disconnecting until either the remote MTA gives up, or the administrator for the remote MTA realizes the problem and stops it.

To prevent this endless cycle, the smtpd_error_sleep_time places a delay of a set number of seconds before Postfix returns the SMTP error code. This is often enough time for the remote MTA to "gather its wits" and realize that something is wrong, preventing the error loop situation.

The smtpd_soft_error_limit Parameter

The smtpd_soft_error_limit parameter attempts to detect when a remote MTA becomes confused. This value is set to represent the number of SMTP errors the remote MTA may create before Postfix inserts a forced delay in the SMTP session. You can control the number of seconds of delay with the error_count parameter.

This is a fairly sensitive trigger that indicates to Postfix that the remote MTA is having problems. If the problems persist, Postfix uses the smtpd_hard_error_limit parameter as an upper limit.

The smtpd_hard_error_limit Parameter

The smtpd_hard_error_limit parameter specifies an upper limit to the number of SMTP errors allowed by Postfix in one SMTP session. When this limit is reached, Postfix automatically disconnects the SMTP client and ends the session.

Outbound Message Controls

Postfix can also control the behavior of outbound messages using parameters in the main.cf file. How Postfix sends messages to remote hosts can also greatly affect the performance of the mail server. You can modify these parameters to change how Postfix delivers messages to remote hosts.

By default, Postfix places restrictions on the number of simultaneous SMTP connections it can establish with a single remote host. This is used to attempt to be a good network neighbor. If a large amount of mail is queued for a single remote host, Postfix prevents the "thundering herd" syndrome, where it bombards the remote host with SMTP sessions until its mail queue is empty.

Instead, Postfix limits the number of initial SMTP connections it establishes. If it detects that the remote host is processing those connections properly, it gradually increases the number of concurrent connections up to a set number, or until the message queue is empty.

The parameters used to set these limitations are located in the `main.cf` configuration file, and you can tweak them to improve overall server performance. The following sections describe these parameters.

The `initial_destination_concurrency` Parameter

The initial number of concurrent SMTP sessions Postfix will establish with a remote host is defined by the `initial_destination_concurrency` parameter. The default value for this parameter is 2.

Postfix starts off with two concurrent SMTP sessions with the remote host. If the remote host handles these sessions without any delays or errors, Postfix attempts to increase the number of concurrent sessions (if it has more mail to send to the host).

The `default_destination_concurrency_limit` Parameter

The `default_destination_concurrency_limit` parameter defines the maximum number of concurrent SMTP sessions that can be established with any remote host. This parameter is related to the `smtp maxprocess` parameter in the `master.cf` configuration file. The maximum number of concurrent SMTP sessions cannot exceed the `maxprocess` value set for the maximum number of `smtp` client processes. Thus, if the default `maxprocess` value of 50 is used, setting the `default_destination_concurrency_limit` greater than 50 has no effect.

You can also modify this parameter to apply to a specific transport type. For example, you can use the `local_destination_concurrency_limit` parameter to limit the number of concurrent messages being delivered to the same recipient. This value should be low since each user's mailbox can only be accessed by one process at a time.

Alternatively, you can set different values for the `smtp_destination_concurrency_limit` and `uucp_destination_concurrency_limit` parameters to reflect different choices for different transport types.

CAUTION

Remember that increasing this value not only affects the performance of your mail server, but it may also affect the performance of any destination mail servers. Do not attempt to flood the destination mail servers with too many SMTP connections.

The `default_destination_recipient_limit` Parameter

Much like the `smtpd_recipient_limit` parameter, you can use the `default_destination_recipient_limit` parameter to limit the number of recipients sent in a single message to a remote host. The default value provided is 50.

You can increase the overall destination recipient limit or increase the value individually for each transport type. Remember that the destination mail server may also limit the number of recipients that it receives per message as well.

Unreachable Hosts

Another performance factor is how Postfix handles undeliverable messages. Postfix uses a set algorithm for handling messages that have been rejected or refused for various reasons. It attempts to determine the cause for the rejection and acts accordingly. A flaw either in the message or in the receiving host causes rejection.

If Postfix thinks that the remote host is having problems, it places the rejected message in the `deferred` message queue with a future timestamp (the amount of time passed since the message arrived is simply added to the current time and assigned to the deferred message). This prevents Postfix from processing the message again until the timestamp is current, thus forcing a delay in attempting to resend the message. The receiving host is marked as being unreachable, so any additional messages destined for it are also deferred for a set amount of time.

If Postfix thinks that the individual message is a problem, it again places the rejected message in the `deferred` message queue with the same timestamp management as outlined above. In this scenario, the remote host is not marked as being unreachable, so any additional messages destined for the host are processed normally.

Each of these functions involves delays that can be controlled by `main.cf` parameters. The following sections describe these parameters.

The `queue_run_delay` Parameter

The `queue_run_delay` parameter sets the time interval (in seconds) that Postfix scans the `deferred` message queue for messages to be delivered. The default value for this is 1,000 seconds.

You can use this parameter to control how Postfix handles deferred messages in general. If your e-mail server handles large quantities of e-mail, you may want to concentrate on processing new messages in the `active` message queue and place a lower priority on messages that have been previously rejected. Often mailing lists contain outdated e-mail addresses that bounce when Postfix attempts to deliver them. Instead of re-trying right away, you can defer these messages to allow Postfix to continue processing new messages.

The `maximal_queue_lifetime` Parameter

The `maximal_queue_lifetime` parameter sets the amount of time (in days) that a message remains in the `deferred` message queue before being returned as undeliverable. The default value is 5 days. Once this value is reached, Postfix returns the message to the sender.

Again, if you are running a mail server that has the possibility of generating lots of bounced messages, it may be beneficial for you to decrease this value so that Postfix does not continue attempting to deliver a message to a bad address.

CAUTION

Use this parameter with caution. It may be tempting to set it to just one day, but that could cause problems. Any messages sent to mail servers that happen to be down for a day for repairs would get returned to the sender as undeliverable. It is best to allow at least two days for delivery attempts.

The `minimal_backoff_time` Parameter

The `minimal_backoff_time` parameter sets one value that has two uses: the minimum amount of time used to hold a message in the `deferred` message queue and the minimum amount of time for which a host can be marked unreachable. The default value for this parameter is 1,000 seconds.

As mentioned earlier, normally the amount of time since a deferred message was first received is used for the backoff time. If this value is less than the `minimal_backoff_time` value, the `minimal_backoff_time` value is used instead.

The `maximal_backoff_time` Parameter

The `maximal_backoff_time` value sets an upper limit to the amount of time a message is left in the `deferred` message queue without a delivery attempt. The default value for this parameter is 4,000 seconds. If you want deferred messages re-processed more quickly, you can decrease this value. If your e-mail environment does not want deferred messages processed quickly, you can increase this value.

The `qmgr_message_recipient_limit` Parameter

The `qmgr_message_recipient_limit` parameter places an upper limit on the size of many in-memory queue manager data structures. This includes values such as the number of recipients that can be specified on a single message. The default value for this parameter is 1000.

This parameter affects several things. It directly controls the amount of memory that the `qmgr` program uses. The more recipients that can be included on a single message, the more memory `qmgr` must have available to it for handling the required data structures. Decreasing this value helps conserve system memory at the expense of generating additional messages.

Tuning the Unix System

In addition to tuning Postfix parameters, the e-mail administrator can use Unix system tuning techniques to attempt to increase the performance of the Postfix mail server. This section describes two common techniques used on Unix systems to increase system performance. They both equally apply to mail servers.

Asynchronous Versus Synchronous Disk Access

Many Unix systems can use several different types of filesystems to store data on hard disks. Each filesystem type has a specific method of organizing and storing files on the hard disk. Linux systems normally use the `ext2` filesystem type, whereas most BSD-based systems (such as FreeBSD) use the `ufs` filesystem type.

The Unix `mount` program initializes the connection between the filesystem and the OS. Once a filesystem is mounted, various processes and users on the machine can access it. When mounting a filesystem, the server can specify different parameters that affect how data is read from and written to the hard disk. The system administrator can modify these parameters to possibly increase disk performance on the server.

The parameter that affects performance the most is the `async` parameter. Allowing a server to use asynchronous disk access increases disk I/O several times over synchronous disk access.

In synchronous disk I/O, each block of data destined for the disk drive is placed in a data buffer and immediately written to the disk. This helps ensure data integrity by minimizing the time the data is vulnerable to system crashes (the time that it is in the data buffer).

In asynchronous disk I/O, each block of data destined for the disk drive is also placed in a data buffer, but the data buffer is not written to the disk immediately. Instead, the operating system waits a set amount of time and allows multiple blocks of data to be placed in data buffers before writing the entire bunch to the disk. This method allows for fewer disk writes that use larger blocks of data.

The downside to asynchronous disk writing is that the data waiting in the data buffers is vulnerable to system crashes. If the data is not yet written to disk and the system crashes, it will be lost and the file it was intended for could become corrupt.

Different Unix systems use different defaults for disk access. Linux systems use asynchronous disk access by default, whereas FreeBSD systems use synchronous disk access by default. Once you decide on the method of disk access that is appropriate for your environment, you can either accept the defaults or change them using the `mount` command.

Different Unix distributions use different `mount` programs. The following section describes the format of the `mount` command found on most Linux distributions.

Using `mount` Interactively

The `mount` command can have many different formats. The most often used format is

```
mount [-fnrsvw] [-t vfstype] [-o options] device dir
```

This format allows the administrator to specify several different command-line options, including the filesystem type with the `-t` option, mounting options with the `-o` option, the specific *`device`* the filesystem is located on, and the specific directory (*`dir`*) to mount the filesystem at. Table 22.1 lists the different options that are available for the mount command.

TABLE 22.1 Command-Line Options Used for the mount Command

Option	*Description*
-f	Performs all background processes but does not actually mount the filesystem
-n	Mounts the filesystem without creating an entry in /etc/mtab
-r	Mounts the filesystem in read-only mode
-s	Tolerates minor mounting errors when mounting a filesystem
-v	Uses verbose mode
-w	Mounts the filesystem in read/write mode
-t <*fs_type*>	Specifies the filesystem type
-o	Specifies various mounting options

Besides the mount command-line options, the -o option allows the administrator to list specific mounting options for the filesystem. Table 22.2 lists these options.

TABLE 22.2 Mounting Options Used for the mount Command

Option	*Description*
async	Mounts the filesystem using asynchronous I/O
atime	Updates the inode access time for each file access
auto	Allows the filesystem to be mounted using the -a option
defaults	Specifies a combination of the rw, suid, dev, exec, auto, nouser, and async options
dev	Interprets character or block special devices on the filesystem
exec	Permits execution of binary files on the filesystem
remount	Attempts to mount an already mounted filesystem (often used to change the mount options)
ro	Mounts the filesystem in read-only mode
rw	Mounts the filesystem in read/write mode
suid	Allows suid or guid identifier bits to be set
sync	Mounts the filesystem using synchronous I/O
user	Allows any system user to mount the filesystem

In addition to these options, you can use the atime, auto, dev, exec, suid, and user options with the prefix no to specify the respective opposite effects.

Once the filesystem is mounted, an entry is created in /etc/mtab to document the mounting (unless of course the -n option is used). These entries allow the administrator to issue commands that display what devices are currently mounted and their status.

Mounting Drives at Boot Time

Unix uses the `mount` command at boot time on all of the filesystems specified in the `/etc/fstab` file. Listing 22.5 shows a sample `/etc/fstab` file from a Mandrake Linux system.

LISTING 22.5 Sample `/etc/fstab` File

```
/dev/sdb1      /              ext2    defaults          1 1
/dev/sda1      /boot          ext2    defaults          1 2
/dev/sdc1      /home          ext2    defaults          1 2
/dev/sdc5      /usr           ext2    defaults          1 2
/dev/sda5      /var           ext2    defaults          1 2
/dev/sda6      swap           swap    defaults          0 0
/dev/fd0       /mnt/floppy    auto    sync,user,noauto,nosuid,nodev 0 0
/dev/cdrom     /mnt/cdrom     auto    user,noauto,nosuid,exec,nodev,ro 0 0
none           /proc          proc    defaults          0 0
none           /dev/pts       devpts  mode=0622         0 0
```

The `/etc/fstab` file lists each device to be mounted on a separate line, along with the related `mount` command options. On this particular Unix system, the `/var` directory, which contains the Postfix message queues and the mail mailboxes, is a separate filesystem and is mounted using the Linux `defaults` option, which includes using asynchronous disk I/O. If the filesystem is not mounted using asynchronous disk I/O, you must add the asynchronous `mount` parameter to the pertinent line in the `/etc/fstab` file.

CAUTION

Whereas using asynchronous disk I/O increases disk performance, it does so at the expense of disk integrity during system crashes. If your e-mail environment requires integrity of all e-mail messages, do not use asynchronous disk I/O to increase performance.

Asynchronous Versus Synchronous Log Entries

As mentioned in Chapter 13, "Postfix Server Administration," Postfix generates log entries that are logged by the Unix system logger program (usually `syslogd`). Each log entry must be placed in a designated text file by the `syslogd` program as messages are processed. Depending on the amount of message traffic, this can become a limiting factor in both sending and receiving messages.

Much like the disk access method described earlier, the `syslogd` program allows for two methods of writing data to files. The *synchronous* method writes the log entries to a data buffer and immediately writes the buffer to the disk, usually after each entry. The *asynchronous* method writes the log entries to a data buffer but waits for a specified amount of time before writing the buffer to the disk. This allows for fewer, more efficient disk writes per log entry.

By default, the syslogd program performs synchronous writes to the designated log file. This can significantly decrease performance on heavily used servers.

As shown in Chapter 13, the /etc/syslog.conf file controls what events are logged and how they are logged. By specifying the mail event and pointing it to a filename, you create a specific log file for all mail events on the server. To allow the syslogd program to perform asynchronous writes to the log file, you can add a dash (-) to the beginning of the log file name. An example of this is

```
mail.*                              -/var/log/maillog
```

After adding the dash to the filename, you must restart the syslogd program by sending it a SIGHUP signal using either the killall or kill programs:

```
killall -HUP syslogd
```

Now all mail log entries will be buffered by syslogd and written asynchronously to the mail log file. This should increase the overall performance of Postfix.

CAUTION

If your Postfix environment requires integrity of the mail log files, do not use asynchronous log file writing. Should the server crash, it is possible for some mail log entries to not get written to the log file.

Testing Postfix Performance

Often when testing different configuration options, you may need to determine the performance of your Postfix server. Venema has included two programs with the Postfix software that you can use to help provide benchmark tests for your configurations.

The smtp-sink program can receive massive quantities of messages sent from a Postfix server, and the smtp-source program can send massive quantities of messages to a Postfix server. The following sections describe these programs.

The smtp-sink Program

The smtp-sink program is included in the Postfix source code distribution to allow administrators to test the e-mail sending capabilities of their Postfix server. The smtp-sink program receives and discards messages sent via either an IP interface or a Unix pipe. Each method has its own format:

```
smtp-sink [-cLpv] [-w delay] [host]:port backlog
smtp-sink [-clpv] [-w delay] unix:pathname backlog
```

The command-line options used with `smtp-sink` are described in Table 22.3.

TABLE 22.3 `smtp-sink` Command-Line Options

Option	*Description*
`-c`	Displays a count of SMTP `QUIT` commands received
`-L`	Uses LMTP instead of SMTP
`-p`	Disables ESMTP command pipelining
`-v`	Verbose mode. Shows the SMTP conversations
`-w` *`delay`*	Waits *`delay`* seconds during the SMTP `DATA` command

In addition to the command-line options, the `smtp-sink` command line specifies either the IP address and port number to listen for SMTP connections on or the Unix pathname of the pipe file. If you intend to use the normal SMTP IP port (25), you must run `smtp-sink` as root.

Also, you can specify a *`backlog`* value to use when calling the Unix `listen()` function. The *`backlog`* value determines the number of concurrent SMTP sessions `smtp-sink` will handle.

When tuning Postfix parameters for sending mail messages, you can test delivery speeds using the `smtp-sink` program on either the local host or a remote host. If using the local host, remember to comment out the `smtpd` process from the Postfix `master.cf` configuration file or Postfix will conflict with `smtp-sink`.

To start `smtp-sink` with 100 SMTP listening sockets, you can use the command

```
/usr/bin/smtp-sink -c :25 100
```

Once `smtp-sink` is started, you can test the Postfix server by using different configuration parameters and sending messages to the `smtp-sink` server. All of the messages received are discarded by `smtp-sink`. You can then compare delivery speeds using different configuration options in Postfix to determine which configuration works best for your environment.

The `smtp-source` Program

The `smtp-source` program is included with Postfix to allow administrators to test receiving messages with various Postfix configurations. The `smtp-source` program can send multiple test messages to a Postfix server in various modes, using either an IP connection or a Unix pipe connection. Again, each connectivity method has its own format:

```
smtp-source [options] host[:port]
smtp-source [options] unix:pathname
```

The smtp-source program has more options than the smtp-sink program, allowing the administrator to control the test environment more precisely. Table 22.4 shows the options available to use with the smtp-source program.

TABLE 22.4 smtp-source Options

Option	*Description*
-c	Displays a running count of SMTP DATA commands sent.
-C *count*	If a RESET command is received, tries *count* times before giving up.
-d	Doesn't disconnect after each message, continues using the same SMTP connection.
-f *from*	Specifies the sender of the test mail message. The default is the address foo@myhostname.
-o	Uses old mode, which doesn't send HELO commands or message headers.
-l *length*	Sends test messages that are *length* bytes long.
-L	Uses LMTP instead of SMTP.
-m *count*	Sends *count* number of messages; the default is 1.
-r *count*	Sends the message to *count* number of recipients. Each recipient address is generated by prepending a number to the given recipient address. The default is 1 per transaction.
-s *count*	Runs *count* number of SMTP sessions concurrently. The default is 1.
-t *to*	Uses the address *to* as the message recipient. The default is the address foo@myhostname.
-R *interval*	Waits a random amount of time no greater than *interval* seconds between sending messages.
-w *interval*	Waits exactly *interval* seconds between sending messages.

To test the receiving ability of a Postfix server, you can run the smtp-source program using a valid recipient address on the Postfix server:

```
smtp-source -c -l 1000 -m 100 -s 20 -t rich@shadrach.ispnet1.net
```

This command sends 100 1,000-byte messages to the username rich on the machine shadrach.ispnet1.net. You can then monitor the server to determine how the Postfix configuration handled the flood of new messages.

To test the Postfix configuration's smtpd settings, you can use the -s option with smtp_source to change the number of concurrently sent messages.

If the master.cf file on the Postfix server specifies a maxprocess value for smtpd processes less than the -s value, you should see that all of the smtpd processes will be used to receive messages. You can then determine how much system load is required to support all of the smtpd processes running.

Summary

Maintaining a Postfix server for thousands of users can be a challenging experience. Fortunately the mail administrator can change things in the Postfix configuration to help speed things up.

The `master.cf` file controls the maximum number of processes a Postfix program can have running at a single time. Servers that process thousands of users (or even just a few users with thousands of mail messages) should be modified to increase the number of processes allowed to run. Servers that accept lots of incoming SMTP connections should increase the `smtpd maxprocess` value. Servers that send out lots of messages to remote SMTP hosts should increase the `smtp maxprocess` value.

Postfix also controls message throughput via several different parameter settings in the `main.cf` configuration file. The mail administrator can fine-tune the Postfix system by modifying both inbound and outbound SMTP session parameters. Postfix also contains configuration parameters to help the mail administrator handle mail for hosts that are not responding.

Besides tuning the Postfix configuration, the mail administrator can also tune Unix system parameters. Many Unix distributions perform synchronous disk writes by default. This method provides the highest level of reliability, but it is also the slowest. In environments where high reliability is not an issue, the mail administrator can use asynchronous disk writes to speed up mail processing on the server.

Likewise, the mail administrator can also configure how the Unix logging program writes messages to the mail log. By default, most systems are configured to perform synchronous writes to the mail log. This requires that each mail log entry be written individually. By using asynchronous writes for the mail log, entries are cached and written in batches to increase performance.

Finally, the Postfix distribution package includes two programs that you can use to test the performance throughput of the Postfix server. The `smtp-sink` program can receive SMTP messages in a quick manner to test SMTP server performance. The `smtp-source` program can send messages via SMTP in a quick manner to test SMTP client performance.

CHAPTER 23

Common Postfix Problems

Sometimes, while using Postfix, problems occur. With the vast number of devices involved with communicating between hosts on the Internet, there's plenty of opportunity for things to go wrong. In addition to delivery problems, self-inflicted problems also occur. Mail administrators must often experiment with configuration options to get Postfix to work just right in their particular e-mail environment. Each new experimental configuration can produce interesting results that might need to be examined and altered.

When things do go wrong for whatever reason, it is good to have a plan on how to troubleshoot the problem. Postfix provides several good methods for troubleshooting. This chapter discusses some techniques to use when experiencing problems with the Postfix package.

Handling Undelivered Mail

One of the biggest problems encountered by Postfix administrators is undelivered mail. This problem can occur for many reasons, but it is often due to strange behavior from a remote SMTP host.

Postfix has some utilities that can be used by the mail administrator to diagnose mail delivery problems. This section describes how the administrator can go about the diagnosis.

Listing Undelivered Mail

You can check the status of messages in the Postfix message queues using the `mailq` command. The `mailq` command reads all messages waiting to be delivered in the various Postfix message queues and prints a brief synopsis of each message. Listing 23.1 shows an example of a `mailq` command session.

LISTING 23.1 Sample `mailq` Session

```
[rich@shadrach]$ mailq
-Queue ID- --Size-- ----Arrival Time---- -Sender/Recipient-------
A0683C352       322 Mon Jan 29 09:52:06  rich@shadrach.ispnet1.net
                  (connect to meshach.isp.net[192.168.1.1]: Connection refused)
                                         rich@isp.net

DD66EC365       329 Mon Jan 29 09:52:57  rich@shadrach.ispnet1.net
                   (connect to meshach.isp.net[192.168.1.1]: Connection refused)
                                         jessica@isp.net

-- 0 Kbytes in 2 Requests.
```

The output from the sample `mailq` command shows that two messages are currently waiting in the Postfix mail queues. Postfix already attempted to deliver both messages, but the delivery attempts failed. The `mailq` command shows the reason for the delivery failures, along with other pertinent information for each message. The next step could be for the administrator to view the actual message that is in the message queue.

Displaying Undelivered Mail

You can display the messages by using the `postcat` command, which can interpret the Postfix message syntax used to store messages in their respective queues. Using the Queue ID name listed using the `mailq` command, you can display the message contents. An example of this is shown in Listing 23.2.

LISTING 23.2 Sample postcat Session

```
[root@shadrach]# ls -al /var/spool/postfix/deferred
total 5
drwx------    2 postfix  root         2048 Jan 29 09:52 .
drwxr-xr-x   17 root     root         1024 Feb  1  2000 ..
-rwx------    1 postfix  postfix       474 Jan 29 10:08 A0683C352
-rwx------    1 postfix  postfix       485 Jan 29 10:09 DD66EC365

[root@shadrach]# postcat /var/spool/postfix/deferred/A0683C352
*** ENVELOPE RECORDS /var/spool/postfix/deferred/A0683C352 ***
message_size:             322              122                1
arrival_time: Mon Jan 29 09:52:06 2001
sender: rich@shadrach.ispnet1.net
recipient: rich@isp.net
*** MESSAGE CONTENTS /var/spool/postfix/deferred/A0683C352 ***
Received: by shadrach.ispnet1.net (Postfix, from userid 500)
        id A0683C352; Mon, 29 Jan 2001 09:52:06 -0500 (EST)
To: rich@isp.net
Subject: test message
Message-Id: <20010129145206.A0683C352@shadrach.ispnet1.net>
Date: Mon, 29 Jan 2001 09:52:06 -0500 (EST)
From: rich@shadrach.ispnet1.net (Rich Blum)

test message
*** HEADER EXTRACTED /var/spool/postfix/deferred/A0683C352 ***
return_receipt:
errors_to: rich@shadrach.ispnet1.net
*** MESSAGE FILE END /var/spool/postfix/deferred/A0683C352 ***
```

The sample session shown in Listing 23.2 first lists all of the messages in the `deferred` message queue. As expected, the two messages shown in the `mailq` command appear in the listing. Next, the `postcat` command displays the contents of one of the messages. As shown, the complete message is displayed, along with the message header information. The administrator can use this information to identify the mail message and determine the next course of action.

By default, Postfix attempts to deliver messages in the `deferred` message queue following a backoff algorithm. This algorithm uses increasing amounts of time between delivery attempts. The more delivery failures, the longer the amount of time between delivery attempts. Eventually (by a time specified by the administrator) Postfix gives up trying to deliver the message and returns it to the sender. If the mail administrator wants to bypass the backoff algorithm, he can decide to manually attempt to deliver the mail message.

Resending Undelivered Mail

By default, Postfix attempts to deliver the messages in the `deferred` message queue following a set backoff algorithm. If you need to attempt the delivery immediately, you can use the `sendmail` Postfix command using the `-q` option:

```
/usr/bin/sendmail -q
```

This command triggers Postfix to attempt to deliver any messages in the `active` and `deferred` message queues. You can then use the `mailq` command to determine whether any messages are still left in the message queues. Postfix then handles any messages left by using the normal backoff algorithm for delivery attempts.

Using the `postconf` Program

Often the source of Postfix problems is a misconfigured `main.cf` configuration file. Items that the mail administrator thought were configured were not recognized by Postfix due to typos and misplaced commas.

You can use the `postconf` command to determine what exactly Postfix thinks its configuration is. The `postconf` command was described in detail in Chapter 6, "Installing Postfix."

By default, `postconf` prints out a complete listing of all the `main.cf` parameter settings used by the Postfix server. This is a lengthy list of parameters, but it might help save you hours of troubleshooting a misspelled configuration word. It pays to go over the parameters to ensure that Postfix is configured the way you thought it was.

The default `postconf` command prints out all parameters, even ones that are initialized from default values. Alternatively, you can display only the parameters that have been changed from their default value in the `main.cf` file. You can use the `-n` parameter to display all of the non-default values. Listing 23.3 shows a sample output from the `postconf -n` command.

LISTING 23.3 Sample postconf -n Output

```
[root@shadrach]# postconf -n
alias_maps = hash:/etc/postfix/aliases
command_directory = /usr/sbin
daemon_directory = /usr/libexec/postfix
debug_peer_level = 2
default_destination_concurrency_limit = 10
local_destination_concurrency_limit = 2
mail_owner = postfix
queue_directory = /var/spool/postfix
```

Again, you should examine each of the non-default values listed for accuracy. Also, not only should you pay attention to what parameters are listed, but also to what parameters are absent from the list. You might realize that a parameter you thought was changed in the `main.cf` configuration file did not take effect. Remember, each time you change a parameter in the `main.cf` file, you must use the reload option of the `postfix` command.

Another useful `postconf` option is the `-m` parameter. This parameter displays all of the database types that are configured into Postfix. Errors often occur from administrators trying to use databases not supported by their compiled Postfix system. Listing 23.4 shows a sample output from the `postconf -m` command.

LISTING 23.4 Sample postconf -m Output

```
[root@shadrach]# postconf -m
nis
regexp
environ
btree
unix
hash
```

The sample output in Listing 23.4 shows that this particular Postfix installation does not support MySQL and OpenLDAP databases. Thus, these database types cannot be used to support alias or virtual tables in the Postfix system.

Troubleshooting Using the Mail Log

Chapter 13, "Postfix Server Administration," described the Unix `syslogd` program and how Postfix uses it to log mail activity. The mail log file is the best tool the administrator has to analyze mail delivery problems. Examining the mail log file can identify most Postfix problems. This section describes how to identify errors in the Postfix mail log and how to selectively increase the capability of individual Postfix programs to produce more verbose mail log entries.

Identifying Postfix Errors

Mail problems are usually marked as such by the Postfix logging facility. Postfix uses four different levels of error flags to identify problems that are encountered with the mail system. Table 23.1 lists the different error levels used.

TABLE 23.1 Postfix Log Error Levels

Error	*Description*
`warning`	Something out of the ordinary has happened that may affect the delivery of a single message, but mail delivery as a whole has not been affected.
`error`	Something has gone wrong with a Postfix program, but Postfix will still attempt to process messages.
`fatal`	Something has gone wrong with a Postfix program that will affect all mail deliveries.
`panic`	Something has gone wrong with the host Unix system that will affect all mail deliveries.

The error level is included on the mail log entry line after the Postfix program that produced it:

```
Feb  2 12:07:32 shadrach postfix/pickup[5591]: warning: 38EF0C352:
➥ message has been queued for 1 days
```

This sample error message indicates that the Postfix `pickup` program generated it. It indicates a warning that a particular mail message has been in the `undeliverable` message queue for a day.

It is always a good idea to scan your mail log file every day looking for one of the error level keywords. You can easily do this using the command

```
egrep '(warning|error|fatal|panic):' /var/log/maillog
```

You need to use the location where your particular mail log entries are being written in place of the `/var/log/maillog` entry. You can even create a Unix cron job to automatically perform this task every evening and e-mail out the results. A sample script to do this could be

```
#!/bin/sh
egrep '(warning|error|fatal|panic):' /var/log/maillog | mail rich@ispnet1.net
```

You can save this script in a file, such as `/root/mailcheck`, and place an entry in root's crontab to run the script at a set time every day:

```
0 23 * * * /root/mailcheck
```

This crontab entry runs the `mailcheck` script you created every evening at 11:00 p.m., checking the mail log and mailing the results to `rich@ispnet1.net`.

CAUTION

Remember that many Unix systems rotate their syslog logs. The existing log is moved to a different location, and the log file is set to zero bytes. You should ensure that the `mailcheck` script runs before the mail log is rotated, or you will not get the desired results.

By running the script as a cron job every evening, you can then simply check the mail message sent to your e-mail account. If no Postfix errors occur for the day, the mail message should be empty.

You should attend to any error messages. Some error messages just indicate a temporary mail delivery failure:

```
Feb  2 09:07:32 shadrach postfix/pickup[5591]: warning: 38EF0C352:
➥ message has been queued for 1 days
```

No immediate action needs to be taken unless the administrator wants to manually attempt to deliver the message. An excessive number of warning messages can mean a larger problem is looming on the horizon.

Other times, error messages point out errors that prevent Postfix from operating properly at all:

```
Feb 2 09:46:13 shadrach postfix/sendmail[23062]: fatal: Queue report
➥ unavailable - mail system is down
```

It is the job of the mail administrator to watch the error logs and determine when intervention is required, such as in the example of a fatal Postfix error.

Using Verbose Logging Mode

When you have determined that there is definitely a problem with the Postfix server but you do not know where or what sort, you can use verbose logging to isolate the problem. As described in Chapter 13, Postfix provides three levels of logging verbosity.

By default, Postfix provides simple informational messages to the server `syslog` program. Each program used in the Postfix server message process logs a message to the system logger. Listing 23.5 shows an example of normal process log entries.

LISTING 23.5 Normal Postfix log entries

```
Feb  5 11:59:21 shadrach postfix/pickup[15182]: 9EFD6C352: uid=500 from=<rich>
Feb  5 11:59:21 shadrach postfix/cleanup[15266]: 9EFD6C352:
➥ message-id=<20010205165921.9EFD6C352@ispnet1.net>
Feb  5 11:59:21 shadrach postfix/qmgr[5592]: 9EFD6C352:
➥ from=<rich@ispnet1.net>, size=334, nrcpt=1 (queue active)
```

LISTING 23.5 Continued

```
Feb  5 11:59:26 shadrach postfix/smtp[15268]: 9EFD6C352:
➥ to=<richard.blum@ispnet2.net>, relay=meshach.ispnet3.net[192.168.1.9],
➥ delay=5, status=sent (250 OK)
```

As you can see in the normal listing, each Postfix process that handles the message logs an entry in the system logger. The `pickup`, `cleanup`, `qmgr`, and `smtp` programs all logged informational entries to the system logger.

As shown in Chapter 13, you can modify the Postfix `master.cf` configuration file to indicate higher levels of verbose logging for the different Postfix programs. By appending one or two `-v` options to the end of the command name, you can increase the verbose logging. Each `-v` added increases the amount of additional text that is logged.

You should use verbose logging sparingly. Turning on verbose logging for every process would result in log files so large they would become useless. Instead, I recommend trying to increase the verbose logging for a single process at a time until you can determine the source of a particular problem.

For example, to increase the level of verbose logging for the Postfix `smtp` program, you can modify the `smtp` entry in the `master.cf` configuration file:

```
smtp      unix  -   -   n   -   -   smtp -v
```

This indicates that the `smtp` program should use the second level of verbose logging. You can add a second `-v` option after the first one to set the program to use level 3 verbose logging.

The results of increasing the verbose logging are dramatic. Instead of a simple, single information entry in the log, the program provides many detailed entries. When `smtp` verbose logging is enabled, a single message to a remote host generates 150 separate entries in the mail log file. Each step of the SMTP process is logged in detail to the log file.

Listing 23.6 shows a partial listing of the 150 entries made using two levels of verbose logging for the `smtp` program. The timestamp and hostname parts of the log entries have been deleted to help simplify the output..

LISTING 23.6 Partial Verbose Logging Log File

```
postfix/smtp[15731]: < meshach.ispnet.net[192.168.1.2]: 220 meshach.ispnet.net
➥ ESMTP Server (Microsoft Exchange Internet Mail Service 5.5.265) ready
postfix/smtp[15731]: > meshach.ispnet.net[192.168.1.2]: EHLO ispnet2.net
postfix/smtp[15731]: < meshach.ispnet.net[192.168.1.2]: 250-meshach.ispnet.net
➥ Hello [192.168.1.15]
postfix/smtp[15731]: < meshach.ispnet.net[192.168.1.2]: 250-XEXCH50
postfix/smtp[15731]: < meshach.ispnet.net[192.168.1.2]: 250-HELP
postfix/smtp[15731]: < meshach.ispnet.net[192.168.1.2]: 250-ETRN
```

LISTING 23.6 Continued

```
postfix/smtp[15731]: < meshach.ispnet.net[192.168.1.2]: 250-DSN
postfix/smtp[15731]: < meshach.ispnet.net[192.168.1.2]: 250-SIZE 5120000
postfix/smtp[15731]: < meshach.ispnet.net[192.168.1.2]: 250-AUTH LOGIN
postfix/smtp[15731]: < meshach.ispnet.net[192.168.1.2]: 250 AUTH=LOGIN
postfix/smtp[15731]: server features: 0x9
postfix/smtp[15731]: lookup ispnet.net type 15 flags 0
postfix/smtp[15731]: dns_query: ispnet.net (MX): Host not found
postfix/smtp[15731]: lookup ispnet.net type 1 flags 0
postfix/smtp[15731]: dns_query: ispnet.net (A):Host not found
postfix/smtp[15731]: > meshach.ispnet.net[192.168.1.2]:
➥ MAIL FROM:<rich@ispnet2.net> SIZE=335
postfix/smtp[15731]: lookup ispnet.net type 15 flags 0
postfix/smtp[15731]: dns_query: ispnet.net (MX): OK
postfix/smtp[15731]: smtp_connect_addr: trying: meshach.ispnet.net[192.168.1.2]
postfix/smtp[15731]: < meshach.ispnet.net[192.168.1.2]
postfix/smtp[15731]: < meshach.ispnet.net[192.168.1.2]: 250 AUTH=LOGIN
postfix/smtp[15731]: > meshach.ispnet.net[192.168.1.2]: MAIL
➥ FROM:<rich@ispnet2.net> SIZE=335
postfix/smtp[15731]: lookup ispnet.net type 15 flags 0
postfix/smtp[15731]: dns_query: ispnet.net (MX): OK
postfix/smtp[15731]: dns_get_answer: type MX for ispnet.net
postfix/smtp[15731]: < meshach.ispnet.net[192.168.1.2]: 250 OK - mail
➥ from<rich@ispnet2.net>; can accomodate 335 bytes
postfix/smtp[15731]: > meshach.ispnet.net[192.168.1.2]: RCPT
➥ TO:<richard.blum@ispnet.net>
postfix/smtp[15731]: < meshach.ispnet.net[192.168.1.2]: 250 OK -
➥ Recipient <richard.blum@ispnet.net>
postfix/smtp[15731]: > meshach.ispnet.net[192.168.1.2]: DATA
postfix/smtp[15731]: < meshach.ispnet.net[192.168.1.2]: 354 Send data.
➥  End with CRLF.CRLF
postfix/smtp[15731]: > meshach.ispnet.net[192.168.1.2]: .
postfix/smtp[15731]: < meshach.ispnet.net[192.168.1.2]: 250 OK
postfix/smtp[15731]: 20546C352: to=<richard.blum@ispnet.net>,
➥ relay=meshach.ispnet.net[192.168.1.2], delay=5, status=sent (250 OK)
postfix/smtp[15731]: > meshach.ispnet.net[192.168.1.2]: QUIT
postfix/smtp[15731]: name_mask: resource
postfix/smtp[15731]: name_mask: software
postfix/smtp[15731]: deliver_request_final: send: "" 0
postfix/smtp[15731]: print string:
postfix/smtp[15731]: print int: 0
postfix/smtp[15731]: master_notify: status 1
postfix/smtp[15731]: connection closed
postfix/smtp[15731]: watchdog_stop: 0x80694d8
postfix/smtp[15731]: watchdog_start: 0x80694d8
```

The verbose log shows the entire SMTP connection details (minus the message body) between the two hosts. This can be extremely helpful when attempting to troubleshoot mail delivery problems with remote hosts.

Using `debug_peer_list`

Often there is just a single remote host that is causing trouble. Instead of having to turn verbose logging on for all SMTP processes as shown in the previous section, you can set verbose logging for a specific group of remote host addresses. This is possible using the `debug_peer_list` parameter in the `main.cf` configuration file.

Instead of using the `-v` parameter on the `smtp` program, you can set the address of the remote host(s) you want to monitor in the `debug_peer_list` parameter:

```
debug_peer_list = ispnet.net
```

To set the level of debugging, you can use the `debug_peer_level` parameter:

```
debug_peer_level = 1
```

This parameter specifies an amount that the normal verbose logging level should be increased by. Thus a value of 1 indicates to use level 2 verbose logging. This is equivalent to using one `-v` option in the `master.cf` file.

With these parameters set, an SMTP connection with the remote hosts specified in the `debug_peer_list` parameter is logged with a higher level of verbose logging.

CAUTION

Remember, if you are using the `debug_peer_list` parameter, do not use the `-v` option in the `master.cf` configuration file.

Troubleshooting Using a Debugger

As a last resort, Postfix allows you to use common Unix system debugger programs to watch exactly how Postfix is behaving during message delivery. This process is not for the novice but can be extremely useful for advanced administrators.

Many Unix systems include code debugger programs by default with their development environments. Common Unix debugger programs are

- `trace`
- `strace`

- truss
- ktrace

One of the most popular tracing programs used on the Linux platform is the strace program, currently maintained by Wichert Akkerman. strace can display all system calls, complete with variables, made by a running program. Most Linux distributions include a binary distribution package for the strace program. You can also download the strace package from the strace Web site:

```
http://www.wi.leidenuniv.nl/~wichert/strace/
```

At the time of this writing, the most current version of strace that could be downloaded is strace-4.2.tar.gz. Once downloaded, you can expand the package into a working directory and compile using the normal methods:

```
tar -zxvf strace-4.2.tar.gz -C /usr/local/src
cd /usr/local/src/strace-4.2
./configure
make
make install
```

This method compiles strace for your Unix distribution and places it in a common executable directory. Alternatively, Mandrake Linux 7.2 includes the strace binary distribution package. It is located in the RPMS directory on the distribution CD and can be installed using the standard rpm command:

```
rpm -Uvh strace-4.2-3mdk.i586.rpm
```

Once installed, you can use the strace command to trace any running program on the system. The following sections describe two different methods that can be used to trace Postfix processes.

Manual Debugging

You can use the strace command from the Unix command line to monitor programs that are already running on the system. The format of the strace command can be complicated:

```
strace  [ -dffhiqrtttTvxx ] [-a column] [-e expr] ...  [-o filename]
➥ [-p pid] ...  [-s strsize] [-u username  ] [command [ arg ...  ] ]

strace  -c  [-e expr] ...  [-O overhead] [-S sortby] [command [ arg ...  ] ]
```

Table 23.2 describes the command-line options and parameters that can be used with strace.

TABLE 23.2 `strace` Command-Line Options

Option	*Description*
`-c`	Counts time, calls, and errors for each system call and report summary
`-d`	Shows some debugging output of `strace` on the standard error pipe
`-f`	Traces child processes as they are created
`-ff`	Stores each traced child process in a separate filename denoted by `.pid`, where pid is the numeric process id
`-F`	Attempts to follow `vfork()` system calls
`-h`	Prints the help summary
`-i`	Prints the instruction pointer at the time of the system call
`-q`	Suppresses messages about attaching and detaching
`-r`	Prints a relative timestamp on each system call
`-t`	Prints the absolute timestamp on each trace line
`-tt`	Includes microseconds on the timestamp
`-ttt`	Includes microseconds and prints the time as number of seconds since the epoch
`-T`	Shows the time spent in each system call
`-v`	Prints unabbreviated versions of environment, stat, and termio calls
`-V`	Prints the `strace` version number
`-x`	Prints all non-ASCII strings in hexadecimal
`-xx`	Prints all strings in hexadecimal
`-a` *`column`*	Aligns return values in a specific column (default is 40)
`-e` *`expr`*	Uses a qualifying expression that modifies which events to trace or how to trace them
`-o` *`filename`*	Writes the trace output to the file *`filename`* instead of STDERR
`-O` *`overhead`*	Sets the overhead for tracing system calls to *`overhead`* microseconds
`-p` *`pid`*	Traces the process with process id *`pid`*
`-s` *`strsize`*	Limits the maximum string size to print (default is 32)
`-S` *`sortby`*	Sorts the output of the histogram by time, calls, name, or nothing (default is time)
`-u` *`username`*	Runs `strace` with the effective user id and group id of *`username`*

The `-e` option allows you to set parameters to limit the output of the `trace` program to specific events. Table 23.3 shows the events that can be matched.

TABLE 23.3 `trace` Event Matching

Option	*Description*
`-e trace=`*`set`*	Traces only the specified set of system calls
`-e trace=`*`file`*	Traces all system calls that use the filename *`file`* as an argument
`-e trace=process`	Traces all system calls that use process management
`-e trace=network`	Traces all system calls that are network related

TABLE 23.3 Continued

Option	*Description*
`-e trace=signal`	Traces all system calls that are signal related
`-e trace=ipc`	Traces all system calls that are IPC (inter-process communication) related
`-e abbrev=`*`set`*	Abbreviates the output from printing each member of large structures (default is abbrev=all)
`-e verbose=`*`set`*	Dereferences structures for the specified set of system calls (default is verbose=all)
`-e raw=`*`set`*	Prints raw, undecoded arguments for the specified set of system calls
`-e signal=`*`set`*	Traces only the specified subset of signals
`-e read=`*`set`*	Prints a full hexadecimal and ASCII dump of all the data read from file descriptors listed in the specified set
`-e write=`*`set`*	Prints a full hexadecimal and ASCII dump of all the data written to file descriptors listed in the specified set

By determining the PID number of the `qmgr` program, you can monitor the Postfix actions as messages are retrieved from the various message queues. You can use the standard Unix `ps` command to determine the PID of a running process:

```
[root@shadrach]# ps ax | grep qmgr
16071 ?        S      0:00 qmgr -l -t fifo -u
16239 pts/1    S      0:00 grep qmgr
[root@shadrach]# strace -o tracefile -p 16071
```

This example shows that once the `strace` program is running, it captures all system calls made by the `qmgr` program and stores the information in the file `tracefile`. Listing 23.7 shows an example of the `strace` output when watching the `qmgr` program while one local user sends a message to another local user.

LISTING 23.7 Sample `strace` Output

```
select(9, [3 4], [], [3 4], {282, 430000}) = 1 (in [4], left {122, 660000})
time(NULL)                              = 981486596
write(3, "\307>\0\0\0\0\0\0", 8)        = 8
read(4, "W", 1024)                      = 1
open("incoming", O_RDONLY|O_NONBLOCK|0x10000) = 6
fstat(6, {st_mode=S_IFDIR|0700, st_size=1024, ...}) = 0
fcntl(6, F_SETFD, FD_CLOEXEC)           = 0
write(3, "\307>\0\0\1\0\0\0", 8)        = 8
alarm(333)                              = 156
getdents(6, /* 3 entries */, 3933)      = 48
lstat("incoming/DD443C352", {st_mode=S_IFREG|0700, st_size=475, ...}) = 0
time(NULL)                              = 981486596
rename("incoming/DD443C352", "active/D/D/DD443C352") = 0
```

LISTING 23.7 Continued

```
open("active/D/D/DD443C352", O_RDWR)     = 7
flock(7, LOCK_EX|LOCK_NB)                = 0
lseek(7, 0, SEEK_CUR)                    = 0
read(7, "C/            320              12"..., 4096) = 475
time([981486596])                        = 981486596
getpid()                                 = 16071
rt_sigaction(SIGPIPE, {0x401152c4, [], 0x4000000}, {SIG_IGN}, 8) = 0
send(5, "<22>Feb  6 14:09:56 postfix/qmgr"..., 115, 0) = 115
rt_sigaction(SIGPIPE, {SIG_IGN}, NULL, 8) = 0
lseek(7, 445, SEEK_SET)                  = 445
read(7, "X\0r\0e\26rich@shadrach.ispnet1.netE\0", 4096) = 30
rmdir("defer/D/D/DD443C352")             = -1 ENOENT (No such file or directory)
socket(PF_UNIX, SOCK_STREAM, 0)          = 8
fcntl(8, F_GETFL)                        = 0x2 (flags O_RDWR)
fcntl(8, F_SETFL, O_RDWR)                = 0
connect(8, {sin_family=AF_UNIX, path=" private/rewrite"}, 110) = 0
time(NULL)                               = 981486596
fcntl(8, F_GETFD)                        = 0
fcntl(8, F_SETFD, FD_CLOEXEC)            = 0
time([981486596])                        = 981486596
time(NULL)                               = 981486596
select(9, NULL, [8], [8], {3600, 0})     = 1 (out [8], left {3600, 0})
write(8, "resolve\0rich@shadrach.ispnet1.net\0", 31) = 31
time(NULL)                               = 981486596
select(9, [8], NULL, [8], {3600, 0})     = 1 (in [8], left {3600, 0})
read(8, "local\0shadrach.ispnet1.net\0rich@sha"..., 4096) = 49
close(7)                                 = 0
time(NULL)                               = 981486596
select(9, [3 4 8], [], [3 4 8], {0, 0}) = 0 (Timeout)
time(NULL)                               = 981486596
alarm(333)                               = 333
socket(PF_UNIX, SOCK_STREAM, 0)          = 7
fcntl(7, F_GETFL)                        = 0x2 (flags O_RDWR)
fcntl(7, F_SETFL, O_RDWR|O_NONBLOCK)     = 0
connect(7, {sin_family=AF_UNIX, path="private/local"}, 110) = 0
time(NULL)                               = 981486596
time([981486596])                        = 981486596
getdents(6, /* 0 entries */, 3933)       = 0
close(6)                                 = 0
time(NULL)                               = 981486596
select(9, [3 4 8], [7], [3 4 7 8], {100, 0}) = 1 (out [7], left {100, 0})
time(NULL)                               = 981486596
fcntl(7, F_GETFL)                        = 0x802 (flags O_RDWR|O_NONBLOCK)
```

LISTING 23.7 Continued

```
fcntl(7, F_SETFL, O_RDWR)                = 0
alarm(333)                               = 333
time(NULL)                               = 981486596
select(9, [3 4 7 8], [], [3 4 7 8], {100, 0}) = 1 (in [7], left {99, 840000})
time(NULL)                               = 981486596
ioctl(7, FIONREAD, [2])                  = 0
time(NULL)                               = 981486596
select(8, [7], NULL, [7], {3600, 0})     = 1 (in [7], left {3600, 0})
read(7, "0\0", 4096)                     = 2
time(NULL)                               = 981486596
select(8, NULL, [7], [7], {3600, 0})     = 1 (out [7], left {3600, 0})
write(7, "3\0active\0DD443C352\000125\000320\0shadr"..., 130) = 130
time([981486596])                        = 981486596
alarm(333)                               = 333
time(NULL)                               = 981486596
select(9, [3 4 7 8], [], [3 4 7 8], {100, 0}) = 1 (in [7], left {99, 830000})
time(NULL)                               = 981486596
ioctl(7, FIONREAD, [3])                  = 0
time(NULL)                               = 981486596
select(8, [7], NULL, [7], {3600, 0})     = 1 (in [7], left {3600, 0})
read(7, "\0000\0", 4096)                 = 3
close(7)                                 = 0
stat("bounce/D/D/DD443C352", 0xbffff6ec) = -1 ENOENT (No such file or directory)
rmdir("active/D/D/DD443C352")            = -1 ENOTDIR (Not a directory)
unlink("active/D/D/DD443C352")           = 0
alarm(333)                               = 333
time(NULL)                               = 981486596
select(9, [3 4 8], [], [3 4 8], {100, 0} <unfinished ...>
```

As you can see, many system calls are used by the `qmgr` while processing just a single piece of mail. You can use this same method to monitor other running Postfix processes.

This example used the `strace` program to monitor an existing Postfix process. Unfortunately, many Postfix processes (such as `smtp` and `smtpd`) are spawned as needed by the Postfix `master` daemon. This makes it difficult for the administrator to monitor them.

Fortunately, Postfix provides an alternative method for using external debugger programs with Postfix processes.

Automatic Debugging

Postfix provides a method to automatically spawn an external debugger program when the `master` program calls a particular Postfix process. This allows the mail administrator to debug individual Postfix programs that are called dynamically by the Postfix system while messages are delivered.

Two things must be configured for Postfix to work with an external debugger. The first is an entry in the `master.cf` configuration file.

When the Postfix program name is defined in the command field, you must add the `-D` option to enable debugging for that program:

```
smtp       unix  -   -   n   -   -   smtp -D
```

Each Postfix program that you want to debug must have the `-D` option included in the command definition.

The second parameter is located in the `main.cf` configuration file. The `debug_command` parameter defines what external debugger program will be run by Postfix when it detects the `-D` option for a program:

```
debug_command = command &
```

While this sounds simple, it often is not. Many times environment variables and/or command-line parameters must be set for the external debugger to function properly. In the case of the `strace` debugger, as seen in the manual example above, the process id of the running Postfix process must be included in the command-line arguments.

Postfix can accommodate these requirements by allowing the administrator to set environment variables in the `debug_command` parameter before the debug command is executed. Also, Postfix provides variable substitutions that can be used as command-line parameters for the debug command. Table 23.4 shows the valid values that can be used in the debug command.

TABLE 23.4 Postfix `debug_command` Variable Substitutions

Value	*Description*
`$daemon_directory`	The configured Postfix program directory.
`$process_name`	The program name of the Postfix process to be traced.
`$process_id`	The process id of the running Postfix program to be traced.

Environment variables and variable substitutions are used within the `debug_command` parameter entry:

```
debug_command =
    PATH=/usr/sbin:/sbin
    strace -o /home/rich/tracefile -p $process_id &
```

The ampersand (`&`) on the command line is important. Without it, the `strace` command will be launched, but the Postfix program being debugged will *not* start until the debugger program exits (which of course it never does). By using the ampersand, the `strace` program is placed in background mode, and the monitored Postfix program can then start as normal.

To verify that the debugger program has indeed started, you can check the mail log entries:

```
Feb  6 14:33:49 shadrach postfix/pickup[20061]: 127DDC352: uid=0 from=<root>
Feb  6 14:33:49 shadrach postfix/cleanup[20067]: 127DDC352:
➥ message-id=<20010206193348.127DDC352@shadrach.ispnet1.net>
Feb  6 14:33:49 shadrach postfix/qmgr[20062]: 127DDC352:
➥ from=<root@shadrach.ispnet1.net>, size=301, nrcpt=1 (queue active)
Feb  6 14:33:49 shadrach postfix/smtp[20069]: running: strace
➥ -o /home/rich/tracefile -p 20069 &
Feb  6 14:33:54 shadrach postfix/smtp[20069]: 127DDC352:
➥ to=<richard.blum@ispnet2.net>, relay=meshach.ispnet2.net[192.168.1.2],
➥ delay=6, status=sent (250 OK)
```

As you can see, the `strace` program started before the Postfix `smtp` program. Notice that the `$process_id` variable has been replaced with the actual process id value (20069) of the running `smtp` process.

Using the `strace -o` option allows the administrator to redirect the output of the `strace` command to a standard text file. After the process is complete, the administrator can view the text file and analyze the resulting system calls made by the Postfix program.

Summary

Although running a Postfix server is often simple, sometimes things can go wrong. Fortunately, you can use several different methods to check for problems.

Mail that is stuck in the Postfix message queue can be displayed using the `mailq` command. Any messages in the message queues that need to be examined can be read using the `postcat` command. If messages in the message queues need to be delivered immediately, the mail administrator can use the Postfix `sendmail -q` command to attempt to empty the message queues.

The Postfix configuration is often a source of problems for novice mail administrators. You can use the `postconf` command to double-check settings to ensure that the running Postfix system is actually using the parameter settings you are expecting. You can use the `postconf -n` command to display all of the non-default parameter values in your configuration. To determine what database types the current Postfix supports, you can use the `postconf -m` command.

Analyzing mail logs is a worthwhile task for all administrators. Often you can detect problems simply by scanning the mail log daily for warning messages. If the mail administrator thinks that a particular problem exists, he can modify the `master.cf` configuration file to add more verbose logging for particular Postfix programs. This enables even more detailed logging of mail events to the mail log. Alternatively, the mail administrator can use the `debug_peer_list` command to log detailed SMTP events when messages are sent to remote mail hosts. This technique is extremely helpful for troubleshooting problems with remote mail servers that the local mail administrator does not control.

As a last resort, Postfix supports using external debugging programs to help debug internal workings of Postfix programs. By using the `debug_command` parameter, the mail administrator can allow Postfix to automatically start an external Unix debugger and analyze internal system calls made by the Postfix program while it is delivering messages.

At this point you should be comfortable installing, configuring, and running a Postfix server. Many different topics have been discussed in the last 23 chapters, but there is always more to know. Mail server technology is improving with new resources and vulnerabilities that must be considered. Wietse Venema has done an excellent job of keeping Postfix current with the latest e-mail features. The Postfix Web site (`http://www.postfix.org`), as well as the Postfix mailing list, are excellent resources to keep you informed and educated on future Postfix features.

Index

Symbols

B

C

D

E

J-K

L

M

N

O

P

S

U

V

X-Z